# SPORT and PHYSICAL EDUCATION AROUND The WORLD

Edited by
## William Johnson

ISBN 0-87563-188-6

Published by
STIPES PUBLISHING COMPANY
10 - 12 Chester Street
Champaign, Illinois 61820

# TABLE OF CONTENTS

Page

# FOREWORD

The allied professions of physical education, health education, recreation, and dance have gradually and steadily placed greater emphasis on international relations over the past three or four decades. Most people within the professions would say that this is a good thing, yet the basis for such statements would undoubtedly vary considerably. The world seems to be in such a turmoil, and only time will tell whether we are moving rapidly enough to promote and help with the assimilation of a sufficient quantity of knowledge, opinion, and understanding to promote lasting world peace.

The large majority of men and women in our allied professions have so little knowledge about what really takes place in--say--physical education and sport in the more than 150 countries presently constituted within the United Nations. But what do we know as well about the programs of health education, recreation, and dance in these countries? It is true, of course, that a number of colleges and universities have added courses in the comparative and international aspects of our professions, but many more have not carried out such additions at either the undergraduate or graduate levels.

The publication of this comprehensive edition of *Sport and Physical Education Around the World* is noteworthy in itself and a most welcome addition to our literature. Those of us with special interest in the area of comparative and international sport and physical education owe a significant debt to Dr. Bill Johnson, Editor, for remaining with this project since the very first volume in this series that has culminated in this "combined" publication. Also, the continuing professional interest of Nick Kellum, and Rudy Schreiber earlier, of Phi Epsilon Kappa Fraternity must be recognized. Further, the interest and support of Bob Watts of the Stipes Publishing Company has now resulted in a fine addition to the excellent series on physical education and sport that Stipes offers. Although we hope that we will see Bill Johnson periodically at the international relations sessions at the AAHPERD Convention, it is true that Bill has retired (at a very "young age," of course) from the University of Illinois, Champaign-Urbana, and this could well be his last effort of this type. Those of us who worked closely with him over the years appreciate what a truly fine professional physical educator he has been. We thank him especially for his many and varied contributions to international relations in sport and physical education.

All of the earlier volumes in this series have been dedicated to Dr. Dorothy Ainsworth, of Smith College, as "Physical Education's 'first lady of the world'." We note with sadness the passing of Dorothy--a warm and friendly person who represented the United States for so long in the eyes of so many physical educators from all over the world. It seemed especially appropriate to continue with the same dedication as before. "Dorothy, we miss you, and we won't forget your example in international relations in the days and years ahead."

There is so very much to be done to improve and strengthen international relations and international education in the years immediately ahead. Having Dorothy, Leona Holbrook, and so many others as examples to follow is a truly wonderful inspiration for others to follow to the best of their abilities and energy.

I must confess that I still feel like a novice along these lines when I realize the effort and devotion that so many have given over the decades (for example, Ray Ciszek and Carl Troester of AAHPERD). In 1974 Mrs. Zeigler and I had an opportunity for an around-the-world trip when the Singapore Sports Council invited me to give a series of lectures there. Then as part of a study leave after completing a term of administrative involvement here at Western Ontario, we had a wonderful opportunity to visit nine different countries during the latter part of the year of 1977. Also, in the fall of 1979 we received an invitation to present a paper on the background and present status of sport science in North America at an international seminar in East Germany (the DDR). It is not possible to thank everyone personally who offered us such unusual hospitality--nor would it be proper to thank a few individuals only--but I do want to take this chance to state that "people simply could not have been nicer," and for this we are most grateful.

As a result of this more intensified international experience over the past fifteen years, we have come away from such involvement with the strong feeling that the need for international cooperation in sport and physical education (not to mention the professions of health education and recreation--and now dance) has become stronger and more urgent. We should be comparing cross-culturally such professional matters as aims and objectives, methods of instruction, the relationship between school and society, and administrative problems of greater or lesser import.

Additionally, and at least as important as those aspects listed above, is the most pressing need for sport and physical education to develop and make available in the form of ordered generalizations a sound body of knowledge upon which to base professional endeavors all over the world. We came to the conclusions rapidly that all sorts of scholarly and/or scientific endeavor are taking place in a number of countries (e.g., Germany the FRG), Japan, Israel, England, the Scandinavian countries, etc.), but we in North America do not have the results of such investigation ready for use as ordered generalizations. For that matter, also, we don't have the situation over here in very good condition either! (Further, we must somehow find out to the greatest possible extent about the results of research on human motor performance in sport, dance, play, and exercise that is occurring in countries within the orbit of communist ideology, because we truly need this knowledge too,) Frankly, as a field we are not in a strong enough position to be able to survive for long under such "incomplete conditions."

Finally, I am impressed by the scope of this volume from the standpoint of comprehensive coverage of the world's various geographical areas. Of course, with the rapid increase in the number of independent countries, to include them all within the scope of one book would be an impossible task. Certainly this fine volume can nevertheless be used in a variety of ways--from usage as a course text (or companion text) on the one hand to a book in one's personal library that makes excellent professional reading on the other side. The writers of the various chapters have been selected most carefully by the Editor--often with supplementary advice from knowledgeable persons--and we are indeed indebted to these people for such fine professional contributions. On behalf of all of us who have had a continuing interest in the "International Relations Wing" of the American Alliance for Health, Physical Education, Recreation, and Dance, we thank Dr. Bill Johnson (Editor) and all those who have contributed in greater or lesser fashion to the success of this important venture.

Earle F. Zeigler
The University of Western
    Ontario
London, Canada
1980

PREFACE

The growth of interest in contemporary sport and physical education world-wide during the first three-fourths of the twentieth century has indeed been phenomenal. From early efforts of the YMCA and YWCA to promote international physical activity, the strong surge of interest in international and comparative sport and physical education may also have been generated by a number of other factors: The revival of the Olympic Games after an absence of nearly sixteen centuries; the ease of movement of participants in the jet age; the promotion of sports by television and other media branches; and finally the desire of individuals and nations to compete and obtain recognition and attention as nationalistic enthusiasm swept the sports scene.

An increasing number of people feel, in this time of international struggle for survival, that cultural and natural barriers to a world community can be broken down by understandings through the medium of education. International sport and physical education, as an important aspect of education, can and does foster a better relationship between peoples and nations and, when properly conducted, can be a very effective means of developing harmony between the countries of the world.

In 1955, Phi Epsilon Kappa's Rho Chapter at the University of Illinois recognized this rapidly expanding area of study and research by selecting "Comparative Sport and Physical Education Around the World" as its program theme for the year. International students presented monthly papers on conditions related to sports and physical education in their homelands. The next logical step was the compilation of the papers into a monograph for wider dissemination. Thirteen years later, seven monographs have been published by Phi Epsilon Kappa including articles on sport and physical education in fifty-one countries written by sixty authors and co-authors.

The authors, editor and publisher of the monograph series were concerned that the articles on sport and physical education in the various countries should be updated to be truly contemporary. It was decided to carry out the project of updating previous articles under the direction of the original monograph series editor and put selected articles into a publication entitled "Sport and Physical Education Around the World." This book is an effort to provide background information, that is, to continue the development of a 'body of knowledge' in international and comparative sport and physical education. Approximately one hundred colleges and universities world-wide offer courses, units, workshops and practicums in this rapidly expanding area of study and some are conducting research from elementary to rather sophisticated levels.

The information on sport and physical education is presented country by country with descriptive and comparative materials included. This method may be classified as area and comparative studies as contrasted to the topical and problems approach. Similarities and differences and possible reasons for them are easily identified in the juxtaposition and comparison stages of the comparative method. A suggested outline permitted comparisons with considerable lee-way offered individual authors as follows:

1. General background or introductory information

2. Historical background of education, sports and physical education

3. Sports programs - in-and-out of school, local, district, national, international, and Olympic Games.

4. Physical education at various school levels

5. Professional preparation of teacher-coaches

6. Special characteristics such as indigenous activities, sports clubs, etc.

The fifty-one articles of the original monograph series were examined closely and twenty-nine of them were selected for this publication. Seven new articles were added to insure adequate representation of the various regions and continents of the world. Seventeen of the original articles were eliminated for several reasons - in many cases political unrest made it impossible to secure updated information; a number of the original authors have since retired; and it was deemed impossible to include more than a representative number of countries in a publication of this nature. Readers wishing to study information on deleted articles may refer to the original monograph series on the following: Cambodia, Chile, Ecuador, Ethiopia, France, Ghana, Hong Kong, Hungary, Iraq, Laos, Lebanon, Singapore, Somali, Spain, Switzerland, Thailand, and Viet-Nam.

We as a profession are deeply indebted to the forty-one authors and co-authors who gave generously of their time to the updating of their original articles or the writing of new articles for this publication. With the cost of publication steadily rising, yet aware of the critical need for such resource materials, each author donated time 'as a labor of love' for this important professional project, receiving no monetary compensation for their efforts.

We with to thank C. O. Jackson, former editor of *The Physical Educator*; R. R. Schreiber, former Executive Secretary of Phi Epsilon Kappa Fraternity; P. N. Kellum present Executive Secretary and Henry J. Montoye, publications chairman of Phi Epsilon Kappa for their assistance and continuing support. The supporting roles of Raymond A. Ciszek and Carl A. Troester, AAHPER and ICHPER officials have been invaluable in making these publications possible.

The foreword is again written by Professor Earle Zeigler, Faculty of Physical Education, University of Western Ontario, London, Canada who was one of the originators of the monograph series. His interesting and stimulating views, and enduring encouragement for the development of background materials for international and comparative sport and physical education have been ever so much appreciated.

Finally, the original seven monographs--were dedicated to Dorothy S. Ainsworth, former Special Consultant in International Relations, American Alliance for Health, Physical Education, and Recreation. Along with her hosts of dear friends around the world, we were saddened by the passing away in 1977 of this great lady. She assisted in identifying and securing authors and gave much encouragement to our efforts in developing information for this area of study and research. We will all greatly miss this true "Pioneer in International Relations."

William Johnson, Editor
February, 1980

# SPORT AND PHYSICAL EDUCATION IN AUSTRALIA

Part I.  Australia's National Sport  -  Winning

by John A. Daly

## Biographical Sketch

*John A. Daly* was born in Australia in 1936.  He received his Diploma of Teaching (Secondary) from the Adelaide Teachers College in 1957 and the Diploma in Physical Education from Adelaide University in 1958.  A Bachelor of Arts degree in History with minors in Geography, Philosophy and Psychology was received from Adelaide University in 1966.

Dr. Daly has been teaching since 1958; first, as a teacher in high schools with the Education Department of South Australia from 1958-1960.  He then became a Lecturer II, Lecturer I, and finally a Senior Lecturer and the Head of the Department of Physical Education at Adelaide Teachers College in 1968.

He started graduate work at the University of Adelaide in 1968 when he began work on a Post Graduate Diploma of Education.  He was awarded an Education Department Scholarship in 1969 (South Australia Teachers Institute Scholarship).  In 1969 he was granted an Assistantship at the University of Illinois, Urbana-Champaign where he completed the M.S. degree and started on the Ph.D.  His terminal degree was completed at the University of Illinois in 1977.

Dr. Daly's sports interests are varied:  Track and field (University 'Blue'; State Champion, Australia; and Senior (Coach), Football, Squash, Badminton, and Tennis.  He was honored as Head Track and Field Coach for the Australian team at the Montreal Olympics.  Presently he has resumed his post as Head of the Department of Physical Education at Adelaide Teachers College.

## Editor's Note

Part II - Physical Education in Australia, was researched and written by Eric L. Stein a member of the Editor's graduate class in International-Comparative Physical Education and Sport at the University of Illinois. Mr. Stein drew heavily on an article written by Jeffery O. Miller on Physical Education in Australia in Monograph #2 of the Phi Epsilon Kappa Series, "Physical Education Around the World." Mr. Stein also secured information on current physical education from many other sources including Dr. John A. Daly, the author of Part I of this article.


## Introduction

Visitors comment on Australia's "Cult of Sport"
"Living in Australia is like living in a gymnasium--there's always somebody practising something."[1]

This is the kind of visitor's comment that appeals to native Australians! It was a comment made recently by Mrs. Ed Clark, the wife of a former United States Ambassador to Australia. It is suggestive of the zestful, athletic life followed by the ancient Greeks in their endeavor for all round individual excellence--the concept of areté. Certainly it conjures up an image of an energetic, sports-loving people occupying their leisure time with purposeful physical acactivity. It is this apparent preoccupation with sport, at the expense of intellectual and cultural endeavor, which has attracted persistent comment from the many overseas visitors. Comment has ranged from amazement, pleasure, even envy to scorn, criticism and/or disparagement from the earliest years of the colonies to the present day. The Scottish pastor, John Dunmore Lang, deplored local interest in sport at the expense of other "more worthwhile" pursuits:

Let the reader turn over a file of the colonial newspapers for 1822 and he will find them stuffed almost to nausea with advertisements and accounts of races, cricket matches, boxing matches and regattas, with challenge to fight or to run or to row. The energy of the native mind of the colony seems of late to have been diverted almost exclusively into this frivolous channel.[2]

It was suggested that the native Australian was too apt to "honor muscle at the expense of mind."[3] It seemed that the Australian climate early encouraged an outdoor life. What else was there to do? Twopenny, commenting on town life in Australia in the 1880's suggested that:

. . . the change to a more genial climate and clearer skies (was) not . . . without effect upon the temperament of the colonists. . . The more ample reward attaching to labor out here leaves the colonist more leisure. And this leisure he devotes to working at play . . . the principal amusements of the Australians are outdoor sports of one kind or another.[4]

In keeping with the observations of later visitors, Twopenny noted that the interest taken in sport would suggest that Australia could "fairly claim to be the most sporting country in the world."[5] The great novelist Anthony Trollope visited Australia in the 1870's and succeeded in capturing the flavor of colonial life of a century ago. His comments on Australian society were among the most searching of any traveller who visited the Colonies in the nineteenth century. Trollope's *Australia and New Zealand* was published in 1873 and despite the author's acknowledged disinterest in physical activity (he was 56 years of age and 17 stone when he visited Australia) he gave a full chapter to the colonists' "Passion for Sport."[6] He suggested that sport in Australia appeared to be a "national necessity."[7] Another noted author, Mark Twain, came to Australia in 1899 and marvelled at the preoccupation of the colonists for sporting involvement. He attended the Melbourne Cup which, at the turn of the century, was attracting even then one-fifth of Melbourne's half million population. "Nowhere in my travels", he exclaimed, "have I encountered a festival of the people that has such a magnetic appeal to a whole nation. The Cup astonishes me!"[8]

The so-called "Australian way of life" placed a premium on energy, vitality and robust individualism--although perhaps paradoxically, individualism was required to take into consideration on the overriding sentiment of "mateship"--and these qualities found natural expression in the "cult of sport."

There were critics and those who surveyed Australian life in the late nineteenth century who were derogatory in commenting about the lack of serious literature and music--on the general thinness of cultural life.[9] Perhaps in retrospect this criticism was a little harsh. Perhaps because classical culture had had such a brief history it was the popular culture (sport) which counted most. However, it is worth noting in answer to these and the later critics that a characteristic Australian school of painting, the Heidelberg, did develop in the nineties. Francis Adams in 1893 suggested though that Australians wore themselves out in all they do, mistaking exercise for cultural activity.[10] This comment was echoed by many other critics of Australian society.

The belief in the active, outdoor, sporting life as the "Australian way of life" continued into the twentieth century and the assumption of the visitors who wrote of their observations were shared by most native Australians. No one corrected Conan Doyle who, when contrasting the spectacular "Victorian" system of football with overseas codes, acknowledged and wrote of the preference of Australians for an active, outdoor life. D. H. Lawrence visited Australia in 1922 and in his subsequent novel, *Kangaroo,* he commented on the energy of Australian men and the manner which they played their sport--as if their "lives" depended upon it![11] Sportswriter Herbert Warren Wind of the United States described Australia recently as "a super California" comparing this country with the sporting American west coast state. Australia to this visitor was seen as a "land completely surrounded by water and inundated with athletes"! Certainly the tangible presence of successful sportsmen and women on the contemporary sporting scene adds conviction to such an idea still and this view of Australians as a race of sportsmen (and women?) is shared and eagerly acknowledged by native Australians themselves. Few Australians in fact would disagree with Mrs. Ed Clark's description of living in Australia as "living in a gymnasium" except to add that as in ancient Greece it is an outdoor one.

## Australian "Passion for Sport" Explained

Australians acknowledge the fact that they do possess a deep affinity for sport and the way of life it encourages. Donald Horne in his provocative book *The Lucky Country* describes "an Australian" and places sport in its accepted context by asserting:

> Sport to many Australians is life and the rest a shadow. Sport has been the one national institution that has had no "knockers." To many it is considered a sign of degeneracy not to be interested in it. To play sport, or watch others and to read and talk about it is to uphold the nation and build its character. Australia's success at competitive international sport is considered an important part of its foreign policy.[12]

National cartoonist Bruce Petty has satirically suggested "after the Australian working week, the citizen is refreshed, relaxed and eager to tackle his leisure and (hopefully) if called upon to give his cartilege for his country"![13] The Austrlian journalist Graig McGregor, in his *Profile of Australia,* accepts the fact that sports furnish a strong, common cultural interest and represent an integrating force vital and important to "the Australian way of life." An interest in sport fulfills a cultural function for vast numbers.

> Flying into an Australian city on a Saturday afternoon can be a revealing experience. There below you, suddenly crammed into a single perspective is Australia at play! There is the race course, stands and paddocks crowded; there are the central sports grounds, the stands full of spectators. There are the beaches strung out one after the other down the coast and disappearing into a haze in the distance each with its crowd of sunbathers and surfers. Every few blocks there seems to be a tennis court, bowling green, park, swimming pool . . . rapid fire race broadcasts drift out of the pubs, surfboards are loaded onto the roofs of old jalopies. . . This

is the life Australians have created for themselves in their leisure hours and in a way it shows them at their best.[14]

That sport does occupy a central position in Australian popular culture cannot be denied. The results of a series of Gallup surveys (1948, 1953, 1963) indicate that playing or watching sport is the favorite way for Australians to spend their leisure time.[15] Real evidence of the place of sport in Australian society is found when one surveys the communications media. Because the Australian newspaper aims at mass circulation in a comparatively small community the papers are shaped for an "ideal" reader. The Sydney Daily Telegraph, for example, aimed to appeal to the "average Australian"--a man who lived near the surf of Bondi Beach, a suntanned out-of-doors character with a cynical sports loving mind.[16] Content analyses of Australian papers indicate a greater percentage of sporting news than either domestic or international reporting.[17] It can be thus assumed that the "average Aussie" gets what he wants and wants what he buys!

This preoccupation of Australians with sport is explicable in socio-historical terms. For almost half the history of the nation there has been an imbalance of the sexes in the Australian population. The masculinity of early Australian life and the paucity of cultural institutiona in a new country accounts for the growth of interest in organized competitive sport (the so-called 'cult of sport'). Sport is basically a masculine interest symbolizing as it does to many, manliness, strength, toughness tested in conflict situations, and incorporating in its inherent structure, process and organization the principle of "mateship." Certainly, this was the case with the vigorous team games of the nineteenth century in colonial Australia. Climate and geography are also as important as the demographic factors. Australians have always been predominantly an urban, peripheral people (despite the legends of the rugged "outback" and the pioneers it cultivated).[18] Large centers of population live in the temperate zones where long, warm summers are guaranteed. There was never a shortage of space or leisure time and very early in Australia's history it was discovered that it was possible to play cricket and football on the same turf (not possible in the colder climes of the northern hemisphere "home.")[19] These factors--masculinity of the early population, urbanization, sufficient leisure-time, a climate inciting to action and limited availability of other cultural institutions--simply help explain the extent of participation, the "way of life"; they do not explain the intensity of that involvement.

The fierce intensity with which Australian pursue their sporting interests cannot be traced back to English origins although the traditional love of games is inherited from the background of Australian colonization by British migrants. The intensity of involvement is only barely related to the nineteenth century English belief that rigorous games and the disciplines associated with teamwork were essential to the "making" of a man. The Australian attitude toward sport and the intensity with which it is followed by large segments of the population was and is a manifestation of the "bushman ethos" which developed in the latter part of the nineteenth century.[20]

The "bush" (or "outback") and the pioneering qualities it encouraged--tough masculinity, lack of affectation, courage, and mateship--were the source of inspiration for a distinctive Australian ethos which permeated many institutions including sport.

A nation's conception of itself is important if only for the influence on the way people act in order to live up to that image. The "bushman" became the symbolic hero figure on whose supposed characteristics many Australians tended, as they still do, consciously or unconsciously to model their attitudes and values. This ethos permeated and colored all sections of the Australian community and was popularized in the literature of the late nineteenth and early twentieth centuries until the tough, aggressive, courageous and athletic outdoor Australian became the presiding model for the nation--"The land of . . . never-give-in . . ."--Henry Lawson, 1902. For the townsman, particularly the common man, sport offered an ideal venue for the expression of these values. Thus Australian sport became an expression of this ethos giving an intensity and sense of purpose to games that was not evident in their British origins for it was, and to a certain extent still is, in sport that the Austraians attempted to live up to this "national myth."[21]

### Australia's National Sport--Winning!

A myth is a kind of historical memory and while the Australian idealized self-portrait was probably always an untrue one in an urban community, the more remote the ideal of national character the more nostalgically it is recalled. Contemporary writers comment on this preoccupation--almost an obsessiveness--with sport and the method of succeeding in it as the Australian "way of life." Horne in his assessment of an Australian (recorded earlier in this paper) suggested of sport that "it had no "knockers" . . . it is considered a sign of degeneracy not to be interested in it. To play sport, or watch others and to read about it is to uphold the nation . . ."[22] Australians exhibit an overt pride in the successful prowess of their international sportsmen who are held up as model representatives of "the national mystique." The win-at-any cost philosophy of these internationals is mirrored in the sporting attitudes of the average Australians who accept unself-consciouly the observations of their own writers, ". . . the love of sport is an abiding influence on the Australian characteristic . . . In their leisure they play and play hard . . ."[23]

Successful participation rather than simply active involvement is the characteristic of Australian sport that amazes onlookers from other lands. Lawrence described it as "playing as if their lives depended upon it." In a land of the anti-hero, the stronghold of the "underdog," only the successful sportsman is accorded and enjoys h hero status. It is in the sphere of sport that the Australian really tries to live up to his "legend." The qualities of the pioneer can all be seen in the sporting arena where keenness and guts is considered as important if not more so than skill. Winning--beating someone--is more important than playing well! Real evidence of this is the fact that radio broadcasts are turned off if Australians are performing poorly--that is, losing--in international competitions such as the Davis Cup or Test matches.

This need to act out a vigorous, successful masculine role through sport is impressed very early upon Australian boys. They are told that they must not be crybabies, must stand up for themselves, must not show too much interest in things which to Australians are unmasculine; they must take their sport seriously and try to be good at it. At schools, games have been coldly organized on impelling competitive principles. In tennis, for example, a promising young player is likely to be pulled into a competitive machine in which the prize is the Davis Cup. Sporting associations organize "kindergartens for champions" to seduce very young children to train while parents exhort youngsters to work hard for the success they themselves never achieved.[24] Donald Horne suggest that competitive sport in Australia can be a ruthless, quasi-military operation. It is the one disciplinary side of Australian life. The elements of loyalty, fanaticism, competitiveness, ambition and drive that are not allowed to show in the "she'll be right, mate'" everyday society are quite precisely stated in sport.[25]

High standards are demanded of Australian sportsmen and this emphasis on success rather than enjoyable participation percolates down to the level of the very young--those who should perhaps be "just playing." The intuitive Australian cartoonist, Bruce Petty, often touches the conscience of the nation with his satirical sketches. He illustrates this preoccupation with success-in-sport-to-prove-Australian identity by correctly portraying Australia's national sport as "winning"!

Conclusion--"Sport" or "Athletics"?

Australians, as a result of the demands of their own mythical self-image seem not to be satisfied with anything but successful (winning) performances from even their smallest children.[27] In fact, sporting prowess appears to be one of the few ways in which the female of the species can be elevated to any level of public approbation. The sports arena in Australia is the true theater of the nation but is reserved for the aspiring young and highly skilled.

Perhaps it is because of this value system--the "beat-some-body," "win-at-all-costs" approach--that sport in Australia doesn't retain active, participating devotees. The term "sport" is really inappropriate to describe Australia's involvement in physical activity. The type of endeavor encouraged in Australia is more inclined towards "athletics"--the agonistic struggle for excellence--even for the very young. The "national mystique" demands that all should do their best, endure the effort and measure their results in terms of success and accomplishment rather than pleasure or exhileration. This emphasis on successful competition ("athletics") contrasts sharply with the true meaning of "sport"--a diversion followed for no other reason than to afford pleasure to those participating in it. The emphasis in true sport is not on winning but the "joy of the effort." Participants play "with" and not "against" and endeavor to maximize the pleasure for all engaged in the activity. Fun, pleasure and delight are the prime motives to "play."

"Athletics", on the other hand, is a serious, competitive activity which has for its end, victory in the contest and is characterized by a spirit of dedication, sacrifice and intensity. The athlete seeks to win, to demonstrate excellence and his pursuit of such an elusive and yet demanding mistress compels him to avoid a "playful" attitude if he is to be successful. Obviously, this type of activity involvement is not for all, yet this is "sport" to the Australian.

Only the few, the exceptionally gifted can succeed and while this approach stimulates international success (and a reputation to go with it as a "country inundated with athletes") for Australia in the "world of sport" it can be inhibiting to average or over-age participants. Perhaps it is the "beat-somebody", "win-at-all-costs", competitive athletics approach which deters Australians from continuing to participate in "sport" as they leave the aspiring age of youth. Perhaps, because the Australian attempts in serious competitive sport to live up to the national myth of the "tough Australian", he is reluctant to enjoy pleasurable activity for its own sake. Perhaps for this reason the average, urban Aussie is "Homo-Sedens"[28] in a land of "athletes"!

## Part II.    Physical Education in Australia

### by Eric L. Stein

I.  History

A.  Country

Australia was discovered in 1606 by the Dutch and was settled by the British in 1788. It is believed that the British decided to colonize in Australia as a result of losing American colonies, and Australia became a country of convict settlements as the British sent their non-desirables to this distant land.

The federal system of government was introduced to Australia in 1901, but prior to this time, the six colonies of New South Wales, Tasmania, Queensland, South Australia, Western Australia, and Victoria were self-governing and under British control. Federal and state governments are now elected by the adult population, and they have a cabinet which represents the majority and is responsible to the two house Parliament and Prime Minister.

Australia is located in the southern hemisphere, and has the Pacific Ocean as an eastern boundary and the Indian Ocean as a western boundary. Her 2,967,909 square miles rank her 6th in total area and the 12,031,000 people rank her 46th in world population. The capital of this basically Roman Catholic and Protestant nation whose leading products are wool, livestock, wheat and factory goods is located in Canberra.

Australia is a progressive nation which is constantly working towards the attainment of a better life for her people. The life expectancy of 72.1 years is increasing within Australia and can be related to the 99% literacy rate which the country has attained. This educational achievement of 99% literacy leads us directly to the focus of this paper which is concerned with another particular aspect of the educational system which is physical education.

B. Physical Education

Australian physical education has its roots in the European culture, and imprints of the English and Scottish physical educational system are still seen today. The European influence continued to dominate until approximately 1942 when Western Australia produced the first non-European program. These early physical education courses bore the mark of the war time emergency and trained quickly through vocational and practical aspects rather than academic. However, this was the basic beginning of which the Australians realized that they wanted to develop their own program.

The physical education programs within Australia are mostly open air activities which depend upon the climate. From the following chart, one can see the effect that the climate has on the physical education system.

| State | Amount of School Time Unsuitable for Outdoor Programs | Adverse Environment Conditions |
|---|---|---|
| New South Wales | 25% Unsuitable & 10% doubtful | Smog, extreme cold, heat and wind. |
| Victoria | 25% - 35% Unsuitable | S.E. has high amount of rainfall. N.W. is hot and dry. |
| Queensland | 20% - 25% Unsuitable | North is tropical, West is hot and dusty and high incidence of skin cancer resulting. |

| State | Amount of School Time Unsuitable for Outdoor Programs | Adverse Environment Conditions |
|---|---|---|
| South Australia | 30% - 35% Unsuitable | Excessive cold, heat and wind. |
| West Australia | 35% - 40% Unsuitable | Severe heat. |
| Tasmania | 55% - 60% Unsuitable and higher in many parts. | Extreme snow, rain and wind. |

Today, each state within Australia has its own physical education branch or department which develops and administers physical education programs in infant-primary and secondary education. The physical education programs are moving a positive direction due to the organization and academic research which has developed. This change in direction has resulted in new trends within the country, and the physical aspect is no longer considered the only important area of concern as the Australian image is changing.

## I. Infant-Primary Physical Education

Infant-primary education within Australia has passed through three phases including the following: Irish national system in which the state provided undenominational and subsidized denominational schools, a dual system was used and abolished, and in the third phase, each state was made uniform and placed under one responsible minister. From this progression, the physical education branch or department has developed for each state.

Formal education begins at age five in the infants department or of the primary or elementary school. The primary school involves the first seven years of school with the first four years being considered the infant aspect. It's within this age group that the physical education program must be constructive and motivating so an individual may obtain a base off of which to work.

Australian physical educators are attempting to develop programs within the first years which will give the children a physical awareness. Areas which are currently being emphasized are movement activities such as skipping, jumping, running, dance, and rhythmic activities as well as basic game concepts. Stress has been placed on swinging apparatus, fixed climbing, variety of small equipment, and free play.

Physical education within the infant-primary schools is coeducational until the fourth or fifth year of the school where a division of the sexes occurs. After these years, there is informal mixed matching in novelty games or some individual sports such as tennis,

golf, or squash.  In the past, playgrounds were segregated due to
policy or custom as boys and girls weren't allowed to play together,
but this division is disappearing today.

The class time during the infant-primary years of physical
education have a different focus of attention.  The program during
the infant grades, (1-4), are involved with 20-40 minute periods
which occur daily.  In the primary grades, (5-7), there are two
forty minute periods each week and sports afternoons are also held
each week with a 60-80 minute duration.

In the infant-primary school, physical education is taught by
the regular class teacher whose techniques of implementation are developed as a part of the teacher's professional training program.
Australian physical educators have recognized their limitations, and
through a qualified staff, a system which involves a better curriculum and professional training, constructive advancements are being
made.

II.  Secondary Physical Education

The first four years of the secondary physical education program are developed towards fundamental skills in games, dance, gymnastics, and other movement exercises through various methods of
presentation.  The last year is directed towards activities which are
used in adulthood with an emphasis on "doing" and developing positive habits and attitudes.  Areas which are commonly covered during
this time include dance, track, aquatic oriented classes, tennis, softball, volleyball, basketball, rugby football, field hockey, and gymnastics.  Though the emphasis concerning physical education varies
in each particular state, it is important that new ideas and methods
are presented so as to give a more realistic and updated picture of
the secondary physical education situation.

One of the most advanced programs is being used in Queensland, and was described quite adequately by Mr. T. Thompson who
is the current supervisor of physical education in Queensland.  The
top grade in primary schools was transferred to the secondary schools
in 1964 which made them include grades 8-12.  This move had numerous positive results including the development of new core programs
in physical education, health education for grades 8-10, and a stabi-
lized time schedule of four periods of forty minutes in length each
week.

The non-status of the subject compared with other areas resulted in a smaller allocation of time for the health and physical education area.  Mr. Thompson and other leaders within Australia believe
that the solution to this status problem is found with the placement
of an emphasis on practical work and the development of a theoretical
base of knowledge.  The pathway towards this base has had positive
results as health and physical education is currently offered at the

senior level, and is given credit for entry into other academic institutions. The following chart is one which shows the relationship between the time being spent in theory and practical work.

| Areas | 11th-12th | 9th-10th |
|---|---|---|
| Theory | 35%-45% | 25%-35% |
| Practical Work | 55%-65% | 65%-75% |

The Radford committee recommended in 1970 that public examinations for junior and senior certificates be abolished, and this was completed in 1972. The board of secondary school studies was developed to control the nature of the awarding of certificates, approval of syllabuses, and the granting of board approved status for new subjects initiated by schools or subject associations.

As the physical education system continued to grow, a conceptual model was developed which included the following organized plan of growth.

KEY CONCEPT — Generalization about complexities of ideas behind curriculum.

CONCEPTS — Major components which delineate the scope of health and physical education as a field of study.

SUB CONCEPTS — Supporting ideas which amplify the concepts in more specific terms.

BEHAVIORAL OBJECTIVES — Guides for selection of content.

CONTENT — Subject matter.

EVALUATION — Determining the relation of the outcome of the objectives.

One can definitely see the effect of the concepts of this model if the 1961 and 1972 constitutions for the Australian Council for health, physical education, and recreation are compared as specific objectives weren't even included in the 1961 constitution.

As the physical education program in Australia has developed, one can definitely see a trend away from the brutal and masculine side of the area. Programs are developed so as to refine skills, devise individual planning programs and fitness schedules and involvement in community service and sports projects. Coinciding with the development of the physical education program has been the health areas as major concerns are involved with the prevention of chronic diseases, accident prevention, personality problems, environmental problems, and meeting standards of the St. John Ambulance First Aid Certificate.

The secondary physical education and health programs are moving in a positive direction in Queensland as well as in other states within the nation. The realization that physical educators with within Australia have a valuable contribution to make towards the advancement of society has made the secondary physical education program one with a purpose to its existence. The positive direction and development is also being seen within the college-university physical education programs.

III. College-University Physical Education

The basic physical education qualification that is met in Australia is a diploma of physical education which is normally granted after three years of training at a State Teachers's College. In New South Wales, two of the eight Teacher's Colleges offer a specialist diploma and the University of Sydney offers a four year bachelor of physical education degree. This program is quite similar to the one currently being offered in Western Australia as there is a three year diploma offered by the Teacher's College as well as a four year bachelor of education degree. In Victoria, the basic physical education training consists of a two year diploma of physical education taken at Melbourne University and one year of professional training at either a primary or secondary Teacher's College.

The three year diploma offered is broken into an organized program in which basic objectives are met. In the first year, a general course plan is followed which allows the individual to experience areas other than his own so as to develop an individual with a well-rounded education. The second year is involved with the physical education curriculum and covers the theory, science, and kinetics that is involved. The third year allows one in the field to specialize in an area of interest such as physical education and society, health education, facilities and applied kinetics. Exceptional students are allowed to participate in "honor courses" which involve original research, and the students are normally determined by their academic accomplishments.

The college-university programs are concerned with physical education, and are moving in a positive direction as constructive undergarduate programs are being developed. Post graduate work is also of importance today as both a masters and a doctorate degree can be obtained from various universities within Australia. Physical educators are also traveling to foreign soil in an attempt to bring back the most beneficial and advanced ideas to Australia as her entire physical education program continues to grow.

Part I. FOOTNOTES

1.  C. Turnbull, ed. *Hammond Innes Introduces Australia.*
    (London: Deutsch Publishers, 1971). p. 100.

2.  A. G. L. Shaw. *The Story of Australia.* (London: Faber
    Publishers, 1969). p. 101.

3.  "Juvenal," (Melbourne, 1892).

4.  R. E. N. Twopenny. *Town Life in Australia.* (London: 1883).
    pp. 202-204.

5.  *Ibid.* p. 204.

6.  Anthony Trollope. *Australia and New Zealand.* Melbourne,
    1873).

7.  *Ibid.* p. 168.

8.  D. L. Bernstein. *First Tuesday in November.* (Melbourne:
    Heinemann Publishers, 1969). p. 1.

9.  A. D. Pringle. *Australian Accent.* (London, 1958).

10. Francis Adams. *The Australians.* (London, 1893).

11. D. H. Lawrence. *Kangaroo.* (London: Heinemann Publishers,
    1950). pp. 83, 387.

12. Donald Horne. *The Lucky Country.* (Melbourne: Penguin
    Publishers, 1971). p. 37.

13. Bruce Petty. *Augstralian Fair.* (Melbourne: Cheshire Publish-
    ers, 1967).

14. Craig McGregor. *Profile of Australia.* (Melbourne: Penguin
    Publishers, 1968). p. 132.

15. Gallup Surveys (1918, 1953, 1963).

16. A. F. Davies and S. Encel. *Australian Society.* (Melbourne:
    Cheshire Publishers, 1970). p. 213.

17. Henry Mayer. *The Press in Australia.* (Sydney, 1961).
    pp. 218, 219.

18. Russel Ward. *The Australian Legend.* (Melbourne: Oxford
    University Press, 1970).

19. C. Turnbull. *op. cit.,* p. 59.

20.  J. A. Daly, "The Role of Sport and Games in the Social Development of Early Australia." *The Australian Journal of Physical Education*. (March, 1972).

21.  *Ibid*. p. 35.

22.  Donald Horne. *op. cit*., p. 37.

23.  James Alexander Allan. *Men and Manners in Australia*. (Melbourne: Cheshire Publishers, 1945). pp. 156-157.

24.  Martion Macdonald, "Catching Them Young." *The Bulletin*. (April 29, 1972).

25.  Donald Horne. *op. cit*., p. 38.

26.  Bruce Petty. *op. cit*.

27.  Marion Macdonald. *op. cit*.

28.  Brian Nettleton, "Homo-Sedens Australis." *The Australian Journal of Physical Education*. (No. 42, February-March, 1968).

Part I.   SELECTED REFERENCES

Adams, Francis.  *The Australians--A Social Sketch*.  London, 1961.

Allan, James A.  *Men and Manners in Australia*.  Melbourne:  Cheshire Publishers, 1915.

Bernstein, D. L.  *First Tuesday in November*.  Melbourne:  Heinemann Publishers, 1969.

Brasch, R.  *How Did Sports Begin?*  Longman, 1971.

Clark, R.  "See It My Way."  *ABC Television Series*.  1971.

*Conference Report*, Australian Physical Education Association.  1966.

Daly, J. A.  "The Role of Sport and Games in the Social Development of Early Australia."  *The Australian Journal of Physical Education*.  March, 1972.

Davies, A. F. and Encel, S.  *Australian Society*.  Melbourne:  Cheshire Publishers.  March, 1972.

Dow, Hume, ed.  *Trollope's Australia*.  Melbourne:  Nelson Publishers, 1969.

Goodman, R. B. and Johnston, G. *The Australians.* Adelaide: Rigby Publishers,1966.

Harris, Max. "Morals and Manners." *Australian Civilization.* Melbourne: Cheshire Publishers, 1967.

Horne, Donald. *The Lucky Country.* Melbourne: Penguin, 1971.

Lawrence, D. H. *Kangaroo.* London: Heinemann Publishers, 1950.

Macdonald, M. "Catching Them Young." *The Bulletin.* April, 1972.

Mayer, H. *The Press in Australia.* Sydney, 1961.

McGregor, C. *Profile of Australia.* Melbourne: Penguin Publishers, 1968.

McLeod, A. L., ed. *The Pattern of Australian Culture.* Melbourne, 1965.

Nettleton, B. "Homo-Sedens Australis." *Australian Journal of Physical Education.* No. 42, February-March, 1968.

Pearl, I. and Pearl, C. *Our Yesterday.* Melbourne: Angus and Robertson Publishers, 1967.

Petty, B. *Australia Fair.* Melbourne: Cheshire Publishers, 1967.

Pringle, J. M. D. *Australian Accent.* London, 1958.

Shaw, A. G. L. *The Story of Australia.* London: Faber Publishers, 1969.

Trollope, A. *Australia and New Zealand.* Melbourne, 1873.

Turnbull, C., ed. *Hammond Innes Introduces Australia.* London: Deutsch Publishers, 1971.

Twopenny, R. E. N. *Town Life in Australia.* London, 1883.

Ward, R. *The Australian Legend.* Melbourne: Oxford, University Press, 1970.

Younger, P. M. *Australia and The Australians.* Adelaide: Rigby Publishers, 1970.

Part II. SELECTED REFERENCES

"AAHPER Fitness Test." *The Australian Journal of Physical Education.* Oct.-Nov., 1962. pp. 32-44.

Auletta, Mary and Dick, "Australia - that boom place 'down under' is a land of contrasting climates and sophisticated informality." *Continental Trailways Magazine.* May-June, 1972. pp. 8-9.

Australian Council for Health, Physical Education and Recreation, "Constitution." *The Australian Journal of Physical Education.* June, 1972. pp. 33-38.

Australian Physical Education Association, "Constitution." *The Australian Journal of Physical Education.* Oct.-Nov., 1961. pp. 40-43.

Australian Council for Education Research. *A Brief Guide to Australian Universities.* 1964.

"Australia: She'll be Right, Mate-Maybe." *Time.* May 24, 1971. pp. 34-38.

Civic Education Service. *Scholastic Magazine.* Scholastic Magazines, Inc., 1969.

Cox, Harvey B., "A Brief History of Australian Football." *Physical Education Journal.* Feb.-Mar., 1955. pp. 13-14.

Daly, John A., "Australia's National Sport-Winning." *Physical Education Around the World Monograph #6.* Edited by William Johnson. Indianapolis: Phi Epsilon Kappa Fraternity, 1973. pp. 1-7.

Fitzgerald, R. T. *The Secondary School at Sixes and Sevens.* Australian Council for Educational Research, 1970.

Garnett, A. C. *Freedom and Planning in Australia.* Lancaster: Business Press, Inc., 1949.

Goodman, Robert B. *The Australians.* Adelaide: Rigby Limited, 1972.

Gray, R. J., "The Development of Professional Training Courses in Physical Education in Australia." *The Australian Physical Education Association Sixth National Conference.* Jan. 15-21, 1966. pp. 15-17.

Hawkes, Ponch; Druden, Robert; Torsh Dany and Hannan, Lorna, "Sex Poles in School Sport and Physical Education: The State of Play." *The Australian Journal for Health, Physical Education and Recreation.* Mar. 1975.

Law, P. G., "The Tough Australian." *Australian Physical Education Association Seventh Biennial Conference.* Jan. 17-24, 1968. pp. 47-56.

MacMillian, David S. *Australian Universities.* Sydney University Press, 1968.

Miller, Jeffery O., "Physical Education in Australia." *Physical Education Around the World Monograph #2.* Edited by William Johnson. Indianapolis: Phi Epsilon Kappa Fraternity, 1968. pp. 1-9.

Nettleton, B., "Adventure Programs - Wither?" *Australian Physical Education Association Seventh Biennial Conference.* Jan. 17-24, 1968. pp. 70-72.

Nettleton, B., "Physical Education in Primary Schools." *The Australian Journal of Physical Education.* March, 1965. pp. 14-17.

Queensland, Board of Secondary School Studies, "Syllabus in Health and Physical Education - Grades 8-12." Sept., 1974. pp. 1-21.

Queensland, Department of Education, Physical Education Branch. *Games Handbook, 1970.*

Queensland, Department of Education, Physical Education Branch. Physical Education for Primary Schools - Gymnastics. May, 1971.

Queensland, Department of Education, Physical Education Branch. *Physical Education for Infant Grades - Book I Gymnastics.* 1972.

Queensland, Department of Education, Physical Education Branch. *Physical Education for Primary Schools.* 1972.

Royal Life Saving Society - Australia. *Manual of Water Safety and Life-Saving.* Melbourne, 1974.

Stewart, Frank, "Australian Government Initiative in Tourism and Recreation." November, 1972.

Stewart, K. B., "A View of the Future of Physical Education in Australian Universities." *The Australian Journal of Physical Education.* March, 1965. pp. 8-10.

Thompson, T., "New Dimension in Physical Education in Queensland Schools." *The Australian Journal for Health, Physical Education and Recreation.* March, 1975. pp. 21-25.

Thompson, T., "Survey of Indoor Facilities for Physical Education in High Schools." *The Australian Journal of Physical Education.* June, 1972. p. 24.

Turnbill, George, "A Look at New Endeavors in Colleges Offering Courses for Primary and Secondary (Specialist) Physical Education in New South Wales." *ICHPER 13.* July 30-August 3, 1970. pp. 104-110.

Wise, Bernard R. *Commonwealth of Australia.* London: Sir ISAAS Pittman and Sons, Ltd., 1913.

Wood, G. L., *Australia - Its Resources and Development.* New York: The Macmillan Company, 1947.

# SPORT AND PHYSICAL EDUCATION IN AUSTRIA
by Nicolaas J. Moolenijzer

## Biographical Sketch

*Nicolaas Moolenijzer* was born in Amsterdam, the Netherlands in 1922. After completing his secondary school school education he received his L.O. degree from the Protestant Teacher College in Amsterdam (1943) and his M.O. degree in physical education from the Academy for Physical Education, also in Amsterdam (1947).

During his collegiate career he represented the Netherlands as a member of the national ice hockey team and was a regular member of one of the Canadia All Star Army teams.

After his immigration to the United States, Dr. Moolenijzer received a B.A. degree from San Jose State College (1949) and continued graduate work at U.C.L.A. where he received his M.S. (1956) and at the University of Southern California where he obtained his Ph.D. (1965).

Dr. Moolenijzer's teaching experience stretches from kindergarten level through the university and includes general classroom teaching as well as physical edu-education, both abroad and in the United States. In addition to a one year's stay in Austria as receipient of a Fulbright Senior Research grant, he has traveled widely through Europe and Asia and has lectured in both Western and Eastern Europe.

Recently he returned to the University of New Mexico after having served almost three years with the United National Educational, Scientific and Cultural Organization (UNESCO) in Paris, France, where he was instrumental in the organization of the "First International Conference of Ministers and Senior Officials Responsible for Physical Education and Sport."

His special interests lie in the areas of international foundations and history of physical education and sport.

# General Background

Austria is situated in the center of the European continent and has formed the link between East and West since its existence. Topographically it is an Alpine country with a great variety of scenery. From all directions the mountains and valleys slope down to the Danube which traverses the country from west to east on its way to the Black Sea. In the east the mountains give way to the Vienna basin which, in turn, leads to the Hungarian plains. Austria has a population of seven million people. In the last census 99% of the inhabitants gave German as their native language and 89% professed to be Roman Catholics. More than one-fourth of the population lives in the capital, Vienna.

Austria's history has been determined by its geographical position, for lying at the very center of Europe it has been on the crossroads of three civilizations, the Roman, Germanic, and the Slavic. Although its civilization goes back to the first Iron Age, Austria did not start flourishing until it became a Roman province. Shortly after its conversion to Christianity it was overrun by Germanic hordes and during the centuries that followed Austria suffered under the domination of Germanic tribes, Hans, Avars, and Magyars (Hungarians). It was not until about the year 1000 that a stable nation could be established. At the end of the 13th century the Royal House of the Habsburgs came in power which maintained itself as an absolute monarchy until the end of World War I. As a result of treaties and marriages the Habsburg empire became so large that it was said that the sun did not set within its boundaries. During the 16th and 17th century Austria formed the Eastern bastion against the incursions of the Turks. Although twice besieged, Vienna never fell. It was during the reign of empress Maria Theresa (1740-'80) that administrative and cultural reforms were initiated which affected early Austrian education. It was in this time too that the first great Austrian musicians such as Haydn and Mozart appeared on the scene.

The defeat in World War I terminated the Austrian-Hungarian monarchy and gave Austria its first taste of government by popular rule. The republic suffered greatly from the damages sustained during the war and from the secession of Czechoslovakia, Hungary, and Yugoslavia which resulted in a very serious economic situation. Between 1918 and 1938 the young republic led a precarious existence marked by a civil war in 1934 and a National Socialistic "Putsch" which led to the murder of its chancellor Dollfuss. In 1938 German troops incorporated the country forcibly into the Third Reich.

Cessation of the hostilities after World War II resulted, for Austria, in a ten year allied occupation during which time it was a pawn in the conflict between the ideologies of East and West. It was not until 1955 that the last foreign soldiers left Austria and that the country could make a fresh start in deciding its own future.

Austria is very popular as a vacation land, particularly during the winter season when numerous ski resorts in the Alps provide excellent facilities and instructors for ski enthusiasts. Although Austrians vary a great deal in many ways, whether in politics, dialect, tradition or national costume, it must be said that they present a solid front with their love for skiing.

## Historical Background of Physical Education

Planned physical education may be first detected in the curricula of the so-called 'knightly academies' of the 17th and 18th century. The programs of these private schools which catered to the wealthy segment of the population included, besides such indigenous activities as running, jumping, stone casting, wrestling and ball games, a heavy emphasis on horsemanship, marksmanship, military drill, fencing, climbing, swimming and dancing. Another activity which was diligently practiced was vaulting which consisted of exercises at the predecessor of the sidehorse. Although some attempts were made in the Austrian-Hungarian monarchy to introduce physical education as an intrinsic part of the school curriculum, the reactionary position of the church generally proved an insurmountable obstacle. Among these exceptions was a law, the *Ratio Educationis,* passed by empress Maria Theresa in 1777. This law granted a daily hour of recreation for the students of Hungary and, in addition, provided for the construction of playgrounds.

The situation was a little more relaxed, too, at the military academies where physical education naturally formed an important part of the program. At the military academy of Milan the ideas of Guts Muths were adopted and were so successful that the school's program is cited as one of the most exemplary of its time. Much of this program has been described by E. Young in his *Elementary Gymnastics* which, translated into German in 1827, became Austria's first physical education manual. In a sense this was a somewhat roundabout way since Young's book is virtually a copy of Guts Muths' *Gymnastics for Youth.*

Another pioneer in this rather sterile era was Eduard Milde (1777-1853) who had a special interest in corrective physical education. Milde, a priest, college professor and ultimately the Archbishop of Vienna favored Guts Muths over Jahn and has been credited with the gradual acceptance of physical education and its eventual introduction in the schools' curricula during the first half of the 19th century.

However, although the opportunity existed, practical implementation of physical education in the schools was still very limited. In 1838 Albert von Stefani opened a private sport school and at the same time accepted a position at the Maria Theresa Academy to teach physical education. In 1848 the University of Vienna opened its gymnasium which was operated by Rudolf Stefani, a brother of Albert. In 1861 the first *Turnverein* made its entree. Due to the political activity of its sister organization in Germany the Austrian *Turner-bund* got a late start and for a long time was watched closely by the authorities. Its activity, however, was partly instrumental in the passage of an education law in 1869 which made physical education obligatory for elementary and secondary schools.

In 1870 the University of Vienna initiated a two-year course for the preparation of physical education teachers. Although the law had made physical education a required subject, it had made no provisions to enforce its implementation. Responsibility for the organization of the program and the operating costs had been delegated to local governments which generally could or would not comply with the federal law. Consequently, physical education remained in many instances a haphazard affair.

Entirely in step with the educational philosophies of the time, directives and courses of study were based on the theories of the Spiesz-Maul system of physical education. Although the *Turners* themselves were rather formal in their approach to physical activity, they none-the-less pressed for a more extensive program, more and better facilities, a more thorough teacher training program and enforcement of the physical education requirement in schools, regardless of their size or location. Other influences such as the Swedish system, various forms of rhythmic gymnastics and modern dance, and the increase in popularity and number of sports activities and clubs were instrumental in creating a public awareness of the need for physical education. Many prominent physicians and orthopedists such as F. A. Schmidt and H. Spitzy, together with such well-known psychologists as Charlotte and Karl Bühler and Edward Spranger took an active part in a movement to convince society of the necessity for physical education as part of the total educational program and gave strong support to attempts for renewal of the existing program.

In 1980 a German, Fritz Eckhardt, published an article, "Physical Education Develops From Natural Movement Patterns" which influenced many Austrian physical educators. Among these was Adalbert Slama (1884-1965), a particularly skilled high school teacher who employed for his time unorthodox methods to stimulate participation. As an eminent practitioner and coach he gained much recognition for his work in tumbling, gymnastics, and track and field. A national survey undertaken in 1910 showed that many physical educators were experimenting with innovations of their own in order to find a method that would prove more satisfactory than the approved formal system. The outbreak of World War I interrupted this process for most physical education teachers were taken into the army and the general emphasis on physical education became of a military nature.

The war turned into a debate for the Austrian-Hungarian monarchy. Separated from most of its territory the once powerful imperium shrank to an insignificant, small republic. Socioeconomic conditions reached an absolute low, and misery and hunger prevailed.

Many children were sent to foreign nations where adequate nourishment would ensure them a healthy future. The social and political changes required modifications in the educational philosophy and its practical applications. Ideologically there was no longer a place for the pre-war educational pattern which had reflected Herbart's theories of the "imaginative mechanism." It was deliberately abandoned by the newly formed government and newer principles of "total education" were formulated to meet the needs of the children of the democracy.

The concept of *total education*, as it developed in Austrian education during the postwar years, stressed four general principles: (1) More emphasis should be placed on character forming than on intellectual forming; (2) the school should offer the child an opportunity to work and create, thus promoting individual achievement; (3) instruction should, as much as possible, be based on the spontaneous interest of children and should depend less on an arbitrary imposition of interest by the teacher; and (4) activity or self-industriousness should be regarded as an essential condition for self-education.

In the process of educational reform Karl Gaulhofer (1885-1941) was appointed as federal consultant for physical education in the Ministry of Education. Together with Margarete Streicher (1891-    ) who had been experimenting independently during the war years when all supervisors were in the service, he developed a new approach to physical education called *natural physical education*. This method soon known throughout Europe as the *Austrian School*, proved a major step forward in the development of modern physical education. Interrupted briefly by the Nazi occupation and slightly modified since then, the principles of Gaulhofer-Streicher are still the guiding tenets of the Austrian physical education program.

In 1932 Gaulhofer accepted employment outside Austria, leaving the local leadership in the hands of Streicher. After his death in 1941 she assumed complete leadership until the end of the war. Despite her age and retirement, Dr. Streicher is still very active. She is much sought after as lecturer and she participates regularly in national and international workshops.

After World War II the leadership of Austrian physical education was entrusted to a very energetic and conscientious educationalist, Hans Groll. Groll (1907-1975), Director of the Institute for Physical Education at the University of Vienna, was a dynamic teacher and prolific writer. A pupil of Gaulhofer and Streicher and, therefore, thoroughly steeped in the principles of the Austrian School. Groll has introduced modifications which tend to emphasize more strongly the moral aspects of physical education.

## Natural Physical Education

The concept of natural physical education can not be thoroughly discussed in a few paragraphs. However, since the approach to physical education, as developed by Gaulhofer and Streicher is still the basis of the present Austria method (and of various other European methods) some familiarity with its principles is required to understand the current Austrian program of physical education.

The military, formal approach to the 'subject' of physical training, which emphasized the development of willpower and self-control, the knowledge of exercises and their execution according to required form and style, is regarded as unnatural, unnatural in the sense that they do not represent activities and movement forms innate to the species of mankind. It is felt that this manner of presentation is in sharp contrast with the needs of the individual as a totality. A dichotomy of mind and body is rejected as it is held that physical education should make itself consciously available to harmonious education in order to contribute to the physical, mental, aesthetical and ethical development of the individual.

By applying the term 'natural' no return to primitive conditions is proposed but rather an adaptation of physical activities to the nature of man in all his biological functions. This includes emotional, intellectual and social as well as physical characteristics. The concept of 'natural' is defined in terms of "how" rather than "what" and does not exclude the use of artificial means to achieve its goals. Implications of the concept of 'natural' may be identified as follows:

1. It implies an approach, a manner of performance, rather than a system or a group of particular exercise.

2. It implies observance of biological principles.

3. As applied to movement, it implies a process of moving from one status of balance to another with minimum expenditure of energy. A natural movement originates at the center of gravity and its action is continued centrifugally; the movement flows from the initial impulse to completion without arbitrary interruption; it utilizes the forces of gravity and applies the exact amount of strength needed as directed by the principle of economy.

4. A natural movement is an integrated mental-physical concept; it is an expression of a personality which reflects the person's individual style of performance.

Each individual needs exercises that are adapted to his needs. Distinguished are (1) needs for everyday life which are similar for all persons of the same age and sex who have followed a natural pattern of development, and (2) special needs which are determined by individual differences. The latter are considered of much importance because of the impact of cultural and industrial influences. Posture or bearing is considered an indicator of the total condition of the individual. Each individual has his own, unique, natural posture and style.

Emphasizing that proper development of the mental functions is as much a biological necessity as effective development of the physical functions, the Austrian School urges the integration of physical education with academic subjects. It stresses that physical education provides many opportunities for developing the emotional and creative powers through play and exercises which offer opportunities for expression and interpretation. In order to develop the intellectual powers, the "problem-solving approach" is utilized in which the teacher assigns the movement problem, leaving the solution to the individual.

Play is regarded as a natural part of the physical education program, as a means of self-development; the acquisition of skills; and, for intellectual challenges in situations where the application of skills, technique and tactics are decisive factors. The necessity to submit to rules and regulations is thought to cultivate moral standards and ethical values, and is believed to stimulate appreciation for the dignity of human performance.

In order to meet the requirements of total education the Austrian School makes use of a systematical organization of exercises, ranked on the basis of educational concepts. In this organization everyday movements, labor movements and physical play are employed, all of which are classified generically in terms of the function they serve in the life of the individual. In relating exercises to human purposes rather than to mechanical considerations, they are distinguished in four categories: (1) Normalizing Exercise, (2) Forming Exercises, (3) Achievement Exercises, and (4) Stunts.

Purpose of the *Normalizing Exercises* is the returning of the body to its theoretically normal, natural condition by employing exercises that aim at flexibility, relaxation and muscle strengthening qualities. They are directed at the development of effective patterns for postural alignment and movement, which they seek to achieve by utilization of structural exercises and adjustment exercises. Adhering to strict principles of functionality and anthropologically correct kinetic principles, the *Forming Exercises* are classified according to their functional characteristics, with emphasis on muscular power, speed, explosive muscular power, and endurance. The aim of *Achievement Exercises* is to stimulate individual optimum performance. Rather than employing activities which tend to lead to standardization and specialization, a wide variety of movement experiences is preferred. Among these are competitive games, self-defense, hiking, swimming and winter activities. Also included are the so-called basic exercises which include running, jumping, climbing, hanging, throwing, pushing, lifting, carrying, and various forms of track and field and gymnastics. Although many of these activities could be measured in terms of time and distance, the optimum achievement is preferred to record setting as is the efficiency of natural movement (individual) to so-called proper form of style.

In addition to the forementioned exercises which are directed at utilitarian goals, the Austrian School also provides activities which are valued for the satisfaction that the performer may find in executing them. These activities, called *Stunts*, are subdivided into acrobatic stunts may be executed with or without equipment and with or without apparatus; the dance-like arts employ movements as a form of self-expression and interpretation in autochthonous circle and folk dances.

Going out from the axiom that man seldom executes individual functions separately but generally groups them together into larger purposeful complexes of coordinated action, the Austrian School stresses the utilization of activities which offer many possibilities for function rather than narrow athletic specialization.

To ensure graduality and harmonious development of the individual as a totality, the Austrian School developed the following outline for lesson plans which it employs as a methodical aid:

A. Introductory Exercises

B. Core
      B-1 Posture improvement exercises
      B-2 Balancing exercises
      B-3 Dexterity exercises
      B-4 Going and running
      B-5 Jumping

C. Quieting exercises

Currently, this lesson plan has been modified and schools have the option to follow models developed by Groll or Fetz. Groll's outline reads:

A. Normalizing and forming exercises,
B. Achievement exercises and stunts,
C. Games and dance,
D. Hiking and camping.

The *introductory exercises* or warm-up exercises intend to pre-prepare the pupil both physically and mentally for the activity to come. Biologically and psychologically they should be related to the preceding activity in intensity and nature. Functioning as a bridge between the foregoing activity and the physical education activity to come it should facilitate the psychological transition and bring the body to optimum temperature for the activity to come. To attain this aim the nature of the activity should be pleasing and recreative.

The *core* forms the nucleus of the instruction period. Its subdivision was established to guarantee specific emphasis on the several functions. The 'posture improvement exercises' may employ both normalizing and forming exercises, placing emphasis on those which promote postural development, particularly of the trunk. They may be executed individually or with the help of another pupil and with or without apparatus. The 'balancing exercises' are mainly concerned with the individual's balance or equilibrium and require a high degree of muscle-sense or coordination. They are considered of great value because of their importance for the development of balance and for their contributions to the proper carriage of the spinal column. Moreover by varying the height or inclination of the supporting plane they may contribute to character building as the danger element will require courage. The 'dexterity exercises' lend themselves well to the teaching of everyday movements and are considered of great value for their carry-over value. Since power and strength might be regarded as an indispensable part of most physical skills, exercises which develop muscular power are included in this section. The dexterity exercises may be executed individually, with the help of a partner, with or without apparatus and in group or team formations. They include sports and stunts as well as exercises. Although 'going and running' have been grouped together in this lesson plan, going is classified as a forming exercise while running emphasizes achievement. The many possibilities of organization, such as running and chasing games, individual running, and relays make it a particularly effective medium for physical education. Due to the many forms and combinations of 'jumping' possible this all-round activity has been considered of so much importance that it has been granted a place of its own in the lesson plan.

The *quieting exercises* are intended as an adaptation period in which intensified organic functions may return to a normal level. Pedagogically they also serve as a means to bring the pupil back to a condition which will allow him to resume his regular class activity.

The discussion of the philosophy and methodology of the Austrian School has necessarily been drastically condensed, of course. Present literature indicates nuances of change, which represent more a manner of formulation than of objectives. The backlash of World War II resulted to some degree in a moral rearmament. Certain circles criticised physical education for having put too much emphasis on the biological aspects of the educational process. Firmly convinced of the righteousness of the basic principles of the Austrian School, Groll has become the chief interpreter for the articulation of the moral aspects of physical education.

General Education

Like most non-American educational systems the Austrian arrangement of educational institutions is a multifarious one which tends to separate and classify students on the basis of ability at an early age. The Austrian educational system may be classified in the following four principal categories: (1) Schools of general education, (2) Technical and vocational schools, (3) Teacher training schools, and (4) Institutes of higher education.

The schools of general education include those which provide a curriculum designed to meet the needs for pupils of compulsory school age. Recently the compulsory school attendance has been extended through grade nine or 15 years of age. The primary school offers in its lower divisions (grades 1-4) an elementary education common to all pupils. In its upper division (grades 5-9) a more extensive and differentiated education is offered, often adapted to local conditions. Qualified pupils who have completed the lower division successfully may transfer to an upper primary school or to the lower division of a secondary school preparing for higher education. The curriculum of the upper primary school provides a more developed general education which prepares the pupils for transfer to intermediate, secondary technical and vocational schools.

Entrance to the college preparatory secondary schools may be granted upon successful completion of the lower division of the primary school and after passing an entrance examination. The secondary schools are comprised of a lower division (4 years) and an upper division (4 years) and provide a general secondary education. In sharp contrast with the American comprehensive high school the Austrian secondary school distinguishes no less than 12 different institutions; each Gymnasium offering a different emphasis on curriculum. Besides the various branches of college preparatory secondary schools there is also a great variety of secondary vocational schools, again, each type preparing for a certain trade or craft.

Admission to the teacher training institutes (who were reorganized in 1976 as Paedogogische Akademien) may be gained upon satisfactory completion of the first eight years of general compulsory schooling. The training for elementary classroom teachers requires completion of four semesters, while the preparation of secondary school teachers takes six semesters.

Admission to the teacher training schools may be gained upon satisfactory completion of the first eight years of general compulsory schooling and successful passing of an aptitude test (14 years of age). Upon completion of the five-year course and passing a final proficiency examination, the graduate (19 years old) can be appointed as a probationary primary teacher. After two years of successful teaching and after passing a teaching diploma examination, this appointment will be confirmed. Additional studies and examinations will enable him to move on to higher levels of instruction or to special areas. However, only those prepared at the various colleges of the university can be appointed to teach in the secondary schools.

## Physical Education at the Elementary Schools

In general, physical education in the elementary schools is taught by the classroom teacher. In 1964 a pilot program was conducted to investigate the possibilities for a daily physical education period. Although this has not been realized, the time allocated for physical education has recently been increased from two to three hours per week. The requirements concerning the teaching of physical education vary at the different teacher training institutes. The general sentiment is that this preparation is still not quite satisfactory; a universal complaint of the profession. Inservice courses and summer school programs are offered regularly to promote interest and to increase the teaching skills of the classroom teacher. Assistance during the school year is supplied by physical education consultants and regional inspectors who are particularly concerned in securing the best facilities available.

The curriculum consists mainly of the activities described in the discussion of the program of natural physical education. It appears that currently there exists no longer the great emphasis on "home-made equipment" as it was customary in the past. This change is not due to an increase of affluency as the purpose of this was never economy oriented, but aimed at fostering an interrelationship between physical education and other facets of education. It also offers an opportunity to place the practice of physical education into a natural setting by employing the products of nature. Tree trunks may be used for climbing and clambering as well as for balancing and coordination exercises; overhanging branches may be used for gymnastic stunts; ditches for jumping and so on. Consistent with the objectives of total education much of the regular subject matter and physical education is integrated. One of the more interesting ways in which this is done is through school hikes. Here, hikes and excursions are combined with lessons in botany, or nature study, history, geography or mathematics. Depending on the grade level, these hikes may last as much as an entire school day. They are conducted in the city streets as well as in the parks or in the countryside. They include excursions to the forests and mountains as well as trips to the lakes and rivers. Walking, mountain climbing, swimming and boating are common activities in these educational ventures. Where the locale permits students also undertake these activities during the winter, thus incorporating winter activities such as skiing and skating.

Save for skiing and soccer, the initiative for after-school sports or any other recreational or competitive program at the elementary school level is left to the individual school administration.

## Secondary School Physical Education

The physical education program for secondary schools is similar in many respects to the program of the elementary schools. Austria has many small towns and villages where the number of students or their diversity often decide the nature of facilities and instructional personnel. In the large cities it is often the lack of space which influences the scope of the program. The Austrian Government supports the education program strongly and budgets for construction and teacher salaries are very adequate by European standards.

Since a recent change in the education code pertaining to physical education, the number of hours for instruction has been increased to three one hour class periods per week. In general practice this usually amounts to two indoor sessions and one period for games and sports. In most instances the students have also the opportunity to participate in a voluntary sports program. This program which is conducted after regular school hours is of an intramural or after-school-sports nature and includes many different ac-activities.

Only recently a limited opportunity for participation in a very loosely organized program of intraschool sports has been introduced. This, however, is mostly restricted to the larger cities. The most popular team sports for this competitive program are: soccer, basketball, skiing, volleyball and track and field.

Although the program has as yet nothing in common with the interscholastic program in the United States it presents an interesting phenomenon. Traditionally the participation in sport was found in non-school affiliated agencies such as sports clubs and associations. Due to the historic development of Austrian society the organization and administration of most of these sport associations have been in the hands of two politically controlled organizations: the "Union" (with a Christian background) and the A.S.K.O. (the Socialist Sport Association), who since World War II have increased their membership to 700,000 and 600,000 respectively.

Realizing the great interest in organized sports programs, physical educators have embarked on an impressive program to meet these needs. Various conditions in the secondary school system, however, prove difficult obstacles. Among these are such facts as: (1) the absence of the concept of a comprehensive school, (2) the prevailing belief that school is a serious business in which there is no place for play.

During the early development of schools sports programs, additional difficulties were created by the absence of student government and coeducational programs. However, since 1974 these conditions have changed. Student government has become an accepted practice and all curricula are now coeducational.

In order to stimulate interest for athletic participation the Department for Physical Education and Sports of the Ministry of Education is instrumental in organizing a type of nationwide Junior Olympics. Representatives of the various states, decided upon through state elimination tournaments, vie for national honors. In order to prevent specialization competition is limited to several events while the choice of events changes each year. In this fashion the national championship in soccer and track and field may be held this year while next year competition may be for the national championship in tennis and swimming.

Competition for school age youth is further stimulated by Austria's membership in the ISF, the International Schoolsport Federation to which approximately twenty-two European countries belong. The organization which was founded in 1972 sponsors, through the national schoolsport associations, international sports competitions for elementary and secondary school students.

The physical education program of the secondary school offers also an opportunity for swimming instruction where it has access to public pools. Besides the regular swimming activities the program includes also a water safety course whose organization, proficiency tests, certificates and badges are very similar to those of our Red Cross swimming program.

Three times per year the secondary school students participate in day-long hikes which are similar in nature to those described in the elementary school program.

Instruction in the national pastime of skiing is so unique a feature that it deserves special attention.

### The Program of School Skiing

Much of Austria consists of mountains which are regularly covered with snow during the winter season. It is therefore not surprising that for practical reasons skiing has become an indigenous activity in these regions. A considerable part of the population, however, is concentrated in the lowlands where snowfall is very unreliable. That, despite this condition, skiing has become a national pastime, is, for the most part, due to the pioneering work of the physical education program of the public schools.

As early as 1890 the Ministry of Education encouraged the promotion of skiing as an extra curricular activity. Many teachers inspired by this break with formalism devoted much of their time and energies to the development of this sport. Plans to incorporate skiing in the regular physical education program had reached a final stage when they had to be dropped as a result of the outbreak of the first world war. In the curriculum design of the Austrian School, skiing was given a prominent place. Despite financial difficulties during the depression years it was possible to develop a uniform systematical approach of teaching techniques. In 1945 Ferdinand Zdarsky became head of the Federal Department of Physical Education. A ski enthusiast who had experienced the development of school skiing from the very beginning, he can be credited with the organization and administration of the national school ski program of today.

At present skiing takes a more important place in the physical education curriculum than ever before. Whatever warranted by local conditions, regular physical education periods may be devoted entirely to skiing. In order to provide for those whose locale does not offer an opportunity for skiing, special arrangements have been made to secure participation in this worthwhile physical activity. Legal provisions allow the organization of ski courses for boys and girls ten years of age and older. To ensure that all secondary school pupils benefit from this program, there is a legal minimum requirement three such courses during the student's secondary school years. Unless the size of the school decrees otherwise, it is recommended that the students be grouped by grade level. If there is enough interest, that is, if more than two-thirds of a classroom participates, additional ski courses may be arranged. However, not more than one ski camp per year may be organized for the same group.

Since the ski courses are organized by the school and during regular school time, the responsibility for the organization and administration lies entirely with the school authorities. Arrangements for transportation, lodging, food, insurance, medical care, recreation, religious services, and various other items are the responsibility of the organizing school. Children who do not partake in the ski course must continue to attend school during this time to meet the legal attendance requirement. Although the ski camp is a pleasurable occurrence, its first aim is to provide the students with a valuable educational experience. Despite the many hours spent in physical activity, regular classes must be conducted. In order to maintain a successful program, the school administration must provide an adequate number of interested and qualified teachers. (The teacher-pupil ratio is about 1 to 10 or 15.)

The integration of subject matter with the skiing program, the opportunity to study the different locale and the social education of a group living which the students, in most cases, would not experience at any other time of the school year, make the ski camp a unique educational experience.

Planning sessions with the parents, and printed materials describing the school ski program furnished by the federal agencies, assure the cooperation of the parents in matters such as medical examinations and proper clothing. Although the cost of these ski camps are minimal, funds are available to guarantee that no student will have to forego participation for the lack of money.

In the ski camps students are grouped according to ability and regular lesson plans are adhered to in order to ensure proper progression of difficulty and technique. Besides the teaching skills of downhill skiing, attention is paid to cross-country skiing and elementary forms of jumping. It is clear that this program is in need of more instructional staff that can be provided by the number of physical education teachers of a given school. In order to prepare sufficient qualified personnel the federal department of physical education organizes special courses for classroom teachers. Participants in these courses receive government support to attend and gain additional financial benefits if they participate in the school ski courses. Additional teaching personnel is obtained by using the services of professional ski instructors who offer their help free of charge or for a minimal fee during the early season. Another source for ski teachers is graduates of a course for volunteer ski instructors who are usually affiliated with various clubs and associations.

The training of ski instructors and their certification is controlled by the Austrian Ministry of Education. Much of the development of the modern ski techniques is a direct result of pioneer work by physical educators. Austrian successes in international ski competition serve as an indicator of the quality of their work and Austrian ski instructors are employed in all parts of the world. Considering this and adding the comparatively low cost of living it is not surprising that Austria has become a mecca for ski enthusiasts par excellence.

In order to guarantee the future of the school ski program, the Austrian government has embarked on the development of a network of ski hostels. At the present there are 11 of these federally operated hostels providing room for 1061 persons. Some are old hotels that have been converted for this purpose, others are brand new modern structures. Depending on the vintage of the hostel, one might find the following facilities: dormitories, dining rooms, kitchen, day rooms, study rooms, bathing and shower facilities, storage rooms for skis, drying rooms for ski boots, living quarters for the staff and office space. Most are equipped with libraries and movie projectors.

Equipment for Alpine skiing has become very specialized and expensive. Although most students either possess their own or are able to borrow the necessary equipment, there still remains a sizable group that has no access to proper, safe equipment. The overriding principle in the development of the School Ski program has been to provide all students with the opportunity to participate in this lifetime sport. To prevent the cost from becoming an insurmountable obstacle the Ministry of Education maintains so-called ski supply centers. Located in the provincial capitals and other large cities, these centers provide students who are going to a School Ski Camp with the necessary equipment at a minimal charge. Each center is provided with a staff that keeps the equipment in excellent condition to minimize possible accidents.

The railroads provide round trip transportation for a fraction of the normal cost. During the ski season trainloads of happy young people, well equipped and well supervised, leave for the healthy clean

air of the mountain areas.  If at one time there was some feeling
among the professional ski instructors and others concerned with the
ski industry that a publicly-controlled ski program might interfere
with their business interests, this notion has rapidly disappeared for
as soon as the students have mastered a minimum of skills they are
instrumental in bringing their families to the ski resorts for more instruction.  In 1947,  8,000 students participated in one week ski
courses; ten years later this number had increased to 40,000 participants.  By 1967 the number had reached 40,000 and in 1976 more
than 206,000 school children had spent one week in School Ski Camps.

In order to be able to improve on practices, organization and
methodic development of ski instruction, the Austrian educators involved in the School Ski program formed an independent organization
in 1964.  In 1965 the 7th INTERSKI (an international organization of
professional ski instructors and operators of ski resorts) met in Bad
Gastein in Austria.  The Austrian School Ski organization attended
and was instrumental in founding an International Study Group for
School Skiing.  Delegations from various countries soon agreed that
they needed to convene regularly and consequently have met every
year since.  Whenever possible these meetings coincide with the
INTERSKI Conferences (1968:  Aspen, Colorado; 1972:  Garmisch-
Partenkirchen, Federal Republic of Germany; 1975:  Strbskeplesov,
Czechoslovakia).

Teacher Training

At the moment there are four Institutes for Physical Education
in Austria (Vienna, Graz, Salsburg and Innsbruck).  As result of the
classical structure of the university, these institutes are affiliated
with the university and form a department in the College of Philosophy.  Since, as in many European countries, education and consequently physical education have not been recognized as fully qualified
academic disciplines, it was not until recently that one could attain the
rank of professor.  Until recently therefore, the responsibility for departmental chairmanship was usually entrusted to professors from
other disciplines.  At present the situation has changed slightly and
Austria can boast on five "ordinary" professors of physical education
(two in Vienna and one each in the institutions of Graz, Innsbruck
and Salsburg).

In general the Physical Education Institutes offer a four year
program preparing for certification to teach physical education.  However, it is not possible to become a specialist in physical education by
itself.  All candidates must qualify to teach one other subject as well.
Where there was formerly a limited number of "Nebenfaecher" (minors)
available, the conditions have improved markedly since 1969 as restrictions on the choice of minor do no longer exist.

Aspirants for the course must meet the regular university requirements and must pass a physical and practical entrance examination. The practical examination is both subjectively and objectively judged and includes:

For men:

I. Demonstration of general motor ability and strength:

| | |
|---|---|
| Jump and reach | 50 cm. |
| Sit-ups (15 sec.) | 12 ea. |
| 20 meter sprint (standing start) | 3.5 sec. |
| Trunk inclination forwards | 8 cm. |
| Locomotion hand over hand (20 sec.) | 4 meters |
| 1000 meter run | 3.4 min. |

II. Skills in tumbling, vaulting, stunts and apparatus of intermediate degree of difficulty.

III. Track and field:

| | | |
|---|---|---|
| 100 m. dash | 13.6 sec. | |
| 60 m. dash | 8.5 sec. | |
| High jump | 1.35 m. | OR |
| Long jump | 4.80 m. | |
| Shotput (7.25 kg.) | 7.75 m. | |

IV. Swimming:

| | |
|---|---|
| 100 m. | 2 min. |
| Dive of 3 m. board. | |

V. Sports:

Demonstration of adequate skills employed in the following sports; Soccer, Federation or Team Handball, Volleyball and Basketball.

For women:

I. Demonstration of general motor ability and strength:

| | |
|---|---|
| Jump and reach | 36 cm. |
| Sit-ups (15 sec.) | 10 ea. |
| 20 meter sprint (standing start) | 4.0 sec. |
| Trunk inclination forwards | 10 cm. |
| Climbing (3 m. pole) | 17 sec. |
| 800 m. run | 3.45.0 min. |

II. Skills in tumbling, free exercise, vaulting and apparatus of intermediate degree of difficulty.

III. Track and field:

| | | |
|---|---|---|
| 100 m. dash | 16.0 sec. | OR |
| 60 m. dash | 9.6 sec. | |
| High jump | 1.10 m. | OR |
| Long jump | 3.40 m. | |
| Shotput (4 kg.) | 6.25 m. | OR |
| Ball throw (80 g.) | 26.0 m. | |

IV. Swimming:

| | | |
|---|---|---|
| 100 m. | 65 sec. | OR |
| 100 m. | 2.20 min. | OR |
| 60 m. | 65 sec. | |
| Free dive from 3 m. board. | | |

V. Sports:

Demonstration of adequate skills employed in the following sports: Federation or Team Handball, Volleyball and Basketball.

VI. Rhythmic gymnastics:

Demonstration of various skills employed in rhythmic gymnastics.


Students who fail the entrance examination may attempt to qualify one more time at the beginning of the second semester. Those who have been conditionally admitted must have corrected their deficiencies by this time.

The course of study for the degree in physical education is regulated by the State Commission on Higher Learning and is uniform for all four campuses that offer a professional program in physical education (Vienna, Graz, Innsbruck and Salzburg).

COURSE OF STUDY FOR PHYSICAL EDUCATION*

A. Required courses:

I. Theoretical training:

| | Hours Per Week Per Semester | | | | | | | | |
|---|---|---|---|---|---|---|---|---|---|
| | I | II | III | IV | V | VI | VII | VIII | Total |
| Foundations of functional anatomy | 2 | 2 | | | | | | | 4 |
| Foundations of physiology of physical exercise (exercise physiology) | | | 2 | 2 | | | | | 4 |
| Hygiene of physical exercise | | | | | | 2 | | | 2 |
| Foundations of adapted physical education | | | | | | | 2 | | 2 |
| First aid | | | | | 2 | | | | 2 |
| History of physical education | 2 | | | | | | | | 2 |
| Methods of physical education | 2 | .2 | 2 | | | | | | 6 |
| Principles of physical education | | | | 2 | | | | | 2 |
| General movement theory of physical education | | | | | | 2 | | | 2 |
| Special theory of movement and methods for specific domains of exercise | 2 | 1 | | | | | | | 3 |
| Seminar in physical education | | | 2 | 3 | | | | | 5 |
| Seminar in biology of physical education | | | | | | 2 | | | 2 |
| Seminar in methods of physical education | | | | | | | 3 | | 3 |
| Seminar (pedagogy, history, theory of movement, etc.) | | | | | | | | 3 | 3 |
| Total hours | 6 | 6 | 7 | 7 | 6 | 5 | 5 | | 42 |

* Description of the courses has been translated as literally as possible as no course outlines are available.

II. Practical training:
(Men and women)

| | Hours Per Week Per Semester | | | | | | | | |
|---|---|---|---|---|---|---|---|---|---|
| | I | II | III | IV | V | VI | VII | VIII | Total |
| General basic training | 3/2 | | | | | | | | 3/2 |
| Free exercise and apparatus | 3/3 | | 3/2 | | 3/2 | | | | 9/7 |
| Gymnastics, modern dance, movement education | 0/2 | | 0/3 | | 0/2 | | | | 0/7 |
| Basketball | | | 2/3 | | 2/0 | | | | 4/3 |
| Team handball | | 2/2 | | | | | | | 2/2 |
| Soccer | | | | 2/0 | | | | | 2/0 |
| Volleyball (Fistball) | | | 3/0 | 0/2 | | | | | 3/2 |
| Swimming | | 3/3 | | 3/3 | | 2/2 | | | 8/8 |
| Track and field | | 3/3 | | 3/3 | | 2/2 | | | 8/8 |
| Ice skating | 2/2 | | | | | | | | 2/2 |
| Practicum methodology of exercises | | | | | | 3/3 | 3/3 | 3/3 | 3/3 | 12/12 |
| Continued exercises | | | | | | | 3/3 | | 3/3 |
| Total hours | 8/9 | 8/8 | 8/8 | 8/8 | 8/7 | 7/7 | 6/6 | 3/3 | 56/56 |

III. Special courses:
(each course counts as one semester week)

Skiing: Two ten-day ski courses (excluding travel time) one in the first and third semester each.

Hiking-Orienteering: One course of seven days (either at one time or any other combination).

Mountain Climbing: One ten-day course (excluding travel time).

B. Optional courses:

During the 5-8 semester students must attend a three semester hour course in an area of concentration. A choice may be made of the following areas:

Free exercise and apparatus
Modern dance and rhythmic gymnastics
Track and field
Swimming
Sport (team sports)

The final examination in the optional area of concentration may be taken at the earliest at the end of the fourth semester.

C. Recommended lectures and activities:
(These are subject to student interest and local opportunities)

Psychological bases of physical education
Sociological bases of physical education
Biomechanics for physical education
Tests and measurement
Construction of facilities
Administration of physical education

In order to obtain a teaching certificate the student must, after completion of his four years of university work, pass a theoretical and practical examination administered by the state. The thus qualified teacher ("professor") may obtain a Doctor of Philosophy degree after completion, acceptance, and defense of a thesis. This degree, however, does in no way compare to the American Ph.D. degree but more to an M.A. degree. To receive a degree comparable to the American doctoral degree much additional study and experience is required and it was not until very recently that physical education was accepted as an academic discipline in university study. Available data indicate that to this date only five physical educators in Austria have "habilitiert," that is, have been granted a degree that permits them to hold a professorial rank in the university.(*)

The Federal Training School for Coaches

The administration of sports rests, in general, not with the schools but in the hands of private clubs and associations. Although many physical educators are, in some way or other, involved with coaching, there is still a great need for personnel. In order to supply qualified personnel Austria instituted in 1946 a two-year course (with a total of 96 hours of instruction) leading to a national coaching certificate. With this diploma coaches may seek employment with private enterprise, clubs, and the government or open their own sport school. As this preparation emphasizes the practical aspects of coaching and has no affiliations with the academic program of the university, the entrance requirements are considerable lower. They include possession of a secondary school certificate and the passing of a medical and practical entrance examination. Although the school emphasizes the athletic ability of its applicants it should be noted that the Institute for Physical Education requires higher scores for identical athletic events.

The two-year study offers a wide variety of courses which deal with the practical aspects of organization, administration and teaching of sport skills. The students must acquire an overall ability in a wide range of activities, but they specialize in two branches of sport which they must master theoretically, practically, and methodically.

Although the original intent to supply qualified personnel for sport activities was very laudable, difficulties did arise in the sixties when many small villages had difficulties in securing physical education teachers. Consequently, there were many instances where with the motto: "Better some than none" coaches were engaged to fulfill the functions of the unavailable physical education teachers. Recent data indicate that the shortage of qualified physical education teachers does not longer exist and fears that the quest for quality academic preparation for physical education teachers had been a waste of effort and money have been laid to rest.

### Sport and the Universities

Although physical education is not required at the universities, facilities and staff are provided for the convenience of those who are athletically inclined. In the past the administration of this service was a function of the Institutes for Physical Education. At present, however, the "Universitäts Turninstitute" (University Sports Institutes) are independent units which are directly responsible to the board of curators. Responsible for all athletic activities that take place in the university, the institutes administer elective physical education programs as well as intramural and varsity sports. Compared to United States standards varsity sports are practically non-existent. As a result of the limited number of universities in Austria (4), and also as a result of the proximity of university campuses in other European countries, competition quite often acquires an international flavor. Participation in competitive athletics is a rather new concept for the European student which is gaining in popularity. Incomplete data available indicate that about 90% of the student body participates in scheduled activities while roughly 10% takes part in varsity athletics.

Present programs can hardly cope with the number of participants. Although Vienna and Innsbruck recently have acquired large, modern facilities, most university complexes still are insufficiently equipped and must rely on public and private facilities to run their programs. Aware of their responsibility to provide adequate opportunity for the maintenance of physical health and recreation, the universities, in conjunction with the Ministry of Education, have embarked on a building program to alleviate present conditions and to provide for the future.

Miscellanea

The organization of sport in Austria is, as in most countries, administered by independent clubs and associations. As discussed previously many of these clubs were extensions of political parties and although the trend is away from this type of association at the moment, there still remain some practices and attitudes in the sporting world that differ greatly with the American concepts of the unifying characteristics of sport.

The Ministry of Education has a special Department of Sport which involves itself with all matters pertaining to sport and recreation. Although it has regulating powers, the department occupies itself mostly with representing the interests of sport on the governmental level in orders to obtain financial support in the form of subsidies. These subsidies are passed on to communities for construction and maintenance of sport halls, swimming pools, stadiums and other facilities. Rather than keeping the administration of these facilities in its own hands, the Department of Sport entrusts this responsibility to the sports organization with the largest membership. Thus control of the sport center, which ought to serve the entire community, becomes a political issue. In large communities duplication of facilities is a natural result.

The discussion of the training of coaches has already indicated that there is a great shortage of experienced personnel. In order to alleviate this condition the Austrian government has created regional Federal Sport Schools. Although operated by the Department of Sport, organization is the entire responsibility of the various sport associations. Provided with choice practice facilities, dormitories, restaurants and lecture rooms these 'schools' are made available for coaching clinics, short courses and special intensive training of athletes who are preparing for national and international competition.

The limited possibility for students to participate in school organized competitive and recreational activities and the current dislike of youth to affiliate themselves with the politically oriented sports clubs have given impetus to a new sports movement in Austria. The initiative of Dr. Hermann Andrecs, Head of the Federal Department of Physical Education, resulted in the creation of the "Open Door Playground" movement. Its function might be compared to that of American recreation departments as it offers an opportunity for youth of all ages to participate in athletic activities without having to belong to a club or a team. The project is barely one year old but is already finding wide acceptance in various parts of Austria.

Dr. Andrecs, who is not only a man of ideas, but who knows how to make them practical experiences, was also instrumental in the creation of a national track event, the "Brückenlauf." Once a year there is an open competition in a running event over a course lying between two bridges spanning the famous Danube. The distance to be run and the maximum time limit to complete the required distance is determined by the participant's age and sex. Similar events are held in other parts of the country and in other branches of sport.

Cross-country skiing, which once was considered the birthright of the Scandinavians, has become popular in the lowlands and the foothills of Austria. Part of this is due to topographical conditions but factors such as the comparatively low cost of equipment and the savings on ski life fares have been important motives, too. As cross-country skiing is an excellent conditioner and easier to conduct than Alpine skiing, physical educators have been very enthusiastic in incorporating it into their program. It has also caught on among the older age groups; so much in fact that open cross-country races have already become a feature in theAustrian sports world.

In contrast with USA national educational policies the educational system of Austria is very strongly centralized. Laws and ordinances regulate educational procedures and supervisory personnel carries out implementation of official policies. The interests of physical education teachers are represented by a teachers' union. However, the general function of this organization is more concerned with the legal aspects that affect the status of the teacher. It is surprising that despite the interest in their profession and their creative abilities the physical education teachers have, as yet, not established a professional organization in the nature of the American national association. The subscription rate of the only professional journal, "Leibesübungen und Leiberserziehung," (Physical Training and Physical Education) is minimal as it is published by the Ministry of Education which bears the cost. The editorial board consists of members appointed by the Ministry (usually the department heads of the physical education institutes of the universities of Vienna, Graz, Innsbruck and Salzburg) and of representatives of the physical education teachers association.

SELECTED REFERENCES

1.     Andrecs, Hermann. "Fuenf Jahre Internationale Schulsport-Foederation (ISF)" in *Leibesübungen-Leibeserziehung.* (July 1977).

2.     Austrian Federal Press Service. *Austria, Facts and Figures.* Österreichische Staatsdruckerei. 1963.

3.     Bundesanstalt für Leibeserziehung. *Die Österreichischer Sportlehereraus bildung.* Vienna: BAfl. 1967.

4.     Bundesministerium für Unterricht. *Provisorische Lehrpläne für die Mittelschulen.* Vienna: Österreichischer Bundesverlag, 1946.

5.     Bundesministerium fuer Unterricht und Kunst. *Educational Careers in Austria.* Vienna: Sven DruckGesmbH. 1977.

6. _____. *Austria: Organization of Education in 1975-77.* Vienna: Druckkunst Wien B. Woiczik. 1977.

7. Burger, Ed. Wolfgang and Groll, Hans. *Leibeserziehung.* Vienna: Österreichischer Bundesverlag. 1959.

8. Council for the Cultural Cooperation of the Council of Europe. *Physical Education and Sport--A Handbook on Institutions and Associations.* Strasbourg: Berger-Levrault. 1964.

9. _____. *School Systems--A Guide.* Strasbourg: Berger-Levrault. 1965.

10. Gaulhofer, Karl. *System des Schulturnens.* Editor Hans Groll. Vienna: Österreichischer Bundesverlag. 1966.

11. _____. "Ubungslehre und Systemkunde des Schulturnens." Unpublished notes on his 1928-1929 lectures, compiled by Hedwig List and edited by Gaulhofer in 1940.

12. Gaulhofer, Karl and Streicher, Margarete. *Grundzuge des Österreichischen Schulturnens.* Vienna: Verlag fur Jugend und Volk. 1924.

13. _____. *Das Neue Schulturnen.* Weinheim: Verlag Julius Beltz. 1962.

14. _____. *Natürliches Turnen I & II.* Vienna: Verlag für Jugend und Volk. 1949.

15. Groll, Hans. *Idee und Gestalt der Leiberserziehung von Heute, I.* Vienna: Österreichischer Bundesverlag. 1952.

16. _____. "Der Schilauf an den Schulen Österreichs," in *Leibesübungen und Leibeserziehung.* (February 1965), pp. 3-6.

17. _____. "Die Leibeserziehung im Neuen Österreich," in *Leibesübungen und Leibeserziehung.* (December 1946), pp. 1-4.

18. _____. *Die Systematiker der Leibesübungen.* Vienna: Österreichischer Bundesverlag. 1959.

19. _____. "Vom 'Turnlehererausbildungskurs' zum 'Institut für Leibeserziehung der Universität'," in *Leibesubungen und Leibeserziehung.* (April 1956), pp. 1-3.

20. _____. "Wo steht das Österreichische Schulturnen Heute? Ist das Naturliche Turnen noch Zeitgemass?," in *Leibesübungen und Leibeserziehung.* (September 1962), pp. 1-5.

21. Groll, Hans and Tschene, Friedrich. *Idee and Gestalt der Leibeserziehung von Heute, II.* Vienna: Österreichischer Bundesverlag. 1961.

22. Institut fuer Leibeserziehung der Universitaeten Öesterreichs. *Studium der Leibeserziehung - Studienplan.* (Date & publisher unknown; probably late 70's).

23. Institut für Leibeserziehung der Universität Wien. *Studienplan und Prüfungsordnung.* Vienna: ILUW. 1967.

24. _____. *Eignungspruefung fuer das Studium zum Leibeserzieher an Hoeheren Schulen am Institut fuer Leibeserziehung der Universitaet Wien.* Vienna: Institut fuer Leibeserziehung. 1977.

25. Jahn, Rudolf, Editor. *Zur Weltgesehichte der Leibesübungen.* Frankfurt: Wilhelm Limpert Verlag. 1960.

26. Moolenijzer, Nicolaas J. "Implications of the Philosophy of Gaulhofer and Streicher for Physical Education." Unpublished Master's Thesis, University of California at Los Angeles. 1956.

27. _____. "The Concept of 'Natural' in Physical Education; Johann Guts Muths--Margerete Streicher." Unpublished Ph.D. dissertation, University of Southern California. 1965.

28. _____. "Playground of the Open Door," in *International Relations Council Newsletter.* (Winter 1968), pp. 9-10.

29. Parker, Beryl. *The Austrian Educational Institutes.* Vienna: Austrian Federal Publisher for Education, Science and Art. 1931.

30. Prossnig, Hans. "Die Organisation des Universitats-sports," in *Leibesübungen und Leibeserziehung.* (April 1965), pp. 2-7.

31. Slama, Adalbert. *Neudeutsches Turnen.* Vienna: Pichlers Witwe. 1923.

32. Streicher, Margarete. *Zur Gestaltung des Madchen und Frauenturnens.* Vienna: Deutscher Verlag fur Jugend und Volk. 1931.

33. _____. "Das Schulturnen," in *Handbuch der Pädagogik.* Langensalza: Verlag Julius Beltz. 1929, pp. 173-190.

34. _____. *Natürliches Turnen III.* Vienna: Verlag für Jugend und Volk. 1950.

35.    _____. *Natürliches Turnen IV*. Vienna:  Verlag für Jugend und Volk.  1956.

36.    _____. *Natürliches Turnen V*. Vienna:  Verlag für Jugend und Volk.  1959.

37.    Strohmeyer, Johannes.  "Untersuchungen zur Entwicklung der Leibesübungen an den Schulen Wiens im 19. Jahrhundert bis sum Beginn des Ersten Weltkrieges."  Unpublished dissertation, University of Vienna.  1959.

# SPORT AND PHYSICAL EDUCATION IN BAHRAIN

by Robert W. Grueninger

## Biographical Sketch

*Robert W. Grueninger* was born in Cleveland, Ohio in 1939, the son of a physical educator. He received his B.S. degree in physical education from Springfield College in 1962 and his M.S. from the University of Illinois in 1963 as an advisee of Dr. T. K. Cureton. He has been overseas a number of times; in 1958 to Western European countries, in 1962 to the United Arab Republic as a participant in the Crossroads Africa summer program, and during the period of 1963-65 in Laos, where he spent two years working with the Ministry of Sports and Youth as a U.S. State Department grantee.

He taught and coached at Frostburg State College in Maryland for two years before moving to the University of Oregon to study under Dr. H. Harrison Clarke. He finished his Ph.D. degree in 1970 and taught at Oberlin College and the University of Wisconsin-Kenosha before accepting the position as Director of the United States Sports Academy (University of South Alabama) program in Bahrain.

Oil, the black gold responsible for the Gulf's being hurled into its present era of frantic development, was first discovered in
1931 in Bahrain. The goal on the island since then, as in the rest
of the Arabian Gulf, has been to create a diversified economy based
on refineries, petrochemicals, and natural gas production. Income
from oil and related materials have enabled the construction of huge
dry docks for giant tankers, new airports with air cargo facilities,
advanced highways, and modern telecommunications systems. Construction is taking place everywhere one looks--houses, multistoried
office buildings, apartments, hotels, hospitals, and banks. In fact,
the development of international, off-shore banking has made the re-
gion--particularly Bahrain--one of growing world significance. For
example, Pan American Airways now boasts the longest possible flight
without refueling, non-stop from New York to Bahrain, which incidentally is a good place to refuel.

## Background and Location

The State of Bahrain comprises an archipelago of thirty-three
small islands in a shallow, protected bay between Ras Tanura in
Saudi Arabia and Qatar. The only island state in the Arab world,
Bahrain has a total area of six hundred square kilometers (255 square
miles). The largest of the six major islands now is linked by cause-
ways to two of the others. Extensive dredging and land reclamma-
tion are underway to extend available land areas for housing construction without interfering with agricultural production.

The population of 260,000 is eighty per cent Arab and is centered in the northern half of Bahrain and Muharraq Islands. There
are many freshwater springs, for which the islands have been famous
from pre-biblical times. Traders have stopped here for centuries to
refill their ships' casks. Three to five thousand years ago, the people of the land called Dilmun were consequently traders of great
wealth and power. According to Babylonian legend, Dilmun was the
location of the Garden of Eden, and--if this were not enough--the
place where writing originated.

The climate is hot and humid during much of the year. May
through October temperatures average $32^{\circ}$ C, and humidity reaches
ninety per cent. During the winter months, a cold northern wind,
"shamaal", makes even Westerners don their jackets. Bahraini men
teaching in unheated school buildings during this time of year wear
wool socks and long johns underneath their customary but heavier,
winter "thobes". Rainshowers occur from November through March,
but are not as common as dust storms.

The language of the Gulf is Arabic. English is spoken widely
in Bahrain and in much of the lower Gulf states, since Great Britain
ruled this area under accord with the Shah of Iran until 1971. English also is necessary for communication with the preponderance of
Indian and Pakistani clerks, waiters, mechanics, and laborers.

## Commerce and Industry

Pearl diving is Bahrain's oldest industry, dating back to 2,000 B.C. when Pliny wrote that the island was "famous for the vast number of pearls." At one time thousands of pearling boats were in the Bahrain fleet, and merchants from East to West met to deal in the world's best pearls. Diving methods are the same now as then, prohibiting use of any apparatus. In either event, the pearl industry found forty years ago that it could not compete with the Japanese cultured variety.

Pottery, however, still is made locally. West coast villagers are known for their weaving. Limestone and other building materials such as gypsum, concrete block, and cement are significant indigenous products. Fishing is a considerable industry, especially for Gulf prawns, and traditional boat building is practiced to this day.

By 1935 there were sixteen producing oil wells in Bahrain. Now their supply nearly is exhausted. A larger quantity of natural gas exists to furnish industrial power, and Bahrain consequently has one of the largest petroleum refineries in the Middle East. The refinery in 1975 was processing 215,500 barrels daily, receiving 154,380 of crude from Saudi Arabia and 61 from the Bahrain field. Aluminum refining is the largest new industry, producing 120,000 tons per year from Australian alumina. An extensive port has been constructed for trading, making Bahrain a significant shiping center for the Gulf.

## Education

In the world of Islam, the first schools were in homes or mosques where mixed groups of boys and girls gathered to read an recite from the Holy Koran. Parents paid nominal fees for this instruction, and hearing that a child had read the entire Koran was an event worthy of celebration.

As education expanded in other Arab countries and as the wealth from the pearl industry produced an upper class, tutors were hired to teach reading, writing, and arithmetic to sons and daughters of the wealthy. From the opening of Koranic schools in 630 A.D., those two types were the only education available in Bahrain until the first public school opened in 1919. Teachers then were recruited from Syria, Lebanaon, Kuwait, Iraq, and Saudi Arabia and a curriculum was established that reflected these diverse nationalities. Since that time there has been a constant stream of progress in education. The first girls' school opened in 1928 and the first secondary school for boys in 1940.

Education is free, from tuition to textbooks, pencils and paper. The system is non-comuulsory, although well over the majority of school-aged children are in attendance. The present education system is as follows:

6 years primary school, ages 6 to 12 years

2 years intermediate school, ages 12-14 years

3 years secondary school, ages 14-17 years.

Advancement is predicated upon successful completion of examinations. Therefore there are many boys 18 and 19 years old who are still in secondary school; there are an equal number who start school late and are behind their age level.

The curriculum is largely British, with more emphasis on rote, recitation, formal instruction, and examination than in the United States. School is held for nine months of the year, October through May, six days per week except Friday, from 7:30 to 12:30 in the morning. The annual expenditure for education is approximately $100 million, on a school enrollment of 65 thousand with some three thousand teachers.

The Ministry of Education has been reorganized into seven equal departments: (1) Administration and Finance; (2) General Education; (3) Higher Education; (4) Technical and Vocational Education; (5) Planning; (6) Examination and Adult Education; and (7) Physical Education and Scouting. Many of the reforms are done through committees. For example, a committee to study and redesign curricula for various subjects has been formed of members from each area.

## Higher Education

There is no four-year institution of higher education in Bahrain. Gulf Technical College began in 1968 as a joint effort between Bahrain, Abu Dhabi, and the United Kingdom to provide advanced technical and commercial education to students from all the Gulf. The campus occupies a fifty acre site near Isatown. Majors offered include two-year courses in business and public administration. There is also a two-year College of Health Sciences that trains nurses and paramedics.

The Teachers' Training College was established in Bahrain in 1966 when the Amir donated the Old Palace for that purpose. Emphasis is on preparation of secondary school teachers, although some aspects of the curriculum are directed to those who will teach in primary or intermediate schools. There are separate sections and facilities for men and women, the latter enjoying the worst of the two. This year, however, a new campus will open and men and women not only will be using the same facilities, but also will have some coeducational classes. The new location near Gulf Tech will see a sharing of facilities between the two institutions, as well.

Admission to the Teachers' College is based on possession of a secondary school certificate, a health examination, Bahraini citizenship, and evidence of promise as indicated by interview. Normally students are between the ages of 17 and 22 years. Enrollment is 100 boys and 320 girls. There are 42 faculty, of whom 30 are men and 12 women.

The curriculum was adapted from Jordan and has changed little since the college was founded over ten years ago. The course of study is two years in length. The general student load is sixteen semester hours, distributed among three sections: general, professional, and special. General studies are the equivalent of all-college requirements and include Arabic and Islamic Culture, Arab Society, Community Development, English, mathematics, science, physical education, and arts and crafts. Professional studies cover the major aspects of the teacher training, our so-called education courses, e.g., Introduction to Education, child development and psychology, class organization and management, and practice teaching. The practice teaching is conducted in government schools and lasts five to six weeks.

Beginning in the second semester, a student at the Teachers Training College chooses a specialty (major) from among the following: Arabic and Islamic Culture, English, Social Studies, Physical Education and Health, Arts and Crafts, or Science and Mathematics. These areas of concentration are selected on the basis of student interest and abilities plus available space.

Recreation and Sports

The horse formerly was essential to Arabic life style and was equally important for transportation and war. Travel on camel always has been preferred for long distances because of its ability to go for long spells without water, but the horse was much better for the quick, agile moves required of a mount during battle.

The Amir of Bahrain, Shaikh Esa bin Salman AlKhalifa, possesses a fine stable of pure desert horses and prides himself on maintaining a strain famed for centuries. The most valued Arabians to be found today in Britain, America, or Poland are descended from Bahrain stock. The typical horse of this lineage is a compact fifteen hands high, with deep girth, excellent legs and magnificent line. Colors prevalent are dark bays with black points, dapple grays, and chestnuts. The riding style still preferred is bareback, although English style is taught at several stables.

Horse racing is popular. The races are held on the Moslem holiday, Friday, during most weeks of the cooler season. They are announced by posting flags around the course on the days races are to be held. About 3 o'clock in the afternoon, motorists will pull over to the side of the road to watch some of the finest, most spirited horses ridden by excellent Pakistani and Arab horsemen. Occasionally, to honor a guest, camel races will be held following the last horse race.

Also popular since ancient times as a sport of the wealthy is hunting with falcons. The birds are highly prized, personal possessions of great expense. The falcon is carried on the forearm of its keeper. A cord is fastened to one of the bird's legs, capable of being released quickly when prey is sighted. The victims often are smaller birds, called bustards, and small ground animals.

Folk dancing is found at festivals and is executed with gusto and skill, to rhythmic drumming and clashing of cymbals.

The desert climate is favorable to outdoor sports during the entire year, although locals feel that the winter months are too cool for swimming. It is over in November as far as aquatic sports are concerned, even though temperatures are still 60 to 80 degrees Fahrenheit. Swimming pools then are drained until April or May.

Bahrain has several large, sandy beaches, the best being on the West Coast of the main island. Inshore the water is very shallow, tapering gradually toward the Saudi coastline 25 kms. distant. There are few sharks or sea snakes. The water is clear, yet the Gulf is one of the world's saltiest seas.

Fishing is a popular leisure time activity. Usually a line and hook are used without a pole, whether from causeway or boat. Fish caught in the waters include the delicious Hamoor, Hagool, Zbaidi, various types of rays and sharks, Chanaad, Queen Fish, Sils, and Barracuda.

The most popular team sport in Bahrain, as in most parts of the world, is soccer, the "real football." There are well over four thousand players and 36 clubs registered with the Bahrain Football Association. Matches are played every afternoon, somewhere, on dirt fields found in or near virtually every community--often with little more than palm tree stumps as goals.

There are a couple of decent soccer fields, however. The Isatown Stadium, completed in 1969, has seating for several thousand and a very nice grass pitch. Recently a Chevron 440 track was laid there, making that the National Training Center and the finest facility in the country. Nearby is a beautiful 50 meter, six-lane swimming pool.

The sports ranking below football in popular appeal are volleyball, basketball, table tennis, and team handball. Combative sports would be non-existent were it not for Tae-Kwon-Do and judo being practiced at the defense force training camp.

There are two golf courses, one owned by the Bahrain Petroleum Company for its employees, and the other started by Bahraini who learned the game as caddies on the oil company's course and who have come to surpass their teachers' skills. Although greens fees may be charged, there are really no greens; browns would be a more fitting description, since the smooth areas surrounding the holes are oiled-down sand. Teeing off is from concrete bunkers, and if grass is desired, the best way is to carry a small patch of astroturf.

## Physical Education

Physical education is a required subject from elementary through high school. Classes meet three times per week during the first and second years of primary school. The third and fourth years meetings are reduced to two hours per week, and then to one hour per week the fifth and sixth years. At the intermediate level, classes in physical education are held twice weekly, and this is also true for secondary school.

There are 115 school days per year. In April attendance becomes less and less regular as boys and girls start skipping in order to study for their all-important annual exams, in May. Say goodbye to organized physical education and sports during this period.

Teachers are not well-trained, although nearly all have a high school diploma. The majority have completed at least two years at the Teachers' Training College. Several have studied abroad, either in Egypt or Iraq. An insufficient number of qualified physical education teachers has led to the importation of specialists from the Arab Republic of Egypt and from Jordan. Four of the women inspectors of physical education are Egyptian, the one exception being the wife of the Director of Physical Education. The majority of male inspectors are also Egyptian, graduates either of the High Institute of Physical Education at Giza, the University of Helwan, or the High Institute of Physical Education at Alexandria. Several of the men are paid through the Embassy of Saudi Arabia as part of the latter's foreign aid program.

The influence on the curriculum is strongly Egyptian and British. Therefore one sees a simulation of educational gymnastics and a preference for the indirect methods. A typical class as explained by Maher Marzouk, Physical Education Advisor, consists of the following:

| 10 min. | Skill | Explanation, demonstration of a new skill by the teacher while the children sit and listen |
| 20 min. | Rotations | Each of the following activities by squad rotation method, every 5 minutes: basketball<br>volleyball<br>handball<br>football and new skill |

The curriculum committe recommended that the intermediate school program be changed to include 10 minutes of calisthenics followed by 20 minutes of games, the remainder of the time consumed by opening and closing formalities. The change, however, was delayed from taking effect because of a conflict of opinion with the views of the physical education director. A compromise was presented when the U.S. Sports Academy submitted a Curriculum Manual and taught the same during a teachers' workshop in the fall of 1977. This manual is now being used as a reference for intermediate and secondary school programs and has some additional guidelines for primary school physical education. Contents include instructions in games leadership, lead-up activities, skills, drills, and tactics for both individual and team sports.

New this year is an interscholastic sports program, with nine schools fielding teams in the following:

Fall:    football, volleyball

Winter:   basketball, cross country

Spring:  team handball, athletics.

In addition, the Ministry of Education will sponsor and conduct interscholastic tournaments in table tennis, swimming, gymnastics, and tennis. Initial response to this innovation has been favorable. Although it is too early to predict the eventual effects the club and school sports programs will have on each other, it is hoped that they will be complimentary rather than competitive.

School physical education facilities vary from dirt and sand fields to smooth asphalt play areas with markings and goals for basketball, football, team handball, and volleyball. Rarely does one find a tennis court at a school, and there are not very many in the entire country. Running tracks exist only at the Bahrain Defense Force Training Camp and at the new Isatown Stadium. Indoor facilities comparable to a U.S. elementary school gymnasium may be found in all of the newer schools, i.e., those constructed during the last decade. None of these have permanent sports fixtures such as basketball backboards, climbing ropes, or stall bars.

Teachers Training College

Required Physical Education. Every student takes physical education for four semesters. Credit is given for classroom work on a par with laboratory credit in other subjects; in other words, two thirty-minute class periods per week are awarded one-half credit hour per semester. Additionally, students are required to practice two team sports and one dual sport while at the college.

The aims of physical education in the required program are as follows:

1. To provide a general knowledge of physical education, including:

   a. its relationship to other subjects;
   b. its development from past to present, especially in the Arab world, and
   c. its significance and modern applications.

2. To acquaint students with folk dance and games in Bahrain, the Arab world, and foreign lands.

3. To help students develop strength, endurance, and courage.

4. To teach personal hygiene.

5. To prepare students for roles of leadership and responsibility.

Required classes in physical education cover the following:

Theory

   Semester I

   1. Nature of physical education
   2. Aims of physical education
   3. Physical education related to other subjects
   4. History of physical education
   5. Folklore and dance

   Semester II

   1. Health education - aims
   2. Relationship between health and physical education
   3. Playground safety
   4. First Aid
   5. History and characteristics of games selected for practice.

Semester III

1. Leadership in physical education
2. Qualities required of an organizer of physical education
3. Rules of games chosen

Semester IV

1. Organization of games and matches
2. Scientific research into games chosen

Games chosen, as mentioned above, refers to the fact that each student must choose two team sports from among basketball, volleyball, team handball, or football, and one dual sport, either tennis or badminton.

Professional Preparation. Enrollment in the physical education section is small. At present there are only eleven girls and six boys concentrating in physical education. The physical education faculty, all of whom were educated in Egypt, numbers two men and four women.

The two-year physical education curriculum is less than a minor in the subject, and leaves considerable gaps in training. Subject matter covered to some extent in the curriculum includes history of physical education, methodology, first aid, anatomy and physiology, health, exercise leadership, and massage. There is little skill practice for majors aside from the general required class. Tests and measurements are neglected and graduates are ignorant of basic procedures for grading and interpreting test percentiles. Beyond basic anatomy and physiology, students receive only a modicum of kinesiology, exercise physiology, or care and prevention of athletic injuries. A basic thrust in future professional preparation will be to improve instruction in the scientific areas, eventually building toward a four-year program.

Physical education has been neglected for awards of scholarships to study abroad, as has music and the fine arts. Not more than four young women and men per year travel to Egypt or to the University of Baghdad to study physical education. The attitude of the Ministry of Education toward physical education, however, is strongly supportive, so improvement is expected.

Physical Fitness

In January 1977, the U.S. Sports Academy and the Supreme Council for Youth and Sports began a physical fitness program through the Ministry of Education. The objectives of this program were as follows:

1. To identify the physical fitness of Bahraini youth, and in turn

2. To counsel each boy and girl to improve physical fitness through specific suggestions that may be carried out on his or her own or through either a school or club program.

3. To select gifted individuals and guide them into those sports for which they appear to be best suited.

4. To motivate youth through a system of incentives and competition to strive for physical fitness improvement.

By the end of April, well over four thousand boys ages eight through 19 years had been tested in the several events of the International Physical Fitness Test.

In the 50 meter dash, performances were average in comparison to Indonesian youngsters tested by Rosandich in 1962 and poor in relation Japanese boys as reported by Hirata, 1972. Japanese boys are also stronger in grip at every age.

The greatest weakness of Bahraini boys was of the arms and shoulders. As many as 45 per cent in any given age group could not do even one pull-up. There are insufficient opportunities in physical education classes and in daily living to provide for improvement in upper body strength and endurance. As a result, the Ministry of Education through the U.S.S.A.-Bahrain Sports Program has begun to install playground equipment at a number of primary, intermediate, and secondary schools. Also, exercises to improve scores in this test item were pointed out at a recent in-service training workshop for physical education teachers.

In the thirty-second sit-up test of abdominal endurance, the boys did extremely well. Perhaps this was due to their linear body type and low fat content, since thin poeple have been shown to perform better in this type of test. Another reason may be the popularity of football, which requires trunk muscle strength and flexibility.

The sit and reach test showed that the average boy at any age can touch his toes with his knees extended, indicating passable flexibility of the hamstring and low back musculature.

Results of the one-kilometer run test indicated a great need for endurance activities in the schools, particularly running or similar continuous, rhythmic exercises.

Some explanation for the poorer physical fitness test performances overall of Bahraini boys is revealed by plotting height, weight, and age data on the Wetzel Grid. Bahraini boys are shorter and leaner than Japanese boys at every age through 11 years, and then show remarkably similar physique except that the Japanese boys are one year advanced in growth and maturation. Improved physical education and sports programs together with improved hygiene and nutrition would be expected to exert appreciable improvement on child growth and development and thenceforth on physical fitness.

It became obvious during the testing that some of these boys were performing skills such as standing long jump, shuttle run, and pull-ups for the first time. They showed a lack of familiarity, furthermore, with pacing in the one-thousand meter run and with the idea of running through the finish line of the fifty meter sprint. Continual coaching and much re-testing was necessary to obtain valid scores.

As the boys become familiar with the test and after the results are more publicized, hopefully they will be motivated to improve their personal fitness. Based on the test norms constructed at the conclusion of phase I physical fitness testing, awards are being given this year to boys who achieve above the 75th. percentile on all five tests. The award consists of an attractive brassard that can be sewn onto a jacket or pennant.

A testing team is now gathering data on the physical fitness of Bahraini girls. Until recently, girls have been denied access to many sports opportunities. Often the best equipment available goes unused because the women teachers lack training in gymnastics and elementary school programs. At the same time, women at other schools are having young girls practice forward rolls on asphalt.

## The Outlook

The future looks bright for Bahrain, but not without difficulties. Whereas a generation ago there were no vehicles other than donkey carts, today Bahrain's roads are choked with automobiles, trucks, and motorbikes. Camels have taken refuge on the West side of the island, and people retire to their airconditioned homes to watch "Bionic Man" on television. The sedentary mode of living is reminiscent of the U.S. a decade ago, with heart disease and traffic accidents being the major health programs and little being done to remedy either situation. Bahrain's leading cause of death in 1975 was disease of the circulatory system, responsible for fully one-third of the total.

Oil may be running out in Bahrain, but money is not. Wealthier neighbors to the north and south and the closeness to Saudi Arabia

---

Further information on physical fitness in Bahrain may be obtained from the Physical Fitness Test Manual or from the Journal of the First Middle-East Sport Science Symposium, both of which are available from the U.S. Sports Academy, University of South Alabama, Mobile, Al. 36688.

portend well for the people's prosperity, even if it may be a threat to their hitherto uniqueness. Rapid construction of the dry dock and dredging have disrupted some freshwater springs beneath the ocean's floor and deprived the island of some of its century-famous sweet water. But while palm trees die in one part of the island due to such an error, thousands of trees are to be imported from Australia to make the South a park and game refuge. Dredging and highway development forge ahead with plans to build an $800 million causeway linking Bahrain with El Saudia across 25 kms. of the Gulf. Estimated traffic over the causeway in 1983 is more than 8,000 cars daily.

Another gift from Saudi Arabia is a $40 million sports city to be completed in 1890, including:

covered stadium seating 30,000

swim hall with 50 meter pool, 25 m. training pool, and separate pools for diving

sportshall seating 3,000, with 3 volleyball, 1 field hockey, 1 handball, and 1 basketball court

rooms for athletic training and sport medicare, gymastics, weight training, and squash

restaurant

tennis courts

four story administration building for the Supreme Council for Youth and Sports

living accommodations for 200 athletes and coaches.

Thus, improved facilities, increased sports exchanges, better care of athletes, research, and instruction in sports education through such organizations as the U.S. Sports Academy are the future transpiring for the State of Bahrain.

SELECTED REFERENCES

Belgrave, James. *Welcome to Bahrain.* Ninth edition. Bahrain: Augusta Press. 1975.

Curtis, Jerry L. *Bahrain: Language, Customs, and People.* Singaport: Tien Wah Press, 1977.

Hirata, Kin-itsu and Tetsuo Meshizuka. "Japanese Standard Physique and Physical Fitness and the Synthetic Evaluating Chart." Unpublished manuscript from the authors. 1976.

Hitti, Philip H. *History of the Arabs.* Tenth edition. London: Macmillan and Company. 1970.

Mehri, Hassan. Director of General Education.

Ministry of Information, State of Bahrain.

Rosandich, Thomas P. *Indonesian Physical Fitness Test Manual.* Djakarta: Published by the author. 1963.

Statistics Directorate, Bahrain. *1975 Statistical Abstract.* Ministry of Finance.

# SPORT AND PHYSICAL EDUCATION IN BRAZIL

by Maurette Augusto

## Biographical Sketch

*Maurette Augusto* was born at Juiz de Fora, Minas Gerais, Brazil. At seven she decided to be a teacher, and at eighteen received her Teacher's Diploma and started to work with feminine adolescents.

Her passion for physical activities inspired all her childhood and youth and in 1949 she received a government scholarship to attend the Escola Nacional de Educação Física e Desportos - Universidade do Brasil - Rio de Janeiro.

Graduating in 1952, she presented herself to a public contest for experts in Physical Education and Recreation in Rio de Janeiro and got her indication to the position.

In 1955 she was appointed as an assistant teacher of Methodology in Physical Education and Sports Training at the Escola Nacional de Educação Física e Desportos; she worked for Larousse Encyclopedia (Brazilian Edition) in 1956, translating Physical Education subjects to Portuguese. She then presented herself as a candidate to that same Chair with a thesis about Modern Feminine Gymnastics in 1958; and in 1960 finally became titular of that Cathedra, with another thesis: "Play - The Hedonistic Theory".

Miss Augusto has been giving all of her efforts to the cause of Physical Education and Recreation in Brazil. She was recommended to be the author of this article on Physical Education and Sports in Brazil by her colleague, Professor Fernanda Beltrão who was a former student of Dr. Dorothy Ainsworth.

Since 1972 Miss Augusto has been in charge of the Department of Educational Sociology at the Faculdade de Educação - Unidersidade Federal do Rio de Janeiro. Presently she also works at the Secretaria Municipal de Educação do Rio de Janeiro - Assessoria de Educação Física - under the direction of Professor Jorge Steinhilber.

# Introduction - General Background

Brazil is a favored country. Its tropical climate makes it possible to practice physical activities during the entire year. Thus, from January to December, people can be out in the open enjoying all the benefits of Nature: the warm shining sun, the pure fresh air, the blue sky, the sea water and the beautiful beaches, or the transparent water of falls and natural pools. The call of the mysterious forest and of the verdant mountains, or that of the fragrant flowered fields, carries one on delightful excursions. As one of Brazil's most celebrated poets once said:

"O, what a peace in nests above!

Nature, here, is a constant feast,

A Mother's breast with overflowing love".

Besides, Brazilians, thanks to their racial heritage, are naturally inclined to intense and varied physical activities. Preferences, as those of Latin peoples in general, are for sports rather than for gymnastics. According to popularity, the order of sports in Brazil is:

| | | |
|---|---|---|
| Soccer | Volleyball | Wrestling |
| Swimming | Track and field | Alpinism |
| Basketball | Tennis | Camping |
| Judo | Handball | Archery |

Some attention, finally, is given to all kinds of gymnastics, stunts and tumbling, and to games and dances.

## Hydrography

Brazil has 8,511,400 square kilometers of area, being placed in the Eastern part of South America, between Parallels 6 degrees North and 34 degrees South and between Meridians 33 degrees West and 75 degrees Greenwich Time.

Its territory is divided in three great hydrographic basins: up to the North, the Amazonas River basin measuring 5,500,000 square kilometers - the biggest river in the world both in length and in water volume. This basin is limted on the North by the Parimá Chain which borders the three Guyanas and with Venezuela.

On the South is found the second important basin, formed by the rivers Paraguai-Paraná, and between the first and second basis is found the Mato Grosso Central Plateau, another ridge of mountains. The third big hydrographic basin is the S. Francisco River which is called "the river of national integration", because its 3,161 kilometers are all in Brazil and link five states. Presently the Sobradinho Dam,

built at the second third of S. Francisco River, is the second bigger
artificial lake in the world.

The Amazonas River originates in Peru. It is navigable in its
whole extension by big keeled ships, except near its sources. It has
inumerable affluents from both shores, many of them 2,000 to 3,000
kilometers long. The Paraguai-Paraná basin springs in Brazilian territory and here being formed, is the natural border with Paraguai
and Argentina, receiving the name of the Prata River in the last
named country.

The S. Francisco River provides electric energy for all of the
Brazilian Northeast Region and is navigable in its whole length, except in the part of Paulo Afonso Falls. Other less important basins
in the Brazilian territory are the Parnaíba, the Doce and the Uruguai
basins.

Orography

Brazil's orographic system is formed by a chain of mountains
in the Atlantic Coast - the Serra do Mar - and by the Central System which divided itself into three branches: the Western, the Amazonas Basin, and the Eastern branch. The heights are not remarkable, the highest summit being 3,000 meters, the Pico da Neblina
mountains in the Paracaima chain; it is the branch of the Andes and
borders Venezuela.

In the center of Brazil lies the Central Plateau, with 600
meters high mountains, which contribute to the milder climate in the
region where temperatures show an annual average of twenty degrees
Centigrade. Here is found the second highest summit of Brazil - the
Pico da Bandeira--2,900 meters high. To the extreme South, as well
as to the Northeastern Region, can be found small elevations, namely,
the Coxilhas range in the South, and the Gerais chain in the Northeast.

Climate

Brazil has all the climates of the Earth, because of its being
in both the Tropical and Temperate zones:

1 - Equatorial climate - warm and humid with annual precipitation up to 2,000 millimeters. The average temperature is around
25 degrees Centigrade during the year, including the States of Amazonas, Acre, Pará and Mato Grosso do Norte; and the Territories of
Roraima, Rondonia and Amapá.

2 - Equatorial half-arid climate - found in the Northeastern
Region, which includes the States of Maranhão, Piauí, Ceará, Rio
Grande do Norte, Paraíba, Pernambuco, Alagoas, Sergipe and Bahia.
Annual precipitation about 600 mm poorly distributed.

3 - Tropical climate - with annual precipitation of 1,200 to 2,000 millimeters. Average temperature: 20 to 25 degrees Centigrade in both Central/Southeastern Regions. The medial temperature is lower in the heights of the Central Plateau. The Central Region and Southeastern Region include the States of Minas Gerais, Espírito Santo, Rio de Janeiro and S. Paulo; the Federal District, with Brasília, belongs to this same Region; the States of Mato Grosso do Sul and Goiás complete the Tropical Climate Region.

4 - Temperate Climate - with annual precipitation of 1,000 to 1,200 millimeters. Annual average temperatures under 20 degrees Centigrade with snowfalls occurring in the mountainous parts of the South. Well distributed rain is also found in this location. The States of Paraná, Santa Catarina and Rio Grande do Sul constitute this Region.

Political Division

Brazil is divided into 23 States, four Territories and one Federal District; Brasília, the Capital, is located at the Federal District. It is a very modern city, especially built sixteen years ago to be Brazil's Capital. Presently living in Brasília are 600,000 people. The largest State is Amazonas, with its 1,200,000 square kilometers, and the smallest is Sergipe, with 29,000 square kilometers. The largest city is S. Paulo, with 9,000,000 people; the most beautiful is Rio de Janeiro. It is known worldwide because of its natural beauties. (Table A).

Economical Items

1. Population - Brazil now has 110 million people according to the last inter-census estimation of the Instituto Brasileiro de Geografia e Estatística. All human races are represented as the country does not have racial discrimination. The three races (White, Black and Mongolian) mix and the result is a great number of half-breed individuals. Proportionally, Whites are 65%; Half-breeds are 18%; Negroes, 15%; and the Mongolians some two per cent.

The White race is represented by Portuguese descendants and by other European immigrants (Italian, German, Spanish, Slavic and Arabian). Negroes are descendants of ancient slaves originally from Angola and from the Ivory Coast in Africa.

In the ancient regions where the sugar cane was cultivated, during the Colonial and Imperial periods, concentrate the Negroes and Half-breeds, mainly in the coast of Bahia and Rio de Janeiro. To the interland, there is a predominance of Whites and, as the Negroes are few, the White mix with the Indians, especially in the States of the Northern and Central Regions.

Table A.

Division of Brazil into Five Geo-Economic Regions.

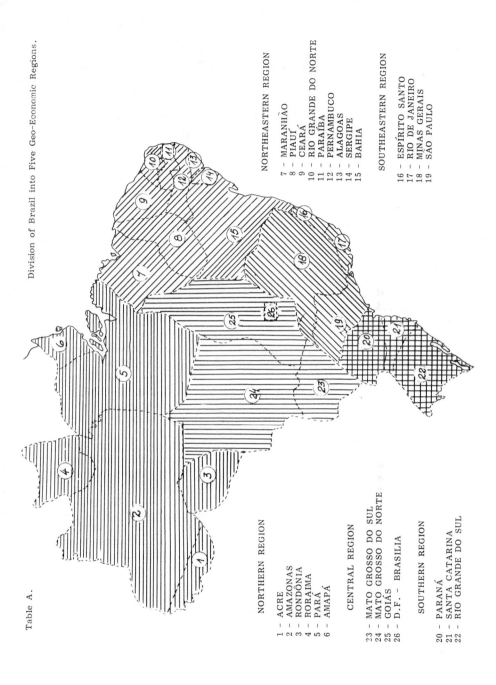

NORTHEASTERN REGION

7 – MARANHÃO
8 – PIAUÍ
9 – CEARÁ
10 – RIO GRANDE DO NORTE
11 – PARAÍBA
12 – PERNAMBUCO
13 – ALAGOAS
14 – SERGIPE
15 – BAHIA

SOUTHEASTERN REGION

16 – ESPÍRITO SANTO
17 – RIO DE JANEIRO
18 – MINAS GERAIS
19 – SÃO PAULO

NORTHERN REGION

1 – ACRE
2 – AMAZONAS
3 – RONDÔNIA
4 – RORAIMA
5 – PARÁ
6 – AMAPÁ

CENTRAL REGION

23 – MATO GROSSO DO SUL
24 – MATO GROSSO DO NORTE
25 – GOIÁS
26 – D.F. – BRASILIA

SOUTHERN REGION

20 – PARANÁ
21 – SANTA CATARINA
22 – RIO GRANDE DO SUL

Completing the racial composition of the population, the Mongolians, represented by the Indigenous people with only 100,000 living primitively in Amazonas jungle as well as in Mato Grosso and in the Goiás forests. It is opportune to relate here that the Indians receive from FUNAI (Fundação Nacio - nal de Assistência ao Indio) social, medical, moral and religious assistance. Their "modus vivendi" is mostly preserved because they get sick and die when under the White Race's way of life. The Mongolian Race is also represented by Japanese immigrants mainly concentrated in the São Paulo State.

2. Natural resources - Brazil is very rich in all three of Nature's Reigns: mineral, vegetal and animal. Minerals will first be considered:

The most important reserves of iron in the world are in the State of Minas Gerais, in the famous Iron Quadrilateral. Recently in the State of Pará just as important iron mines as the first mentioned were found. Brazil also has manganese, copper, zinc, tin, aluminum, etc., and also radioactive minerals. The coal of Brazil's mines is presently not worthy of mention, but some petroleum has been found. Precious and semi-precious stones are known worldwide because of their variety and beauty.

Brazil's hydraulic potential is the second or maybe the third most important in the world; nearly 20 million KVA has already been tapped.

With regard to the Vegetal Reign, the largest forest reserves in all the world belong to Brazil - the Hileia Amazonic Region - comprising of 5,500,000 square kilometers is abundant in long-lasting woods such as mahogany, cedar and paroba (Bignonia similia ropea). It is the original home of Seringueira (Hevea brasiliensis), the rubber tree.

In the State of Minas Gerais, Espírito Santo and Goiás may be found in large reserves of Tropical woods, and in the Southern States are large amounts of Paraná Pine (Araucaria angustifolia). In the Northeast there are great plantations of Carnaúba, Ouricuri, Babaçu (palm trees); these provide oil, wax and other indispensable products in modern industry.

Brazil's Animal Reign has one of the richest fauna in the world being ornithologically the most important of the Universe. Among the land animals the Tapir or Anta is the largest. Brazil has many Rodents, one of which is the useful anteater named Tatu, the most important. Among the Carnivora, the Onca Pintada (the big Brazilian Jaguar) is remarkable because ot its size. Reptilia - Jacarés - and enormous snakes such as Sucuri and Giboia, each capable of swallowing a calf, are very prized because of their pretty skin.

## Agriculture

In the South of Brazil Agriculture is very modern, being in the same rank with that of Europe or the United States in all sectors. In the States of S. Paulo, Paraná and Rio Grande do Sul may be found the largest plantations of soybean, rice, wheat, and corn. The coffee plant, having been destroyed by the frost, is now cultivated in the States of Minas Gerais and Bahia. In the Northeast, cotton and fibers in general, and sugar cane cultures are the basis of the economy. In the South of Bahia there are large Cocoa cultivations, Brazil having the second largest in the world, will reach first place in the next few years. In the North Region, except for the culture of black pepper and jute, the agriculture is empiric and only extractive.

Rearing is also well developed, with Brazil having 100,000,000 heads of bovines, the most important herd; it also has about 50 million swine and 20 million sheep. The bovines are represented from the center of the country up to the North, by cattle originally from India; and from the center down to the South, by European cattle.

## Industry

Brazil is neatly divided in two economic zones according to Industry. The Southeastern and Southern Regions, including the States of S. Paulo, Rio de Janeiro, part of Minas Gerais and part of Rio Grande do Sul, have an excellent development level under modern conception, the steel production reaching 12,000,000 tons a year and from now until 1980, according to the 2nd PND (Plano Nacional de Desenvolvimento) it will raise to 20,000,000 tons. Chemicals, fertilizers, oil refining and the most complex of all - the Automobile industry - with 1,000,000 units a year.

Shipbuilding is located in the State of Rio de Janeiro with a production plan of 7,000,000 tons dead weight. It is worthy of mention the manufacture of textiles worldwide known, also in the Southern and Southeastern Regions. Down to the extreme South there are some basic industries; a few in the Northeast, in Bahia's Capital, Salvador; and in Recife, Pernambuco's Capital; and practically none in the North of the country.

## Economy and Economics of Education in Brazil: A New Strategy in Brazil's Economy

From the end of the fifties to 1963 Brazil has been under very high inflation levels, and that has certainly caused terrible damage to the country.

Since 1964, because of the radical change of the Government regime, a political stability made it possible to operate long lasting strategies.

First of all, a preventable action against the inflationing fo-
cuses was set. In 1964 the inflation had raised at 84,24%, coming
down to 20% per year from 1966 to 1975 (Table I).

Table I.    Inflation in Brazil.

| YEAR | PERCENTAGE | YEAR | PERCENTAGE |
|------|------------|------|------------|
| 1956 | 20,75 | 1966 | 20,58 |
| 1957 | 16,81 | 1967 | 21,66 |
| 1958 | 11,73 | 1968 | 28,75 |
| 1959 | 30,98 | 1969 | 22,01 |
| 1960 | 25,94 | 1970 | 17,74 |
| 1961 | 34,81 | 1971 | 20,99 |
| 1962 | 53,92 | 1972 | 15,73 |
| 1963 | 66,19 | 1973 | 15,55 |
| 1964 | 84,24 | 1974 | 34,52 |
| 1965 | 54,95 | 1975 | 24,48 |

Source:   Relatórios Anuais do Banco Central do Brasil.

Operating a developmental pattern based on an economy in
which prevailed notoriously the primary sector, with possibilities for
exportation, the Government centered greater attention on the secondary sector.

In order to conduct the capital to the secondary sector, the
price of primary products was controlled, to cheapen raw materials.
Meanwhile incentives were created, such as donation of areas and
liberation from taxes for imported technology, as well as many other
financial aids and facilities concerning inputs, because as it happens
in the whole world, the profits from the investment in industry is
bigger than that of agriculture and rearing.   Incentives to the native
production men were also given, as to provide them the basic conditions to compete with the international market.

This strategy was applied aiming at the increase of exportation, and was justified by the slow expansion of the domestic consumer market, and also by the urgent need to generate resources, in
order to face the high level of importation growth.

In searching a way to protect a structure capable to sustain
the high levels of growth, the Government invested directly on basic
sectors as, for instance, the area of mining (Companhia Vale do Rio

Doce) of mineral oil (Petrobrás) and steel industry (Companhia Siderúrgica Nacional - Companhia Siderúrgica Paulista - Usiminas). All these corporations are of mutual capital, the Government being the principal.

From 1968 to 1973 Brazil has reached annual percentages of growth over 9% (Table II). This caused the annual income "per capita" to raise from US $350.00 in 1969 to US $750.00 in 1975.

Table II.   Gross National Product (GNP) Growth.

| YEAR | 1966 | 1967 | 1968 | 1969 | 1970 | 1971 | 1972 | 1973 | 1974 | 1975 | 1976 |
|------|------|------|------|------|------|------|------|------|------|------|------|
| %    | 5,1  | 4,8  | 9,3  | 9,0  | 9,5  | 11,3 | 10,4 | 11,4 | 6,5  | 4,2  | 8,8  |

Source:   Análise a Perspectiva Econômica - APEC, 1967-1977.

Productivity has also been improved thanks to the advanced technology actioned.   A growth of 73,9% in the period 1969-1974 of the real industrial product was observed, and only 32,3% in the employment rate in industry (Table III).

Table III.   Real Manufacturing Product/Employment
In Manufacturing Growth.

| YEAR | REAL MANUFACTURING PRODUCT GROWTH LEVEL IN BRAZIL | EMPLOYMENT IN MANUFACTURING LEVEL |
|------|------|------|
| 1969 | 100,0 | 100,0 |
| 1970 | 111,0 | 102,0 |
| 1971 | 123,5 | 107,0 |
| 1972 | 140,5 | 114,1 |
| 1973 | 162,4 | 125,2 |
| 1974 | 173,9 | 132,2 |

Sources:   Conjuntura Econômica, Fundação Getúlio Vargas Boletim do Banco Central, Vol. 10 n. 8, june/1975.   Basis:   1969 - 100.

In order to minimize the bad effects of past administrations on its development, Brazil has also attracted investments from outside the country, reaching higher levels of profit in enterprises than those usually earned in civilized countries (Table IV).   This high rate of profit has also been maintained thanks to the flattering of the wages (Table V).

Table IV.   Rentability of the Most Important
Corporations in Brazil and U.S.A.

Neat profit /neat patrimony

| CORPORATIONS / YEAR | 1970 | 1971 | 1972 | 1973 | 1974 |
|---|---|---|---|---|---|
| THE 100 MOST IMPORTANT IN BRAZIL | | | | | |
| STATE | 7,8 | 9,3 | 10,1 | 10,0 | 11,3 |
| NATIONAL | 10,1 | 14,1 | 15,5 | 15,8 | 18,4 |
| FOREIGN | 14,8 | 18,3 | 19,4 | 20,1 | 20,4 |
| THE 500 MOST IMPORTANT IN U.S.A. (ONLY MANU-FACTORIES) | | 9,1 | 10,3 | 12,4 | 13,6 |

Source:   Visão - "QUEM E QUEM", Fortune - "500 largest industrial firms".

All this social cost is justified by the idea that the biggest profits within a system are also the biggest inversions it is capable to perform.

Aiming at preventing foreign enterprises from controlling our economy, the Government has opened very special conditions to national corporations (liberations from taxes, better prices, etc.) bringing them to exceptional levels of growth.   This is what explains the quick expansion of Petrobrás, Banco do Brasil and others.   The only negative point in this strategy is the few chances offered to the private national capital.

Simultaneously to this aggressive economical action, Brazil has been fighting for better conditions in Education.   High sums have been invested in MOBRAL (Movimento Brasileiro de Alfabetização).   This institution was founded in 1967 to fight illiteracy, and has already taught 9,000,000 adults to read and write.   The country has invested high percentuals of the Union resources - nearly 7% - in Education (Table VI).

Table V.  Evolution of the Annual Average
of the Real Minimum.

WAGE (at São Paulo and Rio de Janeiro) of the product
"per capita" in Brazil.

| YEAR | (Annual Average of the real minimum wage - Including the 13th - after 1952) Basis:  1952=100. (1) | Real Product "per capita" in Brazil Basis:  1952=100. (2) |
|------|------|------|
| 1952 | 100,00 | 100,00 |
| 1953 | 88,17 | 99,56 |
| 1954 | 107,53 | 106,38 |
| 1955 | 116,13 | 110.36 |
| 1956 | 119,35 | 110,63 |
| 1957 | 131,18 | 116,03 |
| 1958 | 113,98 | 121,35 |
| 1959 | 130,11 | 124,36 |
| 1960 | 115,05 | 132,51 |
| 1961 | 132,00 | 142,07 |
| 1962 | 120,43 | 145,35 |
| 1963 | 109,68 | 143,40 |
| 1964 | 110,75 | 143,49 |
| 1965 | 100,22 | 143,22 |
| 1966 | 94,62 | 146,32 |
| 1967 | 91,39 | 149,07 |
| 1968 | 92,47 | 158,37 |
| 1969 | 89,25 | 167,76 |
| 1970 | 86,02 | 178,56 |
| 1971 | 87,09 | 193,18 |
| 1972 | 89,25 | 207,35 |
| 1973 | 92,47 | 224,52 |
| 1974 | 88,21 | 239,20 |

Sources:   (1) - Conjuntura Econômica - Fundação Getulio Vargas;

(2) - Conjuntura Econômica, vol. 27, n° 12, Dec., 1973.

Table VI.  Resources for Education/Union Budget.

| YEAR | % |
|------|------|
| 1970 | 6,97 |
| 1971 | 6,93 |
| 1972 | 7,17 |
| 1973 | 6,40 |
| 1974 | 6,83 |

Source:  Serviço de Estatística da Educação e Cultura - MEC.


Quantitatively we may see the high growth of enrollment in the three school levels (Table VII).

Table VII.  Brazilian Education From 1965 to 1974.
(thousands of pupils)

| YEAR | ENROLLMENT | | | | | |
|------|------------|--|--|--|--|--|
|      | ELEMENTARY | | SECONDARY | | UNIVERSITY | |
|      | ABSO-LUTE NUMBER | RELA-TIVE NUMBER | ABSO-LUTE NUMBER | RELA-TIVE NUMBER | ABSO-LUTE NUMBER | RELA-TIVE NUMBER |
| 1965 | 11.568 | 100 | 509 | 100 | 155 | 100 |
| 1968 | 14.348 | 124 | 801 | 157 | 278 | 179 |
| 1971 | 17.066 | 148 | 1.120 | 220 | 562 | 363 |
| 1974 | 24,674 | 213 | 1.732 | 340 | 906 | 585 |

Source:  Serviço de Estatística de Educação e Cultura - MEC.


The importance given to Education is a reflection of its economical and democratical values. On one hand there is an expressive improvement of the wages levels of instructed people; on the other hand, better qualification of the population and consequently the enlargement and sophistication of productivity and the constant urge for higher levels of instruction and for specialists. This is demonstrated by the larger growth in the university level than in the secondary school; and also by the larger growth in the secondary school comparatively to the elementary school.

# HISTORICAL BACKGROUND - PHYSICAL EDUCATION

## Synthesis of the Colonial Period (1500-1822)

The indigenous inhabitants of Brasil in the XVI Century, as one can easily imagine, lived in direct contact with Nature. The conditions of the ambient forced them to use their physical strength in order to survive. Thus, only the strong could go on living - that was the natural selection law - winning the bloody struggles against one another or against wild beasts, those which were extremely powerful and dexterous.

The physical condition of Brazil's Indians was excellent, according to the testimony of the historians of that time (Priest Simão de Vasconcelos and Jean de Lery), surprising all Europeans. Vasconcelos said: "They (the savages) are long limbed, strong, well built, healthy and full of strength."

## The Indigenous Sports

Hunting and fishing were among the needs of the Indigenous who got their nourishment from those activities. They were, of course, very skilled with the bow and arrow--their weapons to attack at a distance--and capable, according to Priest Vasconcelos, "to hit a flying mosquito."

Foot races were very popular among the Aborigines whether in hunting or in warfare. Frei Vicente Salvador, observing their war strategy, tells us about, "Their spies, who were very hasty young men. . ."

Swimming and canoeing were very developed among the Indians of Brazil. The Paumaris, one of the best known Aruak tribes of Purus River, were "essentially fluvial, expert swimmers and wonderful canoers", says Joseph Beal Steere. The Taramembes who lived in Maranhao, Beredo assures, ". . . . are the best swimmers of all, crossing miles and miles of water and diving for a long time without any fear."

Horsemanship was also practiced by some tribes of Mato Grosso; one of these tribes was the Guaicurus who practice horsemanship because of war purposes. Francisco Rodrigues Prado tells us: "They ran so violently against the enemy riding their horses that they tore and stamped them, and with the lance killed every living soul. . ."

About canoeing, Jean de Lery writes that the Indian built canoes out of the bark of trees big enough for forty or fifty persons. They used to row standing but in some tribes it was found that they also sat down while rowing. The oars had short or long poles depending upon whether the oarsmen were sitting or on their feet. It seems they didn't use pitchforks on the canoes.

Brazil's Indigenous inhabitants courage and physical strength have been celebrated in many legends, poems and romances. The historians' testimony, however, is the only one worthy of faith. The Indigenous elected as their chiefs those who proved to be the bravest. If those leaders ever behaved as cowards, they were immediately discharged and abandoned.

Lery describes a battle: "At 300 paces from one another, they greeted themselves, throwing many arrows in all directions. If somebody was hurt, as we saw several ones, they pulled the arrow violently out of their flesh and broke it; after that, as if they were wild dogs, they bit those pieces . . . But they went back to fight, as soon as they could."

As can be seen, the Indigenous way of life forced them to take good care of their physical attributes in order to assure life itself. When the Jesuits came to Brazil in 1549, and founded the famous 'Colegios", they understood the needs of physical activities of the young Indians who they taught. The classes were held during the morning and the pupils had the whole afternoon free. To give thorough expansion to their natural instincts towards movement, which the rigid discipline of the priests hampered.

### Physical Education Since Independence

Its Independence being proclaimed on September 7, 1922, Brazil looked forward and started developing on all sides: culturally, economically, socially and industrially. Education experienced, as it had been hoped, a new impulse; and Physical Education gained more importance, its role in general education being better understood.

Father Belchior Pinheiro de Oliveira, deputy for the State of Minas Gerais, presented in 1823, a proposal to stimulate Brazilian intellectualists in order to elaborate a complete educational plan. On July 31st Mariano de Albuquerque Cavalcanti, delegate for the State of Ceara presented, in addition to that proposal, the following items:

Art. 1st--Anybody who presents within one year from now a plan for Physical, Moral and Intellectual Education, if Brazilian, will be publicly declared a benefactor of the Country and, as such, will receive a situation compatible to his rank or profession; if a foreigner, he will have the Nation's gratitude and a monetary prize, and whether foreigner or Brazilian citizen, will be given a distinguished medal.

Art. 2nd--A second prize will also be given to one who presents a plan exclusively for Physical, Moral or Intellectual Education.

Physical Education in Brazil, as one can easily understand, started receiving influence from other countries. The first book published in Brazil appeared in 1828, by Joaquim Jeronimo Serpa, and was entitled a "Treatise on Children's Physical Education and Morals." It had been taken from the works of a Frenchman, M. Gardien. The author conceived education as the health of body and the culture of spirit, considering Physical Education the same as we do today. On the other hand, he called the educator's attention to this in order to fight the common error of comparing Morals to Physical Education, always to the detriment of the latter.

The first national work that is known came to light in 1845. It was presented under the title "Some Considerations on Physical Education" to the Medicine Faculty of Rio de Jeneiro. The author explained thoroughly the importance of physical exercises to obtain the benefits of health and strength and was very explicit about the connection between the moral and the physical parts.

In the following year, to the same Faculty, Joaquim Pedro de Melo presented a thesis: "Generalities on the Children's Physical Education". In 1852 in the State of Amazonas, President Toureiro Aranha determined that "Instruction should include Physical Education, as well as Moral and Intellectual Education" but forbade girls to practice physical activities.

With a thesis under the title "Influences of Physical Education on Man" Antonio Francisco Gomes received his M.D., in Rio de Janeiro's Faculty of Medicine. The author considered Physical Education as an integral part of general education showing a lucid sight of the subject.

Among military classes appears a physical training method which aims at developing soldiers the most important attributes both physical and moral. A German teacher, Meyer, a follower of Jahn, implanted in the Army his influence, until the arrival of the French Military Mission.

The German influence, however, had also entered the schools. Thus, in 1870, the Empire Minister ordered the publication of the "New Guide for Gymnastic Training in Prussia's Public Schools". This was the first official publication of a gymnastic manual that, although never followed, nevertheless influenced remarkably the private publications on the subject.

The most important event in the Empire Period was, undoubtedly, the famous project of Rui Barbosa, one of the most intelligent public men Brazil has ever had. On September 12, 1882, in the Deputy Chamber, a session discussed Project Number 224 "The Elementary and Other Complementary Institutions of Public Instruction Reform." To the distinguished Deputy was given the task to relate the subject and to opine about it. He preceded to a vibrant consecration of Physical Education, giving to it primary importance. He made a general historical picture of Physical Education development since Ancient Greek Civilizations, studying its position in various countries at the time, especially in Sweden. The eminent Brazilian said then: "We do not intend to raise acrobats or Hercules, but to develop in all children the 'quantum' of physical strength which is essential to a balanced life, to the happiness of spirit, to the preservation of all races, and to the dignification of mankind".

*And thus ends the Project:*

1--Institution of a special Gymnastics section in every Teachers' School.

2--Compulsory extension of Gymnastics to both sexes in Teacher's training and in Elementary Schools. In all grades, considering the harmony of shapes and the exigencies of maternity in women.

3--Inclusion of Gymnastics in all school programs as a studying subject, in special schedules, and after the classes.

4--The Physical Education Teachers will be given the same authority and category as the teachers of other disciplines.

In 1888, Pedro Manoel Borges published, "Theoretical-practical Manual of School Gymnastics", for public schools (elementary, high schools, teacher's schools, etc.). This manual was divided in two parts, the first being essentially practical; the second, theoretical-practical. It is preconized freehand exercises grouped in six series for children up to ten years of age--this is the first part; in the second, the Manual gives elementary principles of Anatomy, Osteology, Arthrology, exercises with and on apparatus. This was the heritage that the Republic of Brazil received; it was finally proclaimed in 1889.

In the beginning of the Twentieth Century the Anatomical Concept dominated Physical Education. The more the muscles gained in volume the better according to this concept. The Physical Culture Academies were very popular at the time and names of Triat, Desbonnet, Attila, Sandow, Mercier, Muller, and Ruffier were well known to everybody. The main emphasis was to develop an impressive figure, the physical shape being the most important value.

The influence of French Physical Education through Demeny and Lagrange, brought to Brazilian Physical Education the contribution of Physiology; making clear the importance of doing physical work, as well as distributing the muscular work, in order to obtain harmonical figures. The *Physiological* Physical Education concept then comes to the fore.

A 1907 publication entitled, "Guide for Capoeira or Brazilian Gymnastics", included teaching positions, strokes and defenses of this sport which Banto Negroes brought to Brazil and which became very popular. The author of the guide used a pseudonym.

In 1908 Brazil received the first American influence. Professor Antonio Monteiro de Souza, lecturing in the State of Amazonas in a Physical Education Course, talks about Physical Education in the United States of America, "Where they have the art, the science of building a people", employing all methods, making use of the best procedures each of them could offer to any particular individual.

In the Rio de Janeiro YMCA, founded in 1895, as well as in the YMCA of S. Paulo (1904) and in Porto Algere's YMCA (1901), Calisthenics developed and became official in the State of Minas Gerais.

In 1918 and 1920 methods of German origin were employed in the Military School of Realengo, then in organiztions in Rio de Janeiro. The year of 1921 marks the official French influence in the Army, already known among civilians through the book by Mario Polo and Arnaldo Guinle, published in 1920.

The policial Force of S. Paulo's Physical Education School, whose teachers had been trained by some officers of the French Military Mission in 1905, adopted Ling's method. In 1921 the Army made official the "Military Physical Instruction Rule", inspired in Georges Hebert's method and also in that of Joinville-le-Pont.

In 1929, the "Provisory Course of Physical Education" was organized and several officers and elementary teachers were enrolled, who, having received their diploma, taught the French concepts of Physical Education among the civilians and military as well.

In 1933, on October 19th, the Army Physical Education School was founded. This gave origin, in 1939, to "Escola Nacional de Educação Física e Desportos", now "Escola de Educação Física e Desportos da Universidade Federal do Rio de Janeiro", which graduates more students of Physical Education than ten other schools in all of Brazil as follows:

Physical Education Teachers

Specialized Physicians

Physical Education Technicians

Technicians in Physiotherapeutics

Thanks to the evolution of Pedagogy, helped by Psychology, Physical Education gained one more trait; that of pleasure which should be in all physical activities permitting larger and deeper benefits to the human being. This, then, is the *Psychological* concept of Physical Education.

But one more element was missing, that is, the *Sociological*. In fact, man has to be prepared to become useful to himself and to the community. This, then, is the Sociological purpose of Physical Education.

On the other hand, Physical Education cannot ignore Education's most important aim. This, of course, is the *Philosophical* principle which constitutes Brazil's Education basis--the Bio-Psycho-Socio-Philosophical concept.

Actually, Brazil tends toward electicism utilizing the best of all methods and systems of Physical Education in the world in order to develop all the psycho-physical potentialities of the young pupils. This is aimed when all are given opportunities for a perfect adaptation to the physical, the live, the social environment; assuring, on the other hand, to each and all, freedom which is the only way to happiness.

## Physical Education in Brazil's Educational System

Since World War II Brazil has been undergoing a fast industrialization and urbanization process which is affecting its entire economical and social structure, especially the educational institutions.

One of the most serious problems to be faced is the high rate of demographic growth--3.1--one of the highest in the world (2,500,000 births a year) being the demographic density in cities like Rio de Janeiro, S. Paulo and Recift, doubled every fifteen years. These numbers alone are enough to explain the difficulties to be overcome in order to attend to pressing educational needs.

When planning social and economical development the Government gives top priority to educational projects, emphasizing the elimination of illiteracy and the modernization of the general school system. Education today, as Brazilian people regard it, is important not only regarding social matters, but also is a significant and most rewarding investment. This is reflected in the increase of productivity and improvement of life standards which is the most important aim in the development process of a country.

The important Lei n$^{\underline{o}}$ 6251 of Oct. 8th, 1975, rules the general organization of sports in Brazil. It also establishes a National Politics of Physical Education and Sports which basic objective points are:

*Art. 5th*--

I - Improvement of the population is physical fitness
II - Improvement of sports levels in all areas
III - Implantation and intensification of the practice of popular sports
IV - Raising of the technical-sporting level
V - Diffusion of sports for leisure purposes.

# NATIONAL PLAN OF PHYSICAL EDUCATION AND SPORTS

*Art.* 6th--It will concern the Ministry of Education and Culture the elaboration of the PLANO NACIONAL DE EDUCAÇÃO FÍSICA E DESPORTOS (PNED) following the directives of the Politica Nacional de Educação Física e Desportos.

Unique Paragraph - The PNED will allow priority to the programs of incentive to Physical Education and Sports, to sport for all, and to elite sports.

## RESOURCES FOR SPORTS

*Art.* 7th--The Union financial aid for sports, aiming at the objective points settled by the Politica Nacional de Educação Física e Desportos will be implemented according to the budget outlined to programs, projects and sport activities and will be provenient from

     I - The National Fund for Educational Development
    II - The Social Development Supporting Fund
   III - The financial inputs of sport programs and projects
   IV - The Patrimonial Resources
    V - Donations and legacies
   VI - Any other resources.

Elementary Schools - (1st Grade - 8 series or grades)

Physical Education in Elementary Schools is ruled by a program including:

1. Natural activities
2. Games
3. Stunts and Tumbling
4. Recreational Gymnastics
5. Rhythmical Activities
6. Sports Initiation

Every group receives Physical Education classes of 40 to 45 minutes twice a week and special groups receive daily care, being trained for 20 to 30 minutes in order to improve their physical and mental-moral-social condition.

Although the ideal point in Physical Education matters at this level has not been reached, nevertheless, Brazil is working enthusiastically to give Elementary Schools the facilities and better trained teachers to assure its children a normal thorough development in physical, psychological, and social aspects.

# Secondary Schools

Secondary schools in 1966 were 6,698 in number with an attendance of 2,483,212 pupils, of which 1,230,385 were girls.  Most of these students were concentrated in the States of Guanabara, S. Paulo and Minas Gerais.  In the last ten years, 1958-1967, secondary education showed an increase of 175%; the Southern region representing 75% of the Country's total enrollment.

In 1957, of 905,082 students in secondary schools, 290,567 or 32% were registered in public schools and 614,506 attended private establishments.  In 1966, after a decade, of the total secondary school population (2,483,212), 1,259,156 or 50% attended public schools, whereas 1,224,056 or 49.3% were in private schools.  Such a change is due to the fact that the Government tripled the number of public schools, when its 902 schools in 1957 rose to 2,709 in 1966, and the number of students grew from 290,576 to 1,259,156 in the same period.

The "Directives and Bases of National Education Law" permitted the States to create their own systems and gradually try to solve their particular educational problems, including those of Physical Education.  Each educational district has a Physical Education Supervisor who receives guidance from the Physical Education Department.

Physical Education is receiving very special attention in Rio de Janeiro through the Phsyical Education, Sports, and Recreation Departments.  A major point of these new trends is the placement of a substantial Physical Education Program in all secondary schools, the discipline considered as an important part in the curriculum as well as an essential activity for the pupil's integral education.  That program consists in two parts, namely, a Service Program (regular classes in gymnastics, games and sports, stunts and tumbling and dance) and an Interschool Program (extra-class activities such as intramural, intercollegiate, gymnastics and dance demonstrations).

These are the general procedures:

1.  There will be a minimum of two classes a week for each group of 50 students.

2.  The extra-class activities will be considered as regular work for the teacher.

3.  The Service Program will be carried out on an experimental basis for a period.

4.  There will be a Physical Education teacher responsible for every school who is supposed to attend meetings at the Physical Education Department once a month.

5. There will be a Physical Education Supervisor for each Administrative Region into which the State is divided. He will attend mandatorily weekly meetings at the Department.

6. Each school will organize its own annual Work Program folflowing the lines of the Overall Program of the Department.

A complementary measure was a survey of all the existing facilities and equipment, in order to allow a plan in this area capable of eliminating the previous shortages which were affecting the quality of Physical Education work. The survey revealed that:

1. All schools to be built should have minimum facilities and equipment for Physical Education.

2. A five-year plan to recover the existing facilities should be worked out.

3. A five-year plan to build facilities, in schools which have none, is to be adopted.

On the other hand, the Secretaria Municipal de Educação e Cultura organizes intercollegiate championships aiming at a more significant movement towards athletics for youngsters.

## II JOGOS ESTUDANTIS DO MUNICIPIO DO RIO DE JANEIRO

### 1977
#### (Elementary and Secondary Schools)

|  | PARTICIPANTS |
|---|---|
| 1 - TRACK AND FIELD | 1393 |
| 2 - BASKETBALL | 569 |
| 3 - VOLLEYBALL | 1909 |
| 4 - HANDBALL | 2487 |
| 5 - RHYTHMIC GYMN. | 36 |
| *6 - SWIMMING | 215 |
| 7 - CHESS | 102 |

* Schools without swimming pools.

| | |
|---|---|
| Number of games | 873 |
| Number of schools | 154 |

It is worth mentioning that all the pupils are non-confederate.

# Physical Education in the University

The Brazilian Confederation of the University Sports (Confederação Brasileira de Desportos Universitários) was founded on August 9, 1939 and is a civilian entity constituted by all State entities dependent upon it.

*These are its finalities:*

1. Represent the Brazilian University Sports as its only controller, in all the Republic territory and also in other countries.

2. Rule, divulge and promote all sports in every way.

3. Organize and direct, annually, College Games controlled by special regulation.

*The obligatory sports are:*

| Track and field | Fencing | Rowing |
| Basketball | Swimming | Tennis |
| Soccer | Waterpolo | Volleyball |

Other sports, constituting extra competition, are also conducted.

The President of the Confederation is the Director of the Games and with the Directing Committee indicates all commissions. The technical assistance to the Games is controlled by the Technical Department of the Confederation following the regulations, codes and rules internationally recognized. This year 33 different Superior Schools took part in the Games in Bauru, S. Paulo State, and new records were established in various sports with the Physical Education School of Rio de Janeiro Federal University winning the championship.

It must be said, however, that Physical Education at the University is not a subject in the curriculum nor is it among extra-class ordinary activities. All students bring their physical training from high school and during the University Games fight for their own faculties. The Physical Education Schools always establish all the new records, naturally.

With regard to Feminine Gymnastics, in Brazil there exists a very significant movement toward Modern Feminine Gymnastics oriented by Dalcroze principles, which some Austrian teachers brought to this country in 1952. Several Gymnastics Associations and Federations have been promoting this kind of physical activity for women, which is so close to dance, because of the constant presence of rhythm and music, and which better than any other physical activities permits girls to develop their personality in the fullest extent.

## Teacher Training

Brazil has eighty Physical Edcuation Schools for teacher training. The course at the Physical Education and Sports School of Rio de Janeiro's Federal University is completed in three years and considers several theoretical and practical disciplines. According to the recent reformulation of Brazilian University, each faculty is also undergoing changes in the program and in its regulations. The curriculum includes:

*Theoretical*

| | | |
|---|---|---|
| Anatomy | History | Physiology |
| Hygiene | Methodology | Kinesiology |
| Traumatology | Psychology | Biometry |
| Organization | Pedagogy | |

*Practical*

| | | |
|---|---|---|
| Track and Field | Soccer | Weight lifting |
| Movement Techniques for men | Basketball | Swimming |
| Movement Techniques for women | Volleyball | Tennis |
| Stunts and Tumbling | Boxing | Fencing |
| Dance (Modern and Folk) | Judo | |

Brazil has post-graduation courses for Physicians and Physical Education teachers as well as graduation courses for Physiotherapeutics and many other extension courses are given on Physical Education subjects during the vacations.

The Escola de Educação Física e Desportos da Universidade Federal do Rio de Janeiro has an excellent Dance Group, which have travelled all over the country. Some years ago Mrs. Ainsworth herself invited this same Group for a series of exhibitions in several American Universities and Colleges, including the Smith College.

Both feminine and masculine pupils have Dance classes in the basic curriculum and there is also a post-graduation Dance Course, completed in four semesters, or in 1,440 hours.

The Dance Department head is Professor Maria Helena Pabst Sa Earp. The photos were taken during the Group exhibition on November 18th and 27th, 1977, performed at Sala Cecília Merielles, Rio de Janeiro.

Post-graduation Dance Group Escola de Educação Física e Desportos – Universidade Federal do Rio de Janeiro.

# SELECTED REFERENCES

1. Augusto, M. *Metodologia da aprendizagem motora na Ginástica Feminina Moderna.* Rio. 1958.

2. Augusto M. *O Jogo - Formulação da Teoria Hedonista.* Rio. 1960.

3. Legislação Brasileira De Desportos. Editora Educação Ltda. Rio. 1952.

4. Ministerio Da Educacao E Cultura. *Lei n$\underline{o}$ 6251.* 1975.

5. Penna Marinho, I. *História da Educação Física e dos Desportos no Brasil.* Ministério da Educação e Saúde. Vol. I. Rio. 1952.

6. Penna Marinho, I. *Sistemas e Métodos de Educação Física.* 2a. edição. St. Paulo, Brasil. 1970.

## ACKNOWLEDGMENTS

1. Augusto, Maurício. Brasil. *A Terra e o Povo.* I. Unpublished notes. Rio. 1968. Ibid., II. 1977.

2. Bezerra, Nilton de Amorim. *Economia e Economia da Educação no Brasil.* Universidade Federal do Rio de Janeiro. Faculdade de Educacao. Departamento de Sociologia da Educação. (Co-author of new section - Economy and Economics of Education: a new strategy in Brazil's Economy). 1977.

3. Brito Cunha, Renato. *Educação Física no Brasil.* 1968.

# SPORT AND PHYSICAL EDUCATION IN CANADA
## by Garth A. Paton

### Biographical Sketch

*Garth A. Paton* was born at Stratford, Ontario, Canada on November 12, 1932. He received the Honors Bachelor of Arts degree in Physical and Health Education at the University of Western Ontario, London, Canada, in 1956. The Ontario High School Type "A" Specialist Teaching Certificate in Physical Education was completed in 1957, (Ontario College of Education, Toronto, Canada). The Master of Arts degree was taken at the University of Michigan, Ann Arbor, in 1963, and the Doctor of Philosophy degree at the University of Illinois, Urbana, in 1970.

Teaching experience has included work at the Collingwood District Collegiate Institute Board, Ontario, Canada from 1957 through 1963 (at Collingwood Collegiate, as Head of Physical Education 1957-1961; and at Stayner Collegeiate as Chariman of Physical Education from 1961-1963). High school coaching experience was gained in football, basketball, track and field, wrestling, volleyball, badminton, and school skiing programs. Recreation experience included summer work at the London Public Utilities Commission (1951, 1952, and 1953); the North York Recreation Committee (1955 and 1956); and at the Etobicoke Recreation (1957).

Scholarship and honors received include the University Gold Medal at the University of Western Ontario, 1956 (awarded for highest standing and honors); the Fitness and Amateur Sport Scholarship, Canadian Department of Health and Welfare (awarded for graduate study in physical education); and the Staley Award, University of Illinois, 1965 (awarded by the Phi Epsilon Kappa Fraternity Chapter for outstanding performance as a graduate student).

Dr. Paton returned to the University of Western Ontario, London, Canada where he achieved the position of Associate Dean, Faculty of Physical Education. In the Fall of 1975 he was selected as Dean of the Faculty of Physical Education and Recreation at the University of New Brunswick, Fredericton, New Brunswick, Canada.

Canada, a Western and Northern country, resembles a distorted parallelogram; the location is such that it lies at the crossroads of contact with some of the principal powers and most populas areas of the world. Bordered on the south by the United States, with the southern peninsula of the province of Ontario probing into the heartland of the United States, the people of Canada are strongly influenced by their neighbor to the south. Frequently overlooked are the remaining three borders which provide the closest North American contact with Russia, England and France, and the Far East. Canada's far north brings her into geographical proximity to Russia. The land mass of Newfoundland jutting into the North Atlantic provides the shortest distance between North America and England and France, while the province of British Columbia and the Yukon Territory are the closest North American points to the Far East.

In terms of geographical area, Canada is the second largest country in the world, with only Russia being larger. The 3,851,809 square miles exceeds that of the United States by some 230,000 square miles; yet Canada is less than one-half the area of Russia. There are five distinct geographical regions: The Eastern Maritimes including the four provinces of Newfoundland, Nova Scotia, Prince Edward Island and New Brunswick; the Great Lakes--St. Lawrence River Basin is constituted by the provinces of Ontario and Quebec; the Prairies composed of Manitoba, Saskatchewan and portions of Alberta; the Rocky Mountains and the Pacific Coast Region encompasses the western portion of Alberta and the Province of British Columbia and the Far North region includes the Yukon and Northwest Territories.

The population of Canada is sparse and unevenly distributed; only within the last decade has the population figure attained the twenty-million mark. Canada has only two cities with populations in excess of one million, but the population is distributed such that ninety per cent of the people live on ten per cent of the land. The greatest concentration of population is in the Great Lakes-St. Lawrence Valley region, thus leaving vast areas of thinly populated or unpopulated regions.[4]

The vastness of the country presents problems, but this immensity is also one of its most attractive aspects. The coalescence of the best natural scenery of Switzerland, Norway, France, Scotland, Russia and Romania provides unmatched geographical variation; yet, the great extent of these areas have been one of the influences impeding Canada nationalism. An example is the relatively recent completion of Canada's first coast-to-coast highway. Individual provinces have long had excellent roads, but it was 1962 before the Trans-Canada Highway was completed.

The typical Canadian character is non-existent. As the geography of Canada exhibits infinite variety, similarly does the character of Canadians. The Canadian travelling in Europe is frequently looked upon as an American; yet, the Canadian has basic differences.

The most striking difference is the contrasting views of themselves.
The American has usually looked inward, strong in the belief of what
America means and stands for; the melting pot has forged and tem-
pered the conviction of self-determination. Contrastingly, the Canadian has tended to look outward. The European heritage of Britain
and France runs deep; geography has reinforced regional differences.
The splendid isolation of Newfoundland has developed a determination
and camaraderie in a people forced to wrest a living from the bleak
Atlantic and a ruggedly beautiful landscape, with little arable soil.
The intense regional loyalty of the citizens of the Eastern Maritimes
has developed a reserved, conservative group of Canadians--this in a
region that is most logically a geographical extension of New England
(United States). The "joie de vie" of the French Canadian "habitant"
molded with fine intellectual background of the "colleges classiques"
and the strong bond of religion, has maintained North America's most
unique culture. The tradition of the more than fifty thousand United
Empire Loyalists, who left the Thirteen Colonies and settled in Ontario, parts of Quebec and New Brunswick, perpetuates the British heritage and the British Crown. The Prairie Provinces of Manitoba,
Saskatchewan and Alberta, wheat-growing and oil-wealthy entities,
imprisoned by the Rocky Mountains on one side and vast distance and
the Great Lakes on the other, tend to look to the south, and constitute a distinctiveness and openness of their own. The Province of
British Columbia, isolated by the Rocky Mountains, and thriving on
tremendous natural resources, more closely approximates the American
belief in self-determination than possibly any other region of Canada.[6,16]

## Historical Background of Physical Education[12]

In 1967 Canada celebrated her one hundredth birthday, by
most standards a young country. Typical of evolving countries, organized physical education was virtually non-existent until there was
sufficient urbanization. Early settlers had more than they could do
in coping with the problems of survival. Yet, even in the pioneer
years, there are traces of recreational activity, growing out of the
heritage and environment.

Games and dances were transported from England and France,
and lacrosse, an Indian originated game, later developed into Canada's National Game. Prior to Confederation in 1867, there were evidences of sports clubs influenced strongly by European culture (e.g.
The Halifax Curling Club; The Halifax Yacht Club and the Wanderers
Athletic Club of Halifax, established in 1824, 1837 and 1861 respectively) that reflect the tradition and interests of the people. The
latter group were engaged in lacrosse, soccer, rugby, cricket, lawn
bowling, and track and field. Several athletic clubs were also established in the Montreal area around the mid-nineteenth century, and
in 1881 several of these clubs amalgamated to form the Montreal Amateur Athletic Association.

Egerton Ryerson, an early and influential Ontario educator, promulgated the cause of physical education in the schools. Impelled by his plea, a curriculum of exercises was published in 1852. Within a decade, a normal school was equipped with a gymnasium in order to train treachers.

One of the most illustrious and well-recognized figures in physical education in Canada and the United States, R. Tait McKenzie, assumed the post as Director of Physical Education for Men at McGill University until 1903 when he moved to the University of Pennsylvania where he remained until his death in 1938. He is best remembered for his outstanding sculpture and is commemorated annually by both the American and Canadian Associations for Health, Physical Education and Recreation through the R. Tait McKenzie Memorial Lectures. A lesser known, but equally impressive artistic contribution of Dr. McKenzie's, is the stone plaque that remains in the Houses of Parliament, Ottawa. This plaque was presented to the Government of Canada by former Canadians, who had moved to the United States, as a tribute to their homeland. A national shrine, The Mill of Kintail, stands to his memory at his former home and studio in Almonte, Ontario.

Miss Ethyl M. Cartwright exercised a long and influential force on women's physical education. She served as Director of Physical Education for Women at McGill University from 1906 to 1927 and previously taught at Halifax Ladies College. In 1929 she joined the faculty of the University of Saskatchewan and was instrumental in establishing physical education at each of these institutions.

An unique fund that shaped physical education in the country was established in 1909 by Lord Strathcona. This fund provided provincial grants to establish school curricula for physical training. Instructors from the military were utilized because of a deficiency of civilian teachers. Since the fund also encouraged cadet training, the result was a continuing relationship between cadet corps and physical education instructors in Canada, until after World War II.

As history has so frequently shown, interest in physical fitness increases during a time of war. Canada was no exception after World War I. The depression had its effects on facilities as well as on leisure time. An attempt to utilize leisure time profitably was made by the Federal Government in 1939 through the enactment of a Youth Training Act.

The outbreak of World War II again exposed the unfitness of Canadian youth. The federal government stepped into the breach again and passed the National Physical Fitness Act of 1943. The act aimed specifically at improvement of the physical fitness of Canadians by encouraging extended physical education programs in the schools as well as better facilities. This act improved training as well as recreation development in numerous provinces.

## Kindergarten-Elementary Physical Education

Strong influences in recent years, such as urbanization, improved transportation and communication, and increased population, have thrust education toward the centralization of elementary schools. These same trends exerted their influences on physical education at the elementary school level. In earlier years, the one-room rural districts were common. One teacher, grapping with the responsibilities of teaching the fundamentals of reading, writing and arithmetic to students spanning the grades one through eight, found little time for teaching physical education. Recess periods were regularly scheduled, but physical activity was deemed a diversion and release, not a phase of education. As districts amalgamated and schools consolidated, transformations in physical education occurred. Gymnasia and indoor facilities are essential because of the winter's length and severity and the need is gradually being filled. Several provinces report a staggering increase in new gymnasia in the last few years. In urban centers where elementary schools are large, gymnasia are common.[16]

Most provinces have been reticent to press for improved physical education programs in elementary schools because of inadequate staff. Across the country the typical elementary school teacher has only a general professional training, with little physical education, and the overwhelming proportion of teachers at the elementary level are women. The heavy emphasis has been upon upgrading the secondary program. Elementary programs generally stress fundamental skills of movement, some sport skills, a varying emphasis on physical fitness and teachers frequently allude to the development of attitudes and social skills.

Elementary physical education has been caught in a circular cycle that recently has shown signs of being interrupted. At the bottom of the circle has been a lack of professionally qualified personnel. This lack of professional leadership is responsible for the failure to sell physical education to the public; in turn, lack of public support has strangled program and facility development. Thus, the unappealing prospect of poor facilities and program discourages personnel from entering the field, and the cycle regenerates itself. Even though the profession has long recognized the importance of elementary physical education, it is just beginning to come to grips with the problem. Recently, school boards have begun to appoint coordinators with the direct responsibility for developing the elementary school program.

## Secondary School Physical Education

Secondary school physical education has improved steadily in the past twenty-five years, with progress due largely to the professional leadership and preparation offered by teacher education programs. Women's professional preparation programs antedate programs for men; the first undergraduate major for men in Canada was conceived at the University of Toronto as late as 1940.[19] In the secondary program both male and female programs in physical education are expected to contribute towards the goals of general education. Detailed description of all aspects of the programs are beyond the scope of this brief report, especially since education is a provincial concern. Some generalization is possible and will be attempted; exceptions and unique aspects will be pointed out when possible.

Among the girls, an emphasis on "movement" has been strong. Frequently referred to as "fundamental movement" or "movement education" the aim is to teach the correct and proper use of the body. This inclusive term ranges from the basic locomotor movements through to creative dances. Gymnastics also forms an integral part of the program and basic tumbling provides the foundation that progresses to stunts and apparatus work. Folk and ballroom dancing, as well as the team games of basketball, volleyball, softball, field hockey, and track and field are popular. Where possible, swimming is included in the program; however, schools with swimming facilities are the exception.

Along with the core curriculum in physical education, the girls' program usually includes provision for competitive athletics at both the intramural and interschool level. The scope of the program varies, but in theory and practice the intramural program is much more extensive. Again location and population are factors; urban centers naturally provide the means for competition that is frequently not available in sparsely settled areas. Student bus transportation creates problems in rural areas as well.[3]

Six of the ten provinces have divisions of the Department of Education devoted exclusively to physical education: Prince Edward Island, Nova Scotia, New Brunswick, Quebec, Ontario and Manitoba. The remaining four provinces have agencies at the provincial level that aid school physical education. Initially, the development of these latter departments has been in recreation, but frequently these agencies now offer aid to physical education.[16]

The time allotment for physical education in the secondary curriculum likewise is a provincial policy. Different provinces recommend minimum number of hours on a per-week basis, but this is not always indicative of what actually exists. Local conditions, such as lack of physical education teachers, lack of facilities, overcrowded schools, or administrators unwilling to overcome these difficulties, frequently result in a situation where the actual opportunities for physical education fall below the provincial recommendations. The larger centers of population adhere most closely to the recommendations, whereas the smaller schools tend to deviate. The allotment of time recommended by the provinces for physical education ranges from three activity periods and one health period per week in Ontario to the Province of Newfoundland, where there is no physical education required. Generally, the requirements approximate three periods per week. In all fairness to Newfoundland, it should be pointed out that there are physical education programs in many schools; recent changes by the Government there, bode well for the future of physical education in that province.

The goals of physical education, as well as the means of attaining these goals, show considerable similarity through the country. Concern is shown for proper growth and development; implicit with this concern is the need for some level of physical fitness. A goal of establishing certain basic skills in sports and games has wide agreement. Through the attainment of skills, the assumption is made that sports participation will follow; this in turn leads to situations where the emotional and social characteristics of the student may be developed. The expression of these goals varies widely, but the four goals: physical growth, acquisition of skills, emotional development and social development, form a core that is common throughout the country.

The basis of the activity programs are sports and games. The sports found in the programs are very similar to those found in the schools of the United States such as football, basketball, volleyball, track and field, cross-country, tumbling, gymnastics, wrestling, soccer, softball and swimming. Where facilities, equipment and personnel permit, emphasis is also placed on individual sports such as tennis, golf, badminton and archery. Increased emphasis on the problems of leisure has increased the emphasis on carry-over activities.

Sports and games such as skiing, curling, lacrosse and rugby add uniqueness to the program. Skiing competition between schools, often on a province-wide basis, is growing in popularity. The climate and geography of Quebec, Ontario, Alberta and British Columbia specifically, are ideally suited to the rigorous winter sports. As well as competitive skiing, some programs institute curricular instruction in skiing, school ski clubs, and opportunities for school-sponsored recreational skiing.

The sport that sparks the greatest national enthusiasm and interest is ice hockey. Canadians take a great deal of pride in the fact that the National Hockey league and the more recently established World Hockey League are mostly composed of Canadian players. The hockey program outside the schools is profuse. Age group hockey exists in almost all towns. Secondary schools are extending the broad base upon which hockey operates, and increasing numbers of schools are including the sport in their programs.

Curling is another winter sport that is enthusiastically supported by thousands of Canadians. Originally played outdoors, and in earlier years by older adults only, it is now played in thousands of arenas across the breadth of the land on both artificial and natural ice surfaces. From coast to coast, it is a rare town or village that does not have a curling rink. The secondary schools very frequently include curling in their program. Curling is presently the only high school sport in which a national school boy championship is held annually.

Lacrosse was originally an Indian game. Down through the years it has maintained a modicum of popularity. The vigorous nature of the game, and the skill involved in controlling a hard rubber ball with a lacrosse stick, provide a challenge to many youth. Equipment is negligible, and the similarity between lacrosse and hockey sparks its popularity in many areas of Canada.

Rugby, with its British tradition, minimal equipment, considerable running and body contact has appeal to students in some programs. It is not played as extensively as many other sports presently, but in specific areas its popularity is increasing.

The general philosophy in Canadian school programs emphasizes sports for the masses. Thus, the curriculum program is of paramount importance, followed by the intramural athletic program, and finally by the interscholastic program. The intramural programs are typically coordinated with the curricular program. The extent of intramural athletics is contingent on facilities and student interest. The coordination with the instructional program is based upon an assumption of skill carry-over. Intramural athletics are variously organized, but basically the aim is to provide competitive opportunities for the maximum number of students. Intramurals are frequently conducted prior to school hours or after school. An activity period scheduled into the school day often provides opportunity for bus students to enjoy the same advantage as local students.

Interscholastic athletics provide for those who excel in specific sports, and are often employed as a medium for developing *esprit de corps* in a school. The program base is broadened by organizing two or three teams that represent the school in a particular sport; age is the most common criterion used in determining classification.

The team sports common to interscholastic competition are hockey, football, basketball, cross-country, track and field, wrestling, volleyball and soccer. In urban areas, as well as in selected leagues formed by adjacent small towns, individual sports such as badminton and golf are popular. When schools have the necessary facilities, swimming competition is organized.[16]

The governing of interscholastic athletics shows some differences from province to province. In Newfoundland the St. John's area provides competition in a local league in soccer, basketball and hockey. The provinces of Quebec, Alberta and British Columbia leave the administration of athletics to local or regional authorities. The remaining provinces have provisional associations that coordinate leagues and provide for championship play in ten or more sports.

The outstanding feature across the country is the close sur-
veillance exercised by educators over athletics, Principals and headmasters influence policy; coaches are selected according to their
teaching qualifications and coaches are paid as teachers, rarely receiving remuneration for coaching. Athletics function in and as a
part of total physical education program; the entire program is directed toward the goals of education.

## College-University Physical Education

Basic instruction, or physical education service programs, in
colleges and universities are limited in Canada. Three rather important issues directly affect these programs. The first is the traditional, essentialistic philosophy of higher education found in Canada; the
second is the increased pressure of enrollment in higher education
with a concomitant shortage of staff and the third has been the lack
of graduate programs in physical education and the resulting absence
of teaching assistants. The *fundamental issue* is the philosophical
concept of higher education and it may well affect the other issues.

The essentialistic tradition of Canadian education has had many
ramifications for physical education. This trend, if not completely
propagating a mind-body dichotomy, had certainly left physical education as a second-class citizen in many universities.

Although basic skills courses are rarely available to the general university student, in many universities the physical recreation
and intramural programs provide basic instruction in sports on a non-
credit basis. In addition, there has been an increase in the offering
of disciplinary-oriented introductory courses which attempt to wed
physical education theory with some practical laboratory experiences.
Often this type of course may be available on a university-wide basis.

Intercollegiate athletics were conceived in Canada as far back
as 1881. In 1906 the original Canadian Intercollegiate Athletic Union
was formed. The schools represented were all in Ontario. In 1910
the Maritime Intercollegiate Athletic Union was founded and the year
1920 marked the beginnings of the Western Canada Intercollegiate Athletic Union. However, it wasn't until 1961 that all intercollegiate
associations in the country were united into one body. The original
name, Canadian Intercollegiate Athletic Union, was retained. This
organization is now the governing body for competitive sports in Canadian universities. However, regional differences and the geographical size of Canada has presented enormous problems for the effective
operation of the C.I.A.U.

The shortness of the university academic year in Canada (from
the latter part of September through early May) restricts competition;
however, football, hockey, basketball, wrestling and swimming, in
addition to individual sports such as squash, badminton, tennis and
golf, comprise many college programs. The early termination of
school restricts baseball, and to some extent track and field, although

some institutions sponsor track and field and cross-country competition in the fall.

There are visible efforts to keep athletics within the framework of the educational structure; athletic scholarships, or grant-in-aid scholarships, are infrequent in Canada. There are few full-time coaches, and those who may be classified as such have multiple coaching tasks. Generally coaching goes hand-in-hand with additional teaching or administrative responsibilities.

The "low pressure" athletic programs seemingly result from two factors: (1) the dominant philosophy of "education for the intellect" and (2) the absence of extensive professional athletics in Canada.

Professional football and professional hockey and recently the Montreal Expos in the National League and the Toronto Blue Jays in the American League in baseball, are the sole professional leagues of any consequence. In the case of football, Canadian teams import a significant percentage of their players from the United States, thus limiting opportunities for Canadians; furthermore, the universities have not been prime suppliers of hockey talent.

Intramural athletics exist in most universities. Facilities are often limited, since intercollegiate athletics have tended to take precedence in the time schedule. The variety of activities parallels those of the intercollegiate programs, and in many universities a very high percentage of the student body participates in the intramural program. The newer universities, such as York University, Toronto, Ontario; Trent University in Petersborough, Ontario; and Simon Fraser University in Burnaby, British Columbia, tend to place a heavy emphasis upon the development of the intramural athletic program. There have been increased student demands and a willingness to back the development of facilities primarily for physical recreation in some universities. The University of Western Ontario, London, has recently erected a community centre and a winter sports building with substantial percentages of the costs contributed directly by the students.

### Teacher Education in Physical Education

Teacher education in Canada evolved through gradual government control of the educational system. Initially, schools were operated privately or by churches. Then, as the need for education grew, it became the domain of the provinces. In 1867, the British North America Act established Canada as a self-governing nation, and this act clearly placed education in the control of the individual provinces. Similarities exist among provinces, but there are differences too numerous to discuss.

The earliest institutions for training teachers were the normal schools, with the first being established in 1847. Within a decade normal schools were established in each of the five eastern provinces. There was evident concern for physical training in the normal schools by 1852. The Strathcona Trust Fund (mentioned earlier) was established in 1909. It influenced the development of physical education in the curriculum of the normal schools.

Teacher certification for the elementary school usually requires one year of study at a provincial certified teachers college after completion of high school, but some provinces require a two-year period of training. In the Western provinces teacher education is placed within the university in an education faculty. In the Eastern provinces professional preparation for elementary school teaching takes place in an institution independent from a university.

Where elementary teacher education is obtained through the university, there is an emphasis on basic arts and science courses, as well as on the general and specialized education courses. In the normal schools, or now more appropriately the teachers colleges or faculties of education, as they are contemporarily named, the emphasis is placed on teaching methods, and on psychology, philosophy, and school law. Practice teaching is required in both the teachers colleges and universities.

Two basic approaches are taken to teacher certification for secondary schools, both of which emphasize a broad liberal arts and science background with specialization in a subject-matter area, as well as in professional education course work. The Province of Ontario typifies the one concept; the Provinces of Alberta, Saskatchewan and British Columbia the other. Ontario secondary school teachers complete their undergraduate degree program prior to entrance to a school or faculty. In Ontario universities there are essentially two types of bachelor degrees granted: (1) the honors degree, granted after four years of university work and thirteen grades of high school; and (2) the regular baccalaureate degree is granted for three years of successful study after thirteen grades of high school. The four-year honors degree involves broad liberal arts and sciences study including specialization in a particular major area. The three-year degree is essentially a liberal arts and science degree with an opportunity for limited specialization. Upon graduation from university, the prospective teacher attends a school of education for one year where emphasis is directed to teaching methods, history and philosophy of education, educational psychology, and practice teaching. Teacher certification is granted upon graduation from this education unit. Thus, there is a vertical separation and a consecutive as opposed to a concurrent approach to professional preparation.

The second method, typical of the Western Provinces and some universities in the east, centers teacher preparation in professional education units of the universities. Under this system a concurrent approach is utilized, combining liberal education, special emphasis on teaching subject matter, and teacher education into one curriculum. This approach is analagous to the teacher education programs in the United States.

Undergraduate degree courses in physical education in the universities of Canada have a short history. The first program was established at the University of Toronto in Ontario in 1940.[19] In this decade six other universities instituted programs and by 1964 there were seventeen institutions offering various degrees in physical education. By 1974 there were more than thirty programs in Canada.

The types of degrees and structures of the various curricula show wide variation. Only three institutions offer a Bachelor of Arts degree in physical education. The remaining universities offer a variety of degrees such as Bachelor of Physical and Health Education, or some combination thereof. One can only speculate upon the reasons for this variation.

The structure of the curricula in all universities emphasizes liberal education. In some cases the Bachelor of Arts degree is earned first; in a second approach, the professional phase and the liberal education phase are offered in a parallel manner. A third method is to offer the professional degree first and this is followed by the Bachelor of Arts degree in a succeeding year. The pros and cons of each approach could be debated endlessly.

The curricula context emphasizes arts and science courses, as well as professional theory and activity courses. Depending on the teacher education system in vogue in the particular province, practice teaching and professional education courses may be included.

Graduate programs in physical education have not exhibited the same rapid growth as the undergraduate programs. The only institutions offering work at the master's level are British Columbia, Simon Fraser, Alberta, Saskatchewan, Western Ontario, Windsor, Waterloo, Ottawa, New Brunswick and Dalhousie University in Nova Scotia. At the doctoral level only the University of Alberta offers a program. However, institutions in Ontario, the University of Western Ontario, the University of Windsor and the University of Waterloo, are close to initiating programs. Many Canadians undertaking graduate work in physical education attend universities in the United States. Unless one expects to teach at the college or university level, little pressure exists, and therefore relatively little incentive, for the individual to pursue graduate work in physical education. The educational attainment of most university faculties of physical education has risen sharply over the past decade; yet, there is still room for considerable improvement. Increased availability of graduate programs, as well as increased financial aid for graduate study bodes well for the future. Indeed, the future of graduate education in Canada looks very promising. The insistence on pursuing programs appropriate to the Canadian situation may mean that graduate work in Canada will have an unique orientation that is neither American nor European.

## Special Characteristics

### Canadian Association for Health, Physical Education and Recreation[2]

Dr. A. S. Lamb and Miss Ethel Cartwright were instrumental in initiating action, to form the national association of Canada. Primarily, through the efforts of these individuals, the Canadian Association was established in 1933. The early years were characterized by a small, but hard-working membership. By the early 1940's the Association had a firmer foundation and began influencing developments in physical education. Some credit must go to the Association for early developments in professional preparation programs and CAHPER also helped develop Canada's National Physical Fitness Act of 1943. In 1946 the name was changed to the present one--the Canadian Association for Health, Physical Education and Recreation, Inc.

The Canadian Association had some difficulty earlier in putting a regular publication on a sound footing. Prior to 1950, a bulletin had been published; this was discontinued in 1951. In 1952 another attempt was made to publish a journal, and in 1957 the first printed journal became an entity and has been published regularly since then.

A Research Committee was established in 1961, and it has served as a central group through which researchers in the field could identify. This Committee has undertaken some specific projects, with the most noteworthy probably being the C.A.H.P.E.R. Fitness-Performance Test. The results of this Canadian testing project is being used to establish national norms for children between the ages of seven and seventeen.

The Association was instrumental in developing and has cooperated further in the development of the R. Tait McKenzie Memorial at Almonte, Ontario. Lastly, the role played by the C.A.H.P.E.R. in developing the Fitness and Amateur Sports Act of 1961 was a vital one.

### The Fitness and Amateur Sport Act (Bill C-131)

It is doubtful if any one incident has been more stimulating to the field of physical education than the passage of Bill C-131 in 1961. The objectives of the bill were (1) to assist the development of international and national sport; (2) to aid in training coaches; (3) to provide bursaries for training of personnel; (4) to aid research in fitness and amateur sport; (5) to arrange conferences in this area of concern; (6) to provide for recognition of achievements; (7) to distribute information; (8) and to coordinate interested agencies in the area of fitness and amateur sport. The work was to be coordinated in a national office established in Ottawa.

Since the inception of the Act, many bursaries have been granted to physical educators enabling them to pursue advanced studies in their field. Financial assistance has been provided for many amateur organizations supporting developments in sport, or in underwriting the costs of national teams. The results of the Act have been spectacular, and the benefits accruing to the field of physical education will continue to multiply.

## Sport Canada--Recreation Canada

In an effort to assist the various sport associations in Canada, as well as to encourage mass participation, the federal government has built upon the Fitness and Amateur Sport Act. John Munro, then Minister of National Health and Welfare, outlined the government plan in a speech presented in 1970.[13] The approach was to provide substantial assistance through a national office to help amateur sport, financially and administratively. A parallel unit would function in the same fashion to assist in the recreation sphere.

Since 1970 several reorganizations have taken place and the amount of money has been increased. One of the major tasks of the national office was coordination of the Canadian efforts for the 1976 Olympics in Montreal.

## Physical Education Research in Canada.[7]

Since 1958 when graduate study in physical education began, considerable advances in research facilities, as well as in the quality and quantity of research personnel have been made. The number of research units in physical education has paralleled the rapid growth of professional preparation programs in Canada. With government assistance three fitness research institutes were established in the mid-1960's.[15] Since that time many universities have slowly but surely increased their efforts in physical education and sport research. Indeed, in a submission to the Commission to study The Nationalization of University Research in 1971, the Faculty of Physical Education at the University of Western Ontario spoke of sixteen different areas of interest. As the submission phrased it:

> Physical education and sport will be successful as a profession only to the extent that the field is able to assimilate this knowledge and the resultant ordered generalizations that have meaning for physical education practitioners. It will then be necessary for researchers and scholars in this field to set up tentative hypotheses increasingly--hypotheses based on the findings of scientists in related fields and our own, and to apply all known methods and accompanying techniques of research carefully and painstakingly to problems which belong to physical education and sport (defined above). This task belongs to us alone, and

we must accomplish this goal primarily through our own
efforts if we hope to survive and to serve our fellow
men!  No other discipline will do this for us, except in
a secondary way and belatedly.[18]

## The Province of Quebec:[18],

Deserving of special mention is the province of Quebec and its
uniquely constituted system of education.  There are two distinct
school systems in the Province:  the first encompasses about seven-
eighths of the population and is Roman Catholic; the remainder, non-
Roman Catholic, is predominantly Protestant.  The Roman Catholic
system is patterned after the French system of Education.  The elementary grades stress the basic tools of learning; the secondary level
includes a general section and a scientific section, and in some schools
a special 12th-year course, a commercial course, and a classified section.  The private schools in the province offer equivalent courses,
except at the secondary level there are the classical colleges.  These
classical colleges offer preparation for entrance to the Roman Catholic
universities, and most offer an eight-year classical course through to
the Bachelor of Arts degree.

It was through the "Colleges Classiques" that sports programs
were initiatied in French Canada.  The physical education programs
and facilities in the public schools were slow to develop.  Abortive attempts under the 1939 "Loi Instituant le Conseil Provincial des Sports,"
and through a publication in 1948 by the Department of Public Instruction based on the 1933 British physical education training syllabus, did not stimulate the development of physical education in the
schools significantly.  The progress of intramural and interscholastic
athletes in the classical colleges led the way.  Private organizations
in the Province have given considerable impetus to sports programs
in various localities.  Physical education and sports programs have
now reached the stage where they are considered an essential phase
of education in the schools of the province.

The administrative structure of education in Quebec has just
recently been revised.  Established in 1961, a royal commission has
investigated problems inherent in education in Quebec, and a reorganization within the Province has been effected.  Although the effects
of the reorganization have not been fully felt in physical education,
there are several recommendations arising out of this report that bode
well for physical education in the schools.  Some of these recommendations are (1) at least two hours of physical educaton per week;
(2) summer programs for present elementary school teachers;
(3) physical education specialists to direct programs in school regions
and to teach in secondary schools; (4) the employment of a director
of physical education to prepare curricula and supervise their implementation; and (5) that new schools and existing schools be properly
equipped for physical education.

Construction of physical education facilities has been increased in recent years. Greater availability of qualified personnel, as well as of facilities and equipment, will have a great impact on physical education in Quebec in the immediate future.

## The Olympics - Montreal - 1976

In 1967 Canada was host to the nations of the world through the media of Expo #67, the Worlds Fair. Less than a decade later, in July 1976, Canada again hosted the nations of the world through the media of sport. The attention of the sporting world was focused on Montreal and Canada at the XXI modern Olympiad.

The development of the Olympic site, and the operation of the Games cover over one billion dollars. These costs escalated some four hundred per cent from the original estimates. The financing of the Olympic Games was underwritten by the use of lotteries, the sale of special coins and stamps, as well as other memorabilia associated with the Olympics. However the dramatic rise in costs produced an enormous short fall financially, and resulted in considerable controversies involving various levels of governments. Notwithstanding these problems the Games opened on schedule and proved to be highly successful.

The hosting of a spectacle of the magnitude of the Olympics had great impact on Canada. Many projects were developed utilizing the Olympic theme. For example, the Canadian Association for Health, Physical Education, and Recreation developed an Olympic workbook which received wide distribution in the schools. A commercial interest sponsored a Young Olympians Program which encouraged youth to participate in many of the Olympic events. The 1976 Olympiad for the Physically Disabled hosted in August represents yet another example.

Amateur athletics in Canada were affected very extensively. Sport Canada, an agency of the federal government assisted, and encouraged various sport governing bodies to develop programs preparing athletes for the 1976 games. Although each governing body developed unique programs, some with a broad base of participation, others with a narrower focus on the elite athlete, the overall pattern was much greater opportunity for Canadian athletes.

Hopes remained optimistic and the Olympic spirit assisted Canada in performing well in 1976, but even more importantly the Olympic Games left a legacy of sport enthusiasm in Canada that will be maintained long after 1976.

## Conclusion

The intent of these few brief pages has been to draw some
generalizations on physical education and sport in Canada. Geographical size, variance of population and provincial autonomy in the field
of education limit the similarities. The force that transcends this
uniqueness is the role of physical education and sports in the educational setting. Hence, even though the means may differ, there is
considerable agreement on the ends to be achieved. This core of
agreement has vitalized the field in recent years, and serves as the
basis for optimism about the future.

## SELECTED REFERENCES

1.  Association d'Education Physique et Recreation de Quebec.
    *Le Rapport Parent et L'Education Physique.* (A report pre-
    pared by the Association d'Education Physique et Recreation
    de Quebec, Sillery, Que.)

2.  Blackstock, C. R. "The Canadian Association for Health,
    Physical Education and Recreation," in *Physical Education in
    Canada.* Edited by M. L. Van Vliet, Scarborough, Ontario:
    Prentice-Hall of Canada. 1965.

3.  Bryans, Helen. "Secondary School Curriculum for Girls," in
    *Physical Education in Canada.* Edited by M. L. Van Vliet,
    Scarborough, Ontario: Prentice-Hall of Canada. 1965.

4.  Canada, Bureau of Statistics. *Canada Year Book 1965.*
    Ottawa: Qyeen's Printer and Controller of Stationery. 1965.

6.  Conway, John. "What is Canada?" *The Atlantic Monthly,*
    Vol. 214, No. 5 (Nov. 1964). pp. 100-105.

7.  Howell, Maxwell L. "Physical Education Research in Canada,"
    in *Physical Education in Canada.* Edited by M. L. Van Vliet,
    Scarborough, Ontario: Prentice-Hall of Canada. 1965.

8.  Landry, Fernand and Montpetit, The Reverand M. "Physical
    Education in French Canada," in *Physical Education in Canada.*
    Edited by M. L. Van Vliet, Scarborough, Ontario: Prentice-
    Hall of Canada. 1965.

9.  L'Heureux, Willard J. "Sport in Canadian Culture," *Journal
    of the Canadian Association for Health, Physical Education and
    Recreation,* XXIX, 4, (April-May, 1963). pp. 7-10.

10. Loosemore, J. P. "Intercollegiate Athletics in Canada: Its Organization and Development," *Journal of the Canadian Association for Health, Physical Education and Recreation*, XXVIII, 2, (December, 1961-January, 1962). p. 9.

11. Meagher, John W. "Professional Preparation," in *Physical Education in Canada*. Edited by M. L. Van Vliet, Scarborough, Ontario: Prentice-Hall of Canada. 1965.

12. Munro, Iveagh. "The Early Years," in *Physical Education in Canada*. Edited by M. L. Van Vliet, Scarborough, Ontario: Prentice-Hall of Canada. 1965.

13. Munro, John. "A Proposed Sports Policy for Canadians." Speech presented March 20, 1970. Department of National Health and Welfare, Ottawa, Canada.

14. Passmore, John H. "Teacher Education," in *Physical Education in Canada*. Edited by M. L. Van Vliet, Scarborough, Ontario: Prentice-Hall of Canada. 1965.

15. Shepard, R. J. "Progress and Activities of the Fitness Research Unit, Toronto," *Journal of the Canadian Association for Health, Physical Education and Recreation*, XXXII, 3, (February-March, 1966). p. 12.

16. Spicer, Stanley T. "The Provinces Today," in *Physical Education in Canada*. Edited by M. L. Van Vliet, Scarborough, Ontario: Prentice-Hall of Canada. 1965.

17. Stock, Brian. "Why Young Men Leave," *The Atlantic Monthly*, Vol. 214, No. 5, (November, 1965). pp. 113-114.

18. University of Western Ontario, Faculty of Physical Education. *A Proposal for a Ph.D. Program in Physical Education*. The University of Western Ontario, London. 1972.

19. Wipper, Kirk. "Silver Anniversary--University of Toronto's School of Physical and Health Education," *Journal of the Canadian Association for Health, Physical Education and Recreation*, XXXII, 3, (February, March, 1966). pp. 11-12.

# PHYSICAL CULTURE INSIDE THE PEOPLE'S REPUBLIC OF CHINA

by G. Glassford and R. Clumpner

## Biographical Sketches

*Robert Gerald Glassford* - B.P.E., M.A., Ph.D., received his Doctorate from the University of Illinois in the sociocultural area of sport and physical education. He has been at the University of Alberta for eleven years, five of which as Chairman of the Faculty of Physical Education. He is a member of the American Academy of Physical Education and has traveled and studied sport widely throughout the world, including China. He is considered an expert on the play habits of the Eskimo, having lived in the Arctic doing research on that aspect. He recently completed a year's sabbatical in Europe studying the European Concept of "Sport for All." A highly sought after speaker, Dr. Glassford is a recognized leader in sport and physical education in North America.

*Roy Anthony Clumpner*, B.S., M.A., Ph.D., received his Doctorate from the University of Alberta in the sociocultural area of sport and physical education. Presently he is an assistant professor in Department of Physical Education of Western Washington University in Bellingham, Washington. He has travelled extensively throughout the world and has lived in Germany, Japan and Canada.

# Introduction

Since 1949, the People's Republic of China has been shrouded in mystery, particularly to Westerners. This self-imposed isolationism to greater or lesser extent continued until the early 1970's when a mutually agreed breakdown of barriers occurred between the east and the west involving many facets of Chinese life. Physical Education and Sport was no exception.[1] The visitation by the American table tennis team to China heralded in this new era--and led to the coining of the phrase "ping pong diplomacy." It is significant to note that the selection of the sport media as the initial area for creating cultural exchanges was not, in all likelihood, a mere coincidence. The use of the sport construct in China has been extensively developed toward the ends of improving interpersonal relationships as well as for developing a healthy and physically competent populous.

## Background Data

Fourteen nations border China's 3 3/4 million square miles of land surface area (3rd largest country in the world) which are located in Eastern Asia. Clockwise from the north, these nations are the Union of Soviet Socialist Republics, Mongolia, North Korea, Hong Kong, Macao, Vietnam, Laos, Burma, India, Bhutan, Sikkim, Nepal, Pakistan, and Afghanistan. Within China's borders lie twenty-one provinces, five autonomous regions and two municipalities (Peking and Shanghai). Almost 90% of China's 900 million people (approximately 25% of the world's population) are employed in agriculture, raising the main crops of rice, wheat millet, cotton and tea in a country where mountains comprise four-fifths of the surface area. With the death of Mao Tse-tung and the purge of the "Gang of Four," it would seem that in the future the development and exploitation of China's large deposits of oil, natural gas, uranium, coal, iron and minerals will increase and a greater emphasis will be placed on technical and industrial employment.

## Historical Overview

Unlike many countries, China has remained one country, settled by one ethnic group. The Chinese culture itself dates back over 4,000 years and was looked upon for years as the center of culture and civilization in the far east. However, this advanced culture, which was responsible for the development of the magnetic compass and gun poweder, was markedly influenced by the teachings inherent in Taoism, Confucionism, and Buddhism which led the Chinese toward a non-action orientation, subservience to the authority of emperor and landlords, and mystical beliefs in supernatural processes. As the government structure became weak from corruption, the social structure crumbled. Foreign domination of China during the 19th and early 20th centuries played a large role in revolutionary fomentation within China. An overt act of rebellion occurred against the imperial family in 1911, led by foreign-educated Sun Yat-sen, the upshot of which was the establishment of a republic which soon eroded into a war-lord state.

A rival government, the Kuomintang, evolved in Canton and in 1921 nominated Sun Yat-sen as its president. The Kuomintang formed a coalition with the newly created communist party to fight for the independence of China. However, with Sun Yat-sen's death in 1925 and the ascendency of Chiang Kai Shek as president of the Kuomintang, a split occurred between the parties, and only the Japanese invasion of Manchuria in 1932 and World War II diverted, temporarily, the struggle between the two rival factions. The civil war resumed after World War II and peaked in 1948 when the Red Army, under the leadership of Mao Tse-tung, completely surprised Chiang's Nationalist army by swimming the previously thought unfordable Yangtze River with the use of bamboo buoys. The Nationalist forces were routed and Chiang was forced, in 1949, to seek refuge on the off-shore island of Taiwan. Mao and his party followers structured the government of the People's Republic of China by implementing practices which they had been developing over the years following the split with the Kuomintang.

Chinese society, under the direction of the Communist party, has been completely transformed. Taoism, Confucionism, and Buddhism no longer exist to any great extent. The land reform which Sun Yat-sen originally formulated and pressed for took place during the period of 1949-53. China officially turned to collectivization which evolved into the commune system by 1959. The commune consists of a series of revolutionary or production brigades which control the land and which are responsible for management at the town or village level, with the commune operating major public services and the large scale agricultural coordination or major factories in its region. The building blocks of contemporary China are these revolutionary brigades which are controlled by a revolutionary committee which is the decision-making body for all aspects of life--cultural, educational, social, or economic. The Communist Party still plays the major role in all activities and was instrumental in activating the 1958 Great Leap Forward along with the 1966 Cultural Revolution which redirected the country away from capitalism. By the 1970's, the barriers between east and west had relaxed considerably, due in large part to the admittance of China to the United Nations. As has been noted, the vehicle chosen to pioneer the opening of the "Bamboo Curtain" was sport and the term "ping pong diplomacy" suitably describes the implementation of a sport structure which has been created to generate increased international understanding.

Following Mao's death in 1976, a power struggle ensued which by the late 1970's resulted in China maintaining her path of greater association with the outside world and continuing interest and involvement in technology and industry.

## Pre-Revolutionary Physical Education

Many of the physical activities used in pre-revolutionary China are still in evidence today. These include such activities as swimming, diving, dancing, tightrope walking and ice sports in the northern areas. Other activities such as falconry (3rd Century B.C.) and polo (660 A.D.), while not practiced today, were at one time popular activities, especially among the elite classes. One activity which has had a lengthy history is the traditional sport of Wushu. In the past, Wushu concerned itself with wrestling, fencing, archery, the handling of swords, clubs and spears. Today Wushu activities today is Chinese Boxing (618-906 A.D.), one style of which is Shao Lin or the outer school which consists of 170 movements stressing quickness, leaps and kicks, usually directed toward an invisible opponent. Another branch of the outer school physical training technique is karate. The other style, Tai Chi Chuan (or the inner school) is the more popular form of Wushu and is characterized by slow movements, no jumping or running, a stress on the coordination of breathing with movement. Although both the inner and outer styles were developed as pugilistic disciplines, they are used solely as gymnastic exercises today.

Formal physical education in China began in the 19th century and consisted of two divergent approaches. One approach was characterized by a formal, military-type exercise program such as the one established in 1875 at the Nanking Military Academy. A central part of this program included formal gymnastics usually under the direction of a Japanese or German instructor. The military-style exercise program was later adopted by the government public schools and was generally in evidence until 1949. The second program which developed included western sport, first as a recreative activity and later as a physical education activity. This form of physical education was prevalent in church affiliated missionary schools and the Y.M.C.A. where the mind and body concept was stressed.

The Government's role in physical education became formalized in 1905 at which time legislation was created wherein three to five hours of physical exercise was required initially for elementary schools and later for middle and lower normal schools as well as lower agriculture schools. Since only 5% of all Chinese youth attended schools during this era such a gesture can only be construed as tokenism. Interestingly, the government also sponsored an early form of teacher training for physical educators in Soochou (1903) and Shanghai (1904). Programs were limited in scope and dealt primarily with courses such as anatomy, physiology and some athletic skills under Japanese instruction.

The greatest strides made in physical education, however, were made by the missionary schools. As early as 1890, track and field made its appearance at St. John's University in Shanghai, followed by the introduction of basketball in 1896 at the Tientsin Y.M.C.A. As previously noted, the Y.M.C.A. played an important role, not only in the development of physical education programs, but also in establishing the foundations for China's first national athletic association, and beyond these roles the Y.M.C.A. carried on an extensive training program for its physical directors. In 1918, the Y.M.C.A. School of Physical Education of the Association College of China opened and offered both a two-year program for physical training instructors and a four-year director's program. The programs at the "Y's" like those of the government schools, had limitations. In the case of the government controlled schools only 5% of the populace attended; the Y.M.C.A., on the other hand, placed restrictions in the form of membership thus excluding most Chinese from the programs.

After the turn of the century, the government turned increasingly to the Y.M.C.A. for both in-service training and for the organization of physical education departments in normal public schools. The first of these schools was founded in 1915 in Nanking and was under the leadership of the noted physical educator, Charles H. McCloy. Eventually, the Y.M.C.A.'s influence diminished due to increased feelings of hostility toward foreigners commencing during the mid-1920's and a lack of sound leadership in the organization itself. The control of physical education eventually fell into the hands of the China National Amateur Athletic Federation in the 1920's. With the establishment of Chiang Kai Shek's nationalist government in Nanking in 1928, further legislation was structured which increased physical education in the school programs. As early as 1922, the Chinese Progressive Education Association had recommended the establishment of physical education specialist training schools, new curricula, and the development of research programs. The recommendations had met with no approval. In 1928, however, at the First National Education Conference, all education was forced to conform to the Three People Principles of Sun Yat-sen which focused on the stimulation of a national spirit, a spirit of sacrifice and of self-discipline. Within this framework physical fitness was endorsed. The Kuomintang, due possibly to the Japanese and Communist threat, turned the physical education programs, which had been experimenting with after-school western-type sports programs, to German militaristic-type activities. During the 1930's, a national Director of Physical Education was named and classroom curricula were set up to coincide with the mandatory physical education law passed for all schools. Despite these steps, by the time the Communists came to power in 1949, the vast majority of Chinese had never entered a classroom much less participated in physical education or sport.

## Physical Culture[2] Since 1949

It is necessary at the outset of this section to draw attention to the interrelatedness of all aspects of life in China since 1949. Built upon Marx's dialectical materialism the Chinese system emerges from an economic base with social conditions, theoretical knowledge, political structure and religion emerging from it. It is not surprising, therefore, to find that physical education or physical culture is integrally woven into the fabric of China's social norms.

## Physical Culture - Post Revolution

The term "physical culture" has been used here advisedly in that the intent is to indicate to the reader that the Chinese under Mao Tse-tung view physical education in broad context extending to programs well beyond the formal class instruction periods.

## Administration of Sport and Physical Culture

Before sketching in the programs of physical culture within the formal education domain it seems appropriate to divert momentarily to a brief description of the administration hierarchy within China. There are two organizations which direct and regulate sport and physical culture within China. The major organizational body is the Physical Culture and Sport Commission, a Government ministry, which plans, finances, sets policies and acts as a liaison with other government departments such as public health, national defense, etc. The other organizational body is the All China Sports Federation (the Chinese Olympic Committee) which is responsible for mass organization of sport. Located within the federation is the secretariat with office staff and the national sport associations. The national sport associations basically are involved in three areas: Mass Sport and Recreation which largely involves the mass exercise programs, Competition at the factory, city, national and international level, and the training and support that goes with their programs. Within the latter would be such things as research, personnel training, planning and facilities design.

Each of these two administrative bodies are found within the various provinces, districts, autonomous regions, and major cities. They appear to be carefully and fully interlinked in the upper echelons with leading members of the Physical Culture and Sport Commission also serving in responsible positions with the All China Sport Federation. Physical culture and sport in China seems to be of great significance within the Chinese life-style. A highly efficient organization has been developed to ensure that sport and physical culture continue to remain a viable element in the future development of the nation.

## Primary and Middle School Programs (Grades 1 to 8 or 9)

Since the Cultural Revolution, which began in 1966 a major restructuring of the educational system in China has occurred which has led directly to the paring of three to four years from the standard twelve year program. Virtually all students now complete their middle school program by the age of 15 or 16 years and are, upon graduation, expected to join the work force of the nation. After three or four years of physical labor, a capable individual who wishes to continue with a formal education program must follow a four part application procedure with approval required at each succeeding level; the initial contact and request is made through the leader of his production unit, the applicant then appeals for support from the masses of his unit; the Revolutionary Committee of the individual's production brigade upon request debates the applicant's suitability; and finally the Revolutionary Committee of the institute to which the person applied for admission rules on the request. Decisions at each level are based extensively on the applicant's political ideology, his contribution to the production brigade of which he is a member, and his physical fitness to pursue the program requested. At the present time the evidence would indicate that a very small percentage of the Chinese people continue beyond a middle school education--perhaps as low as 3 - 5%.

The educational policy of China is to develop each individual morally, intellectually, physically, and to produce a worker who has a deep-seated "socialist consciousness." As noted, an integral part of the education program is the physical culture element. To a great extent the Soviet model of physical education or physical culture has been adopted by the Chinese who have translated the Soviet's Physical Culture manuals, their scientific data and approach, their GTO system (Ready for Labor and Defense), and their pedagogical techniques. Beyond that, the similarity of the administrative machinery of sport and physical culture bears striking resemblance to that found in the Soviet Union.

Throughout the eight to nine years of formal education (the actual length varies from district to district and at the moment is in flux) each student receives two hours of formal instruction per week in four basic areas of physical culture: games and dance form one part of the core wherein only a limited stress is placed on competitiveness. Rather, the program emphasizes fun, group consciousness, independence, flexibility, and discipline. A second part of the program incorporates a basic exercise regimen in which utility, repetiticn, and body control in a non-competitive environment is stressed. Sports, which include basketball, track and field, table tennis, volleyball, gymnastics, among many, constitutes a third portion of the program. Competition and a competitive attitude, while still not forming as strong an element as it does in North America, is an integral part of this phase of the physical culture program. The popular motto "friendship first, competition second" is still constantly evident in the schools and is stressed by physical culturists. The fourth component of physical culture in Chinese schools is the military preparation program based extensively on the Soviet GTO system. Route marches of ten to twenty kilometers, grenade throwing, dashes, mock and real rifle training form the core of this program. Although not restricted to the middle school (aged 13 to 16) this part of the program receives limited attention in the elementary grades.

An interesting feature of elementary and middle school physical culture since 1971 is the use of mass exercise programs. In most schools, once and sometimes twice each day students file into the school courtyard where they participate in a set of eight basic exercises (see Figure 1) accompanied by music piped through the ever-present speaker system. It is not uncommon to see 2 - 3,000 students participating in this program at any given time. Most frequently the group is led by a physical culture teacher although from time to time a student is selected to lead. Incidentally, this program forms a part of the life pattern of a large portion of the Chinese populous.

Figure 1. Eight Basic Exercises.

In addition to the above components of the physical culture program, each student is expected, although not required, to participate for at least two hours per week in the extracurricular sports programs. Those who wish to and are capable, participate on inter-scholastic teams; others practice skills learned in the regular classroom program, or develop their prowess in the military elements. Inddor facilities are limited and, as a consequence, many of the organized team and individual sports practices are conducted out-of-doors.

The following itinerary of a primary school physical culture teacher's day might serve to increase the perspective of the topic.

Typically the teacher arises early (6:30 a.m.) and leaves shortly
after so as to be at the school before 7:45 a.m. to assist students in
their extracurricular sports program. She then takes part in the
morning exercise program and teaches two regular physical culture
classes. After 10:15 a.m. she conducts the military training program, has a break for lunch, conducts a third physical culture class
and after 4:00 p.m. coaches youngsters in various sports (in her
case particularly gymnastics) and leaves for home on her bicycle between 6:00 and 7:00 p.m. As with all teachers, this young lady
would also lead the students in a twice daily eye exercise program
which is done to music and structured to reduce eyestrain. Teachers' salaries range from 40 to 90 yuan ($17.80 to $40.00) per month
(as of 1972) with a fixed percentage--3 to 5%--being spent on apart-
ment rental.

Classes are in session between 8:00 and 11:45 a.m. and 2:00
and 3:40 p.m. six days of the week. Core courses are conducted in
themorning and self-study, self-improvement courses are conducted
in the afternoon. Approximately ten per cent of a school day is
given over to industrial or agricultural work which is found at all
levels of education. Similarly, all students must study the writings
of Mao Tse-tung each day.

## Physical Culture in Tertiary Learning Institutions

After the Cultural Revolution a marked decrement in the enrollment of students in tertiary institutions took place within China.
In large part this was due to the motto which derived out of that era
that the youth of the nation must learn from the masses and from
the People's Liberation Army (PLA). Hence, all students were expected to enter the working force after grade 8 or 9 in order to
"learn from the people." An excellent example of the fall-off of enrollment in tertiary institutions was Peking University, which comprised 17 departments with 64 areas of specialization, a faculty of
2,100 full-time faculty, an overall staff of between 6,000 and 7,000
teachers and a magnificent library consisting of over 2.7 million volumes 30 per cent written in foreign languages. From 1970-1973, it
is estimated only 4,000 students were enrolled in programs within that
institution.

After the Cultural Revolution, the length of time required to
earn a degree was shortened and it became possible to obtain a degree in medicine in three years where it formerly took six. This re-
duction was apparently due to the elimination of redundant materials,
extraneous theorizing, and a new approach to teaching. In no small
part it was also due to a year-round study program. Additionally,
whereas the grade orientation had been extremely strong prior to the
Cultural Revolution and cramming a basic study technique, the students after the revolution had to go into the factories, shops and
parks to combine their knowledge with the practicalities and exigencies of the moment. Students and teachers studied together in small
groups rather than stress the lecture method. Above all, however,

only highly motivated students, students who had achieved a strong ideological bent, were permitted to attend such institutions, hence a state-oriented motivation was inculcated and the student supposedly had a strong drive to learn. Today, Chinese education again is going through a period of changes and at this moment it is difficult to ascertain just how much of the post-cultural revolution changes will remain. Indications are that a greater emphasis is being placed on evaluation and the acquisition of knowledge, based more on Western education; however, it really is too soon to make any definite statements on this matter at this time.

Educational costs including fees, medical requirements, and books in China are borne by the state. In 1972, each student received a stipend of 19.5 yuan ($8.75) per month for living allowance and pocket money (this was about half of the base salary of a factory worker or a teacher with limited experience). If the student had worked for five years then they received their normal pay while attending a tertiary level institution.

Physical culture comprises an integral part of the student's life at institutions such as this. Each is required to participate in two weekly classes of approximately one hour duration during which time they study basic physiology as well as participating in activity. Generally the activities are along the lines of what we in the west would term "lifetime sports." In some schools music for the daily exercise program filters through the halls and into the wooden areas where students might be studying. Peer pressure, and habit, among other factors, lead to a high level of participation in this program. Voluntary exercise programs and organized sports such as basketball, soccer, volleyball, table tennis, gymnastics, and track form the equivalent of a North American intramural program. Interdepartmental and interuniversity competitions are held on a regular basis. Military training in grenade throwing, route marches and shooting, comprises a part of the overall structure.

Physical Culture, Mass Sport, and National Defense

The fundamental role of physical culture within the socialist dogma of China's ruling party was established as early as April, 1917 when an article entitled "A Study of Physical Culture" and authored by a young teacher, Mao Tse-Tung, appeared in the journal, New Youth.[3] Although this article was relatively "devoid of political flavor" it set the stage for the creation of an integrated physical culture program which would yield a nation of fit citizens, citizens capable of defending their homeland. Kolatch has made clear the importance of physical culture in the following statement:

> To Mao, when one wishes to remould the outlook of a nation, he must start with one very basic question: What is physical culture? Mao Tse-tung replies that: "Physical Culture is the method employed by human beings in order to prolong their life and develop their bodies in a uniform manner."[4]

With this concept clearly before him, physical culture evolved as a dynamic force in the rebuilding of the Chinese nation.

## Mass Sport and National Defense

As a result of the importance placed upon physical culture, and consequently sport, by Mao Tse-tung a series of programs have been instituted since 1951 the principle aims of which have been to increase sport participation among the people of China. During 1951-1952 a program based to some extent upon the Soviet GTO system (Golov k Trudu i Oborone--Ready for Labor and Defense), was introduced and ratified. Through its inception the Party hoped to achieve the development of a more fit nation. Age and sex group classifications as well as standards of performance were developed in such events as rope climbing, sprints (60, 100, 200 meters), distance runs (500, 800, 1500, 3000 meters), swimming (25, 50, 100 meters), grenade throwing (or a choice of shot put or weight lifting), jumping (Long and high jump), marksmanship, cross country-running, route marches, gymnastics, cycling and the basic labor-defense exercises. Badges and certificates were awarded to encourage participation. The initial program has been reassessed and restructured since its inception but the basic premises appear to hold even today and it is not uncommon to see the Chinese people participating in various activities of the types noted above. The following chart gives some indications of the standards for those 18 and over. (Page 115).

Sports programs comprise an integral part of the daily regimen of most factory workers. The Nanking Precision Instrument Factory, for example, provides their workers with a morning and afternoon exercise break as well as a sports program which begins at 4:00 p.m. each day. Workers may elect to participate and the program includes basketball, volleyball, badminton, tug-of-war, track and field, Wushu, a battledore-like activity, gymnastics, and ping-pong. A participation rate of eighty per cent was cited by the factory officials.

Similar types of programs also exist in the agricultural communes (specifically within each production brigade) where people of all ages join together at designated times during the day to play. Interbrigade and intercommune participation opportunities are an integral component although the highly competitive aspect of play is consciously controlled. This is not to say that all Chinese participate in some type of sport program whether it be on the commune or in industry. Participation generally depends on the circumstances, facilities and the local area. Some places emphasize participation heavily. Recently a decline has occurred somewhat in the number of mass calisthenic programs in factories.

Equipment and facilities are poor by North American standards and it is not uncommon to see an old door used as a ping-pong table or a basketball backboard. Similarly, outdoor facilities are more frequently found than indoor areas. Lighting, as an example, creates something of a problem for the indoor areas. Of significance, however,

# REGULATIONS AND STANDARDS FOR THE NATIONAL PHYSICAL CULTURE TRAINING PROGRAM[5]

## (May 5, 1975)

| | AGE<br>STANDARDS<br>SEX<br>EVENTS/ITEMS | OVER 18 YEARS | |
|---|---|---|---|
| | | MALES | FEMALES |
| 1 | 100 Meter Dash<br>or 1200 Meter Dash (men) | 14.0<br>29.0 | 16.5 |
| 2 | 800 Meter Run (women)<br>1500 Meter Run (men)<br>or 3000 Meter Run (men) | 5:45.0<br>12:50.0 | 3:25.0 |
| 3 | High Jump<br>or Long Jump | 1.25 M<br>4.50 M | 1.10 M<br>3.40 M |
| 4 | Chin Ups (men)<br>Push Ups (women)<br>or Parallel Bar Dips (men)<br>or Sit Ups (women)<br>or Pole/Rope Climb -<br>　　　　(men: 2 hands)<br>　　　　(women: 4 limbs) | 9<br><br>12<br><br><br>3.50 M | <br>9<br><br>10<br><br><br>3.10 M |
| 5 | Hand Grenade Throw -<br>　　　　(men: 700 g)<br>　　　　(women: 500 g)<br>or Shot Put - (men: 5K)<br>　　　　- (women: 4K) | 36.00 M<br><br>7.40 M | <br>23.00 M<br><br>6.00 M |
| 6 | Gymnastics | according to standards* | |
| 7 | Military Outing with Back Pack<br>　- (men: 5k weight for 10 km distance)<br>　- (women: 3k weight for 6 km distance)<br><br>or Swimming - (men: 100 Meters)<br>　　　　- (Women: 50 Meters)<br><br>or Skating or Other Event**<br><br>(* Items are in four categories: vaulting horse, parallel bars, horizontal bar and miscellaneous skills)<br><br>(** Items in this category are determined by conditions in individual provinces, municipal districts and autonomous regions) | 65 min.<br><br><br>any stroke, no time limit | <br>45 min. |

is the Chinese technique of scaling down equipment and facility size to suit the age group. Toward this end they produce three different sizes of basketballs, and several sizes of soccer balls, they reduce the dimensions of the soccer pitch and the goal, they lower basketball backboards to as low as 1.75 meters, and the size of a ping-pong table to suit five-year old participants.

Equally important, they provide interested instructors and workers an opportunity to be re-educated in the local, provincial, or national sports training centers. All expenses as well as the individual's full salary are covered by the state and the in-service training might last as long as six months. Such workers then return to their commune in order to introduce new techniques and training methods.

Beyond the activities noted above the state also provides training in events similar to those developed within the Hitler Youth Program--glider flying, parachuting, navigation and so forth. This program may not be receiving the attention it did in earlier years and our group saw little evidence of its existence.

## Summary

The total integration of the physical culture program that exists in China into other aspects of the socialist state provides an interesting example for analysis. The program was developed to appeal to people of all ages and to encourage participation so as to "build up the people's health."

China's physical culture and sport program, while drawing on Soviet models is unique and tailormade for her own needs. At this writing, China once again is going through a transitional period and it is difficult to ascertain the exact direction she will take in the field of physical culture and sport. Similarly, it is difficult to perceive what impact more leisure time will have on the country in the near future. What is evident, however, is that China does have a well planned program in physical culture and sport meeting the needs of the masses.

# FOOTNOTES AND SELECTED REFERENCES

1.  Surprisingly little material has been published that deals spe-
    cifically with sport and physical culture in the People's Repub-
    lic of China. The following work is among the best that the
    authors were able to locate that was based extensively on pri-
    mary as opposed to secondary source material.

Wee Kok Ann. "Physical Education in Protestant Christian Colleges
    and Universities in China." Unpublished Doctor of Philosophy
    thesis, Columbia University. 1937.

Gunsun Hoh. *Physical Education in China* Shanghai: Commercial
    Press. 1926.

Wu Chih Kang. "The Influence of the Y.M.C.A in the Development
    of Physical Education in China." Unpublished Doctor of Phi-
    losophy thesis, The University of Michigan. 1926.

Jonathan Kolatch. *Sports, Politics and Ideology in China.* New York:
    Jonathan David Publishers. 1972.

Brian Pendleton. "Fitness Standards and Testing in the People's Re-
    public of China." Department of Physical Education and Re-
    creation, Vancouver Community College, Vancouver, British
    Columbia. July 1977.

Kuei Shou Wu. "Physical Education in the Republic of China from
    1880-1965." Unpublished Master's thesis, The University of
    Alberta. 1965.

2.  The term "physical culture" has been used in this and succeed-
    ing sections to denote a broad frame of reference which is im-
    plicit in the Chinese work *t'i yu*. There is a general tendency
    in North America to use the words "physical education" to de-
    scribe a limited kind of activity normally associated with a for-
    mal educational program. It stands apart from organized ath-
    athletics, sports, such as chess and even athletic events spon-
    sored by schools and universities but outside of a regularly
    scheduled, curriculum-oriented program. For the Chinese, the
    term "physical culture" is all-embracive, encompassing competi-
    tive athletic programs, all forms of contemporary and tradition-
    al exercises, factory sports programs, and formal physical edu-
    cation.

    Significantly, one of the first essays to have been
    published by Mao Tse-tung was entitled "A Study of Physical
    Culture" the content of which was focused, among other things,
    upon the need for the Chinese people to be physically fit to
    defend their land. Mao contended that man cannot maintain an
    interest in physical culture unless he fails to grasp the reality

of its relationship to himself. Mao placed substantial responsibility for this on the negative societal attitudes held by Chinese people in general and on several occasions following the establishments of the communist regime in 1949 made public pronouncements in support of sound physical culture program.

3.  Jonathan Kolatch. *Sports, Politics and Ideology in China.* New York: Jonathan David Publishers, 1972. pp. 77-82.

4.  *Ibid.* p. 79.

5.  "Guojia Tiyu Duanlian Biaozhun Tiaoli" in Xin Tiyu (New Physical Culture), No. 5, May, 1975. pp. 10-12. Translated by Brian B. Pendleton, Department of Physical Education and Recreation, Vancouver Community College, Vancouver, British Columbia. July 1977.

# SPORT AND PHYSICAL EDUCATION IN THE REPUBLIC OF CHINA

by Min-Chung Tsai and Daeshik Kim

## Biographical Sketches

*Min-Chung Tsai* received his B.Ed. degree from the National Taiwan Normal University; earned his M.S. degree in physical education and second M.S. degree in health and safety education from Indiana University. He returned to the Republic of China, and taught at the National Taiwan Normal University. He returned to the United States and earned his Doctor of Philosophy degree in educational administration with emphasis on physical education.

Dr. Tsai has taught at the Taipei Normal High School, the National Taiwan Normal University, Indiana University, the University of Minnesota and also served as Fitness Testing Director of the McBurney YMCA in New York City. He has presented papers at several international physical education and sports meetings, and also published numerous articles in professional journals in the Republic of China and overseas.

Dr. Tsai is an Executive Member of the International Council on Health, Physical Education, and Recreation (ICHPER), and is also an officer of many professional organizations in China and overseas. He was a key organizer of the Asian-Pacific Congress of Health, Physical Education, and Recreation, which was held in Taipei in 1975.

Dr. Tsai is the Director of the Department of Physical Education and Sports in the Ministry of Education, Republic of China and is also a Professor of Physical Education at the Graduate School of the National Taiwan Normal University. Presently Dr. Tsai lives with his wife in Taipei.

*Daeshik Kim*, the co-author of this article is also the author of the article on Sports and Physical Education in Korea. He is an assistant professor of physical education at the University of Texas, Austin. A detailed biographical sketch may be found in the Korean article.

Ti-Yi, which literally means "physical education", is an integral part of the Chinese education as well as a vital part of the recreational programs in the Republic of China (Taiwan). The word Ti-Yi encompasses the full spectrum of sports, from physical education, to athletics, to physical recreation and is used broadly and interchangeably by the Chinese.[5]

## Background

The Chinese civilization is one of the oldest and has perhaps one of the most colorful histories of martial arts, sports, and games. The Chinese long before the birth of the Olympic Games in Greece recognized the significant contribution of physical activity to human wealth, and, as a result, Choung Fu was practiced as a form of medical gymnastics by the Chinese about 2,700 B.C.

According to Chinese literature, physical education and sports activities originated at an early stage in Chinese History. Hwang Di, the first emperor in China, taught his warriors archery for use in warfare. This fact evidently marked the beginning of Chinese physical education.[3]

It was during the Chou dynasty that rituals, music, archery, chariot driving, and mathematics were the major courses in the highly organized schools. Dance and poetry were taught in the spring and summer, and the lance and pike were taught in the fall and winter.

During the Han and Tang dynasties, football, dancing, horse-polo, dragon boat racing, and combative sports were very popular with and well participated in by the people. However, regretfully, from the Sung dynasty to the end of the Ching dynasty, physical activity and sports were discouraged and de-emphasized by the ruling class and by scholars. They strongly emphasized literary learning over physical activity. Therefore, people became disinterested in physical activities and this philosophy eventually hindered the developments of physical education and sports.[3]

Sports as we know them today were dormant in China until the early 1800's when foreign powers forced the Ching dynasty to open her doors for trade. It was in 1897 when the first Protestant missionary came to China and introduced western education and modern medical science to the Chinese. From this time onwards, the face of China changed rapidly. In 1862, a governmental school was established in Peking in order to train diplomatic personnel, and in 1870, the government dispatched a group of young scholars to the United States for study.

The government of the Ching dynasty was besieged by the foreign wars of 1834-1844 and 1856-1860, and was put under increasing pressures by foreign powers. From 1860-1894, China was ravaged by the Ching-Japanese War (Sino-Japanese War) of 1894-1895 and the

Boxer Rebellion of 1900. This resulted in the fall of the Ching dynasty in 1912.

As foreign influence increased in China, so did the interest in Western education and sports. By this time, the Chinese leaders had gradually realized the importance of physical education and sports. Eventually, sports were well accepted by the Chinese. Basketball became very popular and spread rapidly from city to city. Calisthenics and soccer clubs were organized also, and local competition became extensive. None-the-less, traditional sports such as Tai Chi Chuan were well preserved by masters and the general public. In 1902, the Ching dynasty issued orders for the remodeling of their antiquated system of education, and by 1903, the department of physical education was established at Chiang Su Senior Normal School in Suchow, Chian Si Province.[4,8] In the same year, The Chinese Gymnastic School was established, and thought was being given to developing a women's gymnastics school in Shanghai which became a reality in 1904. In 1909, the Y.M.C.A. of Shanghai had been established, but China was now torn with internal strife. This had the effect of slowing down the development of western culture and sports in China.

In 1912, the Republic of China was established. May of 1912 was significant in the history of physical education in China because the Ministry of Education ordered all high schools and colleges to initiate a military form of gymnastics in the school curriculum.[8] Seven years later the Ministry of Education ordered physical education in the elementary schools for a minimum of 150 minutes per week and 180 minutes per week in the upper elementary grades. Courses in health education (hygiene) were added in the high school curriculum.

In 1924 and every year thereafter, China had soccer and basketball teams that were sent abroad for competition six times a year.[8]

The government promulgated the National Physical Education Act in April of 1929. The Article 1 and Article 2, of the Act stated that:[3]

Article 1. The prime purpose of the national education program is aimed chiefly at developing good physique and sound stamina in the Chinese people with a view to provide them with the ability for self and national defenses.

Article 2. All Chinese, regardless of sex and age, shall be provided with physical training. Parents, teachers, and organizers work together as a team to teach and supervise physical activities in order to expedite the general development of sports.

As the governmental encouragement and support increased, sports enthusiastically gained popularity in China. By 1936, two hours of credit in physical education were given at all institutions of higher learning in China. In 1941, every 9th day of September was declared to be the official Physical Education Day.

Then on December 8, 1949, due to the increased military pressure of the Communist Chinese, the national government of the Republic of China was obliged to move to Taiwan. After the relocation of government in Taiwan, the leaders in the Republic of China recognized the important role that physical education and sports can play in building a strong nation.[11] The national government has strongly advocated the improvement of physical fitness and health of the people and the use of physical education to impart the elements of Chinese culture to all school age children.

## Administration and Organizations

The Ministry of Education is responsible for the administration of the National Physical Education Act. The Department of Physical Education in the Ministry of Education is the governing department for all physical education programs.[3] Under the Department of Physical Education there are four divisions: 1) school physical education, 2) public physical education, 3) compilation and screening and 4) international sports.

In China there are two central non-governmental sports organizations. One is the Amateur Athletic Federation of the Republic of China (ROCAAF) which officially governs all domestic sports activities. ROCAAF is a government supported federation and is directly supervised and influenced by the Ministry of the Interior. Another one is the ROC Olympic Committee which regulates Olympic sports (23 sports).

The ROC Olympic Committee is an official member of the International Olympic Committee. Taipei, Kimmen and Provincial Associations are under the ROCAAF and the ROC Olympic Committee. Also under their control are three overseas branch associations (Hong Kong, Korea and Philippines), 40 affiliated sports associatons, and two athletic unions.

## Physical Education in Schools

The philosophy and goal of the Chinese educational system is to develop the total individual mentally, physically, and morally. Traditionally, Chinese education encompasses four areas: moral, intellectual, physical, and social education. In addition to these four areas, six arts are also included: manners, music, archery, horsemanship, reading, writing, and mathematics.[10] Education for women was not considered the duty of the public school system until the 20th century. In 1944, the National Physical Education Committee was established in the Ministry of Education. This committee made possible the organized development and progression of physical education.

The purpose of general physical education in China are:[10]

1. To create the spirit of sports, to excite in the people an interest in physical training, and to offer appropriate facilities for such training.

2. To create a spirit of cooperation or team work which can be transferred to other communal works and duties of the citizens.

## Pre-School and Elementary Schools

Pre-school education was not attempted until 1950, and by 1967, there were more than 600 pre-school centers with a total of 88,897 pupils.[3] Free play, simple activities, and supervised games encompass the program at this level. In the same year the government extended compulsory education from six years to nine.

In elementary schools most of the physical education programs were taught by classroom teachers, and the pupils were required to participate in Physical Education for about five hours per week. (Approximately ¼ hours of total class hours per week. Total class hours per week are 25 hours). There were more than 2,376 elementary schools with approximately 2,364, 961 pupils in 1976. Most schools have an annual physical education day where students are encouraged to participate in various games and sports competitions. During this day participation in calisthenics, stunts, and track and field events are common. Gymnastics, combative sports, track and field, soccer, dancing, softball, basketball, and games are offered in physical education programs in elementary schools.

Objectives of Elementary School Physical Education are:[3]

1. To promote the physical well-being of our school education.

2. To instill virtues of justice, obedience, responsibility, honesty, and cooperation as the basis for social life.

3. To develop basic skills in physical education to promote their motor abilities and implant knowledge of safety.

4. To elicit interest in sports for the fulfillment of healthful and happy life.

## The Secondary Schools

The secondary schools in the Republic of China encompasses grades seven through twelve. There were 977 secondary schools with 1,503,953 students in 1976. In most schools, grades seven through nine are classified as junior high, and ten through twelve are considered senior high school. The physical education is taught by professional physical educators. If there are more than eighteen classes in a school, a separate department of physical education is established.[8] Compulsory attendance is required in the physical education program. The students participate in physical education program five hours per week. This is approximately 1/6 of total class hours. (Total class hours per week are 31 hours).

Objectives of Physical Education in the Secondary Schools are:[3]

A. Junior High Schools
1. To develop physical and mental health of the students.
2. To raise the students vitality and to maintain balanced development of body and mind.
3. To cultivate sportsmanship and the love of sports.
4. To increase skills in sports and self-defense.

B. Senior High Schools
1. To develop physical fitness.
2. To cultivate good conduct and morality.
3. To encourage participation in activities.
4. To equip with skills and effiencies for self-defense.

Normal teaching loads for physical educators in the secondary schools are 18-22 hours per week. In fact, total working hours a week are 28 hours because physical educators lead the "morning exercise" and also coach teams for interscholastic competition. There is, however, little compensation for this extra service.[5]

Among popular sports activities (intramural and interscholastic) are basketball, volleyball, badminton, gymnastics, swimming, combative sports, track and field, and dance for girls. This is required in the physical education curriculum for women. Physical education programs in junior high schools and those of the senior high schools are similar. However, a major portion of time for the boys is spent on track and field and ball games. A major portion of time for the girls is spent on dancing.[3] Students in vocational schools are also required to participate in physical education at least 50 minutes per week, and medical and physical examinations are periodically conducted by the government for the students.

## Colleges and Universities

There are more than 100 institutions of higher learning (junior colleges, senior colleges, and technical colleges) with a student population of 289,435. A written physical examination is part of the general entrance examination for colleges and universities.[5] Once a student is admitted physical education is mandatory for a minimum of fifty minutes per week for freshmen and sophomores, and the grades are averaged with the general academic points.[6] Junior and senior students take physical education as elective courses; however, physical education classes are overcrowded at this level.

Each institution offers many sports activity courses, and the student must pass a three sports-proficiency test. These students who do not make a satisfactory score are advised to strengthen and improve their weak area.[5] Competition among colleges and universities is encouraged by the schools and the general public. The objectives of physical education in colleges and universities are similar to those of high schools.[3]

Specific aims of physical education in colleges and universities are:[10]

1. To build up a strong body before attaining adulthood.
2. To cultivate principles, morality, and to light the national spirit.
3. To train individuals for physical usefulness in their personal life and in society.
4. To cultivate a habit of looking upon sports as recreation.

The government enforces the standards for all schools offering physical education which are set by the Ministry of Education. New schools which do not meet the standards for facilities are not accredited.

## Professional Preparation Programs

Prospective major students are required to take an entrance examination which includes a written knowledge of physical education as well as physical fitness, motor ability, and skill tests.[5] In order to teach in high schools and above, a minimum of a Bachelor's degree in physical education is required. However, the shortage of physical education teachers has forced a lowering of the minimum requirement.

In addition, there is a graduate school which offers a two-year Master's degree program in physical education (32 semester hours), and three universities offer a four-year Bachelor's degree program in physical education (128 semester hours). There is also a three-year diploma program in physical education which is offered by two junior colleges (106 semester hours). At present, there are 233 physical education faculty members with the 2,673 major students in professional preparation schools in physical education.[3]

All teaching certificates are issued by the Ministry of Education. The Ministry of Education also designed the programs for teacher education in colleges and universities.

They also have summer in-service programs and/or workshops which are annually conducted for unqualified teachers.[6] Those who do not have an academic degree must have an acceptable research paper or numerous publications to qualify for screening by the Ministry of Education. Colleges recognize and award academic ranks for their faculty members. The ranks of college teachers are: professors, associate professors, assistant professors, and instructors.

Generally, teaching loads are eight hours per week for a professor, nine hours for an associate professor, and nine to ten hours for an assistant professor and instructors. There are also teaching assistantship and graduate assistantship which are available in the programs.

All prospective normal school teachers, regardless of the subject, are required to take physical education. They are required to meet three times per week--one period for theory and two for activity--during their freshman and sophomore years and two times per week during their senior year--one period for theory, teaching methods, practice, and one period for skill activity.

The curriculum of professional preparation for physical education is patterned after the American and European system. However, emphasis is placed upon Chinese education and preservance of traditional sports and games.[6] Dr. Sun Yet-Shen's philosophy, along with Chinese history, and history of Chinese education are also highly emphasized in the curriculum. In addition, traditional martial arts and sports such as Tai Chi Chaun for men and folk dancing for women are both a requirement in the curriculum.

Professional training courses in physical education emphasize teaching methodology, human anatomy, physiology of exercise, kinesiology, motor learning, administration, officiating, coaching of sports, music, history, test and measurement, philosophy, health education, safety education, and research methods. The sports activity courses included basketball, soccer, softball for girls, volleyball, badminton, track and field, combative sports, aquatics, gymnastics, and rythmic activities.

The National Taiwan Normal University in Taipei is the best professional preparation program in physical education.

The objectives of the professional program in physical education at the National Taiwan Normal University are:[5-6]

1.  To furnish physical educators for secondary schools and for community physical education.

2.  To offer adequate scientific knowledge and field experiences in the field of physical education.

3.  To train students for research in physical education.

Special attention and support is given to research and development in physical education by the government and universities. Research assistantships and scholarships as well as grants are available to graduate students and research-oriented faculty members.

The following institutions have professional preparation programs in physical education: National Taiwan Normal University,

Chinese Cultural College, Taiwan Provincial Physical Education College, Taipei Municipal Physical Education College, and Fu Jen University.

In 1964, physical education plans for all schools and communities were published in accordance with the National Physical Education Act which contains detailed regulations of physical education for all school levels, administrative organizations, facilities as well as professional training, and training for athletes.

## Post-School (The Community) Program

The national government promulgated the National Physical Education Act which was aimed chiefly at developing a good physique and the stamina of the Chinese people with an objective view of providing them with the ability for self-defense as well as for national defense.[3]

Physical education and sports programs in the community are well organized. Many financial institutions and industrial establishments have sports activity programs and regular competitions. Many teams of social institutions participate in national and international competition. Amateur sports are the essential element of Chinese sports. Competition in professional athletics are almost unknown in China.[6] Soccer is one of the most popular sports and draws the largest crowds; however, more baseball and basketball games are held in China than are soccer games.

There are, at present, many public stadiums in most of the cities and districts in China. Every stadium has a director and five department heads: research, promotion and development, counseling, maintenance, and general affairs. There are also a number of courses for basketball, volleyball, tennis, and areas for swimming pools; however, facilities and equipment in sports and physical education programs are in need of improvement.[3] In order to fully use the facilities, the government encourages schools to open playgrounds which are not in use by school programs to the general public for their sports activities and games. Today, the national stadium is under construction.

The Taiwan Area Athletic Meet, College and University Athletic Meet, High School Athletic Meet are major athletic events that are held in China. These meets are held annually.

## Armed Forces

The physical education program in the armed forces is also very active and strongly supported. It is carried out by the Physical Education Committee of the Ministry of Defense, which was originally established in 1944. This committee consists of six sub-committees: Army, Navy, Air Force, National Police, Military Police, and

Military Service.[10]  In 1953, the Armed Forces Athletic stadium was opened for military physical education activities.  Chinese Armed Forces Sports Association is affiliated with the Amateur Athletic Federation of the Republic of China (ROCAAF).

## International Sports Activities

International sports activities are considered very important by the Chinese.  Every year, a number of teams participate in international sports competitions abroad, also many foreign sports teams are invited for tournaments in China.

China helped organize the Far Eastern Championship Games in 1913 and actively participated in these games during 1913-1934.

In 1928, for the first time, China sent observers to the 1st Olympic Games at Amsterdam.  Since then, China has sent teams to the Olympic Games.  However, China did not participate in the 15th Olympic Games at Melbourne in 1956 because of possible IOC membership for Red China.  In 1960, China was permitted to participate in 17th Olympic Games at Rome in the name of Taiwan.  She also played a strong role in organizing the Asian Games, and participated in the 2nd Asian Games in 1954.  Since then she has competed successfully in these games.

The Republic of China produced many excellent athletes. Amont them is Mr. C. K. Yan, who is the greatest athlete in modern Chinese sports history.  He formerly held the world's decathlon record.  Miss Chi Cheng has set a world record of 7.6 seconds in the pentathlon in the Amateur Athletic Union of the United States (AAU) in 1966.[2]  It should, at this point, be credited that many Chinese residents who are overseas strongly contributed to the development of sports and physical education in China.  Traditionally, Chinese soccer teams were organized in Hong Kong.  It should also be credited that little league baseball teams and Chinese golfers played outstandingly in many world competitions.

The government, universities and sports organizations sponsor many physical education seminars, conferences and workshops.  These organizations also send a number of delegates and scholars to various international meetings.

## Future Prospects

The Chinese civilization is one of the oldest, yet she has only seventy-five years of modern physical education, many of which were under less favorable conditions when she was engaged in the war of Japanese invasion and World War II.  After World War II, she was unfortunately involved in a civil war between the national government and the Communists.  After the national government relocated in Taiwan, modern physical education programs were successfully developed by the Chinese. New Chinese physical education is one of the most advanced programs in Asia, yet there are a number of problems facing physical education and international sports competitions: 1) strong and effective legislation for the promotion of physical education, 2) strength in the physical education department and programs, 3) better research and development projects in physical education, 4) publications in physical education, 5) expanded graduate programs in physical education-doctoral program, 6) improvement of facilities, 7) scholarships for athletes and physical education teachers, and 8) better and improved relationships with the international sports federations and the International Olympic Committee.

In conclusion, physical education in the Republic of China has come a long way, although it still has many goals to achieve. Therefore, the Ministry of Education has established the objectives for Nationwide Development of Physical Education. These objectives are:[3]

1. To standardize and normalize school physical education.

2. To increase the physical education population.

3. To improve the physical fitness of the people.

4. To promote the quality and quantity of physical education.

5. To popularize sport activities.

6. To intensively train outstanding athletes.

7. Raise the percentage of our country in international sports.

Many educators strongly believe that the Republic of China is making progress and is strong in many areas of physical education. Professional preparation, increase in government support, and public interest have been responsible for the rapid advancement of physical education over such a short period of time.

Acknowledgements: Authors wish to express their deepest appreciation to Professor Wu Wen Chung who kindly furnished professional information and materials concerning physical education and sports in the Republic of China.

# SELECTED REFERENCES

1.  Bartelome, C. C. "Changes in Educational Systems and their Influence on Physical Education in Several Asian Countries before and after World War II." Bulletin, Federation Internationale D'Education Physique, Lisbonne, Portugal. Chapters 3-4. 1968. pp. 60.

2.  *China Year Book* (Physical Education and Sports). 1966-1967. pp. 426-430.

3.  Department of Physical Education. *Physical Education of Republic of China*. Ministry of Education. 1976.

4.  *Educational Statistics of the Republic of China*. Taiwan, Ministry of Education, Republic of China. 1968.

5.  Information obtained from interview by Daeshik Kim with Professor Ming-Chung Tsai at the International Olympic Academy, Greece, in 1969.

6.  Information and materials obtained from Professor Wu Wen Chung, Head of the Department of Physical Education National Taiwan Normal University. 1970.

7.  Kim, Daeshik. "Physical Education in Republic of China", in *Physical Education Around the World*, edited by William Johnson. Monograph no. 4. Indianapolis, Indiana: Phi Epsilon Kappa. 1966. pp. 1-6.

8.  Kyung Hyang Shin Moon Sa, ed. "Chinese Physical Education." *Encyclopedia of Physical Education*. Seoul, Korea: 1961. pp. 784-790.

9.  Tan, George G. and Wu Wen-Chung. "The Present Situation of Physical Education in the Republic of China". *Physical Education Today 7*. 1960. pp. 1-16.

10. Tsai, Min-Chung. "Physical Education in the Republic of China". National Taiwan Normal University, Taipei, Republic of China. 1967.

11. Van Dalen, Deobald B. and B. L. Bennett. *A World History of Physical Education*. Englewood Cliffs, New Jersey: Prentice-Hall, Inc. 1971. pp. 623.

# SPORT AND PHYSICAL EDUCATION IN COLOMBIA
## by Maurice A. Clay

### Biographical Sketch

*Maurice A. Clay* was born May 6, 1911, Waldron, Indiana. After graduating from the Waldron Public Schools, he received an A.B. in Chemistry from Kentucky Wesleyan College in 1932, the M.A. in Physical Education in 1935, and the Ed.D. degree from the University of Kentucky.

He taught and coached in a public high school in Indiana, served as Director of Physical Education at the College of the Ozarks, was a Physical Fitness Officer in the U.S. Air Force, and, following service, was Director of Physical Education, University School, University of Kentucky. He has acted as Director of the Professional Curriculum in Physical Education at the University of Kentucky since 1948.

His major interests include administration, professional preparation, and international physical education movements.

He is past president of the Arkansas and of the Kentucky Associations of Health, Physical Education and Recreation, receiving the Distinguished Service Award from the Kentucky Association in 1955. He is a past president of the University of Kentucky Faculty Club and of the Kentucky unit of Phi Delta Kappa.

He has served as Chairman of the College Physical Education Section, Southern District, and is the immediate past chairman of the Council on Equipment and Supplies of the American Association for Health, Physical Education and Recreation and is the immediate past chairman of the International Relations Committee of NCPEAM. He served as a Fulbright Lecturer to the National University of Columbia in 1960; as a member of a State Department commission on student welfare programs to the same country in 1961; as a Consultant in the Peace Corps, Colombia IV Project 1962, Texas Western College; and, as Consultant to the Foundation of Colombian Universities in Colombia, 1963. He coordinated sports and recreation training for the Peace Corps India Project, University of Kentucky, summer, 1966. In 1957, and again in 1962, he served as a Consultant to The American School Foundation in Mexico.

He has just returned from a visit to Mexico in the interest of the present paper.

Dr. Clay was the Chairman of the National Selection Committee for Fulbright-Hays Scholars for a number of years. In October, 1969, he was a member of the United States Delegation to the First Symposium on "The Importance of Physical Education in the Schools of Mexico."

Presently Dr. Clay has retired from his duties as Coordinator of Physical Education, Department of Health, Physical Education and Recreation, University of Kentucky and has been honored as an Emeritus Professor.

## Editor's Note

Because of the unavailability of Dr. Clay for the updating of his article on Physical Education in Colombia, his original article is presented intact and the current information is included in a special section at the end of Dr. Clay's article. The Editor participated in the ICHPER Congress in Mexico City in 1977 and met Senor Hector A. Mora Rojas, a teacher and teacher educator in Bogota, Colombia. He has written the information on current developments.

## Introduction

The material presented is based upon the literature available, upon extensive interviews and visitation. Problems mentioned were frankly presented by Colombians. A discussion of the problems does not fall within the scope of this paper and is properly the province of Colombians.

## Background

Colombia occupies the northwestern corner of South America, is the fifth largest country on the continent and in 1960 had a population in excess of 14 million people.[9] The climate varies widely from the tropical heat along the coasts and rivers to the snow-capped Andes in the South. Three mountain ranges continue into Colombia from Ecuador dividing the western section into three distinct areas which until recently were largely isolated from one another. Approximately two-thirds of the eastern part of the country is covered by a flat, grassy lowland and jungle. Both a variety and abundance of vegetation is found with plentiful supplies of virgin timber including various oil and gum bearing trees.[8]

The economy is largely agrarian, although manufacturing is steadily growing. Farming methods range from the primitive modes of the Indians to the mass production techniques of modern agriculture and coffee production. Mineral resources appear in abundance. The emerald mines are world famous. Rich deposits of oil have been developed and Colombia is second only to Venezuela in Latin American production of oil.

The population of Colombia is of predominantly European and Indian origin with a small percentage of Negroes and pure Indians. Nearly 70 per cent of the population are of mixed blood, 25 per cent are white, 5 per cent are Negro, the remainder are Indian. Two-thirds of the people live in rural areas.[28]

According to Adams[1] the present life expectancy in Latin America averages about 40 years at birth and Ciszek (Chapter VI) has stated life expectancy in Colombia is 46 years. The result is that the population is relatively young with higher proportions in the younger ages that are unproductive economically and place a heavy burden on education facilities. The effect on the adult worker is explained by Benton:[2] "For Latin America as a whole the proportion of children of school age to adults is *twice* what it is in Europe. Thus the burden of education is potentially twice as heavy on each adult worker."

Spanish is the official language; the social and cultural customs are largely of Spanish origin; Roman Catholicism is the prevailing religion but other faiths are tolerated. The visit of Pope Paul VI to Bogota in August, 1968, the first Papal visit ever to Latin America, and the Eucharistic Congress also held in Bogota were both significant events to Colombia.

> "Colombia is a republic with a popularly elected president and a National Congress (Senate and House of Representatives). Its two major parties--Liberals and Conservatives--were engaged in civil conflict from 1948 to 1958. Following the overthrow of the dictator Rojas Dinilla in 1957, the constitution was amended to provide for a "national front" government in which all government offices would be divided equally between the Liberals and Conservatives until 1974, with the presidency alternating between them every four years during this period."[9]

The government was slow in developing a public school program. Until 1930, the Catholic Church exercised control over the schools. The national government maintains a Ministry of Education with various divisional heads or directors including the Director of

the Section for Physical Education.  The financing and supervision of
education is a joint responsibility, shared by the Ministry of Education, the department or state offices of education, and local boards.

The majority of schools are organized on a 5-6 or 6-6 plan.
The elementary schools are chiefly under the control of state and local authorities.  The National Ministry of Education prescribes the
course of study.  Secondary education has been traditionally an affair
of private enterprise with the National Ministry exercising control.
The national government operates only a few public secondary schools.
Present plans calls for the cooperative establishment of 18 model secondary schools by the Colombian government and the Alliance for Progress.[4]

Presently there are 26 public and private institutions of higher learning with an enrollment of 61,196.[28]  Included are two Pedagogical Universities, one in Bogota, the other in Tunja.  A degree
from one of these allows the graduate to teach at a secondary school
or university.  There are normal schools (for training teachers for
the elementary school), industrial, commercial and agricultural schools

Colombian children attend classes five and one-half days a
week.  Education is free, and compulsory between the ages of seven
and fourteen but distances, a lack of schools and of teachers and
economics have dictated that for most children the elementary school
is a terminal program.

The topography of Colombia has tended to regionalize customs,
attitudes, and loyalties.  It has certainly affected the development of
folk dances and of sports.  While air transportation and improved
roads reduce this effect, it remains strong.

According to the Pan American Union[8]

Colombia is outstanding because of the consistency with which
it has maintained a high cultural level throughout its history,
and for its unusually large number of cultured and professional men who have devoted themselves to public life.  Colombian
literature and writing are noted for their classic purity.  Colonial architecture closely resembles simplicity of exterior decoration.  Colombia's popular music possesses a wealth of original themes and rhythms, influenced by the forms introduced
by the Spaniards and Negro slaves.

## Historical Development

There appears to be no clearly authoritative source on the
historical development of sports and physical education in Colombia.
There are some evidences of competitions or "pruebas" within the
various Indian cultures, in pre-Hispanic times.[9]  Orlando Fals Borda[3]

has written extensively of the place of a game called "tejo" in present rural societies and Harry Davidson, prominent Colombian folklorist, is presently undertaking to trace its historical background.

Colombians who were asked showed hesitancy to credit the Spanish with any real contribution to the active sport life of Colombia. The bullfight is viewed as an "art" and cockfighting, while not uncommon, is not popularly supported, although what is reputedly the finest ring in South America is located in a small town outside of Bogota. Horse racing and fencing were probably introduced by the Spaniards.

Hackensmith[7], referring to European influences on physical education in Colombia states they favored the Swedish system. Swedish and German gymnastics are now being supplemented at some levels by a "modern gymnastics" which comes from Austria through Argentina and Chile.

Physical Education in Colombia is based upon Law 80 of 1925 of the Federal Government. In 1927 the government contracted a German mission and founded the National Pedagogical Institute as provided for in Law No. 25 of 1917. Here was initiated the teaching of techniques and the pedagogy of physical education with appropriate apparatus and rooms for gymnastics and fields for games and sports. Han Gruber, the first national head of physical education was in charge of the courses and according to Hernandex the first head of the Institute was the Chilean professor Candelario Sepulveda Lafuente.[10,19]

After a very brief attachment to the National University the Institute was moved across Bogota to very limited facilities and with minimum support. Repeated conferences and authorities sought its realignment with a major university which was accomplished in 1963 when it became a section in the National Pedagogical University. Physical education has had a representation in the Ministry of Education since 1933.

Hackensmith[7] has mentioned the recommendation of the 1951 Pan American Institute that institutions of higher education provide organized physical education programs. This idea has yet to be fully appreciated in Colombia. Three universities, Valle, Antioquia, and Santander presently have obligatory programs and the faculty of a fourth, the University of the Andes, has approved a program to begin in the next year. Both the Peace Corps and Fulbright Programs have influenced this to some degree. The Fourth Pan American Congress of Physical Education was held in Bogota in 1965. The Pan American Games, first held in Buenos Aires in 1951, were held in Cali, Colombia, in 1961 and will be returned there in 1970.

The term "educacion fisica" has been contracted at times to "edufisica", a term which may appear in normal conversation or in some official documents.

Two physical recreation activities of considerable impact on the social and cultural development of large segments of the Colombian people are mentioned--folk dance and indigenous sports.

Colombia has a rich folk heritage of which they are and should be proud.[21] There is an annual national festival and folk dance comprises a part of the training of the physical educator and of the "official" program for the schools. Some dances are indigenous to Colombia; others show Spanish and Negro influence, the latter especially along the coastal areas. The dances in Colombia may be divided according to regions--the Andes, the coastal, and the "Llanos Orientales" or plains regions.

Among best known dances and their geographic source are: Atlantic Coast--cumbia, porro, mapale, cumbeamba, merecumbe; Pacific Coast--jota chocoana, contradanza, currulao; East Plains--joropo, galeron llanero; Andes Region--bambuco, pasillo, guabina, bunde, sanjuanero. The popular dances are seen most frequently in the carnivals of Barranquilla along the Atlantic Coast and in Pasto in western Colombia.

Tejo, sometimes called "turmeque", is truly a game of Colombian origin attributed to the Chibchas. Played among friends in clubs and always accompanied by the drinking of beer, it is somewhat comparable to horseshoes in the manner of delivery of the disc or "tejo", but there the similarity ends. It becomes a kind of "horseshoes with a bang" and with greater action. Played by teams of one to six, each member of the team in a prescribed order throws his disc weight in approximately two pounds. The object is either to sink the disc in the center of a metal pipe about four inches in diameter and set flush in an inclined mud surface or to explode one of the one to four gun powder-filled triangular "mechas" placed around the perimeter of the pipe. While considered a man's game, we were informed that in some sections of the plains areas of southeastern Colombia, it may be played by women using smaller discs.

## The Control of Physical Education

Education in Colombia may receive national, state and local financial support. Control is divided by law part to the national government and to the state; approximately one-half of the control resides with local authorities.

While the government theoretically supports sport and physical education, some critics say that practically it does not. They believe there are sufficient national laws on the subject though Congrees was said to be studying more laws. As Colombians are prone to say, "hay muchas magnificas layes".[13]

The National Section of Physical Education located in the Ministry of Education is presently headed by Dr. Cayetano Canizares.

The Section is guided by a National Council and has complete authority in the field of physical education. Included on the National Council are the Director of Physical Education, a delegate from the Ministry, from Public Health, the Olympic Committee, Boy Scouts, the
National Sports Association, the Dean of the Physical Education Section of the National Pedagogical University, and an additional func-
tionary from the National Section of Physical Education.[12]

The national office staff presently consists of the director,
technical assistants and secretaries. Approximately three national
inspectors currently offer general supervision to physical education
along with other subjects. By federal law the government is obli-
gated to send certain equipment to the departments for use in the official schools but the extent to which this has been accomplished is
said to be limited by economic resources.[19]

In some but not all of the separate states or departments there
are directors of physical education who are responsible to the national section for the supervision and general level of physical education
in that state. Atlantico, Santander, Caldas, Valle, Cundinamarca are
among states having such directors.

Various efforts have been made to help teachers through seminars, guides and clinics. A guide for physical education on the middle school "ensenanza media" (grades 6-8) was published in 1968 by
the National Ministry in cooperation with the Peace Corps. Among
other things it includes ten units and examinations for them from
which the teacher is able to pick out three sports suitable to his region for a year's program in physical education; a 12 weeks period
with 2 hours instruction per week would be devoted to each activity.
Other materials are presented on types and management of tournaments including round robin, ladder, pyramid, single and double
elimination tournaments.

Among outlined objectives of the program are: a good physical state, development of strength, muscular tolerance, improved
circulation, increased flexibility, reduced fatigue, improved coordination, physical conditioning and warm-up exercises.

One authority[6] speaking of leadership in the National Section
of Physical Education in 1961 was of the opinion that following the
strong national orientation there was emphasis upon championships--
perhaps at the sacrifice of education, particularly at the primary
levels. He was further of the opinion that programs for girls of that
time were dominated by men and presented from a man's viewpoint.

"Official" schools (government sponsored) must by law have a
doctor available and require a medical examination for physical education. The examinations are said to be limited and excuses are not uncommon. In the primary schools most of the students are sent to centers of hygiene for a chest X-ray and limited examination. While the
same requirements exist for private schools, enforcement, possibly for

lack of staff, appears to be more relaxed. Conditions are generally better at the secondary school where the social level represented is generally higher.

It was reported in a local newspaper in 1960 that in the second largest city of Colombia there was a lack of schools of any kind for 40,000 children of school age. In one of the best secondary schools of the city only 10 per cent of the teachers had graduated from or attended a university and between 30 and 40 per cent of the teachers had not graduated from high school.

## Professional Preparation

To this time there has been only one teacher training institution for physical education. The National Director and others have expressed the need for at least five more such programs in view of an estimated shortage of as much as 25,000 leaders if all present needs in Colombia for health, physical education and recreation were met.[19] Ciszek[28] has expressed the hope that second programs will be completely operative at the University of Valle and the Industrial University, Santander, within a year or two (1968).

There are 2 kinds of "normales" or teacher preparation institutions. "Regular" normal schools operating at the secondary level confer the title of "maestro" to their graduates who are prepared to teach in the primary school. The "superior" normal schools, or faculties of education in selected universities, confer a title equal to "licensiado" and prepare their graduates for secondary or university teaching.[11] Professional training in physical education is currently conducted under one of the latter.

The primary purpose of the Section of Physical Education in the National Pedagogical University is to develop teachers of physical education for programs in the secondary, the middle schools, and the normal schools.[25]

Currently the staff of the Section includes the Dean, two professors who teach 25 hours per week and 25 part-time teachers. Of the latter, two Peace Corps Volunteers teach track and field and swimming. The current expenditure per pupil is approximately 6,000 pesos or approximately $360 per year.

The average student enrolls at age 16-17; occasionally a student may reach age 25. The students are either graduates of teacher training programs in secondary schools and are called "normalistas" or are graduates of the college preparatory program and have a "bachillerato" certificate. The "normalistas" are usually better teachers--they know something of teaching and wish to know more and their attitudes toward teaching are better. The normal school student receives approximately 60 credit hours of preparatory work including some information on physical education.[25]

Currently 120 students are enrolled (90 men and 30 women); all are from Colombia. As might be expected, some of the majors are good athletes, but many times the good athletes are not good students. In 1968 there were 23 graduates. Many leave the field immediately following graduation. It must be remembered that these were the only graduates in physical education in Colombia. Current estimates are that approximately 275 graduates with majors in physical education are teaching in the whole of Colombia.

Entrance into physical education as a major is based upon graduation from high school with a "bachillerato" degree, a medical and personality examination and adequate performance in the 100 meter run, the shot put, the high jump, the broad jump and in gymnastics. Philosophically it is felt the prospective teacher must like people, be democratic and not autocratic.

With the transfer of the Physical Education Training program to the National Pedagogical University, the general education requirements were increased. Among the professional courses are anatomy, biology, physiology of exercise, personal and community hygiene, nutrition, community health, history and principles, psychology, body mechanics, sports medicine, physiotherapy and diet, methodology, theory of gymnastics, educational, rhythmic and corrective gymnastics, theory of sports, children's games, organization and administration, program planning, recreation, camping, folk dance, evaluation, ballet, and practice teaching, along with the teaching and practice of a wide range of sports including baseball. There is provision for electives. Certain field types experiences are required; others are elective. English is required four semesters.

Presently the graduate must receive the title of Red Cross Instructor after having served as an aid in such a course. Only three persons in Colombia are said to presently hold the title of water safety instructor--each is a graduate of physical education.[20]

The lack of a graduate program in physical education tends to make grades made at the undergraduate level less important. It is not uncommon for the student in physical education to hold a teaching position in a primary or secondary school while undergoing training.

In an effort to fill a great need special short and vacation courses in physical education are being offered in a number of universities including Pontifica Bolivariano in Medellin where the work has been coordinated by Alfonso Serna and Consuelo Zey; at the University of Valle in Cali under Pablo Julio Porras and at Cucuta under Bonificio Jaime.[21]

There seems to be no general agreement on an author of an authoritative book on physical education in Colombia, but Dr. Gabriel Anzola Gomez is credited with several books of importance to the field. A real restraint on authorship exists in the expense involved and the limited demand for such books. Titles available in English are said to be used little in physical education where the student is said to like the professor to do translations necessary and to hand out material.

The lack of facilities has long been a problem. New facilities were sought in many different ways, elaborate plans have been made but not completed. Presently the offices and classrooms and a court or so are located at a private residence in Bogota. Soccer must be played or practiced across Bogota at one location, basketball games at another, swimming at another.

Since 1959 the graduate in physical education is called a professor (if teaching) and receives the title "licensiado in educacion fisica y salud." It is our impression that such a graduate, if he teaches, is both proud of his degree and of his position as a physical educator. At one time only students in selected subjects were able to secure support for an education under ICETEX, an agency established to support those worthy and needing it. In the past few years, however, we understand this policy has changed. The Fulbright Commission has sponsored short term visits of a number of professional leaders in physical education for instruction in the United States.

The Rectora[23] (woman president, equivalent) of the National Pedagogical University, under whom teacher training in Physical Education has been located for four years was asked to suggest how the problems of teacher preparation in physical education differ from those encountered in other fields. It is her opinion: there is a lack of understanding of the physical education teachers' place and function in the community of scholars; and, while many students seek to be teachers in other fields, few choose to become teachers of physical education; students choosing physical education as a profession tend to come from a lower social strata than those choosing other fields; except for those written in English, there are few books available to support physical education as a field of merit; and, the lack of a physical plant or facilities that could indicate support for physical education as a field is a factor. Finally, there is a general lack of orientation to the importance of physical education at the secondary level.

### Research

Research in physical education in Colombia is practically unknown. This is highly understandable, however, in view of the lack of a graduate program, the limited number of students and professors and professionally trained practitioners.

Pond, a Fulbright lecturer to Colombia with the help of Colombian educators, completed a comprehensive "national research project" to determine the fitness of the children of Colombia in a report published by the Commission for Educational Exchange in 1962.[6] The Kraus-Weber Test was used as a measure of fitness and a detailed record of diet and sleep was compiled on more than 12,000 children.

Colombian children "were found to have poor stomach muscles, 'surprisingly strong' back muscles and a near absence of flexibility as judged by the tests. Colombian children with a diet regularly including milk appeared much more apt to pass the test than otherwise. While only 8.7 of European children tested failed the test, 57.9 per cent of U.S. children failed and 78 per cent of Colombian children failed. Colombian girls were slightly more successful than Colombian boys. Children in the capital city, Bogota, had the poorest test record: of city groups tested, 83.2 per cent failed. Cali (Cauca), Colombia's sports' capital, had the best performance--66.1 per cent failed. Records of other cities' performers reported and the state in which they are located follow in descending order of performance: Puerto Tejada, (Cauca); Cartagena (Bolivar); Medellin (Antioquia) 70.9; Copacobana (Antioquia) 76.6; Barranquilla (Atlantico) 81.6.

The IV Pan American Physical Education Congress held in Bogota in 1965 officially adopted the AAHPER Fitness Test and Peace Corps Volunteers have assisted the National Section of Physical Education in giving the test and assembling data (Ciszek, p. 96).

David A. See, a Fulbright lecturer, participated with the Colombian delegation to the Congress at their request and in his final report (1965) stated that AAHPER had given consent to use and reproduce the AAHPER Fitness Test.[6]

Opportunities for further research in Colombia are practically unlimited in the history and background of sports and physical education. In addition to the various statistical studies and comparisons commonly found in some countries, studies should be undertaken on the relation of art and sport; literature and sport; folk tales and sport; and of sports indigenous to Colombia.

## Teaching as a Profession

In the opinion of Adames, the position of the teacher of physical education who is a "licensiado", or graduate, is equal and sometimes better than that of other teachers of the school. He may be closer to the students because he is with them in classes, in recreation, in games and in championships; he is often the source of many answers to many questions. If he studies and reads, he may be looked upon as the equal of other teachers. Most graduates with majors in physical education teach in secondary schools. The opposite is the unprepared teacher who is likely to have been a good athlete or to have held some rank in the army or the police and now teaches. Teachers of physical education commonly do not teach another subject.

Tenure is given the first year except if the teacher commits errors or is immoral (drinking, etc.). Teachers cannot participate in political meetings. They may express themselves on politics to friends but never to the students nor can they be involved in political controversy.[11]

While tenure may be granted at the public school level, strikes or repeated student complaints may make it meaningless for a particular professor in a particular university. In one instance complaints were made in the form of "letters to the rector" or president as many as nine times and with as many as 300 signatures in one instance before the sports council decided it had had enough and dissolved the section and then rehired the director on a temporary basis. By comparison this man was lucky.

It is extremely difficult to find a school program of physical education or sports to which one man has devoted a lifetime and to whom the program owes its being. Positions seem more fluid than this and program development seems definitely to be hampered through this fact.

There is a National Association of Professors of Physical Education but concensus of opinion suggests it is not very active or effective. Currently there are no professional journals devoted to physical education. The National Association of Professors of Physical Education print a newsletter distributed to its membership.

Coaching as a profession as it is known in North America does not exist in Colombia and with rare exceptions a full time coach is not encountered. Miguel Zepata, coach of the national basketball team, is an exception. A number of coaches of the professional soccer league are foreigners. A rather common attitude has developed over the years that the foreigner knew more about sports than the Colombian and often was given a leadership role whether he deserved it or not. Perhaps the greatest weakness revealed in sports and in the coaching of sports is in fundamentals.

Both the Fulbright and Peace Corps programs have lent various assistance including clinics and exhibitions in this area. Ciszek has treated this aspect of the Peace Corps program extensively and there is general recognition of its effectiveness. In locating Peace Corps Volunteers an effort was made to locate him with a Colombian counterpart. Castrillon[13] spoke approvingly of their work in some sports. One such coach has had exceptional success with girls volleyball championships and continues "volunteer" coaching though now in business. Dedicated to coaching, he is seeking to organize a team at a girls' school for the deaf and dumb.

A top level coach in Cali was said to earn as much as 8,000 pesos, or $480.00 per month. A basketball coach may handle teams for both men and women during the same season.

Physical Education in the Schools and Universities

Ciszek has described the slow development of physical education in Colombia and the influences of European systems as previously referred to in this article. A regular part of the program at the primary school level--grades 1-5, physical education varies from school to school, is affected by such factors as the teacher, the equipment and facilities available. In the opinion of the physical educators of Colombia, their field is not recognized for its true value as an integral part of education.

Required for one-half hour daily at this level, it generally includes simple games, singing games called "rondas", and gymnastics. Facilities, for reasons of planning or topography, may be limited, but provision is being made in some of the newer schools for playrooms. Covered gymnasiums are in very limited supply at any school level. Parks where available in the neighborhood may be used.

In grades 6-9, or the middle school, there is a three hour requirement each week; classes are generally segregated--boys and girls. A shortage of women teachers forces the use of men to teach girls classes in some schools.

At the secondary level in the "bachillerato" program there is a three-hour requirement (with the teacher) but in the last two years for boys, military science may be substituted. Programs vary widely but programs for boys include educational gymnastics, games, volleyball, softball, basketball, soccer, track and field. The programs for girls include rhythmics, educational gymnastics, folk dance, games and selected sports.[28]

There is little difference in programs of sport and physical education in public as contrasted to private schools; they may be good or poor in either. It was said a few schools meet the requirement by having a coach handle a single team representing the school or by training for a single exhibition of gymnastics for the school.

The capital of Colombia, Bogota, is located in a special district within the Department of Cundinamarca. While physical education here is not representative of its general status, it is presented because capital cities in Latin America have a special significance as the seat of national government, the site of authority and of the greater part of support for education.

The number of pupils attending the first five grades in Bogota (primaria) has jumped from 89,646 in 1964 to 127,460 in 1968.[16] Only 18 teachers who graduated with majors in physical education ("licensiados") are available for work with this number. Fourteen and five-tenths per cent of 127,460 students in classes, averaging 50 to a class, have physical education three times a week under qualified teachers. In the judgment of the Director they have a very good program for 14.5 per cent of the children, but the remainder have irregular classes under poorly prepared teachers or teachers without preparation.

In-service conferences are held seeking to upgrade the programs. Individual teachers make out an annual teaching plan before

the school year starts.  Considerable attention and effort are given
to the sponsorship of track and other championships for both boys
and girls.  An exhibition of physical education activities is sponsored
by the District Director each year at either the Plaza Bolivar (central
plaza in Bogota) or in the Plaza de Toros (bullfight ring).  Twenty-
five hundred boys and girls participated and 22,000 spectators attended the Recreation Festival in June, 1968.

A five-year development program has been started which would
allow for progression.  Twenty-two additional teachers are being
sought at the moment.  The city has been divided into 4 zones and
special teachers would work a circuit of schoools within one of the
zones.  It is hoped for the future that no more than 1,500 students
would be assigned to a single teacher during a week's period of work.

While the lack of teachers is the biggest problem found in the
Federal district, space and facilities along with a lack of equipment
are also difficult.  Presently a budget of 500 pesos each--or about
$30.00--is sought to provide 1 basketball, 1 volleyball, 1-2 soccer
balls, some 20 small balls and some wooden circles (for girls gymnastics) for schools which average 1,200 students.

Each Professor of Physical Education in this system is currently checked out with 1 basketball, 1 volleyball, 2 footballs (soccer
balls), 1 softball bat and ball, and 1 1-inch rope for climbing, at the
beginning of the year.

At the secondary level the school population drops to 22,000
children who attend a total of 6 "public" schools of various types and
purposes including a normal or teacher training school, a technical
school, a "bachillerato" or college preparatory program and a commercial education program.  A special departmental regulation requires
that each of the Physical Education teachers must have been professionally prepared.

In this special district the director indicates there is little
difference in the quality of programs directed by men and women.

One teacher of Physical Education in the federal district is
chosen as "Professor of the Year" and receives 1,000 pesos (about
$60.00) in books as a reward.  It is a highly valued award.

While there is general knowledge of the Socratic philosophy
"mens sans en corpora sano" it was not until 1965 under Fulbright
Commission sponsorship that a unifying philosophy supporting physical education and sports in university life was available to which all
universities could subscribe.  To that time only three universities
had been able to overcome the lack of tradition, facilities, equipment,
staff, heavy student schedules and other problems to establish required programs.

Educational radio and more recently television broadcasts are helping develop an understanding and climate for recreational activities in the primary and secondary schools, the universities, and the community generally.[21]

Reference has previously been made to project INEM, sponsored jointly by Colombia and the Alliance for Progress. Hopefully, schools established under this program will extend horizons and method. Physical Education will have an integral place in these programs under plans presently being studied. Policies and practices established would provide examples for other schools. Present thinking calls for physical education to be required two hours weekly in segregated classes for each of grades one through six at the secondary level.

## Sports

Colombians like sports. Reference has previously been made to "tejo"[26], Colombia's own sport. Competitions are held at all levels. The present Olympics have added interest in sport but are not as important to Colombia as the Pan American games which were held in Cali, Colombia, in 1961 and will be sponsored there again in 1970. The strongest influences on sports presently come from the United States[13] (through visiting specialists, and teams, through the Peace Corps, the Commission for Educational Exchange). In time past soccer coaches were imported from other Latin countries in efforts to develop improved professional soccer.

Sports clubs of two types are common in Colombia. Memberships in the more exclusive clubs are limited by cost which may be more than $6,000 for a club membership plus established fees. Since there are no public pools in Bogota, participation in swimming for example remains with "limited exception, limited." This is also true of golf and tennis. In the second type of sports club fees are nominal and are not generally a block to participation. Such clubs are members of a league, and its by-laws are subject to approval by the league. Membership in such clubs is fluid.

The air force, the military police, the Colombian navy and army have a sports meet each year in Bogota with teams represented in track and field, basketball, soccer, volleyball, swimming and possibly chess. A nice spirit is shown. Events winners are rewarded appropriately to accompanying music and the pinning on of a medal by a selected celebrity.

The National Association of Atletissmo controls sports at the top level. Leagues including 24 sports are formed at the local level from clubs. Each state may have a separate association.

Percy Wynne[10] stated in 1960 that 11 of 12 universities in Bogota, the capital, did not have a director of sports. At that time there was not a single full time director of sports and physical education in any university in Colombia. In 1968, however, most universities appointed as a director of sports a professionally prepared person, a student or another person. Such persons generally hold the title of Director of Sports or Director of Sports and Physical Education.

Presently the program at the National University is limited to intramural and interuniversity sports. Included are soccer, basketball, volleyball, track, weight lifting, gymnastics and cycling. It is faced with an increasing number of students (reportedly 18,000) and increased costs for equipment but operates without an increased budget.[13]

C.O.D.U.C. or the University Sports Council, headed by an elected student president, establishes policies for interuniversity sports at the national level. Each university and the Association of Colombian Universities--the parent administrative body for Colombian unversities, are represented. The individual university at the state level must have permission of the state organization to participate in any event.

The national interuniversity games are supported by funds supplied by the Ministry of Education and are supposed to be scheduled annually. In 1960, for example, the Ministry supplied 150,000 pesos or approximately $15,500.

Regulations for the games are established at a national congress of university representatives. There is general agreement that Colombian sportsmen and physical education teachers make full use of the opportunity to establish rules and by-laws. There is a popular saying to the effect that in Colombia there are laws for everybody.

Eligibility for teams in leagues is generally established at three age levels in either the secondary schools, where applicable, or in open leagues as follows:
Infantiles--up to 16
Juvenile --16 to 18
Mayores --18 and over

While eligibility rules may be tightening up, the idea of "amateur" status is by some standards, on the basis of information received, rather free. For example, a professional football player may still play amateur basketball and need only to be matriculated to be eligible for a university team; that is, he must take one or more courses. One man is said to have played ten years with a university team. Secondary school eligibility is also reported to be difficult to enforce.

The size of the country, high mountains and other geographical barriers and the limited number of universities (outside the state in which Bogota is located) make scheduling of university games a problem. Most transportation is by bus though airplanes are used increasingly over long distances.

The lack of well defined sports seasons results in an inability to plan training and the problem is worsened by overlapping seasons for the various sports.

At the high school level scheduling of games may be done between friends; such arrangements are called "partidos amistosos" or friendly games. Most games, however, are scheduled by a "Junta Deportiva" or sports committee council representing a "department" or state. Open teams are organized into leagues which sponsor all games and organized tournaments, collect all monies and pay for authorized travel of teams representing it. Since attendance at an average game is light, the leagues may be sponsored in part by wealthy patrons. Such people like sports and are indulged by publicity attendant to being elected president. It has been said that administrative positions in sports in Colombia are at times held more because of politics than by administrative acumen.

Both officiating and pay for officiating are considered poor in Colombia. Despite this there is little turnover in officiating and referees are generally older than encountered in the United States. Officials need not have had (as is true in the U.S.) extensive participation as players. Membership in an officials' associaton is based upon an examination of both theory and practice. Efforts have been made to improve officiating through clinics.

Sports events may be extensively advertised and run with great flair including engraved invitations to special guests, Olympic-type parades and ceremonies conducted in connection with the games. A fencing meet might combine cocktails, the meet, and a dance.

The conduct of competitions[17] at the departmental or state level and at the national level, are often comparable to an Olympics on a small scale. Tournaments may start with a parade of the teams followed by an Olympic salute and pledge to sportsmanship. Each team may have a queen and flowers are presented to the directors. The national anthem is played followed at times by songs of the various schools.

Similar to the Olympic practice, school flags may be exchanged between competitive teams at the beginning of each game. School banners and small lapel buttons with school symbols are common. Flags may be exchanged between schools or between representatives of different leagues. It is not unusual for a banquet and dance to follow the competitions. In rural areas the banquet may be replaced by an open air buffet-type event with such colorful and imaginative tropical innovations as the use of banana leaves in lieu of tablecloths. Such events as described here were witnessed at two national inter-university competitions and at two departmental competitions at the secondary level.

The North American is often impressed by both the extent and quality of chess played in Colombia. Considered a sport, it is commonly included in school and university sports meets or championships. Colombia has produced some excellent chess players including internationally recognized Cuellar Gucharna.

Billiards are very popular in Colombia; billiard parlors are common and generally appear neat and well run. Bowling, while nationally known, is largely if not entirely limited to a few private clubs. Championships are held.

American football has never been played in Colombia although an exhibition game was said to have been played without equipment.

Cali is generally considered the sports capital of Colombia. Located in the land-rich Cauca Valley they have, as one informant put it, great interest in sports, good organizational ability, the money needed to establish various programs and a desire to do so. Cali won 9 national sports championships in 1964. Having hosted Pan American Games championship in 1961, it is now planning for the 1969 games. Though its facilities presently rank among the best in Colombia, it hopes to establish new sports facilities for this event. Its present sports center includes a coliseum or basketball arena, a soccer stadium, a track, and large swimming installation.[6]

Colombia was represented in the 1968 Olympics in track, bicycle races, swimming and diving and soccer. Included on the team were two athletes most frequently mentioned by the professional physical educators and others interviewed in the present study, they are currently the popular sports figures of Colombia. Their names are "Cochise" Rodriguez, a cyclist of international repute, and Alvaor Mejia, a successful distance runner.

### Facilities and Equipment

Some cities in Colombia, Cali and Medellin for example, have extensive facilities for sports. In Medellin state law is said to require industry to put a limited per cent of profits into facilities for sports. Their sports center may be the best in Colombia today and includes a "velodromo" for cycle racing, a coliseum, a soccer stadium, a nice baseball field, Olympic pool and tennis courts.[6]

However, as expected in a country of many high mountain ranges, some locales have limited areas for courts and here basketball and volleyball are more frequently found than games requiring large areas. Lacking play space, it is not uncommon for a street to be used for classwork. Students are stationed at either end to signal a car or other traffic. Perhaps the problem of limited facilities for sports in some of the recognized universities in Colombia may be illustrated by the University of the Andes. One of the most advanced universities in Colombia, this relatively young school is situated near the center of Bogota on a mountainside.  Its faculty has voted a one year requirement in physical education beginning January, 1969.  Its facilities for sports include one basketball court and room for weight lifting, judo, chess and ping-pong.  For basketball contests they use the courts of Javeriana University, north of them; and, they travel across Bogota to the National University to play baseball, for example. An energetic young director, however, is trying to conduct a full program of interuniversity and intrauniversity sports in addition to the one-year requirement soon to be added.[25]

Equipment for physical education and sports is also a major problem to physical educators.  With the possible exception of balls for basketball and soccer, equipment is either of poor quality or expensive; equipment for track is practically non-existent; basketballs and some other equipment may be imported as contraband or through social cooperatives.  The problem of importing materials has long been a problem because of a high import tax; some items for gymnastics are in particularly short supply.

## Other Influences Affecting Physical Education

In the opinion of Angel Humberto Vaca the effects of an original Chilean delegation on the inclusion of gymnastics in the program and the United States' influence on sports patterns have been most significant in shaping present interests and programs in Colombia. Three additional forces are identified and treated in this paper.

## The Y.M.C.A.[18]

As contrasted to Argentina and to Mexico where Y.M.C.A.s have existed for approximately six decades, the first Y.M.C.A. in Colombia was established in Bogota in 1964.  Governmental permission was finally given and the "Y" received a letter from the Catholic Cardinal granting permission for Catholics of Colombia to belong.  Prior to this, it is reported that some felt the "Y", which is non-sectarian, "gave an image of Protestantism", and there were others who reportedly did not understand the attitude of the "Y" in helping the poor with sports.

Financial support and facilities remain in critically short supply for the "young" "Y".  Presently operating from a private residence in Bogota, they hope to secure land from the government agency known as "Beneficia de Cundinamarca" and they are seeking money from North America for a new building.  Despite these problems the "Y" has undertaken and accomplished a lot in pushing physical education during its brief existence[12]

     1.    it has worked with both the Section of Physical Education in the Ministry and with the Peace Corps.

2.     it has been instrumental in bringing a number of top-flight foreigners to Colombia to conduct clinics.

3.     a long range clinic program has been established for coaches and teachers who are permitted to "place" themselves on either an A, B, or C basis in the clinics. They may later repeat the clinics at a more advanced level.

4.     they work with various employees of businesses and industry in forming sports teams.

5.     they offer a varied program for young adults which includes sports one night each week.

One of the principal goals of the "Y" is to become a center of interest in sports. They began their sports program with a secondary school level interscholastic league held in the Nueva Granada (a private school) gymnasium. Tourney fees were used to pay officials and for other costs. Industrial leagues were also formed for workers in both Colombian and North American owned plants.

Instruction of "drown proofing" in swimming was started in 1968; and the "Y" brought in author Orestes Volpe of Uruguay to conduct a highly successful course on recreation leadership and games for: police who worked with juveniles, workers in centers, mothers, and teachers of physical education. In the judgment of its sponsors this work had its greatest impact on workers in correctional institutions. Original interest is said to have lapsed quickly among leaders in the separate regions of the city (barrios).

The "Y" has also organized softball tournaments. Players in such tournaments have usually been either North Americans or Colombians from the Atlantic Coast area where baseball is highly popular.

The "Y", cooperating with the Physical Education Section of the Ministry of Education in 1967, brought the Director of Physical Education of the Instituto Technico of Montivideo to conduct an intensive course in evaluation and in swimming instruction for teachers. Lacking a pool, they used the Military School pool for instruction.

It has established a camp, some 35 miles from Bogota, in the Department of Santander on a site bought from a construction company. In 1966 and again in 1967, 120 boys and girls from Bogota paid 200 pesos, or approximately $12.00, to attend this camp for a period of ten days. The activity most appreciated by the parents appeared to be training in first aid. (Also taught by the Boy Scouts and or Girl Scouts or "Guias."). During the past year, with the help of 16 people from the Duncan "Y" in Chicago, they launched a special camp leadership training program. Though there are no official seasons in Colombia it was called a traditional "summer camp". North

Americans worked with Colombian counterparts in classes in crafts, swimming, hiking, picnics, outdoor cooking and nature study.

## Peace Corps

Raymond A. Ciszek, Director of the AAHPER Peace Corps Project has thoroughly described the work of the Peace Corps in Colombia. This cooperative effort with Colombia in health, physical education and recreation was begun in 1963. The program is described as among the most successful of all Colombian Peace Corps projects. While AAHPER supervision has been discontinued, work in physical education continues. Ciszek's summary of the major efforts and accomplishments between 1963 and 1968 are quoted:

1. At the university level, Volunteers have developed a compulsory physical education service program for all first and second-year students at two universities. Nine universities have established organized intramural programs to afford their students greater opportunities for participation. Athletic competition has increased as have the number of participants and the standard of performance.

2. In the normal schools (teacher training) a concentrated effort has been made to upgrade the physical education programs and to improve the quality of teaching. It is hoped that because of this effort the elementary school programs will continue to improve.

3. Rural units have been formed in which three or four Volunteers travel from village to village in the interior of the country to conduct in-service meetings for teachers of physical education at all school levels. The units travel by jeep and spend from two to five days or longer in a village working with the personnel responsible for the program to improve the knowledge and skills in physical education.

4. Volunteers have been working throughout the country administering the AAHPER Physical Fitness Test to thousands of boys and girls. The test, officially adopted by the IV Pan-American Physical Education Congress held in Bogota, Colombia, in May 1965, is being used throughout Latin America to determine the physical fitness of school-age children. The Volunteers have accepted the responsibility of assisting the National Department of Physical Education gather the necessary data.

5. Development of the summer school courses and other professional meetings has been received enthusiastically by teachers and school officials. Improving the qualifications of the teachers of physical education through summer courses, in-service meetings, conferences, and clinics and

working in the teacher training institutions has been of
some assistance in alleviating the shortage of qualified
teachers.

6.  A joint effort between this project and a Peace Corps Edu-
    cational Television Project has promise of making one of
    the most significant contributions of any phase of the pro-
    ject to date. The cooperative assignment is under way,
    with a pilot project in which the physical education Volun-
    teers are developing a series of television programs in
    health education and physical education for children and
    youth throughout Colombia. If as successful as antici-
    pated, the series could become a regular part of the Edu-
    cational Television Project program."[28]

According to Steve Dachy[15], Deputy Director of the Peace
Corps of the ten Peace Corps Volunteers presently in physical education, three will work as members of integrated teams at the elementary level. The remainder may work in some aspect of teacher training. Team composition will vary but might include some combination
of mathematics, science, counselling, library, physical education and
recreation. The object would be to aid in improving the level of
teaching and to use the initiative of students.

Whether the influence of the Peace Corps program was greater
in the field of sports or in physical educaton remains unsettled. Some
Colombians were reluctant to say. Apparently, from our investigation, more help was asked for at times than was given. The overall
appraisal is that they have been successful--that "they worked with
heart" and in all parts of Colombia. The volunteer had to prove his
technical knowhow, or, as a coach he had to prove his performance
ability. And, as must have been expected--"sometimes they just
didn't"--the selection process just didn't guarantee complete success.
As with Fulbright and other programs of similar intent--the end product must be viewed in terms of objectives, problems and long term
results. One trainee expressed his position in this way: "Enthusi-
asms seem to wax with ease, and wane with little difficulty."

"Joy of Effort" medals have been presented by AAHPER to
those Colombians (both men and women) whom it was thought made a
special contribution to the development of physical education as a
worthwhile effort. [22]

Commission on Education Exchange<br>(Fulbright)

Dr. Jaoquin Pineros Corpas, Director of the (Fulbright) Commission in Bogota, Colombia, has outlined and evaluated the work of
six North American professors of physical education who have worked
in cooperation with various university, school governmental, and
sports groups in the promotion of the Fulbright Commission's programs.[5] He is of the opinion that great progress has been made in

the acceptance of physical education and sports as in integral part of the total education.

Working with Colombian experts and coaches, the Fulbright professors sought to study the principal problems of physical education in Colombia in relation to their social and economic setting. They helped in the development of a concept and philosophy of sports acceptable to Colombian governmental and educational authorities in the development of clinics, seminars for Colombian teachers, and in the evaluation of the fitness and nutritional status of a large sample of Colombian children (as previously mentioned). The reports of two of the Fulbright lectureres to Colombia have been bound and published by the Fulbright Commission in Bogota.

Conclusions reached in the seminar on "Philosophy of Physical Education and Sports"[27], sponsored by the Fulbright Commission, were accepted by the National Olympic Committee and by the Olympic Committee of the Universities of Colombia (CODUC). In the seminar professors of philosophy and the humanities deliberated with coaches, professors and experts in physical education and sports; concurring "on the importance of sports and physical education within the framework of educational institutions", and "on the necessity of giving them a sound academic foundation".[25]

The Commission has also provided partial support for study in the United States of a number of Colombian leaders and students in physical education, including: Numael Hernandez, who studied at Ohio University; Angel H. Vaca, who studied in New York; and Marco V. Mejia, who studied at Iowa State University.

### National Council of Youth and Sport

What may emerge as the greatest current influence on both sport and physical education in Colombia is the National Council of Youth and Sport. According to an announcement appearing in the newspaper *El Tiempo*, November 9, 1968, Bogota, the National Government has provided approximately 2.5 million dollars for a joint venture between the Ministries of Education and of Health to broaden and to stimulate physical education and sports. Working under an executive director and a council it will give technical assistance and will work cooperatively with the various sports associations.

### Colombian Sport and Physical Education Updated - 1978

#### by Hector A. Mora Rojas

In General
_____

Colombia is a country trying to escape underdevelopment at a slow pace while politically, educatively, administratively and culturally influenced by the United States. It has approximately 30 million inhabitants and continues to be Catholic and conservative with little concern for change in its structures.

## Education

The determining factor in the progress of a nation and every government's problem does not reach all sectors because of a number of factors such as the lack of teachers (from inadequate renumeration in the form of salaries and social considerations), inadequate budgets, lack of educational centers and precedence of other interests. Colombia is, for this reason, a country with a high incidence of illiteracy in which education has been considered another privilege of a certain social class. It is surprising the number of children who are left without education even in the capitals where there is an influx of teachers. Education is controlled by the government under the direction of the National Ministry of Education which is the body that supervises, organizes and controls the curricula and areas of study in schools, colleges and universities of official or private concern; these last ones have high tuition and board rates. 90% of the Colombian population is comprised of people with few resources and whose salaries are inadequate for a comfortable life. For this reason public schools and high schools are swamped with children wishing to study. It is disappointing to see the conditions under which those who manage to gain admission in one of these centers have to study.

The inadequate funding for installations, teaching materials, teacher education, books, audio visual materials, furniture, etc., contribute to make the education actually received an incomplete and inadequate one (In UPN, foremost University in the country graduating teachers of physical education, the facilities at their disposal consist of three patios for the practice and teaching of basketball, volleyball, and it must serve more than 500 students, teaching candidates). Lack of investigation, bad planning, and poor distribution of academic buildings and other socio-academic considerations impedes the development in all areas of education.

## Physical Education in Colombia

In spite of its 40 years of establishment and its recognition as an indispensable part of a people's culture and even more, of the development of the whole person, physical education in Colombia finds (just as education in general does) serious social, political and economic difficulties. It has attained recognition from a government which (on the other hand) has deprived it of its due participation and support in any continuous and efficient manner.

Professionally, physical education is a new career that could bring a good income when compared with other areas of teaching because the country has less than 2,000 licensed teachers, with the majority concentrated in Bogota, it being the city which offers advancement in the cultural-economic area.

Colombian children are the ones who receive the least orientation in recreation and physical education since the directors of primary and secondary schools do not recognize the central value of physical education in the attainment of a perfectly developed youth. Moreover, in many educational centers a teacher of physical education is not indispensable and in order to comply with a requirement of the M.E. Nal., the work is entrusted to retired police officers, athletes or any person who may be ignorant of the subject.

## Sports and Recreation

There is a body of government (Coldeportes) whose function is to promote sports and recreation. This body receives tax monies but its work doesn't reach even five per cent of the Colombian population for lack of planning and inadequate distribution of its budget. Our athletes are persons who without receiving any technical help, support or advice, have become outstanding through the rudimentary practice of their efforts. Also, the athletes who have managed to become champions came from a poor environment and with their individual study of tactics and exhausting practice have gained worldwide acclaim as in the case of Colombian boxing with its two great stars: Rodrigo Valdes and Antonio Cervantes "Pambele".

In Colombia athletes don't have, as they do in developed countries, dieticians, teams of doctors, masserus and all the personnel to which athletes should have access for their physical betterment.

The universities shaping physical education teachers work very independently of (Coldeportes) and their objectives are completely different. Coldeportes tries to popularize sports but in a manner that goes against the teaching philosophy of physical education itself; all because of a lack of preparation in the matter of technical directives and trainers. Now Coldeportes is getting ready to enter the world soccer championships in 1986 by teaching the sport to some groups of children centered in Bogota.

Because of all this, physical education, sports and recreation cannot show fast development in the field of scientific investigation, so important an area suffering from discrimination in the majority of Latin American countries.

These comments are given by a student and teacher of this field whose sole purpose is to inform and offer positive criticism of the progress and development of physical education in my country.

Hector A. Mora Rojas

# BIBLIOGRAPHY

1.  Adams, Richard and others. *Social Change in Latin America.*
    Vintage Books. 1960.

2.  Benton, William. *The Voice of Latin America.* New York:
    Harper and Brothers. 1961.

3.  Borda, Orlando Fals. *Peasant Society in the Colombian Andes:
    A Sociological Study of Saucio.* Gainesville: University of
    Florida Press. 1965.

4.  *Curriculum, Framework for Comprehensive High Schools.* INEM.
    (Translation-mimeographed). Bogota. 1967.

5.  *Diez Anos De Intercambio Educativo.* (1957-1967). Commission
    for Educational Exchange Between Colombia and the United
    States. Bogota. 1967.

6.  *Final Reports.* Exchange Professors: (a) Pond, C.
    (b) Clay, M. A.; (c) Price, H. D.; (d) Furman, D.;
    (e) Twardowsky, E.; (f) See, D. Commission for Educational
    Exchange Office, Bogota. 1960-1965.

7.  Hackensmith, C. W. *History of Physical Education.* New
    York: Harper and Row. 1965.

8.  *Introduction to the Latin American Republics.* Washington,
    D. C.: Pan-American Union. 1965. pp. 65, 66.

9.  *Other Lands, Other Peoples.* National Education Association.
    Washington, D. C. Revised 1962.

10. Personal Correspondence, Percy C. Wynne, Director, Physical
    Physical Education and Sports, National University, Bogota.
    1960.

11. Personal Interview, Luis Carlos Adames, Inspector, Physical
    Education, Bogota. August 1968.

12. Personal Interview, Dr. Cayteano Canizares, National Director
    of Physical Education, Ministry of Education, Bogota. August
    1968.

13. Personal Interview, Escalon Castrillon, M.D., Director, Sports
    and Physcial Education, National University, Bogota. August
    1968.

14. Personal Interview, Dr. Joaquin Pineros Corpas, Director,
    Commission for Educational Exchange Between Colombia and the
    United States, Bogota. August 1968.

15. Personal Interview, Steve Dachy, Deputy Director of Peace Corps, Colombia, Bogota. August 1968.

16. Personal Interview, Alvaro Sierra Espinel, Director, Physical Eeucation. Special District of Bogota. August 1968.

17. Personal Interview, Richard Gorrell, Daniel Margolis, former Peace Corps Volunteers, Bogota. August 1968.

18. Personal Interview, Alberto Guzman and Steve Bolton, Asociacion Critians de Jovenes, Bogota. August 1968.

19. Personal Interview, Numael Hernandez, Former National Director and Dean of Faculty, Physical Education, Bogota. August 1968.

20. Personal Interview, Judith Jaramillo, Professor; Miriam Riviera, Secretary, National Pedagogical University, Bogota. August 1968.

21. Personal Interview, Martha Moncado, Programadora, Physical Education, INEM, Bogota. August 1968.

22. Personal Interview, Amparo Reynosa, Secretary to the Peace Corps, Bogota. August 1968.

23. Personal Interview, Irene Jara Solarzano, Rectora, National Pedagogical University, Bogota. August 1968.

24. Personal Interview, Luis Sotan, Director of Sports and Physical Education, University of the Andes, Bogota. August 1968.

25. Personal Interview, Angel Humberto Vaca, Dean, Physical Education and Health, Universidad Pedagogica, Bogota. August 1968.

26. *Reglamento de Tejo*. Bavarian Company, Bogota.

27. Report of Fulbright Commission Seminar on "Philosophy of Physical Education and Sports". Mimeographed, the Commission Office, Bogota. 1965.

28. Vendien, C. Lynn and John E. Nixon. *The World Today in Health, Physical Education and Recreation*. Englewood Cliffs, New Jersey: Prentice-Hall, Inc. 1968. (Chapter VI). "Colombia ———", Raymond A Ciszek.

## SELECTED REFERENCES

*Physical Education and Games.* ICHPER Questionnaire Report, Part I, International Council on Health, Physical Education, and Recreation, Washington, D. C.

*Quick Colombian Facts.* Instituto Colombiano de Opinion Publica, Bogota. 1960.

*Teacher Training for Physical Education.* ICHPER Questionnaire Report, Part II, International Council on Health, Physical Education, and Recreation, Washington, D. C.

# SPORT AND PHYSICAL EDUCATION IN CZECHOSLOVAKIA
## by Luis Bisquertt, S. M.D.

### Biographical Sketch

*Luis Bisquertt*, S. M.D., the co-author of an article on Physical Education in Chile, visited Czechoslovakia. He had a number of good friends who provided the information for this article. The primary contributor of this article requested anonymity for personal reasons.

We are deeply distressed that Dr. Bisquertt passed away shortly after co-authoring the Chilean article with Dr. Clyde Knapp of the University of Illinois.

The monograph editor is responsible for some minor editing changes in the original manuscript which was forwarded through Dr. Bisquertt for publication in the present monograph series.

### Editor's Note

In 1976, while on a sabbatical study visit to the USSR and selected Eastern European Countries, the Editor visited Czechoslovakia, and in Prague, conferred with the primary contributor of this article. Later when it was decided to update all of the PEK monograph articles the primary contributor was contacted and the following reply was received:

> I have read carefully the present article which was published in monograph #6 and found that even after four years it is quite good and no part needs updating or rewriting. There were no substantial changes since its first publishing and - according to my opinion - the mentioned article is fit to print in its original version again.

# General Background Information

The Czechoslovak Socialist Republic is the most westernly situated member of the socialist group of countries. Czechoslovakia is located in the center of Europe and has common frontiers with the German Federal Republic, German Democratic Republic, Poland, Soviet Union, Hungary and Austria.

Czechoslovakia covers an area of 127,860 sq. km., and has around 14,000,000 inhabitants. In terms of nationality, the population of the country comprises over 9,000,000 Czechs and 4,000,000 Slovaks, with small Hungarian, German, Polish and Ukranian minorities. Prague, the capital, has over 1,000,000 inhabitants.

Under the Constitution, promulgated on July 27, 1960, Czechoslovakia is a Socialist State, based on alliance between workers peasants and intellectuals. After January 1, 1969, Czechoslovakia became a Federal Republic, composed of the Czech Socialist Republic and the Slovak Socialist Republic. It is a country of two equal nations, the Czechs and the Slovaks. Each nation has its National Assembly. The Federal Assembly is the supreme body of the State power and the President of the Republic is the head of the State. The leading political party and the chief power in the State from 1948 is the Communist Party of Czechoslovakia.

# History

The first inhabitants of the territory of present Czechoslovakia were Celtic tribes of Boii. In the 4th to 6th centuries A.D., the territory of Czechoslovakia was occupied by Slavonic tribes coming from the north, the forefathers of the Czechs and Slovaks. At the beginning of the 9th Century Christianity began to spread to this territory and the Great Moravian Empire was formed. In the 10th century this empire disintegrated and Slovakia was separated from Moravia and Bohemia. Bohemia became the political center of the new state and was ruled by the dynasty of Premyslides, of the Luxembourg dynasty and dynasty of Jagellons. Slovakia was occupied in the 11th century by the Hungarians who subjugated its Slav inhabitants for a full ten centuries until 1918.

After the extinction of the dynasty of Jagellons (1526) the Czech nobility elected to the throne of their kingdom the Habsburgs who also ruled over the Alpine Lands and Hungary. The Hapsburgs tried to suppress the sovereignty of their individual lands and to form a centralist, absolutist and strictly Catholic State. The persecuted Protestants left the country in exile. The Czech Kingdom, only a short time before an important factor in European politics, gradually sank to the level of an insignificant province of the Austrian Empire. The Czechs attempted, though unsuccessfully to regain their political rights in 1848. The Habsburgs were finally defeated in

World War I, and the Czechs and Slovaks received their national freedom in a common state, the Czechoslovak Republic, proclaimed on
October 28, 1918.

In 1938 Czechoslovakia fell victim to aggression by Nazi Germany. At Munich, by an agreement between the Western Powers and
Hitler, Czechoslovakia was deprived of Sudentenland which was annexed to Germany, and on March 15, 1939 was forcibly occupied by the
Nazi Wehrmacht. The so-called Protectorate of Bohemia and Moravia
was set up in the western half of the country and a puppet Slovak
State in Slovakia. Two million Czechs served as slaves in the German
was industry and about 360,000 people fell in the struggle or were
tortured to death in German concentration camps and prisons. The
year 1945 brought the Czechs and Slovaks liberation by the Red Army.
Liberating Czechoslovakia the Soviet Union won the gratitude of
Czechoslovak citizens and also the Communist Party of Czechoslovakia
enlarged its power when many new members entered directly after
World War II.

In 1948 the Communist Party took over the control of the state
and became the leading political power in the country. The Communist party nationalized all private properties in business, industry
and agriculture. The number of members organized never exceeded
one-tenth of the Czechoslovak population, but the Communist Party
has strong support of the Soviet Union and other socialist countries.
Since 1955 Czechoslovakia has been a member of the Warsovian Pact
which was established as an economical, political and military union of
the USSR and other Eastern countries against NATO. The Warsovian
Pact is the most important criterion for all activities in Czechoslovakia
and controls both international and home politics of the country. A
crystal clear example of this was August 21, 1968 when the troops of
the USSR, Poland, Bulgaria, Hungary and the German Democratic
Republic occupied Czechoslovakia to help the Czechoslovak Communist
party keep her sovereign position in the country.

## Historical Background of Physical Education

A. Development of school physical education through 1945.

The first Czech pedagogue who recognized physical education
as an important element not only in the physical but also in moral upbringing was the great educationalist and "Teacher of Nations" Jan
Amos Komensky (Comenius), 1591-1670. In his leading work, the
"Orbis Pictus" described and illustrated the games and exercises
known in the XVII century, and never ceased to point out in his
writings the great pedagogic value and influence of these games and
exercises, especially the effect of physical exercises upon the mind
of the child. Komensky's ideas was to introduce the game as the
main principle to all education, both psychic and physical, which
were to be carried out like a children's game (using the games). His
main idea was expressed in the following slogan "Schola ludus" (School
by Game).

Komensky was not given a chance to apply his modern pedagogic methods and ideas in his native country, because he soon left the Czech kingdom in exile when the period of persecution of Protestants began.  However he could apply all his knowledge in Poland, Hungary (Saropatak), England, Sweden and Holland, where he later died.

Unfortunately, Komensky and his educational methods did not find any followers for a very long time.  Physical training was carried out quite exceptionally in some Czech elementary schools and noble private schools as in the other countries of the Austrian Empire where the regulations of physical education were the same.

The very first time when physical education was introduced to all secondary schools was the year of 1849.  This new school subject was non-compulsory and again the regulations were common for all countries of the Austrian Empire.  These regulations were valid in Czech schools until the end of World War I.  Physical Education was compulsory by law in 1869 for elementary schools, in 1870 for training colleges and in 1874 for secondary schools.

The first elementary school program of Physical Education was issued in 1870 and both secondary school and training college programs in 1875.  They were common for all countries of the Austrian Empire and were based on German exercise methods by Spiess and Maul including rank exercises to increase discipline, geometrically stylized exercises and apparatus gymnastics.

A very important public inquiry concerning the physical training of the youth was organized in Vienna in 1910, where many experts from the whole Empire took part and expressed their opinion. This action brought many reforms.  Based on this inquiry the new program for secondary schools was issued in 1911 for boys and 1913 for girls, where some exercises from Swedish gymnastics were applied as well as track and field athletics.

After World War I the physical exercise system by Spiess and Maul was replaced in the newly established Czechoslovakia by Tyrs' Sokol system, supplemented in turn by exercises from Swedish and Danish gymnastics, natural exercises by French reformer Georges Hébert, rhythmic gymnastics for girls by Emile Jaques Dalcroze and and Georges Demenyi, track and field athletics and sport games (soccer, handball, basketball, volleyball).  An eclectic system of physical education was propagated and the teachers had many possibilities to select from.

Capable teachers of physical education were sent to foreign countries (Germany, France, Denmark, Sweden, USA, etc.) to study there and to learn the newest trends of modern physical education. The most important works of foreign reformers were translated into Czech and published, e.g., the works of Hébert, Thulin, Niels Bukh, etc. Recently the program of Czechoslovak schools has been supplemented with the Austrian natural physical method by Dr. Karl Gaulhofer and Margarete Streicher (See Nicholaas J. Moolenijzer's excellent description of this method in Monograph 3, pp. 4-7). In addition to two compulsory hours of physical training per week, since 1890, non-compulsory minor games were introduced to elementary schools and team sport games to secondary schools.

After World War I, the secondary schools organized various competitions (contests) in track and field events and games every year on an intramural, district and national basis. The youth from primary and secondary schools had their own independent competition and even mass drill displays organized at the time of the All-Sokol-Festivals (Rallies).

### Physical Education at Universities and Colleges

Physical education at higher levels of education was introduced as a non-compulsory subject since 1908. The introduction and propagation of non-compulsory sport and physical training at universities and colleges is due to Dr. Frantisek Smotlacha, the first lecturer of physical education at Charles University in Prague. After World War I he established "University Sport" (Vysokoskolsky sport), where the full opportunity to pursue all possible sports and games was offered to all college and university students. He also organized various competition in many sport events for excellent sportsmen, who had risen from students starting their membership in "University Sport" together with their studies. The competitors coming from the university and college campuses were the best Czechoslovakia had at that time.

B. Development of the voluntary physical training organization.

Czechoslovakia is a country with an old and glorious tradition in physical training. It is more than 100 years since a voluntary physical training organization was founded in this country. In 1862 Dr. Miroslva Tyrs and his friend Jindrich Fügner were the founders of the first Czech Gymnastic Society and called this organization the *Sokol*. The word Sokol translated literally means falcon, the bird, symbol of swiftness, activity and freedom of Slav Nations.

Dr. Miroslav Tyrs (1884-1932), professor of art history at Charles University in Prague, was the creator of the Sokol idea and the founder of the Sokol system of physical training. This ardent desire to free the small Czech nation, with a glorious past, from the foreign yoke and to preserve its forces for the future cultural life induced him to seek a suitable way for the physical and moral development of the nation.

The model for this he discovered in ancient Greece. Dr. Tyrs came to the conclusion that physical training can make a small nation able to withstand the attacks of more powerful peoples. According to his conception physical training was a means of reeducating the nation. He had seen the best method of education in the Greek motto of "Kalos Kai Agathos." A nation so weakened in its physical and its moral substance as was the Czech nation, subjugated by the Austrian monarchy, must renew that physical substance, restore health and strength, reform its character and regain its national pride and self-confidence.

Freedom he considered humanity's greatest possession. Every unfree nation must be prepared to fight for its freedom and every free nation to defend it. If a citizen is to defend his nation, he must be physically and spiritually well-equipped, healthy and strong, morally firm, ready to make sacrifices, disciplined and courageous. This whole view of the nation was incorporated by Tyrs into the ideological base of the Sokol Movement. He worked out a gymnastic system of his own, in which esthetic elements play a very significant role, prepared an original Czech gymnastic nomenclature, and laid the foundation to the organization of Sokok associations.

Tyrs' system of physical training covered all gymnastic exercises known in his time which were logically divided into 4 groups: 1) the exercises where no help of another exercising person is needed and no apparatuses are used, 2) the apparatus gymnastics, 3) the exercises where the help of another exercising person is needed, and 4) combative exercises. This system was satisfactory enough during Tyrs' life. Later, in the period of extreme development of new sports and games, the new young generation was not satisfied with it any more. The Sokol Organization kept in mind the piety to Tyrs as a person and his many merits and refused for a very long time all attempts to amplify Tyrs' system by new sports and games. Finally the Sokols had to accept the demands of the youth and to modernize their physical training system.

The Sokol was a national organization in the broadest sense of the word. Sokol training was conducted in the national spirit. From the first Tyrs' aim was to gather within the organization members belonging to all classes of society, so one could find tradesmen and professors, factory hands and land workers, students and clerks training side by side. Membership in Sokol organization was open to both sexes, to all political parties and all religious confessions. Jinrich Fügner, the co-founder of the Sokol, gave to the organization the character of brotherhood. Members used "thou" forms among themselves and addressed one another as "brother" and "sister." Equality, freedom and brotherhood, discipline and morality were the first and main elements of the Sokol idea. All the work done by the functionaries and by the instructors was done free of charge, out of love for the cause. No one received any rewards, grants of assistance or compensation whatsoever. Nor did the Sokol Union receive any grants from the Czechoslovak State, all the expenses being paid entirely by the members themselves.

The Sokol Physical Training Unit formed the basis of the Sokol organization. The Units of a given Region associated in the Sokol Regional Group, and all the Regional Groups were associated in the Czechoslovak Sokol Community (Ceskoslovenska Obec Sokolská - COS) with its head offices in Prague.

The Sokol Units organized in foreign countries outside Czechoslovakia were associated in the Sokol Foreign and Overseas Group (in Poland, Yugoslavia, Russia, Sutria, France, etc.). The first Sokol Unit in the United States was founded in 1865 where Czech and Slovak Sokols were associated in the Union of Czechoslovak Sokols.

It is very interesting to note, that after 1948, when Czechoslovak Sokol Community and Sokol Physial Training Units were broken up because of their political undesirability in Czechoslovakia controlled by communists, the Czech minorities abroad still kept the tradition and organized Sokol Units there. Many large Sokol Units still exist especially in large cities, e.g., Vienna, Paris, New York, Chicago, and others.

## "Slet"--The Sokol Festivals

The most joyous manifestations of the Sokol movement and the most inspiring surveys of Sokol achievement were the All-Sokol Festivals. Eleven Sokol Festivals have been held during the whole period of Sokol organization's existence. The first one was held in 1882 and Dr Tyrs in person directed it. The number of participants taking part in exercises was 720. This number has extended Festival by Festival so that in 1948 at the last one the number of participants reached 516,000. The Sokol Festival arena prepared for some last Festivals had the dimensions of 300 x 200 meters with seating for 250,000 spectators and dressing rooms for 150,000 gymnasts. The mass-drill-displays presented in 1938 included 286,000 gymnasts simultaneously. The program of the Sokol festival contained a great variety of Youth, Men and Women contests of all kinds, public gymnastic mass displays and a parade through Prague.

Before World War II the Czechoslovak Sokol Community had approximately 760,000 members, 1,200 Sokol-halls (gymnasiums) and 1,800 playgrounds. On October 8, 1941, the Sokol Organization was liquidated by Nazi Germany, its property confiscated, the leading personalities and more than 20,000 Sokol members were executed or sent to prisons or concentration camps.

## Physical Training Associations (Federations) Politically or Religiously Founded

Although Sokol Organization members, many of whom were workers never separated according to social classes to which they belonged, since 1897 new Workers Physical Training Units have been established by Social Democratic Party members. In 1903 the Association of Workers Physical Units was founded to be the head organization. There were two reaons for establishing the Workers Physical Training Units:

a. The Sokol Organization strictly propagated the nationalistic ideas while the Social Democratic Party inclined to internationalism.

b. Physical training was an excellent item of propaganda helping the Social Democratic Party to increase the number of new members who usually opened their membership very soon after they started their physical training in the Workers Physical Training Units. The Association of Workers Physical Training Units copied entirely the Sokol Organization, accepted also Tyrs' system and organized three Workers Olympiads--festivals not very different from the Sokol Festivals.

When the Communist Party of Czechoslovakia was established in 1921, the communists separated from the Social Democratic Party and its other organizations. Thus they withdrew from the Association of Workers Physical Training Units also and established a new Federation of Workers Physical Training Units. In the same year they organized their own festival called a Spartakiade. In 1926 the name of this organization changed to the Workers Proletarian Physical Culture Federation. This federation accepted the physical education system and organization system from Moscow as it was carried out there at that time. Its sports clubs called "Red Star" went in for games and scouting as a special program for their members.

Since 1896 Catholic Physical Training Units had also been separately established which united themselves in 1908 in an all-Moravian organization and in 1920 throughout the country in an organization named OREL. The OREL organization had quite a different ideology but the physical training program was similar to the Sokol organization. The OREL organization also held two festivals where the members throughout the country took part.

These three political physical training organizations never reached the same importance and level of the Sokol organization, either by number of their members or by professional standards of physical training.

## Y.M.C.A. and Y.W.C.A.

After World War I the American Young Men's Christian Association (YMCA) started its activity in Czechoslovakia being later followed by the Young Women's Christian Assocaition (YWCA). These organizations built up sports centers in Prague and other big cities. Instructors in these centers were the pioneers of popular American games, especially volleyball, basketball and baseball, which were previously unknown in Czechoslovakia. American instructors found their followers in Czech physical education teachers who had received degrees at Springfield College, Massachusetts, U.S.A. They became the propagators of American games and succeeded, especially in the case of volleyball which became the most popular game in Czechoslovakia. In the course of time Czech players got ahead of their American teachers.

## Development of Sports

The oldest sports in Czech country were fencing and horse riding. They are reported to be important subjects of a knight's education and army training in the Middle Ages. Other sports came into existence in the second half of the nineteenth century, usually according to English example. All sports, with the exception of a few soccer professional players and boxers, were organized and done on a strictly amateur basis.

Single sports had unions which were associated since 1896 in the Czech Olympic Committee (after 1918 in the Czechoslovak Olympic Committee) and since 1928 in the Czechoslovak All-Sports Committee. The Czech Professor Dr. Jiri Guth-Karkovsky (1861-1944) assisted Baron Pierre de Coubertin in reviving the Olympic Games and became a founding member of the International Olympic Committee. Since the second Olympiad in 1900 at Paris the Czechoslovak athletes participated successfully at all Olympic Games.

## Present Physical Education in Czechoslovakia

The political dependence of Czechoslovakia on the Soviet Union after World War II appeared to be significant also in the field of physical education. The development of the organization of present physical training in the schools, as the voluntary physical training in the sports clubs, was profoundly influenced by the Soviets. Physical education gained an important place in the educational process evolved in all Communist States. Physical culture is defined as the systematic and all-sided development of the working people in the interest of preparation for labor and defense of the country. Socialist society gives physical training the greatest possible support. In postwar Czechoslovakia the government also promoted physical training and sports with generous subsides.

## School Physical Education

Physical education is an integral part of the Communistic education and therefore it is compulsory in all schools. The basic objectives of physical education in the schools of all socialist countries are in fact very similar: to improve and ensure the correct physical development of the school children and students, to make them handy, to develop agility, speed, strength and endurance, to accustom the children and pupils to habits of personal and social hygiene, to train them to be bold, disciplined and develop their sense of friendship and comradeship.

### Preschool Physical Education for Children Up to Six Years of Age

*Nursery school* is an educational institution for the care of children ranging in age from 3 months to 3 years. These schools are assigned for children whose mothers are employed and cannot take proper care of them. Children are cared for by qualified nurses and physicians. Physical activities in the first year: children learn to creep, sit, stand and walk; in the second year: children's games with running, jumping and throwing.

*Kindergarten* for children in the ages from three to six years. Physical education in these schools provides active out-of-doors exercise for children to develop their motor abilities, to teach them basic hygiene habits and to help them develop good body posture. Physical education represents one-third of the total period children spend in school. It is applied with small breaks all day long. It consists of morning exercise from 10 to 15 minutes, organized and controlled by the teacher; free playing and children's games in the course of the day, and of a short walk in the school neighborhood.

The program of physical activities in Kindergarten: rhythmical movements and singing games; imitation of animal life; basic skills of running, jumping, throwing, climbing and playing games to develop all these activities; playing with the ball. The physical program is supplemented by periodical physical examination by the teacher and the physician. Going to nursery school and kindergarten is not compulsory in Czechoslovakia. All Czechoslovak children may visit these schools, but usually only those families where both parents are employed send their children there.

### Elementary School Physical Education

All children from 6 to 15 years of age receive their basic education at a nine-year primary School. Physical Education at these schools is a compulsory subject. The time allocated for physical education is two hours per week. The schools in which personnel and material conditions are especially good have increased this time from two to three compulsory hours per week.

The pupils from the grades 3-9 may participate in voluntary courses of games which are 1-2 hours per week. Pupils from the grades 3-5 have minor games in their programs while those from grades 6-9 have sports games. In the spring and autumn each class has an excursion of 3-5 hours combined with outdoor exercises and games.

Elementary schools organize swimming courses for the pupils in grades 4-6. Unfortunately some schools in the countryside are not able to provide swimming courses because no swimming pools or even a river are available. Ski courses are also organized by the school for the pupils from the grades 7 and 8. These ski courses are usually held at some mountain area because most of the schools locale do not offer an opportunity for skiing.

Some schools conduct morning exercises for the pupils before the lessons start and games or exercises during the main interval. The "exercise-break" is a very short period of exercises provided during the lesson, usually from 2-3 minutes. Its aim is psychical and physical recreation for the pupils who stay in the class and exercise according to the teacher's directions. Morning exercises, main interval exercises, exercise breaks and other exceptional kinds of exercises were introduced to Czechoslovak schools according to the Soviet Union's example, but there were many organizational difficulties, and only a few schools accepted them.

The older pupils (grades 6-9) often take part in various intramural, district or regional sports competition organized by school physical education teachers and volunteers. Physical education in lower divisions (grades 1-5) is taught by the classroom teacher, who also teaches all other subjects. In higher divisions (grades 6-9) it is taught by qualified physical education teachers. Grades 1 and 2 have coeducational physical education while grades 3-9 have separated lessons for boys and girls.

Pupils suffering from various diseases (spine or foot deformities) or those whose physical development is irregular (mainly heart diseases or obesity, etc.) participate in special lessons of correctional or remedial exercises. These lessons are conducted by specialized qualified teachers. Children are divided into groups of 10-15 pupils according to their diseases as assigned by the school physician.

*Programs* of physical education in lower divisions (grades 1-5): class formations; introductory, preparatory and corrective exercises; rhythmic activities and basic forms of national dances; running, sprinting for short distances and relay games; jumping--long and high jump, jumping across obstacles; tumbling, climbing and hanging; minor games and ball games with simplified rules--soccer, basketball, handball, and volleyball.

*Programs* of physical education in higher divisions (grades 6-9): class formations, preparatory and corrective exercises; rhythmic activities and national dances; track and field events--sprinting, relays, long and high jump, shot-put, grenade throw; basic skills of apparatus gymnastics; sports games--basketball, handball, soccer, volleyball, ice-hockey; and swimming.

## Sports Schools--Research Schools

There are also some experimental sports schools or sports classes in Czechoslovakia for the instruction of the most talented pupils between 12-18 years of age in the particular sport in which they show an aptitude. There are sports schools for track and field athletics, sport gymnastics (apparatus exercises), swimming, ice-hockey, soccer, and basketball. These sports schools develop a high level of performance in their pupils and prepare them for contests and championships. They are well staffed with the best teachers, specialized in their field, and have excellent facilities. The sports schools have more hours of physical training and sports than ordinary schools.

## Secondary School and Physical Education

Secondary schools in Czechoslovakia can be divided into four principal categories: 1) High schools of general education called "Gymnasiums" to prepare pupils for university study, 2) Vocational schools--industrial, commercial, agricultural, 3) Schools for apprentices and secondary schools for workers, and 4) Art academies. The term of study at these schools is about 4 years.

Physical education at secondary schools is compulsory. The average number of hours for physical education is two one hour class periods per week. The school of general education where personnel and material conditions are especially good have increased this number from two to three compulsory one hour class periods per week. The average of 2 hours of physical education per week is absolutely unsatisfactory. The increase of the number of hours for physical training from two to three as it is permitted at the present time by the Ministry of Education has met with many difficulties and therefore the majority of the schools have not yet increased the number of required hours.

In addition to the compulsory class periods the pupils may participate in voluntary outdoor sports and games in the afternoon which adds another two hours per week. Actually only a low number of pupils may participate in these voluntary sport hours because of an insufficient number of qualified teachers and coaches, and lack of money for their salaries, deficiency of gyms, athletic fields, playgrounds and equipment.

The best conditions for compulsory physical education can be found in high schools of general education (Gymnasiums) where almost all the teachers are qualified professors of physical education, who have graduated from the Faculty of Physical Training and Sports. Most of those schools have sufficient equipment. The worst conditions can be found at schools for apprentices and workers where the absence of qualified teachers, gyms and sports equipment occurs very often and where the number of hours for physical education has been decreased to one hour per week for grades 1 and 2 and pupils from grade 3 do not have any physical education at all.

The secondary school students participate in week-long skiing courses organized by the school and are similar to those described in the elementary school program. There is also the possibility to execute morning exercises, main interval exercises and exercise-breaks for secondary school students, but the reality is identical with that of of elementary schools, i.e., only a minimum of them realize these additional physical exercises. Special lessons of correctional or remedial exercises are organized at secondary schools for the students suffering from various diseases. They conform with those previously described in the elementary school program section.

The physical training program for secondary schools is divided into three groups: 1) basic exercises--all students learn them, 2) supplementary exercises--more difficult exercises taught to students who have already mastered the basic exercise, and 3) choice exercises--certain specialized exercises for any sports event, i.e., track and field, basketball, for the excellent students. Groups 1 and 2 are taught during the regular compulsory lessons of physical education while group 3 takes place in the program of voluntary physical education lessons held afternoons after school. These lessons are organized for groups of 15-30 students separately for each sports event. The groups are further classified according to each student's performance and ability.

The physical training program includes basic gymnastics exercises--class formations, preparatory exercises, calisthenics, and folk dances for girls; sports events--track and field, sports gymnastics, modern gymnastics for girls, combative exercises, basketball, volleyball, ice-hockey, swimming, skiing and eventually also skating.

Each school practices specifically such sports for which it has specialized teachers, sufficient gymnasiums and sports grounds as well as sport equipment. For example certain schools might be specialized in track and field and others in apparatus gymnastics or basketball.

Sports training oriented toward talented individuals has now almost replaced natural physical education as it was practiced in Czechoslovakian secondary schools by the method of Hébert and Gaulhofer. In physical education programs we now find unnatural artistic exercises on apparatus which may be good for specialized sports gymnasts but which are much too difficult for the majority of students. The trend of physical education in recent years differs from previous many-sided training working toward average level performances. The practice from the pre-World War II period has been replaced by specialization with emphasis on the best performances. In Czechoslovakia as well as in the USSR, the German Democratic Republic and other socialist countries, competition is considered the best way in the school physical education.

To reach the best performances the school physical education uses the methods customary for top competitiors and sports clubs, e.g., weight lifting for increasing the muscle force, and circuit-train-ing. Physical education teachers very often give all of their time to a few talented students in the class to the detriment of average students. To increase students' interest in competitive sports many intramural, district or regional sports competitions are organized. The top competitors take part in all-state championship.

Experimental sports schools were recently established for talented sportsmen among secondary school students. These schools are being established on the same basis and with the same conditions as experimental elementary schools were, but there are very few at the present time.

Secondary school physical education is supplemented by Civil State Defense. This subject had been classified as the third physical education lesson per week. Now it is taught in specialized lessons out of physical education lessons. It includes basic knowledge of pre-military training: drill, the use of small arms, tactics and map read-ing; civil air-raid precautions; war-gas and A-weapons precautions.

## University and College Physical Education

There are 48 universities, polytechnical colleges and special-ized institutes in Czechoslovakia, comprising altogether 107 faculties.

All college and unversity students are required to take classes in physical education for the first seven terms ($3\frac{1}{2}$ years) of their studies. After this period the classes in physical education are non-compulsory. Students may register for gymnastics, soccer, swimming, track and field, basketball, volleyball, tennis, rowing and canoeing, cycling, skiing, according to their interests. In the case of younger students for whom physical education is still compulsory, their presence is required and often controlled but they do not have to pass any tests of physical fitness. The minimum hours of instruction is two fifty minute periods per week.

After accomplishing their third term all students take the ski-ing course organized by the school. Arrangements for transportation, lodging, food, insurance, and medical care are the responsibility of the organizing college or university. The stay on the ski campus is about eleven days. The first aim of the skiing course is to give stu-dents a chance to learn or to improve their skills in it.

After accomplishing their fourth term all students take the summer course staying 10-14 days with their physical education teach-ers in some famous Czechoslovakia recreational area. They live in tents, prepare the food themselves and meet other facilities of camp-ing in summer nature. Hikes and excursions are combined with les-sons in various sports, track and field, games and especially swim-ming and canoeing. The arrangements and organization are very similar to those of winter ski courses.

Each college or university faculty has its department of physical education officially called Chair of Physical Education, which takes care of the organization of compulsory physical education and provides necessary material conditions. This department also provides voluntary sports courses for those who are athletically inclined. An expert is elected to be the head of the Chair of Physical Education.

There is a staff consisting of professional assistants qualified for teaching general physical education or specialists who teach just one sports event. The staff represents the best of the secondary school physical education teachers who besides practical teaching also do research work on a certain problem. The teachers are required to spend a certain number of working hours on their research and to publish their theoretical works and conclusions. This target undoubtedly helps the increase of the theoretical basis of physical education, but on the other hand the target of scientific work leads to certain formalism and perfunctory results because not every good teacher is always a good scientist.

The most obvious difficulty in providing university and college physical education is the lack of adequate gymnasiums, sports halls, swimming pools and outdoor facilities of their own. Since physical education became compulsory at universities and colleges in 1945 they have had to rent public sports facilities or facilities belonging to other schools or clubs, which are often far from the school itself.

## Voluntary University and College Physical Education

The administration of this service is a function of the University students clubs called "SLAVIA VS" which all are members of the Czechoslovak Union for Physical Training. Student competition is organized on an intramural, district and national basis. The national championship of all universities and colleges in Czechoslovakia is held every year under the name of the Czechoslovak University Games (Czechoslovak Universiad). Winners of these games represent Czechoslovakia at the World Academic Games which are organized by FISU. All students in higher education who have not served in the army forces are required to take several hours per week of military training for 2 years. This training includes drill, the use of small arms, tactics and map reading on a professional level taught by specialized army officers.

## Teacher Training

From 1870 to 1945 elementary school teachers received four years of education at the Teacher Training Colleges where physical education was generally one of many compulsory subjects. After World War II the training of elementary school teachers was provided at Pedagogical Institutes and now at Facilities of Pedagogy, which offer a four-year study program. Elementary school teachers with specialization in lower divisions and who will be teaching all subjects in their classes must qualify to teach all of them, one of which is physical education. Teachers with specialization for higher elementary school divisions teach only two subjects, one of which may be physical education. Extramural study is possible, but it takes five years instead of four years of regular study.

Secondary school teachers of physical education were trained from 1891 to World War II at the "Course for Training of Physical Education Teachers" founded as an institute in conjunction with Charles University in Prague. In the beginning this course took two years, was then lengthened to three years and in 1936 extended to four years. Its educational program has also been profoundly changed in the course of time. In 1945 the name of the course was changed to "Institute for Training of Secondary School Teachers of Physical Education." In 1953 the "Institute of Physical Training and Sports" was founded as part of Charles University in Prague and in 1960 a second Institute as part of Comenius University in Bratislava. Since 1960 Czech students attended Prague Institute and Slovak students attended Bratislava Institute. In 1965 both institutes were reorganized and changed to independent university faculties called Physical Training and Sports Faculty.

Tasks of the Faculty were: 1) Training of teachers for physical education at secondary schools, colleges, universities and all other schools; 2) training of professional trainers and coaches for competitive sports at sport associations and clubs; 3) Scientific research in all the field of physical training and sports as well as preparation of qualified experts in the scientific research institutes. The dean is the head of the faculty. There are four vice-deans who run the faculty affairs.

The faculty has now 12 departments (chairs): 1) theory and methodology of physical education, 2) history, pedagogy, psychology and administration of physical education, 3) philosophy and sociology, 4) anatomy and biomechanics, 5) physiology, 6) sports medicine, 7) gymnastics and combative sports, 8) track and field athletics, 9) sports games, 10) tourism, cycling, rowing, canoeing, skating and skiing, 11) swimming, and 12) military physical training (men only).

The most significant problems of scientific research or of education are advised by the Scientific Council of Faculty led by the dean. The other members are the vice-deans and representatives of individual departments.

In 1968 the Physical Training and Sports Faculty in Prague had the following qualified staff: 5 university professors, 22 associate professors, 79 senior lecturers, 9 lectueres. The faculty had approximately 570 fulltime students and 380 extramural students.

Full time study of physical education takes 5 years while extramural studies takes 6 years. The studies can be divided into two groups: 1) students who want to be physical education teachers at the secondary high school must study two subjects, physical education and one other subject in the following combinations: Physical Education + Czech, Physical Education + Russian, Physical Education + English, Physical Education + Geography, Physical Education + Biology, Physical Education + Mathematics. The combinations offered to university freshmen are not the same every year. They are set down before entrance examinations take their turn according to forecasts of recent or expected future requirements for new teachers; 2) students who want to be specialists in physical education by itself or become research workers in some of Czechoslovak sports institutes or to train athletes and teams of a high level of performance, they study physical education by itself with a specialization in certain sports.

An entrance examination is required of all aspirants (men and women) before they are admitted to the Faculty. All aspirants must have a secondary school certificate, pass a medical examination, a written test of biology (anatomy, physiology, hygiene) and also a practical examination of performances in various activities. The practical examination includes track and field events (to run 100 m. and 1000 m., high-jump, shot-put), apparatus-exercises, swimming and team games--basketball, soccer, volleyball.

Aspirants must meet not only practical and physical entrance examinations but also show a positive attitude toward the communist system, policy and cooperation with USSR and other socialist countries is required. Their political opinion is checked as well as that of their parents.

There are about 500 aspirants for the studies at the Faculty every year but only 100 of them may be admitted. The main reason is that the Faculty does not have its own building and sport facilites yet. It is provisionally located in the former Sokol organization property--Tyrs' house which is very old and its sport facilities and equipment do not satisfy the modern requirements of the Faculty any more.

Study Program

The following courses are offered:

Political Science, Philosophy of Marxism-Leninism, Political Economy, Social Function and Problems of Physical Education, Sociology, Psychology, Sport Pscyhology.

Anatomy, Anthropometry, Biomechanics, Kinesiology, Human Physiology, Physiology of Sport, Biochemistry, Hygiene.

History of Physical Education, Theory and Principles of Physical Education, System of Physical Education, Pedagogy, Principles of Teaching, Methodology of Physical Education, Methods of Physical Education, Teaching Practice in the Schools.

Theory, Practice and Methods of Following Sport Branches: Gymnastics (preparatory, physical condition, health, correctional and remedial exercises), modern gymnastics and folk dances for women, sports gymnastics (apparatus exercises), combative sports (boxing, judo), minor and team games (basketball, handball, ice-hockey, soccer, volleyball), swimming, tourism, camping, cycling, rowing, and canoeing, skiing, facultative special training in a sport branch of own choice.

Organization and Administration of Physical Education, Sport Facilities and Equipment.

Courses of 12 days: tourism, hiking, cycling, canoeing, skiing--2 courses, skating and ice-hockey.

General knowledge: training in foreign languages (Russian and an occidental language) training in drawing exercise pictures.

## Examinations

Each student must pass partial examinations from individual main subjects in each term which are the only condition for admission to the next term. Completing their studies students must pass a final examination administered by the State. The students may pass this examination after completing and defending a special "diploma-thesis."

The graduates may obtain the doctoral degree (Ph.Dr.) after passing a rigorous examination. The candidates have to complete with the help and advice of an academic tacher, a Doctor's Dissertation on a theme of sports science as well as to pass examinations in philosophy and in the subject of their specialization.

## Trainers (Coaches) School

A three-year extramural school for trainers is attached to the Faculty of Physical Education. Graduates of this course may work as professional trainers of the first grade to train top athletes and teams not only in Czechoslovakia but also abroad. Students of the trainers school are mainly former top competitors who finished active sporting life in competition but who want to work as professional trainers using all their knowledge and experience. The Central School of the Union for Physical Training in Prague provides also courses for voluntary trainers, instructors, and referees, who in turn look after registered athletes and top sportsmen.

# Research in Physical Education

The Physical Training Faculties in Prague and in Brasislava have essentially contributed to the creation of the fundamentals for Sports Science as an independent scientific branch. Several teachers of these faculties are active members in the commissions of the International Council of Physical Education and Sports with UNESCO. For many years, the scientists of Physical Training Faculties have also participated in an International Congress of Sports Sciences. They are also members of the Scientific Council of the Czechoslovak Union for Physical Training.

The Documentation and Information Service of the Physical Training Faculty in Prague is recognized by international experts. Summary of Physical Education publications and articles is published quarterly by the Faculty.

The Library of the Physical Education Faculty possesses nearly 140,000 indiegenous and foreign books and an extensive service of journals.

The Teachers of Physical Education Departments at Pedagogy Faculties and at all other Colleges and Universities in Czechoslovakia deal with a multitude of research themes.

In 1953 the Research Institute of Physical Training in Prague was founded. It is an independent center of research of physical training with the main accent on the research of the influence of physical training on the strengthening of the health of the nation. At present 37 employees (7 Candidates of Science) work in this Institute.

The Institute of Sports Medicine was founded in Prague in 1946 by Professor MUDR. Jiri Král does not only ensure the solid sports medical training of the future sports doctors and sports pedagogues but is developing more and more into a center of sports medical science in Czechoslovakia.

The Scientific Council of the Central Committee of CSTV is an advisory body of the Czechoslovak Union for Physical Training. It is the representative of scientific research in physical training. The task of the Scientific Council is the planning, organizing and coordination of these activities. In close connection with the physical training movement, the Scientific Council applies scientific research results in the solution of basic problems of physical training. It is the initiator of research, transfers its results into practical life and studies the experience gained. The Scientific Council organized some international Congresses on problems of Physical Education in Prague.

The Czechoslovak Union for Physical Training publishes monthly a scientific journal *Theory and Practice of Physical Culture*. Scientific work is reflected also in numerous publications.

## Medical Care and Control in Physical Education

The first Czech physician and surgeon who became a well known propagator of physical exercise was Jan E. Purkyne (1797-1869). Professor of physiology. He was a member of the Sokol Organization, trained himself and also did various scientific tests--for instance he observed the graduation of muscles exertion by various exercises (swarm up a rope, jumps) when carried out with a weight on the back.

After World War I MUDr. Karel Weigner, Professor of anatomy at Charles University based physical education on scientific principles.

Professor MUDr. Jiri Král was the founder and the first worker on the field of sporting medical care and the first teacher of it. Now he is vice-chairman of FIMS (Federation Internationale de la Medicine Sportive).

Sports Medicine is a compulsory subject for medical students in their 9th and 10th term. It consists of a one-hour period of theoretical lecture and one practical training per week. Students must pass an examination at the end of the 10th term. Physicians who want to specialize in sports medicine must pass an extra professional examination after they have accomplished a 3 years medical practice in a sports medical center.

Medical control in physical training is provided by state institutions and voluntary personnel. Everybody who wants to do actively some sport in a club must first pass a medical examination. Active competitors must pass this examination every year in a specialized medical control and consulting center and get a physician's confirmation to his competitor's registration card. According to their health condition and efficiency, the competitors are divided into four groups. Those who didn't pass medical control can't take part in any competition. Top sportsmen and competitors who are important for the state representation at international meetings have special medical care of their own. Sports clubs and unions usually have their own voluntary working physicians and other medical personnel.

## Physical Education and Sports in Czechoslovakia Today

After World War II the Sokol Organization and other Physical Education organizations stopped during the Nazi occupation were re-established with an exception of the small Workers Proletarian Federation.

In 1948 when the 11th Sokol Festival was finished in the course of which Sokol members showed that they did not have a great liking for the new communistic Government, Sokol Organization was re-organized and later Czechoslovak Physical Education was united in one all-state organization which adopted the Soviet Physical Education System.

On the basis of a new law in 1949 the state assumed the care of Czechoslovak Physical Education. Thus the State Bureau for Physical Education was established which changed to the State Committee for Physical Education in 1953. Finally in 1957 a new Czechoslovak Union for Physical Education was established.

It is a voluntary united sports organization based on the union of two national physical education organizations--the Czech and the Slovak--having equal right units on an autonomous basis are 44 independent sports associations (of track and field, basketball, soccer, etc.). The Czechoslovak Union for Physical Training (CSTV) had in 1964 1,758,000 members (expressed in percentage in relation to the number of inhabitants this represents 12.3%). They may be divided:

1. Basic Physical Education including gymnastics, most popular recreation sports and hikes, with 605,000 members.

2. Competitive sports with 982,000 members.

3. Tourism with 171,000 members.

The total number of trainers, coaches and referees--152,000. The most popular sports are:

1. Soccer 367,000 accredited players in 5,788 clubs.

2. Ice-hockey 77,700 accredited players in 1,718 clubs.

3. Volleyball 70,000 accredited players in 2,962 clubs.

4. Track and field 60,400 accredited members in 1,000 clubs.

5. Table tennis 56,000 accredited members in 2,715 clubs.

6. Skiing 52,500 accredited members in 1,447 clubs.

In addition, there exists in the country a number of technical sports branches, especially of military character, which are controlled by the Union for Cooperation with the Army (SCAZARM).

These sports are: aviation, aeronautic model making, gliding, parachutism, motoring, shooting, radio fan club, etc.

Spartakiad: Similar festivals to former Sokol ones were organized in 1955, 1960, and 1965 by state sports authorities. The 4th Spartakiad prepared for the year of 1970 was postponed for political and economic reasons. These new festivals called "Spartakiad" have had mass-displays and contests similar to Sokol Festivals but the effort for the most possible attractivity of mass gymnastic displays was remarkable: 700,000 gymnasts took part in each Spartakiad on the average.

Physical Fitness Badge:  Soviet Physical Fitness badge GTO
was the pattern for adopting this contest in Czechoslovakia and establishing of the Physical Fitness Badge PPOV (Ready for Labor and Defense of the Country) for boys and girls.

In 1965 the fitness badge was gained by 61,880 adults and
248,200 boys and girls.  The relatively high number of boys and girls
is due to the fact that fitness award contests were carried out even
during the compulsory lessons of Physical Education, because Physical Education teachers were merit-rated according to the number of
students who were awarded the mentioned fitness badge.  This caused
the contest to become formal and students interest in it is now very
low.

The item of great interest among young people are the "Sports
Games of the Youth" organized every year, where many competitors
take part in various events--e.g., track and field, sports gymnastics,
soccer, basketball, volleyball, etc.

The sportsmen of Czechoslovakia, especially football, handball,
volleyball, and ice-hockey players maintain extensive sports relations
with foreign countries.  Also the Czechoslovak coaches and experts
of these sports have been highly respected and in demand abroad for
many years.

### Characteristic Development of Czechoslovak
### Physical Eduucation in 1945-1970

Since 1948 when the united Physical Education organization was
established according to the Soviet pattern, its representatives propagated the motto "Soviet Physical Education--our exemplar!"

Communists completely reorganized the ancient system of Physical Education based on the Sokol national ideology to conform to the
materialistic and dialectical principles of Marxism-Leninism.  Soviet
methods have been consistently adopted to sports organizations and
training methods where very often the original Czechoslovak organization, training methods and corresponding results were much better.

Former Sokol instructors or Trainers who were unacceptable
for their anti-communist political opinions were replaced by young
trainers politically acceptable by the communists but very inexperi-
enced in Physical Education.  This caused a professional level decrease and even a decrease in the number of members in physical
training units and clubs.

In contrast, after World War II the results of top sportsmen
representing the country abroad, improved exceptionally because these
competitors also received full support according to the Soviet Pattern.

In the course of the last 25 years Czechoslovakia entered the
arena of world sport.  The Czechoslovak sports had the essential

condition for its development which has produced such remarkable world champions as Emil Zátopek and Vera Cáslavská. Czechoslovak sportsmen have won (registered till August 1969) in total 36 Gold, 38 Silver, 29 Bronze Olympic Medals, 198 first, 220 second, 244 third places in World championships and 74 first, 94 second, 273 third places in European championships, and have held 120 World records, 27 European records and 14 Olympic records.

On the other hand, these really excellent Czechoslovak achievements, which place as small a country as Czechoslovakia among the most successful countries in sports competition, have their short-comings.

The training and all preparation of Czechoslovak athletes as well as the costs tied up to international representation represent large sums of money. These funds might be used to support public recreation and physical education.

Top sportsmen and National team representants must train many hours every day. They have reserved many gym halls, swim-ming pools, and other sports facilities for almost whole days which means that public admittance is minimal. Thus, the real public phys-ical recreation and sports recreation is cut down in contrast to the prewar (W.W. II) period.

Finally there are moral and ethical defects too. Top sports-men who are the members of the teams representing the country need many hours of training every day to reach splendid sporting condi-tion. From the point of view of how many hours per day they spend with training, it is very hard to understand how they can be employ-ed and earn their money too. As a matter of fact, it is quite impos-sible for these people to have a regular job and to be the top sports-men at the same time. Because in Czechoslovakia, as well as in other socialist countries, pure professionalism in sport isn't permitted for ideological and other reasons. The only solution of this problem is pretended amateurism. A competitor is formally employed somewhere but he doesn't work there at all because he has to train. Many of such competitors serve in the Army where they have only one duty--training and good sports performance. Also the method of timeless studies of active sportsmen at the University has been adopted.

This understanding of amateurism isn't new and an isolated case in the world's competitive sport scene and perhaps the above mentioned way of successful state representation has been more or less adopted in some other countries, especially in those where inter-national sport successes belong to their political program.

## SELECTED REFERENCES

1. *Appui apporté par l'Etat en Tchécoslovaquie à la culture physique et au sports.* Prague, Orbis. 1949.

2. Bisquertt, Luis, Dr. Sobre educación física en Europa. *Revista Chilena de Educación Física.* 1968. No. 135-138, pp. 6-10.

3. Bures, Karel Dr. *Les sports et l'éducation physique en Tchécoslovaquie.* Prague, Orbis. 1926.

4. Chysky, J. *Guide to Czechoslovakia.* Prague, Artia. 1965.

5. Czechoslovak Sport. *Sports Review of the Czechoslovak Olympic Committee.* Prague, CSOV. 1967-69.

6. *Information Bulletin of Czechoslovak Sport.* Prague, CSTV. 1967-69.

7. Milne, Armour. *Le sport tchécoslovaque 1945-1955.* Prague, Orbis. 1955.

8. Moolenijzer, Nicolaas J. *Physical Education in Austria,* in "Physical Education Around the World. Monograph No. 5, Phi Epsilon Kappa Fraternity, Publishers.

9. *Prague the Olympic City.* Prague, Olympia. 1968.

10. Scheiner, Josef Dr. *The Sokols.* Prague, COS. 1968.

11. Seurin, Pierre Dr. *L'Education physique dans le monde.* Bordeaux. 1968.

12. *Sokol Czechoslovak.* Prague, COS. 1932.

13. *Systeme de gymnastique Tyrs.* Prague, Grégr. 1920.

14. *Tenth Sokol Festival Praha 1938.* Prague, COS. 1938.

15. Tyrs, Miroslav Dr. *Introduction to the Foundations of Gymnastics.* Chicago.

# SPORT AND PHYSICAL EDUCATION IN ECUADOR

by Jaime Paz y Mino M.

## Biographical Sketch

*Jaime Enrique Paz Y Mino Merino* was born on May 13, 1939, at Riobamba, Ecuador. His primary education was received at the Escuela Hermano Miguel De San Blas De Quito; secondary education at the Colegio Nacional Montufar in Quito; and the Estudios Seperiores at the Universidad Central in Quito. Additional study in sports and physical education was received at Ecuador institutions and at St. John's University, New York; at Denver, Philadelphia, Boston, and Washington, D.C.

Professor Paz Y Mino M., has been an Inspector, Professor of Physical Education and Recreation at the Normal Juan Montalvo from 1962 to 1966; Professor of sports, physical education and recreation and director since 1972 of the Centro De Coordinacion Docente De Education Fisica Y Deportes (The Alfred Perez Guerrero). He has been honored by positions as delegate, vice president, president, secretary-general and director of physical education and sports societies in Educador. In addition he has been very active in futbol, basquet, and gimnasia sports and has numerous articles on sport and physical education published over the years. Space does not permit inclusion of Professor Paz Y Mino Merino's extensive biographical sketch.

## Editor's Note

In Monograph #4 of the Phi Epsilon Kappa series, "Physical Education Around the World" may be found an article written in 1970 on Physical Education in Ecuador by Dr. Celso Torres (former Director of the Institute of Physical Education at Central University, Quito) and Dr. Maurice A Clay of the University of Kentucky. The background information on Ecuador is excerpted from their article and the present current information has been submitted by Professor Paz Y Mino M., in response to my letter requesting updated information.

## Part I

## General Background

Ecuador is situated on the northwest coast of South America. Its size and relative area are shown elsewhere in this article.

Quito, the capital, is located just 10 miles south of the Equator and is considered one of the most beautiful cities in the New World. As is commonly true in Latin America, the capital city is the political and cultural center. Guayaquil is Ecuador's principal port, largest city, and financial center.

Ecuador's population is a mosaic of races and cultures. Approximate percentages of the population follow: Indian, 50 percent; mixed blood, 30 percent; negroes, 10 percent. The remaining 10 per cent are of European origin, largely Spanish.

A republic with a directly elected president and a bi-cameral National Congress and a Supreme Court, Ecuador has 19 provinces and one national territory, The Galapagos Islands. It has only recently begun to manufacture other than consumer goods.

Bananas, coffee, cacao and rice are grown for export. Ecuador is among the world's largest exporters of bananas. Though agriculture is the largest and most important economic activity, less than five (5) percent of the land is cultivated.

Ecuador shares with its neighboring states and with Mexico a common (in part, at least) heritage of Spanish or Iberian culture, a common religion, and what Benton refers to as "the frontier freshness that is still the mark of the Americas." Ecuador is one part of what Benton calls Indian Latin America.

Ecuador, as is its neighbor Peru, is divided into three kinds of land mountains, with a strip of lower land extending down to the west coast and with tropical valleys and lowlands east of the mountains.

Regional differences have long had a decisive effect on Ecuador. "Guayaquil, the country's commercial center and principal seaport, is brisk and progressive despite the tropical climate. It is politically liberal and has little in common with and almost no sympathy for Quito, the old conservative and mountain bound capital." Ap proximately 16 percent of the total population of Ecuador live in the two cities of Guayaquil and Quito.

One of the centers of the vast, highly developed Inca empire was in Quotio, Ecuador. More than one half the 1950 population were Indian, many of whom were direct descendents of the Incas and spoke the Quechuan language of the Incas.

About the size of Colorado (the highest state in the U.S.),
Ecuador is the smallest of the Andean countries but in Ecuador even
the mountain valleys (many are higher than 9000 feet) may be as high
as the highest Rocky Mountain peaks in the United States.  Many of
its people live in tight clusters in the valleys between high mountain
peaks.  Transportation across the mountains, long next to impossible,
is still difficult but has been improved by airplane travel.

The eastern side of the Andes in Ecuador is rainy, and water
flowing down its rivers to the Amazon (across the entire breadth of
South America) has carved incredibly steep canyons) some nearly
twice as deep as the Grand Canyon.

Commenting on the adaptations made by the Andean Indian (including those of Ecuador, Bolivia, Chile and Peru) who live at altitudes of up to 17,000 feet it is stated that "he has developed certain
physical characteristics to get the most use of what oxygen exists at
those heights"--his lungs are larger than normal, the sacs of the
lungs are permanently dilated providing maximum surface for oxygen
transfer; there is a modification of the blood supply ("the Indian living at these altitudes has about two quarts more blood than do the
lowlanders, the red oxygen carrying corpuscles are considerably larger and the heart is larger by as much as 20 percent.").

Farming in mountains as high as the Andes poses problems not
known in the United States.  Crops must be grown where they "will
grow," not where they "will grow best"--potatoes for example will
grow at a height of 14,000; barley at a slightly lower altitude; wheat
and corn will grow at altitudes of up to 10,000 feet.

The Incas had sought to use every available land area for
growing food staples and other products to feed a concentration of
people which in some instances was greater than it was in 1940, approximately four and one half million.  Terracing was practiced and
water supplies were brought at times from great distances.  They
built a remarkable system of roads along which food stores were placed
which extended from as far away as Argentina through Ecuador and
to Colombia.

With the Spanish conquest the people of Latin America, including Ecuador, were brought under the yoke of the Spaniards-- it was
a conquest not only of their possessions, but of their souls and minds
as well.

The Indian has tenaciously resisted the encroachments of the
white man--he has steadfastly held onto his own language, mode of
dress, culture, and behind a thin facade of Christianity, his own
religion.  Thought inscrutable by the white man the degree of which
he is in scrutable is a matter of his own choice.  In those areas where
the Indians remained savages the Spaniards found it impossible to
subdue them.

Most of the Negroes live in the tropical coastal areas of Ecuador. The mixture of European national groups with the Indian nations began with the arrival of the Europeans around the 1530's. Later there was intermixture of European and Negroes with the arrival of Negro slaves. Both the Mestizo (Indian-White) and the whites have played an important role in molding contemporary Ecuador. It was among the Mestizo and the whites that nationalism found its strongest adherents; revolution and other movements for social change found particularly strong support among them.

Ecuador is among the countries of Latin America in which great numbers of Indians still live under conditions roughly equivalent to those of medieval serfdom. Those folk work their master's land, render him personal service and depend upon him almost entirely for whatever rudimentary "social services" and money income they may receive.

## Education in Ecuador

With both free and private schools in the educational system the constitution of Ecuador states that "education shall be free." Presently, municipalities may subsidize free private schools, but "such subventions shall not exceed 20 percent of the total set aside for education." The same constitution states that special attention shall be given to moral and civic education.

The national government supports the educational system in Ecuador. The National Ministry establishes national schools called "escuelas fiscalis," and municipalities may organize schools when funds are available. The cost of textbooks and personal school supplies is borne by the student. There are no tuition fees at the state universities, but there are small enrollment, graduation and examination fees.

Geographic, demographic and economic factors affect education, communications are often inadequate in Ecuador and widely different characteristics of the mountain and coastal areas have brought about considerable difference in customs and in the availability of schools. There are few secondary schools in the rural areas of Ecuador.

The population is predominantly rural, is very unevenly distributed and there is a marked population drift. Many children of school age are reported to suffer from disease and malnutrition. In some areas young child labor is extremely important so that children from age seven may be expected to contribute to family income.

Direction and control of education in Ecuador is under the Minister of Public Education whose responsibilities are discharged through the various technical and administrative departments (including the Department of Physical Education and Sport).

The administration of pre-primary and primary education is the responsibility of the provincial (state) directors of education. School inspectors are responsible for reporting to the director. The administration of secondary schools is the responsibility of their principals and board of governors. Private schools in Ecuador, most of which are maintained by religious groups, are expected to conform to official curricula and are subject to government control.

The educational system is formed at four levels--pre-primary (3-6); primary (6-12); secondary and higher. The "complete" primary schools are organized in three cycles each of two years. Many rural schools, however, provide only the first two cycles. Primary education is compulsory from ages 6-14.

At the secondary level (both state and privately run) are found both modern and classical general secondary schools. Other teacher training schools and technical and vocational schools, most of which offer a six year course leading to the "bachillerato" degree or secondary school certificate. Some rural teacher training schools offer four, others offer six years of secondary education.

## Sports and Physical Education

Professionally physical education is considered to be an integral part of the development of young men and women. It includes gymnastics, the natural activities--running, walking, jumping, throwing, climbing, etcetera; sports; and, for girls and women, dance. In Ecuador as in the greater part of Latin America, Modern Swiss gymnastics is the form of work most highly developed at the present time.

The effect of the increased school populations on the conduct of sports and physical education is much like that encountered in the United States or in Colombia or anywhere else unless additional facilities are made available. For example, at the Central University the facilities currently available are essentially the same as those available for many fewer students a few years back. Plans have been made for extensive additions including a new gymnasium and an Olympic size swimming pool.

Physical Education is required in the schools by law. In the "primaria" or elementary school, the first 6 years; and, in the secondary schools, it is required 3 days each week for 1 class period. In the universities, it is required for three hours a week for one year. At the Central University, the student may take the same activity for the full year or he may change at the end of one of the trimesters.

Increased population has forced an increase in the number of teachers and supervisors needed, in the number of events sponsored, and especially in larger numbers of tournaments. This has called for additional planning and organization and has led to a shortage of teachers of physical education.

The private schools are reported more apt to permit a teacher to teach without a degree than are public schools with whom regulations may be more closely enforced. Teachers in private schools are paid by the hour and hence are said to make less than teachers in public schools. Coaches are commonly hired because they know and practice a sport, not necessarily because they are graduates or professionals.

In the public schools the teacher of physical education may also be the "inspector," a position involving duties somewhat similar to that of attendance officer in the United States.

The most popular sports and activities among those of preschool and school age are: for the pre-schoolers--games; for those in the elementary school--juvenile soccer; in the high school--soccer, track and field, Olympic Gymnastics, and basketball; at the university level--soccer, track and field, basketball, volleyball, and tennis.

Alexander has noted that one aspect of the popular culture of Latin America is sports--the people of the region are "ardent fans." He commented that "no sport of importance has originated in the area, but the Latin Americans have taken avidly to several imports. Probably the most popular sport in the region as a whole is soccer. . ."

Some understanding of the true place of soccer in the early lives of the average Ecuadorean boy is given by a common statement that he learns to kick a soccer ball almost as soon as he can walk. Three stadiums in Quito have been constructed primarily to accommodate the popular acclaim of this as both a participant and spectator sport. Many of the professional soccer players found in Ecuador have been recruited from Argentina, Uruguay and Paraguay.

Volleyball is approximately equal in interest to basketball among sports activities. It is not unusual for soccer teams to be sponsored by textile industries or any other business. Basketball and volleyball rank almost equally in favor as sports among girls.

The swimmers from Guayaquil, Ecuador's chief port city, have traditionally excelled . . . they frequently are unfavorably affected by the altitude of Quito when they leave their coastal area to visit there. Similarly, athletes going to Guayaquil from Quito may suffer from the heat encountered there.

The temperature of Quito, the capital city, is usually low; swimming is, therefore, generally limited to heated club pools, or privately owned pools. Nearby Quito, however, are located natural thermal (hot) waters, which are used to fill pools which are quite popular.

Ecuador was represented in the 1968 Olympics with support from the national government. Interest in the Olympics served to stimulate physical activity in children and young men and women and

igher marks and performances were registered as the young sought
ɔ reach the heights of their heroes.

The World Zone semi-final matches in chess were held in Quito
uring this year. Tennis is a popular activity in some groups and is
ell played. Public tennis courts are extremely rare. Pancho Segura,
ɔrmer world champion in this sport, is from Guayaquil.

Bicycle races are popular in Ecuador. A principal race has
een a long distance one across extremely rugged terrain running
rom: Ibarra -- Quito -- Latacunga -- Ambato -- Riobamba -- Cuenca
- Guayaquil and Manta. Considering the mountainous terrain of Ec-
ador this may well be one of the most difficult courses in the world
ɔr a bicycle race.

In the more remote areas where communications are very limit-
d competitions in sports are largely confined to soccer and volleyball,
ut topography is less a problem than money in the development of
ports and physical education.


## Part II

### Current Information on Sport and Physical Education in Ecuador

Professor Jaime Paz Y Mino Merino, Director of the Centro De
'oordinacion Docente De Education Fisica Y Deportes (Alfredo Perez
'uerrero) of Quito, writes as follows: "Yesterday, we received your
ɘtter requesting current information on sport and physical education
ı Ecuador. This letter is satisfying to us because it allows us to
cquaint ourselves with the institution which you represent and to be
ble to exchange information, and possibly an exchange at a profes-
ional, athletic level." He then provides the following photos and
ʻritten information for this publication.

The Center has its own building in which all the sections plan
wo gymnasia operate (judo and weightlifting). Besides this, there
re an athletic and soccer field, these facilities being within the
esar Anibal Espinoza Stadium. There is a tennis court and construc-
.on of larger and more functional facilities has already begun. Con-
truction is being finished on a covered basketball and volleyball
ourt with seating capacity for 1,000 persons. Besides these, there
; an alternate soccer field and another is being built at 3,000 meters
ltitude. There are three basketball and four volleyball open-air
ourts. There is also a local covered court for dance and karate.
his year the construction will begin on an Olympic-size covered and
eated swimming pool built in accordance with international regula-
ʻons, a water polo court and ornamental falls.

Edificio (facilities) del Centro de Educación Física, Deportes y Recreación "Alfredo Perez Guerrero" Quito

Cancha de Fútbol, pista Atlética del Estadio Universitario, al fondo a la derecha el Edificio del Centro

The Center of Physical Education, Sports and Recreation, "Alfredo Perez Guerrero", was founded as an institute on May 3, 1955, with Dr. Alfredo Perez Guerrero being Rector, Dr. Cesar Anibal Espinoza Vice-Rector and Mr. Genaro Fierro the first Director.

At the present time, the Center of Physical Education, Sports and Recreation, "Alfredo Perez Guerrero" consists of a Director, an Assistant Director and heads of the Physical Education, Sports, Recreation and Athletic Medicine sections.

The Physical Education Section, directed by Dr. Ana de Maggio, works with first-year students from the twelve university faculties, that is to say, with 30 schools with an annual average of 10,000 students--6,500 men and 3,500 women--served by 21 male professors and four female professors.

The Athletic Section is directed by Dr. Celso Torres and is connected with the University Athletics and coordinates with the LDUA and LDUP[1]. It consists of two major areas: 1) Intramurals, under the direction of Coordinator Prof. Washington Santos, whose principal activity is the Juegos de Novato[2] for first-year students, and the coordination of the Interschool games for all the university athletes; and 2) Extramural athletics for which the Center furnishes coaches for all the sports in which the University participates locally, nationally and internationally.

The Recreation Section is directed by Mr. Edison Suarez and concerns itself with providing an opportunity to those students who have finished their obligatory sequence of Physical Education and wish to maintain the activities. For them, we have excursions, long weekend hikes in the countryside and resort areas in the vicinity of Quito and surrounding provinces.

The Athletic Medicine Section attends to all which is connected with this field and has a resident physician, Dr. Hugo Mora G., who is also head of this section, besides a kinesiologist, Mr. Milton Cervantes, and a licensed physical therapist, Jorge Reyes. This section maintains medical files on all the sports and handles investigative matters.

The majority of the faculty of the Center are distinguished ex-athletes in their activity, most are professional graduates, and a few are technicians who were qualified before their respective schools existed.

The director of the Center, Jaime Paz y Mino, professor of physical conditioning, is directly responsible for the accomplishments of each of the members of this faculty.

The assistant director, Hector Pino H., professor of volleyball, is in charge of the academic portion and the utilization of sites and materiale.

Professors - The Center of Physical Education, Sports and Recreation.

The operational chart of our organization is provided below:

CENTRO DE
EDUCACION FISICA
DEPORTES Y
RECREACION
"ALFREDO PEREZ GUERRERO"

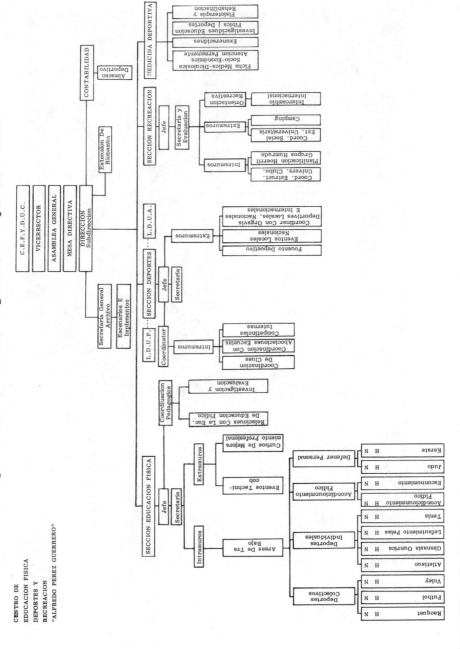

Presentación Masiva

The Board of Regents is a technical advisory body made up of full-time professors that, besides their class schedules (which are reduced according to a physiological age curve), complete their designated hours directing sections and coordinating activities.

The Center performs identical functions in the University Extension in the city of Riobamba located 200 kilometers from Quito and at which approximately 500 students attend. The coordinator is Tarquino Saltos.

The Center depends directly upon the Vicerectory of the University, whose head now is Professor Edmundo Rivadeneira, who has been one of the Vice-Rectors to have shown a major concern for physical activity.

Besides this, we are also involved in the presentation of large-scale gymnastic productions as an extension to the general public.

The most popular sport in Ecuador--as in all of South America --is futbol, or soccer. Quito has a huge Olympic Stadium where soccer is played every weekend, and many of the smaller cities have their own teams and playgrounds. Pelota de guante (gloveball), is often called the national game. It is played using a heavy bat, ball, and leather glove. Bullfighting is popular the year round, but the most important fights are held in Quito's large bullring on Sunday afternoons in December. Almost every small town in Ecuador has a pit for cockfighting.

Professor Paz Y Mino M., concludes his letter with the following statement: "As indicated at the start of this letter, I would like to continue correspondence with you. Allow me to express my sincere appreciation for your interest in corresponding with us."


FOOTNOTES

1.   LDUA and LDUP: the exact translation is unknown, but are equivalent to "leagues." Literally, University Sports League of "A" and of "P".

2.   Juegos de Novatos: Literally, "Games of Novices." American equivalent would probably be "Junior Varsity."

# SPORT AND PHYSICAL EDUCATION IN ENGLAND
by Mike Dunetts and E. Keith Milner

## Biographical Sketch

*Mike Dunetts* was born in Sherborne, Southwest England. After graduating from Yeovii Grammar School in 1973, he attended St. Luke's College of Education and was awarded a Bachelor of Education degree in 1977. In the fall of 1977, he entered the University of Illinois as a graduate teaching assistant. He is currently working towards the Master of Science degree in physical education.

*E. Keith Milner* was born in Chesterfield, England. After graduating from Chesterfield Grammar School in 1960, undergraduate work was taken at Worcester College of Education. After teaching for three years in Tamworth, England he was awarded sabbatical leave to attend Carnegie College of Physical Education where he obtained a diploma in physical education. In 1969, he accepted a graduate assistantship at the University of Wisconsin-LaCrosse where he obtained a Master of Science degree. On returning to England in 1970 he taught for Sheffield Education Authority and then returned to the United States in the same year to the University of Iowa where he received a Ph.D., in 1975. Dr. Milner is now an Assistant Professor and Director of the Physical Education Activities Program at the University of Illinois.

## General Background

In England during the nineteenth century, the public schools played a major part in the development of games and physical activity. The public schools had originally been founded for the education of the poor, but gradually these schools became institutions for the education of the upper classes. By the beginning of the nineteenth century, public schools had become education establishments for only the upper class. The reasons for this change are unclear, since for hundreds of years the nobility had not sent their sons to school at all. However, it is possible that the improvement of the transportation system, which occurred during the eighteenth and nineteenth centuries, allowed the ruling classes to attend distant schools of well repute. Education for the poor was thus entrusted to the church schools, each one of which was devoted to teaching reading, writing, arithmetic, and religion. These schools were self-sufficient and received no aid from the government until 1833, when a grant of Ł 20,000 (1 = $1.80) was given to them.

Sport and games played a large part in the life of any public school, and by the end of the eighteenth century cricket, boating, hunting or poaching (illegal fishing), and riding had become fairly well established. Association football was also played at all schools but unlike cricket had no written code of rules. It was played enthusiastically but outside school; it was not considered to be a gentleman's game. Although these sports were fairly well established, the attitude of headmasters (principals) towards them was one of reluctant tolerance rather than active encouragement. Pupils' attempts at inter-school competition were usually doomed to failure simply because of the lack of interest and hostility of the masters (teachers).

Such a situation did not last and by the 1860's the hostile attitude shown by the masters had given way to an attitude of active encouragement. Cricket matches and boating became popular competitive activities and rugby football (where the ball is carried in the hands) became an acceptable pastime for the gentry. With the advent of the industrial revolution, a new middle class of people rose to power. The educational needs of these people could not be satisfied by the existing public schools because their curriculum was too restricted. The curriculum of the poor schools organized by the National Society of the Church of England and by the British and Foreign School Society was also considered inadequate. Thus, a number of new schools came into being, the earliest of which were King's College School (1829), University College School (1830), Blackheath (1830), and Liverpool College (1840).

Some of the more wealthy members of the middle class sent their children to the old public schools, a fact which was resented by some. However, their intrusion influenced developments within these schools and as a result the Royal Commission on Public Schools (subsequently known as the Clarendon Commission) was initiated in 1861. Its purpose was to examine the management of public schools. Nine were examined: Eton, Winchester, Westminister, Charterhouse, St. Pauls, Merchant Taylor's, Harrow, Rugby and Shrewsbury. The results of the inquiry were published in 1864 and among the findings was the conclusion that public school education was an institution for character training. The importance of organized games for character training was stressed, but unfortunately there was a lack of emphasis on skilled performance. In association football, it was considered more important to show courage, stamina, and an ability to withstand knocks rather than to exhibit good ball control. Professional cricket coaches were sometimes employed by schools, but such moves were accepted with reluctance by many people, including those of the Commission. It was more important to be able to stand up to a fast bowler in conditions of bad light and poor ground conditions than to show skill in wielding a bat.

The emphasis on character training aspects of games led to a decrying of those activities which did not appear to produce the desired qualities. Thus, gymnastics was not thought to have much value and drill never established itself in the majority of schools. Gymnastics and drill were considered inferior due to the fact that the teaching of both activities was handled by Army sergeant instructors. This position was in direct contract to that of the elementary schools organized by the church, where gymnastic exercises and drill were the basic physical training activities.

The gymnastic approach to physical exercises had been initiated in Germany from the educational theories of Rousseau. On the practical side, J. C. G. Guth Muths was responsible for developing and publishing manuals of physical education. His first English edition was published in 1800 and included a wide range of activities: running, jumping, walking, wrestling, throwing, lifting, dancing, military exercises, and swimming. In 1822 P. H. Clias, one of Guts Muths' disciplies, was appointed to organize gymnastic courses at various military and naval establishments in England. In 1823 he produced a book containing his own gymnastic exercises and although based on Guts Muths' exercises, the emphasis was on artificial rather than natural activities. Being an Army officer, Clias approach consisted of military drill exercises and hence were very regimented. Nevertheless, his educational gymnastic exercises appeared in many elementary schools and persisted throughout the century.

Until 1870, there had been no national system of elementary education in England. The public schools catered to those people who were wealthy and the poor schools were open to the rest of the people. However, the latter schools were dependent upon voluntary contributions and the meager fees of their pupils. When Parliament made the first grant of ₤20,000 to the poor schools, an administrative system was necessary to monitor the monetary allocations. Thus, in 1839 an education department was established for this purpose and inspectors of schools were appointed to insure an unbiased judgement was made. These inspectors have ever since been known as His (or

Her) Majesty's Inspectors (HMI's) and from the beginning the Education Department took a great interest in physical education. They encouraged schools to build recreation and exercise areas and judged the competence of teachers to take classes in physical education. However, the department's attempt to promote physical education was not very successful. The lack of good teachers, lack of books and equipment, and the poor physical conditions of most schoolrooms presented more urgent problems than the lack of physical education.

In 1870, the Forster Education Bill was introduced into the House of Commons, and as a result a revised code of regulations came into operation. Drill attendance for not more than two hours a week and 20 weeks in a year was permitted. However, this regulation was not compulsory. Military drill was the only activity and this was used hopefully as a carry-over to maintain discipline. Military drills were instructed by drill sergeants, who took the exercises from the War Office's "field Exercise Book". Critically such an activity was for boys only, but after reports and recommendations by HMI's, girls were allowed to participate.

After the passing of the Forster Education Act, the School Board for London had decided to promote physical education. In 1877, the playgrounds of eighteen schools were equipped with gymnastic apparatus and a Miss Lafring was appointed by the Board to introduce Swedish Gymnastics. This style of gymnastics was developed by Ling and was a scientific adaptation of Guts Muths' informal, naturalistic gymnastics. Her work was well supported and developed rapidly. The Swedish system was suitable for boys as well as girls, but it was only in 1883 that the Board agreed to its adoption for boys. Meanwhile, Miss Martina Bergman (later to become Madame Bergman-Osterborg) had replaced Miss Lafring in 1881 and had set up the first teacher training college for women in Hampstead in 1885. After her departure from London in 1888, the Swedish system continued to be used for girls, but physical education for boys took a different approach. Physical exercises involving the use of apparatus-dumbbells and horizontal bars were introduced toward the end of the century.

In 1902, the Balfour Education Bill was introduced into the House of Commons. This bill appeared at the time of the Boer War when army recruitment figures were most important. These figures showed that a large number of volunteers for the Army had been rejected due to physical disabilities and hence, attention was focused on the physical state of the population of Britain. To meet the public calls for action and to improve the physical fitness of the population, the Board of Education and the War Office drew up a physical training course based on Army practices. Schools were encouraged to appoint ex-Army drill instructors to initiate the physical training course. As a result, men's physical education suffered a major setback and the military system of physical education was once again in operation.

After the war, in 1919, a "Syllabus for Physical Training in Schools" was issued by the Board of Education (formerly the Education Department). This new syllabus was less formal than the old syllabus and adopted a wider approach. At this time, organized games were encouraged since it was felt these would contribute to the total education of each pupil.

The post-war interest in physical education also affected the training of teachers; the short training courses which were in progress throughout the war now continued. The Board of Education became reluctant to employ men who had been trained by the Army Physical Training Staff because of the brief nature of their training and their inexperience in handling children. Arrangements were therefore made with the City of Sheffield for a three month training course and then later for a one year course for certified teachers who had served on the Army Physical Training Staff. This was the first of such programs.

Thus, the immediate post-war period was one of expansion for physical education in elementary schools; boys physical education now included games and girls physical education was progressing under the Swedish system taught by teachers trained from Madame Osterberg's college. No such expansion was evident in the public schools. An attempt to introduce the Swedish gymnastics system into Eton and Harrow had failed and games still maintained great prestige, even if their main objective was to prepare the pupils for leadership in society.

By 1933, the first college for training specialist men teachers of physical education was founded. Carnegie College accepted would-be physical education teachers provided they were already qualified in another academic subject area. The college provided a one year course in physical education initially for sixty students with the emphasis on gymnastics. With the initiation of this course, both the standard and the status of physical education began to rise. Until this time the only specialist physical education colleges had been for women.

Another major development was the institution of "keep fit" classes. Initially, these classes were confined to the northeast area of England, but their ideas quickly spread throughout the rest of the country. By 1935, the growth of recreative physical training necessitated the forming of a coordinating body and the Central Council of Recreative Physical Training (CCRPT) was born. Although this organization depended upon volunteer workers and voluntary subscriptions, it was widely supported by the physical education profession. It was not until 1936 that the CCRPT received its first grants: £1,000 from King George's Jubilee Trust and £1,000 from the National Playing Fields Association. 1935 also saw the opening of an additional one year course in physical education at Loughborough College to supplement a three year course which comprised of games and athletics.

Two years later, the fitness campaign coordinated by the CCRPT had moved well away from the physical training approach and as a result, the Physical Training and Recreation Act was introduced in the House of Commons. The emphasis was still on the health aspects of physical education but such a view came under some criticism from a Mr. Aneurin Bevan (member of Parliament). He claimed that the emphasis on health was a mistake and that the desire to play should be a justification in itself for playing. In spite of the criticism, the Act was passed and Ł2,000,000 was made available to the National Fitness Council for distribution to sports clubs and sporting and athletic organizations. Unfortunately, war broke out in 1939 before most of the money could be allocated.

In 1944, the Butler Education Act reached the statute books and as a result it became compulsory for local education authorities to provide physical education in schools. The school leaving age was raised to fifteen; hence, more mature forms of physical education had to be initiated. Another result of the act was that the Board of Education was replaced by the Ministry of Education which took over the functions of the National Fitness Council. The CCRPT changed its name to the Central Council for Physical Recreation (C.C.P.R.) and as a result much useful work was done with regard to planning and the breaking down of the old social class barriers which had previously been associated with some sports.

The end of the war also saw a change in the training of teachers and the recommendations of the McNair Report 1944 stated that physical education should be regarded as a school subject for the training of physical education teachers. As a result, year specialist training courses were opened at Exeter, York, Cheltenham, and Cardiff in addition to those at Leads (Carnegie) and Loughborough. In 1946, Birmingham University accepted physical education as a subject which could be studied together with other subjects for a general degree in the Faculty of Arts. There was no practical examination and game tactics were considered not to be worthy of inclusion. This was the only such degree course in the country at this time. When teacher training was increased from a two year to a three year program in 1960, seventeen colleges ("wing" colleges) were designated by the Ministry of Education to offer specialist courses in physical education. Ten of these colleges were for men, seven for women.

The Crowther report published in 1959 was concerned with the education of fifteen to eighteen year olds. This report recommended that physical education should be taken in school by all students of this age range. This counteracted a tendency in some schools to omit physical education for those students due to examination pressures. The report also felt that the Outward Bound Schools and Duke of Edinburgh's Award Scheme should be recognized and used in high school programs. In the latter system launched in 1956, each boy had to satisfy certain conditions in fitness, community service, individual pursuits and an outdoor expedition test. Girls were admitted to the scheme in 1958. Both the Outward Bound Program and the Duke of

Edinburgh's Award Scheme gained rapidly in popularity and many local education authorities were sending boys and girls to mountainous areas not only in England but also abroad to participate in outdoor activities.

In 1960, the Wolfendon Committee issued a report entitled "Sport and the Community". This committee recommended the establishment of a sports development council which should be responsible for the distribution of £5,000,000 per annum to various sports organization. The government did not accept the Committee's advice and it was not until 1965 that an Advisory Sports Council (formerly the C.C.P.R.) was established. This council made a number of important recommendations and among them were recommendations that competitors representing their country should receive financial support from public funds and that school facilities should be available for use by the whole community.

The Newsom report published in 1963 expressed concern over the lack of facilities for physical education in urban areas and the lack of participation by boys and girls in sport and physical activity. Consequently, some local education authorities built a variety of facilities for many large comprehensive schools in order that such activities as squash, horse-riding, and golf could be introduced to older boys and girls.

The most significant report regarding teacher training colleges was the Robbins Report which was published in 1963. It stated that such colleges should offer an internal Bachelor of Education (B.Ed.) degree which should have a standard comparable to a university degree. The course should be of four years duration and should provide a base for graduate study in physical education. This report was subject to much discussion by all interested in education and eventually thirteen universities in England agreed to implement its recommendations. Seven universities did not accept the report and gave such reasons as lack of staff, no existing university department of physical education and the reluctance to accept physical education as a discipline. However, by 1968 most universities had accepted physical education as a subject which could be offered for the B.Ed. degree and thus a new era in the history of physical education had begun.

The Comprehensive School System

With the advent of the labor government in the late 1960's, the educational policy in England underwent a rapid change. The system whereby the pupils went from a primary school (five to eleven years of age) to either a secondary or grammar school, depending on their eleven plus examination results, was abolished. The eleven plus examination was a compulsory exam taken at eleven years of age toward the end of primary school education. It was used to determine the eligibility of the student to enter either the secondary or grammar school. In its place came the comprehensive system of education.

The transition from the old system to the new comprehensive system did not always occur smoothly and indeed there are still a few areas today which have retained the old grammar school tradition. The basic premise behind the comprehensive system is that every child should have access to the same educational opportunities and that there should be no educational segregation for elitism as occurred with the grammar school system.

In the comprehensive system a child would progress from a primary school entered at five years of age, progressing through a middle school and then finally to a comprehensive school from thirteen to eighteen years. In some areas of the country, the latter two schools are combined in the same buildings, while the primary school would be on a different site. Some education authorities provide sixth form colleges for students aged sixteen to eighteen years. Here specialist pre-entrance degree programs are studied prior to attending a college or university. The physical education curriculum in the comprehensive schools tends to be fairly consistent from school to school, although it is not centrally governed. Each school usually has an indoor games lesson lasting for 60 to 90 minutes each week. During the first two or three years in a comprehensive school, a male student will usually be taught gymnastics in the physical education lesson, while the games lessons will consist of rugby, soccer or field hockey plus cross country in the fall and spring terms and cricket, tennis and track and field in the summer term. Swimming is also taught in most schools throughout this time period. It must be realized that this is a generalization and that the exact subjects taught will depend on the facilities available, teacher's skills, and philosophy of the school and physical education teachers. Girls are taught educational dance, gymnastics, field hockey, net ball, tennis, track and field, and swimming in their curriculum.

An options program is available in the latter years of the comprehensive school. During this time the pupil can elect to take one or more options in the physical education and games lessons. Again, the exact options available are governed by facilities and equipment that are available and the physical education teacher's personal skills and philosophy. Such options might include soccer, rugby, Olympic gymnastics, volleyball, tennis, track and field, cricket, swimming, canoeing, sailing, squash, badminton, golf, field hockey, basketball, table tennis, archery, horse-riding, skating, and trampolining. During these years in many schools there is a strong bias towards outdoor pursuits (camping, sailing, canoeing, rock climbing and skiing) and education towards leisure time and life-time activities.

Throughout the comprehensive school, classes are taught on a single sex basis. The male physical education teacher has been specifically trained to teach physical education to boys; likewise the female teacher is concerned mainly with girls. It is usually only during swimming and some optional programs that classes become co-educational. Most, if not all classes are taught on a mixed ability basis. Consequently, there is often a wide variety of skill level within each class, although games classes may be taught in ability groups. For many who want additional practice in a particular activity, there often exists after school practice and sports clubs during which time school sports teams are often organized.

Inter-school sport is quite popular; however, a major difference between England and America lies in the philosophy behind this type of competition. In America, winning is the objective of every team; yet in England this is not so. The emphasis is not so much on winning but more on participation and enjoyment. However, it cannot be denied that by participating in a competitive event, one team is seeking to establish its superiority over another. For this reason there has been much discussion as to whether or not inter-school competition is beneficial.

The traditional "house system" of grouping pupils within the school has, to some extent, been dropped in favor of the year group system. Under the old grammar/secondary system, a pupil would be assigned to a particular house on entering school. The pupil would remain in this particular house throughout his or her school life. Intramural competition would then consist of competition among houses to find the best house in a particular sport.

The new year group system is rather different, basically the comprehensive school is split into an upper and lower school. Each particular school has a head teacher and year tutors responsible for each year. The class tutor is responsible for a particular class within the year and any competition within the school would be inter-class competition.

The comprehensive system of education is now generally established in England; however, there still exist some independently financed schools (private and public schools). These are financed by tuition fees paid by parents, gifts from patrons interested in the school, and endowments. These schools place a high value on physical education and sport and consider it an important part of a student's education. Students very often will devote two afternoons each week to sport. These schools have flourished over the past few years because a number of parents are not in favor of sending their children to the comprehensive school.

Teacher Education

In order to study physical education at the undergraduate level, a student almost inevitably has to attend a college of education. The main aim of such colleges is to train teachers and all courses are oriented toward this goal. Usually, physical education is studied together with the theory of education and in addition, a second subsidiary teaching subject of the student's choice is studied.

At the present, colleges of education and universities are being reorganized, mainly because of the shortage of money available for education. Hence, the exact syllabus of each college is probably subject to change. A good example of two differing syllabi is to be found at St. Luke's College, Exeter.

Until 1973, St. Luke's College had a three year course in physical education, the end result of which was the awarding of a Certificate in Education, which was the basic teaching qualification in England. A fourth year of education was available to students who were suitably qualified and this led to the awarding of a Bachelor of Education Degree (B.Ed.).

In 1973, the government and teachers' unions agreed that the teaching profession should ultimately be an all graduate profession and hence, teacher preparation programs underwent a big change. The new three year course led to the awarding of a B.Ed. (ordinary) degree and if a student was suitably qualified at the end of this course, the student could stay on for a fourth year which would ultimately end in the awarding of a B.Ed. (honors) degree. This new syllabus has only recently been initiated and hence, it has yet to be thoroughly evaluated.

Figure 1 illustrates the main content of the old three year certificate plus one year B.Ed. degree at St. Luke's College. During the first three years the physical education course is studied together with the theory of education. The physical education curriculum is initially biased in favor of the practical with only 40% of one's program devoted to the academic aspects of physical education but by the third year the ratio is reversed. Each theory and practical course is assessed continually throughout a student's career. There is a written exam at the end of each theory course, and also at the end of most practical courses. The latter courses are also subject to subjective and objective tests. Each course is oriented towards teaching, and practical courses are assessed not only on knowledge of the sport or activity techniques, but also much time is devoted to methodology.

During the first year of the second term (January to March), students are sent out into schools for teaching practice. Here the student will teach for five weeks; during this time students are expected to also teach their subsidiary (minor) subject. Students are assessed by their college lecturers and also by the teaching staff of the school in which they teach. Final teaching practice is carried out between September and December of the third year. This lasts for ten to eleven weeks and because of the time element, it is much more realistic to the actual teaching situation.

In order to be awarded the Certificate of Education, the student must have passed the theory and practical aspects of physical education and must pass a final examination in the theory of education. All students have to pass the practical teaching aspect of their program.

PHYSICAL / PRACTICAL

| | | OPTIONS |
|---|---|---|
| Track and field | Track and field | Track and field |
| Basketball | Educational Dance | Trampolining |
| Gymnastics | Gymnastics | Gymnastics |
| Sports Hall Techniques | Field Hockey | Field Hockey |
| Outdoor Pursuits | Physical Conditioning | Swimming |
| Soccer | Rugby | Tennis |
| Swimming | Swimming | Squash |
| Tennis | Tennis | Volleyball |
| Cricket | Volleyball | Cricket |
| | | Badminton |
| | | Soccer |
| | | Rugby |
| | | Adaptive P.E. |

SELECT 3

EDUCATION / THEORY

| | | |
|---|---|---|
| Biomechanics | Physiology | |
| Physiology | Anatomy | |
| Anatomy | Sociology | |
| Tests and Measurements | Tests and Measurements | SELECT TWO |
| Research Methods | Growth and Development | OPTIONS from: |
| Growth and Development | Philosophy of P.E. | Anatomy, Physiology, |
| Acquisition of Skills | History of P.E. | Biomechanics, Growth |
| | 40 hr. P.E. project | & Development, Soci- |
| | | ology, Philosophy, |
| | | Comparative Educ., |
| | | Acquisition of Skill |
| | | (compulsory). |

THEORY of EDUCATION

| | | |
|---|---|---|
| Theory of Education | Education psychology | One from:  Psychol- |
| Teaching practice | Teaching Practice | ogy, Sociology, Com- |
| (5 weeks) | (5 weeks) | parative, Philosophy, |
| Selected options | | Human Relationships, |
| | | History of Educ., |
| | | Teaching Practice |
| | | (10 weeks). |

A second subsidiary subject is studied throughout the three years, e.g., Physics.

B.Ed. year in P.E. 1976-77
(Fourth Year)

Physical Education Options
   (Theory)
Acquisition of Skills
Current ideas and issues
   in P.E.

SELECT TWO
OPTIONS from:
Biomechanics, Phys-
iology, Anatomy,
Growth & Develop-
ment, Comparative
Educ., Sociology,
Philosophy.

Education Options
Curriculum Theory
Dissertation

SELECT ONE
OPTION from:  Psy-
chology, Sociology,
Comparative, Philos-
ophy, History of
Education.

Figure 1.  St. Luke's College, Exeter.  Three Year
Course in Physical Education 1973-75.

The final B.Ed. year is devoted purely to theory. Time is equally split between the theory of education and the theory of physical education. A thesis within the field of education is also required. With the exception of the final examinations (which are held in May) work within the year is not assessed. Examinations are taken in physical education options, Current Ideas and Issues Within Physical Education, Acquisition of Skill, Educational Options, and Curriculum Theory.

The new syllabus differs from the old syllabus in that throughout the first year a double main subject is taken (e.g., Physical Education/Physics) plus the theory of education. Both main subjects are taken for equal time and at the end of the first year either one can be dropped to a subsidiary subject level. At the end of each year, should the student's grade falls below the minimum required level, the student will be religated to a lower level; i.e., from B.Ed. (Hons) to the B.Ed. (ord) level, or from the B.Ed. (ord) to the Certificate of Education.

Teaching practice is carried out from January to March in the second year and again from September to December in the third year. B.Ed. (ordinary) exams are taken at the end of the third year, while those candidates for the B.Ed. (Hons) take examinations at the end of the fourth year. This syllabus is still relatively new and hence, little feedback is available in order to evaluate its progress. Whether or not this course will continue in its present form remains to be seen.

## Higher Degrees in Physical Education

At present, Birmingham University is the only university where physical education can be studied for the purpose of obtaining a B.A. degree. In 1946, the Faculty of Arts accepted physical education as a subject in the B.A. (combined subjects) course. Physical education could be taken as one of two subjects to be studied for three years, with one other Arts subject taken for an additional year. In this course, physical education was studied in its own right, and was not studied for the purposes of obtaining a teacher's qualification.

At the University of Aberystwyth, education is studied together with three other subjects for the B.A. or the B.Sc. degree. Physical education can be chosen as an accessory course with the education course. At Sussex University, physical education can be chosen as an arts topic by science students who are taking a B.S. under the combined Arts/Science scheme. This course consists of seminars and tutorials, and a dissertation.

At this time, there are only four universities in England which offer a M.A. or M.Ed. course in physical education, where the awarding of such degrees is determined by an examination. Birmingham University offers a M.A. course which is an extension of its B.A. course. This course was initiated in 1972 and lasts for one year. Three main areas are covered in the syllabus: Research Methods in

Physical Education, Physical Education in Contemporary Society, and Skill in Athletic Performance. Also required are studies of either statistics or the Mechanics of Physical Skills and a short dissertation.

A similar one year course has been offered at Leeds since 1969. This course was an outgrowth of the Leeds University Institute of Education advance study in physical education which lead to the Institute Diploma. The latter course was provided by both the University Department of Physical Education and Carnegie School of Physical Education, and was open only to those physical education specialists who had had considerable teaching experience.

In 1973, Manchester University offered a course in physical education which led to an M.Ed. program. Physical education can be studied as a subject for a part time two year course, with the additional requirement of a dissertation.

Liverpool also offers a M.Ed. degree, where two physical education courses have to be selected. The student has a choice between two different methods of study: he may opt for either two physical education courses plus a long dissertation, or for one physical education course, plus three education options, plus a shorter dissertation.

The above courses are the main Master's degree courses in physical education; however, there are other courses in which physical education makes some contribution. At Loughborough University a M.S. in recreational management is offered which contains sections on physical education topics.

Current Issues in Physical Education

Throughout the last decade the educational system in England has undergone a variety of changes. The major change was undoubtedly the introduction of the comprehensive school system and the near abolition of the grammar schools. The introduction of new teaching methods, new teaching aids and in some cases, new school facilities have all had their effect upon the way different subjects are taught. Physical education is no exception and perhaps it is only during these past years that people have come to question much of the material that had previously been taken for granted.

At the present time the physical education curriculum is subject to much discussion. The current economic crisis in England has resulted in a severe cutback of monetary funds available to schools. Consequently, equipment is in short supply and the Local Education Authorities (LEA's) are often unwilling to take on any more teachers. Indeed, in some cases teachers' contracts have been terminated due to lack of funds. Thus, many people are questioning the value of the physical education curriculum. Is it doing what it is supposed to do? Unfortunately, the answer to the last question is not apparent, since many people have differing ideas as to the value and purpose of physical education in schools.

In an effort to enhance the status of physical education, several new ideas have been introduced. The traditional way of assessing the success of a physical education course has been through the subjective evaluation of the teacher. A pupil's grade would thus be purely subjective in nature and as can be imagined, such a method is not without its faults.

## Examinations in Physical Education

Recently, however, examinations have been introduced for those pupils who wish to take an examination in physical education. At Holly Hall County Secondary School, Dudley, a formal examination system has been in operation since 1971. The scheme involved the integration of physical education, the history of physical education, and games with basic physiology and its relationship to physical activity.

The purpose of the course was to give a wider range and choice of physical activity, and therefore enable particular skills to be developed and credit to be given for them. It was felt that at sixteen years of age a pupil's Certificate of Secondary Education (C.S.E.) or General Certificate of Education (G.C.E.) results would be enhanced by the inclusion of a subject which would establish the student as a person who has achieved a standard in sportsmanship and endeavor as well as obtaining an academic qualification in physical education.

In the final year at school, a student can obtain either a Certificate of Secondary Education or a General Certificate of Education examination. The latter examination is considered to hold a higher standing than the former. Depending on the school, an examination is taken in five to eight subject areas.

The Holly Hall examination is a C.S.E. mode 111 exam, (mode 111 allows the teacher to determine the syllabus) and it is divided into two sections:

1.  Theory (science, history of P.E.)

2.  Practical gymnastics (Olympic or Educational), games, and Outdoor Pursuits

Four theory and four practical lessons are held per week. The theory examination consists of written papers under four section headings (20% of the total mark) combined with course work assessment based on the work covered over two years (30%). The practical exam is marked under headings of gymnastics, games and a selected activity (50% of the total mark).

When this plan was presented to the C.S.E. board of examiners, difficulty was experienced over a method of assessing the practical activities. However, with the help of physical education specialists within the L.E.A. and C.S.E. board members a satisfactory plan was eventually adopted.

The above example is only one of a number of C.S.E. mode 111 exams. As yet there is no standard examination format in physical education; the syllabus may take a variety of forms depending on the area of the country yet not everyone is sure that examinations in physical education are beneficial. While it is possible that examinations may enhance the status of physical education, provide more motivation for pupils, and allow them to gain credit in a subject in which they excel, it could be argued that it is not possible to enhance the status of a subject simply by giving an examination in that subject. In fact, a physical education examination would inevitably mean more administrative work for an already overburdened teacher. Some people would argue that physical education is performed mainly for enjoyment and that examinations would destroy this essential intrinsic nature of the subject.

The use of a common examination in physical education also poses one other problem; that of a core curriculum. A core curriculum consists of basic material which is taught in every school. There is no core curriculum officially at the present, but in fact it could be argued that one does exist, since most schools teach soccer, rugby, track and field, cricket and swimming. The use of a common examination might require the use of a common curriculum, which in turn would require that every school have the same facilities and equipment. In the present economic climate, however, such an idea is not feasible.

In conclusion, the number of schools offering examinations in physical education is growing. Whether or not this is beneficial still remains to be seen, but it is clear that some teachers are turning to an objective means of assessment in preference to the old subjective analysis.

## Integration of Physical Education with Other Areas of Study

The integration of physical education with other areas of study is another idea that is growing in popularity. The basic concept behind integration is that the subject boundaries which are presently in use impose artificial limits to the study of knowledge; an individual should be able to study within and among various disciplines.

In some schools, physical education is studied within a General Studies Program. For example, at Burleigh Community College in 1972, the physical education department initiated a course which was part of the general studies course for the sixth form (sixteen to eighteen years of age). This course was distinct from the normal games lesson. The overall aim was to extend the insight of the student into the whole society; its make-up, problems, and values, and also to extend his knowledge outside his own academic discipline.

A scheme of work was developed which was pertinent to the timetabling, staff interest and expertise, the proximity of a college and university laboratory facilities and the availability of resource material. Three two-lesson units per week were assigned and each unit was assigned a different teacher but arranged in order that one teacher be able to take all three units in any one week. There were three parts to the course so each staff member could utilize his or her expertise to the full.

The areas of study are:

Human Performance: Comprising laboratory, practice, seminar, tutorial sessions. This section is concerned with the importance of the body in modern society and includes physiology and psychology. The course is based on the scientific examination and assessment of physical fitness; fatigue; attention and arousal; perceptual and motor skills; motivation. Also included are the variation of these factors with age, sex, body size, the effects of training, environment, drugs, tobacco, alcohol and nutrition on the body.

Sport and Society: Studying the interaction of sport and society in the modern world. Comprising discussion and seminars in:

1. Olympic games - origins, history, nationalism
   - importance to countries and spectators
   - uses made of the games by various groups
   - arguments for continuation, abandonment, and change

2. Spectators & Sport - the rise of the spectator to the level of chief importance in professional sport
   - influence of television and the general effect on society

decorative phrase in the program of the schools. However, at this time Georgios Pagon, a teacher of history in München, was asked to attend the Gymnastic School of Massmann there, and when he returned to Greece he was appointed to the newly established School for Teachers on the island of Aigina.[3] At that time Pagon wrote the book *Summaries of Gymnastics* based on Guts-Muths' and Jahn's writings, which is considered the first guide text for school teachers. The last chapter of this book, "Problems on the Application of the Gymnastike, Oppositions, Rejections," gives a clear picture of the conditions under which Pagon carried out his pioneer work among conservative-minded school teachers and ministry officials.

2. *The Rebirth of the Olympic Idea*--To the simple, open-minded Greeks of this period, newly freed from a hateful tyranny, the rememberance of any event of the glorious past awakened anew the enthusiasm and the initiative for noble undertakings. Thus in 1838, 56 years before Coubertain's step on the Olympic movement, we have the interesting declaration of the Latria community, by Olympia, about "the reorganization and opening of the Olympic Games" on the occasion of Independence Day." In 1848, Evangelos Zappas, one of the heroes of the War of Independence, perhaps influenced by the initiative of the Latrian people, made a most generous donation for holding Olympic Games in Athens every four years.

It is very sad that the responsibility for the fulfillment of the will of the utilitarian-minded Minister succeeded in changing the primary purpose of the donation, and only a small portion of it was given to the Games. These first Olympic Games finally took place in 1859, and then irregularly in the years 1870, 1875, and 1889. The meager means and the lack of interest on the part of the appointed Olympia Committee caused their failure. In the book *Philostratos Traite Sur la Gymnastique* (1858) and in the chapter dedicated to Zappas' donation, Menas Minoides, a bright scholar of that time, makes a severe criticism of the misuse of the donation, "which caused the loss of a great opportunity for the development of the Hellenic athletics...."[5]

3. *The First Physical Education Teachers' Training Seminars* --Up to 1880, due to the prevailing ideas and poverty in the country, very little progress had been made in Physical Education both in and outside the schools. It was in 1882 and 1884 that for the first time seminars were held for teachers with gymnastics as a subject. These seminars were developed later into the Normal School of Gymnastike. The seminars were carried out under the leadership of a most gifted education man, Phokianos, the father of Greek Physical Education whose untiring efforts and inspiring initiative created great enthusiasm among young men giving new impulse to the field.

In his work, Phokianos mainly used the system of Adolf Spiess the German gymnast light exercises with movable gymnastic instruments. Phokianos was also a great supporter of the Olympic ideology, revived again in those years by Zappas' donation. In 1889, when the

Olympia Committee refused to hold the Games, he carried them out by his own meager means.[6]

4. *Basic Physical Education Laws - The Introduction of the Swedish System of Gymnastics*--At the period of the last Zappas' Olympic Games, three steps in the imposing personality of Ioannes Chrysaphes. He was one of Phokianos' enthusiastic youths. Soon he became his successor and later the actual organizer of Hellenic physical education. In 1899, through his proposals the first basic laws of physical education were issued, and thereafter the Swedish System of gymnastics was introduced in the schools. In 1929, the already existing Normal School of Gymnastike took an additional third year and became an Academy, today's National Academy of Physical Education.

In his latter years, the broad-minded Chrysaphes, influenced by the ideas of Lewis Riess, a Springfield College man working then as Physical Education Directors at the Thessalonike YMCA[7] and by the program and philosophy of the International School of Physical Education in Geneva[8]--a daughter school of Springfield College--was ready to bring changes to the system applied in the Greek schools; but his sudden death prevented him from taking steps in that direction.

5. *Period of Stern Scholasticism and Inactivity*--After Chrysaphes, for decades Greek physical education suffered an undistributed stagnancy. His successors, both at the Ministry and at the Academy - the two poles of school physical education - mediocrities in thought and in conception, remained attached to the letters of the pre-World War I rigid form of the Swedish System. Ideas beyond their conceivability or elements of foreign trends were not allowed to come into their domain. They were usually appointed by political criteria, had little sense of professional responsibility, and were mainly concerned with their own positions and power. Thus, their intelligence was chiefly directed to create obedient adherents. Even the teachers of the Academy were appointed by personal choice, not by the code of competency. So the courses given conformed to the teachers' ability, not to the real needs of the students, with the result the professional background of the graduates was very poor. However, a number of open-minded gymnasts did everything to raise their level and modernize their work, sometimes paying dearly for their heresy. To these bright colleagues we owe the first steps toward the emphasis on sports and athletics, as well as on the use of free movements in gymnastics, already in application long before 1964 when the official changes occurred.[9]

1964 A New Era - Educational Reform

As mentioned in the previous lines, for decades Greek Physical Education, along with the whole education, had remained almost stagnant.[10] Only small steps had been taken from time to time; conservatism always stands against progress. With the ascent to office of the Democratic Party, in 1964, the problems of Education took priority. The Prime Minister himself took charge of the Ministry of Education, and an elaborate Reform Law was passed.[11]

### Outline and Philosophy of the Reform

1. A scientific body of 52 most qualified men of education, under the name "Pedagogical Institute", was established. The Office of this body was to carry out research work; prepare new school books; do the programming of the curricula in all school levels; help and train the teachers for the new programs, and face, as the supreme power, all matters concerning education.[15]

2. Public education of all levels become free. "We inaugurate free education not to favour the rich but to avoid humiliating the poor," were the words of the Prime Minister.

3. Education became compulsory up to the age of 15; previously it was up to the age of 12. This meant: six years of education in Elementary School; and three years in the Gymnasion, the Secondary School.

4. The professional training of the Elementary school teachers was increased from two to three years.

5. Four new Universities, besides the ones in Athens and Thessalonike, were to be established, so that more opportunities might be given for higher studies.[14]

The above cardinal plan for changes was in the process of being fulfilled in accordance with the spirit of the following two main principles:

1. The education of the new generation must be grounded on sound humanism, bringing humane values into harmony with the scientific spirit of our time.

2. The chief aim of education is character building; creating the free man, the brave cultivated individual who realizes what his duties to country and to humanity are.

### The Reform in Physical Education

Diagrams showing the frames of the Physical Education administration in the pre-Reform and Reform periods, for comparison follow:

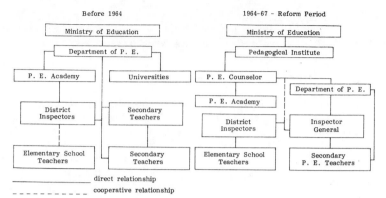

| Before 1964 | 1964-67 - Reform Period |
|---|---|

Ministry of Education — Department of P. E. — P. E. Academy / Universities — District Inspectors / Secondary Teachers — Elementary School Teachers / Secondary Teachers

Ministry of Education — Pedagogical Institute — P. E. Counselor / Department of P. E. — P. E. Academy / District Inspectors / Inspector General — Elementary School Teachers / Secondary P. E. Teachers

————————— direct relationship

— — — — — — — cooperative relationship

Administration rigidly authoritative; all powers concentrated in the hands of two men: the Director of the Physical Education Department at the Ministry, and the Dirctor of the Physical Education Academy.

Here also, at the Pedagogical Institute; the authority is in the hands of two men: the Counselor and his Assistant; but all the plans and steps of these men were examined and approved by the other 50 members of the Pedagogical Institute.

1. *The Physical Education Administration at the Reform Period*

   a.  Responsible for the whole program of the school physical education is the Physical Education Counselor's office.

   b.  The Department of Physical Education, housed at the Ministry of Education, carries out and administrates the lines drawn by the Physical Education Counselor's Office at the Pedagogical Institute.

   c.  The supervision of the physical education program in schools is done by six Inspectors General, each one having under his office a certain section of the country.  Another duty of the Inspectors General is to evaluate the work of the physical education teachers regarding the following six points of efficiency:  scientific knowledge, teaching ability, leadership, professional consciousness, social behavior, and activities performed.

   d.  Under the Inspectors General are the 48 District Inspectors.  Their duties are:

      1)  To help the Elementary school teachers with their physical education work.[15]

      2)  To organize district games and championships[16] in the two cycles of the Secondary School:  Gymnasion and Lykeion.

3) To supervise the sport activities of the outside school organizations, and superintend the city and communal sports grounds as well as the National Stadia.[17]

2. *School Curricula*

   a. Physical education is compulsory: six times of 30 minutes weekly in Elementary Schools; three times of 45 minutes weekly in Gymnasion and two times of 45 minutes weekly in the Lykeion.

   b. The activities in the daily schedule at the Elementary Schools vary and include, according to the season and the means available, rhythmical exercises, relay races, simplified track and field events, games, folk dances, swimming. In the two cycles of the Secondary School, Gymnasion and Lykeion, the activities include: free exercises, gymnastics of the Olympic program, track and field events, basketball, volleyball, handball, folk dances and swimming. Football (soccer), was excluded from the schedule.

3. *School Athletics and Competitive Games Outside School Hours*

   a. At the Elementary School level there are no games and championships outside school hours.

   b. At the Secondary School level there are basketball, handball and volleyball championships between schools of the same district. There are also meets in track and field as well as in cross-country and swimming. At the end of the school year the champion teams of the districts meet for the National championship.

   c. Toward the end of the school year there takes place, in each town, the traditional Gymnastic Festival, a demonstration of gymnastic exercises, games, folk dances and athletic events. However, due to the fact that these Festivals tend to cultivate the spirit of the "circenses," the show, and that their value, in terms also of the time spent and the upsetting of the whole school program, becomes too doubtful, there was thought that they be eliminated and replaced by more constructive meets.

4. *The Reform Spirit - Supplementary Steps*--The growth of personality of a child, a solid character, a creative, useful individual for society, is the main objective both of education in general and physical education.[18] To achieve this objective, the new schedule transposes the emphasis from the one-sided exercises of the static,

old-fashioned Swedish Gymnastics to many-sided competitive activities, in which the freedom in movements, the spontaneity and self-expression of the child are the basic characteristics.[19]  To conduct the program more effectively, the following supplementary steps were introduced:

    a.    The use of a personal card system by which one could have, at any time, a picture of the physical development of each boy or girl as well as the picture of his progress in athletics and other events.

    b.    The awarding of a Sportsmanship Badge for evidence of high ethos.

    c.    The awarding of an Athletic Badge for special records and attainment.

    d.    The creation, in each school unit, of a Student Athletic Association, which, by its own initiative, will carry out all the intramural sport activities and championships.

## Athletics and Sports Outside the School

    1.    *"Segas" and the Other Sport Associations*--The athletic and sport associations are private.  However, the State has a kind of supervision and sees that they function toward their established purposes.  Today, there are over 2500 clubs in Greece, and they are under one or another Federation.  The oldest federation is SEGAS, the Hellenic Amateur Athletic Association, which was founded in 1895, one year before the first Olympic Games, and which included all sports.[20]  Gradually some sports gained ground, which led to the establishment of new Federations with hundreds of clubs under their power.  The main ones today are the Federation of Soccer, the Federation of Swimming and the Federation of Wrestling-Boxing-Weight Lifting.  SEGAS is still the best organized Federation and stands on a relatively high amateur level.  Under its power, besides track and field, it has also the sports of basketball, volleyball, gymnastics, cycling and fencing.

    2.    *The Secretariat of Sports*--Today, SEGAS as well as the other Federations are under the Office of the Secretary General of Sports who is a political person (and in a way with political aims). The Secretariat of Sports has an immense financial income, collected by the Soccer Lottery (Pro-Po), and the Horse Races.  Its "declared purpose" is to assist the Sport Federations and Clubs, and raise the level of athletics and sports in the country.[21]

    3.    *The Hellenic Olympic Committee*--The Hellenic Olympic Committee is the oldest of the Olympic Committees in the world.  It was the one to organize the first revived Olympic Games, in Athens, with the Greek scholar Vikelas as President and de Coubertin as Secretary.

Although this Committee had unlimited means and prestige, being the nearest to the royal family institution, it did not expand its initiatives beyond the ordinary assignment of getting ready, each time, the National Team for the Olympic Games, and only lately has been able to bring into reality the long discussed project among Olympic ideologists,[22] the Academy in Olympia.

4. *The International Olympic Academy*--Established in 1961 at Olympia, owes its foundation mainly to the untiring efforts and enthusiasm of Carl Diem of Germany and the late President of the H.O.C., Ioannes Ketseas. It is run and administered by the H.O.C., in cooperation with the International Olympic Committee. The purpose of the Academy is "to promote the Olympic ideology" by holding courses on historic and other Olympic themes, for selected physical education students and physical education men. The courses are held in the summer and the enrollment of the candidates is done through the National Olympic Committee of each country.

5. *The Hellenic Alpine Club*--Before doing this article it is only fitting to mention here the invaluable service the Alpine Club and its branches render to the nation in the area of physical culture. Almost all mountain tops are endowed by well-organized shelters, built up mostly by the toils of its members in the highest amateur spirit. Besides other activities, the Club regularly gives out a notable and very scholarly publication, which keeps its members informed of world alpine news and the progress and activities of mountaineering within the country.

6. *The Association of the Gymnasts*--Up to 1967 there also was functioning the prominent Association of Greek Gymnasts. Its special monthly publication served as a very helpful and creative medium in keeping the colleagues of the profession united, and in informing them of the progress achieved in the field. Unfortunately this Association is actually now in silence, "The water of speech is quenched."[23]

### Four Years After the Dictatorship

Concluding the article of Physical Education in Greece at the period of the military dictatorship (1967-74):

Thus far was the state of Physical Education and Sport in Greece until 1967. How things have developed since then for obvious reasons, it is not the time to put on paper.

To cover today the gap of that period a few lines are necessary. Dictators have never been friends of any ideology. The only thing they are interested in is to gain friends to relieve their wild isolation. Often this is attempted through athletics and sports. By organizing grand festivities and well paid football matches, in the spirit of the old Roman "panem et circenses", they also attempt to withdraw the attention of the people from the prevailing political situation.

Fortunes of money from Pro-Po (the soccer lottery) and other sources were spent even by the supposedly apolitical institutions, as the Hellenic Olympic Committee and the Segas, to organize impressive moetis in order to promote the image of the Junta.

School physical education was downgraded to a lower level, the main attention being given to demonstrations and parades. The man behind this movement, a major in the army, is now known as a petty thief,[24] was chased by the Interpol in foreign countries.

The period of the dictators is over, but the essence of their trails and corruption is still here. In almost all key positions, in schools and outside the schools, are men who had served the dictators in the best way. The capable men, usually free thinking individuals, are kept out of the picture. Evidently the party that now governs the country is controlled by the powers that had enforced the dictatorship and no substantial change can be expected.

Due to the pressure of the time a reform program, a substitute of the 1964 educational reform, was announced. However, the program lacks the faith and the free will of the men involved, so necessary to make any change. But the disquieting voice demanding a sound structure of education and physical education becomes stronger every day; and this is the positive hope for the dawn of a better day.

A few lines from recent publications on the subject will give a clearer picture of the situation - From AN OPEN LETTER TO THE SECRETARY GENERAL OF SPORTS:[25]

.....The natural nursery of athletics everywhere is the school. Some day we have to comprehend this plain fact. Only the millions of young boys and girls in the Elementary and High Schools will give us the broad foundation to raise the high pyramid of our national sports. Consequently the only ones who can be of positive help for our aims are the thousands of sports teachers scattered in schools throughout the country. Pity that you actually ignore them.

As the Physical Education Counselor at the Ministry of Education I feel it my duty to state openly that we do not need modifications in the proposed new draft of sport regulations, but a radical change in our thoughts and in the contents of the planned work. The pre-Junta and Junta methods of "showcase" in athletics should be put aside if we don't want to build our athletics on sand.

From a second OPEN LETTER TO THE SECRETARY GENERAL
OF SPORTS:[26]

In all advanced countries it is the official sports teachers who
study, plan and draw the guiding lines in matters of physical
education and sports. In our country it is the contrary. As
a result, a whole year after the fall of Junta we are still experimenting and have nothing substantial to show.

If we really want to have results, the first concern must be
the reorganization of our physical education and sport program in a radical way. This must be done by men and women
who had dedicated their lives to the field, not by employing
personal or party friends; and above all we must use those
people who have remained firm in their ideology during the
Junta period. In terms of the reorganization, the reestablish-
ment of a high athletic standard and sportsmanship should have
the priority. Only men with true hearts and ethical standards
can inspire the youth and accomplish this delicate task.

From an interview on ATHLETICS:[27]

After the total failure of the national team in the Balkan Games
and in Montreal, new decisions had been taken for the advancement
of school athletics: a two-hour weekly program was dedicated for
athletic training of the high school pupils:

QUESTION: What is your opinion as Physical Education Counselor?

ANSWER: Even if there was the necessary number of sports teachers in the schools and the necessary facilities, we could
not expect a substantial result if at the same time we
don't start applying a serious physical education program in the Elementary schools. As things have been
planned we just put the cart before the horse. That is
how I see the case.

A LAST QUESTION: We have heard on the TV, from a representative of the government, that the people responsible for
holding back the progress in sports are the sports
teachers. Is it true?

ANSWER: Certainly not. The real responsible ones for the lack of
progress in sports is the State itself. For the government there is only the champions' "show-case" and Football. For Physical Education and Sports of the schools
the authorities have never shown a real interest. Sports
grounds and sports facilities in schools are still in an
almost primitive state. And the main reason for the situation is certainly not the lack of money, as there is always ample money for constructing Stadia and financing
Athletic Clubs and Football.[28]

Also in another case the policy of the government is reprehensible, that of the Sport Academy. For years there had been a plan to raise the Academy to a University level so that the future sport teachers might get a better and a more scientific education. Their work might be of the highest possible quality. The State has never given serious attention to this possibility.

Part I.  FOOTNOTES

1.  G. Kurkeshkin, "Sport and Culture Activity", in UNESCO Helsinki Conference. 1959. p. 101.

2.  Diehl: Anthologia Lyrica Graeca. Frag. 10.

3.  Ilias XXIII, pp. 257-897: in Odysseia (xxiv 85-93) we have a very touching account of the funeral agones held by the pyre of Achilleus himself. Those had been set up by the Goddess Thetis, his mother. It is Agamemnon's spirit, in Hades, that gives their report to Achilleus. There, in the dark rooms of the underworld Homeros wants their beauty to be heard.

4.  Odysseia XXIV, 14-204.

5.  Ilias XXIII, 630-640.

6.  Ilias XXIII, 679-680.

7.  Ilias VI, 208; XI, 787. For the English version of both Ilias and Odysseia in this paper the translation of Richard Lattimore has been used.

8.  E. N. Gardiner, "Athletics of the Ancient World". 1930. p. p. 28.

9.  Odysseia VIII, 100-284.

10.  Odysseia VIII, 147-148.

11.  Odysseia VIII, 159-164. It is here that we meet the word athlete for the first time in the Greek Literature.

12.  Odysseia VIII, 186-193.

13.  Thoukydides, "The Peloponnesian War" (I, 69-70).

14.  Herodotos VII, 228.

15.  Ploutarchos: Lykourgos, 16.

16.    From 18-20; two year term of military service.

17.    Palton: Nomoi, 6330.

18.    Xenophon: Pol. Laked. I 4; Ploutarchos: Lyk. 14.

19.    Strabon II, 3, 7.

20.    H. Harris, "Greek Athletes and Athletics". 1967. pp. 220-223.

21.    Thoukydides II, 41, 1.

22.    C. M. Bowra, "Classical Greece". 1965. p. 93.

23.    Xenophon, "Pol. Athen." II, 10.

24.    Aischines: Timarchos, 9.

25.    Platon: Nomoi, I 630B.

26.    Loukianos: Ancharsis. The translation to English has been adapted from the book "Sources for the History of Greek Athletics" of R. S. Robinson.

27.    Thoukydides II, 45, 4.

28.    Platon: Polit., 452A-456E; Phaidr. 239C.

29.    Loukianos: Anacharsis, 9-10.

30.    Pindaros: Olympia, 8, 1.

31.    Xenophanes: (fragm. 2).

32.    H. J. Rose, "Greek Literature". 1964. p. 77.

33.    Xenophon: Apomn. III, 5, 15.

34.    Aristophanes: "Frogs". 1069-70.

35.    Euripides: Autolykos (fragm. 282) Nauck.

## Part II.  FOOTNOTES

1. I. Chrysaphes. *The Modern Olympic Games* (gr.). 1930. p. 15.

2. Ibid.

3. I. Ioannides. *Die Kontinuitat der Korporkultur in Griechenland.* 1939.

4. I. Chrysaphes. *The Modern Olympic Games* (gr.). 1930. p. 17; The Declaration bears the Number 313 and the date March 25, 1938.

5. K. Kitriniares. *Phrostratou Gymnastikos* (gr.). 1961. pp. 143-144.

6. Akropolis (gr. daily paper). May 6, 1896.

7. L. W. Riess, "The New Physical Education Movement in Greece", in:  JOHPER 2 (1932) 42.  "The Modern Delphic Games", in:  JOHPER 5 (1931) 14-15.

8. In 1930 Chrysaphes visited the School of Geneva as a lecturer.  The author of this article had the rare privilege to be with him there, as his scholarship student, and I attend his course on the "Homeric Heritage".

9. I. P. Ioannides, "The Elementary School Basis of Athletics", (gr.), in:  Deltion SEGAS 9 (1965) 5-8; "Program of Athletics in Place of Demonstrations", (gr.), in: GYMNASTIKE 10 (1965) 4-5, 1 (1965) 2; "On Physical Education", (gr.), in:  GYMNASTIKE 8 (1956) 3-4.

10. Since 1913 the Elementary Education; since 1931 the Secondary.

11. Legislative decree 4379/1964.

12. Taken from the speech of E. Papanonsos, the mind behind the Reform, given at the UNESCO assembly in Paris, October 26, 1964.

13. In the Pedagogical Institute, the field of Physical Education was represented by two physical education men--it was the first time that physical education was represented in high office--one as Counselor of physical education, the other as Assistant.

14. There were also plans for the creation of Physical Education Institutes of four years of studies attached to the Universities so that the education and status of the physical education

teachers could be raised to the university level, the same level as that of the other professors.

15. There are no Physical Education teachers in the Elementary School.

16. In track and field, including cross-country; in swimming, basketball, volleyball, handball, and mountaineering.

17. By this last office the District Inspector acts as a bridge between the school physical education and the outside school sports.

18. See Report at UNESCO Assembly; footnote No. 12.

19. See footnote No. 9; "On Physical Eeucation", "The Elementary School Basis of Athletics", "Program of Athletics in Place of Demonstration"; guidelines of the Physical Education Counselor at the Ministry.

20. I. Chrysaphes. *The Modern Olympic Games* (gr.). 1930. pp. 257-258.

21. During the Reform Period, Minister G. Mylonas had set down plans to have this Secretariat General of Sports, along with the whole of Physical Education, into a sub-Ministry.

22. Delendas-Broneer, "On the Plan of Reviving Olympia". Athens. 1948.

23. The line quoted, only as a symbolic notion, is from the last oracle of Pythia to Oreibasios, Emperor Julian's envoy to Delphoi: "Tell the King, the fairwrought hall has fallen to the ground, no longer has Phoibos a hut, nor a prophetic laurel, nor a spring that speaks. The water of speech even is quenched."

24. Der Spiegel. 49 (1973) 120.

25. GYMNASTIKE. 1 (1975) 8.

26. GYMNASTIKE. 2 (1975) 3.

27. TA NEA. November 11, 1976. GYMNASTIKE. 6-11 (1977) 1-3.

28. N. KARAYIANNIDES: We gild the recordmen and stay indifferent for the depth. In ELEUTHEROTYPIA.

# SPORT AND PHYSICAL EDUCATION IN INDIA

## by William Johnson

### Biographical Sketch

*William Johnson* was born at Clatskanie, Oregon
and received his B.S. degree from the University of
Oregon, Eugene in 1936. Additional graduate work was
taken at Stanford University, San Francisco State University, The University of California at Los Angeles,
and the University of Southern California before the
M.S. and Ed.D. degrees were finally conferred at the
University of Oregon in 1942 and 1955 respectively.

After twelve years in secondary teaching and
coaching at Hillsboro and Eugene, Oregon, Johnson
entered college instruction first as a graduate assistant
at the University of Oregon in 1954; as Principal of the
College of Physical Education, East Pakistan in 1955-
1957; as coordinator of student teachers at Los Angeles
State University from 1958-1962; as department chairperson and athletic director at the College of the Desert,
Palm Desert, California in 1963; and at Minot State College, North Dakota in 1963-1965; and presently on the
staff of the Department of Physical Education, University of Illinois as an Associate Professor.

He has travelled extensively, first as a member
of the U. S. Navy during World War II; then on the
AAHPER Olympic Games tour to Helsinki, Finland in
1956; as an employee of The Asia Foundation working in
East Pakistan and attending the Melbourne Olympics with
the Pakistan Olympic Team; to the Mexico City, Munich,
and Montreal Games; as a Fulbright-Hays Grant recip
ient to the University of Dar es Salaam, Tanzania, East
Africa in 1973-1974; and finally on a sabbatical leave to
the USSR, Romania, Czechoslovakia, and East Germany
in 1976.

As a followup of this international interest he
has been Newsletter Editor of the International Relations
Council of AAHPER for a period of ten years; served
two three-year terms as a Contributing Editor for
*JOHPERS* in the area of international relations; three
years on the Editorial Board of *The Physical Educator*
and is currently the Editor of the Department, "Elsewhere in the World" of the same publication. Seven
monographs entitled, "Physical Education Around the
World" have been edited by Dr. Johnson covering fifty-

one countries. Monograph articles are being updated for inclusion in the present book.

Dr. Johnson has been Chairperson of the International Relations Sections of the States of California and Illinois; of the Midwest District International Relations Section; of the International Relations Council of AAHPER; of the NCPEAM International Relations Committee and of the Comparative Section of ICHPER.

## General Background

The Asian subcontinent of India is a country of extremes. From the towering Himalayan Mountains in the north and the lowland plain formed by the valleys of rivers, India extends 2,000 miles south to the Deccan Plateau and the Eastern and Western Ghats (hills) of the Indian peninsula. India is bounded on the east by Bangladesh, Burma, and the Bay of Bengal; on the west by Pakistan and the Arabian Sea; and on the north by the People's Republic of China, Nepal, Bhutan, and the protectorate of Sikkim. The island of Sri Lanka lies to the south.

Many rivers provide fertile land (and religious significance), but some parts of India are arid desert. Her southern tip lies only eight degrees north of the equator, and her climate varies from extremes hot to deadly cold. India depends on the tropical monsoon which usually comes in June and lasts until September. Without a regular monsoon season, India's agriculture (about 70% of the country's occupation) suffers. The hot season usually lasts from March to May or June, and winter occurs from October to February, during which time many people die of the cold in the north. India has both the richest and the poorest people in the world. She has the second largest population of any country but is only one-third the size of the United States.

A general comparison between India and the United States:

| Country | Pop. in Millions | Birth Rate per 1,000 | Death 1,000 | Literacy | Avg. Income | Life Expectancy | Food Consumption Cal. |
|---------|-----------------|---------------------|-------------|----------|-------------|-----------------|----------------------|
| India | 600 | 38.6 | 14.0 | 29% | 53 | 52 | 1880 |
| USA | 220 | 17.7 | 9.7 | 98% | 4000 | 70 | 3150 |

# Historical and Cultural Background

Studies indicate that a high degree of civilization was apparent in the cities of Harappa and Mohenjodaro (now in Pakistan) by 3,000 B.C. The occupants of these cities were known as the Dravidians. Theories as to why these cities disappeared range from a flooding of the Indus River to an invasion by Aryans. Since that time, historians have recorded at leat 26 invasions of India. The Aryans (noblemen) who first appeared in India were probably from Persia and were cultivators and cattle raisers who had mastered the use of iron. From these people came the Vedas, old religious hymns. Hinduisim was based on these hymns. The caste system originated about 1,000 B.C., dividing people into four groups (Brahmins or priests, Kshatriyas or warriors, Vaisyas or artisans, and Sudras or slaves). Jainism was an offspring of Hinduism which resulted from a revolt during the 16th century B.C., led by Vardhamana Mahvira. Complete non-violence and no caste system were their beliefs. Gautama Buddha led another religious revolt at this same time. He also believed in non-violence, the elimination of the caste system, the peaceful coexistence of mankind and the ultimate peace within himself (Nirvana).

Alexander the Great invaded India in 326 B.C. The Gupta period brought a system of law and order to India and is considered the golden age of history when the arts flourished and agriculture and commerce were developed. Buddhism was the main religion, although Hinduism was regaining influence. With the end of the Gupta period in 480 A.D., Huns invaded and were absorbed into India.

Mahmud of Ghazni extended his Muslim empire into the Punjab and converted many people to his religion around the year 1,000 A.D. The Mughul empire began in 1526 with Babar and ended with Aurangzeb in 1707. During this time, Shah Jahan built the Red Fort in Delhi and the Taj Mahal on the banks of the Jumna in Agra as a memorial to his wife, Mumtaz Mahal. It took 22 years and the work of 20,000 men to complete it.

India was invaded by many European explorers: Vasco de Gama, the Dutch, Denmark, France, and England. Britain finally dominated over the other European forces and worked mainly through her East India Company. Many British people made India their home. British rule did bring better transportation, communication, education (fashioned after the British educational system) and a judicial system.

Indian independence was achieved in August 15, 1947 by the British Parliamentary Indian Independence Act which partitioned India into India and Pakistan. England had ruled India for over 200 years and Indians had struggled long for their final independence. The partition saw much slaughter as Muslims tried to flee to Pakistan, and Hindus and Sikhs tried to move to India.

Present India is a country of many cultural and social differences because of the many invasions it has endured. No ruler before independence was able to unite all of India, and at present the national government is trying to keep the country from splintering off into regional cultural factions. There are many different languages in India, with only 15 being recognized regional languages. At present, Hindi and English are official languages. Although officially abolished, the caste system has been neatly woven into everyday life.

## Physical Education and Sports Historically

As the dominant cultures of India changed in times past so did the peoples' practice of physical education and sports. The Aryans (2,000 to 1,400 B.C.) participated in archery, mace fighting, riding, running, swordsmanship, and wrestling. Hinduism stressed the fact that the human soul passed through several reincarnations before being united with Brahma, the supreme goal. The quickest and most certain way to attain this goal was to refrain from catering to the body and enjoying worldly things. The person who desired to be holy ignored the physical needs of the body and concentrated on spiritual needs. It can readily be seen that physical activity had little place in the culture of this religious people.

Buddha's prohibitions of games, amusements, and exercises in ancient India did not totally prevent participation in such activities. Evidence is available as to such pastimes as dice, throwing balls, plowing contests, tumbling, chariot races, marbles, riding elephants and horses, swordsmanship, races, wrestling, boxing, and dancing. Yoga, an activity common in India and involving exercises in posture and regulated breathing, was popular. This discipling of mind and body required the instruction of experts, and a person fully trained in this activity followed a routine involving eighty-four different postures.

The English arrived in India in the early 1700's and by the 1850's governed virtually all of India. They tried to introduce physical education into high schools by 1875 without much success. The English introduced German, Swedish, and Danish gymnastics, military marching and barbell exercises. They also introduced such games as field hockey, soccer, cricket, and lawn tennis. The games became very popular especially in the urban areas. With the increase of the British population, track and field, golf, boating, swimming, rowing and archery became popular. Although the British did not favor organized indigenous games, they encouraged sports clubs, particularly those patronizing the British games.

In 1920, Harry C. Buck of the Y.M.C.A. founded the first Physical Education College in India at Madras. Also in 1920 physical education classes were introduced in India. In 1947 the Indians became independent of British rule and three years later formed an advisory board of physical education. Physical education was made compulsory in the schools and a national plan was drawn up. Games which did not require a great deal of space, time, or money became more popular, such as volleyball and indigenous Indian games such as Kabaddi, which is also popular in all of Southeast Asia.

KABADDI

Playing area:

Outdoors or indoors.

Players:

10 to 20, divided into two equal teams.

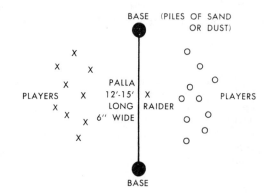

PROCEDURE:

Teams take positions on each half of the playing area. Captains toss to determine which team will raid first. The teams alternate raids; only one player raids at a time. The raider assumes a position on or near the *Palla,* or center line, takes a deep breath and begins loudly repeating the word "Kabaddi, Kabaddi, Kabaddi, Kabaddi," etc. At the same time the raider advances into the opponent's area attempting to touch (tag) as many of the opposing players as he can, before running out of breath. If the raider loses his breath and stops saying Kabaddi before he returns to the *Palla* the opponents may catch him. Points are scored according to the number of players that are touched by each raider and the number of raiders that are caught. Usually the game is supervised by a referee. The game may be played with two 20 minute halves with a rest interval of 5 minutes after the first half.

A very similar game is played in Thailand, where it is called Tee Jub. The players hum, loud enough to be heard, instead of saying the word "Kabaddi."

General Education

Education is viewed as a way to solve many national problems. There are basically two major aims of the educational system: 1) to provide better educational opportunity for more children in order to achieve economic development, technological progress, and a common social order founded on the values of freedom, social justice, and equal opportunity, and 2) to develop each individual to his full potential. There are four levels of education: primary (five years), middle schools (three years), high schools (three years) and colleges-universities. For rural children, education is being developed in relation to other phases of village modernization. In secondary education more emphasis is being placed on vocational and technical training. Over one-half of India's 46 universities have been established since Independence, and a variety of new institutes for higher technical training also have been developed.

## Physical Education in Schools

Physical education is compulsory, and the ideal sought after is the fullest development of the individual. The objectives are physical fitness and health, development of motor skills, discipline, character and a sense of patriotism. Each state sets minimum standards regarding periods in the schedule, facilities to be provided, and personnel to be employed. Physical education has not reached all of the educational institutions. Primary school programs are poorly run due to the lack of facilities, play areas, and poor training of the classroom teacher who is in charge of the program. High school physical education is run by a qualified teacher but facilities here too are inadequate. Activities include:

Primary School

Girls - Free exercises, story plays, small area games, stunts, and rhythmics.

Boys - Free exercises, story plays, initiations, singing games, small area games, stunts, and rhythmics.

Intermediate/Middle School

Girls - Calisthenics, marching, light apparatus, rhythmics, small area games, relays, leadup games, skills of team sports, and track and field.

Boys - Calisthenics, marching, gymnastics, light apparatus, rhythmics, small area games, relays, leadup games, skills of team games, and track and field.

Secondary School

Girls - Calisthenics, light apparatus team games (net ball, throw ball, badminton), rhythmics and relays.

Boys - Calisthenics, team games, gymnastics, light apparatus, relays, and track and field.

In primary and intermediate schools there are five class periods a week and between three and four in secondary schools. Classes last 30 minutes in primary and 45 minutes in intermediate and secondary schools. In primary and intermediate school there is some mixing of girls and boys in the same class, but none in secondary school. Students are not required to change to a uniform for class. Physical education is comparatively well developed in secondary schools, but is weak at the primary and university levels of education. On the whole physical education has not been able to take its rightful place in the scheme of education. There are several reasons for this unfortunate state of affairs:

1. "Traditional" practices of older physical exercise systems still persist in India while other countries discarded them years ago.

2. Physical education was viewed by educational commissions as a student welfare program.

3. Educators were concerned with rapid economic growth and loaded the curriculum with academic subjects.

4. Teachers had diverse and many times inadequate backgrounds in the professional preparation required to teach physical education.

5. Physical educators have been weak in organization and apathetic about building good public relations.

6. There has been a lack of vitally needed research in problems that are peculiar to the profession in India.

7. Physical education has failed to become recognized as a discipline by other educators, political leaders and the public.

Despite the negative aspects of the above seven points, there have been some recent steps taken to help improve the programs of physical education in India. In the primary school program some schools have appointed physical education specialists to oversee and guide the overall activity program of that entire school as well as teaching a general subject. Grades 6-9 receive five periods of physical education each week and grades 10-11 at least three to four periods per week - fairly new standards that reflect significant improvement over past practices. Recently the government integrated the physical education program for secondary schools under one unit, The National Fitness Corps Program. Another recent development is to include physical education as an elective subject in secondary schools with high standards.

## Physical Education at the College
and University Level

College students are not required to participate in physical
education, but all universities have their sports board and compete
in inter-university competitions. The professional college is the unit
used for organizing teams - the physical education director organizes
the college teams which compete against other colleges within the university. The best players from the college teams then will play on
the university team against other universities. The Inter-University
Sports Board sponsorship enables the university teams to play in
tournaments organized by sport federations. Universities may obtain
a sports coach from the National Institute of Sports and federal money
can be obtained to help pay salaries. Intramurals are held, mainly
in soccer, cricket, hockey, kabaddi, basketball, volleyball, tennis,
badminton, table tennis, weight lifting, carrom, and chess. College
Annual Sports Days which involve track and field competition usually
marks the end of the physical education program for that session.
Facilities are usually adequate, although city colleges have problems
with room for playgrounds.

College students are able to volunteer for participation in the
National Service Program which is composed of the National Cadet
Corps, National Social Service, and National Sports Organization
(which is only for top college students).

## Professional Preparation in Physical
Education

The education of teachers of physical education dates back to
the year 1920. The same general educational pattern was used for
more than thirty-five years in regards to professional preparation.
The government allowed for professional training colleges to offer a
certificate course (one-half a year for high school graduates) or a
diploma course (one year for college graduates) to students to be
educated as physical education teachers at the elementary and secondary school levels respectively. The short courses did not produce
highly qualified teachers, and as a result the National Laxmibai College of Physical Education was established in Gwalior in 1957. This
college offers a three year professional course in physical education
after which time a bachelor's degree is conferred. Its curriculum includes general education, preprofessional subjects such as anatomy,
physiology, psychology, and professional subjects such as principles,
organization, and methods of physical education. By 1963 this college was offering the master's degree with more advanced professional
subjects being taught and students introduced to research in health,
physical education and recreation.

More colleges offered degrees - the Government College of
Physical Education, Patiala, and the University of Punjab (Chandi-
garh made similar arrangements. Presently five universities offer
post-graduate courses in physical education. There are 53 training

colleges with most of them offering certificate or diploma courses in physical education. About 4,500 teachers in physical education are graduated each year. With the exception of a few, teacher training institutes are ill-equipped and poorly staffed.

Efforts to upgrade leadership in the field include government grants-in-aids to physical education colleges and the founding of physical education professional organizations including the All India Association of Colleges of Physical Education and the Indian Association of Teachers of Health, Physical Education, and Recreation. Physical educators and others can also obtain coaching qualification in a sport by joining the National Institute of Sports at Patiala.

## Status of Physical Education Teachers and Coaches

Physical education is not thought of very highly as a profession, and many physical education teachers do not get a good education. Library facilities are limited, research is scarce, facilities are poor, and the curricula needs to be revised. Teaching in general is regarded as an unattractive profession and the salaries are much lower than other professions. Physical education teachers do not have the status of academic teachers and are allowed little if any influence in formulating or regulating educational policy. In the colleges and universities, physical education instructors are not considered as full faculty members. This situation is gradually improving as individual instructors attain qualifications similar to those of other faculty members. Women are paid the same as men and receive the same benefits. Although this salary is not very high, it is definitely higher than the per capita income.

## Sports Competition

The All India Council of Sports was established in 1954 to advise the national government on sports programs in the country. Concern over poor representation in international athletic competitions produced the National Institute of Sports in Patiala in March 1961. The National Fitness Corps was launched in 1965-66. It recommends that where facilities exist after school intramural and interscholastic sports and games and a weekly period of mass physical training activities be conducted. The departments of education of the various states organize state level competitions in certain sports for students of the secondary schools. Also the All-India Games Federation conducts annual national competitions for representative teams from the states. These tournaments are quite popular and help to improve the standards in school sports. A strong interest and emphasis on academic studies deters an interest in sports at the university level with many students receiving little physical activity in either sports or physical education. Recently though the Union Ministry of Education and Social Welfare instituted a number of national sports scholarships for students who achieve high standards in national competitions.

Likewise the state governments offer some scholarships for their out-standing athletes in schools and colleges. Nevertheless, India draws most of her athletes for international games from the armed forces, police, and railways, rather than from the schools or universities.

In 1924 the first country-wide track and field competition was held, and a token team was sent to the 1924 Olympics. In 1928 the Indian Olympic Association was established and charged with regulating international competition. India dominates the field hockey world in international and Olympic Games competitions. International success has also been attained by cricket and football (soccer) teams. National Federations promote their particular sport, and each association has its own state and district unit. India participates in international competition in the following sports: field hockey, football, basketball, volleyball, track and field, cricket, swimming (few), gymnastics (few), wrestling, shooting, polo, tennis, badminton, table tennis and boxing. Women have not participated in sports for long due to their socially restricted role. Track and field is one sport in which some women are beginning to excel. Uniforms have restricted their participation in some events in the past.

Native indigenous activities are dands (prone calisthenics), baithaks (squatting exercises), asanas (prone positions), malkhamb (pole exercises), lezium (a form of rhythmics), regional folk dances, kho-kho (a vigorous team tag game), kabaddi (a native running and breath-holding game), langadi (a hopping game), lathi (a combative activity), and jambia (a self-defense activity).

## Recreational Sports

Organized recreational sports are actually just getting started. The people still participate in traditional activities such as dancing, music, and indigenous games. They also take part in many festivals. There are many forms of traditional games and pastimes especially popular in certain seasons - marbles in one season, top-spinning in another, and kite flying in another. Kabaddi, a combative game, is popular with some young people. Various kinds of ball games are played, the balls being made of wood or stuffed with leather.

In 1952 the Committee of the National College of Physical Education and Recreation reported: "If any country needs a recreation program that would cheer the people and bring them joy, it is India." Little has actually been accomplished in this area in the last twenty-five years. An organization entitled the Indian Recreation Association, which is voluntary, has been working to publicize the need for recreation. The central government is extending assistance to this group. Their main emphasis is to revive traditional forms of recreation and to emphasize activities inherently appealing to the people of India.

## Acknowledgements

The writer is indebted for background information for this art article to a number of Directors of Physical Education Institutes visited in India while on a two-year tour with The Asia Foundation in Pakistan. The assistance of various graduate students at the University of Illinois, especially Harsharan Singh Ahluawalia, a former physical education teacher-coach at Rajasthan, India and Patricia Riddle, who spent many years in India as a child of Missionary parents were most helpful. Other students providing informative materials include Karen Richards and Greg Roarick.

## SELECTED REFERENCES

1. Ahluwalia, Harsharan Singh, "Physical Education and Sports in India." Unpublished paper, University of Illinois. 1971.

2. "Background Notes on India." Department of State Publication #7847, Government Printing Office, Washington, D. C. 1973.

3. Bennett, Bruce L., Howell, Maxwell L. and Simri, Uriel. *Comparative Physical Education and Sport*. Philadephia, Pa.: Lea & Febiger. 1975.

4. Chopde, Sadanand, "Curriculum and Professional Preparation for Physical Education in India." *Proceedings of the 15th International Congress of ICHPER*. Washington, D. C. 1973.

5. Chopde, Sadanand, "Physical Education in India." *Proceedings of the 9th International Congress of ICHPER*. Washington, D. C. 1967.

6. Haggerty, William J. *Higher and Professional Education in India*. Washington, D. C.: U. S. Government Printing Office. 1969.

7. ICHPER, International Questionnaire Report Part III. *Status of Teachers of Physical Education*. Washington, D. C. 1967-68.

8. Publications Division. *About India*. Government of India. 1958.

9. Puri, Balraj. *Recreation and Social Education*. Bombay, India: Vora and Company Publishers PVT, Ltd. 1963.

10. Richards, Karen, "Indian and Physical Education." Unpublished paper, University of Illinois. 1977.

11. Riddle, Patricia., "India." Unpublished paper, University of Illinois. 1972.

12. Roarick, Greg, "Physical Education in India." Unpublished paper, University of Illinois. 1977.

13. Thomas, J. P. *Organization of Physical Education*. Madras, India: Gnanodaya Press. 1967.

14. Thompson, Elizabeth. *Other Lands Other Peoples*. National Education Association, Washington, D. C.

15. Van Dalen, Deobold B. and Bennett, Bruce L. *A World History of Physical Education*. Englewood Cliffs, N. J.: Prentice Hall, Inc. 1971.

16. Vendien, C. Lynn and Nixon, John E. *The World Today in Health, Physical Education and Recreation*. Englewood Cliffs, N. J.: Prentice Hall, Inc. 1968.

# SPORT AND PHYSICAL EDUCATION IN INDONESIA
by Nicolaas J. Moolenijzer and Sieswanpo

## Biographical Sketches

*Nicolaas Moolenijzer* was born in Amsterdam, the Netherlands in 1922. After completing his secondary school education he received his L.O. degree from the Protestant Teacher College in Amsterdam (1943) and his M.O. degree in physical education from the Academy for Physical Education, also in Amsterdam (1947).

During his collegiate career he represented the Netherlands as a member of the national ice hockey team and was a regular member of one of the Canadian All-Star Army teams.

After his immigration to the United States, Dr. Moolenijzer received a B.A. degree from San Jose State College (1949) and continued graduate work at U.C.L.A. where he received his M.S. (1956) and at the University of Southern California where he obtained his Ph.D. (1965).

Dr. Moolenijzer's teaching experience stretches from kindergarten level through the university and includes general classroom teaching as well as physical education both abroad and in the United States. In addition to a one year's stay in Austria as recipient of a Fulbright Senior Research Grant, he has traveled wide widely through Europe and Asia and has lectured in both Western and Eastern Europe.

Recently he returned to the University of New Mexico after having served almost three years with the United National Education, Scientific and Cultural Organization (UNESCO) in Paris, France, where he was instrumental in the organization of the "First International Conference of Ministers and Senior Officials Responsible for Physical Education and Sport."

His special interests lie in the areas of international foundations and history of physical education and sport.

*Sieswanpo* was born in 1927 on the Island of Java. He received his B.S. degree in 1953 and subsequently his special credential in physical education in 1954 from the University of Indonesia in Bandung. In 1960 he received the equivalent of the *Sardjana* degree from the University of Indonesia in Jakarta. In 1964 Dr. Sieswanpo came to the United States where he obtained his M.A. degree at the University of Minnesota in 1965 and his Ph.D. degree at the University of Missouri-Columbia in 1971.

His teaching experience ranges from the elementary school level through the university. In addition, Dr. Sieswanpo has been commissioned with various responsible administrative positions among which: Secretary General of the Indonesian Council for Physical Education (1957-'64), Secretary of the Indonesian Olympic Committee (1955-'57), Secretary of the Asian Congress on Physical Education (1962), Project Director of the Indonesian Sports Science Center (1975-'76), Advisor/ Assistant to the Director General of Sports and Youth (1971-'75), Vice-President of the Indonesian Coordinating Body for Physical Education, Health and Recreation (1972-'76), and many others.

Currently Dr. Sieswanpo is back in the United States where he is Sports Therapist in the Department of Adjunctive Therapies of the Middle Tennessee Mental Health Institute in Nashville, Tennessee.

# General Background

Indonesia consists of more than 2,500 islands, lying between the mainland of Asia and Australia and separating the Indian Ocean from the Pacific Ocean. The principal islands and island groups are Sumatra, Java and Madura, Nusa Tenggara (Lesser Suda Islands), West Irian (West New Guinea), the Moluccas, Sulawesi (Celebes) and Kalimantan (Borneo). The chain of island from east to west measures about 3,000 miles which is approximately the same distance as between the west and east coasts of the United States and covers a total area of 732,748 square miles. A large part of Indonesia is mountainous. The great number of active volcanoes (about 150) makes the country the most volcanic area in the world. The elevation ranges from 6 to 2,300 feet above sea level. Grouped along the equator the islands experience little changes in temperature, which may vary from 74 to 78 degrees. Depending on the location the annual rainfall may vary from 57 to 213 inches per year, accounting for a relative humidity ranging from 73 to 85 per cent.

In 1968 there was an estimated population of almost 115 million people, making Indonesia the fifth most populous nation. More than 60 per cent of the people live on the islands of Java and Madura which, with 1,230 people per square mile, are among the most densely populated areas in the world. Geographical conditions and historical development are partial causes for the great variety of ethnic and linguistic differences and cultural patterns. The people are predominantly of Malay stock and have, through the years, used Malay as a *lingua franca* between the ethnic sub-groups. Since independence this language, with some modifications, has become the official Indonesian language of all written communcation, education, government and business. Some 60 per cent of the population is literate; the rate is about 70 per cent in the 6 to 16 age group.* Almost 90 per cent of the population is Moslem; the remaining 10 per cent, save for a small number of disciples of Buddhism and Hinduism, is Christian. The constitution guarantees freedom of religion and Christians as well as Moslems are represented in Parliament and occupy high places in the government, civil service and armed forces.

When the Portuguese and Spanish came to Indonesia in the sixteenth century, they met with an advanced civilization which had existed for almost 1,000 years. Beginning in the early 1600's the entire archipelago was brought progressively under Dutch control. During the 300 years of Dutch rule (interrupted only by a brief British interregnum during the Napoleonic occupation of Europe) Indonesia, or the Dutch East Indies as it was known, was developed into one of the world's richest colonial possessions.

The independence movement began in the early 1900's and had expanded greatly by the end of the Japanese occupation during the second World War. The leadership for this independence movement

---

* According to 1971 census.

The independence movement began in the early 1900's and had expanded greatly by the end of the Japanese occupation during the second World War. The leadership for this independence movement came largely from those educated in the Netherlands. Three days after the Japanese surrender a small group of Indonesians proclaimed independence and established the Republic of Indonesia. After four years of warfare and political negotiations an agreement was reached with the Dutch who, in 1949, recognized Indonesian independence. As with many other young developing nations, Indonesia lived through years of political and economic difficulties. At present a new post-revolution generation has come into its own, a generation which is no longer preoccupied with the problems of the past but which has focussed its attention and energies on the problems of the present and the future.

## Historical Background of Education

Prior to the sixteenth century education was influenced primarily by the Hindu and Moslem faiths which aimed predominantly at a religious education. The institutions established by the Hindus were called *pesantren*, and those by the Moslems *langgar* or *surau* and were maintained by the community. The first European-type schools were organized by the Portuguese and Spanish in the Moluccas. In contrast to the *pesantren*, reading, writing and arithmetic formed part of the curriculum.

The first contact with Dutch education occurred during the reign of the Dutch East India Company. This organization was a private enterprise which controlled the entire arhcipelago from the early 1600's until after the Napoleonic period when it sold its interests to the Dutch government. As the main purpose remained religious education, the East India Company established only schools in such areas as the Moluccas, some of the Lesser Sunda Islands, Jakarta and Semarang where the population had adopted Christianity. The first regulations governing education were enacted by this company. Among the terms of the School Act of 1684 no school could be established without the company's consent; school hours were fixed; coeducation was prohibited; holidays and school fees were set and a biannual school inspection was instituted. A School Act of 1778 dealt with matters of admission (Christians only); organization of grade levels; curriculum; and teaching methods.

It was not until 1848, after Indonesia had become a part of the Dutch empire, that the Dutch government assumed responsibility for providing education for the native population. In order to meet the need for teaching personnel several teacher training institutions were established, the first one in Surakarta (Java) in 1852. The Dutch settlers as well profited from the educational reforms. In the period from 1860 to 1878 the first public secondary schools were organized: among them a technical high school in Surabaja (1860), a general high school in Jakarta (1867), and teacher training schools in Jakarta (1871), Surabaja (1875) and Semarang (1877). In 1867 a Department of Education was organized to facilitate administration of the increasing number of schools. A Royal Decree of 1871 increased the number of training schools for native teachers; prohibited the teaching of religion in the public schools; discontinued financial aid to denominational schools; and, most important of all, eliminated all class restrictions for admittance to the public elementary schools. In 1890 the restriction on financial aid to parochial schools was lifted, thus qualifying for government subsidies any school that advanced the intellectual capabilities of its pupils. Although the native elementary schools had been divided into 'first class schools' and 'second class schools' (for the Indonesian aristocracy and the masses respectively) there had been until the end of the nineteenth century little or no practice of segregation and Indonesian pupils had been admitted to the Dutch public schools rather freely. New regulations in 1894, however, limited the admission of Indonesian pupils drastically by the introduction of an age limit, an increase in tuition, a Dutch language proficiency requirement and a preference policy which gave priority to Dutch pupils.

At the beginning of the twentieth century an attempt was made to upgrade the educational practices in the native schools by a greater emphasis on Western science and culture and a greater usage of the Dutch language. In 1911 the program of the 'first class schools' was extended to seven years the Dutch language to be taught from the second grade on. One year later Dutch instruction was introduced in the first grade. In 1914 the name of the school was changed into *Hollands Inlandse School* (Dutch-Native School). As the Chinese population in Indonesia showed much interest in receiving a Dutch education, a parallel school, the *Hollands Chinese School* (Dutch-Chinese School), was organized along the same pattern. A greater demand for elementary education and a larger supply of native teachers was responsible for the creation of the so-called village schools which provided an education for grades 1 through 3. Although most pupils limited their education to the program of the village school there was a possibility to continue one's education for two more years in the so-called 'extension schools' which were organized in 1915. The old 'second class schools' gradually merged with the village and extension schools.

Around the 1920's the secondary school system evolved into a pattern similar to that in the Netherlands, i.e., a diversified arrangement in which some schools provided a terminal or vocational education while others prepared for college entrance. During the same period a limited number of special secondary type schools were established including: the *Technische School (School of Technology)* at Jakarta in 1906; the *Rechts School* (School of Law) at Jakarta in 1909; the *Landbouw School* (School of Agriculture) at Bogor in 1911; the *Technische School* at Surabaja in 1912; the *Handels School* (School of Commerce) at Surabaja in 1912; the *Cultuur School* (School of Agriculture) at Malang in 1918; and the *Handels School* at Jakarta in 1935. To the special secondary schools belonged also the teacher training institutions. The program of these training institutions was limited to the preparation of teachers for the elementary schools. In the same fashion as the elementary schools themselves, these institutions were divided into *Hollandse Kweekschool* (Dutch Normal School); *Hollands Inlandse Kweekschool* (Dutch-Native Normal School); and *Hollands Chinese* Kweekschool (Dutch-Chinese Normal School).

The number of institutions of higher education was very small and offered a very limited choice. Among them might be mentioned the *Technische Hogeschool* (Institute for Technology) at Bandung; the *Rechts Hogeschool* (School of Law) at Jakarta; the *Geneeskundige Hogeschool* (School of Medicine) at Jakarta; and the *Militaire Academie* (Military Academy similar to Westpoint) at Magelang.

During the Japanese occupation many existing educational institutions were abolished or replaced. The public elementary school offered a dual program: three-year elementary schools covering grades 1 through 3 and six-year elementary schools providing a complete elementary education leading to secondary education. Secondary education consisted of a three-year Junior High School and a three-year Senior High School program preparing for admittance to the institutions of higher learning. Besides these schools there were also vocational high schools which were mostly a continuation of the vocationals schools established by the Dutch and which prepared for a terminal education.

During the interim of Dutch administration following the Japanese surrender very little was actually accomplished. The political and economic conditions were highly unfavorable and the time too short to warrant great results. In essence the Dutch attempted to re-establish the old system, though on a larger scale and on a much broader non-segregated base.

After independence Indonesia was faced with the enormous task of reorganizing its educational system. In order to develop an educational program that would be in conformity with the national ideals, a Ministry of Education, Instruction and Culture was established which was charged with "the forming of capable persons with a high moral character, democratic citizens with a sense of responsibility for the welfare of society and the country as a whole." To the most urgent items of its program belonged (1) the eradication of illiteracy; (2) an intensified program of education of the people at all levels with equal opportunity and free choice for all concerned; and, (3) the in introduction and enforcement of compulsory education. Naturally the Ministry was faced with a monumental task. The war conditions and its aftermath had left the country without qualified manpower and the economic picture was far from encouraging. To meet the need for elementary school teachers the ministry established a four-year junior high school for teacher training called the *Sekolah Guru Bawah* which prepared teaching personnel for grades 1 through 3. To this school were admitted those pupils who had completed the sixth grade of the elementary school and who had passed the entrance examination successfully. In addition the *Sekolah Guru Atas* (Senior High School for

Teacher Training) was created. Here students who had completed
the junior high school were prepared to teach all grade levels of the
elementary school. The duration of the course was three years. One
of the strongest motives for this approach had been the financial aspect. It had been reasoned that more teachers would be needed for
the primary grades than for the upper grades and that lower requirements for teacher education would result in a lower salary scale.
However, experience soon proved that the primary grades needed
teaching personnel with equal if not more qualifications and experience. It did not take long, therefore, before the *Sekolah Guru Bawah*
was phased out (1958).

Originally all secondary school teachers had been educated in
the Netherlands. Although many of them stayed on after independence there soon developed a great need of additional personnel. It
is remarkable that the Indonesian authorities adopted the identical
process which the Dutch had practiced. Here qualified elementary
school teachers attended extension courses to specialize in certain
secondary school subject matter. Successful completion of the course
requirements concluded with a state examination that qualified the student to teach this subject at a secondary school. Although the extensive development of Higher Education has included Education as
one of its disciplines and although it is at the present possible to obtain various degrees in education, the state still maintains certain requirements of the procedures described above in its certification of
secondary school teachers.

At the present the educational organization in Indonesia might
be summarized as follows:

### Kindergarten Level:

Save for some schools operated by private groups there are no
kindergartens in Indonesia.

### Elementary Level:

All public elementary schools now cover grades 1 through 6.

### Secondary Level:

*Junior High Schools.* As in the United States, the junior high
schools comprise grades 7 through 9. Contrary to the American concept of the comprehensive school there are two types of junior high
schools. One, the *Sekolah Menegah Pertama* offers an academic program. Specialization starts in the ninth grade when the students
have the option of going either the direction of the liberal arts or that
of the sciences. Parallel to this school there are various vocational
junior high schools. Among these are the junior high schools for commerce, home economics, elementary school teacher training, religion
(Moslem), fishery, merchant marine, agriculture, and forestry.

*Senior High Schools.* The senior high schools comprise grades 10 through 12 and are divided into college preparatory schools which offer an academic program and schools which specialize in a vocational orientation. The first one, the *Sekolah Menengah Atas*, offers a threefold program with specializations in the arts, sciences or social studies. The main purpose of the *Sekolah Landjutan Kedjuruan Atas*, or vocational senior high school, is to prepare manpower for specialized vocations and professions. In the United States most of these professions would require a general secondary education, on the job training and the completion of some special courses. Among the vocational senior high schools are those which specialize in business, elementary school education, home economics instruction, social work, mechanics, physical education and sports, pharmacy, practical nursing, fishery, merchant marine, agriculture, forestry, and legal administration. It should be clearly understood that the programs of most of these vocational schools are directed toward training personnel for *supporting* functions in the various professions. A limited number of students graduating from these vocational schools who can meet certain requirements have the opportunity to continue studies in their area at an institution of higher learning.

Higher Education

Although the development of higher education in Indonesia is almost entirely a post-war development, much of its structure has been caught in the web of the classic approach to higher education and has been patterned after European design. One of the main reasons for this is the fact that in the beginning most of the Indonesian faculty had been trained in the Netherlands. There is, therefore, still some duality in the structure which leads to duplication of functions and the preservation of traditional practices. In this structure the following institutions might be distinguished:

*Universities*, with schools of medicine; law and social sciences; psychology; technical sciences; natural and pure sciences; language, arts and philosophy; educational sciences; agriculture; veterinary medicine; and dentistry. Both undergraduate and graduate studies are available at the various schools.

*Institutes* might be regarded as independent schools which are wholly autonomous and degree granting. Among these are the Institute of Technology; the Institute of Teacher Training and Educational Sciences; and the Institute of Agriculture.

*Sekolah Tinggi*, or Schools of Higher Learning, are also specialized institutions with both undergraduate and graduate programs. One of these is the School for Health, Physical Education and Sports.

*Academies*, such as the Military Academy, the Naval Academy and the Air Force Academy.

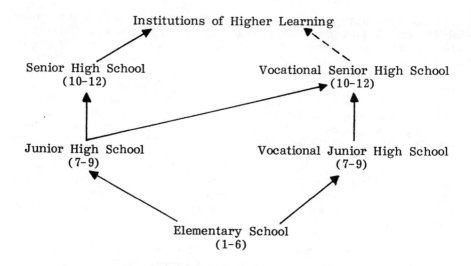

Institutions of Higher Learning

Senior High School
(10-12)

Vocational Senior High School
(10-12)

Junior High School
(7-9)

Vocational Junior High School
(7-9)

Elementary School
(1-6)

Structure of Indonesian Education

### Historical Background of Physical Education

During the pre-war administration of the Dutch, little attention was paid to the development of a physical education program in the public schools. This was not a purposeful neglect but a reflection of a similar educational philosophy held in the Netherlands. It was not until the 1920's that physical education was introduced in some places. This haphazard scheduling was not a matter of administrative preference but was solely dependent on the availability of military personnel who did the teaching. Consequently the approach was army-like, formal. At that time the Dutch army, as many other European forces, was committed to the Swedish system. The first inspector for physical education, a Mr. F. H. A. Claessen, seems to have been appointed in 1922. A two-year training course leading to certification for the elementary and junior high school levels was instituted in 1937. Shortly after, in 1940, the administration opened the *Gouvernements Instituut voor Lichamelijke Opvoeding* (Government Institute for Physical Education), a four-year college preparing for a complete certification of physical education teachers. The Japanese invasion in 1942 prevented anyone from graduating. Thus it happened that when the Dutch disappeared into the Japanese concentration camps, only fourteen Indonesians were qualified to teach physical education on the elementary school level; none for the secondary levels. The Japanese, who aimed at enlisting Indonesian manpower in their war effort, overemphasized physical development. Not only school children, but also the older youth and adults were forced to participate in taiso (physical exercise) which consisted mostly of calisthenics and military drill. All over the country special training courses were held for teachers and high school students who, upon completion of the course, were assigned as leaders in their own schools and communities.

Much of this physical training program was carried over during the interim following the Japanese surrender. Although the Dutch had re-established themselves in Indonesia and had commenced with the restoration of the administration, there existed at the same time an Indonesian government which was in control of part of the territory. Where the latter was the case, physical education was a required subject of the school curriculum and military drill and calisthenics were the main aim of the physical education program. In the area occupied by the Dutch the Department of Education, Arts and Sciences created an Inspectorate for physical education which was charged with the overall development and administration of physical education programs. One of its efforts was the establishment of the *Academisch Instituut voor Lichaamsoefeningen* (Academy of Physical Education) at Bandung in 1947. The main responsibility of this academy was the preparation of a teachers corps for the secondary schools. The Indonesian authorities established a similar institution, the *Sekolah Olahraga* at Sarangan in East Java around the same time. However, due mainly to lack of qualified personnel, the latter closed its doors in 1950.

When in 1949 Indonesia was recognized internationally as an independent nation, Dutch specialists in almost all professions stayed on as advisors and instructors, particularly in education. However, due to the social and economic instability of the country there was a persistent lack of funds which made it impossible to realize many of the proposals adopted by the First National Conference on Physical Education in 1957. One of the main actions of this conference was to appoint a council, the *Madjelis Pendidikan Djasmani*, which was composed of: representatives of the Ministry of Education; the various institutions concerned with physical education, including the universities; the National Advisory Council of the Republic of Indonesia; the Indonesian Medical Association; the Indonesian Olympic Committee; and various other organizations representing students and youth. The council was very active until 1960 when all forces and funds of the Indonesian nation were mobilized for the organization of the Fourth Asian Games to be held in Jakarta in 1962. Although the interest in developing the area of physical education remained, the continued social, economic and political instability prevented the following of a steady course. Many schemes and stop-gap measures were developed to qualify adequate teaching personnel. Various degree granting institutions and courses were established to train the necessary manpower.

As a result of a political rearrangement the responsibility for the development and organization of physical education was withdrawn from the Ministry of Education, Instruction and Culture and placed under the authority of the Ministry of Sports, or *Departemen Olahraga*. To the functions of this department belonged the organization, coordination and supervision of:

All physical education and sports activities in the nation, including intra- and extramural activities at the public schools and at the institutions of higher learning;

Construction and maintenance of sports facilities throughout the nation;

Preparation and training of teachers and specialists for physical education and sports;

Development of national sports industries and responsibility for importation and distribution of sports equipment of foreign origin;

Exchange of athletes and/or coaching personnel with foreign nations;

International contests, meets and competitions;

Research activities in the areas of physical education and sports, including sport medicine.

At times the Ministry of Sports would appoint special task forces or *Komando Gerakan Olahraga* to assume responsibility for special events. As a result of the political situation sports, and consequently physical education, became more and more a tool to be manipulated for the purposes of national and foreign policy. International relations with the foreign sports world deteriorated so much that Indonesia withdrew from the International Olympic Committee. Its National Olympic Committee was dissolved and replaced by a new national sports body, the *Dewan Olahraga Republik Indonesia.* In an attempt to create an international contest of Olympic dimensions of its own, the Indonesian government organized the First Games of the New Emerging Forces (GANEFO) at Jakarta in 1964. These were held in the hyper-modern 12.5 million dollar sport complex which the Russians had built previously to accommodate the Fourth Asian Games in 1962.

Aware of the great need for assistance, the Indonesian government invited a contingent of 50 Peace Corps volunteers on condition that their major effort was to be concentrated in the area of sport and physical education. Although the Peace Corps volunteers were highly popular and effective and although their efforts contributed greatly to the development of sport and physical education in Indonesia, they had to be withdrawn in 1965 when political relations with the United States reached an all time low.

Since the abortive communist coup of 1965 the country has experienced a reassuring interest in social and economic matters which in turn has influenced educational conditions. Drastic changes in foreign policy made the politically oriented Ministry of Sports obsolete.

It was dissolved and replaced by a Directorate General for Sports*
which forms part of the Ministry of Education and Culture. In 1966
a new national sports committee, the *Komite Olahraga Nasional Indonesia*, was created to function as a coordinating body for the various
sports associations. International relations were re-established and
Indonesia rejoined the International Olympic Committee.

## Physical Education Today

In a relatively short span of time the educational system of
Indonesia has been subjected to the influence of different political
philosphies. As a consequence the objectives of physical education
were changed to suit the goals of the educational program in vogue.
Today physical education and sports still play an important part in
the lives of the Indonesian people. Its status is a major concern of
the Indonesian government which recently passed legislation which en-
sures the Directorate General for Sports representation in the Indonesian Parliament and National Assembly. Indonesia is still a young
nation and the period of independence has been too short to properly
develop an autochthonous philosophy of physical education. It should
not be surprising, therefore, that much of the accepted philosophy
and methods reflect earlier Dutch influences. After all, many members of the established teacher corps were Dutch trained and, save
for short intervals, have continued to practice what they have learned. Although slight adaptations have been made, the Indonesian system still employs the method of the Austrian School of Physical Education. This is very evident in the Directorate's formulation of the ob-
objectives of Indonesian Physical Education, which states in part that
the program should be geared to the psychological, physiological,
sociological and cultural needs of the child; furthermore, that in order
to guarantee the harmonious development of the individual as a psycho-
somatic totality, use should be made of the so-called 'natural' physical
exercises.

The administration of education in Indonesia is of a centralized
nature which implies that the responsibility for coordination, implementation and supervision of programs and policies has been channeled in
a hierarchical fashion from the Ministry of Education down to the
smallest community. The Directorate General for Sports administers
its program in a similar fashion, which means that even the smallest
villages have access to teaching or supervisory personnel. Due to
lack of qualified specialists most physical education on the elementary
level is taught by the classroom teacher. Although the situation on
the secondary level is better, particularly in the larger cities, there
is still a shortage of trained personnel.

Presently the law required a minimum of three physical education periods per week for boys and girls in grades 1 through 12. Although the Directorate has furnished a general outline for the course

---

* In 1968 it became the Directorate General for Sports and Youth.

of study to be followed, much of its implementation has been left to the local level in order to provide an opportunity to adapt the physical education program to ethnic and geographical conditions. The program on the secondary school level has much in common with that of the elementary schools. Unlike the American secondary schools, neither the junior high schools nor the senior high schools engage in intra- and extramural athletic programs. Contests between schools are incidental and depend largely on the schools' administration and teaching staff. It is customary in Indonesia that most celebrations include activities of a sportive nature. These events, however, take more the form of tournaments or sports days.

There exists in Indonesia a National Championship for Secondary School Students in the Pentathlon. Participants are selected in regional qualifying meets. In addition there are national championships for various team sports. It is customary to vary the program each year; the activities scheduled depend largely on location and preferences of the organizing committee of the region.

## Teacher Training

As in other aspects of education, the training of physical education teachers has passed through various, sometimes greatly different, stages of development. The traditional position of higher education, which did not recognize education as an academic discipline, had already exercised its influence before the establishment of a university system in Indonesia. As a result various arrangements of extension courses prepared teachers for special credentials in physical education for the elementary and/or secondary level. In 1963 a law was passed which endeavored to create order in this confusion. Degrees and credential requirements were standardized and various training programs were consolidated. Although the certificates earned before 1963 are still honored, there are at present only two avenues of enrollment in a major program. One of these is the *Sekolah Menengah Olahrage Atas* (Senior High School for Physical Education) which offers a three-year program leading to certification for the elementary and junior high school levels (grades 1 through 9). Although the law states that graduates of the junior high school qualify for admittance to the senior high schools there is often not enough room to accommodate all applicants. It has, therefore, become customary to apply some criteria for selection of candidates. The emphasis of this process is slanted toward physical proficiency and competency in skills. At the moment there are sixty-five institutions of this nature scattered throughout Indonesia. As secondary education is administered centrally, these schools all follow a uniform program which is coordinated by the Directorate General for Sports.

A typical program offers the following:

| | Course Title | Year I | II | III |
|---|---|---|---|---|
| 1 | Gymnastics (incl. 'natural exercises') | x | x | |
| 2 | Track and field | x | x | |
| 3 | Sports and Games (incl. games of low organization) | x | x | |
| 4 | Aquatics | x | x | |
| 5 | Self Defense Sports | x | x | |
| 6 | Pedagogy | x | x | x |
| 7 | Psychology | x | x | x |
| 8 | Human Anatomy (incl. Applied Anatomy) | x | x | x |
| 9 | Human Physiology | | x | x |
| 10 | Hygiene and First Aid | | | x |
| 11 | History of Physical Education | | | x |
| 12 | General Theory of Physical Education | | x | x |
| 13 | Methodology of Physical Education | | x | x |
| 14 | Scouting and Camping | | | x |
| 15 | Indonesian Language | x | x | x |
| 16 | English Language | x | x | x |
| 17 | Student Teaching | | | x |

The educational authorities in Indonesia have been aware for some time that the *Sekolah Menengah Olahraga Atlas* forms only a stop-gap measure in the acute shortage of teaching personnel. Plans are in progress to establish an undergraduate and graduate professional program which will meet the needs of secondary and higher education. Part of these plans were realized when an agreement was reached on the requirements for higher education in physical education. Prior to 1963 various departments of individual universities had organized 'institutes' of physical education. Departmental and regional rivalry had created an atmosphere of competition and had precluded any coordination in matters of requirements and the granting of degrees. The situation was further complicated by the legal provision that all candidates for credentials must successfully complete a state examination regardless of degrees earned previously. The final outcome of the overall revision resulted in the creation of an independent school of higher learning for physical education, the *Sekolah Tinggi Olahraga*. The entrance requirements for this institution are identical to those for any other branch of the university. Again as the number of applications usually is five to six times the number of open-ings available, the institutions utilize a selective process for admission. It seems a little contrary, however, that the graduates of the *Sekolah Menengah Olahraga Atas* do not receive preferred treatment. The three-year program leading to the *Sardjana Muda* or Bachelor's degree is identical at all institutions so far as the course of study for physical education is concerned. The coordinative efforts here are performed by the Directorate General for Sports. However, each institution has its own board of curators and is fully autonomous in all other decisions concerning the academic program and its operations. Depending on the availability of qualified teaching staff the *Sekolah Tinggi Olahraga* may also offer the *Sardjana* or Master's degree with an additional two years of study. At this date, however, only three of the eleven* institutions have been able to realize their program through the Master's level. Although the projected program envisages the granting of a Doctoral degree, none has been awarded as yet. As there is not possibility at this moment to prepare person-nel qualified to assume the responsibility for directing graduate studi-es locally, efforts are being made to have this personnel groomed in foreign countries.

The undergraduate program does not offer electives. On the graduate level there is an opportunity to choose the following areas of specialization: (1) General physical education, (2) Coaching indivi-dual branches of sport, (3) Community recreation and sports, and (4) An area of 'sportshealth' which, depending on the emphasis, may lean toward the direction of either sports-medicine or health educa-tion. If compared to our approach of college education, it should be noted that the Indonesian program, particularly the undergraduate program, appears to have been organized much more in a high school fashion. Although many hours are spent in required activity courses the Indonesian students student seem to carry a heavier load than ours. The following course of study is utilized by the *Sekolah Tinggi Olahraga* at Bandung:

---

* Jakarta, Bandung and Jogjakarta offer a Master's degree. The others, Semarang, Surakarta, Surabaja, Medan, Padana, Makassar, Menado and Bandjarmasin offer at the moment an undergraduate program only.

# CURRICULUM OF THE SEKOLAH TINGGI OLAHRAGA*

A. General Courses
   1. Religion
   2. "Pantja Sila"**
   3. Philosophy
   4. Modern & Ethnic Dance
   5. Jeugdwerk***
   6. Anthropology

B. Basic Courses
   1. Paedagogy (General)
   2. Psychology
   3. Health Education
   4. Anatomy
   5. Physiology
   6. Administration
   7. Statistics
   8. Methodology & Didactics
   9. Audio Visual Aids

C. Core Courses
   1. Physiology of Physical Education
   2. History of Physical Education/Sport
   3. Coaching (theory & practice)
   4. Research Methods
   5. Construction & Maintenance of Physical Education Facilities
   6. Guidance & Counseling
   7. Tests & Measurements
   8. Evaluation & Construction
   9. Kinesiology
   10. Body Mechanics
   11. Planning and Programming of Curriculum
   12. Practicum Anatomy & Physiology
   13. Theory & Techniques
   14. Teaching Skills
   15. Recreation
   16. Training
   17. Sport Physiology
   18. Physical Conditioning
   19. Professional Preparation
   20. Prevention and Care of Athletic Injuries
   21. Public Relations

D. Supplementing Courses
   1. "Bahasa Indonesia"****
   2. English
   3. Mathematics
   4. Chemistry
   5. Thesis Writing

---

* Source: Sekolah Tinggi Olahraga, Bandung. January 1974.
** Ideological Foundations of the State.
*** Youth Work.
**** Indonesian Language.

# UNDERGRADUATE STUDY

| First Year | Semester I | Semester II |
|---|---|---|
| 1. Religion | 1 | 1 |
| 2. "Pantja Sila" | 2 | – |
| 3. Jeugdwerk | – | 2 |
| 4. Anatomy | 2 | 2 |
| 5. Physiology | 2 | 2 |
| 6. Paedagogy | – | 2 |
| 7. Introduction to Philosophy and Principles of Physical Education | 2 | – |
| 8. Psychology (General) | 2 | – |
| 9. History of Physical Education | – | 2 |
| 10. Health Education (General) | 1 | 1 |
| 11. Bahasa Indonesia | 2 | 2 |
| 12. English | 2 | 2 |
| 13. Theory & Practice: | | |
|     Track & Field | 2 | 2 |
|     Play & Games | 4 | 4 |
|     Gymnastics | 2 | 2 |
|     Swimming | 2 | 2 |
|     Dance | 1 | 1 |
|     Self Defense | 2 | 2 |
| 14. Mathematics | – | 1 |
| 15. Chemistry | 1 | – |
| 16. Training | 4 | 4 |
| | 34 | 34 |

| Second Year | Semester I | Semester II |
|---|---|---|
| 1. Philosophy (Introduction) | 2 | – |
| 2. Anatomy | 2 | 2 |
| 3. Physiology | 2 | 2 |
| 4. Modern & Ethnic Dances | – | 2 |
| 5. Anthropology | 2 | – |
| 6. Health Education (Hygiene) | 2 | – |
| 7. Didactics | 2 | 2 |
| 8. Administration | 2 | – |
| 9. Psychology (Child & Adolescent) | – | 2 |
| 10. Kinesiology | – | 2 |
| 11. Theory & Practice: | | |
|     Track & Field | 2 | 2 |
|     Play & Games | 4 | 4 |
|     Gymnastics | 2 | 2 |
|     Swimming | 2 | 2 |
|     Archery | 2 | 2 |
| 12. Training | 4 | 4 |
| 13. Term-paper writing | – | – |
| | 30 | 28 |

| Third Year | Semester I | Semester II |
|---|---|---|
| 1. Administration & Organization | 2 | 2 |
| 2. Health Education (Practices) | 2 | 2 |
| 3. Introduction & Principles of Coaching | 2 | 2 |
| 4. Tests & Measurements | 2 | 2 |
| 5. Recreation & Youth Leadership | 2 | – |
| 6. Body Mechanics | – | 2 |
| 7. Sport Psychology | 2 | – |
| 8. Health Education | – | 2 |
| 9. Statistics (Descriptive) | 2 | 2 |
| 10. Practicum Anatomy & Physiology | 2 | 2 |
| 11. Teaching Skills | Pro Men | Pro Men |
| 12. Theory & Practice: | | |
| Track & Field | 2 | 2 |
| Games & Play | 2 | 2 |
| Gymnastics | 2 | 2 |
| Swimming | 2 | 2 |
| Self Defense | 1 | 1 |
| 13. Training | 2 | 2 |
| | 27 | 27 |

## GRADUATE STUDY

| Fourth Year | Semester I | Semester II |
|---|---|---|
| 1. Philosophy Logic | 2 | – |
| 2. Statistics (Inferential) | 2 | 2 |
| 3. Public Relations | – | 2 |
| 4. Research Methods | 2 | 2 |
| 5. Sport Physiology | 2 | – |
| 6. Care & Prevention of Athletic Injuries | – | 2 |
| 7. Mental Health | 2 | – |
| 8. Audio Visual Aids | – | 2 |
| | 10 | 10 |

| Fifth Year | Semester I | Semester II |
|---|---|---|
| 1. Construction & Evaluation of Tests | – 2 | 2 – |
| 2. Construction & Maintenance of Facilities | 2 | – |
| 3. Professional Preparation | 2 | – |
| 4. Guidance & Counseling | 2 | – |
| 5. Physical Conditioning | 2 | – |
| 6. Nutrition - Dietetics | 2 | – |
| 7. Thesis Writing | Pro Men | – |
| 8. Seminars | Pro Men | – |
| | 12 | 2 |

Concerned with the need for expansion and upgrading of existing physical education and sports programs, the Indonesian Government explored ways in which the training program of prospective physical education teachers could be improved. In 1974, under auspices of the United Nations Educational, Scientific and Cultural Organization (UNESCO), Dr. Moolenijzer of the University of New Mexico assisted the "Directorate General of Sports, Health Education, Physical Education, Recreation, Community Development Education and Youth" in designing a master plan for a proposed Development Center for Health, Physical Education and Recreation and curriculum development.

## Sports and Athletics

The organization of sport in Indonesia is, as in most countries, administered by independent clubs and associations. Indonesians are very fond of sports and have participated in organized competition for many years. In the beginning all sports organizations were affiliated in the *Persatuan Olahraga Republik Indonesia* (Sport Federation of the Republic of Indonesia). When Indonesia became interested in participating in the Olympic Games, an administrative organization, the *Komite Olympiade Republik Indonesia* (Olympic Committee of the Republic of Indonesia) was established. In 1951 the two committees merged into the *Komite Olympiade Indonesia* (Indonesian Olympic Committee) which administered all national and international events until 1964, when it was dissolved. Its functions were later assumed by the *Komite Olahraga Nasional Indonesia* which was formed in 1966. One of the national events is the *Pekan Olahraga Nasional* (National Sports Week) which is held every four years. At present there are more than twenty-two sports associations which compete in various leagues and divisions for national championships. Since independence the participation of girls and women has increased significantly.

Most popular sports are those which form part of the Olympic program, such as soccer, field hockey, track and field, swimming, basketball, volleyball and tennis. Soccer and badminton are very popular and draw many participants. Badminton in particular is a favorite among the Indonesians. This year the national team clinched the Thomas Cup and the international championship for the third time. Lesser known sports such as marching and *pentjak* have a large following in Indonesia.

Marching is a team sport. Depending on its division, the team participates in marches over shorter or longer distances. The team's achievement is not decided by its recorded time only but depends also on its appearance and team work (synchronization). *Pentjak* is an indigenous art of self defense. It is a ceremonial sport, dating back to the eleventh century and is usually performed to the accompaniment of *gamelan* music. The name is derived from *tjak,* meaning step. The activity consists of a series of elaborate steps and kicks. The kick, the offensive weapon, is generally blocked by the hands. Some times the elbows constitute an offensive weapon. There are about as many forms of *pentjak* as there are regions in Indonesia but attempts to organize *pentjak* competitions have not been very successful. Recently, after many years of inactivity, girls have resumed the practice of *pentjak*. The sport requires, besides dexterity, strong concentration and considerable courage. Since Indonesian independence the armed forces have introduced a combination of *pentjak* and bayonet drill.

Another traditional and ritual sport on West Java is Indonesian archery; here one shoots with bamboo bows and arrows at straw pigeons placed on top of poles. One more remnant of the past is the exciting and colorful water buffalo races on the island of Madura.

One remarkable aspect of Indonesian sports life is the interest displayed by the government. Generally speaking the standard of living in Indonesia is still low and it is self-evident, therefore, that the population would not be able to participate if they were to defray all expense themselves. As there is no athletic program to speak of on the secondary school level all youth must depend on the opportunities that private sports associations have to offer. In order to make this feasible the government supports these sports programs to a large extent. Facilities, equipment and other support are often provided by the Directorate General for Sports. These subsidies are partly recouped by the gate receipts of important (international) athletic events and by the government's share of the income of the Totalizator. Athletes who have been selected to participate in international meets often receive special training at the national training center in Jakarta. The cost for these programs is also defrayed by the Directorate General's office.

As indicated previously, the universities do not offer programs or even facilities for participation in intra- or extramural sports. All athletic contact between universities is organized by the student organizations themselves and is coordinated by the *Badan Keolaragaan Mahasiswa Indonesia* (All Indonesian University Student Sports Union) which was established in 1953. Competition is organized in the following sports: soccer, volleyball, tennis, track and field, federation (team) handball, badminton, basketball, fencing, field hockey, water-polo, judo and baseball. For the latter the women substitute softball. Though the student associations receive some financial support from the Ministry of Education to assist them in the administration of their activities, all organization and administration is done by volunteer labor. In some instances this has included the installation of sport fields. Most of the moneys are used to defray the cost for leasing public or private facilities for practice and for equipment. Except for participation in the *Pekan Olahraga Mahasiswa* (University Students' Sports Week) there is no set varsity roster for competition. Various contests between university teams are held as a result of university celebrations or local festivities. At such occasions it is customary that the host team provide board and lodging while the visiting teams furnish their own traveling expenses which they earn through the organization of local projects. For participation in the University Students' Sports Week traveling funds are usually provided by local sponsors while the hosting community and the Ministry of Education and Culture defrays the expenses for board and lodging and other expenses that may accompany local organization.

## Miscellanea

*Dance.* Throughout the Indonesian archipelago many of the traditional dance forms have been preserved. Men and women participate in elaborate, characteristically stylized traditional dance movements. On Java the best known are the Javanese (Central Java) and Sundanese (West Java) styles. Central Sumatra is known for the intricate movements of the *Tari Piring* (saucer dance) which is performed with lighted candles affixed to saucers placed on the palms of the open hands. Most famous of all, of course, are the Balinese dance dramas which reflect the ancient influence of the island's Buddhist-Hindu heritage. In sharp contrast to the stately dance patterns executed to the melancholic music of the *gamelan* the *Gali-gali*, a Chachacha-like modern social dance of Indonesian origin, is danced to the tunes of Western music. In order to preserve the cultural heritage the Indonesian government encourages all efforts to maintain and expand local and regional folk dancing.

*Sport, Education and National Development.* As in other developing nations Indonesia's leaders have relied in many instances on physical education and sport as tools to stimulate national consciousness and national pride. Through sport it has been possible to reach a large section of the population which otherwise might have remained indifferent to educational programs. Indonesians are very fond of competition and sports events, both as participants and as spectators. Although the Asian Games and the GANEFO Games were overshadowed by political overtones, they nevertheless have produced positive results by stimulating national involvement in matters of international proportions. Education-wise the area of physical education, through its hierarchy of inspectors and teaching personnel, offers more possibilities for incidental education in matters other than physical education than any other government service. In situations where different government agencies, jealously guarding their own dominance, are not able to communicate, the physical educator often serves as the go-between in matters of local interest. The great interest for intra-regional and extra-regional sports events is partly stimulated by the opportunities for social education derived from the interchange of ethnic and geographically different peoples.

Indonesian sources proudly claim that no newly developed nation in the world shows a greater concern for the development of physical education and sport. A quantitative comparision of the ratio of population and the institutions for the training of specialists in the area of physical education and sports among various nations, other than the United States, ranks Indonesia highest.

Ratios of Institutions for the Training of Specialists and
Teachers in Physical Education and Sports in Various
Countries Per 1,000,000 Population

| | | Population Estimate 1966* | | Number of Insti-tutions | Institutions Per 1,000,000 Population | |
|---|---|---|---|---|---|---|
| | Country | All Ages | Ages 5-24 Years | | All Ages | 5-24 |
| 1. | INDONESIA | 107,000,000 | 39,001,508 | 76 | .710 | 1.949 |
| 2. | Austria | 7,290,000 | 2,097,293 | 4** | .549 | 1.907 |
| 3. | United Arab Republic | 30,147,000 | 10,927,410 | 10*** | .332 | .915 |
| 4. | Brazil | 84,679,000 | 32,038,343 | 11** | .130 | .343 |
| 5. | Venezuela | 9,030,000 | 4,068,800 | 1*** | .111 | .246 |
| 6. | India | 498,680,000 | 187,119,234 | ca. 50*** | .100 | .267 |
| 7. | Thailand | 31,508,000 | 11,995,459 | 3*** | .095 | .250 |
| 8. | Nigeria | 58,600,000 | not available | 4*** | .068 | |
| 9. | Colombia | 18,650,000 | 8,253,197 | 1— | .054 | .121 |
| 10. | Ethiopia | 23,000,000 | not available | 1** | .043 | —— |

  * United Nations. *Demographic Yearbook.* 1966.
  ** Phi Epsilon Kappa Fraternity. *Physical Education Around the World.* Monograph No. 3. 1969.
  *** Vendien, C. Lynn and Nixon, John E. *The World Today in Health, Physical Education, and Recreation.*
     1968.

# REFERENCES

1.    Academiach Instituut voor Lichaamsoefeningen. *Programma Cursus 1949–1950.* Bandung: AILO. 1949.

2.    Balai Perguruan Tinggi R. I. *Lembaga Akademi Pendidikan Djasmani.* Bandung: LAPD. 1951.

3.    Baudet, H. and Brugmans, I. J. (Eds.). *Balans van Beleid.* Assen: van Gorcum & Comp. N. V. - Dr. H. J. Prakke & H. M. Prakke. 1961.

4.    Biro Pusat Statistik. *Statistical Pocketbook of Indonesia 1961.* Jakarta: BPS. 1961.

5.    Department of State. "Republic of Indonesia." *Background Notes, No. 7786.* Washington, D. C.: U. S. Government Printing Office. 1969.

6.    Dewan Olahraga Republik Indonesia. *Mengapa Indonesia Menarik Diri dari Olympic Games Tokyo?* Siaran No. 1. Jakarta: DORI. 1964.

7.    Djumali, Moh. "Pentjak-Silat, Sedjarah dan Manfastnja bagi Pendidikan Djasmani dan Rochani," in *PUSARA*. (January 1961). pp. 21-31, 37.

8.    Games of the New Emerging Forces. *Documents of the First GANEFO Congress*. Jakarta: GANEFO. 1963.

9.    _____. *Documents on the Preparatory Conference for the GANEFO*. Jakarta: GANEFO. 1963.

10.   Games of the New Emerging Forces, Komite National. *Dokumen-Dokumen Kehahiran GANEFO*. Siaran No. 3. Jakarta: GANEFO. 1963.

11.   _____. *GANEFO*. Siaran No. 2. Jakarta: GANEFO. 1963.

12.   Indonesian Olympic Committee. *Indonesia and the International Olympic Committee*. Jakarta: IOC. 1963.

13.   Indonesia, Republik, Departemen Pendidikan dan Kebudajaan, Direktorat Djenderal Olaraga; Keputusan Direktur Djenderal Olahraga No. 57, Tahun 1967, tentag Peraturan Dasar Sekolah Tinggi Olahraga.

14.   Indonesia, Republik, Direktorat Djenderal Olahraga. *Kertas-Kerdja Direktorat Djenderal Olahraga pada Musjawarsh Nasional Olahraga Ke I di Jakarta pada tgl*. 26 September, 1967.

15.   Indonesia, Republik, Keputusan Menteri Pendidikan, Pengadjaran dan Kebudajaan. No. 66437/Kab., ttgl. 2 Nopember, 1955.

16.   Indonesia, Republik, Keputusan Presiden No. 94, Tahun 1962, tentang Departemen Olahraga.

17.   Indonesia, Republik, Keputusan Presiden No. 131, Tahun 1962, tentang Tugas dan Fungsi Departemen Olahraga.

18.   Indonesia, Republik, Keputusan Presiden No. 23, Tahun 1963, tentang Pendirian Sekolah Tinggi Olahraga.

19.   Indonesia, Republik, Keputusan Presiden N. 176, Tahun 1964, tentang Pembentukan Dewan Olahraga Republik Indonesia.

20.   Indonesia, Republik, Undang-Undang Dasar Sementara R. I. (1950).

21.   Indonesia, Republik, Undang-Undang No. 12, Tahun 1954, tentang Dasar-dasar Pendidikan dan Pengadjaran di-Sekolah, Lembaran Negara Tahun 1954, No. 38.

22.  Instituut Pendidikan Djasmani. *Prospektus*. Jogjakarta: IPD. 1950.

23.  Komite Olahraga Nasional Indonesia, Keputusan Sidang KONI PARIPURNA I, tanggal 26 s/d. 29 Februari, 1968, di Jakarta.

24.  Lembaga Akademi Pendidikan Djasmani. *Lembaga Akademi Pendidikan Djasmani*. Bandung: LAPD. 1950.

25.  Moolenijzer, Nicolaas J. "Physical Education in Austria," in *Physical Education Around the World*. Monograph No. 3. Indianapolis: Phi Epsilon Kappa Fraternity. 1969.

26.  _____. *Indonesia - Physical Education and Sports Development*. (Serial #3035/RMO.RD/ESM). Paris: UNESCO. 1974.

27.  Oen, B. T. A letter dated March 31, 1969 in "Physical Education and Sports in Indonesia." Unpublished paper by Swanpo Sie: University of Missouri - Columbia. Winter 1968/1969. p. 93.

28.  Sekolah Tinggi Olahraga Bandung. *Kurikulum Sekolah Tinggi Olahraga*. Bandung: STO. 1967.

29.  Sie, Swanpo, "Perkembangan Gerakan-gerakan Keolshragaan Mahasiswa Indonesis Sedjak 1950," in *Kenang-kenangan Pekan Olahraga Mahasiswa IV*. Jogjakarta: Panitia Penjelenggara POM IV. 1958. pp. 13-19.

30.  _____. "A Proposed Curriculum for the Undergraduate Study at the Sekolah Tinggi Olahraga in Indonesia." Unpublished paper, Madjelis Pendidikan Djasmani, Jarkarta, Indonesia, May, 1964.

31.  _____. "The Problem of Administration in Physical Culture and Sports in Indonesia." Unpublished paper, School of Health Education, Physical Education and Recreation, University of Minnesota, Minneapolis, 1965.

32.  UNESCO. *Studies on Compulsory Education, Compulsory Education in Indonesia* by M. Hutasoit. Paris: UNESCO. 1954.

33.  United Nations. *Demographic Yearbook 1966*. 18th Issue. New York: Statistical Office of the United Nations, Department of Economic and Social Affairs. 1967.

34.  Universitas Gadjah Mada, Fakultas Pendidikan Djasmani. *Pedoman Fakultas 1962-1963*. Jogjakarta: Universitas Gadjah Mada. 1962.

35.   Universitas Padjadjaran, Fakultas Keguruan dan Ilmu Pendidikan. *Pedoman, Tahun Akademi 1957-1958.* Bandung: Universitas Padjadjaran. 1957.

36.   Universitet Indonesia. *Lembaga Akademi Pendidikan Djasmani.* Bandung: LAPD. 1952.

37.   Vendien, C. Lynn and Nixon, John E. *The World Today in Health, Physical Education and Recreation.* Englewood Cliffs: Prentice-Hall. 1968.

# SPORT AND PHYSICAL EDUCATION IN ISRAEL

by Moshe Schneider and Larry Horine

## Biographical Sketches

*Moshe Schneider* was born at Rishon Le Zion, Israel in 1938 and received his teacher certificate in 1964 and the high school teacher certificate in 1972 at the State Teachers College, Beer Sheva. His Master of Arts Degree was taken in 1977 at Appalachian State University in Boone, North Carolina. Mr. Schneider's major was in physical education with a minor in education.

Mr. Schneider held positions of teacher of physical education in the Elementary School of Beer Sheva from 1964-72; was an instructor in physical education at the State Teachers College, Beer Sheva in 1968-75; an instructor in physical education at Ben Gurion University, Beer Sheva in 1972; a supervisor of physical education in the Ministry of Education in 1973-76; a graduate assistant in the Department of HPER, Appalachian State University, Boone, North Carolina, 1976-77; and presently is Chariman, Department of Physical Education at Beer Sheva Teachers College, Beer Sheva, Israel.

*Larry Horine* is chairman and professor, Department of HPER, Appalachian State University, Boone, North Carolina. In part the information and documentation of this article on Sport and Physical Education in Israel was submitted in partial fulfillment of the requirements for the M.A. Degree in Physical Education at Appalachian State University by Mr. Schneider under the supervision of Dr. Horine.

Dr. Horine received his B.S., M.A., and Ed.D., degrees in 1953, 1957 and 1966 respectively at the University of Colorado, Boulder. His teaching experience includes: Cheyene Wells High School, Colorado, 1953-54; Sports Officer, Ramey A.F.B., Puerto Rico, 1954-56; Graduate Assistant, Athletic Department, University of Colorado, 1956-57, Balboa High School, Canal Zone, 1957-61; Supervising Director of HPERSA, U. S. Canal Zone Schools, 1961-68. He has been in his present position for the past nine years.

Dr. Horine has published widely; holds many professional offices; and has made major presentations at important professional meetings. He has visited eleven

countries in Europe; most of the countries in the West
Indies; and to many Latin American countries. He has
attended the Munich and Montreal Olympic Games. He
was selected by AAHPER as a sports consultant to Mexico in 1976. He is editor of the North Carolina International Relations Newsletter and has just been appointed
as editor of the "Elsewhere in the World" Department of
*The Physical Educator* of Phi Epsilon Kappa Fraternity.

## General Background

This dynamic country of about three million population has
existed as an independent state only since 1948. However, the Land
of Israel comprising roughly the same region has been in existence
since the conclusion of WWI as a result of the Balfour Declaration
which was a mandate received by the British from the League of Nations to govern the area and ultimately establish a homeland for the
Jewish people. Although Hebrew is the official language, English
and other languages are used widely since a substantial number of
the citizens are recent immigrants. Because Israel is surrounded by
seven countries that are generally hostile, the constant need to prepare for war has greatly influenced education in general, and physical
education in particular. While the socio-political exigencies have im-
peded the growth of physical education and sport because of restric-
tive budgets, the same forces have supported the continual expansion
of physical education to assist in preparing a citizenry of high physical fitness qualities[24:40; 23:9; 29:7].

## History of Physical Education

Physical education was formally established in the Land of
Israel early in the Twentieth Century largely through the efforts of
Abraham Zvi Goldsmith, who was on the faculty of the General Teacher's College *Ezhra*, located in Jerusalem, and Zvi Nishri, who began
teaching physical education at Hertzeliha High School in 1906. At
that time, a gymnastics sports club called *Bar-Giora* was started which
later became the first Jewish sports organization in the country entitled the Maccabi[24:38; 29:7-10].

The first physical education textbook in Hebrew, *Gymnastics
Lessons*, written by Nishri was published in 1920. In 1927, there
were about ten physical educators in Israel who originated a Physical
Education Teacher's Organization. The international athletic competition similar to the Olympics in Israel, the Maccabiha Games, was first
held in 1932[24:49-50].

An important stage in the history of physical education in the
Land of Israel was the origination of the first Physical Training Department of the *Va'ad Le Ummi* in 1937. The director was Dr. Immanu-
el Simon, a sports physician. The department was responsible for all

physical education and employed the first supervisor of physical education in 1938, Mr. Joshua Alouf(24:36, 49-50; 30:12; 1:16).

## General Education Organization

The administrative structure of education in Israel followed during the British Mandate was continued until 1966 at which time it was reorganized. The following is the new structure:

| | | |
|---|---|---|
| Pre-kindergarten | - | one year |
| Kindergarten | - | one year |
| Elementary | - | six years |
| Middle school | - | three years |
| High school | - | three years |
| Higher education | - | three or more years |

Because of budgetry and facility restrictions, not all programs have yet changed to this new structure(23:149).

In Israel, education is further divided into general state education and religious state education. Students have a choice of which they attend. Education through the middle school is free and compulsory while tuition is charged for high school. Following the British system, students must pass a qualifying examination to be admitted to the academic tract(11:1; 23:149).

To be admitted to colleges or universities, students must earn a "Bagrut" certificate, as well as graduating from high school. To earn this certificate, students must pass examinations in four core subjects: *Bible*, Hebrew, English, and mathematics. In addition, two elective areas must be selected such as history, physics, a foreign language, physical education, etc.(23:150).

## Aims and Objectives

The aims of physical education in Israel is defined as the development and cultivation of physical education, improving health, shaping of personal and social behavior; and the preparation for efficient performance of functions in society, learning situations, work, and in defense and leisure.

Objectives promulgated to achieve these aims include the following: (1) The physical; (2) Knowledge and understanding; (3) Social; (4) Emotional and personal. Included in the physical area are physical fitness (including cardiovascular, strength and power, neuromuscular, and flexibility), physical skills, and good posture. Within the knowledge and understanding area, are learning the basis facts, terms, and rules. Included in the social area are learning to participate in a group to achieve a common goal, sportsmanship, and to develop habits of participation. Under the emotional and personal area, students learn to enrich life through achievement, employ creativity and express movement, gain aesthetic experience from movement and enhance body image; develop habits of discipline, punctuality, and personal hygiene; and encourage characteristics such as courage, persistence, and intuition.

Those students attending religious schools also have additional objectives to the above(11:8-9; 12:5-7; 13:5-9; 26:5-6).

## Physical Education for Elementary School

Generally, the classroom teacher is responsible for the physical education classes on the lower elementary level, however, there is a trend for physical education specialists to be assigned to do this. Specialists trained at a teachers' colleges now teach the physical education classes in grade four and higher. The classes are coeducational through grade six and thereafter segregated and taught by an instructor of the same sex. The first three grades receive two hours per week in the general state schools and one hour per week in the religious schools. Starting in 1971, time was added for physical education, and by 1976, there were three hours per week for grades four through eight in the general schools and two hours per week in religious schools(25:11; 14:2-3; 7:9; 5:3; 20:par. 148; 8:86; 22: par. 268).

The physical education curriculum was revised in 1969 as a result of a council of 40 members being appointed through the curriculum center of the Ministry of Education. Dr. Dov Aldoby from Wingate College was named chairman of the committee. The study resulted in new curricular guides for all levels although the program for the early grades are in non-specific terms since these grades are generally taught physical education by the classroom teacher(11:1; 14:1A; 26:3).

The new curriculum stipulates the number of classes per year that must be devoted to each activity or skill starting with grade three and it is mandatory to follow the guide. The areas included for elementary physical education are as follows: fitness, motor learning, basic skills, movement games, swimming and water activities, dance, jazz, folk dance, track and field, gymnastics, soccer, basketball, volleyball, team handball, racquet games, and cross country. In the early grades (grades three and four), the emphasis is on fitness, track and field, and volleyball. However, time for tests, basic skills, motor learning and dance and other such activities are still stipulated (18:par. 123; 11:12-14; 6:34).

All students in grade six were required to complete the fitness test unless excused. Until 1976, the test items for boys and girls are similar except for sex adjustments and include the following: (1) sixty meter sprint; (2) long jump, high jump, and stand long jump; (3) throwing field hockey ball, shot putting for boys, and throwing a "Telly-Ball" for girls; (4) sit-ups in thirty seconds; (5) push-ups, chin-ups for boys, and bar hang and movement to side for girls. A special small lapel medal is awarded to all students who score at the outstanding level in all sections(7:10; 14:15).

## Middle School Physical Education

This level of education has been the slowest to become fully implemented of the revised curriculum. By 1973, only 127 schools with about 40,000 students were organized under the new structure. The physical education classes in the middle schools are designed to be separated sexually; however, depending on facility and staffing problems, many classes are still held with boys and girls together(12: 20-21; 25:11; 8:95). All students are required to take a swimming test in grade seven and complete the physical fitness test during grade nine.

The physical education curriculum for middle schools for girls is based on two classes per week. On all three grades (7-9) about thirty per cent of the total time (2880 minutes) is devoted to each of the following: basic skills, track and field, gymnastics, and, on grade seven, team handball. Lesser time is spent on dance, testing, and racquet sports. In grades eight and nine, more time is devoted to basketball and volleyball(12:20).

The boys have physical education two times a week (2880 minutes), of which about twelve per cent of the total time is devoted to fitness on all three grades. Approximately fourteen per cent of the time is used for gymnastics and nearly half of the total minutes is devoted to track and field, basic skills, and fitness. A small amount of time is used for racquet and movement games, and dance with the remaining approximate thirty-seven per cent of time allowed for team games of basketball, volleyball, team handball, and soccer. The new curriculum suggested a future program of three classes a week(13:17).

## Physical Education in High Schools

High school physical education classes are held twice per week and are required every year for both men and women. The curriculum revision committee suggested three classes per week, gymnastics, track and field, basketball, volleyball, team handball, and swimming if facilities permit. The women had additional areas in dance (modern dance and jazz) and movement, while soccer is included in only the men's curriculum. A substantial amount of time (almost thirty per cent) in grade twelve is structured for elective activities(12:21; 13: 15-17).

Until 1976, physical fitness testing in high school was mandatory and students were required to complete the test annually. The test, which was based primarily on track and field events, included sprints, middle and long distance running, jumping events, shot putting, and strength exercises such as chin-ups and pull-ups(16:1-3; 33:16).

The lack of appropriate facilities has adversely affected both the physical education curriculum and after school competition. In 1973, it was reported that slightly less than half the high schools in Israel had a gymnasium. Many of the existing facilities are small and without sufficient dressing and storage space or showers. In 1975, a new law required the inclusion of a gymnasium in every new school built(15:4; 7:10).

Although there is no "varsity interscholastic" type of competition with paid coaches and expansive budgets, there are regularly scheduled sports days, intramurals, and local district, and national competitions in such sports as basketball, volleyball, team handball, track and field, and cross country. Israel is a member of the International Sports Federation of Schools (I.S.F.) and has been represented recently by Mr. Shalom Hermon, the chief supervisor of physical education in Israel(12:87-88; 33:16; 16:34; 17:10; 30:53-54).

During the school year 1976-77, a new complete battery of skill and fitness testing was implemented. This battery starts with a skills test at the conclusion of grade four; track and field and swimming test in grades six, nine, and twelve; track and field in grade seven; track and field and gymnastics in grade eight; abilities in team games in grade ten; and, a recreational activities test in grade eleven (11:7-62).

## Physical Education in Higher Education

In Israel, higher education is differentiated into college and universities. In 1976, there were 60 teachers' colleges, and eight universities. Physical education is required in both types of institutions usually meeting twice a week. There is no prescribed curriculum or tests. The instructors are graduates of teachers colleges in Israel or institutions abroad(19:par. 219; 32:153; 29:6-9; 31:1-10).

The instructors in the teachers colleges continue some of the high school curriculum activities, and many of the university instructors emphasize their particular specialties. For example, the following courses were offered at Ben-Gurion University for the 1976-77 school year: fencing, swimming, basketball, shot put, karate, fitness, and firing range supervision(31:5).

## Teacher Preparation for Physical Education

There are four teachers colleges for professional physical educators in Israel. Wingate College and State Teachers College in Beer-Sheva were independent colleges from their inception, while the other two, Seminar Ha' Kibbutzim College in Tel-Aviv, and the religious college in Givhat Washington were organized as physical education departments in general colleges. The entrance requirements, curriculum, and certificate received are all similar(7:10; 19:31-32; 25:12).

The general requirement for admission to the four special physical education teachers colleges is to have completed twelve years of study and have a "Bagrut" certificate. All students take examinations in skill ability, knowledge, and sometimes psychological evaluation(32:2; 32:5).

The school year runs from early September to mid-June and subjects generally are scheduled to be taught all year rather than by terms. The course of study was two years long from 1953 to 1968 at which time it was expanded to a three year program. Included in the curriculum are the following subjects: Hebrew language and culture, pedagogic, psychology, geography, statistics, history of sports and physical education, phonetics, track and field, swimming, tumbling, dance, folk dance, team handball, volleyball, basketball, soccer, first-aid, movement games, physiology of exercise, psychology of sports, biomechanics, organization and administration, planning facilities in schools, and practicum teaching(9:52; 32:2; 34:4, 13-15; 2:4; 5:8; 27:17).

Wingate Physical Education Teacher's College was the first physical education institute in Israel and is perhaps the best known institution related to physical education in Israel. It opened in 1944 in Tel-Aviv and until 1953 the course of study was for only one year. Although the college started out with very limited facilities, it now has the best in the state including classrooms, weight room, fitness rooms, swimming pool, stadium, outdoor fields and courts, and track and field facilities. Since all teacher college programs are three years or less, one earns a certificate rather than a Bachelor's Degree; however, since 1973 the Tel-Aviv University has recognized the three year course of study at Wingate College as the equivalent to a minor subject of the first academic degree. Several international conferences on such topics as motor learning have been held at Wingate and it also serves as a training center for national teams of Israel(9:51); 32:6; 31:9-10; 2:4; 5:8-18; 27:17; 22:13; 33: 15; 7:10; 34:1).

Through the encouragement of Dr. Elly Friedmann, the State Teachers' College of Physical Education of Beer-Sheva was established in 1963. The primary aim of this institution was to supply physical education teachers to the southern district of Israel which was in short supply. In 1972, the duration of study was increased from two years to three years. By 1977, there were ten classes with 300 students in attendance(5:8; 32:1; 7:10; 29:1). *Seminar Ha' Kibbutzim* was a general teachers' college in Tel-Aviv in which a physical education section was founded in 1944 under the guidance of Mrs. Judith Bineter as a private school. Programs in dance, movement, and free gymnastics were emphasized. *Givat Washington* was founded in 1963.

It became a department in a religious college and its course of study has paralleled the other three in length and content except for the added religious component(15:8).

## Supervision and Teacher Status

The organization of physical education in Israel is centralized and in 1938 Jehoshua Alouf was selected as the first supervisor(1:16). The structure was revised in 1970 and Mr. Raphael Penon was named chief supervisor and served in this capacity until 1975. Following his retirement, Mr. Shalom Hermon was promoted to the post. The country is divided into six districts and there are sixteen supervisors (part-time and full-time) to cover all levels in all districts. Many supervisors are responsible for 100-250 elementary, middle and high schools involving 250-300 professional teachers(7:9; 21:1).

Although originally physical education instructors were not compensated on the same pay schedule as regular teachers, they are now. Reimbursement is based on degrees and experience with automatic increases for 21 years familiar to classroom teachers. As in most countries, students are required to attend more school days per year in the lower schools thus requiring teachers on the lower levels to work more days per year. Thirty paid sick days are allowed annually(10:41, 50, 60).

## National Defense and Physical Education

For the purpose of preparing the young men and women of Israel for defense of their country, there has been strong support for physical fitness. The origina name for the national military preparation was *Gadna*. In 1975, this was changed to *Shelack*, the combination of the words *Sadee* (field), *Leom* (nation), and *Chevra* (society). *Shelack* is an active program in and out of schools whose purposes are to develop fitness and shooting ability, activities in the field, discipline habits, leadership, loyalty to the country, awareness of security, and friendship and teamwork(15:10-11).

## Physical Education Teachers' Organization

About 2,800 teachers belong to the organization which was founded in 1927. The organization is administered by a national conference of 137 members who are elected in districts. The national conference elects a national council of 32 members which in turn elects a management committee of seven. The organization published information bulletins for physical education teachers such as *Igeret* and the physical education journal, *Hachinuch HaGufany*. A profoundly worded statement of 18 ethical principles is promulgated by the physical education teachers' organization which calls for the highest of professional standards(14:46-48; 2:3; 5:21; 6:3; 24:50; 28:58).

# History of Sport

As in many nations, the origin of sport in Israel grew out of gymnastics. The first sport clubs formed in 1906 were primarily gymnastics oriented; Bar-Giora club in Jerusalem and the Rishon-Lezion club in Jaffa. Subsequently, in 1909 the Bar-Giora was replaced by a club called Shimshon and in 1911 by the Maccabee club. The later club was expanded in 1912 to the National Maccabee Association which grew to twenty clubs and about 1,000 members by the start of World War I(29:2).

As a result of British influence, by 1928, soccer replaced gymnastics as the most popular sport. Through the Maccabee club and the Hapoel club working together, a soccer association was formed which led to eventually competing in the 1934 World Cup Games. The Hopoel club, which was organized by workers, concentrated its efforts on mass activities as well as soccer joining the International Association of Labour Sport (SASI) in 1927(29:3).

These two clubs have continued to stimulate and organize much of the large sporting events and festivals of the country. The Hapoel club had held its first national festival in 1928 and in recent years has staged this festival of competition every five years. The Maccabee club formed the Maccabiah in 1932 which has become widely recognized as the Jewish Olympics. The Maccabiah is scheduled every four years following each Olympics Games(29:3). The last Maccabiah Games was held in July, 1977.

## Olympic Competition

The National Olympic Committee was formed in 1935 and the nation entered competitions in the 1952 Olympic Games for the first time. Probably because a substantial percentage of the population are immigrants, there has been intense interest in international competition. Naturally, invitations to compete in the 1936 games in Berlin were rejected and a team could not participate in the 1948 games because Palestine no longer existed and the new Olympic Committee of Israel was not yet recognized(29:3).

In the continuing development of Olympic involvement, a milestone was achieved in the 1960 games in Tokyo. Thirty-two athletes represented Israel(29:4). In Munich, the strong team from Israel was decimated by the despicable act of a terrorist gang resulting in the deaths of eleven athletes and coaches. With the typical resilience of these people, another strong delegation was sent to the Montreal Games in 1976 with many fine athletes.

## Sport Federations

Since soccer is the most popular sport in Israel, it is not surprising that the oldest organization is the Football (soccer) Association which was founded in 1928. Sponsored by the Association are over 550 teams and 15,000 players. The national soccer team has competed favorably in World Cup, Olympic, and Asian Games(29:4). The writer had the privilege of witnessing a fine Olympic contest in 1976 in Montreal between Israel and France which concluded in a one-to-one tie.

The organization which controls the largest number of sports is the Sports Federation which was founded in 1931. This organization controls 16 sports through over 400 clubs with over 22,000 active members. The sports with the largest number of participants are: (1) Volleyball with about 6,000 members; (2) European handball with about 3,000 members; and (3) Fencing, Table Tennis and Swimming(29:4).

More recently popular sports in Israel are Tennis and Basketball. The Tennis Association was formed in 1950 and now number over 60 clubs and Israel has competed in the Davis Cup regularly since 1949. Basketball has become very popular recently following the origination of the Basketball Union in 1968. It now has about 500 teams with about 15,000 players and among all sports appears to have the best record in international competition(27:7). The Basketball team of Maccabi Tel Aviv won the European Basketball Cup of 1977.

## Sport and Minorities and the Kibbutzim

There is a trend of increased participation in sport by Arabian minorities in Israel, and to probably a greater degree for women. Perhaps due to the males being involved in military duties, but more likely due to gradual awakening of abilities and opportunities, the women in Israel are expected to become more involved in sport in the future.

Although only about five per cent of the population live within the Kibbutzim, a much greater proportion participate in sport. A large majority of the volleyball teams in the nation are from the Kibbutzim. About one-third of the basketball teams and a majority of the swimming teams are also from the Kibbutzim(29:7).

## Sport and Youth

Although most of the sport organizations are associated with political parties, the Academic Sport Association is politically independent. This organization (A.S.A.) was founded in 1953 and represents Israel in international student competition(29:4).

In addition to the extensive opportunities for students to engage in competitive sport through clubs and associations, there are programs associated with the schools. Competition on the secondary level are held on the local, district, and national levels.

### Number of Competing Teams 1972-73

|  | Total | Boys | Girls |
|---|---|---|---|
| Basketball | 250 | 160 | 90 |
| Volleyball | 130 | 90 | 40 |
| Handball (Europe) | 95 | 70 | 25 |
| Football (soccer) | 90 | 90 | |
| Track and Field (Athletics) | 430 | 230 | 200(29:9-10) |

### Sports Schools

Through the Sports Authority, special summer camps for outstanding athletes are arranged for elementary and secondary school students. In addition, special courses for referees and sport leaders are also held during vacations(29:10).

### SELECTED REFERENCES

1.    Alouf, Joshua. Memories of the first physical education supervisor. *Kovetz*. Wingate Institute, Netanya. November-December. 1965.

2.    Alouf, Joshua. *Sports and Physical Education in Israel*. Wingate Institute, Netanya. 1971.

3.    Ben-David, Asael. The sports and physical education authority. *Physical Education and Sports in Israel*. Wingate Institute, Netanya. 1968.

4.    Farhi, Asher. Physical education teacher's college in Israel. *The Physical Educator*. Vol. 22, No. 1, March, 1965, pp. 39-41.

5.    Glasberg, Glill. *The Sports and Physical Education in Israel*. Wingate Institute with the Sports and Physical Education Authority. Segal, Tel-Aviv. March, 1973.

6.    Ha'Chinuch, Ha'Gufany. *The Supervision of Physical Education in Schools*. Wingate Institute, Netanya. January-February. 1971.

7.    Hermon, Shalom. Physical Education in Israel. *Sports and Physical Education in Israel.* Wingate Institute with the Sports and Physical Education Authority. Segal, Tel-Aviv. January, 1974.

8.    International Council on Health, Physical Education and Recreation. *Physical Education in School Curriculum. International Questionnaire Report, 1967-68 revision.* Part I, Washington, D. C., USA. 1969.

9.    International Council on Health, Physical Education and Recreation. *Teacher Training for Physical Education. International Questionnaire Report, 1967-68 revision.* Part II, Washington, D. C. USA. 1969.

10.   International Council on Health, Physical Education and Recreation. *Status of Teachers of Physical Education. International Questionnaire Report, 1967-68 revision.* Part III, Washington, D. C. USA. 1969.

11.   Ministry of Education and Culture. The Curriculum Planning Center Committee. *Physical Education Curriculum for General and Religious Kindergarten and Six Grades in Schools.* Jerusalem. 1974.

12.   Ministry of Education and Culture. The Curriculum Planning Center Committee. *Physical Education Curriculum for Girls in Middle and High Schools.* Jerusalem. 1974.

13.   Ministry of Education and Culture. The Curriculum Planning Center Committee. *Physical Education Curriculum for Boys in Middle and High Schools.* Jerusalem. 1974.

14.   Ministry of Education and Culture. The Curriculum Planning Center Committee. *A Planning Guide in Teaching Physical Education.* Jerusalem. 1975.

15.   Ministry of Education and Culture. *Gadna Teaching in High Schools.* Jerusalem. 1971.

16.   Ministry of Education and Culture. *The Physical Education Tables Test in Ninth-Twelfth Grades.* The Sports and Physical Education Authority with the Supervision of Physical Education.

17.   Ministry of Education and Culture. *The New Physical Education Test in Fourth-Twelfth Grades in Schools.* The Sports and Physical Education Authority with the Supervision of Physical Education. Tel-Aviv. 1976.

18. Ministry of Education and Culture. The New physical educa-
    tion curriculum. *A Circular Letter From the General Director
    of the Ministry of Education and Culture to Schools.* No. 34/6,
    par. 123. February, 1974.

19. Ministry of Education and Culture. The list of colleges in
    Israel. *A Circular Letter From the General Director of the
    Ministry of Education and Culture to Schools.* No. 36/8, par.
    219. April, 1976.

20. Ministry of Education and Culture. Addition of one physical
    education hour per week to the fourth grade. *A Circular Let-
    ter From the General Director of Ministry of Education and
    Culture to Schools.* No. 32/7, par. 118. 1972.

21. Ministry of Education and Culture. Addition of one physical
    education hour per week to the sixth grade. *A Circular Let-
    ter From the General Director of the Ministry of Education
    and Culture to Schools.* No. 33/8, par. 181. 1973.

22. Ministry of Education and Culture. Addition of one physical
    education hour per week to the eighth grade. *A Circular Let-
    ter From the General Director of the Ministry of Education and
    Culture to Schools.* No. 36/10, par. 168. June, 1976.

23. Ministry of Information in Israel. *Facts About Israel.* Jeru-
    salem. 1975.

24. Nishri, Zvi. *The History of Physical Education.* The Ministry
    of Education and Culture, and the Supervision of Physical Ed-
    ucation. Tel-Aviv. 1953.

25. Panon, Raphael. *Physical Education in Elementary Schools
    and Physical Education Teacher's Training.* Wingate Institute,
    Netanya. 1968.

26. Raskin, Hillel. The new physical education curriculum in ele-
    mentary schools. *Ha'Chinuch Ha'Gufany.* Wingate Institute,
    Netanya. January-February, 1973.

27. Raskin, Hillel. The beginning of the two year course study.
    *Ha'Chinuch Ha'Gufany.* Wingate Institute, Natanya. May-June,
    1970.

28. Simri, Uriel. A dissertation, physical education and sports in
    Eretz-Israel prior to World War I. Wingate Institute with the
    Sports and Physical Education Authority. 1971.

29. Simri, Uriel (Editor). *Sport and Physical Education in Israel.*
    Wingate Institute for Physical Education. 1974.

30. Simri, Uriel and Bnajahu Mair. *Physical Education and Sports in Eretz-Israel Prior to World War I.* Wingate Institute with the Sports and Physical Education Authority. 1969.

31. Simri, Uriel and Paz Isrea. *Sports - Anything That You Want Wanted to Know About Sports.* Wingate Institute and the Sports and Physical Education Authority. February, 1975.

32. The Physical Education and Sports Department. *Information Pamphlet, 1976.* Ben-Gurion University, Beer-Sheva. October, 1976.

33. The Physical Education State Teacher's College in Beer-Sheva. *Information Pamphlet.* The State Teacher's College, Beer-Sheva. 1975.

34. Wein, Chaim. *Physical Education and Premilitary Training in High Schools.* Wingate Institute, Natanya. 1968.

35. Wingate Teacher's College. *Information Pamphlet, 1975.* Wingate Institute, Natanya. 1975.

# SPORT AND PHYSICAL EDUCATION IN ITALY

## by Michele Di Donato

### Biographical Sketch

*Miehele Di Donato* was born at Torre del Greco, Italy on January 15, 1915. He attended the Academy of Physical Education in Rome and received his diploma in 1936. Presently he teaches physical education in the Secondary Schools and is a professor of History of Physical Education at the Superior Institute of Physical Education in Rome.

As a member of a Ministerial Commission, Professor Di Donato was instrumental in reforming the secondary curriculum in physical education (Lido di Camaiore 1965-66). He also was appointed by the Minister of Public Instruction to the board of the Children's National Center for Physical Education and Sport Education and to the Institute of Neuropsychiatry of the University of Rome.

He collaborated from 1947-1960 with the Catholic Encyclopedia and with the Encyclopedia dello Spettacolo (show). From 1953 to 1960 he was directly responsible for news of physical education for the National Physical Education Association of Italy.

Professor Di Donato has written widely as follows: *Physical Education, Gymnastics, and Sports*, Firenze 1954 (Catholic Encyclopedia, Vol. 1950-51-53); *Fundamental Elements to the Modern Physical Education*, Rome, 1962; *A Way to Teach Physical Education in the Elementary Schools*, 3rd Edition, Florence, 1969. *Girolamo Mercuriale—M.D. and Professor of Humanities of the 16th Century*, Naples, 1964; *Exercise With the Ball in the Classic Times*, Trapani, 1965; *The Use of Physical Exercise in the "City of the Sun" of Tommaso* Campanella, Trapani, 1966; and the *First Chronological Collection With Eight Letters from the Call of Letters from Girolamo Mercuriale*, Trapani, 1969.

Physical Education

Historical Development and School Laws:

Physical Education has been taught in Italian education institutions since the beginning of the 19th century. Three regions, Cam-
pania, Lombardy, and Piedmont are pioneers in this field but following the political and military events of that century the region of
Piedmont took the lead. Between 1833 and 1844 through the efforts
of Oberman (called from Zurich in 1833) gymnastics was introduced in
the military and civilian circles. Later Count Richard di Netri joined
Obermann and their combined campaign and work brought about the
introduction of gymnastics in the kindergartens of Turin. In 1849
the Gymnastics Association of Turin was founded; it was the first of
its kind in Italy.

With the Casati Law (1859) which was to give a permanent
structure to the organization of the schools in Italy, physical education was officially introduced in the state-school-system. The "Mini-
stro alla Pubblica Instruzione" Francesco De Sanctis (1861) provides
for the establishment of a special school for the training of physical
education teachers connected with the Gymnastic Association of Turin.
Another De Sanctis Las (No. 4442--July 7, 1878) makes "ginnastica
educativa" (educational gymnastics) compulsory in the elementary and
secondary schools.

Two schools were in contention at this time to influence the
choice of methodology in the field of physical education. The school
of Turin (Ricardi di Netro, Valletti, Gamba) supported a "ginnastica
educativa" and "militare" begun by Obermann (who died in 1869,
while the school of Bologna (Reyer, Baumann, and Gallo) favored a
"ginnastica educative" and as the same time "razionale".

The programs of 1878, slightly modified in 1886 when Valletti
and Baumann came to a compromise, were completely revised in 1893
following a strong campaign for renewal on the part of scientists and
educators (Todaro, Mosso, Celli, Baumann, Abbondati and others).
The use of heavy apparatus (side horse, parallel bars, rings, etc.)
widely employed at that time was discontinued and in their place was
introducee the use of games of many kinds. It was a victory for
Mosso and Baumann at the time, but the practical results were negligible. The new programs could not be applied due to the lack of
facilities and scarcity of adequately trained teachers. The only
accomplishment was a change of name from "educazione ginnastica" to
"educazione fisica". With the law No. 805 of December 26, 1909 the
structure of physical education underwent a complete reorganization,
thus fulfilling the wishes expressed by many during the years 1892-
1893. The law restates that physical education is a compulsory subject in all schools, elementary (1/2 hour daily) and secondary (not
less than three hours a week). A semester of physical education is
also to be taught at the University schools of medicine for all medical students and all university students working toward a degree in

education in the secondary schools regardless of their major. The roles of school personnel were also reorganized and the schools for the training for physical education teachers were renamed "Istituti de Magistero di Educazione Fisica" (Rome, Turin, Naples) and were open only to students who had obtained the diploma of a secondary school, 2d degree (level). Also the position of "Ispetore centrale" for physical education was created. This law couldn't be practically enforced due to the national and international events of those years (Lybian War, World War I) and for lack of a responsible directive body.

After World War I three new concepts developed in the field of physical education teaching: Romano Guerra, new director of the Magistero in Rome favored a "rational" and at the same time "sport-influenced" physical education outside the schools. Giuseppe Monti aimed at a compromise between the traditional programs of Turin and the new ideas of Buamann, programs to be developed in the school. General Luigi Gasparoto supported a program of physical education under the direction of the military.

The Gentile Law of 1923 which aimed to change completely the structure of the school put an end to the controversy. The teaching of physical education was entrusted to an organization outside the school, the "Ente Nazionale per l'Educazione Fisica" (E.N.E.F.) (decree No. 684 of March 15, 1923 and No. 3039 of December 31, 1923). This plan proved to be a complete failure.

In 1927 the task of teaching physical education in the schools was taken over by a new organization, the "Opera Nazionale Balilla" (O.N.B.), a typical organization of the fascist regime. The President of the organization automatically became the Undersecretary of State for the education of the youth and for physical education at the dependence of the Ministero della P.I. (decree No. 2341 of November 20, 1927, and decree No. 1661 of September 12, 1929 and No. 1992 of November 14, 1929). A dyarchy (school and youth organization) had thus taken place in the field of physical education. At this same time two new Academies of Physical Education were instituted in Rome and Orvieto to replace the Magisteri which had been closed in 1923 when the E.N.E.F. was founded. Physical education was expanded and assumed an eclectic character. New facilities for physical education and sport activities were built in large numbers. Eugenio Ferrauto defines the purposes of physical education as being "gymnastic, educational, rational, recreational, preparatory for sport, and sport influenced." Little by little physical education assumed a strongly militaristic physiognomy.

In 1937 (law No. 1839 of October 27) the job of the O.N.B. was passed over to the "Gioventu' Italia del Littorio", (G.I.L.) the new youth organization of the regime, and with the law No. 1361 of December 14, 1941 the rapport between school and G.I.L. in the field of physical education teaching was regulated. Physical education had a role equal to any other subject in the school curriculum of Italy.

With the fall of Fascism all youth organizations were dissolved (decree No. 704 of August 2, 1943) and the activities of the G.I.L. were taken over by the Ministero della P.I. and the Defense Department. Thus came to an end the 10 year period in which physical education had been taught by an outside organization.

By the Decree No. 816 of September 7, 1945 physical education remained a compulsory subject in the school curriculum and new programs were drawn up (1962). On October 19, 1950 (Gonnella, Minister of P.I.) negotiated between school and C.O.N.I. bringing about new regulations in regard to sport activities to be developed in the school along with the existing physical education programs. Thus was born the "Gruppi Sportivi Scolastici"; sport remains optional. In 1958 (law No. 88 of February 7) a complete revision of the physical education programs took place, and this represented a big step forward even if it didn't completely satisfy the teaching body. In 1969 thanks to a closer collaboration between school and C.O.N.I., sport activities in the school have greatly increased and an even closer collaboration in the planning and carrying out of the "Giochi della Gioventu" is expected in the future.

## Structure of Physical Education

The law No. 88 provides for the compiling of a complete role of physical education teachers to be kept in the offices of the Ministero della P. I., and for the creation of several positions for physical education teachers. A central organ, the Ispettorato per l'Educazione Fisica e Sportiva" has been established, and a coordinating office has been formed in every city under the supervision of the "Provveditore agli Studi (School Superintendent in the Provinces), who can delegate a school Principal or a physical education teacher to carry out the work involved. The teaching of physical education is compulsory. In the elementary schools it is taught by the regular teacher for 1/2 hour, four times a week. In the secondary schools there is also a two hour a week program; in the upper level students are grouped by grade and sex, in the lower level, by sex only. There must be a group of at least 15 students. Only for health reasons are the students excused from physical education instruction. The students of the "Istituti Magristrali" (secondary schools for the training of elementary school teachers) cannot be exempted from attending classes of physical education (Theory) but only from the actual performance of physical education exercises. Provisions are made for some kind of sport--non-compulsory--as an extracurriculum activity (2 hours a week in the lower level, 4 hours a week in the upper level). Courses of "ginnastica differenziata" are provided for the students who can't attend regular physical education classes for health reason. The pupils are divided in groups of 10 or 15 at the most and are taught at the end of the school day. Accident insurance is available and covers the students during physical education classes, sport activities, field trips, outings, etc.

Gruppi Sportivi--Unions (Associations)
of Gruppi Sport--in the Provinces

All sport activities are organized by the "Gruppi Sportivi", an association of students, on a voluntary basis, formed in each school (the principal is the chairman), and governed by a committee on which are represented the parents of the students and the student body. The purpose of these clubs is to train the young people for different kinds of sports and athletic competition on a local and regional level. Technical assistance is provided by the "Unioni Provinciali" with the Superintendent of Schools as presiding officer. Their goals are to further recreational and sport activities in the schools, to offer technical assistance to the various groups, and to help organize special courses in regard to some activity which can't be carried out in each separate school. The Superintendent of Schools coordinates the various services of the surrounding towns with the assistance of a physical education teacher "di ruolo" (with tenure). There are separate groups for each level of the secondary schools.

## Sport Organization in the School

In 1968 there was 93 "Unioni Provinciali", 3,163 "Gruppi Sportivi", of which 981 in the first level of the secondary schools, and 2,182 in the second level with 1,382,863 members in all (853,341 male and 529,522 females), organized into squads as follows: male and female squads--5,028 for track, basketball and volleyball; 168 skiing; 105 for gymnastics on apparatus; 89 for tennis; 49 for fencing; 47 for swimming. Male only--13 for beginning football, 12 for rugby. Male and female--57 for other various sports, like canoeing, horseback riding, ice hockey, handball, sailing, etc.

A sample of the 1969 calendar of recreational activities and sport competition

### Winter Sports:

Skiing--to end by Feb. 15--training courses, competitions and selection of finalists (male and female), championship in the provinces.
Feb. 27-28--Selection of finalists (male) on the regional level in collaboration with the "Centro Sportivo Italinao".
Feb. 20-21--Selection of finalists (women) on the regional level.
March 11-12--Final competition on the national level.

Ice skating--various activities and competitions on the local level.

Track--by Feb. 23--Cross country championship on the local
and interprovincial level.
By May 11--various competitions for women on the
local and provincial level.
By May 18--interregional selection of finalists.
By April 29--various competition for men and cham-
pionship in the provinces.
By May 1--qualifying competitions in the provinces.
May 4--final competition.
By May 15--interregional selection of finalist for the
national champion.
May 25--national championship.

Gymnastics--by April 30--various exhibitions and competitions
(men and women) on the local and provincial level.

Fencing--by April 2--competitions (men and women) on the
local and provincial level.
April 12-13--selection of finalists (in 3 localities) for
the national championship (men only)
April 19-30--national championship.

Tennis--by May 20--selection of finalists (men and women) on
the local level and championship in the provinces.
June 1, 2, 3--Selection of regional finalists--men only
(in 3 localities).

Swimming--by May 28--qualifying competitions (men and women)
on the local level and championship in the provinces.
June 4-5--interregional semifinal (men) for the national
championship (in 3 localities).
June 14-15--national championship.

Other sports--May 16-17-18--regional competitions for the
"coppa Siciliana" (Cup Sicily).
By March 31--tournaments:  volleyball, basketball, etc.

Summer Activities (July and August)

Recreational and sport activities continue during the summer
vacations under the supervision of school personnel (camping, swimming, track, etc.) in the "Centri Estivi di Perfezionamento" (Summer
training centers).

Swimming--free courses for secondary school students (boys
and girls) (several).

Camping--Local, provincial, interprovincial (3), national camping grounds.

Track--several national training centers in cooperation with
C.O.N.I.

# Physical Education Programs Now in Force

*Elementary School* (decree No. 503 of June 14, 1955). The elementary school is divided into 2 levels: I (grades 1 and 2), II (grades 3, 4, and 5).

Group I--During each regular school day games and physical exercises are to take place, possibly in the open, which while amining to develop friendly group work will also help to improve and refine the motor ability of the child and enable him to fully express himself through song and rhythmical movements, thus working toward a harmonious development of his physical and intellectual abilities.

Group II--Physical Education is to be considered closely connected with moral and civil education, and viewed as a means of developing respect and control of the body, of channeling the exuberant energies typical of this age group, and of teaching auto-control, auto-discipline and sociability. The teacher will see to it that the pupil executes properly the exercises connected with walking, running, jumping, etc. In teamwork priority will be given to rhythmic motion aimed to develop agility, and expressive and harmonious movements. In this phrase of work, as in choral singing, the teacher can avail himself of local folkloristic elements. Orderly group games are to find their place in this age group not only for their recreational value, but also for their educational value in developing loyalty, kindness and friendliness. Games and physical exercises are to take place as much as possible in the open. The teacher will carefully watch the physical development of the individual pupil and consult a physician as soon as he suspects some anatomical and functional changes. He'll keep in mind that physical activity requires as much energy as study.

## Secondary School (Decree of April 24, 1963)

The teaching of physical education must conform to the biophychological characteristics particular of this age group. Physical education must stimulate, through rational movements, the harmonious development of the body and its vital functions and thus help prepare the individual to better adapt himself to society. The teacher must recognize and discuss with his colleagues the individual constitutionsl differences and characteristics of the pupils and provide adequately for their needs. Physical education contributes to the total formation of the pupil by developing his psychomotor abilities through exercises which serve not only as an outlet for his repressed energy and a balance for the long hours of sedentary work, but also as a means of developing in him a healthy behavior. Therefore the teacher will encourage and support indvidual initiative, promote group work to which each pupil may feel free to contribute, and suggest ways of utilizing the exercises beyond the framework of the school. The teacher will also give as much as possible practical demonstrations. Any activity performed in the open air will offer the opportunity to draw attention to the benefits of the outdoors and to teach appreciation of nature.

The programs are the same in all three grades and consist of basic exercises for general body development, integrated with graded exercises suitable to the various age groups and the capabilities of the two sexes. In classes for boys the exercises will be characterized by the use of natural movements aimed at a rational development of the body and stressing self-confidence and self-determination. In classes for girls the choice of exercises and the manner in which they are performed will aim to bring about a graceful self-confidence. Rhythmic gymnastists will find an eminent place in these classes since it stresses control of movements and imparts good posture and composure. Exercises on small apparatus may be incorporated in the classes as long as they remain in the framework of the basic technical and didactic guidelines for physical education teaching.

Istituti di istruzione classica, scientifica,
magistrale ed artistica[1]

(decree No. 1226 of July 25, 1952)

General Guidelines: The teaching of physical education has its basis in the recent studies in the field of biology and pedagogy and utilizes the laws on human growth and the constitutional differences of this age group. The purpose of physical education is the integral formation of the person by means of an adequate somatopsychic activity and a harmonious balance between the mental activity and the normal physiological needs of all organic systems (nervous, cardiovascular, respiratory, endocrine, etc.), in order to safeguard and develop rationally the healthy energies of body and mind.

Guidelines: In the schools physical education must:

1. *educate* the body, psychologically and physiologically to respond exactly to the power of the will.

2. stimulate through motion the rational development of all muscles and the normal functions of vegetative life.

---

[1] These programs will remain in force until the present law regarding the secondary schools of II degree will be revised. See: Ministero della P. I. Ispett. per l'E. F. and S. "Phys. Ed. and Sport in the the sec. school of II degree. Proposals and conclusions. Lido di Camaiore, Lucca, 1966.

3. compensate, through motion, the harmful effect of sedentary work.

4. teach self-discipline without suppressing personality.

5. help to overcome timidity, instill courage and all other moral qualities.

6. arouse interest in physical activity and in the practice of the same, acquaint young people with the benefits of physical activity and stress the importance of hygiene as a basis of good health.

7. aim, in physical education for girls, at the development of the female body through a wise choice and performance of suitable exercises avoiding those exercises which are more suited for males.

8. guide and counsel those young people particularly gifted for a specific kind of sport activity.

The "Instituti Magistrali" have both theory courses and practical classes. Student teaching programs are also provided. In the Conservatories of Music special physical education courses are provided. All programs are grouped by grade and sex.

The structure of physical education, as it appears from the programs now in force, remain eclectic, and the programs are fundamentally educational and ortogenic. The technique and methodology are undergoing a radical evolution particularly in regard to physical education for girls.

The new trend in the teaching of physical education in boys classes is to group the activities according to the objectives, with the aim at developing the whole person through natural movements (Lido di Camaiore, 1966). Technique and didactics are changing at a slow pace.

In the field of physical education for girls a change of technique was brought about thanks to Andreina Gotta Sacco of the school of Rome, by passing gradually from "static gymnastics" to "dynamic gymnastics" which applies the modern biopedagocial principles. The value of rhythmic movements has been recognized and has effected the technique. The prevailing "metric" performance of exercises has been changed into a "rhythmic", softer, more graceful and beautiful performance through continuous action, fluidity and body displacement in which muscle contraction are of short duration and even if prolonged, of light intensity (alternating contraction and decontractions). The participation of the various muscles and the perfect adherence of rhythmical movements to the rhythm of the music makes for a more "economic" movement. An adequate use of games and pre-sport activities completes harmoniously the existing programs.

## Training of Physical Education Teachers

The training takes place in the "Instituti Superiori di Educazione Fisica" (law No. 88 of Feb. 7, 1958).

*Instituti Superiori di Educazione Fisica.* The State Instituto di Educazione Fisica in Rome is a university type school with the following purposes:

1. to train both young men and women as physical education teachers for all types of schools through a series of theoretical and practical courses.

2. to prepare them for all kinds of activities related to physical education and sport.

3. to improve the education of the future physical education teachers in the technological and scientific field.

4. to promote the study of sciences applied to physical education.

The Institute is a three year coeducational school. The candidates must have (a) completed the secondary school (I and II level), (b) passed a strict physical examination by an appointed medical commission, (c) successfully completed a series of tests of practical nature and passed a comprehensive written examination on general culture. Attendance is compulsory. The curriculum comprises two groups of courses:

a. Scientific and Cultural:

1) Anatomy as applied to physical education--1st and 2nd years.

2) Anthropology and anthopometry--2nd and 3rd years.

3) Biology and Chemistry applied to physical education--1st year.

4) Endocrinology--2nd year.

5) Hygiene general--2nd year.

6) First aid--2nd and 3rd years.

7) Physiology--3rd year.

8) Corrective physical education--3rd year.

9) Italian language and literature--1st year.

10) General methods of teaching--2nd and 4rd years.

11) History of physical education--2nd and 3rd years.

12) Institutional civil law--2nd and 3rd years.

13) One of three foreign languages--1st and 2nd years.

b. Technical Training:

1) Methodology of teaching motor activities--1st, 2nd and 3rd years.

2) Technique general of physical education--1st and 2nd years.

3) Technique of gymnastics--1st, 2nd and 3rd years.

4) Rhythmical gymnastics--modern femminile--1st, 2nd and 3rd years.

5) Technique of sports--1st, 2nd and 3rd years.

6) Student teaching--1st and 2nd years.

7) Corrective gymnastics--2nd and 3rd years.

8) Legislation and organizations of physical education and sport--1st and 2nd.

9) Musical exercises--Men - 1st year, women - 1st and 2nd years.

10) Gymnastics for low intelligence and physical defective groups--3rd year.

11) Use of Visual materials for physical education and sport--3rd year.

At the end of the three years the students must pass a final comprehensive examination before being granted the diploma. Fully accredited institutes for the training of physical education teachers have been established at the Universities of Turin, Naples, Bologna, Florence, Milan State University, Milan Catholic University, Palermo, Perugia and L'Aquila. (Law No. 88 of February 7, 1958).

Fencing Academy

With an ordinance of the Ministero of P. I. of December 15, 1962 the Fencing Academy in Rome was reactivated to provide for the training of professional fencing teachers according to modern techniques and didactics.

## "Centro Didattico" for Physical
## Education and Sport

The "Centro" was established with decree No. 412 of November 20, 1969 with the following purposes:

a) to promote interest in physical education and sport in the Nation and especially among educators.

b) to gather and publish data on events in the field of physical education and sport both on the national and international levels.

c) to promote through courses of study, publications, conventions and a closer collaboration between Italian and foreign experts.

d) to encourage experimentation of new techniques, teaching aids and apparatus.

e) to promote and organize courses of "aggiornamento", study-trips, exchange of teachers and experts.

f) to promote personal involvement in some kind of sport as a worthy and educational use of leisure time.

g) to train supervisory personnel for permanent and seasonal "colonie" (resorts at the seashore or in the mountains) where children, especially needy children are sent free of charge or at a minimal charge.

The "Centro" organized an International Convention (Canedabbia, 1959), an International Seminar on Cinematography, Television, and Audio-visual Aids used in sport (Roma, 1968), hundreds of courses for physical education teachers in elementary and secondary schools with particular emphasis on the Instituti Magistrali, and specialization courses for various sports (tennis, swimming, gymnastics, basketball, etc.). The "Centro" has produced films and edited didactic materials and owns a library and a well equipped film library.

## "Aggiornamento" of Teachers

In compliance with the decree of the Ministero of P. I. (February 10, 1962) the "Ispettorato" for Physical Education organizes every year courses of "aggiornamento" in the fields of methodology and didactics in corrective gymnastics and sports in the schools. Courses include track, skiing, gymnastics, swimming, fencing, tennis, basketball, volleyball, etc., and camping. The courses are taught in the various provinces and as "state-courses."

National Association of Physical Education

Since March 1949, the Association of Physical Education to
which practically all physical education teachers belong, has been in
operation in Rome. The purpose of the Association is to promote
study, research and publications and experimentation with new ideas
aimed at improving physical education methodology. The Association
provides social assistance, coordinates all services of labor groups
and is a non-profit organization--it also has instituted an annual prize
for literature (A.N.E.F.).

## Sport

### History Development, Laws and Structure

Sport developed during the second half of the 19th century a
and gradually became more organized and gained in popularity. The
first "Societal Ginnastica" was founded in Turin in 1844. The first
Federation was the "Federazione Ginnastica" founded in Venice in
Mercy 1869 by Costantino Reyer of Triest, Pietro Gallo and Domenico
Pisoni of Venice, and was named "Federazione di Ginnastica."

At the end of the 19th century sport developed greatly through
the efforts of Angelo Mosso, eminent physiologist, and other scientists
and politicians. In 1904 during the 4th Olympics (London) a group of
sport enthusiasts founded the first "Comitato Olimpico Nazionale"
(C.O.N.I.) to coordinate the activities of the "federazioni sportive"
between Olympics. In 1927 the "comitato" underwent radical changes
and was renamed "Confererazione delle Confederazioni." With law No.
426, February 16, 1942 (amended by the decree No. 704 of August 2,
1943) C.O.N.I. passed under the supervision of the "Presidente del
Consiglio dei Ministri" (Prime Minister). With another decree (No.
362, May 5, 1947) C.O.N.I. was reorganized on a democratic basis
and the officers were elected--C.O.N.I.s permanent structure.

C.O.N.I. channels its activities through the Federazioni Sportive "Olympic" and "non-olympic", controls and furthers sports activities, coordinates and disciplines all sport activities, supervises and
protects all sport organizations, ratifies the statutes and regulations
directly or through the National Sport Federations, finances the athletes participating in the Olympics and other National and International Sport Exhibitions. Some changes were made in the administration
of CONI (law No. 1379, December 22, 1950) with the addition of two
new members appointed by the Secretary of Treasury and the Finance
Minister.

The law No. 617 of July 31, 1959 provided for the establishment of a "Ministero del Turismo e dello Spettacolo" (Ministry for
Turism and the Performing Arts) with supervisory functions over
CONI previously exercised by the Prime Minister. To carry out its
work CONI avails itself of the National Sport Federation, which is its

legal "organs" and whose administrative staff is elected every four years by the members of the Socital Sportive.

The Sports Federations are:

Aeronautica, Mounting Climbing, Atletica Legera, Atletica Pesante, Automobilismo, Baseball, Bocce, Hunting, Canottagio, Cronometristi, Ghiaccio, Ginnastica, Golf, Hockey, Medici Sportivi, Motociclismo, Motonautica, Swimming, Pallacanestro, Handball, Volleyball, Pentathlon Moderno, Fishing, Boxing, Rugby, Fencing, Water Skiing, Horseback Riding, Winter Sports, Tennis, Target Shooting, Pigeon Shooting, and Sailing.

Other "organs" of CONI are: The National Council, a deliberating body; the President and his council; the Executive Board; the Secretary General, and the Board of Auditors.

The National Council is composed of the Presidents of the National Federations with each having a vote. The National Council elects by secret vote, the President and two Vice Presidents and six other members who, together with the Secretary General constitutes the Executive Board.

With the decree of April 24, 1961 (article No. 2 of the law No. 259 of March 21, 1958) CONI passed under the direct control of the "Corte dei Conti" (Court of Auditors) CONI receives the necessary funds for its operation and for the operational expenses of the federations from the "Concorso Pronostici Totocalcio" (a national football contest in which one "predicts" the winning teams). The law No. 1117 of September 29, 1965 is better known as law "fifty-fifty," provides that 38% of the total gross be used to pay out the prizes, and 26.5% be given each to the State Treasury and to sport, and the remaining small amount given to cover operating expenses. Therefore the only source of revenue for sport is the amount alotted by CONI. In the 1967 budget of CONI ordinary and extraordinary outlay amounted to 7,642,593,161 lire.

CONI has provided for construction of new sport facilities and the modernization and maintenance of existing facilities with an outlay of over 40 billions. To schools CONI has contributed considerable sums for sport activities and for the construction of athletic fields reserved for students. Up to July 1968 there were sixty-five such facilities.

Sport in the universities is organized and directed by a national association called "Central Universatario Sportivo Italiano" (C.U.S.P.) whose goals are to promote and encourage physical education and sports in the universities and to organize sport exhibitions at the local, national and international level. For this purpose CONI appropriates substantial sums which are divided among the various C.U.S. (University Sport Centers).

In regard to the Armed Forces, each branch has established a "Centrao Sportivo (Centro Sportivo Army, C. S. Air Force, C. S. Carabibieri, C. S. Navy, C. S. Fiamme Oro, C. S. Fiamme Gialle). These centers are regular sport associations affiliated with the National Sport Federation. They train contestants for the Olympic Games and for the motorcycling races. The instructors are military personnel trained in the Military School of Physical Education (S.M.E.F.).

Nearly four million people are members of the federation and sport groups in the schools (3,382,863). To them must be added the members of the other associations, like the "Centro Sportivo Italiano", the "Unione Nazionale Sport Popolari" (more popular sports), the "Centro Nazionale Sportivo Libertas" and the students of the youth centers of CONI (55,000).

## "Scuola Centrale dello Sport"

The school was founded and financed by CONI and was dedicated on December 22, 1966. Its goals are to train a well qualified and specialized group of instructors for the CONI. Admission in the school is by competition. The applicants must have the diploma of a secondary school (II degree) since the courses are at the university level. The course of study lasts 3 years and the students must live in the school. The students who have satisfactorily completed the course of study and passed the prescribed examination receive the diploma of "Maestro di Sport". After a two year "tirocinio" (apprenticeship) with CONI or in one of CONI controlled organizations the students receive a diploma of higher degree and become permanent employess of CONI.

Admission to the Scuola Centrale is open also to national athletes or former athletes if sponsored by a National Sport Federation, provided they have the necessary qualifications and aptitude. These students are called "auditori" and after the three years they receive the title of "Sport Instructors". After a one year "tirocinio" they become technical advisers of CONI.

## Youth Training Center

In 1954 CONI established on an experimental basis the "Centri di Addestramento Giovanili", to recruit young people who show a particular aptitude for some kind of sport. Since 1963 several centri "Pulcini" (chicks, pullets) are in function for children from 6 to 8 years of age. About 20 sports are practiced: track, football, canoeing, bicycling, horseback riding, gymnastics, lawn hockey, swimming, basketball, volleyball, water polo, ice skating, modern pentathlon, rugby, fencing, skiing, tennis, diving, archery, sailing. The Center is open to boys and girls between 7-15 years of age. The federation determines the age group for the different kinds of sport. The candidates must undergo a strict medical examination and aptitude test. The course of training lasts from 3 to 5 years beginning and ending

as the regular school year.  Classes are held 2 or 3 times a week depending on the sport and lasts from 1 to 1½ hours.  In order to pass
from one level to the other the students must take an examination of
"brevetto" which becomes gradually more difficult.  During the summer special courses are organized in suitable localities and the best
students are invited to attend them.

In order to expand its activity CONI has sought the collaboration of the "Enti di Propaganda" which are sport organizations connected with social or political movements, and has promoted the establishment of centers for track competition and for the "Pulcini" which
are called "Centri Olimpia."

## Giochi della Gioventu'

In order to help with the education of young people, acquaint-
ing them with sports and therefore building a solid foundation for the
sport in the nation C.O.N.I. has promoted the "Giochi della Gioventu'
with the collaboration of the National Federations, the Enti di Propaganda, and the School.

Of the 8,055 "comuni" about 6,000 have responded ... 600,000
boys and girls have taken part in the games.  Participants must be
between the age of 10-15.  The first phase of the competition takes
place in the "comuni," and it is the most important since it involves
a large number of competitors, and the cooperation of all local organizations.  The second competition takes place in the "provinces" and
it is here that the work of the comuni is recognized.  The national
competition takes place in Rome at the end of June.

The basic sports are:  track, cycling, gymnastics, swimming,
basketball, volleyball, skiing.  In the competitions in the "comuni"
other sports may be added, (but not more than four), chosen among
the following:  bocce (a form of bowling done on a sand court), football, motocross, canoeing, lawn hockey, judo, wrestling, tennis, target shooting, archery, sailing, fencing, rugby, etc.

The members of the Gruppi sportivi della Scuola who have
proved to have the required qualifications may participate in the Giochi della Gioventu'.

## Italian Sports Updated[7]

"Although sport is a spontaneous and natural expression of
human behaviour it still requires some form of organizational structure.  In Italy, the task of coordinating and supervising all sporting
activities is the responsibility of the National Olympic Committee
(C.O.N.I.).  The law instituting the Committee was approved in 1943
and it authorizes this body to undertake the training and preparation
of athletes for the Olympic Games as well as all national and international meetings and competitions, to supervise equipment and facilities

and to control the various clubs and organizations that exist. With such a wide range of activities to cover, C.O.N.I. performs its task through 32 national sports federations--enjoying wide discretional powers--and over 20,000 sports clubs.

The task of C.O.N.I. has been a particularly arduous one in recent years because of the many complicated problems with which it has been faced, chief among them being the preparation and equipping of sports grounds and gymnasia, of such importance to the younger generations. Assisted by the authorities, the Committee has managed to provide many Italian regions with sports grounds, swimming pools and stadia and some of the most outstanding achievements include the Sports Palace at Bologna, the Velodrome at Ferrara, Athletics Stadium at Palermo, the covered swimming pool at Trieste, the stadium at Pescara and a number of sports grounds and gymnasiums for schools in different localities. To these must be added the installations and buildings for the 1960 Olympic Games at Cortina d'Ampezzo and Rome. Indeed, those at Cortina were started in 1956 for the Winter Olympic Games and consist of the magnificent ice rink, the "Italia" trampoline and a bobsleigh run. The Rome complex includes the Olympic Stadium, holding 100,000 spectators, a large swimming pool, the Palace of Sport, the Little Palace of Sport, the Velodrome, the Sports Centre in the EUR district and sports installations at Acqua Acetosa (Rome). The Olympic Committee is also responsible for encouraging sport as a pastime in which the competitive spirit is not always necessary. It has introduced new methods and techniques whereby students are given more opportunities for such activities while at school, given assistance to the Armed Forces (which have become a source of many of the present-day champions) and organized centres where training is given in swimming, tennis, cycling and winter sports.

The question of training the younger generations in different branches of sport is a responsibility that no government can avoid. Under the general five-year development plan, the Italian government attributed a new role to physical training, allocating Lit. 30,000 million for the five-year period 1966-70. Parliament has also approved what has been termed the "fifty-fifty" law which alters existing regulations on tax levied on the State Football Pool and allocates C.O.N.I. fifty per cent of the weekly receipts. Now exist also a "Central School of Sport" at the Sports Centre of Acqua Acetosa in Rome. This school is necessary because of the high level of specialiation and and skill now reached, trains an elite corps of instructors and provide refresher courses for those already qualified.

Development of sport and all its connected interests, meaning the enthusiastic and competitive participation of the younger generaation, seems to be assured in Italy. With the victories and laurels it won at the Olympic Games, this country has become one of the favored nations. From 1896 to 1968, from the first Olympic Games at Athens to those which were held at Montreal, nearly 3,000 Italian activities have taken part in twenty-one of these international meetings and have won over 110 gold medals, 95 silver medals and as many bronze medals, covering all branches of modern sport.

The original approach of Maria Montessori to work with pre-school children has been an inspiration for the growth of nursery schools over the world. Angelo Mosso's experimental work in physiology of exercise, especially with fatigue, is a classic in its field.

## SELECTED REFERENCES

1. *Chirone*. Rassegna trimestrale (quarterly) di studi psico-pedagogici e technico-metodologici sull'educazione fisica e sportive, Casella postale 135, Trapani.

2. *Educazione Fisica e Sport Nella Scuola*. Rivista bimestrale: organo ufficiale del Centrao studi per l'educazione fisica di Bologna, strada Maggiore 46, Bologna.

3. *A Glimpse at Italy*. Instituto Poligrafico dello Stato P.V. (4211301). Rome. 1977.

4. *La Ginnastica Medica*. Organo ufficiale della Societa Italiana di ginnastica medica. medicine fisica, e riabilitazione, Istituto orotpedico "Rizzoli", Bologna.

5. *Notiziario del Centro didattico nazionale* per l'education fisica e sportiva, via Guidubaldo del Monte 54, Rome.

6. *Notiziario di educazione fisica*, organo ufficiale del'Associazone nazionale di educazione fisica, via Ridolfino Venuti 10, Roma.

7. *Traguardi*, Rivista bimestrale (bi-monthly) di studi sull'eduzazione fisica e sportiva, piassale Marconi 25, Rome.

# SPORT AND PHYSICAL EDUCATION IN JAPAN

by Souichi Ichimura

## Biographical Sketch

*Souichi Ichimura* was born at Mito, Japan, on January 27, 1939. He graduated from the Mito First High School in 1957 and from the Tokyo University of Education (Department of Physical Education) in 1961. He received the Master's College degree from the Department of Psychology, Tokyo University of Education in 1963 and additional study was carried on in Psychology during the 1963-1965 period.

While pursuing his studies a Thesis was presented entitled, "The Psychological Organization of Stage Fright in Sports." This research was presented at the International Congress of Sports Science in Tokyo, in 1964.

While attending the various preparatory schools and colleges, Mr. Ichimura participated in interscholastic and intercollegiate athletic meets in Japan and at the Japan National Sports Festival.

He studied towards his Master's Degree in Physical Education at the University of Illinois in 1965-66 and was a graduate assistant teaching in the basic service instruction program.

Upon his return to Japan, Mr. Ichimura graduated from the Doctor's College in Psychology in 1967 and was a full time assistant at the Department of Psychology of Adolescence and Psychological Measurement. During this time he contributed to the Japanese Journal of Physical Education on the topic of mathematical research methmethods.

Presently, Mr. Ichimura is an Associate Professor, Tokyo University of Education, Department of Physical Education, teaching sports psychology, statistics and computer application for physical education. He is also interested in cultural anthropological study of sport.

## General Background

Lying in an arc off the eastern coast of Asia, Japan is a chain of four large and many small islands. Northern Japan is roughly 500 miles from the Russian port of Vladivostok, while southern Japan is about 120 miles from the tip of Korea and about 200 miles from the coast of China. With a total land area of around 150,000 square miles, Japan is somewhat smaller than California. Most of Japan is covered by hills and mountains; little more than fifteen per cent of the land is suitable for cultivation. Weather conditions across Japan are varied, ranging from semi-tropical in Okinawa to semi-Arctic in northern Hokkaido in which The Winter Olympic Games were held in 1972. The main island, Honshu, experiences four distinct seasons which blend moderately into one another. The highest and the lowest average temperature in Tokyo is 26 and five degrees centigrade respectively. Japan has about half the population of the United States (statistics show Japan had 104 million people in 1970), with its largest cities and major industrial areas located on the central island of Honshu. Tokyo, the capital, has over eleven million people.

The traditional Japanese way of life bears the imprint of early cultural borrowing from China, partly by way of Korea. The Buddhist religion, the Confucian pattern of family relationship, and the characters for writing Japanese language all were acquired from China. These borrowed elements, however, were absorbed in relative seclusion from the Asian mainland and the Japanese created a distinctive civilization of their own. However, it is difficult to describe the characteristics of modern Japanese culture tersely. Japan is a melting pot of varied types of culture. Traditional culture influences customs, ethnic customs, moral consciousness, the shape of human relationships and so on. Western European culture has brought systematized morality and economic system through Christianity, democracy, and capitalism. Arts, liberal arts and technological arts from western European countries and the United States also have had civilizing influences upon Japan's culture. The third element which can not be overlooked is the civilizing influences of the socialist states. It has influenced the labor movement, the social security system, literature, criticism, movies and musical movements. The fourth element of Japanese culture is the mass culture which has been facilitated by the development of the mass communication media. The influence of American culture upon the mass culture in Japan has been quite remarkable.

Japanese culture is open to foreign influences and tends to assimilate them readily into its organic tissue. For example, those who have an inclination for Japanese traditional music can still appreciate music by Samual Barber and Leonard Bernstein (for example) even though they do not know their names. Most of those who have no special interest in music can also feel something comfortable in music by Richard Rodgers. In the same manner, Judo players can be enthusiastic baseball fans, and Karate fans are often Rugby fans at the same time. In consequence of this feature of Japanese culture many various kinds of sport can be seen. If Japanese began playing English cricket and polo, then for something new, they would have to invent an altogether new game to play. Of course, American football is also becoming popular among young people.

The Japanese Gross National Product reached the 4,090 billion dollar mark in 1973. This was second only to the United States (12,949 billion) and above the Federal Republic of Germany (3,482 billion). In 1974 four million passenger cars were produced and 1.7 million cars were exported. Seven million TV sets were produced and six million were exported. On the other hand raw materials are imported from almost all over the world. 99.7 per cent of the oil, 99.5 per cent of the iron ore, 97 per cent of the copper, 96.4 per cent of the wheat and 55.7 per cent of the lumber used in Japan were imported in 1973. In trade with the United States in 1974 Japan exported 485 million dollars worth of radio sets and 840 million dollars worth of motorcycles and imported 324 million dollars worth of airplanes and 725 million dollars worth of Indian corn (mostly from Illinois). These are typical examples of the trading relationship between Japan and the U.S.A. The surprising growth of the GNP has been supported by the low price of oil and the domestic and international monetary policy. Giving cheap labour as a reason for Japan's growth is to show ignorance of modern Japanese economy.

The growth of wealth has given people more leisure time and facilitated the learning and practice of various leisure habits. The development of an industrial society, however, has produced new problems. These are the flowing of people into urban areas and environmental pollution and inflation. Besides these, rapid changes of the international economic situation has begun to affect the daily life of the Japanese people.

Educational opportunities are provided in various forms all through life from infancy to old age in the home, schools and society. Schools, however, are the main educational institutions which provide these opportunities systematically and with definite objectives. After the Second World War, schools shifted to a 6-3-3-4 "single-track" system, in order to equalize educational opportunities. Under this new system, Japan has attained, during the quarter of a century since the end of the Second World War (1945), a high status among the advanced countries of the world in terms of educational expansion. In recent years, however, the necessity for reappraising the existing system has been increasingly pointed out with the aim of realizing the fundamental ideal of educational opportunities as well as meeting the requirements of a modern industrial society. One of the biggest problems has been to provide educational institutions which can meet the diverse abilities and aptitudes of those who are going on to upper secondary educational institutions in increasing numbers every year. In light of this, technical colleges were established in 1962 to provide lower secondary school graduates with five consecutive years of technical education. Moreover, need has recently been seen to adjust the structure and curriculum of the school system to match better the stages of child development.

Compulsory education in Japan begins at the age of six and its length is nine years. The proportion of compulsory school graduates going on to upper secondary school has increased rapidly from 43 per per cent in 1950 to 55 per cent in 1960, 82 per cent in 1970 and 91 per cent in 1974. The proportion of compulsory school graduates going on to junior colleges and universities has also increased; from 16 per cent in 1966, 24 per cent in 1970 to 35 per cent in 1974. Figures for 1975 show that Japan has 410 universities and colleges, 505 junior colleges and 203 graduate schools.

## Historical Background--Physical Education

Physical education was made a compulsory subject in elementary and secondary schools, with the enactment of the educational legislation of 1872. The type of physical exercise practiced at first was gymnastics, introduced by Daigaku-Nanko, at the Tokyo Higher Normal School, the predecessor of Tokyo University of Education. In 1878 the Ministry of Education created a gymnastic training center, with G. A. Leland (U.S.A.) as invited consultant, to train leaders in this field for the general promotion of school physical education. He introduced to Japan the gymnastic system developed by Dio Lewis (U.S.A. 1823-1886). Since then, an organized set of physical exercises including free exercises and apparatus gymnastics came to be the nucleus of physical education in the schools of Japan.

School physical education at the beginning of the 20th century was largely composed of educational gymnastics, and military style gymnastics. At the same time public opinion gradually determined that games should be given a more central place in the physical education program of elementary schools, and that sports should be formally introduced in the physical education program of the secondary schools. Opinion was also favorable to the introduction of traditional sports in the regular physical education class. Swedish gymnastics (N. Posse's gymnastics) were introduced to Japan during this period.

In the years between 1915-1925 some urban schools opened summer schools in the mountains or at the seaside for the promotion of children's health. Some schools had become progressive enough to apply the project method or Dalton plan to the teaching of physical education. In this period sports from overseas, baseball, basketball, volleyball, soccer football, Rugby football, tennis and so on, became popular. It was in the 1910's that Japanese sport circles first joined into international competitions. The Japan Amateur Sports Association was founded in 1911 as a non-governmental organization to secure liaison and coordination among all the sports in Japan. In 1912 Japan sent a delegation to Stockholm as the first country in Asia to participate in the Olympic Games.

About the time when World War I broke out, however, there was once again a strong current of opinion in favor of military gymnastics. In the 1920-1930 period physical education came to be considered in the wider context of promoting physical education for all the nation.

The traditional military arts came to be encouraged from the standpoint of cultivating national spirit. In 1913 the syllabus of military arts at the elementary school was adopted to encourage the teaching of Judo and Kendo. In 1941, or nine months before the breakout of the Pacific War, the National School Ordinance was enacted to reorganize elementary school education, and the previous physical exercise course was renamed the physical training course.

It was in 1947, or two years after the termination of World War II, that the course of school physical education was re-baptized "physical education." This change in the name of the course offered in the schools was not merely nominal, but implied an intrinsic change in the concept of physical education, as well. The teachers guidebooks of the Ministry of Education which details the standards and basic principles of Japanese education advocate that the objective of physical education is to promote balanced development of pupils' minds and bodies and to develop customs and attitudes for pupils to enjoy healthy and safe lives.

## Kindergarten--Physical Education

Physical education at the Kindergarten level is not conducted systematically, but some physical exercises are given according to the children's ages to help the balanced development of mind and body. Low iron bars, trapeze, jungle gyms, sliding beds, sand boxes and other apparatus are installed on the playgrounds of the kindergartens. Eight areas of education are included at the kindergarten level: health, community life, nature, language, music and rhythms, drawing and handicrafts. Physical education is integrated into the two areas of health, and music and rhythms. The following activities are taught in the kindergarten program of physical education: 1 - walking, running and jumping in various forms; 2 - throwing, pushing, pulling and rolling; 3 - competitive play in running, jumping, target throwing, etc.; 4 - group games, such as tag; 5 - playing on slides and swings; 6 - playing with balls, ropes, carts, etc.; 7 - rhythmical movement; 8 - understanding of how to use various sports equipment, adapting the materials to use and putting them away after use; and 9 - keeping on good terms with others and observing the rules.

Recently a strong interest has been aroused in physical education for kindergartens and nursery schools and study of this problem is now underway.

Elementary School--Physical Education

According to a course of study published by the Ministry of
Education, the objectives of the physical education course in the elementary school are:

1.  To develop fundamental motor ability of elementary school
    pupils through the practice of adequate physical exercise
    of various types.  The plan aims at promoting the develop-
    ment of a sound mind and body and at enhancing the
    physical vitality of children of this age group.

2.  To develop the attitude of fair play through the practice
    of sports and games and to foster the type of attitude
    which will be necessary for later social life; a willingness
    to observe rules and agreements and to cooperate with
    others and fulfill one's own assigned responsibility.

3.  To develop the attitude and ability to engage in sports
    with proper attention to health and safety and to cultivate
    the attitude and ability to live a healthy life with a funda-
    mental knowledge of health.

The content of the course of physical education consists of
seven subject areas:  1 - free exercise gymnastics; 2 - apparatus
exercises (horizontal bars, horses, and mats); 3 - athletics (running
and jumping); 4 - games (baseball, basketball and soccer type games);
5 - folk dance and creative expression; 6 - other exercises (games of
tag, rope-skipping, sumo, swimming, skiing, and skating; and
7 - knowledge of exercise and health.

The number of periods allocated to the physical education
course are three hours per week through all elementary school grades.

Lower Secondary School--Physical Education

Essentially the objectives of the lower secondary school physical education program are the same as those of the elementary school.
The content of the course is divided into eight areas:  free gymnastics, apparatus gymnastics, track and field, traditional sports, ball
games, dancing, swimming and theoretical knowledge of physical education and sports.  The physical education course of the lower secon-
school, which is a continuation of the elementary school, is designed
to advance various motor skills as well as the development of attitude
that will be useful in social life.  The maintenance of health and safety
through the learning and practice of physical exercises are also objectives designed to assist students to make good use of physical education and sports in their present and future lives.  In the teaching
of sports, pupils are required to develop the necessary skills to such
an extent that they may organize sports as well as practice them
under the regular rules.  For this purpose, guidance is made in such

a way as to allow the pupils themselves to work out plans of exercise and organize and operate athletic or other sport contests.

The traditional sports of Judo, Kendo (the art of defense with a sword or swordmanship) and Sumo (Japanese traditional standing wrestling) are also included, and more than one of the three activities must be taught. The number of periods per week allocated to the course of study of physical education in the lower secondary schools is as follows: 1st grade (7th), three hours of physical education; 2 2nd and 3rd grade (8th and 9th), two hours of physical education and one hour of health education.

### Upper Secondary School--Physical Education

The health and physical education course of the upper elementary school consists of two separate subjects--physical education and health education. The objectives of physical education are:

1. To develop the abilitis and attitudes conducive to the practice of various physical exercises and to promote the development of sound minds and bodies.

2. To improve skills by rational practice based on a scientific understanding of sports and to deepen the understanding of the significance of sports in human life, thus cultivating the abilities and attitudes to make life healthier and richer.

3. To develop the attitude of fair play through the experience of competition and cooperation in sports, and to cultivate the ability and attitude to make efforts for individual or group attainment, to the utmost of one's power and in cooperation with others, thus enabling pupils to acquire certain patterns of behavior desirable in social life.

The objectives of health education are:

1. To deepen the scientific understanding of basic matters relating to health and illness, and, on the basis of this understanding, develop the individual's ability to solve problems relating to the promotion and maintenance of health.

2. To cultivate attitudes conducive to the promotion of the health of the group and the nation, by imparting systematic understanding of public health.

Subject areas in the physical education program are: apparatus exercises (horizontal bars, horses and mats); athletics (running, jumping, and throwing); traditional sports (Judo, Kendo and Sumo); ball games (basketball, volleyball, tennis, table tennis, handball, badminton, softball, soccer and rugby football); swimming (swimming, diving and life saving); dance; and theoretical areas.

The content of the theoretical physical education program is as follows: (a) Development and physical exercises; (b) Practice of physical exercises, and (c) Social life and physical education. The content of teaching in health education is as follows: (a) Physiological study of the human body; (b) Pathological study of the human body; (c) Mental hygiene: (d) Labor and health and safety, and (e) Public health.

The number of periods allocated per week to the physical education course at upper secondary school increased a little in 1969: 1st grade--comparable to sophomores in American system (males - four hours, females - two hours); 2nd grade--juniors (males and females - three hours); 3rd grade--seniors (males and females - three hours). For the first and second grades, one additional hour per week is set aside for the teaching of health education.

## College-University--Health and Physical Education

A new university system came into existence in 1947 and physical education was formally brought into university education. Students are required to take two lecture credits in health theory and physical education theory and two credits in practical work. In the lecture course the following subjects are taught: Theoretical principles of health (hygiene concerning food, clothing and housing, sports hygiene, disease prevention, mental hygiene, sex education, first aid, environmental hygiene, national welfare, racial hygiene, hygienic policy, population problems, hygienic statistics); Kinesiology and physiology of sports and physical fitness; Psychology of physical education (psychology concerning physical exercises, sports and recreational activities); Cultural and social problems (history of physical education, sociology of physical education, administration of physical education, management of physical education).

The objectives of physical education activities are as follows: To maintain and promote health and improve physical fitness as well as to develop awareness of this objective; Activities should be interesting enough to stimulate the student's desire to participate in sports; and, an atmosphere conducive to the development of desirable social attitudes should be created during the instruction period. Nearly all of the physical exercises already mentioned for the high school programs are also practiced at the university level.

The most popular part of the physical education program among students is sports events, tennis, softball, volleyball, skiing, ping-pong, golf, and soccer. They tend to prefer recreational activities to vigorous exercise. After lengthy preparatory study for the entrance examinations of colleges and universities most young people are exhausted. Their fitness as a group is far lower than the average upper secondary school students. Physical education at colleges and universities has many problems awaiting solution. Shortage and deficiency of facilities caused by the crowding of universities in urban areas where land is extremely expensive and the general and financial situation in physical education prevents students from participating in physical exercise. The basic ideals and principles of college and university physical education also need to be set out and clarified.

## Extracurricular--Physical Education

Each school (from the elementary school to the universities) has various sport clubs as well as cultural clubs. Most of the students belong to these sports clubs and enjoy the practice of sports after school hours. In the upper secondary high school, the average number of students who belong to sport clubs was 254 per school in 1962. This represents about 30 percent of the total number of students enrolled in the schools. The kind of sports popular among upper secondary schools are: track and field, judo, table tennis, and soft tennis (more than 90 per cent of the schools have these clubs); volleyball, basketball and baseball (70-80 per cent) and Kendo 50-70 per cent), for male students. The program for female students includes volleyball, basketball, table tennis, soft tennis (more than 50 per cent), and track and field (more than 40 per cent).

National contests are organized in the respective sports. The National Sports Festival which is organized annually on a large scale has an Upper Secondary section, in which national contests in various sports are staged. Practically all the national sport contests are sponsored by the Physical Education Federation of the Upper Secondary School with the marked exception of baseball, whose national tournament is organized and operated by the All Japan High School Baseball Association.

## The Training of Physical Education Teachers

Students who want to be physical education teachers at the Upper Secondary High School level must study at the faculties of physical education for at least four years. Only for Elementary and Lower Secondary School physical education teachers is a two year's junior college program available. The students are expected to take the following courses besides practice in physical exercises: (1) The Principles of Physical Education; (2) Psychology of Physical Education; (3) Administration of Physical Education; (4) Sociology of Physical Education; (5) Kinesiology; (6) Physiology of Sport; (7) Introduction to Medicine; (8) Hygiene; (9) Applied Anatomy, and (10) Practice Teaching.

There are fourteen universities with faculties of physical education, from which 4,300 students graduate every year. Education faculties of some other universities also have a physical education major. Graduates from education faculties must have a minor also and teach both in elementary or lower secondary schools. Teachers of physical education at upper secondary schools must be graduates of physical education faculties, and they teach physical education and health education full time. In recent years universities graduated not only physical education teachers but also physical education leaders and recreation administrators for communities and enterprises. Teacher's license examinations are arranged by the Board of Education of each province.

Tokyo University of Education which has one of the most outstanding courses in physical education in Japan is moving from Tokyo to the Tsukuba area, thirty miles north of Tokyo, to obtain a better educational environment, changing its name to the University of Tsukuba. The faculty of physical education will graduate 200 students a year. The University of Tsukuba is going to start the first doctors course in physical education in Japan in 1976. There are three universities which have masters courses in physical education and 142 students are working for masters degrees in Japan at this time (1975).

## Traditional Sports

Traditional sports may be distinguished as follows:

(1)　Sports that are not performed today except on certain ceremonial occasions, e.g., Kemari (a kind of kick ball), Yabusame (equestrian archery), and Dakyu (equestrian ball-hitting). These are of very ancient origin and highly formalized.

(2)　Sports that are still performed by many people today, e.g., Judo, Kendo, Kyu-Jitsu (Japanese archery), and Sumo. Judo and Kendo acquired their present forms during the age of the Tokugawa Shogunates (1603-1867) when they were predominantly military arts, although, doubtless their origins date back much further. Modern Judo was organized by Jigoro Kano who established the Kodakan Training Center of Judo in Tokyo in 1882. Soon after this time modern Judo spread all over the world.

The important objective of Judo is, not only to acquire skills, but also to develop sound minds. Judo players are strongly inhibited to use their skill as a weapon of combat.

Kyu-Jitsu which uses bamboo bows also has begun to attract the attention of some western European people.

## Research in Physical Education
## and Sports

Research studies in physical education and sport in Japan are carried on at the universities and research institutes. The results of these studies are released through the Japanese Society of Physical Education and the Japanese Fitness Society (the head offices of these societies are in the University of Tokyo).

The Japanese Society of Physical Education is an academic institution with a membership of 2,000. Its general meetings have been held once a year; since 1950, when the first meeting was held, there have been fourteen such general meetings. This Society publishes quarterly the *Research Journal of Physical Education*, which includes original articles in Japanese and English. The Japanese Physical Fitness society had its first general meeting in 1949. It publishes the *Japanese Journal of Physical Fitness*, including proceedings of the general meetings on the occasion of every general meeting. The publications are printed both in Japanese and English.

Some Statistics on Health and
Physical Education

1. The nationwide survey of health and physical education was carried out by JASA, entrusted to Professor T. Asada at Tokyo University of Education in 1974. The following are some of the results:

   a. Question: Are you afraid that your health might be affected through lack of exercise?

   b. Question: Are you afraid that you are putting on flesh?

   c. Question: Do you have the habit of exercise for keeping your fitness?

   The following are percentages of "YES" responses to the questions.

| Age | (a) Males | (a) Females | (b) Males | (b) Females | (c) Males | (c) Females |
|---|---|---|---|---|---|---|
| 15-19 | 19.3 | 26.7 | 18.6 | 54.0 | 69.6 | 57.1 |
| 20-24 | 36.8 | 36.2 | 21.3 | 46.9 | 69.7 | 55.4 |
| 25-29 | 42.9 | 37.1 | 22.0 | 42.8 | 63.7 | 68.0 |
| 30-34 | 35.1 | 30.3 | 35.0 | 55.3 | 69.4 | 67.3 |
| 35-39 | 33.3 | 33.9 | 28.3 | 49.2 | 70.4 | 78.1 |
| 40-44 | 31.3 | 25.0 | 35.5 | 46.8 | 67.5 | 72.4 |
| 45-49 | 26.8 | 25.0 | 34.8 | 48.6 | 73.9 | 80.6 |
| 50-54 | 22.1 | 28.7 | 31.7 | 42.6 | 74.0 | 79.1 |
| 55-59 | 28.4 | 25.0 | 26.3 | 43.8 | 81.1 | 75.0 |
| 60-64 | 21.1 | 19.5 | 21.1 | 27.3 | 83.1 | 74.0 |
| Total | 30.7 | 29.8 | 27.7 | 47.1 | 71.0 | 69.8 |

2. Statistics of the nationwide survey of physical fitness of pupils are presented annually by the Ministry of Education. The following are some of the data of 1974. Figures show averages.

| Age | Sex | (cm) Height | (kg) Weight | (sec) 50 Meter Run | Grip (kg) Strength | Vertical Jump (cm) |
|-----|-----|-------|--------|-------------|----------|--------|
| 6 | M | 115.2 | 20.5 | | | |
| 6 | F | (114.5) | (20.1) | | | |
| 8 | M | 126.4 | 25.7 | | | |
| 8 | F | (125.8) | (25.2) | | | |
| 10 | M | 136.4 | 31.6 | 9.1 | 18.6 | 33.8 |
| 10 | F | (137.4) | (32.0) | (9.5) | (17.0) | (31.1) |
| 12 | M | 148.3 | 39.9 | 8.5 | 25.0 | 40.9 |
| 12 | F | (149.5) | (41.6) | (8.9) | (22.8) | (36.7) |
| 14 | M | 161.9 | 50.7 | 7.7 | 37.3 | 53.3 |
| 14 | F | (154.7) | (48.4) | (8.7) | (27.7) | (41.4) |
| 16 | M | 167.7 | 57.6 | 7.4 | 44.9 | 60.1 |
| 16 | F | (156.1) | (52.0) | (8.7) | (30.3) | (43.4) |

SELECTED REFERENCES

1. "Educational Standards in Japan," Ministry of Education. Japan. 1970.

2. "Japanese Sports Behavior," Japan Amateur Sports Association. Tokyo, Japan. 1975.

3. Physical Education and Sports in Japan. Ministry of Education. Japan. 1964.

4. Report of the survey of physical fitness of pupils. Physical Education Bureau, Ministry of Education. Japan. 1975.

5. Taishukan, Y. Imamura. Health and Physical Education in High Schools of Japan. Tokyo. 1958.

6. Thompson, E. M. Other Lands Other Peoples. (National Education Association of the United States, Washington, D. C. 1964).

7. "The Youth of the World", Youth Bureau, Prime Minister's Office, Printing Bureau of Ministry of Finance. Japan. 1974.

Note: Numbers two and four above are written in Japanese.

# SPORT AND PHYSICAL EDUCATION IN THE REPUBLIC OF KOREA

by Daeshik Kim

## Biographical Sketch

*Daeshik Kim* was born in Seoul, Korea in 1934. He graduated from the Korean Yudo College with a major in physical education specializing in martial arts sports. He then served in the Republic of Korean Army and taught martial arts to the officers and men in the ROK Army and the United States Armies. In 1960 he came to the United States to continue his education.

Dr. Kim received his diploma from Georgia Southwestern College; earned his B.A. in Political Science at Georgia State University; M.Ed. degree from Emory University and his Ed.D. degree at the University of Georgia. He also studied at Teachers College, Columbia University, and Concordia University in Canada.

Dr. Kim has taught at Georgia State University, University of Georgia, City College of New York and Yonsei University in Seoul, Korea. From 1971-1975, he was a director of the Korean Amateur Sports Association and an officer in several other sports and professional organizations in Korea and the United States.

Dr. Kim is presently employed as an Assistant Professor in the Department of Physical and Health Education, the University of Texas at Austin. He holds seventh degree black belts in both judo and tae kwon do. Dr. Kim has published numerous articles for professional journals and magazines. He has also authored and co-authored the books *JUDO*, and *KARATE* in Wm. C. Brown Publishers' physical education activity series. He is a member of the International Advisory Council of the Institute of Comparative Physical Education at Concordia University in Montreal, Canada. Presently he lives in Austin, Texas with his wife and two daughters.

Physical education is a vital part of the present Korean education system as well as an important part of the Korean way of life. "Che Yook" means physical education and this term encompasses in its full meaning sports, athletics, and physical education. Koreans use the word CHE YOOK broadly and interchangeably.

The Korean peninsula, stretching almost directly south from Manchuria, is approximately 500 miles in length, and includes some 3,300 islands scattered along the coast. The territory is bounded by Manchuria and Siberia on the north: and by the East Sea (Sea of Japan) on the east; by the narrow Korean Strait on the south; and the Yellow Sea on the west. Lying between 124.11 and 131.52 degrees east longitude and between 33.06 and 43.00 degrees north latitude, Korea encompasses 85,000 square miles. The area of Korea north of the Military Demarcation Line, commonly known as North Korea, is 47,203 square miles and that of the south, the Republic of Korea, 37,996 square miles.[3]

The population of the Republic of Korea is approximately thirty-five million. The Republic of Korea is a democratic republic and the capital city is Seoul (population is approximately 7 million). Korean has a relatively temperate climate and the climate of Korea is very similar to that of the Middle Atlantic States (Virginia - New York). Due to the influence of both continental and oceanic weather, there are four distinctly different seasons in Korea. Koreans have their own language, and their own alphabet (14 consonants and 10 vowels), called HANGUL. Due to its scientific efficiency and usefulness as phonetic symbols, it is regarded as one of the best alphabets in the world.

BACKGROUND

The civilization of Korea is more than 4,310 years old, and has its own traditional games and sports. Basically, Korean games and sports are classified into three categories.[16] These are (1) the martial arts, such as YU SUL (a form of Korean Jujitsu), TAE KYON*

---

* The most ancient of Korean martial arts had their beginning hundreds of years before the birth of Christ, and generally included the use of many kinds of weapons. All forms of combat developed as a part of military training. Consequently Tae Kyon (Tae Kwon Do) developed as a part of the martial arts limited to combat with fists, hands and feet. Tae Kwon Do literally means the way of fist and feet fighting. In May, 1973, the World Tae Kwon Do (Federation (WTF) was organized, and currently this Federation has 78 national member organizations. Recently, the WTF has become affiliated with the General Assembly of the International Sports Federations (GAIF). Thus Tae Kwon Do has become a truly international sport, and there has already been three successful World Tae Kwon Do Championships held.

(the forerunner of Tae Kwon Do), GOONG SUL (archery), SSIRUM (or Si-room, a form of Korean wrestling), SUK CHUN (stone throw fighting), KUM SUL (a form of swordmanship), MA SUL (horseman-ship) and others; (2) general sports activities such as CHOOK KU (a form of soccer), CHANG CHI KI (a game similar to the present field hockey), SUL MAE TA GI (sleigh riding), JOOL DA LEE GI (a game of Tug of War) and others; (3) recreationa activities such as YON RAL LEE GI (kiting game), NEU NAE (swing), NUL DEU GI (a form of see-saw games where two women stand at the end of each edge of a board and jump alternatively) and others.

## 1.  Brief history of Korean martial arts[6]

The legendary soldier-king DAN GOON forged the various tribes into a unified kingdom 23 centuries before the birth of Christ; this kingdom lasted more than 12 centuries.  Next, the Three King-doms emerged: KOGURYO (37 B.C. - 668 A.D.) located in Southern Manchuria and northern Korea; PAKJE (18 B.C. - 600 A.D.) along the Han River and in Southwestern Korea; and SILLA (57 B.C. - 936 A.D.) is the southeastern part of the peninsula.

Archaeological findings such as mural paintings on the Royal tombs of the Koguryo Dynasty, the stone sculptures of pagodas in temples produced during the Silla dynasty, and documents written in the Pakje dynasty show many studies of fighting stances, skills, and formalized movements.  Therefore, it can be inferred that people in the three kingdomes practiced an art very like the one Koreans prac-tice today.

The Silla dynasty (670 A.D.) reunified the three kingdoms and held control for three centuries.  This unification was made possible by the HWA RANG DO.  Hwa Rang Do was a noble youth organization instituted approximately 1,300 years ago by King Jin Heung of Silla dynasty.  The purpose of this organization was to develop indidivuals physically, intellectually, socially, and mentally, as well as to develop and to improve military proficiency for the nation.  Eventually, Hwa Rang Do vitally contributed and played a significant part in unifying the three kingdoms.  Hwa Rang Do Chung Shin (the spirit of Hwa Rang Do) was essentially based on the ethical code of honor and con-duct which incorporated five principles:  (1) loyalty to the nation, (2) respect and obedience to one's parents, (3) being faithful and honorable to one's friends, (4) courage in battle, and (5) avoidance of unnecessary violence and killing.  Philosophically, Korean martial arts and sports activities were strongly influenced and enriched by the spirit of Hwa Rang Do.  Thus the spirit of Hwa Rang Do became not only a part of the Korean way of life, but also the essence of Korean physical education.

It was during the Koryo dynasty (935 A.D. - 1392 A.D.) that Korean martial arts gained its greatest popularity, and it was prac-ticed both by military personnel and the general public.  It was dur-ing this period that the martial arts were first scientifically organized and systematized by the leading masters. Unarmed-combat armed became recreational activities. Military officers and masters of arts were invited by the Royal family to present demonstrations and matches annually at the Royal Court.

Under King Taejo, founder of the Yi dynasty (1392 A.D. - 1919 A.D.), Buddhism was replaced by Confucianism as the state religion, and that change strengthened the Chinese influence, not only upon official functions, but also upon the private lives of people. This was because the ruling class strongly emphasized Chinese classical learning, and discouraged and despised physical activity as well as martial arts. As a result, people grew disinterested in the forms of unarmed combat, and the technical development of the martial arts was hindered. The decline of the military skills continued. Martial training and the armed forces were neglected while the ruling engaged heavily in factional strifes.

As a result of the victory in the First Sino-Japanese War (1894-95) and the Russo-Japanese War (1904-05), Korea was annexed by Japan in 1910. The Japanese government not only banned cultural activities but also martial arts and team sports in order to destroy the Korean identity, however, they emphasized physical training in order to control the Koreans through physical training and discipline. Korea was liberated from Japan in 1945 and the Republic of Korea was established in 1948. Tragically, however, the Korean War broke out in 1950 which lasted three years. Since the war, Korea has strongly rebuilt the country and at present, Korea is doing very well politically, culturally, and economically. She participates in international sports competitions, and has achieved records in sports events. Furthermore, Korean martial arts sports in general have progressed rapidly. It has been noted that Tae Kwon Do, a Korean art and sport, has become a truly international sport.

## 2. Modern physical education and sports

Korea, in 1876, began culturally intermingling with Western civilization, and by 1886 American missionary teachers were invited into newly opened schools; natural science and foreign language courses were added to the school curriculum. From 1894-1897, the Korean Military Academy of the Yi dynasty and all levels of schools were established, and privately supported secondary schools were also established with the assistance of the American missionaries during this time. It was during this period that gymnastics were for the first time introduced as a physical education activity in school by the Japanese. From 1881-1886, Korea diplomatically entered into treaties with the United States, Great Britain, Germany, Italy, Russia, France, and Japan. This introduced Western culture, and especially sports, in Korea. One time, King Ko Chong of the Yi dynasty made a royal decree which encouraged and emphasized participation in sports and athletic competitions.[15] In 1903, the Young Men's Christian Association (YMCA) was established in Seoul and introduced physical education and sports. This marked the beginning of modern physical education in Korea.[17]

Due to the great popularity of Western sports and the encouragement of King Ko Chong, Koreans enthusiastically participated in sports meets and interschool competition. Unfortunately for Korean physical education, however, the rapid growth of and the public enthusiasm for sports brough them to the attention of old government officials and conservatives. They were stubborn scholars of Chinese classical learnings who seriously opposed Western sports activities. Because of this strong antagonism, the Minister of Education of the Yi dynasty prohibited the participation in athletic competitions in 1910. In the same year, Korea under the Yi dynasty was annexed by Japan.

Apparently the Western sports program was introduced into Korea during the period from 1890 to 1924. Among the activities initiated (with approximate dates in parenthesis) were soccer (1890), track and field (1896), competitive swimming (1898), cycling (1900), basketball (1904), skating (1905), tennis (1909), weight lifting (1920), rugby (1923), and table tennis (1924).[7]

During the Japanese occupation, the Y.M.C.A. was the only organized institution for producing leaders in physical education and sports, and it maintained a number of sports programs for Koreans.

In spite of the limited scale and opportunity of physical education during this period, other sports were introduced either by the YMCA or by Korean students who studied abroad. The Chosun Amateur Athletic Association (the predecessor of the present KASA) was organized by Koreans in 1920. Its first president was Chang Too-Hyun.[22]

SONG Ki-jong, a Korean marathon runner, won first place for the Japanese team at the 11th Olympic Games of 1936 in Berlin, Germany, and another Korean marathon runner, NAM Soung Yong, won the bronze medal in the same race. A number of excellent Korean athletes also participated in many international competitive events as members of Japanese delegations.

During the World War II, the objective of physical education was rigid and strict; physical education was for military preparation and combative proficiency.[5]

In 1945, World War II had brought about the independence of Korea and Koreans began to restore and rediscover the true values of physical education. The Korean Amateur Athletic Association (KASA) was reformed and reorganized in September, 1945, under the leadership of YO Woon Young, who served as its first president. The First National Athletic Games were held in October, 1945, and Korea participated in the 14th Olympic Games of London in 1946, where the Korean team placed 24th on an overall rating which was, in fact, the highest place attained by an Asian nation.[22]

## ADMINISTRATION AND ORGANIZATION

On March 1, 1968, three major sports organizations in Korea, the Korean Amateur Association, the Korean School Athletic Association and the Korean Olympic Committee, were consolidated to become the Korean Amateur Sports Association (KASA). The Korean Amateur Sports Association is the only government supported organization which officially governs and directs all levels of sports activities, including domestic and international competition. There are thirty-two sports associations and eleven provincial and city sports presentations (each association has at least 4 sub-associations such as elementary school federation, secondary school federation, collegiate federation and provincial association), which are affiliated with KASA. Administratively, the KASA is under the supervision and direction of the Ministry of Education. The Bureau of Physical Education and the Ministry of Education handles administrative matters for sports organizations as well as physical education and athletic programs in schools. The Korean Olympic Committee (KOC), established in 1946 became a member of the International Olympic Committee in 1947.[10]

## GOVERNMENTAL POLICY

Beginning in 1961, the government reformed their educational policy and placed the highest emphasis on health and physical education, and encouraged all Koreans to participate in physical fitness programs and sports activities.[8] The government also increased required number of hours in physical education from elementary schools to graduate schools. Methods of teaching in physical education were changed from theoretical study to a program of practical and active participation. Physical and medical examinations (including chest x-rays) are administered to students and teachers in schools under governmental sponsorship.

Following the educational reforms of 1961, the government enacted the Kook Min Che Yook Jin Heung Bup (National Physical Education Promotion Law) in 1963 and stated its objectives as: (1) to achieve improvement of physical fitness, (2) to prepare physical educators, (3) to improve the old and build new facilities, (4) to provide for proper guidance of outstanding athletes, and (5) to encourage schools to emphasize the social aspects of physical education.

In early 1970 the city government of Seoul established a Junior Physical Education High School and a Senior Physical Education High School to educate and train young athletes.

In March 3, 1970, the National Physical Education Council was created by the government, and the Prime Minister served as the Chairman, with twenty members. This council studies and evaluates physical education policy and related problems, and makes recommendations to the government.

In 1973, the Seu-Po-Tsu So-Nyun Dan (Sports Youth Groups) were organized in every elementary and junior high school and annual National Sports Youth Competitions have successfully been held in Korea.

There are several types of scholarships available to outstanding athletes, as well as, several kinds of physical education awards by the government, the press and private organizations. Of them, the Physical Education Award of the Republic of Korea is the highest award (service, leader, research and athlete) which is awarded annually. Recently the government also initiated the Physical Education Medal which has five different degrees, and this awards leaders in physical education and sports, and outstanding international players. In 1977, the government established the National Physical Education College which primarily educates and trains elite athletes and future leaders in sports. The government also designates "Physical Education Day" and "Physical Education Week", and encourages people to sponsor and participate in sports programs and events.

## PHYSICAL EDUCATION IN SCHOOLS

The basic principle of Korean education was clearly indicated in the Constitutional Law which states "the foundation of Korean education is a democratic philosophy which guarantees equal opportunity for education and respect of individual ability."

The general objectives of Korean physical education are to develop the individual physically, mentally, emotionally, and socially, and to develop recreational and fitness concepts and a safe attitude toward activities.[5]

The Korean school system consists of pre-schools (kindergarten), elementary schools (grades 1-6), junior high schools (grades 7-9), senior high schools (grades 10-12), institutions for higher learning (colleges and universities), and graduate schools.[12]

1. Pre-Schools. There are more than 600 kindergarten in Korea, and there is no official syllabus for kindergarten physical education program. However, educational laws state that physical and mental development of children are primary purposes of pre-school education. Most children participate in simple calisthenics, free play, and simple individual and team games.

2. Elementary Schools. In 1950, compulsory and free elementary education was instituted, and there are now more than 6,150 elementary schools in Korea with approximately 5.8 million children enrolled. Physical education in elementary schools is required and is a vital part of the school program. Most of the programs are taught by classroom teachers and 2,600 specialists in physical education. The pupils meet an average 3-5 hours per week (45 minutes per session).[8] Each school has a "play day" or "Physical education day" and annual physical education sports meets where pupils are encouraged

to take part in the programs; parents are also invited to participate in certain races. The physical education program mainly consists of simple gymnastics, play, low organized games and activities, dance, health and hygiene.

Basically, the Ministry of Education permits interschool athletic competition at the elementary school level. However, the government allows only 5th and 6th grades to participate in interschool competitions in the following sports: gymnastics, track and field, basketball, skating, badminton, soccer, swimming, table tennis, tisrum, and baseball. Recently Rae Kwon Do has become a popular sport in the elementary schools. [10]

3. Junior High Schools. There are approximately 1,810 schools with 1,600,000 students. During the 7th grade through 9th grades, the English language is introduced (some private elementary schools teach English in the 5th grade) and physical education program is taught by specialists who encourage participation in athletic programs. Participation is required in the physical education program for six hours each week (45 minutes per session). In the girl's program, one period of physical education is for dance. Most of the students participate on teams of their own choice as co-curricular activities. Physical education teachers also coach teams, but there is no extra compensation for the service. Most physical education teachers serve as student counselors. A great number of schools require YUDO (judo) or Tae Kwon Do as a part of their physical education programs. A great majority of schools participate in interschool competitions and every junior high school has a Sports Youth Group. There are about 2,500 physical education specialists and 300 coaches in junior high schools.

The physical education program mainly consists of gymnastics, sports, dance, recreation, health and hygiene, and the theory of physical education. The following sports are offered at this level: track and field, swimming, soccer, baseball, basketball, volleyball, table tennis, handball (German), gymnastics, tennis (lawn and soft), rugby, football, Tisrum, Yudo, Tae Kwon Do, Kum Do (Oriental fencing), hockey, and fencing.

4. Senior High Schools. There are about 900 senior high schools with 680,000 students, and over 1,100 P.E. specialists and 300 coaches. A physical education examination is a part of the general entrance examination to high school which consists of physical fitness test and basic knowledge in physical education. All students are required to meet three hours per week (50 minutes per session). Most students participate in and enjoy co-curricular activities. The following sports activities are popular among students: Boys - gymnastics, soccer, track and field, baseball, basketball, volleyball, table tennis, tennis, badminton, yudo, tae kwon do, boating, skating, tisrum, wrestling, fencing, cycling, weight lifting, handball, and others; girls enjoy almost all of the sports except the combative sports; dance programs are very popular for girls. Classical, modern, and

traditional Korean dancing are taught in the dance programs. In physical education lecture classes, theory, history, hygiene, health, and safety, and sports rules are taught. Students participate in interscholastic competitions and parents and teachers encourage their participation in such competitions.

5. Colleges and Universities. At the present time, there are more than 100 institutions for higher learning with approximately 172,100 students and 350 full time physical education faculty members. Physical education is mandatory and students are required to meet twice per week (50 minutes per session) and must earn 4-6 semester hours for graduation. Intramural programs and athletic competitions are very popular and there are a number of intercollegiate contests. Some outstanding college teams compete with professional teams or go abroad for international competition, and some colleges and universities encourage and emphasize interscholastic competitions more than regular physical education. The best known intercollegiate contest is "Yon-Ko Chun" or "Ko Yon Chun" (Yonsei University vs. Korea University or vice versa) which their two teams compete in soccer, baseball, rugby, basketball and ice hockey annually. It should be noted that the Ministry of Education encourages every college or university to have at least five different sports teams. At the present, there are more than thirty sports activities avilable to college students in Korea.

6. Graduates Schools. There are about 67 graduate schools in Korea, and graduate students are also strongly urged to take part in the physical education program[1] (once physical education was required for graduate students).

## PHYSICAL EDUCATION IN THE COMMUNITY (Post-School programs)

Korea has a long and proud history of traditional sports and games. Nevertheless, she has only sixty years of modern physical education and thirty-six of those years she was under foreign occupation. Being a physical education-oriented people, the Koreans love sports and actively participate in sports and physical education programs, as well as athletic competition. The following official creed indicates the Koreans' belief in honorable sportsmanship and in the value of sports' education.

### ATHLETES' PLEDGES

Athletics is a process of physical and mental development which makes man useful to human society through intensive and balanced conditioning of body. Athletics forms the basis of wholesome human life, and contributes to social development by enabling man to behave with courage, perserverance, and a sense of self-sacrifice. We hereby

pledge ourselves to fulfill the following in order to participate actively in athletic activities and to elevate the
general standards of culture:

1.  Participants in games shall be devoted to these
    games, shall do their utmost with sportsmanship un-
    affected by self-interest and shall never be over-
    elated in victory or feel humiliated in defeat.

2.  Participants in sports shall accept rulings by judges,
    pay due respect to opponents, and compete in the
    fairest manner without inordinately concerning them-
    selves with outclassing their adversaries.

3.  Those charged with officiating shall administer
    games according to pertinent rules and ensure an
    amicable atmosphere throughout the games.

4.  Athletic leaders shall possess amateur personality,
    always endeavoring to stress scientific development
    of playing techniques and imaginative approaches
    and instruction.

5.  Spectators shall not spare admiration and recognition
    at each display of sportsmanship and outstanding
    performance by players, refraining from assuming
    too partisan an attitude.

Athletes abiding by these principles will be looked upon
as model citizens for others to emulate and will develop
themselves cadres in carrying out just and salutary activities.

Koreans consider post-school physical education programs to
be very important. Today, many social institutions and industrial
establishments have sports and recreational activity programs and
regular competition. Major industrial and/or business companies sponsor sports teams. Most all banking institutions have basketball,
volleyball, and baseball teams which have produced a number of outstanding men and women players for international competitions.

Other community organization and manufacturing establishments
have teams and programs which are of interest to administrators and
employees. A number of community teams actively and successfully
participate in domestic and international games.

There are a great number of YUDO and TAE KWON DO practice halls throughout the country. These practice halls are under
the direction and supervision of the Korean Yudo Association and the
Korean Tae Kwon Do Association of the KASA respectively. Soccer,
table tennis, swimming, volleyball, and basketball are popular sports

in the community programs.  However, soccer draws the highest number of spectators.

The YMCA of Korea in Seoul, the birthplace of Korean modern physical education is still strongly contributing to the development and improvement of Korean physical education.  YMCA, Korean Recreation Association, Boy Scouts, Girl Scouts and other institutions also offer excellent sports and physical education programs for children and the general public.  Their contributions to the development of physical education are tremendous and valuable.  Wrestling is also a popular sport among students because YANG Jung Mo, a featherweight wrestler, who for the first time represented the Republic of Korea, won a gold medal in the 21st Olympic Games in Montreal.  The Korean Amateur Sports Association also strongly sponsors and develops post school physical education programs.  Recently Hapkido, an art of self-defense, has also gained in popularity in Korea.

The Pan National Sports Festival includes thirty-two sports, and usually more than 12,000 athletes participate.  This meet is more than fifty years old, draws the largest crowd of spectators and contestants, and is the highest level of national competition.  This festival is organized and directed by the Korean Amateur Sports Association.  It should be noted that the Pan Sports Youth Festival is also held annually in Korea.

## PHYSICAL EDUCATION IN THE ARMED FORCES AND POLICE

The Republic of Korea armed forces is the fourth largest army in the world and second in size only to that of the United States in the free world.

Each Military installation has well organized physical and recreational programs and relatively fine facilities.  In addition to military training, Tae Kwon Do and Yudo are emphasized and special training is given to the officers and men of the Korean armed forces.  The Service Academies (the Military Academy, the Naval Academy, and the Air Force Academy) offer a modern physical education and sports program for cadets.  In the academy physical education programs, they emphasize Yudo and Tae Kwon Do which are required programs for cadets.  All cadets must attain the rank of black belt or brown belt either in Yudo or Tae Kwon Do or both prior to their graduation.

Administratively, the physical education program for the Armed Forces is directed and supervised by the Section of Physical Education, the Ministry of National Defense, and competitive sports are the responsibility of the Armed Forces Sports Association which was established in 1951.  The Army Sports Association, Naval Sports Association and Air Force Sports Association are each responsible for sports competition in its respective branch.  In 1954, the inter-academy physical education competition was instituted and the three service academies annually hold this competition which draws one of the largest groups of spectators in sports.[14] The Services compete against one another not only in sports but also in military review, marching, and cheerleading activities during the intermission of the games.

Most top flight athletes are in the Armed Forces and there is inter-unit athletic competition in all levels of military units. Physical education officers who are specialists in sports direct the programs. The Armed Forces Sports Association of Korea became a full member of the International Military Sports Council (CISM) in 1957 and regularly and successfully participates in CISM Championships.

## PROFESSIONAL TRAINING PROGRAM

Korean colleges and universities are under the direct administrative jurisdiction of the Ministry of Education. However, each institution has the right to design and formulate the curriculum for its institution subject to approval by the Ministry of Education.

More than one hundred and twenty-eight semester hours are required for a bachelor's degree and at least one-third of these credits must be in general education. The government establishes a quota of students for a specific department in each college or university and the college and universities must observe this quota number. There are, at present, approximately 4,000 students in professional undergraduate programs in physical education and also about 100 students at the graduate level. However, there is no doctoral program in physical education available yet.

In order to obtain a teaching certificate in physical education for junior high schools, a minimum of two years of college education (junior college) is required and additional education courses are necessary. However, in fact, it is almost impossible to get employment for a physical education teacher with only a junior college diploma. For senior high schools, a Bachelor's degree or equivalent diploma (issued for a specific activity) is needed. Five differently classified teaching certificates are issued by the Ministry of Education which range from special instructor for a particular activity or course (one holding a diploma) to a fully qualified teacher in physical education.

For college teachers, at the least a Bachelor's degree is required, and those who do not have graduate degrees but who have engaged in teaching for a long time must have acceptable research papers or publications. Their qualifications are screened and evaluated by colleges and also by the Ministry of Education which determines their academic rank and control promotion to another rank. There are four academic ranks in college teaching positions: instructor, assistant professor, associate professor and full professor. The curriculum of the professional training programs in physical education has been primarily patterned after the professional programs of the United States and Japan. However, the needs of Korean education and some of the better points of other national programs were incorporated into the program.  Physiology of exercise, anatomy, kinesiology, research methods, measurement, methodology, psychology of sports, history, sociology of sports, and administration, as well as sports activities, are emphasized in the program.

The following institutions offer the professional programs in physical education:  Seoul National University, Korea University, Yonsei University, Ehwa Women's University, Dan Kook University, Dong Kuk University, Kon Kuk University, Cho Sun University, Soo Do Women's Teacher College, Don Ah University, Kyung Buk University, Choong Buk College, Myung Ji College, Kyung Gri College, National College of Physical Education and Korean Yudo College (which offers a unique program in martial arts, sports and physical education), and others.

There are a number of seminars or summer training courses annually available to physical education teachers as in-service training.  Training for coaches is conducted by the Coach Academy (founded in 1965) which is an institution of the Korean Amateur Sports Association and primarily teaches the science of coaching and advanced training techniques for coaches.

There are two professional physical education organizations in Korea, the Korean Association for Health, Physical Education, and Recreation (KAHPER) and the Korean Society of Physical Education (KSPE).  KSPE publishes The Journal of Physical Education annually.

CONCLUDING STATEMENT

Koreans love sports and enjoy participating in almost all sports and games.  Koreans believe that physical fitness is a very important part of their way of life.  Koreans also participate in international physical education conferences, clinics, seminars, and the Olympic Games, and international sports competitions.  The Korean government strongly supports physical education programs in schools and encourage people to actively take part in physical fitness programs and sports.  Norms and standardized physical education tests have been constructed for all levels of schools and athletes.  Official textbooks for professional programs in physical education have been published and special scholarships program for outstanding athletes were instituted a long time ago.  The government placed physical education in top priority list in the national policy.  President Chung-Hee Park of the Republic of Korea stated that:[22]

"Sportsmanship should be regarded as the guiding
principle to be practiced by the democratic citizen.
It is one of the major sources of energy essential
to national and social development.  Therefore, I
am calling on all citizens to step up their efforts
to further promote our athletic programs."

There is a strong tendency in Korean physical education and sports today for Korean leaders to overemphasize athletic competition, particularly at the collegiate and international levels. While the success and production of good results in international competitions and in the Olympic Games are very important, it is not the most pressing need for Korean physical education and sports. The primary emphasis should be placed on physical fitness, research, innovated curriculum of physical education, sports medicine, improved facilities for school and community, governmental support of finance, security and employment of sports leaders and elite athletes, men and women. Without these areas of emphasis, the Korean physical education and sports program will be delayed and perhaps before long even regress.

Korea apparently needs and should organize an Office of Physical Education and Sports at the cabinet level in the government and/or should establish a Presidential council on Physical Fitness and Sports with selected professionally qualified physical educators as its members who actively and scientifically participate in formulation of national policy for physical education and sports in general. Furthermore, consolidations of present organizations and the establishment of a central administrative office (needed for efficiency and proficiency) should be taken into consideration.

Korea is striving to build a true welfare society in the 1980's in which all people will be able to fully live their lives and also fully enjoy sports and recreation activities.

SELECTED REFERENCES

1. Chang, Juho. "A Study of Current Problems and Proposed Solutions in Effective Administration of Physical Education." (Unpublished Master's Thesis in Public Administration), Seoul National University, Seoul, Korea (Korean edition).

2. Chei, Kihong. *Kyo Yook Sa.* Seoul, Korea: Kyong Sul Chool Ban Sa. 1965.

3. *Guide to Korea, 1969.* Washington, D. C.: Korean Information Office, Embassy of Korea. 1969.

4. Kim, Daeshik. "Korea's Physical Education: Today and Tomorrow." *Che Yook.* Korean Amateur Sports Association. 1972.

5. Kim Daeshik. "Physical Education in Korea." *The Physical Educator.* Vol. 26, No. 2. 1969.

6. Kim, Daeshik. "Tae Kwon Do - Brief History of Tae Kwon Do and Korea." *The Third Tae Kwon Do World Championship Program.* Chicago: September, 1977.

7. Kim Daeshik and R. T. Bowen. "Physical Education in Republic of Korea," in *Physical Education Around the World.* Edited by William Johnson. Monograph No. 4. Indianapolis, Indiana: Phi Epsilon Kappa. 1970.

8. *Korea, 1968.* Ministry of Information, Republic of Korea, Seoul, Korea. 1967.

9. *Korea Today.* Seoul, Korea: Kookjo Hong Bo Sa. Seoul, Korea: Vol. 16, No. 5. 1968.

10. Korean Amateur Sports Association. *Che Yook Paik Suh.* Seoul, Korea: KASA. 1972.

11. Korean Amateur Sports Association. *Che Yook Chung Suh.* Seoul, Korea: KASA. 1973.

12. Korean Education Federation (ed.). *Han Kook Kyo Yook Nyun Kam.* Seoul, Korea. 1965.

13. *Korean Report.* Washington, D. C., Embassy of Korea. 1968.

14. Kyung Hang Shin Moon Sa (Ed.). *Encyclopedia of Physical Education.* Seoul, Korea. 1961.

15. Lee, Byungku. *Che Yook Jak Tong Ron.* Seoul, Korea: Yook Min Sa. 1964.

16.    Lee, Byungwi, "Han Kook Che Yook Eui Bal Chun Sang Ko Chul." *Che Yook*. Korean Amateur Sports Association, Vol. 27, Nos. 3 & 4. March-April, 1968.

17.    Lee, Dong Soo and C. P. Yo (Eds.). *Che Yook Ke Ron*. Seoul, Korea: Dong Nyung Sa. 1964.

18.    Lee, Hongsek and K. B. Lee. *Kook Sa Yo Hae*. Seoul, Korea: Min Kye Sa. 1961.

19.    Nam, Dong Yong. *Kook Sa Chung Sul*. Seoul, Korea: Dong A Chool Ban Sa. 1960.

20.    Paik, N. U. *Dae Hak Che Yook*. Seoul, Korea: Il Shin Sa. 1963.

21.    *Sports*. Seoul, Korea: Han Kook Che Yook Moon Wha Sa. 1968.

22.    *Sports in Korea*. Korean Olympic Committee. 1973.

23.    Yon Hap Shin Moon Sa (Ed.). *Che Yook Dae Kam*. Seoul, Korea. 1957.

# SPORT AND PHYSICAL EDUCATION IN KUWAIT
## by Mesaed Al-Haroun and Jim Stillwell

### Biographical Sketches

*Mesaed Al-Haroun* was born June 10, 1953. He received his B.S. from The Higher Institute of Sports Education in Cairo, Egypt in 1972. He received his M.A. in 1976 from San Francisco State University. He served as Sports Supervisor at Kuwait University for one year. He is currently a doctoral student in the School of Health, Physical Education, and Recreation at Indiana University.

*Jim Stillwell* was born on the 26th of September 1947. He received his B.S. and his M.S. in Education, both with a major in Physical Education, from Western Illinois University, Macomb in 1969 and 1973, respectively. Between those dates he taught in the public schools of Illinois. At present he is a doctoral student in the School of Health, Physical Education, and Recreation at Indiana University.

# INTRODUCTION

Kuwait is located on the northwestern shore of the Arabian Gulf. It is bordered on the southwest by Saudi Arabia, on the east by the gulf, and on the north and west by Iraq. The area of Kuwait is approximately 7,000 square miles, somewhat smaller than New Jersey. The country is roughly rectangular in shape and includes five off-shore islands.

Located in the desert zone, Kuwait has a continental climate. The summer months are hot and quite humid. The temperatures reach their highest peaks during July and August, when it is common for the temperature to surpass 110°F. The winter months are generally warm, but temperatures occasionally drop below freezing.

Kuwait is a constitutional state ruled by the Sheikh Sabah al Salim al Sabah, the Head of State or Emir of the country. The Emir holds executive power and holds office for live. The Emir appoints the Prime Minister who in turn has the power to both appoint and dismiss the remaining 15 ministers. Legislative power is vested in the National Assembly. There are 50 legislative members who are elected by the people to a four year term. Judicial power is vested in the Supreme Court whose members are appointed by the Minister of Justice.

Kuwait is regarded as one of the richest countries in the world. Oil was discovered in 1936 and was first exported in 1946. Kuwait is a true example of a welfare state, with a free and comprehensive health service program plus a free educational system from kindergarten to the university level. The population of Kuwait in 1975 was 994,837 (See Table 1). Because of the vast number of job

Table 1. Population Information

| | Kuwaiti | | | Non-Kuwaiti | |
|---|---|---|---|---|---|
| | Number | Per Cent of Total | | Number | Per Cent of Total |
| Male | 236,600 | 23.8 | Male | 307,168 | 30.9 |
| Female | 235,488 | 23.7 | Female | 215,581 | 21.6 |
| Total | 472,088 | 47.5 | Total | 522,749 | 52.5 |

opportunities in Kuwait, there are more non-Kuwaities than Kuwaities residing in the country. Kuwait City, the capital city, is located on the Arabian Gulf. The official language is Arabic, with English the second language. The official religion is Islam, with 95% of the population being Moslem.

## GENERAL EDUCATION

Passage of a 1965 law made education compulsory for all Kuwaities between the ages of four and 16. The educational system is administered by the Ministry of Education who is appointed by the Prime Minister. As stated previously, education is totally free. Students are not only provided with textbooks, meals, and uniforms, but when the situation warrants they also receive transportation and lodging. The Ministry of Education establishes standardized curricula, administers school achievement examinations, writes and approves textbooks, trains and hires teachers, regulates teacher salaries, prepares the budget, and approves all expenditures. The Ministry also determines how many and what types of public schools are to be constructed.

The 1961 school year found more than 51,000 students in the public schools of Kuwait. By 1975 this total had increased to more than 201,900 students. Of this student enrollment, 109,900 were male and 92,000 were female. This disparity is due to the fact that Kuwait is predominantly a male society. However, women are rapidly approaching both educational and social equality. There has been a change in the attitudes toward the role of woman, they are being increasingly liberated from the restraints of custom.

In comparison to the increase in student enrollment, the number of teachers increased six-fold during the same period, from 2,500 in 1961 to 15,500 in 1975. This statistic indicates a very handsome pupil-teacher ratio of 13 to one. A Pan-Arabic flavor to the teaching fraternity exists in Kuwait, with many of the public school instructors coming from Egypt, Jordan, Lebanon, Palestine, or Syria.

Kuwait University is the country's only university. It is an imposing complex and quite modern. The university provides both undergraduate and graduate education for all Arabs. In 1975 there were 583 graduates from the schools of commerce, law, literature, science, and economics and political science. Many of the Kuwaiti graduates follow-up with advanced study in the western world, primarily in the United States or Great Britain.

Following a two year nursery school, public school education is separated into four levels, each consisting of four years of study. (See Table 2). The emphasis during the first two levels of public

Table 2. Public School Education.

| School Level | Age of Student |
|---|---|
| Elementary | 6-9 |
| Intermediate | 10-13 |
| Secondary | 14-17 |
| University | 18-21 |

schooling is placed upon both the mental and the physical development of the individual, with mastery of reading, writing, and arithmetic mandatory. The secondary level is separated into two categories: (1) academic and (2) vocational. These two categories are broken down further. An academic course of study is either literary or scientific, whereas the vocational course of study is either technical or commercial. In Kuwait there is a large and very well equipped institute which provides training for special education students at all levels.

## PHYSICAL EDUCATION

Two Ministeries are responsible for physical education in Kuwait Kuwait: (1) the Ministry of Education within the schools and (2) the Ministry of Social Affairs and Labor outside the schools.

### Ministry of Education

The physical education program in all public schools is under the central control of the Physical Education Department, which is under the leadership of the Ministry of Education. Physical education is required in the three public school levels, elementary, intermediate, and secondary. Physical education is taught three times per week at the elementary level and two times per week at both the intermediate and the secondary levels. Individual class periods are 45 minutes in length. In addition, there is a special sports' period conducted each school day following regular class work. This period allows for maximum participation by a large number of students. In an attempt to avoid overexertion and to provide ample time for school work, the students are allowed to participate in no more than two sports. All students dress accordingly and participate in both the physical education and the sports' program. Excuses from participation in either of these programs are uncommon.

The physical education curriculum, extending from the elementary level to the secondary level, follows a natural progression. The elementary physical education program offers various modes of exercise and movement, including initiative, creative, and repetitive. As the students progress, the elementary program includes tumbling, apparatus activities, and team sports. The intermediate and secondary physical education programs consist primarily of the following activities: aquatics, basketball, dance, gymnastics, soccer, team handball, track and field, and volleyball. Although comprehensive examinations are administered at the end of each school year in all other course work no physical education examinations are administered. The physical education grade is not included in the student's overall average. There are no physical education textbooks, however the instructors use a handbook prepared by the Department of Physical Education.

Athletic competition in the public schools begins at the elementary level. Interscholastic competition is an integral part of the total physical education program. The physical education instructors are solely responsible for coaching the athletic teams and receive no monetary compensation. There is no general admission price for athletic events. There are no bands or cheerleaders and it is unusual to find more than 30 spectators in attendance at any athletic contest.

There are extracurricular activities during the spring and summer months. The Department of Physical Education organizes scout jamborees and allocates funds for secondary sports' teams to travel to Arabian and European countries to participate in various competitive events. The department has also established a number of sports' centers which are equipped to instruct beginners, enabling them to participate in such sporting events as the Arab School Tournament, which is held every four years.

## Ministry of Social Affairs and Labor

The Department of Youth Affairs within the Ministry of Social Affairs and Labor is responsible for physical education outside the public schools. This department has established 13 sports' clubs whose functions are to (1) encourage youths to participate actively in sport, (2) raise the standards of sports' participation, (3) control juvenile delinquency, (4) sponsor various athletic events, (5) help athletes who are in special need, and (6) discourage professionalism in all sports.

The activities sponsored by these sports' clubs include aquatics, basketball, boxing, fencing, gymnastics, judo, soccer, squash, table tennis, team handball, track and field, volleyball, and weight training. Each activity is categorized into levels according to the participants' ages. Funds needed to sponsor these sports' clubs come from four sources: (1) the Ministry of Social Affairs and Labor, (2) membership dues, (3) private contributions, and (4) ticket sales.

The competition between and among these 13 sports' clubs is organized by individual athletic associations, which are totally funded by the Ministry. These associations function to organize, administer, and supervise tournaments for the sports' clubs within the country. The activities organized by the athletic associations are governed by the Kuwaiti Olympic Commission. The commission was founded in 1961 and functions to assist the athletic associations in their duties, supervise all association activities, and prepare Kuwaiti teams for Olympic competition.

The Department of Youth Affairs also finances and supervises neighborhood youth centers. These centers conduct recreational activities for those children, 18 years or younger, who do not participate in the sports' clubs. The department also sponsors periodic lecture and in-service seminars for the physical educators.

## CONCLUSION

Physical education and sport hold a place of importance among the Kuwaiti people. Kuwait, being a small country surrounded by larger countries, wants to be outstanding in its many areas. The people of Kuwait consider physical education and sport an important approach to achieving this goal.

## SELECTED REFERENCES

1. *Annual Statistical Abstract*. Central Statistical Office - Ministry of Planning, Kuwait. 1976.

2. *Area Handbook for the Peripheral States of Arabian Peninsula*. Sanford Research Institute. 1971.

3. *International Yearbook of Education*. UNESCO, Vol. 30. 1968.

4. *The New Encyclopedia Britannica*. Kuwait, Vol. 10. 1974.

5. *Who's Who in the Arab World*. Lebanon. 1971-1972.

SPORT AND PHYSICAL EDUCATION IN MEXICO

by Maurice A. Clay


Biographical Sketch


*Maurice A. Clay* was born May 6, 1911, Waldron,
Indiana. After graduating from the Waldron Public
Schools, he received an A.B. in Chemistry from Ken-
tucky Wesleyan College in 1932, the M.A. in Physical
Education in 1935, and the Ed.D. degree from the Uni-
versity of Kentucky.

He taught and coached in a public high school
in Indiana, served as Director of Physical Education at
the College of the Ozarks, was a Physical Fitness Officer in the U. S. Air Force, and, following service, was
Director of Physical Education, University School, University of Kentucky. He has acted as Director of the
Professional Curriculum in Physical Education at the
University of Kentucky since 1948.

His major interests include administration, professional preparation, and international physical education movements.

He is past president of the Arkansas and of the
Kentucky Associations of Health, Physical Education and
Recreation, receiving the Distinguished Service Award
from the Kentucky Association in 1955. He is a past
president of the University of Kentucky Faculty Club
and of the Kentucky unit of Phi Delta Kappa.

He has served as Chairman of the College Physical Education Section, Southern District, and is the
immediate past chairman of the Council on Equipment
and Supplies of the American Association for Health,
Physical Education and Recreation and is the immediate
past chairman of the International Relations Committee
of NCPEAM. He served as a Fulbright Lecturer to the
National University of Columbia in 1960; as a member of
a State Department commission on student welfare programs to the same country in 1961; as a Consultant to
the Peace Corps, Colombia IV Project 1962, Texas Western College; and, as Consultant to the Foundation of
Colombian Universities in Colombia, 1963. He coordinated sports and recreation training for the Peace Corps
India Project, University of Kentucky, summer, 1966.
In 1957, and again in 1962, he served as a Consultant
to The American School Foundation in Mexico. He has

just returned from a visit to Mexico in the interest of
the present paper.


## Editor's Note

Because of the unavailability of Dr. Clay for the
updating of his fine article on Sport and Physical Education in Mexico, his original article is presented intact
and the current information is included in a special section at the end of Dr. Clay's article. The Editor participated in the ICHPER Congress in Mexico City in 1977
and secured considerable current information from Mexican leaders in Sport and Physical Education. Sr. Mario
Vázquez Rãna, President of the Mexican Olympic Committee and Professor Miguel Meneses Cabrera, Director
of Physical Education, Mexicali were especially helpful
in providing current informational materials. George
Zigman, basketball coach at a suburban Chicago High
School and a student in the Editor's Extramural Class
in International Sport consolidated this and other current information into a class research paper.


The material presented is based upon the literature, visitation
and personal interviews. Physical education in Mexico cannot be
separated from sports, though they are not syonymous. The more
troublesome problems of Mexican physical education, it mentioned, are
best known to Mexicans and discussion does not come within the scope
of this paper.


## Background

Mexico lies between Central America and the United States, is
the third largest of the Latin American countries with a land mass
approximately one-fourth that of the continental United States. Its
population of 34.6 million (1962) is fast increasing with one of the
highest birth rates in the world.

The land is characterized by a high interior plateau averaging
from 3,000 to 4,000 feet in the north to 7,000 to 8,000 feet farther
south. The plateau is flanked by a range of mountains along the
east and west with a fringe of lowlands along the coast. The southern end of the plateau near Mexico City is crossed by broken ranges
of mountains including snow-clad Popocatepl (17,887 feet) and other
high volcanic peaks. The lowland peninsula of Yucatan in the southeastern tip was the seat of the ancient Mayan culture.

The largest cities are Mexico City, the capital and site of the
Aztec capital before the Spanish conquest, with a population now

approaching 8 million; Guadalajara; located in a rich mining and agricultural area; and Monterrey, the Pittsburgh of Mexico. Other important cities are Puebla, Merida, San Luis Potosi, and Vera Cruz.

The people of Mexico are largely of mixed Indian and Spanish descent. Approximately 20 to 30 per cent are Indian, some 10 per cent are white. Spanish is the official language and Mexico is the most populous Spanish-speaking country in the world. The people are largely Catholic; there are approximately 1 million Protestants. Church and State are separated and there is complete religious freedom. No religious body can acquire landed property.

A federal republic of 29 states, 2 territories, and one federal district, Mexico has executive, legislative, and judicial divisions of government. The Partido Revolucionario Institucional Party (PRI) has been the majority political party since 1928, with four opposition parties registered. Independence from Spain was effectively achieved in 1821, eleven years after Hidalgo's declaration of 1810.

Over half of Mexico's population is engaged in its basic economic activity--agriculture, with the principal corps being corn, wheat, beans, cotton, coffee and chicle. The country is now self-sufficient in most foodstuffs though agriculture accounts for only one-fifth of the gross national product. Mining and petroleum production are important sources of national wealth. The national income is approximately ten times higher than it was 25 years ago and in recent years has expanded more than the population. Since the 1930's Mexico has been embarked on an extensive program of economic development, rural education and public works which represent an extension of the social and political revolution which began prior to World War I. According to Dwight S. Brothers, the per capita income in Mexico is $350 per year.[2] Other sources list it somewhat higher.

Primary education (1-6) is free and compulsory, but lack of schools and teachers and great distances with inadequate transportation lead to problems in enforcement of the law. Enrollment at the primary level has more than doubled since 1930 and despite tremendous efforts school facilities have not kept pace with population growth. At the secondary level the student may prepare for entry into a teacher, commercial or vocational school or for one of the universities. In addition to the National University in Mexico City, founded in 1551 and currently one of the largest in the world, there are 16 state universities.

## Historical Development

Hackensmith[3] has treated the historical development of sports in Mexico at length. He reported that Culin was convinced that the oldest existing games among primitive peoples of the Americas originated in the southwestern United States; and that the games and sports of all such peoples in the Western Hemisphere were remarkably similar, with variations restricted to differences in design or materials used in the construction of playing equipment affected by environment and by the skill of the craftsmen.

He quotes Goellner to the effect that the Mayans played a court game which may have been invented as early as 700 A.D. (Mexican sources suggest that such a ball game was played in Tehotihuacan earlier than this.) Goellner located approximately 40 courts, thirty in and about Yucatan (others were found in Guatemala, Honduras, and southeastern Arizona). He described the typical court as recessed in the ground with the floor, sides, and ends paved with stone and typically shaped like an "I". The target for the probably three players to each side was a 9-inch hole in a stone about four feet square and one foot thick at an elevation of 25 feet above the court. The ball (made of rubber) could only be touched with the knees, thighs, hips, buttocks, and head. He concluded that it was a fast, furious, painful game inasmuch as the players wore leather hip and loin aprons and helmets. Furman[4] indicated that a similar game had been found in Puerto Rico.

A well-illustrated book on pre-Hispanic sports has recently been published in Mexico--*Deportes, pre-Hispanica*--as one of an *Arte de Mexico* series.

The development of physical education in Mexico is not clear. According to Gayou[5], physical education was fostered officially in the government schools as early as 1890. The salaries of 18 teachers of physical education on the government payroll represented 6 per cent of the total salaries that year for national education.

Hinojosa[6], however, is of the opinion that before 1921 the subject known today as physical education did not exist in Mexico. The closest thing to it, he says, was called Gimnasia--based upon the Swedish system of Peter Ling--and supplemented by cable exercises, navy climbing ladders, and other apparatus. Most of the people, however, knew of sports such as soccer, basketball and swimming. The YMCA was considered a leader and innovator.

Luis Bisquertl[7] in a report to the Sixth International Congress of Health, Physical Education and Recreation has stated that in the development of sports and physical education in the Spanish-American countries the opinion that has counted is that of the sports leader, the sportsman, the amateur, the journalist, or the military, rather than that of the educators.

Before Dr. Jose Peralta became the Director of Physical Education in secondary schools their programs were taught by unprepared professors, and classes were held during the students' free time. With the Mexican Revolution everything was subject to change and physical education became an important part of the educational program. To promote and give life to physical education, the Office of

Physical Education was created as a division under the Minister of Education.

Dr. Peralta, who studed in the United States and was familiar with physical education in that country, introduced many ideas relative to physical education and is credited by some with introducing basketball into physical education in Mexico. Dr. Peralta's plan of physical education was presented to the then President of Mexico, General Alvaro Obregon, who gave it effective support and appointed Peralta as the first Director of the new office of Physical Education.

Members of the Office of Physical Education did not have professional preparation in physical education. The majority were young men who had distinguished themselves in different sports; and their academic preparation was in fields such as engineering, agriculture, and law. Nonetheless, they were appointed as professors after taking a comprehensive examination on physical education.

The first Director of the Elemental School of Physical Education was Jose U. Escobar. The program offered in the school changes in some degree in each of the years 1912 and 1926. The National School of Physical Education was founded in 1936.

## Professional Preparation

The professsional preparation of teachers of physical education is effected in four special schools; the National School of Physical Education in Mexico City, and others at Puebla, Tabasco, and Chihuahua. The relationship between the schools is a moral one only. The National School in Mexico City feels a responsibility for and has strongly influenced the other institutions.[8] Preparation follows the general patterns of other teaching fields--lasting three years, and beginning immediately after completion of the secundaria (grade nine) or normally between the ages of 15 and 22.

Present practice supports an earlier observation by C. H. McCloy that greater attention is given to skills and less to theory and to a background of general education than in the United States.

Dr. David Juarez Miralda and his staff at the National School of Physical Education in Mexico City have had a new curriculum of preparation approved by the National Council of Education, effective in November, 1967.[8]

Included will be the establishment of the school on a military basis to encourage discipline; the division of the school year into semesters with courses normally calling for the completion of 100 clock hours of work. The student will receive three times as much Spanish as formerly, and English--presently taught for two hours each week for a year--will be extended to six hours each week for one year.

The psychology of teaching physical education; the history of philosophy, including logic and ethics; observation in the public schools; and tests and measurements (statistics) will be introduced.

The objectives of the new program are: to prepare specialized professors to teach in public and private schools; to contribute to improvement of the professors already in the field; to be a center for research and discussion promoting new ideas and methods and the application of modern techniques in physical education; to establish orientation programs and public crusades to educate the public toward physical education.

Presently the teacher of physical education has no direct responsibility for teaching health, but an effort is being made to advance this responsibility. The plan of study includes general subjects and related activities.

General policies for teachers seek wider student participation, use of audio-visual devices, seminars and workbooks. Every effort is being made to avoid the strict lecture method with the student as a passive element. A serious attempt will be made to schedule all classes on two-hour blocks of time, three days each week.

There are three major student organizations at the National School, along with special clubs. They are: Student government, an alumni club, and a third (or senior) year club which serves as "a generator of improvement."

Lacking facilities, very little research is being done at the National School, but the Director has asked for funds to establish laboratories for social, psychological, and biological research. The current staff includes some professors with a medical and other research background (for example, Dr. Aniceto Ortega in the physiology of exercise).

Attention is being given at the National School to preparing the teacher to cope with the lack of equipment and facilities through training in improvisation of equipment, working with a minimum of equipment, to adapt games, and to work through the equivalent of the P.T.A. (Padres de Familia).

The program of studies includes:[9]

Economic, Social and Cultural Problems of Mexico

> Introduction to Philosophy (History, Logic, Ethics, and
>     Aesthetics)
> Spanish (Techniques of Written and Oral Expression)
> General Psychology
> History of Physical Education
> Applied English
> School Observations

Basic Gymnastics I, II
Track I, II
Swimming I, II
Volleyball
Organized games
Exercises de order
Regional dances
Applied Anatomy
Child Growth and Development
Science of Education
Physiology I, II
Educational Sociology
Educational Psychology
Techniques of Teaching and Student Teaching I, II
Basketball I, II
Soccer
Music Education
Biolipologia and Kinesiology
Psicotechnica and Physical Education
Organization and Administration
Hygiene and Nutrition
Statistics Applied to Physical Education
Prevention and Treatment of Sports Injuries
Softball and Baseball
Fencing
Olympic Wrestling
Dance

For the fourth or optional year of specialization, in addition to preparation for the examination there will be a year-long class of 10 hours weekly. The options for specialization include:

Sports Application of Gymnastics--Artistic gymnastics with
    Olympic application
Track
Swimming
Diving
Basketball
Soccer
Volleyball
Baseball
Fencing
Boxing
Wrestling
Racquet sports
American football
The Organization of Sport
Regional Dance
Dance
Recreation

## Teaching As A Profession

Of a total of 2500 teachers of physical education[10] 90 per cent hold certificates which are given on a basis of minimum preparation. Approximately 10 per cent of the teachers hold the title of Professor given after the preparation of a thesis on a special subject plus other requirements. In some schools there are helpers or teaching assistants, called "monitores."

There is a limited amount of moving around in positions after assignment is made by the Office of Physical Education to one of eight geographical areas. Each year a particular school is assigned a specified number of teachers and teaching hours. The basic salary for 12 hours work per week is $96. Whether one makes more or less depends upon living costs and conditions and upon advancing to receive more than the basic 12 hours work. The "basic" salary in Lower California is reported as double the basic amount due to two factors—higher living costs near the United States and, in this instance, distance from the capitol.

The teacher may retire after 30 years of work and a minimum age of 55, or after 25 years of work and a minimum age of 65. A proposal has been made that retirement should be possible after 30 years of work, regardless of age.

Government employed teachers and their famililies receive free medical and dental care, insurance, discounts on food, drugs, et cetera, at special stores; and may receive loans on houses, trips, and cars. Similar benefits are available to those working for private agencies, schools and clubs through the Social Security Institute.

Written questionnaire reports on teachers come to the national office each two months from the directors in the several states, with the approval of the director of the school where the teacher is employed.

The teacher must reach age 25 before receiving more than the minimum work assignment of 12 hours. He may advance to 22 hours of teaching; inspectors receive 30 hours; state directors and regional inspectors in the 8 geographical zones receive more. The reported maximum weekly assignment was 42 hours.

Advancement is reported based upon a table of points allowing 12 to 14, 16, 18, 20, 22 hours of work, et cetera. Consideration is given to recommendations by school directors, outstanding success in competitions, and to reported punctuality, discipline, conduct, cooperation and other activities.

Lacking full employment with a government school, many of the physical educators work at private clubs or private schools. One such person is reported to hold five jobs.

The apparent effect of an extended teaching day in several schools or clubs is to make planning difficult and to limit the opportunity for good programs. Further, it tends to limit professional improvement and advancement through reading and study because as it is often said, "you simply do not have the energy to do more."

The teacher of Physical Education is considered a full faculty member at all educational levels. They have the same rights and they participate in the foundation of schedules and policy.[11]

The Association of Professors of Physical Education of Mexico is currently said to be defunct. It had state associations. In theory the Association worked for professional improvement and for an increase in social and cultural status for Physical Education. It made occasional contact with the Ministry of Education to settle matters of interest to the Association's members. It was reported that neither the teachers of physical education nor their organizations participated in the development of teaching standards nor in the development of inservice education and short courses. Teachers of physical education are eligible for membership in a general teachers syndicate--some participate.

There is no generally recognized professional magazine devoted to physical education in Mexico. One very good one privately published had a life of six issues (Educacion Fisica). There are numerous magazines devoted to professional sports and to physical culture, and sports receive wide newspaper coverage.

### Physical Education in Schools

Physical Education in the schools is under the direction of a National Office in the Ministry of Education, which generally establishes standards and policies, issues directives, assigns and oversees personnel.

The major objectives of physical education are:[12]

> "Harmonious and balanced development of the human body; development of physical, intellectual and moral abilities; training of the individual to make maximum efforts and to behave."

According to the Director General of Physical Education, Juan Figueroa Peralta,[13] in the Ministry of Education, emphasis is being placed upon "sports education" and upon six basic sports--track, basketball, soccer, swimming, volleyball, and gymnastics. The student will be allowed to make his choice of activities and it becomes the responsibility of the teacher to make participation possible at all times rather than on a seasonal basis. The basic philosophy is that they want participation "with liking and vigor,"--a good sportsman is one who engages in sport for pleasure and "a person who respects people, women, his city, his country, and the law."

There was formerly a belief that a sportsman was only that--now they seek to maintain an equilibrium between sport and education, with consideration in sport being given to those who are also good students. An effort is also being made to call attention to cleanliness.

Under a plan being advanced now, the teacher will teach six hours at the school and will take his students after school to the parks to make use of the facilities there, and will then return them to the school.

Physical education classes are scheduled twice each week for 50 minutes and are in the program of the student each year, though it is not uniformly required at the university level. While administrators and some professors have not fully accepted or supported physical education, the problem is largely limited to the older generation. Regardless of subject field, each new teacher prepared in the normal schools has physical education and sports training each year--including volleyball, track, either soccer (men) or softball and rhythms.

The content and source of syllabi and of physical performance examinations are a responsibility of the teacher, of the school administration and of the National Office and are available (ICHPER Report #1 op. cit. pp. 10, 16) at each grade level. School gymnasia, playrooms, and hard surface play areas of varying size and parks may be available.

As is known there may be considerable gap between activities listed as possible of inclusion in the physical education program and those which commonly are included.

Generally speaking, the early hours of each day are considered the best for learning and are reserved for academic classes. In inclement weather space for indoor activities is commonly lacking, and physical education classes are not held.

With burgeoning populations class sizes for regular classes may approach 60,--two shifts a day are common. In public primary schools the girls may attend the first shift, the boys are second. Increasingly in the public schools boys and girls attend school together at the secondary level (grades 7, 8, 9); this may also be found now in some primary schools.

In a National Office of Physical Education communication dated April, 1967[14] the values of recreational type games were listed and guides outlined. Teaching points commonly found in the Unites States appear here: developmental values should be stressed, instructions should be brief, groups equalized, the timid encouraged. Stress seemed placed on playing according to the rules, forbidding blasphemy or boastful language, and on the indispensability of a carefully used whistle.

Many activities known to North American elementary children such as "cat and rat," "poison ball" and "relays" are found here, too, but it is significant that a strong effort is made in the Federal District (including Mexico City), through instruction and competitions called "Juegos Escolares," to encourage games traditional in Mexico and activities called "rondas," including Mexican singing games, marbles, rope jumping, gymnastic games, and top spinning. High degrees of skill and interest are developed in each and awards are given. Game competitions under the same program are held for the secondary school.

Great importance is given in girls physical education to rhythmic activities with a strong folkloric background--rhythmic exercises, dances and regional dances.[12] Dance as defined in Mexican physical education includes folk or regional dances and ballet.

The North American will be impressed by the interest of the Mexican government in preserving this aspect of their culture, and likely will join the rest of the world in admiration of the famous Ballet Folklorica of Mexico. He may also reflect the disappointment of Kate Simon[15] that Mexican folk dances are done largely in the schools, by professionals, or by limited groups, on special occasions.

Interschool Competitions

There are no regular school-sponsored sports competitions as known in the United States though some schools have sports teams and belong to a sports league. One school was known to belong to five such leagues. The leagues have lacked central control, may be formed around a particular school or individual with organization and re-organization common. Participation in sports associations and isolated clubs is voluntary. The Office of Physical Education in the Ministry of Education has established basic rules for special competitions sponsored by it.[14]

As outlined, competition begins in the fifth year and extends through the secundaria, the technological, industrial, and commercial schools (for those who are not academically oriented), and through the "Preparatoria," or preparatory schools for those who will go into a technological institute or to a university.

The "five basic sports" included in such competitions are volleyball, basketball, soccer, track and swimming; the sixth activity is gymnastics.

It is stated that professors who do not carry out the rules will be punished, particularly if they do not follow age limits established. Age limits are fixed within grades; for example, in the fifth grade of a particular year the age limit was for those students born in 1953 or after.

The physical education teachers serve as advisers in their assigned schools. The rules indicate there are to be no elimination trials for team members. That is, a certain number of those who come out at a set time are to be used. Entries are sent in on forms established by the physical education section.

Time limits and specifications for games vary with sex and age. In volleyball, boys in the fifth year of primary school use a net two meters (approximately 79 inches) in height; the net is raised about 3.2 inches in each succeeding grade. For girls the nets are approximately 2 inches lower than for boys the same age. The Mexican physical educator works in a metric world.

Final competitions in these school sports contests become real spectacles and in one instance 1200 separate volleyball teams competed in the final elimination for the championship.

Strong efforts are being made to develop an extensive intramural program for both boys and girls.[16]

## Sports and Physical Education in
## Private Institutions

The program at the privately supported Instituto Technologico in Monterrey represents one of those most recently organized. There are three branches--a varsity sports program, intramural sports and an elective sports instruction opportunity.[17]

The varsity program includes competition under regularly assigned coaches in soccer, basketball and American football, and without such benefit in baseball and track. Competitions are largely in city leagues though the Instituto is a member of an American football league which includes six teams, playing at least one game across the border each year.

An extensive intramural program, including ten sports, follows the playing seasons of the sports. Representative groups of students may choose their teams and compete for individual sports championships and for an all-sports trophy awarded on a point system. Round robin and double elimination tournaments are popular with this program. All sports are supported financially by the Institute, but there are gate receipts in basketball and American football; the latter is the most expensive sports sponsored.

## Official and Semi-Official Agencies

Two official institutions--the Office of Physical Education in the Ministry of Education and another called Accion Deportiva del Districto Federal--sponsor programs of sports and physical education. Cognizance must also be taken of two semi-official agencies--the Social Security Institute and the National Institute of Mexican Youth

(INAHUM)--which have established installations and programs; and of a third agency for government workers--popularly known as ISSTE-- which is reported moving in a similar dissection. One unit is given as an example, which may or may not be truly representative.

The sports and physical education program at the Morelas Social Services Unit (for family welfare) in Mexico City is the first of a number of such programs sponsored by the Mexican Social Security Institute (Seguros Sociales). It is an example of tremendous facilities and programs being developed by government-approved, but separately funded, Social Security ventures. Incorporating the first Social Security Youth Center built by the Institute, it was approved by former President Lopez Mateos and represents a new conception of social welfare,--extending beyond insurance, medical assistance, and old-age benefits.

The physical education and recreation program is one part of a comprehensive, preventative effort to improve the social milieu and to improve the physical, mental, emotional, social and psychological welfare of the masses of people. The program has five basic functions: Preventive medicine, improvement in diet, elevation of home life, general culture, civic education, and recreation or the utilization of leisure time.

Included under the physical education and recreation aspect of the program are: (1) military training, (2) national military service, (provided by instructors of the ministry of national defense under its direction), (3) sports and sports hygiene, (4) hiking, (5) indoor games, (6) movie clubs, (7) dramatic stands, music and choral singing, (8) Social Security brigades, (9) first aid techniques in accidents and disasters, (10) community aid social service, including active participation of all youth in civic ceremonies and celebrations.[18]

Among sports facilities provided are basketball, volleyball, track, soccer, American football, and swimming. A heated, Olympic size pool with a shallow addition is open year round from 6:00 a.m. to 8:00 p.m.

As in the Y.M.C.A. and in the Ministry of Education, there seems here to be a strong, underlying philosophy stressing mass participation and improvement; and competition, though sponsored, is secondary.

As many as four classes were observed going on simultaneously in swimming. Other programs included three age leagues in American football, comprised of forty terms.

Dr. Manual Barroquin, Director of the Unit at Morelos,[19] observed that--in a country where Indian runners had daily brought Montezuma fresh seafood from the coast or information on the advance of Cortez; where the Spaniards had forbidden the Indian population to bathe--there were now being revived attitudes of approval toward physical performance and cleanliness. Kids were being taken off the streeets and clinical records on more than 15,000 participants had been established. Juvenile delinquency was being forestalled and physical health improved. There were changing parental attitudes toward children who were now participants. There was a developing community pride in an area of very low income; which had, contrary to all expectations, sent three participants to the Pan-American Games in Winnipeg and presently has twenty-five representatives in training for the Olympic Games of 1968.

## The YMCA and Physical Education

There are presently three YMCA's in Mexico; the oldest is in Mexico City, the second was established in Chihuahua, and the newest is located at Torreon. The YWCA is separate, but, as in the United States, the physical education programs in the YMCA's include extensive activities for women. While physical education is the most popular, it is but one part of the program.[20]

Goodwin, using files available in the International Committee of the YMCA, New York office, has completed a chronological study of the YMCA in Mexico.[21]

In the early 1900's, with the exception of a few private clubs sponsoring limited sports, the YMCA was about the only place where an organized program of physical education could be undertaken, and with the exception of school programs the same situation still existed as late as 1950. The unique position of leadership begun by the YMCA in the early 1900's and held until recently is now shared by other groups.

Mr. R. Williamson arrived in Mexico in 1903 to serve as a physical director to the YMCA, bringing with him the first basketball seen in Mexico.

Enrique P. Aguirre, presently a member of the Mexican Olympic Committee, graduated from Springfield College in 1916, and between 1916 and 1921 is credited with laying the foundation for the modern type of physical education found in the YMCA in Mexico,--a program which has strongly influenced both government schools and private institutional programs. Mr. Aguirre and a Mr. Underwood made a goodwill tour of twenty-five cities in the eastern and southeastern United States with a basketball team, with good results. In December, 1924, Mr. Aguirre conducted a two weeks institute for physical directors.

Political and financial problems beset the "Y" in 1930-31 and leaders of physical education, many trained in the "Y" and now working for the government, began taking leadership in physical education.

The first modern camp in the Republic of Mexico was established by the Mexico City "Y" and inaugurated at Camohmila in 1917.

The "Y" started its American football program in 1946-47. President Manuel Avila Camancho personally recognized the "Y" football team by donating new uniforms and issuing free railroad fares to the team so it could travel and play games. Professor Gonzalo Corrdero of the Mexico City YMCA is credited by the present director-- Mr. Villanoweth--with leadership in the development of American football in the "Y" program, a sport which it no longer sponsors.

In 1949 the Federal Pensions and Retirement Agency of the Mexican government asked the "Y" to take over the recreation program in the first large-scale multi-family housing project for federal employees. The next change in government did not include this in its budget and the program was dropped.

Taylor Reedy reported in 1953 that the "Y" was recognized as the agency in Mexico with the consistent "know-how" to develop an organized, orderly, and effective program of sports and physical education. YMCA secretaries at the time were represented in federations of every sport conducted in Mexico.

Mr. Goodwin, a Springfield graduate currently secretary of the Torreon YMCA, has introduced the game of paddle rackets in Mexico; first at the Mexico City "Y" and later at Torreon and Chihuahua.

Currently basketball is the most popular activity sponsored by the YMCA in Mexico.[20] Soccer, as adapted for the gymnasium in Montevideo and called "baby football," is increasingly popular. It is played with six players on each team, using a modified ball and a 4 meter by 2 meter goal. There is added emphasis upon apparatus gymnastics, which is most popular with boys and girls aged 15 to 23. Volleyball is considered interesting, but not excitedly so.

A highly organized physical program in Mexico City is currently directed by Mr. Federico Villanoweth, a graduate of the Technical Institute of the South American Confederation of YMCA's in Montevideo (Instituto Technico de la Confederacion sur Americana de YMCA). Emphasis is upon mass participation rather than upon competition, and from 80 to 85 per cent of those who attend the Mexico City program receive instruction as well as play.

The Montevideo Institute will figure prominently in the fourth year of a training program being established for greatly needed YMCA workers who are to meet expanding needs and dwindling supply.

Extensive use of YMCA volunteer leaders is now hampered by increasing industrialization, employment and economic conditions. The first three years of training of physical directors will be undertaken in Mexico; present plans call for the fourth year either at Montevideo; at George Williams College, or at Springfield College.

## Sports Facilities and Sponsorship

Sports facilities of the Social Security Institute are mentioned elsewhere in the paper. Comparable developments are being processed by the government workers syndicate referred to as ISSTE, in government sponsored parks, in the New Olympic facilities.

There is belief that the sports facilities available and being built in Mexico will excel those of any other city in the world.

Writer W. Berge Phillips of Australia has seen no better facilities available to sportsmen. He describes the Magdalena Mixhuca Sports Center,[22] authorized by President Ruiz Cortines and built in 1942 to replace 500 acres of slum (Hackensmith, p. 301), as including 70 football fields, four hockey fields, two Olympic pools, 50 basketball courts, a stadium for 30,000, a velodrome, 5 kilometer track for cars and motorcycles; gymnasia, auditoriums, theatres, children's playgrounds and parks, fountains and landscaped areas. This area is serviced, he says, by 500 sports specialists who teach full time. On Sundays the facilities are attended free by upwards of 30,000 people.

But it is not everywhere the same--Mexico has long been distinguished by its great contrasts. For example, the beautiful modern designs of cities' sports facilities may be contrasted with the powder-dry village soccer or volleyball court. There is the historical contrast of the ancient ball court found in Yucatan and other areas of Mexico with the new Aztec Stadium which seats 105,000 for the Olympics and where spectators may drive their cars to the immediate area of rug-lined boxes. While facilities of 10 to 20 years ago showed greater architectural ingenuity and creativity than attention to provision of essential comforts of the participants or to the necessities of the spectators, present design is both imaginative and functional.

Truly creative developments and playground apparatus are found in recent centers and parks. Representative of these are those at Oceania--a housing project, play and sports center--and at a new gymnasium found at the Instituto Technologico in Monterrey; and of course the Olympic structures.

Limited space in Mexico City around the schools presents obstacles to both programs of physical education in the school and to after-school sports. These limited areas will be supplemented with facilities, where available, developed by the Social Security Institute and other agencies.

It is not unusual for the better established industrial plants of Mexico to have sports facilities and programs for their employees, and

the facilities for sports provided at private clubs such as the Club
Israelita and Club Deportiva de Chapultepec are outstanding.

## American Football in Mexico

American football, as contrasted to "futbol soccer," was probably played at the end of the last century in Mexico, but it was first
played seriously in 1904 in Jalapa.[23]  Little information was available
until 1927, when the first solid organization of sports for youth began
in Mexico.

It was played with various success for years; there were a lot
of teams but they were disorganized, and handicapped by size, by
poor nutrition, and by lack of experience in sports.  It was predict-
ed, therefore, that American football would disappear.  Contrary to
this, however, the boys practiced, they played, and finally it was
adopted by the National University, by Colegio Militar, C. A. M.,
Club Suizo, Universidad Obrero, Politechnico, Mexico City College,
Normal and Pentathlon.

There were no regulations, no special divisions, and rules
were made up by judges on the field.  Spectators might be called on
to play or to help make decisions.  Despite this, American football
prospered, probably because of its techniques.  It improved year by
year, probably reaching its height in the years 1945 to 1950 with the
"T" formation, which gave the small Mexican players an opportunity
to prove themselves.  They were able to use their heads and their
speed to help to consolidate American football as a sport in the Aztec
medium.

In 1956, there were youth, intermediate, and major leagues of
American football.  That which was thought impossible, then, developed.  They anticipated that in ten years their football would become
the best in the world, through strategy and speed.

The American School in Mexico City has currently revived its
football program for the third time.  Appropriate league opposition
and varying interest have made it impossible to maintain over the
years.  Football equipment is not manufactured in Mexico and must be
imported over great obstacles from the United States.

There is a national league of six teams in American football.
This includes the National University, the Politechnical University A
and B teams, Chapingo., University of Nuevo Leon, and Institute
Technologico of Monterrey.

Though traditional games between the giant Politechnico and
National Universities are among the most colorful and noisy in all of
football's tradition, it can be fairly said that--to this point--"American" football has caught and held the interest of the players to a
greater extent than that of the spectator in Mexico.  (Villanoweth)

## Mexican Olympic Participation

Mexico has participated in each Olympics since 1924 and as is well known, the 1968 Olympics will be held in Mexico City.

According to an editorial appearing in Deporte Ilustrado,[24] Mexican sport has been declining since 1959. To support this contention the writer made comparison of Mexican preparation in the Pan American Games in 1959, 1963, and in 1967.

|  | Chicago 1959 | Sao Paulo 1963 | Winnipeg 1957 |
|---|---|---|---|
| Gold Medals | 6 | 2* | 5 |
| Silver | 11 | results not given | 13 |
| Bronze | 12 | results not given | 24 |

* Lowest number of medals ever won by Mexico in the Pan American Games.

In 1967, though Mexico sent 100 more athletes to Winnipeg than it had sent to Chicago, they were by passed by the Cubans and by Brazil and Argentina, viewed as the Latin American leaders in sports progress and representation. Cuba's progress is made though they have no more people than are to be found in the single Federal District of Mexico.

Mexico was fourth in the number of medals won in the Pan American Games in 1951 and 1959. They were third in 1955, fifth in 1963, and sixth in 1967.

Medals obtained by Mexico, Cuba, Brazil
and Argentina in Winnipeg
1967

|  | Mexico | Cuba | Brazil | Argentina |
|---|---|---|---|---|
| Gold | 5 | 8 | 11 | 9 |
| Silver | 13 | 14 | 10 | 14 |
| Bronze | 24 | 26 | 5 | 11 |
| Total | 42 | 48 | 26 | 34 |

The editorial stated that Mexico was again late in the preparation of its athletes, that they began in 1963 but only after they had received the Olympic Games for 1968. It takes exception to the position taken by the Mexican Olympic President, who wished to compare the performance at Winnipeg with that at Sao Paulo where--the Editor stated--Mexico was not well represented. Mexican prospects in the 1968 Olympics were held not *to be good.*

We Could Learn From Mexico:

to more carefully plan the promotion and retention of indigenous and traditional folk dances, songs and games;

by planning and more fully utilizing park facilities as supple-
ments to school facilities for sports;

by more fully coordinating school programs in physical education and recreational opportunities in after-school programs;

by considering a concept of social security which goes beyond
insurance and assistance to include a responsibility for the improvement of cultural opportunities including sports and fitness;

through the establishment of a national "core" of activities in
which every youngster would theoretically find a place;

through greater effort at a national level in overcoming geographical, economical, and educational difficulties in providing
programs and facilities available for participation in physical
activities.

# SPORT AND PHYSICAL EDUCATION IN MEXICO
## UPDATED

### by George Zigman


Mexico, because of its fine climate has always been an all year sports country.  Its 6210 miles of coastline along the Gulf of Mexico, the Caribbean, the Pacific and Gulf of California make it a top sports attraction.  Visitors can be above or under its waters; big game fishing, sailing, water skiing, parasailing, and diving; but its ball playing traditions date back more than a thousand years before Columbus took up sailing.

One of the first things the Mayans are believed to have done when they built their city of Chichin Itza in Yucatan in the mid-fifth century was to put in a ball court formed by two parallel stone walls 272 feet long.  You can still see the stone rings embedded in the center of each wall about twenty-four feet above the ground.

Here the Mayans played a sort of combination of basketball and soccer, the idea was for the players to drive a small hand rubber ball through the eighteen inch ring openings, using only their elbows, knees, and hips.  The Mayans played for keeps too; at the end of the game the captain of the winning team got to chop off the head of the losing captain.  In the Mayan league, it seems, nice guys were finished first.

Soccer is still something of a national mania in Mexico, even though murder and mayhem have been ruled out, the only participant whose life might be seriously endangered is an occasional referee.  Big time soccer is centered at Mexico City's Azteca Stadium, seating 100,000 spectators and site of the world championship matches five years ago.  Soccer season lasts from June to January, with games at noon on Sunday and nine p.m. on Thursday.  Admission is $2.00.

Mexico has a triple A baseball league.  Baseball is played nightly from March through August in Mexico City, Guadalajara, Montorez, Poza Rica, Puebla and Regnosa.  There is hope in Mexico City of eventually acquiring major league baseball status.

Mexico is very much horse country.  The army still has mounted cavalry units and Mexican military rides are always very much a part of the scene at the National Horse Show at Madison Square Garden in New York.  Saddle horses are conveniently seen all over the country and on the beaches in front of the Acapulco Princess Hotel. The best place to watch the horses run is at Mexico City's handsome Hipodrome Je las Americas, where tourists are admitted free--a practice that has so far eluded the management of Belmont Park.  Races start at two p.m. on Sunday, Tuesday, Thursday, and Saturday and the minimum bet is ten pesos--80¢.

If one would like to do a little nighttime betting, there's jai alai at the Mexico City's fountain in the Plaza de la Republica, open every day except Friday at 7:30 p.m.

For a uniquely Mexican spectacle, there are the *Charreadas* in Mexico City, Monterey, Guadalajara, Chihuahua, and other Mexican cities. There are equestrian exhibitions by gentlemen cowboys dressed in the colorful charro costumes--changing horses at full gallop, roping and tossing bulls by the tails, all backed by the unmuted grass and the guitar strings of the mariachi bands.

Despite the fact that there are few public courses in Mexico, golfers have plenty of chances to play because most of the beautiful private clubs extend temporary membership privileges to foreign visitors. They include the top rated Club de Gold Mexico, scene of the 1967 World Cup and International Trophy matches in 1967. Five other 18 hole courses in Mexico City are affiliated with the Mexican Golf Association and there are two 18 hole courses in Guadalajara and Monterey and one 18 hole course each in Tampico and Tijuana. Newest and one of the finest courses in Mexico is the 18 hole championship course at the luxurious Los Hedas resort near Manzanillo.

After Mexico City itself, Acapulco is the golfing capital of Mexico. There are two neighboring 18 hole courses at the Acapulco Princess and its country club and another 36 hole layout at the Tres Vidas Golf Club; plus the course at the Club de Golf de Acapulco.

Other sports which are catching the fancy of Mexican youth is American type football. Mexico City has hundreds of youngsters who play football through various sports clubs.

Sports are practiced outside of school hours in addition to the regular physical education programs at school. This is mainly geared to the schools which received the best grades. It also enables the same students to follow classes much better. The number of these pupils gradually increases in school games, especially in the last two years of elementary school and in secondary school. They participate in various competitions: gymnastics, a sport considered to be a basic activity, basketball, track and field, volleyball, swimming and soccer.

Eighteen sections of pupils from elementary and eighteen from secondary schools have been organized for competiton. In each section championships are held between eight teams of each school year and branch of teaching. About 55,000 pupils take part in these school games, aside from the 500,000 who take physical education at schools. The members of the federation total, at the beginning of the selections, 2,000,000 candidates, out of which 5,000 will be picked for the national events. All pupils follow this sports plan outside of classes.

Mexican Sports Confederation Program:

To improve sports in Mexico, a few years ago the Mexican Sports Confederation in conjunction with our National Association for Sports and Physical Education, started a project to help upgrade Mexican Sports and Physical Education programs. They began to select United States coaches and physical education educators to travel to Mexico and put on clinics and workshops in various sports and areas of Physical Education.

This past summer, 1977, the program was scheduled for cities including such enchanting names as Tampico, Matamord, Michoacan, Chihuahua, and Vera Cruz. Clinics vary from city to city, depending on requests from various cities and qualifications of personnel selected.

NASPE sends credentials of candidates to the Mexican Sports Confederation and President Jose Garcia Cervantes and his staff make final selections and assignments.

One such clinic given at the Veracruz Technological Institute Track and Soccer Stadium shows how the clinics are carried out.

The Veracruz Sports Complex has a swimming facility good enough to hold a national championship (warm up pool, diving tower). The center also had several outdoor basketball and tennis courts, plus some courts with one high wall which was used for a game like handball, only tennis racquets were used. Down the street were the professional teams' soccer stadium and baseball fields.

The sessions were well attended; the groups ranged from 150 to 200 men and women. Those in attendance were Physical Education majors from the University of Veracruz and teachers and coaches from the surrounding city schools.

The type of topics discussed in this clinic was the Administration of Physical Education and Athletics, swimming, track and field, and basketball.

## MEXICO OLYMPIC SPORTS PROGRAM

The Mexican government has helped to support the Mexican Olympic Committee. It was founded on the 23rd of April in 1923.

The objective of the Mexican Olympic Committee is the development and potential of the Olympic movement and amateur sport in the Mexican Republic.

The Mexican Olympic Committee recognizes some twenty-one sports. Mexico has been participating in Olympic games since 1924; and they hosted the games in 1968. The have also hosted several Latin American games and Pan American games.

The Mexican government has created the Mexican Olympic Sports Center. It was established with the object of developing a sports ensemble that would serve as a place for intense training for the Mexican athlete. It is located in the Northwestern section of Mexico City. The facilities are found around the track and field area and they are composed of the following specialities: A gymnasium for basketball, volleyball, gymnastics, handball, judo and wrestling. There is a stage for fencing and weight lifting. There are swimming facilities, and a cycling track.

The athletes selected to participate in the Olympic Center are attended by coaches of high caliber. The athlete can live and train at the Sporting Center for a period of no more than 60 days.

The athlete must cover the following basic requirements:

1. Be a member of the Mexican Athletic Organization.

2. Compete for a National championship.

3. Birth certificate, three recent photographs, proof of schooling, permission from parents or guardians.

The food service to the athletes is quite elaborate. Food is given to all athletes who enroll. Expert nutritionists help to prepare the food, and they take into account the basic points of nutrition, hygiene and taste. There are some thirty basic menus, including several international dishes, and the average meal consists of 4500 calories. The athlete is able to select his own menu according to the sporting specialty that the sport and body demands. The facility is able to feed up to 1000 in one day.

The following medical services are provided for the athletes: general medicine, preventive medicine, psychiatry, cardiology, nursing, dental laboratories, X-ray, ambulance and pharmacy. Each athlete must go through a clinical study. The study includes: clinical analysis, psychological tests, socio-economic tests, X-rays, and electrocardiograph readings.

The facility provides for housing of foreign competitors or the national teams. There are some buildings that are constructed at the west side of the track and field area. Near the cycling auditorium is the housing for men. It has 32 rooms and 128 beds. The housing for women has three floors consisting of 18 rooms and 72 beds.

There are a variety of vehicles to transport and satisfy the needs of the athletes which are readily available for the athletes' use.

The facility has a recreation center so the athletes can relax and play less active sports. T.V. rooms, movie houses and a library with some 1300 volumes are available.

One also finds a complete audiovisual department. It has a variety of technical equipment: cameras, projectors, videotape machines, closed circuit T.V. Other services are as follows:

Auditorium that can seat 100 people.
Printing press room.
Postal.
Tailor ship for athletes clothes.
Sauna.
Parking.
Sporting Goods Store.
Cafeteria at Recreation Center.
A sports school for young athletes.

FOOTNOTES
Dr. Clay's article

1.  National Education Association. *Other Lands, Other Peoples.* Washington. Revised 1942.

2.  Brothers, Dwight S., "Mexico's Economy, A New State". *Current History.* December 1966. Vol. 51.

3.  Hackensmith, C. W. *History of Physical Education.* Harper and Row. New York. 1966. pp. 6, 11.

4.  Furman, David C., "Physical Education and Athletics in Mexico." *Proceedings,* the College Physical Education Association. 1958. p. 201.

5.  Gayou, Lamberto Alvarez, "A National Sports Program." *Journal of Health and Physical Education.* January 1943. Vol. 14, No. 1. pp. 8-10.

6.  Hinojosa, Ruben Lopez. Unpublished paper "Education Fisica en Mexico 1921-1926." Office of the Direccion General de Educacion Fisica. Mexico, D. F. August 1967.

7.  Bisquertl, Luis, "Physical Education in Latin American Countries." *A Report on the Sixth International Congress.* International Congress on Health, Physical Education and Recreation. Washington. 1963.

8.  Personal Interview, Dr. David Juarez Miralda, Director. National School of Physical Education. Mexico City. August 1967.

9.  Unpublished Curriculum, National School of Physical Education. Mexico City. 1967.

10. Personal Interview, Abraham Ferreira, Office of Director General of Physical Education, Ministry of Education. Mexico City. August 1967.

11. ICHPER. *State of Teachers of Physical Education.* International Council of Health, Physical Education and Recreation. Washington. 1963.

12. ICHPER, Questionnaire Report #1. *Physical Education and Games in the Curriculum.* International Council of Health, Physical Education and Recreation. Washington.

13. Personal Interview, Juan Figueroa Peralta, Director General de Educaccion Fisica. Mexico City. August 1967.

14. Unpublished Directive, Direccion General de Educaccion Fisica "Juega Recreativos." Mexico D.F., April 1965.

15. Simon, Kate. *Mexico, Places and Pleasures.* Doubleday and Company, Garden City, N. Y. p. 119.

16. Unpublished Directive, Direccion General de Educaccion Fisica "Juegos-Deportivos-Escolares." Mexico, D. F. March 1967.

17. Personal Interview, Antonio S. Gonzales, Director of Sports and Physical Education, Instituto Technologico. Monterrey. August 1967.

18. Mexican Social Security Institute. *"Morelos" Social Services Unit.* San Juan de Avagon, D. F. 1962.

19. Personal Interview, Dr. Manuel Barroquin, Director, "Morelos" Social Services Unit. San Juan de Avagon, D. F. August 1967.

20. Personal Interview, Federico Villanoweth, Physical Director. Mexico City Y.M.C.A. August 1967.

21. Personal Letter, Seth A. Goodwin, Director, Y.M.C.A. Torreon, Mexico. August 2, 1967.

22. Phillips, W. Berge, "Mexico." *The International Swimmer.* Vol. III, #12. May 1967.

23. "El Futbol Americano en Mexico." *Educaccion Fisica.* Ano 1, Numero 3. Julio, Agosto. September 1959. Mexico, D. C. pp. 16-18.

24. Editorial. *Deporte Illustrado.* #190. 9 de Agosto, 1967. D. F.

## SELECTED REFERENCES
### Zigman's Updated Materials

*Esquire.* (October 1975, Vol. 84, No. 4).

Joseph, Richard. "Mexican Sports Roundup." *Esquire.* (Oct. 1975, Vol. 84, No. 4).

Killian, Michael, "Summing Up Mexico: Rich Land of Poor People." *Chicago Tribune.* (Tuesday, November 22, 1977).

Mexico. *International Council on Health, Physical Education and Recreation.* "Physical Education in the School Curriculum." (1968).

*Mexico Olympic Committee.* (October 1976).

"Mexico, the Amigo Country." *Chicago Tribune Supplement.* (October 16, 1977).

*The Physical Educator.* "Elsewhere in the World," William Johnson, Editor. (May 1977).

*Social Change in Latin America Today.* "Mexico Since Cardenas," Lewis Oscar. Vintage Books, New York, New York.

Welty, Paul. *Latin American Cultures.* J. B. Lippincott Co., Philadelphis, Pennsylvania.

Yanez, Augustin. *Mexico Sports Education.* (October 7-9, 1968).

SPORT AND PHYSICAL EDUCATION
IN THE NETHERLANDS

by Jan Broekhoff


Biographical Sketch


*Jan Broekhoff* was born in Maarssen, The Netherlands, in 1935. After graduation from the classical
high school in Utrecht, he completed his undergraduate
studies at the Academy of Physical Education in Amsterdam in 1958. Until May, 1960 he served in the Royal
Dutch Army as an officer of sports and recreation. In
the fall of 1960, Broekhoff started his graduate studies
at the University of Oregon in Eugene. He received his
M.S. from the University of Oregon in 1963 and his
Ph.D. in 1966. During his stay at the university, he
rose from teaching and research assistant to the rank of
Assistant Professor of Physical Education. Broekhoff
served as supervisor of H. Harrison Clarke's "Medford
Boys' Growth Study," as laboratory supervisor, and as
project director of a Title III project aimed at innovations in curriculum design. He also coached the University of Oregon Soccer Club and helped found the Oregon Intercollegiate Soccer Association.

In 1967, Broekhoff joined the physical education
staff at the University of Toledo. He was involved with
the preparation of elementary school physical education
teachers and conducted longitudinal research in the
growth and development of children. In 1973, he was
promoted to Professor of Physical Education. That same
year Broekhoff returned to the University of Oregon to
succeed his mentor H. Harrison Clarke. At present he
is Director of Microform Publications, conducts research
in the physical and social development of children, and
teaches graduate courses in growth and development,
statistics, and experimental design.

Broekhoff has been active in national and international professional organizations. He is a Fellow of
the American Academy of Physical Education and is a
member of the Executive Board of the I.C.H.P.E.R. In
1976, he became an American citizen. Broekhoff has
edited two books and has contributed chapters to various
texts in physical education. He is the author or co-
author of some twenty articles in American and foreign
journals. Besides his teaching and research assignments,
Broekhoff's scholary interests lie in the cultural, historical, and philosophical aspects of physical education.

For many Americans The Netherlands may be little more than a dot on the globe, a tiny country associated with windmills, tulips, dikes, and wooden shoes. Although these quaint stereotypes contain a shade of truth, the visitor to modern Holland will find a highly cultivated and industrialized country with bustling metropolitan areas connected by numerous highways. In an area the size of Massachusetts and Connecticut combined live more than fourteen million people, making The Netherlands the most densely populated country in the world.

The geographical location of The Netherlands--at the edge of the North Sea and on the lower reaches of the river Rhine--has put a definite stamp upon Holland's development. The flat country and the absence of natural barriers has invited the exchange of products and ideas with neighboring countries, and the sea has proved the gateway to even wider horizons. As a result, the Dutch people have never lived in isolation and have always had an open window to the rest of the world. This may in part explain the liberal attitude of the Dutch toward people of different race, religion, or political conviction, which prompted many illustrious foreigners to seek refuge in The Netherlands.

The scattered windmills in the Dutch folders are the symbol of a long lasting internal struggle to turn vast stretches of water into new land. Modern stations using electric power have long since taken over the water-pumping task from the windmills and now more than twenty per cent of The Netherlands lies below the level of the North Sea. The climate of Holland emphasizes the battle of the Dutch against the elements. Officially, the Netherlands has mild winters and cool summers, but actually the weather is very unpredictable and is a never failing topic of conversation.

Education in The Netherlands is based on the principle that parents should have the possibility of giving their children the kind of schooling which is in agreement with their way of living and their religious beliefs. The government and the municipal councils not only provide public education, but also subsidize denominational and non-denominational schools run by private institutions or organizations. At all levels of instruction, the private schools outnumber the public schools.[7]

This freedom in the choice of education, guaranteed in the Constitution, has resulted in a great variety of types of schools and educational methods. Although public education is fully regulated by law and the requirements of efficiency and thoroughness for private education are clearly defined, the Minister of Education has delegated great power to the governing organizations of the schools. Educational reform and innovation often originate, therefore, in the schools themselves and in the pedagogical centers and private institutions where teachers are trained with the aid of the government. It is only

since 1968, with the passing of a new school law, that the government has taken a more active role in educational reform.

## Historical Background--Physical Education[14]

Until 1920 the theoretical and practical development of physical education in The Netherlands showed a strong German influence.
In the middle of the nineteenth century the German Carl Euler introduced in Holland the exercise method of his teacher Eiselen, a close
associate of "Turnvater" Jahn. Although the method of Jahn and
Eiselen did not find its way into the Dutch schools, it helped pave
the way for the acceptance of the gymnastic lesson. Later in the
century a systematized form of Jahn's "turnen" adapted to the school
situation by the Germans Spiesz and Maul proved acceptable to the
Dutch schools. Modifications of the German method by such early
Dutch physical educators as Disse and Labberte resulted in a genuine
Dutch-German system of physical exercises.

For the Dutch physical educators the appeal of the German
method lay especially in its pedagogical emphasis. The geometrically
stylized exercises, classified according to the movement possibilities
of the body, aimed at creating discipline and making the body the
obedient servant of the mind. Within and beyond this rather rigid
systematic framework the apparatus gymnastics offered opportunities
for wider pedagogical and psychological aims. When in 1910 the
Dutchman-German Hubert van Blijenburgh wanted to replace the
Dutch-German system with Swedish gymnastics, it was precisely the
lack of pedagogical intent which made the physical educators reject
the Swedish system. The Swedish exercises with their emphasis on
movement utility and their use of anatomical and physiological principles were, however, officially adopted by the Dutch army.

After World War I the Teachers College in The Hague (Haagse
Kweekschool) propagated an eclectic system of physical education
which combined Swedish and German gymnastics with games, and
track and field. By that time reforms in general education were reflected in the practice of physical education and the German and
Swedish systems had lost much of their initial rigidity. The increased interest in sports on the European continent and the spread of the
rhythmic gymnastics movement also influenced physical education programs. Of even greater importance for an understanding of modern
physical education in The Netherlands was the development of a new
system by the Austrians Gaulhofer and Streicher. Dutch interest in
the methods of the "Austrian School" was evidenced by the appointment of Gaulhofer as Rector of the Academy of Physical Education in
Amsterdam in 1932.

The "Austrian School" regarded physical education as an integral part of a child-centered education which should be sensitive to
the psychological and biological needs of the pupils. In contrast to
the stylized, isolated movements of the older systems, the "Austrian
School" emphasized "natural," functional movements resulting from

games, movement exploration, concrete tasks, or expressive imagination. On the basis of the concept of "exercise intention," Gaulhofer distinguished the following four groups: normalizing exercises, forming exercises, performance exercises, and exercises leading to complete and artistic control of movement. This systematic classification and its methodological consequences provided the Dutch physical educators at least with a tentative theoretical model, and also promoted consistency and unity in the practical situation.

The development of physical education after World War II consisted partially in a differentiation and elaboration of the Austrian system. At the same time, however, the work of the leaders in physical education at the academies and teacher colleges pointed to more independent directions. In a theoretical sense, this was apparent in the writings of academy rectors Groenman at Groningen, Gordijn at Arnhem, and Rijsdorp at the Hague, which focused upon the philosophical and anthropological foundations of physical education. A practical result of the renewal was the "Basic Teaching Plan," prepared under the leadership of Rijsdorp on the initiative of the Royal Dutch Association of Teachers in Physical Education. Within the variety of theory and method so characteristic of Dutch education, the "Basic Teaching Plan" formed a blueprint of modern Dutch physical education and lent support to the renewal efforts of a group of physical educators at the teacher colleges charged with the preparation of the elementary school teacher.

## The Basic Teaching Plan[19]

In the "Basic Teaching Plan," physical education is presented as an aspect of education which shares its point of departure and ultimate aim with total education. The planning committee lists the following specific objectives of physical education: 1) maintenance and improvement of health; 2) development of organic strength, muscular strength, and mobility; 3) development of good posture; 4) forming of movement; 5) development of performance; 6) integration of the individual; 7) advancement of social behavior; 8) maintenance of the desire to move; 9) teaching of valuable carry-over activities; and 10) advancement of hygienic attitude and proper health habits.

To reach the objectives of physical education, the teacher should approach the practical situation with a definite purpose in mind. The planning committee distinguishes three fundamental exercise intentions: body development, forming of movement, and increase of performance. During body development the teacher aims at the development of the functional and structural prerequisites for good movement, posture, and performance. The main purposes during the forming of movement are to have the students experience their movement possibilities, to help them in gaining confidence and control, and to guide them in finding proper ways of movement and posture. In the performance phase, finally, physical fitness and versatility of movement are directed toward optimum performance and the awareness of the students' potentials and limitations.

In contrast to the Austrian system, the "Basic Teaching Plan" does not classify the actual physical exercises on the basis of the exercise intentions. It rather offers a generic classfication in which the exercises are presented in the progressive development of functional movements such as walking, running, jumping, climbing, pulling, pushing, throwing, catching, rolling, and tumbling. The teaching plan describes the stages of development of these movement forms from the first through the twelfth grade and also presents short sections on the progression of games, track and field, and swimming. According to the planning committee, gymnastics along the lines of the functional movements should be the central part of physical education in the schools, but adequate time should be reserved for games, swimming, and track and field and to a lesser degree for hiking and skating. It is the task of the teacher to select from this variety of possibilities the movement forms that fit his exercise intentions.

This freedom of physical education teachers to select their own programs has resulted in an increased emphasis on the use of games in physical education classes, at least at the secondary school level.

## Teaching Plan in Progress[1]

As mentioned above, the Dutch government started to take a more active role in educational innovation during the late sixties and early seventies. This development was not without importance for physical education. In 1974, the Minister of Education appointed a committee to modernize instruction in physical education with a special emphasis on the evaluation of teaching plans. Fifteen such curricula committees had already been appointed in other subject areas. Although the Committee to Modernize the Teaching Plan in Physical Education was not directly related to the development of the "Basic Teaching Plan," a certain continuity was guaranteed with the selection of Rijsdorp as committee chairman. The members of the committee formed a cross-section of the world of physical education and related educational institutions and agencies.

The final committee report to the Minister of Education was published in August, 1977, in three volumes, including the results of a survey of junior and senior high school students.[1] The committee reaffirmed most of the objectives of physical education stated in the "Basic Teaching Plan," but couched some of these goals in language more attuned to societal values. There is, for example, the intimation of physical education's role in the "affirmation and encouragement of desirable attitudes, values and norms," and the accent is on the development of movement behavior which is meaningful qua function as well as expression.

The survey of 4,567 junior and senior high school students forms an indication that the Teaching Plan Committee was interested in the experiences and reactions of the client population. This in itself was a change from previous curriculum evaluations. The students showed a clear preference for physical education over a host of other school subjects. Nearly 44 per cent would like to have more hours of physical education instruction, whereas only 2.2 per cent indicated that they preferred to have fewer hours than the present number. Students as well as parents mentioned the health aspects of physical exercise as the most important benefit of physical education. Among the many areas that were investigated, the survey revealed that the appreciation of co-educational instruction increased with age.

Other parts of the Committee Report gave evidence of an increasing awareness of the need to integrate physical education within the whole of Dutch education. Special chapters were devoted to movement education for exceptional children, remedial physical education, and school sports and movement recreation. The relationship between physical education and extramural sports became especially important as half the students indicated that they were a member of a sport club. Thus, the work of the Committee to Modernize the Teaching Plan in Physical Education underlines the more active role of the Dutch government in shaping the physical education and active recreation of its citizens.

## Elementary School--Physical Education[11,13]

In comparison to the United States, physical education in the Dutch elementary schools is in a rather fortunate position. Since 1890 physical education has been a required subject in the primary schools and at present the physical education program in most of the big cities and many of the rural communities is in the hands of expert teachers. Most of these teachers have had a thorough professional training and are well acquainted with modern principles and methods. Many Dutch children, therefore, participate in a well rounded, enjoyable physical education program throughout their entire elementary school period.

It is only appropriate to point out, however, that despite this seemingly favorable situation, physical education at the primary level faces some persistent problems. The most obvious difficulty is the lack of adequate gymnasiums, swimming pools, and outdoor facilities. In The Netherlands, space is at a high premium, and although some progress has been made in the planning and building of accommodations, the situation is far from ideal. Of even greater concern to the profession is the preparation of the classroom teacher, who still occupies a central place in elementary school physical education.

Elementary school teachers receive their training at teacher colleges which deal exclusively with elementary education. To teach physical education the students have to pass an examination at the end of their senior year. Without a passing grade for the physical education examination the classroom teacher will not be able to get tenure. The preparation for this examination involves a study of three hours per week during the junior and senior years in which the student is expected not only to acquire a sufficient level of personal skills but also the theoretical and practical knowledge necessary to conduct a responsible physical education program. In spite of the best efforts of the physical education staff at the teachers colleges, the general contention is that the classroom teacher is inadequately prepared for his physical education task. The Royal Dutch Association, for example, has continuously urged that physical education in the elementary schools be given by professional teachers.

The lack of facilities and trained personnel has held back physical education in the elementary schools from the day of its requirement. Until 1939 it was relatively easy for school boards to get permission to drop the physical education requirement for lack of gymnasiums or personnel. This is no longer the case, partly because of a change of attitude in the Ministry of Education. Since World War II, the number of expert teachers has increased greatly through the influx of physical educators with secondary certification who could not find employment in the high schools. At the same time, elementary school teachers with a strong interest in physical education are encouraged to take special courses leading to an elementary school certificate in physical education (Akte J). When changes of the Secondary School Act in the late sixties opened up positions for people with secondary certification, many of these physical educators left the elementary schools to be replaced by teachers with Akte J. By the middle of the seventies, however, this trend had run its course and once again teachers with secondary certification applied for positions at the elementary level.

Ironically, the program leading to elementary certification in physical education has received some criticism and will probably be phased out when changes in the preparation of secondary teachers go into effect. There is concern that the number of elementary teachers with Akte J is too large in proportion to the number of qualified secondary physical educators who want to teach at the elementary level. Another point of concern is that due to the changes of the Secondary School Act many elementary teachers with Akte J are now teaching physical education at the secondary level. Critics maintain that the Akte J was never meant for certification at that level.[18]

## Secondary School--Physical Education

Education in The Netherlands is compulsory from six through sixteen years of age. After the six grades of elementary school, therefore, all Dutch children pursue some form of secondary education. Many attend four-year high schools which prepare them for administrative or vocational jobs in industry, agriculture, or business. After graduation, employed youths from sixteen through eighteen years of age must attend school one day a week for extended general education, including physical education. This schooling is fully paid by the employer and is in addition to job training programs.

Students who want to be admitted to higher vocational schools, such as Academies of Physical Education, Teacher Colleges, and Art Academies, must graduate from five-year high schools providing a general education program. Finally, a rather select group of students enters the unversity preparatory schools: the Atheneum and the classical high school (Gymnasium). These six-year high schools offer a variety of courses in modern languages, mathematics, history, and the sciences. In addition, the Gymnasium offers courses in Latin and Greek.[7]

Physical education is a required subject at all secondary schools and has a minimum time allotment of two hours a week. In recent years there have been few openings in physical education at the secondary school level, and as a result, the competition has been strong. In general the high schools have better facilities than the elementary schools, but even here the situation leaves much to be desired. Physical education in the high schools is mainly taught by teachers who graduated from an Academy of Physical Education with secondary certification. As mentioned earlier, however, many of the four-year administrative and vocational high schools have teachers with elementary certification.

In the highly intellectual climate of preparatory education, physical education has long been regarded as a subject that "does not belong in the school." When physical education became a required subject for the citizens' high schools in 1863, the government did not specify the number of hours. It was therefore rather convenient for the high school principals to "forget" the physical education program. In classical high school circles, where the requirement was only accepted in 1920, the opposition was even greater. As recent as 1947 there was a proposal to reduce the number of physical education hours in the school type which ironically derives its name "gymnasium" from the Greek verb meaning "to exercise in the nude." Fortunately the time of discriminiation is past and physical education now enjoys a good reputation, not least because of the continuous activity of the Royal Dutch Association of Teachers in Physical Education.[14]

## University--Physical Education and Sport

Traditionally, the Dutch universities and institutes of higher learning have left the student with a great deal of responsibility. In Holland the student has indeed, as Koningsberger expresses it, the "freedom to go to the devil." It is, therefore, hardly surprising that the institutes of higher learning do not have a physical education requirement. The structure of the universities was until recently largely determined by the venerable faculties of theology, law, medicine, and the humanities to which the physical and behavioral sciences were added as relative newcomers. In this academic universe, one would look in vain for departments of athletics and undergraduate programs of physical education.

In recent years, however, some important developments for physical education have taken place at the university level. In 1969, Dr. Klaas Rijsdorp was appointed as Professor Extraordinarius to the Chair of Physical Education Sciences at the State University of Utrecht.

In connection with this appointment, the Society Study-center of Physical Education, Sport, and Movement Recreation founded the Gymnologic Institute at Utrecht. With Rijsdorp as its director, the Institute offers courses in movement therapy, physiotherapeutics, gerontology, and various other domains.[9]

While the scientific aspects of physical education were recognized in Utrecht with the appointment of Rijsdorp, the Minister of Education established an Interfaculty of Physical Education at the Free University of Amsterdam in 1971. This interfaculty, lodged between the Faculties of Medicine and Behavioral Sciences, was the natural outcome of the work of Professor C. C. F. Gordijn, who had established a Department of Physical Education within the Subfaculty of Education at Amsterdam since 1963. The Interfaculty has the task to gain scientific knowledge in the domain of physical education with an aim to apply this knowledge to the practical situation. To this purpose, the Interfaculty offers programs in applied anatomy, exercise physiology, motor learning, and various directions of movement education. These programs can lead to a doctorate degree and the first graduates of the Interfaculty obtained their degrees in the past few years.[2,10]

Although the other universities in The Netherlands do not have graduate programs in physical education, there are several "work groups" in other departments at these universities conducting research in growth and development of children, exercise physiology, motor learning, and the physical and psychological development of handicapped children. All in all, the developments of the last decade have seen an important recognition of the scientific aspects of physical education and sport. The training of teachers in physical education is still separate from the Dutch universities, but the established graduate departments should give an impetus to the study of physical education as a discipline.

After World War II, there has been an increasing interest among university students in sport as a form of recreation and in physical exercise as a means to stay physically fit. A change in the attitude of the university administrations with regard to sport was evident during the dedication of two modern sport halls at the University of Nijmegen and the Free University of Amsterdam in 1966.[22] These sport complexes continued a trend that started earlier with the accommodations at the Technological Institute of Delft and the Economic Institute of Tilburg. In the last decade substantial improvements have been made in the sport facilities of most Dutch universities.

The Dutch government has actively supported the building of sport facilities for the universities. The sport center of the Technological Institute of Delft, for example, was sponsored jointly by business and government. The administration of the sport hall, gymnasiums, tennis courts, and fields is in the hands of a sport director aided by a staff of physical educators, coaches, and maintenance personnel. This entire staff is paid by the government. The students, who contribute ten per cent of the total yearly budget, play an important role in the organization of all activities. Many are members of the sports and activity sections organized by the sport center, whereas others participate in more independent sports clubs which are entered in local or regional amateur leagues.

It is difficult to obtain recent figures on the participation of students in university sponsored sports. Estimates go as high as fifty per cent. The most popular sports are tennis, swimming and water polo, crew, table tennis, soccer, judo, badminton, field hockey and volleyball. Training and conditioning courses always enjoy high enrollment. Participation in university courses does not include membership in university sports clubs. In 1976, the Dutch Students' Sport Foundation listed 30,000 active members of university sports clubs competing in amateur leagues.[16]

The sport centers at the Dutch universities must not be confused with the athletic departments of the American colleges. The task of the sports director and his staff is in the first place to give all students an opportunity for participation and recreation. Although the universities compete against each other in a variety of sports during the yearly Intercollegiate Games, there are no collegiate leagues or conferences with regularly scheduled games in any of these sports. The control and organization of the Intercollegiate Games is entirely in the hands of the students themselves. The only sport in which the universities have provided important leadership and outstanding performances is crew. The rivalry between university crews has traditionally been fierce and many a university team has represented The Netherlands at European and World championships and at the Olympic Games.

## Teacher Training--Physical Education

Physical education at the elementary school level is often the task of the classroom teacher, especially in the primary grades. The preparation of the classroom teacher during the junior and senior years at the teachers colleges is far from adequate, which is the main reason why so many elementary schools employ specialist teachers. As mentioned before, the teacher colleges now offer special programs leading to certification in physical education. Even though the quality of these programs has improved consistently, there remains considerable doubt about their adequacy. With the anticipated reforms of the educational system, the elementary certification in physical education will probably be discontinued and teachers with secondary certification will take over, eventually.[15]

The preparation of physical education teachers at the highest professional level takes place at the academies of physical education. These four-year institutions prepare their students for the secondary teaching certificate, which in fact enables them to teach at all levels of the Dutch educational system. At present there are five academies in The Netherlands: three private ones in Amsterdam, The Hague, and Groningen, and two denominational ones (the Catholic Academy of Tilburg and the Protestant Academy of Arnhem). Students must have graduated from a five-year high school or a college pre-school to be admitted to the academies. Because of the great number of applicants, the academies are highly selective in their choice of students.

The curriculum of the academies is partly determined by the examination requirements for the final diploma which are set by the government. During the practical part of these examinations the students have to prove their personal skills in gymnastics, track and field, swimming, and a variety of sports and games. They must also demonstrate their teaching ability in these areas in the practical situation. During the oral and written parts of the examination the students are thoroughly questioned in the areas, among others, of anatomy, physiology, physiology of exercise, educational psychology, theory and history of physical education, and methodology and didactics. Consequently, the academies devote ample time to the required practical and theoretical subjects and student teaching.

The academies, however, extend their activities beyond preparation for minimum requirements. Through publications and practical demonstrations, each academy expresses its own philosophy and contributes important ideas to the development of physical education. The Academy of 's-Hertogenbosch, for example, is oriented toward the "Austrian School," whereas the Academy of The Hague represents the ideas that led to the formulation of the "Basic Teaching Plan." The Academy of Amsterdam requires its juniors to pass a "Candidates Examination" in such "non-required" subjects as sports medicine, sociology, general psychology, and philosophy. This diversity of ideas and methods, which is nevertheless guided by a unity of purpose, is characteristic of Dutch education in general.[8]

As was intimated earlier, the academies do not offer degree programs or graduate studies. The secondary teaching certificate is a diploma, however, which in many respects is comparable to a bachelors degree in the United States. Graduates from the academies who are interested in furthering their education at the university level have now access to the Interfaculty of the Free University of Amsterdam or the course in the Pedagogical Faculty of the State University of Utrecht. As in the past, there are also opportunities for graduate studies at the universities of the neighboring countries of Belgium and Germany.

At the date of this writing, wide-reaching changes in the training of teachers for secondary education are being contemplated by the Ministray of Education. One of the more important implications for the academies of physical education is that physical educators may be required to seek certification in a second subject area.

This would no doubt effect the curricula of the academies since certification in physical education might be obtained at various levels. The impact of these changes can only be assessed after new regulations have gone into effect and this seems to be linked very much to the political atmosphere of the country.15

Eighty per cent of all physical education teachers are members of the Royal Dutch Association of Teachers in Physical Education. This association started in 1862 with seven members and now, after more than 115 years has a membership of more than 6000. Another 1200 physical education teachers are members of the Catholic Association St. Thomas Aquinas. Since approximately 700 of them are also members of the Royal Dutch Association, there are some 6,500 "organized" physical educators in The Netherlands.

## Physical Education and Sport

After World War II, school sports have enjoyed increasing popularity. The participation in interschool sports at the regional and state level became so large that it necessitated instituting the Foundation Dutch School Sports, in 1972. This Foundation now organizes regional and state meets in soccer, volleyball, European handball, basketball, swimming, skating, track and field, judo, skiing, field hockey, softball, and orienteering. Besides the thousands of participants in Foundation-sponsored sports, there are also the tournaments run by the Royal Dutch Soccer Association and the Royal Dutch Track and Field Union. Many cities, moreover, organize their own interschool competition in a variety of sports during the Easter and Christmas holidays. The school sports have thus beyond doubt become an important part of school life.12

It would be entirely wrong, however, to compare the Dutch school sports with the American interschool athletics. The primary and secondary schools in The Netherlands do not have athletic budgets, athletic directors, or coaches. The selection and organization of the school teams in the different sports rests mainly with the students aided by the physical educator. The preparation for the tournament games is somewhat haphazard and the players perform without the benefit of bands, cheerleaders, and throngs of spectators. The emphasis is on participation, and often a school is represented by six or seven teams in one sport. In the tournaments all these terms are classified in appropriate pools so that the competition remains fair.

School sport in The Netherlands has a distinctly pedagogical character. For the physical educator it forms ideally the realization of the performance intention in a competitive situation. As such, sports and games have an important place in the actual physical education program, intramural meets, and the annual sport day. The value of this educational emphasis in school sport is clearly recognized by the government. The Minister of Education, for example, has repeatedly refused to employ the graduates of the Central Institute for Coaches (C.I.O.S.) in the schools, although in many respects the coaches have a better understanding of physical exercise than the classroom teacher. Physical education and athletics are thus clearly separated and in a sense the school sports form a bridge between the two areas.

For athletic participation in amateur league competition, students at all levels of the educational system have the opportunity to join the public sport clubs that are associated with the regional divisions of the national sport associations. In 1976 nearly three-and-a-half million youths and adults belonged to a sport club. The Royal Dutch Soccer Association alone had nearly one million members (See Table 1). In most sports, competition is organized according to age

Table 1. Membership of the Ten Largest Sport
Organizations in the Dutch Sport Federation.

| Organization | 1966 | 1972 | 1976 |
|---|---|---|---|
| Royal Dutch Soccer Association | 537,027 | 769,000 | 924,388 |
| Royal Dutch Gymnastics Association | 203,047 | 275,197 | 269,155 |
| Royal Dutch Lawn Tennis Association | 77,089 | 138,880 | 249,300 |
| Royal Dutch Speed Skating Association | 217,335 | 170,000 | 160,000 |
| Royal Dutch Swimming Association | 87,302 | 115,000 | 140,000 |
| Dutch Catholic Gymnastics Association | 89,589 | 92,092 | 85,000 |
| Dutch Volleyball Association | 35,372 | 60,950 | 82,000 |
| Dutch Handball Association | 41,425 | 68,125 | 81,450 |
| Royal Dutch Korfball Association | 43,626 | 66,169 | 77,000 |
| Royal Dutch Field Hockey Association | 39,537 | 52,325 | 76,000 |

and skill levels so that participation is possible for nearly everyone. Most sport organizations require their members to take a medical examination. The majority of these physicals is monitored by the

Federation of Bureaus for Medical Exams in Sport. The Federation
started with the first medical bureaus in 1927 and saw its number increase to 213 in 1973. In 1976 the Federation provided medical examinations to nearly 400,000 athletes of all ages.[3]

One of the indigenous sports of The Netherlands recently made
its appearance in the United States. The Royal Dutch Korfball Association sent teams of international repute to America to demonstrate
before the membership of the American Alliance of Health, Physical
Education, and Recreation during the national convention in Milwaukee
in 1976. Korfball, which resembles basketball but is played co-edu-
cationally, was introduced by a Dutch school teacher, Nico Broek-
huysen, in the beginning of the twentieth century. The game blos-
somed and the Royal Dutch Association now has a membership of
77,000. The demonstration in Milwaukee was a success and Americans
in various parts of the country have begun to play basketball "Dutch
style."

Although in league play the competitive aspect is paramount,
sport leaders in The Netherlands show a great awareness of the educational values of amateur sports, especially in their work with the
youth sections. In this respect it is interesting to note that many
physical educators serve as coaches or sport leaders in their free
time. The most recent survey of the Royal Dutch Association of
Teachers in Physical Education indicated that 70 per cent of its membership held one or more positions in the world of sport. These
positions varied from technical advisor to trainer and coach.[4]

The various sport associations in The Netherlands form the
membership of the Dutch Sport Federation, which has become the
powerful nucleus of the Dutch world of sport. The Federation receives a considerable income from the Foundation National Sport Lotto.
This foundation runs the professional football lottery and distributes
the receipts to the various sports organizations. In its distrubiton
plan for 1978, the Foundation allotted more than 20 million dollars to
sport and recreation.[17] The Dutch Sport Federation resides in a
National Sport Center 'Papendal' and has its offices in The Hague.[16]
The Federation sponsors research in sport and physical education and
has an excellent documentation and information center. Through the
lottery, professional soccer for which The Netherlands is known, indirectly helps support the broad base upon which amateur sports
thrive.

## Summary and Conclusions

From a diversity of viewpoints, physical education in The
Netherlands emerges as a profession with a well defined image and a
unity of purpose. In the development of this image, the Royal Dutch
Association of Teachers in Physical Education, which celebrated its
centennial in 1962, has played an important role. Through its continuous activity under such eminent leadership as the last J. M. J. Kor-
pershoek and its present executive J. P. Kramer, the Association,

with more than 6000 members, has become a powerful influence in the Dutch teachers world. The acadamies of physical education have also contributed much to give the profession its own identity. In cooperation with the teacher colleges, the academies continue to give leadership in the way they relate innovation and educational reform to past heritage. Although the government has left great freedom to the teaching profession, it is undeniable that it has provided structure for the preparation of physical education teachers by establishing minimum requirements. The government has also given valuable guidance and advice to elementary as well as secondary school teachers through a group of inspectors of physical education.

Indirectly, physical education has gained its identity also through the structure of the Dutch educational system. This has remained so during the last decade in which the Dutch government is taking a more active role in educational reform and innovation. Although impending changes undoubtedly will change the face of physical education of the future, the separation of physical education and athletics is bound to stay a feature of the Dutch schools. It has prevented much of the confusion so prevalent in the United States, where it is often hard to distinguish between the two. In this connection, it must be mentioned also that health and recreation have not yet developed as separate fields of study in The Netherlands.

The unity of purpose in Dutch physical education is clearly reflected in the school programs. In general, the physical education programs in The Netherlands give evidence of a more systematic approach and greater uniformity than those in the United States. A study of the "Basic Teaching Plan" and the new efforts in curriculum development would confirm this observation. Undoubtedly this difference can be explained partly by the emphasis on local autonomy in America. Especially in the elementary schools, the physical education programs in The Netherlands are ahead of those in the United States, not least because of the many expert teachers employed by the Dutch schools. Compared to the American schools, the Dutch schools offer only limited possibilities for athletic participation to talented young athletes. These youngsters, however, will find ample opportunities in the civil sport organizations. The elaborate system of sport clubs, moreover, has the advantage of enabling young men and women to engage in vigorous competitive activity long after they have graduated from high school or university.

One of the most gratifying developments of the past decade is the inroads physical education has made in the university. American physical education has always been fortunate in that it had a place in the universities and colleges, where it could establish sound educational and scientific bases in interaction with other departments working at the summit of the educational system. In 1967, Rijsdorp expressed the hope that physical education might find incorporation in the Dutch universities.[21] With his appointment at the State University of Utrecht and the establishment of an Interfaculty of Physical Education at the Free University of Amsterdam, that dream has now partially come true. Hopefully, these graduate islands in the universities will maintain strong bonds with the academies where the teachers are prepared and with the schools where physical education really happens.

## Acknowledgements

I want to express my gratitude to Professor K. Rijsdorp for his initial assistance in obtaining background information. The publication *History of Physical Education in The Netherlands* by J. P. Kramer and J. Kugel was a valuable source for the historical section in this chapter. Finally, I should like to thank my colleague Freek Stam for his invaluable help in updating the information about physical education in The Netherlands.

## SELECTED REFERENCES

1. Commissie Modernizering Leerplan Lichamelijke Oefening. *Leerplan in Beweging*. Delen 1, 2, 3, 's-Gravenhage. Augustus 1977.

2. Crum, B. J. "Interfaculteit en Academie: een Kwestie van de Lamme en de Blinde?" *De Lichamelijke Opvoeding*. 10:333-337. Juni 1977.

3. De Heer. H. A. W. "Medische Sportkeuring." *De Lichamelijke Opvoeding*. 3:95-97. Februari 1975.

4. "De Plaats van de Leraar Lichamelijke Opvoeding in de Sportwereld." *Richting*. 11:264-265. August 1965.

5. *Digest of the Netherlands*. Publication by the Ministry of Foreign Affairs. January 1959.

6. Dutch Korfball Magazine, "Special Issue for the U.S.A." *Royal Dutch Korfball Association*. P. O. Box 1000, Zeist, The Netherlands. March/April 1976.

7. *Dutch Schoolsystem*. Publication by the Ministry of Education, Arts and Sciences. 1960.

8. Gerdes, O. "Eenheid en Verscheidenheid." *De Lichamelijke Opvoeding*. 19:635-638 ff. October 1966.

9. "Het Gymnologisch Institute." *De Lichamelijke Opvoeding*. 5:129-131. Maart 1975.

10. "Interfaculteit Lichamelijke Opvoeding V. U. Amsterdam." *De Lichamelijke Opvoeding*. 1:30-31. Januari 1975.

11.  Kappinga, L. L.  "Quo Vadis? . . ."  *De Lichamelijke Opvoeding*.  11:309-314.  June 1967.

12.  Kramer, L. D. E. J.  "Relate School en Sport."  *De Lichamelijke Opvoeding*.  16:460-462.  September 1965.

13.  Kramer, J. P.  "De Noodzaak van het Vakondervijs in de Lichamelijke Opvoeding op de Lagere School."  *De Lichaemelijke Opvoeding*.  10:277-286.  May 1967.

14.  Kramer, J. P. en Kugel, J.  *Geschiedenis van de Lichamelijke Opvoeding in Nederland*.  Jan Luiting Fonds.  No. 24.  1962.

15.  Loopstra, O.  "Opleiding Leraren Lichamelijke Opvoeding in Discussie."  *De Lichamelijke Opvoeding*.  10:326-332.  Juni 1977.

16.  Nederlandse Sport Federatie.  *Jaarverslag 1976*.  's Gravenhage.  1976.

17.  Nederlandse Sport Federatie,  "Ontwerp Eerste Deel Bestedingsplan 1978 van de Stichting De Nationale Sporttotalisator."  *Flitsen*.  5:6.  1977.

SPORT AND PHYSICAL EDUCATION
IN NEW ZEALAND

by Grant and Penni Cushman


Biographical Sketches


*Grant Cushman* was born in Hamilton, New Zealand, in 1948. He received the Diploma of Physical Education from the University of Otago, Dundein, in 1970,
and after being awarded a Teacher's Diploma in 1971
from Christchurch Teachers' College he taught science
and physical education at Rotorua Boys' High School for
nine months. He received his M.S. degree in 1973 from
the Department of Leisure Studies at the University of
Illinois in Urbana-Champaign. In 1975 he was awarded
an Avery Brundage Scholarship for his involvement in
amateur sport. Currently he is Head of the Department
of Leisure Studies at Preston Institute of Technology in
Melbourne, Australia. He will return to the U.S.A. in
November 1977 for a three months period to complete
work on his Ph.D. degree.


*Penni Cushman* is a graduate of the School of
Physical Education in Dunedin, New Zealand, and received a Teaching Diploma from Christchurch Secondary
Teachers' Training College in 1971. Before coming to
the United States in 1972, she taught physical education
and science at Western Heights High School in Rotorua.
Penni completed an M.S. in Health Education at the University of Illinois in 1973. She is currently employed
at the Preston Institute of Technology in Melbourne,
Australia as a teacher of pre-school Downs Syndrome
children.

## Introduction

Since Edward J. Wright's article "Physical Education in New Zealand", was written approximately ten years ago, a number of important and timely developments have occurred on the New Zealand scene. The major purpose of this article is to describe and analyze these developments. A special effort is made by the authors to avoid presenting descriptive information contained in Dr. Wright's article, which is not directly relevant to this discussion.* In this way, repetition and redundancy is prevented. It will be necessary however, for purposes of orientation and introduction, to present a general description of New Zealand.

## General Background

New Zealand is situated in the southwest section of the Pacific Ocean, far removed from any continent, and 1200 miles from its closest neighbor Australia. New Zealand's total area of 103,000 square miles is divided between two major islands, the North Island and the South Island which are separated by Cook Strait, and a number of smaller islands.

The country features an infinite variety of landscapes. A group of volcanoes, both active and extinct, are found in the center of the North Island, and in the South Island the rugged Southern Alps run along the western coast and reach heights of over 12,000 feet. Gently rolling hills are found over most of New Zealand and these are inundated with numerous lakes and streams. The coastline is frequented by deep, natural harbors, rocky outcrops, and endless miles of sandy beaches.

New Zealand's climate is influenced by the proximity of the sea to most areas. In fact, no part of New Zealand is more than 70 miles from the sea. The climate of the North Island is subtropical with average temperatures rarely below 50 degrees Fahrenheit in Winter, and even in the most southern part of the South Island temperatures seldom dip below freezing for any appreciable length of time.

Obviously the geographic features and climate have a great bearing on physical education and sporting activities in New Zealand. The climate, especially that of the North Island, encourages year-round outdoor activities, and the abundance of lakes and rivers make aquatic sports such as fishing, boating, water skiing and swimming, popular. New Zealand's endless miles of coastline - rocky and sandy

---

* For a more extensive coverage of this descriptive information, refer to Wright, Edward J., "Physical Education in New Zealand." *Physical Education and Sport Around the World*. Monograph 1.

- make surfing, surfcasting, deep-sea fishing, swimming, snorkelling, skin diving, sailing and boating an accepted part of the New Zealand way of life. The temperate climate allows for a long swimming season, and many of the above activities are participated in year round.

New Zealand's population of just over 3 million includes a wide range of religions; the majority of the population however is Protestant and there is an absence of religious conflict. Racially, most of New Zealand's European population are of British descent. The Maori population, or New Zealand's Polynesian race, is estimated to be 240,000, and is increasing at a greater rate than the European population. English is the only language widely spoken in New Zealand, and the language of New Zealand's native race, Maori, is rarely used.

New Zealand was not settled by Polynesians until thousands of years after most sizeable lands had been inhabited by humans. And it was discovered by Europeans and settled late in comparison with most places to which they emigrated.

New Zealand has a social democratic form of government which is based on the British system. The New Zealand government is elected by universal adult franchise and operates under a cabinet representing the elected majority party, and is responsible to Parliament. New Zealand is a member of the British Commonwealth with Queen Elizabeth II being the reigning Monarch. The Queen is represented in New Zealand by the Governer General.

General Education

The educational system is centrally controlled by the Department of Education headed by the Director General of Education. The Department distributes funds, controls school inspections, supervises staffing, and plans curricula, although local school Education Boards now have a lot more power in these areas. Educational concerns amounted to 18% of Government spending in 1973-74, and in these same years, 31% of the population was enrolled in schools, colleges and universities.

Education is free and secular in state primary and secondary schools in New Zealand, and compulsory from the age of six to fifteen years. There are a number of primary and secondary schools conducted by religious bodies and private groups, and financial assistance is provided by the State subject to certain conditions. In addition, children living in more inaccessible areas of New Zealand are enrolled in the Correspondence School. These children receive their lessons through the mail, and radio time is set aside to assist them each day.

Almost all children in New Zealand attend kindergartens or play centers before they enter primary school at the age of 5 years. For the next six years the children attend the primary school and then, depending on whether intermediate schools are present in the area (they are comparatively recent phenomena) the children will either attend an intermediate school for two years or remain a further two years in the extending primary school.

At approximately 13 years of age, all children enter secondary school. Testing or channelling into different schools according to aptitude, is not common practice, although once in the school, students are frequently grouped according to ability. After three or four years of secondary schooling, all students throughout New Zealand take the School Certficiate Examination. Success in this permits them to take University Entrance exams the following year and this exam must be passed before students are permitted to enter the university. Both exams may be taken more than once; therefore failure does not necessarily prevent a student's progress.

There are six universities scattered throughout the North and South Islands, and most of these are found in the large cities. Community colleges and technical institutes are the newest components in New Zealand's tertiary education system. Their growth rates have been extremely rapid over recent years, even more rapid than those of the universities. This increase in enrollments nationwide in part reflects the greater emphasis given to, and the popularity to, continuing and adult education. Government grants, scholarships, and bursaries bring tertiary education within the scope of all students qualified to be admitted to a tertiary institution.

## Historical Background of Physical Education and Sport

The first organized sporting activities in New Zealand may well have developed in accordance with the lifestyles of the gold rushers of the 1860's. At this time recreation was centered around the bars, with activities such as billiards, darts and cards most popular. Sportsdays, held close to, and sponsored by, the public houses developed with visiting shows and entertainment provided alongside a variety of sporting activities. The influence of the English settlers was also evident and the game of cricket was popular both for the activity it afforded and for its potential for increased social involvements.

The physically demanding life of the early settlers provided all the activity necessary to maintain some degree of fitness, and therefore it was mainly the social opportunities that sport offered which made it attractive. In these years it was the games of English heritage that featured most prominently, and thus in addition to card, dart and billiard games, rugby, cricket and croquet were found in most settlements. With the development of communications and transport, games between towns became popular, and the competitive aspect of sports became increasingly important. More recently, with sports becoming more highly organized, more competition-oriented, and more serious, the small settlement type activities have decreased or died out.

Physical education itself was not compulsory in the schools until the late nineteenth century, and when introduced, the memories of Maori Wars, the Boer War and trends in other countries influenced the choice of a military-type program. The 1877 Education Act stated:

In Public Schools, provision shall be made for the instruction in military drill for all, and in such of the schools as the Board shall from time to time direct, provision shall be made for physical training. (Van Dalen, 1971).

As well as training students in military drills, it was thought that such a program would have a strong disciplinary effect and make children "more obedient, more tractable, and therefore more willing to absorb school education" (Wright, 1964).

In 1912 a parliamentary report on the poor postural habits of many children, and pressure from critics of the inflexible military-type program, were able to bring a favorable change to the rigid system of physical education, and in 1913 the English Physical Training Syllabus (1909) was officially adopted. This provided a more balanced program of Swedish exercises as well as the military exercises. The classes were still formal, however, and the cadet corps remained in secondary schools. In 1920, the 1919 English syllabus was introduced and this furthered the strong tendency to follow English trends. This system lapsed, however, during World War II.

During these early years of formal physical education, facilities were limited and equipment hard to come by. In fact it was not until 1946 that physical education equipment was first issued to the schools, and subsidies for playground equipment became available.

## Recent Trends

In the 1950's and 1960's a major upsurgence in the number of school facilities has been witnessed. The majority of schools in New Zealand, both primary and secondary, have swimming pools, and few secondary schools are without gymnasia. The proliferation of gymnasia has led to the growth and popularity of many indoor sports such as badminton, volleyball, indoor basketball, creative dance, weight lifting and gymnastics, all of which experienced obvious difficulties when only outdoor play spaces were available. Also, the increased quantity and wide variety of equipment in almost every school now provides for a more varied range of activities.

The total physical education program emphases are in the midst of major changes. Part of this must be attributed to a greater willingness on the part of administrators to experiment. It must also be due to a greater appreciation of the potential and possibilities that physical education has to offer. Changes that have been seen in other areas of teaching have also been carried over into the area of physical education. Emphasis has changed from more formal teaching procedures to a discovery-type approach, as administrators and teachers have come to recognize the benefits of intrinsically over extrinsically-motivated learning.

Sport in the schools is no longer viewed as "sport for sports' sake". Rather, other aspects of sports are being promoted and individuals are encouraged to participate for the other benefits afforded. The 1960's have witnesses a drift away from team sports, which until then, in true British tradition, had held the major place in the physical education program, and were thought to promote all the qualities desirable in man. Some more liberal schools have now completely eliminated compulsory sports and have instituted more recreational-type activities in their place. This reflects a desire to educate students in a variety of activities that may be pursued during leisure time for a longer period than adolescence.

Another recent trend in physical education and sport in New Zealand is the pooling of facilities by schools and communities for recreational use. In fact, not only are facilities now being shared, but programs are also being planned jointly, and the benefits of these changes, especially in smaller communities, cannot be underestimated. There is still a great need for further liaison between schools, voluntary clubs and community agencies to avoid duplication of facilities but present, favorable changes appear to be moving in this direction. Just recently, a bill was passed in parliament giving education boards and the governing bodies of high schools the power to grant licenses so that school grounds, buildings and facilities can be used for recreational, sporting and cultural purposes.

Thus, the development of physical education and sport in New Zealand has seen a gradual change from a traditional and rigid military-type approach, to a more flexible, humanistic approach designed to provide people with a greater variety of physical education, sport and recreational opportunities, and to educate people on the possible benefits and costs of physical education, sporting and recreational activities.

## Elementary School Physical Education

In the elementary school, twenty minutes daily are normally devoted to physical education, and this is taught by the classroom teacher. Very few physical education specialists are found in primary schools although physical education advisors are available to help teachers in the planning and administering of programs.

Traditionally, the New Zealand primary school curriculum in physical education emphasizes basic movement activities involving the large muscle groups. This includes running, jumping, throwing and games, as well as the introduction of team sports such as rugby, netball, cricket, and softball in the later years. A noticeable emphasis is placed on swimming instruction; few children leave primary school without some degree of competency in the basic swimming strokes.

Because no part of New Zealand is more than 70 miles from the sea, and children are continually exposed to the sea, the lakes and the rivers, swimming and lifesaving are considered very important skills for all ages.

A unique feature of the physical education program is the inclusion of Maori activities: poi skills, stick games, knucklebones, hakas, hand games, dances and songs. These are very popular with primary school children, and in addition, they represent the Maori culture, of which most New Zealanders are justifiably proud.

Interschool competition in the various major games begins in the primary school. Competition may well have been too strongly stressed in the physical education program, but recent trends indicate that participation and enjoyment are more strongly emphasized than winning. However, as already mentioned, the teaching of compulsory team sports has in recent years been de-emphasized, and changes are apparent even in the primary school curriculum.

Secondary School Physical Education

Recent years have witnessed an examination of the major goals of the secondary school physical education programs and consequently, dramatic changes have become apparent.

The New Zealand secondary school system is now characterized by increasing flexibility and willingness by administrators to experiment with intrinsically motivated approaches, and, to include more, and a wider variety of, leisure experiences (Howat, 1975).

Rather than team games alone, the physical education program now extends to experiences oriented towards later life such as judo, yoga, self-defense, weight control, jogging and golf. A much greater diversity of activities is offered in order that students can experience a wide range of activities during their school years. Rather than spending long periods of time developing high standards of performance in a small number of activities, students are now encouraged to join community programs if they wish to specialize in any area to which they have been introduced in the school physical education program. With a view towards health and fitness in later life, the schools are accepting the responsibility of providing an extensive program as possible to increase the possibility of students finding an activity, or activities, which may then be pursued beyond school hours.

New Zealand's natural environment abounds with opportunities for outdoor enthusiasts, and schools have taken advantage of this by developing programs in outdoor education, often in association with geography, biology and science classes. Courses in camping, canoeing bushcraft, first-aid and climbing are covered theoretically in the classroom and put into practice in the outdoors. As a result, many schools have their own mountain lodges where several areas of the school curricula are explored during the school week. These lodges are also used by extracurricular clubs at other times.

With the blending of school and community facilities and programs, many Saturday sports teams previously organized by the schools have become more closely affiliated with clubs, or completely taken over by them. Schools are making greater use of community resources and are not only using facilities such as golf courses and squash courts for physical education classes, but are bringing in specialist persons from the community to teach activity units.

The physical education program in New Zealand secondary schools is administered by physical education specialists who are also responsible for coaching sports teams, although assistance is frequently given by other teachers. In the past, two forty-five minute periods of physical education have been required each week, in addition to thirty minutes of organized games. More recently, the trend towards greater flexibility in program offerings has ensured greater flexibility in scheduling and timetabling. In the last two years of schooling physical education is not compulsory, but most schools offer a physical education or recreation program for the senior school.

## University Physical Education and Sport

Physical education opportunities vary greatly between universities. Only two universities - Victoria and Otago - have modern well-equipped facilities; two other universities - Auckland and Canterbury - have plans for building large sporting complexes. Sporting and recreation officers are being employed to program for, and administer these facilities.

There is no physical education requirement at the university level. The only courses in physical education at the university level are at the University of Otago where physical education specialists are trained. No students other than physical education specialists can take the courses which the School of Physical Education offers. However, club sporting and recreational activities are popular within the universities, and annual unversity tournaments provide the opportunity for sporting teams from each university to compete against each other in a wide range of activities.

## The Teacher Education Program

There is only one university in New Zealand offering courses in Physical Education, and this is the University of Otago in Dunedin. The courses offered at the University of Otago are a Diploma in Physical Education and a Bachelors Degree in Physical Education. No graduate programs in physical education are offered in New Zealand, and many students travel to the United States and England to pursue graduate studies. After studying at the University of Otago, many physical education graduates then spend a year at a secondary teachers' training college, either in Auckland or Christchurch, where they spend a large amount of time student teaching before they take up positions in secondary schools.

About 120 students are admitted each year to the School of Physical Education, and in the past ten years the competition for acceptance into the courses has increased. In 1975, only 43% of the applicants were accepted.

A major disadvantage of the absence of any graduate programs in physical education is that many of the better students leave New Zealand to gain higher degrees overseas. At the moment no plans for graduate programs in physical education in New Zealand have been proposed although there is a Masters Degree in Recreation Management offered at Victoria University.

## Special Characteristics and Current Trends

The New Zealand Physical Education Society (now called the New Zealand Association of Health, Physical Education and Recreation) was formed in 1938 and has active branches throughout New Zealand. It is administered by a National Council and publishes the New Zealand Journal of HPER triennially. The National Council, through a Board of Examiners, administers qualifying examinations for members wishing to be approved for Diploma, Associate or Fellow status. Recipients of these qualifications gain credit towards teacher training. The NZAHPER is affiliated with other international physical education associations and is regularly represented at international conferences.

## Educational Development Conference

In 1973 the New Zealand Government convened three working parties to examine various fields of education in preparation for a public seminar which was held in 1974. This consisted of the Educational Development Conference. The three working parties reported on aims and objectives, on improving learning, and teaching, and on organization and administration. Major recommendations which are relevant to the school physical education curriculum include: that importance be given to a wide variety of skills and talents for all individuals along with the pursuit of academic excellence; that emphasis be given to the participation of people of all ages in worthwhile activites; that there be increased involvement of staff, students and the community in the process of policy and decision-making in education; that provison be made for continuity by removing as far as possible the present barriers between the various educational levels and institutions; that action be taken to provide special opportunities for children in educationally disadvantaged localities; that action be taken to provide learning environments which meet the needs of Maoris and other Polynesians.

## Administration

The Physical Education Branch of the New Zealand Department of Education is administered by the Superintendent of Physical Education and he is responsible to the Director of Education.

Recently, and as a result of the Educational Development Conference, unification of primary, secondary and tertiary education has been proposed. If effected, this will mean greater continuity and unity of physical education programs across these institutions. Other major recommendations involve attempts to bring about greater flexibility, variety, and suitability of programs to local circumstances. This push for decentralization should encourage local school districts to develop and orient their physical education programs to more closely fit in with the interests and demands of their clientele.

## New Zealand Government Assistance to Recreation and Sport

In 1973 the New Zealand Parliament passed the Recreation and Sport Act which aims to assist all types of recreation and sport. An Advisory Council was appointed by the Minister of Sport to make recommendations on local, regional and national recreation and sports projects. To date, the Council has favored assistance in the areas of leadership and coaching, administration, the development of incentive schemes, and the purchasing of equipment and buildings. The Minister of Recreation and Sport services the Council and processes the many applications for assistance. In the period 1973-74, over 6 million dollars were distributed to national associations, local authorities, youth agencies and community groups.

Other schemes include a 'Come Alive' campaign to increase involvement in recreation and sport, the development of the Diploma of the New Zealand Council for Recreation and Sport to train recreation leaders, and the promotion and development of research into recreation participation patterns of New Zealanders. With regard to the training of recreation administrators, supervisors, leaders and programers, the Ministry is actively encouraging Otago University to include a major study of recreation in the existing Diploma of Physical Education. Also, Victoria University, the University of Auckland, and Lincoln College have expanded their present offerings to include recreation administration and leadership.

## Sport and Outdoor Recreation

Sport is an important part of the lives of most New Zealanders. Every sport has its own national body which now receives administrative and financial support from the Ministry of Recreation and Sport as do the local clubs. The clubs are based on the British tradition of amateurism and these are a notable feature of the New Zealand sporting scene.

The Commonwealth Games were held in Christchurch in 1974, and apart from being host to a magnificent sporting festival, the city is now endowed with a very large sports complex. Following from this, the Ministry of Recreation and Sport have indicated their support of developing large regional sports and recreation complexes similar to the facility developed in Christchurch. The argument proposed here is that regional facilities would be much more efficient and productive than a multitude of facilities scattered throughout local areas.

An issue which is of much concern to New Zealanders is whether to continue sporting contacts with South Africa. In 1974 the Springboks (the South African Rugby Team) was scheduled to tour New Zealand, but this tour was stopped by the New Zealand Government because of South Africa's apartheid policies. This issue is of much concern to New Zealanders because of the moral issue involved and also because Rugby Union is New Zealand's national sport and a strong competitive rivalry has developed between the two countries.


## SELECTED REFERENCES

"Educational Aims and Objectives", Educational Development Conference 1973-74, A. R. Shearer, Government Printer. Wellington, New Zealand. 1974.

Howat, Gary. Personal Interview. July 1975.

"Improving Learning and Teaching", Educational Development Conference 1973-74, A. R. Shearer, Government Printer. Wellington, New Zealand. 1974.

Jackson, Keith and Harre, John. *New Zealand.* London: Thomas and Hudson. 1969.

Kurney, Jack. An Overview and Report from the Chairman of the Examination Board. NZAHPER. February 1974. *New Zealand Journal of HPER.* 6:4. April 1974.

Larkin, Rovert N. "New Zealand Government Assistance to Recreation and Sport." June 1975.

*New Zealand Yearbook.* Wellington, New Zealand: A. R. Shearer, Government Printer. 1974.

"Organization and Administration of Education". Educational Development Conference 1973-74, A. R. Shearer, Government Printer. Wellington, New Zealand. 1974.

*Recreation and Sport Act 1973, No. 36.* Wellington, New Zealand: A. R. Shearer, Government Printer. 1973.

Scholer, E. A. "Teacher Training in Physical Education in New Zealand". *The Physical Educator*. 23:1. March 1966.

Siers, James and Aberdein, Keith. *New Zealand*. Wellington, Millwood Press. 1973.

Van Dalen, Deobold B. and Bennett, Bruce L. *A World History of Physical Education--Cultural--Philosophical--Comparative.* Englewood Cliffs, New Jersey: Prentice-Hall, Inc. 1971.

Wright, Edward J. "Physical Education in New Zealand". *Physical Education Around the World*. Monograph No. 1. Indianapolis, Indiana: Phi Epsilon Kappa Fraternity. 1965.

# SPORT AND PHYSICAL EDUCATION IN NIGERIA

by Awoture Eleyae

## Biographical Sketch

*Awoture Eleyae* was born in Nigeria and took his grade school, high school, and undergraduate education in the schools of Nigeria. Since graduation, he has attended a number of colleges and universities in other countries. Three months were spent in each of the following institutions: (a) The Carnegie College of Physical Education in Leeds, England; (b) Loughborough College of Physical Education, England; and (c) The Scottish (Jordan-Hill) College of Physical Education, Glasgow, Scotland. He also attended the British Summer School for senior coaches and obtained the coaching award in the Sprints, Hurdles, and the Relays. He received his M.S. degree in 1971 and the Ph.D. in 1974 in Physical Education at the University of Illinois, Urbana-Champaign Campus.

Dr. Eleyae has taught at all levels--grade school to the university. He was the Nigerian national record holder in the 880 yards run in 1956 and a member of the relay team that set the West African one mile relay record in 1959. He later became the Nigerian Olympic Head Coach in 1964 and 1968, and was a member of the Nigerian research team that travelled to Mexico City in 1967 to study the effect of altitude on Nigerian athletes. He was also the Nigerian Head Coach to the All-African Games at Congo Brazzaville in 1965; and to the British Commonwealth Games in Jamaica in 1966; and in Edinburgh, Scotland in 1970. He served as the Assistant Team Coach to the combined British Commonwealth team that competed against the U.S.A., track team in Los Angeles in 1967. He was also the coach of the Pan-African track team that competed against the U.S.A., in Durham, North Carolina in 1971.

Dr. Eleyae is presentedly employed by the National Sports Commission, Lagos, Nigeria.

## Introduction

It is quite a task to try to compress what ought to be said about Physical Education in Nigeria into less than thirty double-space typed pages. Yet this is what is attempted in this study. The obvious result is that the subsections are treated in a very sketchy form. However, the preparation of teachers and the program of physical education is given more "flesh" than other aspects.

The purpose of this study is to review and enrich the literature on Physical Education in Nigeria that is presently found in the Physical Education Library of the University of Illinois at Urbana-Champaign Campus. It is intended to provide up-to-date information which will serve as a source of reference for future studies on Nigeria. It is different from other reviews in that very little can actually be found on Nigerian physical eduation anywhere in the world, including Nigeria itself. Very little has actually been written on the subject.

A good attempt was made by Vendien and Nixon in *The World Today in Health, Physical Eduation and Recreation*,[16] to devote a section to 'physical education' in Nigeria. Nevertheless, this special study has brought up-to-date a great deal of the deficiencies in Asikiye Kiri's presentation in Vendien and Nixon's book.[5] The changes have been primarily due to the rapid developments going on in Nigerian Phyical Education. For example, free primary education has been extended to all parts of the country--a situation which did not exist in 1960. Where there were four political regions in the country up to the middle of 1967, Nigeria now has twelve states (See Figure 1), and this means that more coverage and attention is given to education including physical education. Supervision has improved due to the more compact demographic delimitations of operational zones (states). This has come to imply also that whereas governmental sports organizations existed in only four regions in 1966, twelve such organizations now exist to fund and promote the growth of sport and recreation--an integral part of the physical education program.

This special study, therefore, has not only appraised physical education in Nigeria as documented by a few people, but it has also attempted to restate physical education as it is in 1971 Nigeria. Another obvious change is the name, function and sphere of influence of what used to be the National Sports Council of Nigeria referred to by Van Dalen and Bennett.[15]

General Background Information: Nigeria is located on the West Coast of Africa. It is bounded on the south by the Gulf of Guinea, on the northwest and north by Niger, on the northeast by Lake Chad, on the east by Cameroon and on the west by Dahomey. It received its name from the River Niger.

Generally, there are two seasons, the dry and the wet. While these are clearly marked in the north, they are less so in the south.

## Nigeria

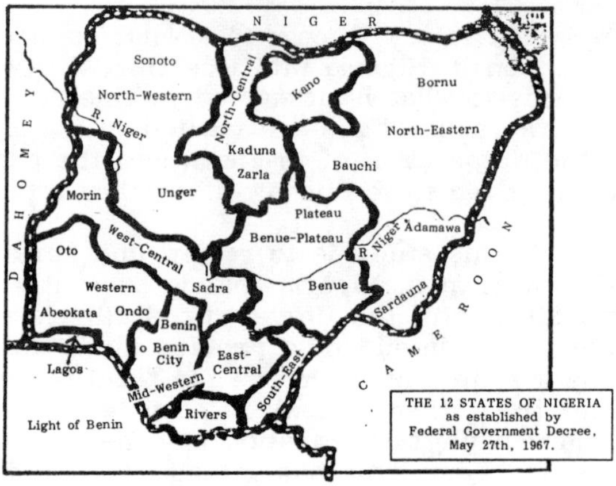

THE 12 STATES OF NIGERIA
as established by
Federal Government Decree,
May 27th, 1967.

Figure 1. Each of the 12 states has a Ministry of
Education which recommends the curriculum
adopted in the elementary, secondary and
teacher training institutions.

Topographically, the land rises from the sea level in the extreme south
south to some 6,000 feet above sea level in parts of the Benue Plateau
State. The south is riven, pretty uneven to the east and west, con-
caving into the Niger Delta. The north is flat in most parts except
the Benue Plateau and The Cameroon border of the whole east.

Vegetation: Mangrove forests at the Coastal areas merge into
equitorial, tropical, deciduous trees and grassland which occupies
most of the Northern States. As the northern boundary is approach-
ed (about 60 miles) the vegetation changes rapidly into scrub land.
The areas is 356,569 square miles.[8] The population is about 60 million people--about 160 inhabitants per square mile.

The Government: A Republic. At the moment it is ruled by a
military government. There are twelve states (See Figure 1). The
states center around tribal groups.[14] Population distribution is about
23% urban and 77% rural. It is advancing very rapidly toward urbanization.

There are about 15,000 primary schools with some 2,900,000
pupils[4] and some 1,000 secondary (post primary) and technical schools
with about 234,000 students. Higher education: about 20 out of
every 100,000 of population.

History: Nigeria's earliest known culture NOK, flourished
around 700 to 200 B.C.[7] During the 12th Century, Nigeria's next
culture grew around Ife an ancient Yoruba City and later Benin City.
In the medieval times northern Nigeria had contact with the large

- 462 -

Kingdoms of the western Sudan and by the end of the 14th century Islam was firmly established in the north. This is important when considering the physical education program in the Northern States which are predominently Islam. Between the 15th and the 18th centuries, the Portuguese and the British engaged in Commerce and slave trading on the coast. Trade across the desert was also a possibility. There are more than 150 tribes (cultures) with distinct languages and customs. English is the linqua franca.

Education: About 80% of all six year olds go to school--more boys than girls. In the South, about 98% attend primary school while in the Northern states the percentage is lower. One in every ten students who enter primary school gets some form of post primary education, particularly secondary Grammar and Technical education.

## Natural Physical Education

Before the influence of the European Countries, and the Arab world on the cultures that constitute most of Nigeria, each had their local games. These local games and sports were varied and many of them formed the core of the different cultures. Some of these are still dominant particularly, the dances and what the present physical education specialists call "minor games."[2] In the typical rural areas, physical education as we understand it is undertaken by the children and the teenagers. The adults have their physical activities in their everyday life pursuit on the farm, lake, or river, etc. This is why the average Nigerian is slim and wiry. In fact most of Nigerian successes in international sports bear a relation to this natural hardy upbringing. Both the young and the old do have recreational games, such as ayo, draft, and eko. They engage in these late in the evenings, after their normal occupations; and also on Sundays, and during "market days." Many of those games are coming into the school programs. Furthermore, both adults and the young prepare for local festivities. These entail a variety of physical activities in any given locality and there is usually the need to prepare very elaborately for these activities.

With more of the population going to School there has been increasing need for well guided programs of activity to replace what was was naturally obtained in the daily pursuit of means of livelihood.

## Physical Education in the Schools

Primary Schools:

The first formal schools started after 1840, in Southern Nigeria.[11] Since these schools were started by the missionaries, not much of physical education went on at the beginning. However, this has changed completely.

It is a requirement by the Ministries of education that physical education should be provided. In some states it is throughout the five school days in the week. In others it is provided three times a week. In general physical education lessons are provided at this stage for upward of 120 minutes per week. Additional game periods are provided every day for those who have the time. The school teams schedule their practices in the afternoon so that the players have time to participate in normal classes. (See Table 1 for a normal Physical Education Table for average age range 6 to 12).[6]

Table 1. The contents of the table changes according
to the age of the children. In general the pattern
remains the same.

---

Physical Education Lesson

Class:  Standard I.

Age:  8 to 9 years.

Time:  20 to 25 minutes.

Preliminary Activities:
Pick up any piece of apparatus and play with it (the teacher could indicate the number of activities she expects from each child.)

Introductory Activities:
1. Grow as tall as possible;
2. grow as small as possible;
3. jump like a frog;
4. fly like an aeroplane/eagle, etc.

Rhythmic Jumps:
1. In 3s skip-jump over a swinging rope;
2. astride jumps over backs;
3. jumping from hoop into a hoop (hoops arranged in any form the teacher chooses);
4. landing from varied heights.

Trunk Activities:
Imitate a cow running very fast;
walk like a very big lizard;
form a very big circle with your body;
make a bow with your body in any way you like.

Balance:
Walking on low beams erected for the purpose;
Walking fast on the toes.

PART TWO

MINOR GAMES OR DANCE.

1. Fire is on the mountain;
2. Onomiroro;
3. ubiaka.

---

The level of work to be done is directed by the State Ministry of Education. But the resourceful teacher modifies the syllabus to the the need of the class. Every class teacher handles the physical education lessons at this stage. In some Big Schools in the large cities such as Lagos, physical education teachers are designated to handle physical education in some specified classes of the Primary School.

The children play games such as football, netball, volleyball, table tennis, deck-tennis and track and field (Figure 2). Interschool competitions are a common feature. There is usually the gamesmaster and or the gamesmistress whose responsibility it is to coordinate the intramurals and the extramural sports.

Figure 2. The game of netball. A typical scene in Elementary and Secondary Schools--in all the states of Nigeria. In most of the secondary schools the girls wear prescribed uniforms for physical education lessons.

Health education takes the form of health practices. Practical lessons in how to brush the teeth (with a chew stick), how to take care of toe and finger nails, how to sweep and dispose of refuse, etc., are given. In the upper classes some community projects are undertaken (more in the villages and small towns than in the big cities). The theory of simple health habits is given.

Secondary and Technical Schools: The practice of physical education at this level is very different. The ministry of education stipulates that there should be at least eighty minutes of physical education during regular school hours. But since these schools vary in staffing, the practice is varied. Generally, the gamesmaster, takes all classes. In some areas, the monitorial system is still encouraged-- boys from the senior classes handle the physical education lessons of the junior classes.

But in the Government institutions and some well established mission schools, trained physical education specialists are employed to be responsible for the physical education program. A normal table of activities will look like this (See Table II).

Table 2. The activities increase in their degree of difficulty as we go up the classes. In Part II, skills in track and field, soccer and other sports are often included.

---

### Physical Education Table

Class: Form III.

Age: 15 to 16 years.

Time: 35 minutes.

Introductory Activities:
1. General play with apparatus;
2. Tails (pupils make tails with braids). In a given time children try to catch as many tails as possible;
3. Corners (pupils touch the four corners of the playing area. The first to come back.)

Leg Exercise:
1. Skip Jumps;
2. skipping (could be with ropes);
3. landing from a height.

Trunk Exercise:
1. In twos, using a bean bag or rubber ball, with two hands pass the ball from side to side over head; or between your legs to your partner.

Strengthening or contest activity:
1. Cork fight;
2. knee boxing;
3. back wrestling, etc.

### PART TWO

CLASS ACTIVITY: handspring.

GROUP ACTIVITY:
1. forward roll;
2. headstand;
3. headspring;
4. handspring.
   (the teacher stations himself near the most recently taught activity. From there he does most of the supervision of the other groups.)

QUIETING EXERCISE: Breathing in and out accompanied by by heelraising and lowering. (this could be done in a variety of ways).

---

Intramurals, intermurals, and extramurals are very common particularly in the government institutions and some of the popular mission and privately owned schools. Since most of the schools are residential, it is easy to organize the intra- and intermural programs. The popular practice is for the physical education specialist, through the cooperation of the principal, to involve every member of staff in the afternoon programs.

The outdoor physical education programs include soccer, track and field, lawn tennis, field hockey, swimming, volleyball, cricket, netball, basketball and camping. The indoor program includes dancing, table tennis, many card and local recreational games. The intensity of the secondary school program is seen in the number of juniors who represent Nigeria in international competition.

## Physical Education in the Universities and the Advanced Teacher Training Colleges

The program of physical education has been least successful in the institutions of higher learning. The reason is that until recently, no coaches or sports coordinators were employed who could take care of the sports programs. The British club system worked when these institutions were predominantly staffed with British lecturers. But since independence when Nigerian lecturers have increasingly taken up responsibilities, physical education programs deteriorated because physical education specialists were not encouraged to take over from the former European tutors and lecturers. In part this is because there is the inherited deep-seated bias that physical education is not academic, and sports is play which should be left for the "kids."[17] But with interuniversity competitions becoming increasingly popular all the six Universities have now employed coaches. It should be noted that the institutions of higher learning have not contributed significantly to Nigeria's national and international teams. Many of these Universities lack adequate facilities. However the University of Nigeria at Nsukka started off in the right direction. It has a first class stadium, a good number of various courts for tennis, basketball and volleyball and also a swimming pool. The gymnasium is small. The University of Ife is fast improving its facilities. It is hoped with improved facilities more opportunities will be given for competitive and recreative sports in these institutions than the situation is presently. The Nigerian Universities Games Association (NUGA) arrange annual Interuniversity Games.

## Training of Physical Education Teachers

The training of teachers for physical education takes three forms. The teachers who teach in Primary Schools are produced in Grade II and Grade III Teachers Training Colleges. Since these teachers handle every subject on the time-table including physical education, the Grade II Teacher Training Colleges feature a very active physical education program. They are taught various forms of stunts, agilities, vaulting, minor and major games. Then they learn to teach during the period of two to five years that they remain in training. They are also encouraged to play these games. There are national inter-teacher training competition in different sports which bring the best teacher/competitors from all over the country together one or more times every year in about four sports. The competition which begins at the institutional level, gives practice to the student-teachers on how to organize meets.

The Advanced Teacher Training:

This group of institutions are patterned after the British system. Since physical education was generally considered a non-academic discipline, it was felt the training should belong to the teacher training institutes of the Universities. And all that was awarded was either the Nigerian Teacher's Certificate or a Diploma in Physical Education.

The first of these Colleges was established in Ahmadu Bello University in Zaria in 1957. Until then, the few specialists who were trained went to Britain's, Loughborough, Jordan Hill or Carnegie College in Leeds. Only one came to the United States for 9 months. The Physical Education Course in Zaria was patterned after Jordan Hill in Scotland, but various aspects of it were moderated by the Universities of London and Leeds.

The Program was as follows:[1]

| | |
|---|---|
| P.E. 101 | Anatomy--3 terms. |
| P.E. 102 | Principles of Physical Education--9 terms. |
| P.E. 103 | Theory of Games--9 terms. |
| P.E. 104 | Theory and Practice of Athletics (Track and Field)--9 terms. |
| P.E. 105 | Theory and Practice of Basketball--9 terms. |
| P.E. 106 | Theory and Practice of Soccer--9 terms. |
| P.E. 107 | Theory and Practice of Vaulting and Agility--9 terms. |
| P.E. 108 | Theory and Practice of Hockey (Field Hockey)--9 terms. |
| P.E. 109 | Theory and Practice of Cricket--9 terms. |
| P.E. 110 | Primary School Teaching Practice--3 terms. |
| P.E. 111 | Physiology--6 terms. |
| P.E. 112 | History of Physical Education--6 terms. |
| P.E. 113 | Secondary School Teaching Practice--6 terms. |
| P.E. 114 | Kinesiology--3 terms. |
| Ed. 101 | English Language--8 terms. |
| Ed. 102 | English Literature--8 terms. |

| Ed. 103 | Speech Training and Phonetics--8 terms. |
| Ed. 104 | Principles of Education--7 terms. |
| Ed. 105 | Philosophy of Education--4 terms. |
| Ed. 106 | Psychology of Education--4 terms. |
| Ed. 107 | History of Education and the Organization and Aims of Education--3 terms. |
| P.E. 115 | Extended Essay--not less than 10,000 words on a chosen and approved topic. |
| P.E. 116 | Personal Performance. |
| P.E. 117 | Coaching Ability. |
| P.E. 118 | Testing Methods. |
| Ed. 108 | Teaching Practice. |

There are three terms in an academic year. Altogether every student was expected to receive lectures for 232½ hours in the three years. This was apart from the time spent on physical education (115 to 118 hours). The successful students received a diploma or the Nigerian Teacher's Certificate.

There are five of these Advanced Teacher Training Colleges, since 1965. Although the programs are not as intensive as the one in Ahmadu Bello the principle is the same. The products from these institutions teach in Grade II Teacher Training Colleges and in Secondary Schools. They also work in the Sports Councils, and some other corporations and industries. Some of them serve as coaches in the Universities (this is a very recent practice).

Preparation of Physical Education Teachers
in the Universities

The first University to award Bachelor degrees in Physical Education is the University of Nigeria, Nsukka. This institution which is modelled on the United States pattern, "aims to develop the knowledge, skills, attitudes and appreciation necessary for successful teachers of Physical Education, Health Education and Recreation, for coaches and organizers of physical education and for workers in related fields. The degree program also makes provision for students from other departments to minor in Physical Education or Health Education."[3]

Similar to the courses in Zaria mentioned above, the program in Nsukka is more detailed and more theory oriented. The Health Education aspect is taken into a higher level. Since 1968 the University of Ife has started to workd toward producing graduates of Physical Education. Products of these two institutions go into Grade II Teacher Training Colleges, Secondary and Technical Colleges and Sports Councils, as the products of the Advanced Teacher Training Colleges.

Since 1959, many Nigerians who had obtained their degrees and diplomas from these institutions have been coming to the United States of America to work for their Master's and Doctoral degrees. With the introduction of these people with advanced degrees into the Nigerian Universities, the Nigerian Government is gradually recognizing Physical Education as a worthwhile academic discipline. There are two other degree programs in the offing--at Ahmadu Bello University and Lagos University.

## Competitive Athletics and Sport Administration

There are two types of competitive sports--The Amateur and the Professional. It is expected by the casual sports enthusiast that the National Sports Commission of Nigeria should cater to both types; but presently the sports commission directs its main efforts to the development of amateur sports. One of the main reasons is that professional sport is expected to support itself. At the moment this does not happen to any enviable extent. It is true that Nigeria has produced two world champions in boxing (Hogan Kid Bassey and Dick Tiger); but like other Nigerians who are now in Europe, Bassey and Tiger had to leave Nigeria for Britain before they had promoters and the quality of competition that enabled them to achieve their ambition.

Professional sport is not popular. Its administration is handled by individual non-committed groups of interested persons. Boxing is handled by the Nigerian Boxing Board of Control; Wrestling by the Nigerian Professional Wrestling Association, and Golf by the Nigerian Association of Golfers. Among these three, boxing is the most popular. Yet it does not pose any major threat of "seducing" amateur boxers to the Nigerian Amateur Boxing Association.

Basically amateur sports in Nigeria thrives on the club system. There are two major levels of competitors at the National and State levels--Senior and Junior competitors. Both can be found within the same club. Senior males are all males who are 19 years old and over by the day of the competition. While senior females are all those who are 17 years and over by the day of competition. See Figures 3 and 4. There are national associations which are affiliated to international federations. The clubs are affiliated to the district committees while the districts are affiliated to the States and the States in turn, are affiliated to the National Governing Bodies (the associations).

Apart from the competition organized by the associations (Table 3), the various units like the Secondary Grammar Schools, the Technical Schools, the Universities, the Teacher Training Colleges, the Police, the Army, organize competitions ranging from club level to national level in their particular categories. In that way many competitions are provided all the year round.

The unit of training and competition is the club. But the national governing bodies directly or through the state committees organize coaching clinics for honorary coaches and organizers. The

Figure 3.  The Nigerian team participating in Dakar
Senegal in 1963 during the Dakar Friendship Games.
Twenty-four countries including France participated
in twelve different sports.

Figure 4.  Since 1966 the Men and Women Track and Field
Association form a single Amateur Athletic Associations.
Competitions feature both men and women.  In this
photograph a woman athlete is throwing the discus
during National Championships at the National Stadium
Sururlere-Lagos.

Table 3. This fixture changes from year to year.
Usually some major event like the Olympic Games and
the British Commonwealth Games determine the end of
the season in the years that they feature.

---

Amateur Athletic Association of Nigeria Approved
Programme of Events for 1968/69 Season

1. November 16, 1968.
--Interstate Cross Country for Boys, Girls and Men. KADUNA.

2. December 14, 1968.
--Interstates Marathon. KADUNA.

3. January 25, 1969.
--Interstates Relay. LAGOS.

4. February 21-22, 1969.
--Junior States Open Championships in the various States
Capitals.

5. March, 1969.
--State Police Athletic Championship.

6. March 14-15, 1969.
--Senior States Open Championships in the various States
Capitals.

7. March 27-29, 1969.
--All Nigeria Junior Open Championships. LAGOS.

8. March 31, 1969.
--All Nigeria Police Championships.

9. April 10, 11 and 12, 1969.
--Grier-Powell Cups Competition. LAGOS.

10. April 24-26, 1969.
--All Nigeria Senior Open Championships. LAGOS.

11. April 25-26, 1969.
--Hussey Shield Competition. IBADAN.

12. May 23-24, 1969.
--International Athletic Meeting. ACCRA.

13. June 21, 1969.
--First Trials for 2nd African Games. IBADAN.

14. July 26, 1969.
--Second Trials for 2nd African Games. LAGOS.

15. August 9, 1969.
--Third Trials to select Athletes for Camp. KADUNA/LAGOS.

16. August 29-30, 1969.
--Interstates Competition. BENIN CITY.

17. October 11-15, 1969.
--2nd African Games in Bamako. MALI. Following fixtures are
yet to be confirmed:

18. ? ? ?
--Interuniversities Championships.

---

associations raise money from private donations, fines, gate receipts, sales of handbooks, programs, and entry fees. Since this money is usually inadequate for costs of travelling and other competition expenses, the Governments of the Federation and the States set up Sports Councils commissions. These are government agencies that are responsible for the development of sports. They employ coaches and qualified organizers that assist the associations in their coaching programs. In the states these councils help both individuals and clubs. They also provide up-to-date facilities.

The national coaches employed by the National Sports Commission serve as advisors to the national governing bodies and to the National Sports Commission. They help to draw up programs for coaching and for national championships. (See Table 4). They run clinics for State Coaches and also assist the State Coaches in conducting coaching courses.

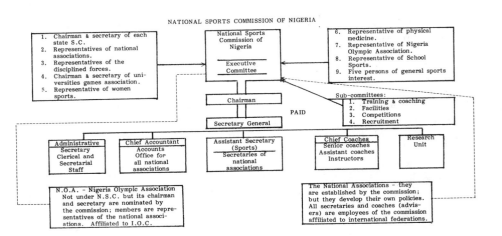

The Sports Councils get their revenue from the governments. They also help the associations to collect money at the gates and keep the accounts of the associations. With Government grants the sports councils assist governing bodies that are unable to organize enough competitions because of money. The National Sports Commission through the national governing bodies finance national and international programs in Sports with national associations.[10] These sports are: (a) Soccer, (2) Track and Field, (3) Boxing, (4) Lawn Tennis, (5) Table Tennis, (6) Swimming, (7) Field Hockey, (8) Cricket, (9) Basketball, (10) Netball, and (11) Volleyball. On the average, the governments of the twelve states and the Federal Government through the National Sports Commission spend some N₤800,000 ($2,400,000) of taxpayers' money on sports every year. This is besides what the Associations raise through diverse means including gate tickets, entries, and membership dues.

Nigeria's Participation in International
Amateur Sport

Nigeria has had a long experience at international amateur competition. The first attempt was in 1948 when an observation team for track and field athletics left for Great Britain to watch the 1948 Olympic Games, but with specific design to participate in local meets while in Britain. Since then, Nigeria has taken part in all Olympic and British Commonwealth Games, except the 1962 Commonwealth Games in Perth.

Furthermore, the range of sports in which Nigeria takes part internationally has widened ever since. Nigeria is now regularly represented in Track and Field, Boxing, Soccer, Lawn Tennis, Table Tennis, Volleyball, Basketball, Swimming, Cricket and Field Hockey. As the result of reports on these international engagements, the Nigerian sports public has grown nervously critical of the growth and development of competitive amateur sport.

At a time when training was not as intensified as it has been through the sixties, Nigeria was one of the leading African nations in track and field athletics. The meritorious performances of a small Nigerian team in 1954 at the Vancouver Games in Canada was a testimony of this.[12]

In the early sixties, the drop in standard of Nigerian performance internationally was due to the problems connected with early independence (1960) and associated problems of adjustments to new responsibilities. There was a marked rise in the quality of performance in 1966 and 1967. But with the outbreak of the Nigerian Civil War--August 1967 to February 1970--the exigencies of the war precipitated the drop in performances of Nigerians in international amateur sport. Since the end of the war the Governments of the Republic have stepped up the arrangements for promoting the growth of sport and improving the quality of performance in international competition. The establishment of a revitalized "National Sports Commission" by Federal Military Government Decree No. 34, is a vindication of this awareness at the national level.[9]

General Trends and Conclusion

Until the Civil War, the governments of Nigeria did not think seriously about the place of physical education in a nation. Nigeria has always participated in the Olympic Games and the British Commonwealth Games since 1950, yet there was no accepted relationship between a healthy physical education program and participation in national and international competitions. Physical fitness, recreation and general leisure time sports pursuits have still not been given serious thoughts.

The hope is that the people in the field who are now gradually getting better qualified from all over the developed world, U.S.A., in particular, are attempting to project the profession more than it had been done before. It is heartwarming that in the very recent past the quality of physical education programs at all levels is fast improving because of more specialists that are graduating from the advanced teacher training colleges and the universities. Although the number of pupils reached by this "quality work" is limited because of the shortage of qualified personnel in this field, the consciousness and need generated in the schools is a good indication for the future of the profession.

It is also reassuring that the universities are gradually accepting physical education into their academic programs. Out of the six university in the country two have established physical education departments, and two are on the verge of doing so. This will help to develop the body of knowledge which will in turn aid research and the healthy growth of the Physical Education profession in Nigeria.

## NIGERIAN SPORTS UPDATED[17]

"Traditional Sports

Nigerians have always taken keen and active interest in sports. In traditional times they devoted the season following the harvesting of crops to wrestling, archery, hunting, racing, swimming, canoe racing, and even horse racing and acrobatics, which have become an integral part of the culture. A good number of these sports suffered temporarily from the activities of the missionaries and the pursuit of the R's in Nigerian educational institutions.

New Approach

Today, there is a new approach to sports and recreation. Nigerians are participating fully in sports and their development. Before 1930, the main strength of Nigerian sports lay in athletics which was favoured by the Army and the teachers' training colleges. For many years, primary schools competed in sports every Empire Day. The diversity of the sports programme depended on the various localities and the knowledge of the organisers. With the advent of the Grier Cup and the Hussey shield competitions starting from 1933, secondary schools began to take a more serious interest in the development of athletics. The Hussey shield competition is now the premier athletics championships for secondary schools in the country. It has grown to become an interstate secondary school athletics competition. There are other national school competitions in other sports such as the Morocco cup contest in cricket and for football, the Adebajo cup competed for at national level.

## International Competition

The need for responsible organisation of athletics in the country led to the formation of the Amateur Athletics Association of Nigeria in 1944. But it was not until the Nigerian Olympic and the British Empire and Commonwealth Games Associations, (NOBECGA) was founded that Nigeria officially entered the international fields of sports, and in 1950, participated for the first time, in sports of international calibre - the British Commonwealth in Auckland, New Zealand - and returned home with a silver medal in the high jump. Four years later, Nigeria won a gold medal in the same Games - the British Commonwealth Games that took place in Vancouver, Canada.

Although Nigeria sent a team of observers to Britain in 1948 during the London Olympics, the country's first official appearance in the Olympic Games was in Helsinki, in 1962. Thereafter, Nigeria has participated in all Olympics and British Commonwealth Games since 1950 with exception of the 1962 Commonwealth Games in Perth, Australia.

## All-Africa Games

Nigeria took part in the first All-Africa Games in Brazzaville in 1965 in which she came out an overall third (behind Egypt and Kenya) with twenty medals; nine gold, six silver and five bronze. Of these, the women athletes won four gold, two silver and two bronze medals. In the second All-Africa Games which took place in Lagos, in 1973, Nigeria showed a mark of improvement by placing second to Egypt.

## National Competition

Keen interest and participation in national sports meetings provide the opportunity for selecting top athletes to represent the nation at international games. Important national competitions include the Grier cup competitions and its zonal counterparts among secondary schools; the All-Nigeria Police Athletics Championships; the Armed Forces Competitions; the N.U.G.A. Games which is a competition among the Nigerian Universities, the bi-annual State and National Sports Festivals introduced in 1973 and the All-Nigeria Athletics Championships. It should be said also that other sports such as football, swimming, boxing, basketball, cricket, hockey, lawn tennis, table tennis also have their national open championships as well as their national closed championships for well defined groups of participants.

## National Sports Commission

Sponsorship of competitions is the responsibility of the National Sports Commission, though some firms and industries and even private individuals have taken keen interest in the promotion of sport.

The National Sports Commission (NSC) which was established by Decree No. 34 in August 1971, is in charge of the coordination of the activities of all the governing bodies of sports in Nigeria. Its function is to organize sports at the national level. The Commission appoints a governing body known as the National Association for each sport and each body advises it on technical matters related to its particular sport. The Federal Military Government set up the Commission because it realized the very valuable role that sports play in the promotion of national unity, the promotion of good health and the building up of cordial international relations.

Sports Councils

In each state of the Federation, there is a Sports Council - a state government agency similar to the National Sports Commission - which is responsible for the administration and the organisation of sport in its state. The Sports Councils are responsible to the N.S.C. and they cater for as many sports as they consider necessary. These include football, cricket, athletics, table tennis, lawn tennis, boxing, hockey, basketball, netball, swimming, judo, polo, handball, squash racket and badminton.

Over the years, some of these sports have become more popular than others; some have been identified with some social rankings, while others were only recently introduced into the country.

International - Standard Stadia

Each Nigerian city or town has at least a football pitch where sporting activities take place. In more recent years, efforts have been made in all state capitals at building some standard stadia. So far, only four of these stadia - the National Stadium at Surulere, in Lagos, the Liberty Stadium at Ibadan, the Ahmadu Bello Stadium at Kaduna, and the Ogbe Stadium at Benin - are of international standard. The University of Ife stadium compares favourably with all non-synthetic stadia anywhere in the world.

Nigerian National Sports Festival

In the effort to whip up competitive interest in sports at all levels in all Nigerian communities, the first ever National Sports Festival in Nigeria was organised in Lagos from August 18 to 27, 1973. Competitions were held at village, district, zonal state and finally, at national levels. This helped to ensure that all sections of the country felt the impact of the festival.

Over 6,000 competitors from all over the Federation participated in this mammoth festival. There were three categories of competitors - the Juniors (13 years and under), the intermediate (18 years and below), and the seniors (above 18 years of age).

During the first National Sports Festival, eleven sports were competed for. These were football, athletics, volleyball, boxing, basketball, lawn tennis, table tennis, swimming, cycling, hockey and cricket. The second National Sports Festival was held in August 1975, and participants vied for honours in 15 sporting events, including judo, handball, squash racket and badminton.

The theme of the first Sports Festival was "Talent Hunting Through Mass Participation". The all-embracing sports festival enable the country to discover new talents as a first step toward building up a massive sports reservoir from which Nigeria hopes to field the potential medalists at future international competitions. In the first National Sports Festival, the Mid-Western State were the overall winners with 68 gold, 64 silver and 59 bronze medals.

Some of the spectacular performances recorded during the 1973 festival included those of Vincent Ekunwen from the Mid-Western State who emerged as the Champion of the Festival by winning 10 gold medals, and the performance of Master Abdullahi Garba, a 9-year old boy from the North-Central State, who participated in the intermediate category in the 5,000 meters race and impressively finished it.

In all, Nigeria has gained recognition internationally through sports, in recent times, several international teams in different disciplines of sports have visited Nigeria. Such teams have come from Europe, China, America, the West Indies, and other parts of the world while Nigeria too has sent sportsmen and women abroad on several occasions as goodwill ambassadors.

Sports Institute

The National Sports Commission, in its pursuit of excellence in sports, is building a national sports training institute, in which coaches, sports administrators, sports broadcasters and sports medicine specialists, will be trained. The Institute will serve as the source of manpower for the growth of sports in Nigeria.[11]

SELECTED FOOTNOTES AND REFERENCES

1. "Ahmadu Bello University, Zaria, Department of Education: Physical Education Program. Mimeographed copy (1964).

2. Eleyae, Awoture. "A Comparative Analysis of Amateurism in Track and Field Athletics in Nigeria and in the United States of America." (Urbana: M.S. Thesis, 1971). p. 29.

3. "Faculty of Education, Department of Health and Physical Education: University of Nigeria Nsukka. Degree Requirement February 1971." (Mimeographed copy sent on request).

4. Federal Ministry of Education. "Statistics of Education in Nigeria 1968." (Series II, Vol. I. Federal Ministry of Information Printing Division, Lagos, Nigeria).

5. *Ibid.*

6. Kay, N. C. *Physical Training for West Africa with Special Reference to Nigeria.* (2nd enlarged ed. London: Macmillan and Co., Ltd., 1958).

7. Kurlz, Seymour (Chief Editor). *op. cit.*

8. Kurlz, Seymour (Chief Editor). "Nigeria," in *Encyclopedic Almanas 1970.* (New York: Book and Educational Division of *The New York Times,* 1969). pp. 816-847.

9. "National Sports Commission Decrees 1971." Nigerian Official Gazette (No. 41, Vol. 58, 12th August, 1971).

10. "National Sports Commission Decree 1971." *op. cit.*

11. Nduka, Otonti. *Western Education and the Nigerian Cultural Background.* (Ibadan: Oxford University Press, 1964). p. 21.

12. New York Times, The. (October 4, 1954).

13. *Nigeria Handbook.* Lagos, Nigeria: Published by Federal Ministry of Information and printed by Modern Publications Nigeria, Limited. 1976-1976. Chapter 7, Sports. p. 156.

14. Temple, O. and Temple, C. L. *Notes on the Tribes, Provinces, Emirates and States of the Northern Provinces of Nigeria.* (10 Woburn Walk London W.C.I.: Frank Cass and Co., Ltd.).

15. Van Dalen, Deobold B. and Bennett, Bruce L. *A World History of Physical Education.* (Englewood Cliffs, N. J.: Prentice-Hall, Inc., 1971). pp. 607-610.

16.   Vendien, Lynn C. and Nixon, John E. *The World Today in Health, Physical Education and Recreation.* (Englewood Cliffs, N. J.: Prentice-Hall, Inc.). pp. 284-296.

17.   Wade, Michael A. "Teacher Education in England--Canada, U.S.A." Published in Monograph No. 3, "Physical Education Around the World" by Phi Epsilon Kappa Fraternity (1969). p. 16.

# THE CONCEPT OF SPORT IN NORWAY

by Thor Volla

## Biographical Sketch

*Thor Volla*, Director of the Norwegian College of Physical Education and Sport has a long background as a a sports participant and has been active in ICHPER (the International Council on Health, Physical Education, and Recreation) Congresses. He has presented papers at recent Congress mettings at Dublin, Ireland and at Mexico City.

## Some Facts About Norway

In an European scale, Norway is large by size, with a land area greater than the United Kingdom or Western Germany. The length from south to north is more than 2,500 kilometers.

On the other hand, with a population of only four millions, Norway is one of the smaller countries in Europe. It is sparsely populated, with an average of 10 inhabitants pr. km.$^2$. Only three cities have more than 100,000 inhabitants.

Some 150 years ago, Norway was one of the poorest countries in Europe. Living far to the north, with long and cold winters, Norwegians from days of old have learned to work hard in order to survive.

Today, Norway is a rich country. Compared with many other countries, the political situation must be characterized as stable and peaceful. The basic goals of the "welfare state" have to a large extent been reched, with almost no social distress and unemployment.

The policy for the post-welfare society attach higher importance to the standard of life than to the economic standard of living. In this connection, increased priority is given to the "soft values" of society.

## Sport as Part of a General Cultural Policy

The Norwegian Government regard the work in the cultural field as one of the most important of all the tasks which will face society in the years ahead. The guidelines for the work related to questions of cultural policy in the years ahead have been drawn up in three large reports which have been submitted to Parliament.

The reports are based on a wide concept of culture, which in addition to the traditional field of culture includes youth work, sport activities and other recreational pursuits. Through this, sport has been given a new formal base in Norway. The government has accepted a public responsibility for sport activities, which goes much further than previous system of friendly support.

One of the prime aims of the reports is to promote cultural democracy. The intention is to decentralize not only the activities themselves, but also the decision making process in such manner that regional and local authorities become responsible for cultural development in their areas.

Another and not less important objective is to do away with the social barriers which surround, and sometimes repress, many forms of cultural activity, and to build up instead a society in which each individual may develop his talents and inclinations in an environment where he is free to make his choices on his own premises. Words such as "participation" and "self-directed activity" are significant in this connection.

Underlying the work of cultural policy there will always be certain values, whether explicit or implicit. All cultural policy is and must in some way be an assessment of qualitative values. An extension of the concept of culture laying more stress on self-activity does not alter this fact. But a decisive factor in a great deal of cultural work is that the evaluation of qualitative values is carried out within each individual community.

One important statement in the report is that there is a need for a greater effort on the part of the authorities in the sphere covering sport, physical training and outdoor recreation. Activities in the field of sport are, and should be, an important public responsibility, and the authorities attach great importance to the transfer of sufficient funds to work in this field, so as to make it available to all population categories throughout the country.

State support of the sports movement should first and foremost be directed at efforts which will benefit the largest possible number of of people. But the goal SPORTS FOR ALL also entails that the champions should be supported as far as resources are sufficient. Professional sport, however, is not covered in the term cultural activities.

Sport Organizations in Norway

That sport has become a part of an official, cultural policy, with public responsibilities for sport activities, does not mean that the State directs and take part in the practical work in the same way as you find in Eastern Europe.

The Ministry has in general stressed that an important task is to bring about the best possible cooperation with all the voluntary

# Organizational structure and channels of cooperation

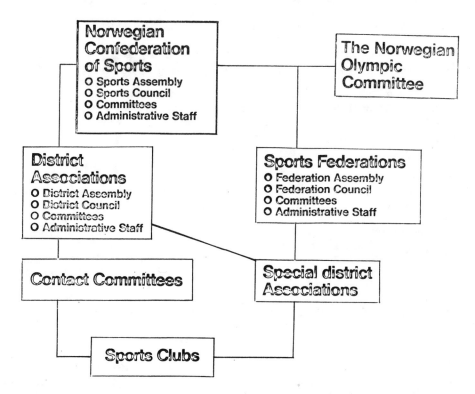

organizations in the cultural field, and it is pointed out in particular that a simultaneous strengthening of both public bodies and voluntary organizations is the best way of avoiding undesirable direction from both central as well as local authorities in cultural affairs. The Ministry assumes that no tasks will be transferred to public bodies if these tasks are being solved or can be solved better by voluntary organizations.

Democratic traditions have long prevailed in Norway, in politics and administrative measures as well as in well-developed voluntary organizational activities. Within sports there is only one central organization, Norges Idrettsforbund (The Norwegian Confederation of Sports) which was founded 116 years ago and today has more than one million members, that means more than 25% of the population. The confederation is divided regionally into 20 sports districts, technically into 40 special federations, while the elementary units are more than 8000 sports clubs.

The sport organizations are entirely free and independent in the sense that they choose their boards and representatives without any interference from political authorities.

In many countries the National Olympic Committee are in charge of the whole spectrum of sports. In Norway, the Olympic Committee is responsible for selecting teams and organizing the participation in the Olympic Games, but has little influence beyond that.

The system of sport as part of an official cultural policy and a voluntary organization to carry out the major part of the practical work, may cause problems, if the government and sport organizations don't agree on important issues.

It has been - and still is - a problem, that the special sports federations may put more of their resources into efforts to raise the level of elite performance than the governmental priority of "sport for all" indicates.

However, the sport federation in Norway has worked out a program for the future that to a high degree is based on the same ideas we find in the report of New Cultural Policies. In fact, the General Assembly of the Norwegian Confederation of Sport worked out this program some years before the cultural report.

It was in 1971 that the Norwegian Sports Assembly presented a declaration that has proved to be of great importance for the relations between the government and the sports organizations. The assembly accepted in this connection responsibilities which go far beyond high level competitive sport. In this connection, only two points will be mentioned, that the sports organization promised to participate actively in the district and environment policy and that the total sports offer must be developed at a rate and on a scale which will correspond to the demand of the Norwegian people for active athletic participation.

The Sport Assembly of 1971 stated that competitive sport must be included in the "sport for all-concept", and that talented athletes still must be taken care of. The Assembly strongly emphasized, however, that the ethical rules of sport must be adhered to, and that there must be a healthy balance between the means and the goal in competitive sport.

TRIM

Already some years before the declaration in 1971, the Norwegian Confederation of Sports had taken steps to prepare to sport organizations for this policy.

The Sports Assembly of 1965 inaugurated the project "Sports for All", and 3 basic conditions were then agreed upon:

1.  that the preparation and implementation of Sports for All
    should not result in establishing any new organization out-
    side of or parallel to the Norwegian Confederation of Sports,
    or superimpose upon it;

2.  that any form of participation ought to be voluntary, as
    far as participation and leaders were concerned;

3.  that in the field of motivation, the pleasure of practicing
    sport should be stressed.

The Norwegian Confederation of Sports launched TRIM for the
whole population in 1967. This was done in recognition of the fact
that a large part of its members were passive, and that organized
sports therefore must assume greater responsibility for activating the
general public. In Norway, TRIM is neither "action" nor "campaign",
not even an independent section of the sports movement. It is based
on the recognition - expressed in its program - that there is only one
sports movement, though its aims, forms and activities may differ.
Therefore TRIM has no separate organization or administration. TRIM
provides clarification of the many-sided image of sports, and its purpose is that the sports movement should intensify efforts toward the
goal of sports for all.

TRIM may be called Norway's part in pioneering the concept of
"Sport for All".

A long term plan for TRIM in Norway has been established.
An introductory period of five years (1967-72) is completed, and the
present work is going on through a ten-year executive period of programs and concrete projects. TRIM-offers, well-known sports in
modified forms, are made available to club members and the population
at large.

Three types of activitiy offers have been outlined:

a)  Organized activities, limited by time, place and group.
    The sports club is usually responsible for the events (ball
    games, gymnastics, family cross-country "orienteering"
    hikes, long distance cross-country skiing, etc.), but other
    societies, firms and various institutions also take part.

b)  Prepared but unorganized activities on TRIM trails, flood-
    lit ski trails, "orienteering" hikes, etc. These are ar-
    ranged jointly by clubs and local authorities. Hundreds of
    thousands participate in the three activity forms mentioned.

c)  Unorganized activities in open-air natural surroundings at
    all seasons. There characteristic key words of Norwegian
    natural environment are topical in this connection: moun-
    tains, forests and coastline. There is enough of this for

everybody, and open-air activities will always form a basis for physical activities in Norway.

TRIM in Norway is non-commercial. Its means are derived from government and municipal contributions, in order to avoid becoming dependent on commercial enterprises. That means that the financing of TRIM is to take place within the existing financial framework for the sport organizations.

This poises obvious problems in the relations between championship sports and traditional competitive sports on the one side, and non-committed sports for all (TRIM) on the other side. Spokesmen for giving elite sports a higher priority have already appeared, while the Board of the Norwegian Confederation of Sports has expressed a preference for greater attention to decentralized projects for the general public. In most countries this problem has not yet arisen, but we would like to offer the advice that it is an advantage to be well prepared.

## Physical Activities and Sports Interest in the Norwegian Population

Long range planning and development of concrete working programs for physical activities in a society, must take place in accordance with actual demands and with due consideration for interests, traditions and qualifications.

In the last 10 years, that means since TRIM was introduced, about 30 investigations dealing with the recreational physical activity of the Norwegian adult population have been carried out. The strong increase in the number of investigations may partly be due to the strong interest shown by the State and to the fact that the new Norwegian College of Physical Education and Sport, which operates on a university level, was established in 1968.

Of particular interest is an investigation from 1973. On request from the Working Group TRIM in the Norwegian Confederation of Sports, a research group at the Norwegian College of Physical Education and Sport conducted a nationwide investigation based on personal interviews with 3098 women and men fifteen years old or more. The purpose of this investigation was to study physical activities and sports interest in the Norwegian population.

It was established that 65.1 per cent of the adult population (62.2% of the women and 68.1 of the men) engage in some form of sport or open-air activities in their leisure time. Hobby-type work like gardening, or walking to and from work have not been included, nor holiday activities. Translated into figures this means that about 2 million persons of the adult population engage regularly in physical activities.

The investigation showed that outdoor life - or open-air activities was most popular. About 55% participated fairly regularly, and approximately 90% had participated in these activities at least once a year. On an average the persons participated 62 times per year in the outdoor life activities.

The activities which the population most often took part in were walking/hiking (64%), outdoor swimming (52%), and skiing (51%). Hiking, outdoor swimming and skiing occurred on an average 100 times per year among the people most involved in these activities. This means that these activities occurred frequently in their seasons.

Competitive activities like track and field athletics, football (soccer), handball, had 10% or fewer adherents.

The investigation collected information about the age, sex, place of residence, socioeconomic background, distance to areas for practicing and motivation for the different kinds of activities.

Reasons for non-participation is recorded as well. Not having sufficient time and lack of initiative are the reasons most often mentioned.

It was considered particularly desirable to figure out the general effect of TRIM campaigns and projects of several years duration. It appeared that 67.6% of the adult population had accepted and appreciated the information, and 14.9% expressed the view that TRIM had directly inspired them to participation in physical activities. It can thus be stated that more than 300,000 persons have been encouraged to engage in sports activities at a time when TRIM is still in an early phase of the executive period of programs.

Teacher - Education

Norway has only one college of Physical Education and Sport. It is located in Oslo. The college operates on university level. The college's course options include:

"Grunnfag" (basic/minor - 2 semesters)
"Mellomfag" (intermediate - 1 or 2 semesters after completion of "Grunnfag")
"Hovedfag" (major - 4 semesters after completion of "Mellomfag")

Sport studies can be combined with university studies in other fields for an academic degree (embetseksamen).

The "mellomfag" provides opportunities for choice. Up to this time it has been three main categories of study at this level - among them a one-year study in the field "physical activities for disabled". Teacher training is included in two of the categories.

Norway has 19 teacher-education colleges that prepare teachers for work in the elementary school. As part of the three-years teacher education, it is possible to choose up to a one-year course in physical education.

# SPORTS AND PHYSICAL EDUCATION IN THE PHILIPPINES

by Mrs. Josefina J. Ruiz

*Josefina Jainga Ruiz* finished her elementary and secondary education at Central Philippine College in Iloilo City. She obtained her Bachelor of Education degree with a major in physical education from the University of the Philippines in Manila, where she was captain of their volleyball team and a varsity letter-woman in tennis. While still a junior, she became captain of the champion Philippine women's volleyball team during the Far Eastern Games held in Manila in 1934. After graduation she taught for three years in a public high school, six years at the Iloilo Normal School and the summer before the war at the Cebu Normal School.

In 1948 she went to Hamline University in Minnesota for a semester of refresher courses in health and physical education then went on to work for an M.Ed. degree in physical education at Boston University. At Boston University she became a member of the Pi Lambda Theta, a national honor society for women in education. On returning to her country in 1950, she taught in a private college founded after the war by her husband and a few public school teachers. The summer of 1954 she taught at the National College of Physical Education in Manila. In 1956 she organized and became Chairman of the Health and Physical Education Department of Central Philippine University, where she still works at present. She also served as acting dean of the College of Education for three years.

She is a chartered member of the Girl Scout Council, Family Planning Organization of the Philippines, YWCA, and the Quota Club all in Iloilo City. She has held high positions in these organizations. She has traveled all over Southeast Asia, the United States, in South America and Europe in her capacity as Vice-President of the Asian Baptist Women's Union and member of the Executive Committee of the Women's Department of the Baptist World Alliance. She received honors and citations from the YMCA and the Iloilo Rotary Club for her services in their recreation programs. She was honored as one of the Outstanding Athletes of her province and voted the Outstanding Baptist Woman Leader for Community Leadership and Service at their Golden Jubilee 1975.

# Acknowledgements

In 1971 Dr. Robert H. McCollum, Director of the Department of Recreation at the University of Pennsylvania, wrote an article on "Physical Education in the Philippines" for Monograph No. 5 of the Physical Education Around the World in collaboration with Professor Emeritus Candico C. Bartolome of the University of the Philippines and Mrs. Josefina J. Ruiz. Some of the recent information here has been supplied by Prof. Bartolome.

## General Background[1]

The Philippines consists of 7,107 islands, which sprawl in a north-to-south direction beyond the fringe of the southeast side of the Asian mainland, studding the China Sea. Eight hundred islands are inhabited, with only forty-five of the eight hundred accounting for 98 percent of the land mass; Luzon and Mindanao comprise two-thirds of the total land area of 300,000 square kilometers. The latest estimate of the population (1975) was 41,457,000 with a density of population of 123.3 (1970) to the kilometer. This makes the Philippines sixth in density in Southeast Asia, next to Taiwan. It is exceeded by only fifteen of the more than 125 countries of the world, population-wise. The population is essentially "young" with about 47.5 percent being children below fifteen years.

Often referred to as the show-window of democracy in the Far East, the country is characterized by diversity. It is geographically fragmented; there is linguistic diversity, with 87 major languages and dialects, including Filipino (the national language), with English and Spanish as second languages for most Filipinos. There is religious diversity with 92 percent Christian distributed among 84 percent Roman Catholics, 5 percent Philippine Independent Church, 3 percent Protestants. Five percent of the population embraces the Islamic religion while 3 percent is distributed among other minority religions.

But amidst this diversity there is latent unity. This unity has found its flowering in the rise and development of nationalism in the body politic among its present inhabitants in 67 provinces and 60 chartered cities.[2] The culture is indigenously Malayan, but it has been enriched through commerce and trade by the Great Traditions of the Orient, like Arabian, Chinese, and Hindu; and by Occidental influence through colonization by the Spaniards for nearly four hundred years and by the Americans for three-quarters of a century.

Latest figures (1970) showed a literacy rate of 83.4 percent. As of 1973 the total school population was about 10.5 millions, with nearly one in every four Filipinos in school. The people have a strong desire for education because it is a potent force for social and economic mobility. This obsession for education is given impetus by the fact that primary education is free and compulsory and that the total expenditure for education was 22.47 percent of the total national budget in 1971-71 and 16.53 percent in 1972-73. Generally speaking, elementary education is handled by the government and the secondary and higher education by the private sector. About 82.5 percent in the secondary schools and 76 percent of the total enrollment in colleges and universities were reported enrolled in private schools (1972-73).[3]

Early History[4,5]

Physical Education in the Philippines can be divided into seven stages or periods, namely:

| | | |
|---|---|---|
| 1st. period | - | Before the coming of the Spaniards in 1521 |
| 2nd. period | - | Spanish Occupation from 1521 to 1897 |
| 3rd. period | - | Short lived Philippine Independence under Gen. Emilio Aguinaldo, 1898 |
| 4th. period | - | American regime, 1898 to 1941 |
| 5th. period | - | Japanese occupation, 1942 to 1945 |
| 6th. period | - | Republic of the Philippines, 1946 to 1972 |
| 7th. period | - | Republic of the Philippines, New Society, 1972 to present |

Before the coming of the Spaniards, the Filipinos were fond of swimming in the rivers and sea coasts, Because of economic necessities they indulged in strenuous hunting and fishing. They travelled from one place to another either by walking or canoeing. Although these physical activities had specific purposes, they also served as their body-conditioning activities. The children had few games since they had to work at an early age. They played blindfold games and walking on stilts. A favorite game among small boys was for one of them to be a horse, cow, or carabao, while the others tried to lasso him.

When the Spaniards came, they introduced their national dances, sports and some races. Ateneo Municipal (1860) was the first college in Manila to include drawing, vocal and instrumental music and and gymnastics in its curriculum. Dr. Jose Rizal, in his "Modern School" mentioned gymnastics, fencing and swimming.[6] During the latter part of the Spanish occupation, soccer, which has supposed to have been introduced by the English during their short sojourn in Manila and nearby provinces, was played at the Sunken Gardens between sports clubs during Sundays.

The secondary school curriculum, which was classical in nature and content, aimed to provide the student with a liberal education with an end in view to prepare him for the university. The curriculum in 1870, for instance, included such subjects as Latin and Spanish grammar, Christian doctrine, sacred history, descriptive geography, universal history, history of Spain, arithmetic, algebra, rhetoric, poetry, Spanish and Latin composition, geometry, trigonometry, and ethics. Physics, moral philosophy, chemistry, natural history, and French were also a part of the program of studies.[7] Physical education as a subject was generally ignored. What physical education there was consisted in "walking" when with pupils, especially those studying for the priesthood, were given some "airing" by their mentors. Other forms of physical activities were considered a sheer waste of time and energy, not conducive to moral and spiritual discipline, and distracting to contemplative and meditational pursuits.

During the short-lived Republic under General Emilio Aguinaldo, his soldiers were required to exercise every morning to keep them physically fit. Physical exercise was included in his manifesto.

When the Americans came they had soldiers who were former students and college graduates. Later these became the pioneers in the new educational system, as teachers and administrators. They introduced baseball, track and field, volleyball and basketball. When competitions became keen in the schools, the interschool, interdistrict and provincial meets were organized, followed by the interprovincial and regional meets. The Bureau of Public Schools Interscholastic Athletic Association (BPSIAA) and the Philippine Private Interscholastic Athletic Association Meet (PRISAA) evolved from this interest in competition. The oldest athletic associations were the following:

Southern Luzon Athletic Association    -   1904
Central Luzon Athletic Association    -   1908
Manila Interscholastic    -   1909
Visayan Athletic Association    -   1909
Ilocos Athletic Association    -   1910
Southern Tagalog Athletic Association    -   1910

The secondary curriculum was academic, at first with inadequate provision for physical education. Patterned after the American model at the time, the curriculum aimed "to give the student basis of a liberal education and to fit him for a college or university of the American type."[8] The ideal of "A sound mind in a sound body" must have permated the thinking of the early American teachers, for as early as 1903, a system of physical exercise was prescribed for all the grades. There were recess periods which served as breaks of the routine of academic instruction and continuous study. There was little of specialized athletics; American games were gradually introduced but as for a well-rounded program of health and physical education, there was none. Monroe, in his survey of the educational system of the Philippines, highly "commended the emphasis" in physical education and urged that "it be continued."[9]

The schools gave more emphasis on specialized athletics than on physical education. In 1919, the Bureau issued an official bulletin of 374 pages that gave "the essentials for a systematized course in physical education for all Philippine public schools."[10] The manual gave attention to games and athletics, folk dancing, by grades, including the music therefor, formal gymnastics, marching and dancing. Graded lessons were also included, as were formal calisthenics. The program as outlined in the manual became more varied and meaningful, and although it was not free from imperfections, it was a help materially. But the manual was given to untrained teachers, who could read the instructions but who could not execute them accurately. The report of the Director of Education in 1920 declared that "it is now being planned to required as many teachers as possible to study the new course in division normal institutes during the coming vacation."[11]

Because of lack of qualified teachers and of the financial difficulties, physical education was assigned as an extra or minor load. Since it was not a requirement for graduation, the teacher was thus assigned to handle as many as 200 to 300 students. In 1937, physical education became a required subject in the school curriculum. Since the objective of many administrators in the provinces was to win provincial athletic meets, physical education was mostly geared to procing and developing good athletes.

Little by little changes were introduced in the organization and subject matter of physical education. The Bureau of Education created a Division of Physical Education which was charged with the responsibility of improving the work in the field through the preparation of syllabi or memorandums, bulletins on methods, regular supervisory visits of Central Office personnel, and institutes for teachers. Some colleges and universities offered physical education as majors or minors. In 1941, the secondary school academic curriculum outlined specific semester requirements for physical education. Department Memorandum No. 5, s. 1945, made changes to include at least one period a week devoted to health instruction. The description of the course is now given as "Health and Physical Education."[12] Preparatory military training was eliminated from the first and second years and five days a week were devoted to health and physical education. There has been a move to reduce the number of students taking physical education to the same number as those in academic classes.

The YMCA was another entity which promoted physical educations, especially in the elementary schools in Manila. Mr. Fred O. England, who was associated with city schools, introduced freehand calisthenics, gymnastic dances and pyramid building to boys in the elementary schools. Annual playground day was held at the Nozaleda Park. His syllabus on freehand calisthenics was the first to be distributed and used in the elementary schools in the Philippines.

When Dr. Jorge Bocobo, former president of the University of the Philippines, became Secretary of the Department of Public Instruction, he emphasized the teaching of Philippine Folk Dances in physical education classes in all educational institutions with the view of nationalizing, preserving and keeping alive this phase of Philippine culture. Mrs. Francisca Reyes Aquino, who was at the University of the Philippines at the time, became the outstanding pioneer and promoter of the movement. She traveled all over the country and collected folk dances, published them and taught them in her classes. Soon after all playground days included mass demonstrations of Philippine folk dances.

During the Japanese occupation schooling practically stood still; however, games like basketball and baseball were not discouraged. In Manila all government employees were required to take part in "radio taiso" (some sort of exercises) in the morning and afternoon during working days.

When independence was granted by the Americans in 1946, the education system was one of the government's functions that was strengthened.

Health and Physical Education

The health and physical education program in the Philippines has developed from simple, aimless "body training and physical exercises" before the 1920's, through "mass calisthenics" coupled with "school ground improvement" up to and including the 1940's, to a planned program of activities after World War I.

A. General Objectives:

Bulletin No. 17, s. 1960, issued by the Director of Public Schools to all Division Superintendents of Schools in the country, outlines the general objectives of physical education as follows:

1. To develop and maintain optimum physical fitness,
2. To develop specific neuromuscular skills,
3. To develop proper ideals and desirable attitudes toward physical activities,
4. To provide opportunities for wholesome recreation and harmonious associations,
5. To impart knowledge and develop skills on varied physical activities that have carry-over values in life, and
6. To revive, propagate, and preserve Philippine culture.[13]

The same bulletin also includes suggested activites in the elementary schools from which teachers in the field might evolve their own action programs:

1. Posture education
   a. Skills relating to locomotion,
   b. Skills essential to games,
   c. Skills related to athletic team games, and
   d. Body conditioning and corrective exercises.

2. Self-testing activities
    a. Activities on horizontal bars and balance beams,
    b. Rope skills, and
    c. Stunts, tumbling, pyramids.

3. Quickly organized games and relays.

4. Athletic team games preparatory to sports and athletics.

5. Rhythmic activities
    a. Fundamental rhythms,
    b. Rhythmic interpretations,
    c. Dramatized rhythms,
    d. Singing games and action songs, and
    e. Folk dances and creative work.

6. Individual and dual games of target and bandy type games.

7. Swimming (where facilities are available).

In further recognition of the importance of elementary school physical education in the curriculum, the National Board of Education, the policy-making body on educational matters, ordered that physical education shall stand as one subject area in Grades I to III and should be given a time allotment of twenty minutes a day, five days a week. In Grade IV it is combined with health, thirty minutes a day, four days for physical education and one day for health. In Grades V and VI, it is forty minutes, four days for physical education and one day for health. Among other things, the Department Order states states:

.....The present physical fitness program of the Government underscores the need for increased emphasis on physical education in the early formative stages in the development of the Filipino child. The emphasis in the primary grades will be on the acquisition of good posture and of developing and maintaining one's health, strength, and grace. To further pursue a balanced physical education program in the higher elementary grades, increasing opportunities shall be given to pupils to participate actively in games and other group athletics and contests including such wholesome activities as club work, hiking and boy and girl scouting...[14]

B. Secondary School

In the secondary schools, physical education received greater attention than in the elementary schools, first, because of the requirement that majors should handle the subject and second, because detailed guides have been issued by the

Department of Education. One such guide was the "Guide in Physical Education for Secondary Schools," Department of Education 1951.[15] Girls from first year to fourth year and first and second year boys take physical education four days a week and one day a week for health, forty minutes a day. Third and fourth year boys take physical education, two days, preparatory military training two days and health one day a week, forty minutes a day. The Guide gives the following objectives:

1. To develop sportsmanship, leadership and citizenship,
2. To develop skills in the fundamental knowledge of physical education activities,
3. To inculcate health habits and to develop organic fitness, and
4. To create an intelligent and healthful interest in games that will carry-over into adult life.

Some of the suggested activities listed in the Guide are:

1. Games - group games, relays, lead-up games, recreational games,
2. Gymnastics - marching, freehand exercises, light apparatus, balance beam activities, stunts, tumbling and pyramids,
3. Rhythms and dances - square dances, Philippine folk dances, foreign folk dances, modern and rhythmic activities,
4. Specialized athletics,
5. Projects - posture week, intramurals, play days, folk dance clubs, student leaders' clubs.

With reference to pre-military training, it has been observed that many of the boys are too young to be subjected to a very strict type of discipline. The Survey Team (1960) pointed out that most of the activities in PMT were military drills on the school campus and recommended that more emphasis should be shifted from drilling and marching to the development of attitudes and military skills. This has been difficult to implement because the Philippine Army is, by law, authorized to plan out activities in connection with military training, ostensibly to prepare for the ROTC in college.[16]

In 1972 under the New Society concept, Physical Fitness and Sports Development programs became a national concern. The Department of Education was changed to Department of Education and Culture (DEC). In 1973 the DEC revised the physical education and health and PMT programs in the secondary schools. These activities were divided into two areas, namely:

1. Youth Development Training (YDT) to include physical education, health and scouting. Time allotment was two days physical education, two days scouting and one day health for boys and girls from first to third years.

2. Citizen Army Training (CAT) for all fourth year boys and girls. This basic citizen training should be administered by a qualified high school faculty member in consultation with the Superintendent of the ROTC or PMT units in the area. Each period is forty minutes.[17]

This was further revised when the time allotment was changed from forty minutes to one hour a period each day. The revision stated:[18]

1. First semester: I, II, III year boys and girls

   2 days scouting, one day each for health, physical education and music.

2. Second semester:

   2 days physical education, one day each for health, scouting and music.

3. Fourth year boys and girls:

   2 days of Citizen Army Training, one day each for health, physical education and music.

The most common problem in secondary schools today is the lack of equipment and facilities. An activity room is rare in most schools, especially in public schools, so that little work is done during the rainy season. Some schools take up their health and music units during the rainy months and reserve their physical education and scouting units during the non-rainy months.

C. Colleges and Universities

Traditionally, the rationale behind the inclusion of physical education in the college curriculum was the liberal education concept. "A sound mind in a sound body" has been the guiding philosophy. It is for this reason that physical education is required of all college students for graduation. The National Board of Education rendered a ruling on April 25, 1961 that ROTC cannot be substituted for Physical Education in partial fulfillment of the requirements of a college title or degree. Physical education is considered a part of education and aims to develop physically, mentally, emotionally and socially integrated individuals.[19]

Circular No. 7, s. 1957 of the Bureau of Private Schools prescribes the time requirements for physical education in college: thirty-three to thirty-six hours per semester for the first two years, or a total of 132 to 144 hours. Schools could spread the required total number of hours over the four years, at the convenience of the students.[20]

Private schools are free to design their basic programs, so that the kind and direction of such programs depend in no small measure, on the attitude of the administrators towards the subject, and, in a greater degree, on the teacher's initiative and within the limits of the resources which the administrators allot to this subject.

D. Professional Preparation

The early American classroom teachers were the pioneers of physical education in the Philippine schools. They taught young boys and girls the skills and techniques of the newly introduced Western sports. To implement the "play for everybody" policy of the Bureau of Education, Filipino teachers were given special training during the Teacher's Vacation Assembly in Manila in 1914 so that they could conduct various physical activities. They taught other teachers at the provincial normal institutes. Since then, courses for the training of teachers for physical education had been offered in normal institutes, vacation assemblies in Baguio, in the University of the Philippines, the National College of Physical Education held at Rizal Memorial Complex during summer. Summer courses in physical education, without credit, but leading to appropriate certificate was started in the University of the Philippines on February 7, 1915. On December 19, 1928, major courses in physical education initiated by the Department of Physical Education for the College of Education, University of the Philippines, leading to the degree of Bachelor of Science in Education was instituted.

On October 11, 1930, a Certificate in Physical Education was given to students who completed 28 units in four summers. On March 14, 1933, the Board of Regents of the University of the Philippines, approved the courses leading to Bachelor of Physical Education. On January 30, 1976, the Board of Regents approved the elevation of the Department of Physical Education into a degree-granting unit and called it the U. P. Institute of Sports, Physical Education and Recreation (SPEAR). The Institute hopes to answer the need for a training center for sports specialists, physical educators, and recreation leaders.[21]

Other large colleges and universities offer a major and minor in physical education as part of their teacher-education programs. Requirements[22] for majors range between twenty-four to forty-two units and between twelve to eighteen units for minors; however, because of the admittedly too heavy requirements for graduation, unit-wise, there is a general trend to reduce the over-all total number of units for graduation, necessarily, the number of units apportioned to physical education for major purposes would also be reduced. Among the most common theory subjects are History of Physical Education, Anatomy and Kinesiology, Physiology and Physiology of Exercise, Principles and Philosophy of Physical Education, Organization and Administration, Methods and Materials, and First Aid and Massage. Among the practical courses are Dance Fundamentals, Philippine and International Folk Dances, Modern Dance, Children's Rhythms, Coaching Courses in Volleyball, Basketball, Soccer, Softball, Track and Field, Individual Sports, and a course in Recreation and the Conduct and Practice of Group Games. Among the Universities that offer majors and minors in Physical Education are Central Philippine University, Far Eastern University, Philippine Normal College, Silliman University, University of the East, University of Santo Tomas.

E. Certification

In theory all graduates of recognized colleges who have majors in physical education are qualified to teach in the secondary schools, although no graduate can be employed as a regular public school teacher unless he has passed the civil service examination and no teacher may be employed unless he has passed the annual teacher selection examination which is conducted by the Division Office. There has been a dearth of physical education majors, specially among the men; so that it often happens that unqualified teachers conduct classes in physical education. The current degree requirements include:

Bachelor of Science

Education subjects . . . . . . . . . . . . . . 79 units
Pedagogical courses . . . . . . . . . . . . . 27 units
Physical Education subjects . . . . . . . . 36 to 42
                                                       units
Electives in sciences . . . . . . . . . . . . . 3 units
Electives in field of concentration . . . . . . 13 units
Service Physical Education . . . . . . . . . 4 units
                                 Total: 164-170
                                     units

Masters of Physical Education

Foundation courses. . . . . . . . . . . . . . 9 units
Major field of concentration . . . . . . . . . 18 units
Electives. . . . . . . . . . . . . . . . . . . . . 9 units
Thesis . . . . . . . . . . . . . . . . . . . . . . 10 units
                                 Total: 46 units

## F. The National College of Physical Education[23]

The National College of Physical Education (NCPE) was started as a professional class in physical education for principals and supervisors at Teachers' Camp in Baguio in 1932. It was followed by similar classes in 1933 and 1934. In 1935, Mr. Serafin Aquino, Superintendent of Physical Education in the Bureau of Education, organized classes for teachers in physical education at the Philippine School of Arts and Trades on an experimental basis. The courses were not given any academic credit until 1937, when Physical Education was made a curricular subject in the public schools.

In 1938, arrangements were made with Dr. Regino R. Ylanan, then National Physical Director and Executive Secretary-Treasurer of the Philippine Amateur Athletic Federation (PAAF) for the use of facilities in the Rizal Memorial Stadium with payment of a minimal rental.

In 1940, there was a movement among officials of the Bureau of Education, University of the Philippines, and the PAAF to combine their efforts and jointly conduct a summer school of Physical Education. The PAAF agreed to provide the necessary facilities and equipment and qualified pesonnel to serve as instructors, while the Bureau of Education agreed to provide instruction and supervision and to encourage the teachers to attend summer classes. To give added incentive to teachers, the Director of Education secured authority from the Secretary of Public Instruction to award a Certificate in Physical Education (CPE) to teachers who earned twenty-eight units of credit in these summer classes. Teachers with Bachelor of Science in Education degrees who were already in the service and who had earned their CPE would be considered by the Bureau of Education as having majored in physical education and, therefore, eligible for full time assignment in the secondary schools.

The Japanese occupation of the Philippines during World War II disrupted the summer classes. In 1947, when these summer classes were reopened, the United States Army still occupied the major portion of the Rizal Memorial Stadium. Classes were held in the war-torn buildings of the Philippine School of Arts and Trades. The limited income derived from fees was used in the purchase of needed equipment.

When Rizal Memorial Stadium was returned to the PAAF in late 1947, the PAAF and the Department of Education resumed dual responsibility for conducting the summer school. The Executive Committee of the PAAF agreed to underwrite the expenses of the summer school and to buy the essential equipment.

Hon. Jorge B. Vargas, President of the PAAF, made it possible to secure the services of foreign leaders in Physical Education to serve as instructors in the summer school. The first three foreign instructors were Prof. Elise N. Nelson of Sargent College, Boston University, USA, 1950; Mrs. Aase May Anderson of the National Institute of Copenhagen, Denmark, 1951; and Dean Bartlett Cromwell, track and field coach of the University of Southern California and the U. S. Olympic Team, 1952. By 1952, a total of 1,976 attended the courses from every province and city in the Philippines. Other instructors who came later were:

1. Prof. Renate Scholtsmethner - Denmark - gymnastics
   1955
2. Mr. Jesse Owens              - USA        - track and
   field - 1957
3. Mr. William Miller           - USA        - track and
   field - 1960
4. Mrs. Ginko Chiba             - Japan      - gymnastics
   1965
5. Mr. Thomas Jarvis            - USA        - track and
   field - 1967
6. Mr. Donald Smith    1968
7. Mr. John Gregory             - Australia - swimming
   1968
8. Maj. James P. Hall           - Clark Air Base -
   track and field lecture - 1968
9. Mr. Juji Tsuchiya            - Japan      - volleyball
   1969
10. Mrs. Mary Griffith          - Great Britain -
    creative rhythms - 1970

In 1953, the Secretary of Education expressed desire to discontinue the arrangement for dual responsibility with the PAAF for the conduct of the summer school. The Department of Justice upheld the right of the PAAF under its charter to conduct courses in physical education.

During the school years 1948-49 and 1949-50, in answer to popular demand, Saturday classes for teachers in Manila and nearby provinces were held in the Rizal Memorial Stadium. By mutual agreement, the PAAF and the Philippine Normal College authorities conducted these classes at the Philippine Normal College and concentrated the summer classes at the Rizal Normal Stadium. Saturday classes continued until 1951-52.

In 1960 a curriculum committee composed of members of the faculty who finished graduate studies abroad, recommended fusion of allied subjects to permit introduction of new and important subjects and graduate courses leading to Masters in Physical Education.

Upon urgent demands from teachers who desired to complete the requirements for CPE or Masters in Physical Education (MPE), Saturday classes were again resumed in June 1962. An MPE degree was first awarded in 1963. In 1970, the Executive Committee of the PAAF approved the conversion of the National College of Physical Education into a full fledged College of Physical Education.

G. Research and Evaluation

Very little scientific research is being conducted in the field of physical education. A university, may occasionally, initiate a research project in physical education done by a graduate student studying for a master's degree. The Bureau of Public Schools has a Research Evaluation Center, which has started one project on the physical fitness of Filipino children. The reasons for the lack of research activity in this discipline include the lack of trained researchers and financial support.

## Athletic Facilities

Each provincial capital has sports facilities for its citizens. These normally include areas for participation in track and field, soccer, basketball, volleyball, baseball, softball and sometimes swimming.

The most complete facility is the Rizal Memorial Stadium complex in Manila which includes track oval where field events and soccer football are held, baseball stadium where softball and volleyball may be played, a swimming pool 20 by 50 meters, 12 tennis courts, basketball stadium where boxing, tennis, badminton, and table tennis may be held, gymnasium for gymnastics, weightlifting and an archery field.

In Marikina, Rizal, is located the finest track facilities including a Tartan running surface. The Pagla-um Stadium in Bacolod, Negros Occidental is another useful complex.

## Sports Development

The first American teachers introduced their games to the Filipinos. Governor William Cameron Forbes was the first official who gave impetus to the development of athletics by providing equipment to schools that showed the greatest progress.

Mr. Elwood S. Brown, YMCA Secretary and Physical Director was the most outstanding pioneer in athletics in the country. The YMCA came to the country with the American forces during the Spanish-American War in 1898. On November 10, 1911, the YMCA was incorporated and the famous Filipino philanthropist, Don Teedore M. Yangos, became its first president. Mr. Brown also helped organize athletics in the Bureau of Education. Through his efforts an open meeting was called on November 10, 1910 to discuss the menace of professionalism in Philippine sports. On January 1911 the Philippine Amateur Athletic Federation (PAAF) was created. Under its guidance the Far Eastern Athletic Association was organized and the first Far Eastern Games were held in Manila in 1911 with China, Japan and Philippines as participants. The events were track and field, pentathlon, tennis, swimming, volleyball, basketball, baseball, and soccer. In the 1924 Olympics in Paris, the Philippines for the first time sent a lone representative in track. The PAAF also took a leading role in the formation of the Asian Games. The first Asian Games were held in New Delhi, India in 1951.[24]

The YMCA is credited with having launched the first training program for Physical Directors for Public Schools in 1910; the first law school in English which is now the College of Law of the University of the Philippines, and the first Far East Athletic Meet in 1911. Subsequently it built for the country its first gymnasium and swimming pool in 1914, formed the first Boy Scouts Troop for Filipinos in 1916, and organized the first student conference in 1914. It launched the first boys camping program in 1923, initiated the first Inter-Scholastic, Inter-Dormitory, Inter-Commercial and Inter-Bank Leagues from 1912 to 1932.[25]

Because of the great interest in competitive sports, colleges and universities in Manila under the leadership of Dr. Regino R. Ylanana, Physical Director of the University of the Philippines, formed an athletic association the summer of 1924. Representatives from Atenee, La Salle, Jose Rizal College, San Beda, Letran, University of Santo Tomas, National University and the University of the Philippines attended the meeting. They agreed to form the National College Athletic Association (NCAA).

In 1930 the universities seceded from the association and formed their own associated called the "Big Three". In 1934 this was expanded and the association became the University Athletic Association of the Philippines (UAAP). Up to 1974, the member universities were all in Manila. In 1975, the universities of Northern and Central Luzon formed their own group and joined the one in Manila. In 1977, universities from Bicol, the Visayas and Mindanao formed their own association.

Act No. 3236 of the Philippine Legislature empowered the PAAF to promote and encourage the development of all recreation and amateur athletics in the country. It had 19 national amateur sports associations as members:

1. Archery (men and women)
2. Basketball
3. Baseball
4. Badminton
5. Athletics (track and field)
6. Cycling

7. Boxing
8. Football
9. Gymnastics (men and women)
10. Golf
11. Judo
12. Swimming (men and women)
13. Shooting
14. Table tennis (men and women)
15. Tennis (men and women)
16. Volleyball (men and women)
17. Weightlifting
18. Wrestling
19. Softball (men and women)

Other associations which became members later were yachting, karate, sipa (a tennis-type game using a rattan ball kicked across the net) and arnis (a sort of fencing game).

After the World Olympics in Rome in 1960, it was felt that the PAAF set-up was outmoded and obsolete. The result was Republic Act No. 3135 which approved a new charter for the PAAF on June 17, 1961. The new act decentralized the promotion of sports associations. After the World Olympics in Germany in 1972 the national sports associations were heavily criticized by the press and the public so that on December 10, 1974, Presidential Decree No. 604 abolished the PAAF but not its national sports associations. It was replaced by the Department of Youth and Sports Development (DYSD) which was directly under the President.

The Department of Education and Culture did its part in mobilizing the school system in implementing the new program. Department Order No. 35, s. 1973 described the broad features of the program as:[26]

1. A physical fitness program to make sports accessible to the broad mass of the population and provide for active participation for the greater number of our youth in competitive sports, recreation and physical fitness activities.

2. A sports development program encompassing public, vocational and private schools, colleges and universities except state colleges and universities.

3. A sports development program which provides ample opportunities for participation of all sectors of youth, both those in school and out of school.

It provided for a National Council for Physical Fitness and Sports Development (PFSD) to organize, plan and administer the national program. Provincial and city councils would likewise be created to administer the program in the provincial and city levels.

The Athletic Regional Organization will, more or less, follow the Public Schools Interscholastic Athletic Association pattern to insure a more balanced representation and strength in athletic competition. As usual, the school superintendent of the host division is the president of the Regional Athletic Association. The National Council of the PFSD is composed of:

Chairman - Secretary of Education and Culture
Vice-Chairman - Undersecretary of the DEC
Three directors of promotional bureaus
Eleven regional directors (designate)

The rationale of the program comes from Article II, Section 5, of the Constitution of the Philippines: "The state recognizes the vital role of the youth in the nation - building and shall promote their physical, intellectual, and social well-being."

A brief description of the program includes:

October    - Intramurals in the barrios, towns, districts and cities for elementary and secondary pupils and the out-of-school youth (12 to 21 years).

November - Unit meets among the 4 to 6 districts in a province for the elementary and secondary pupils. The out-of-school youth shall enter as an independent team.

December - Provincial meets. The Division Superintendent shall run the meet. There shall be two divisions:
1.  Junior - elementary and secondary units
2.  Senior - college and university units
The out-of-school youth shall join the Junior division with their mayor as managers.

January    - Regional meets of nine athletic associations. Only one athletic delegation composed of the selected best athletes from each association.

February - National Meet (NIAA) National Interscholastic Athletic Association composed of nine regional associations. This shall be conducted by the Board of Directors headed by the host superintendent.

As of 1975 seven-man soccer was included in all meets of the DEC.[27] In 1976 boxing was included for two groups. Group I was for the 12 to $14\frac{1}{2}$ year-olds and Group II was for the 14 to 7 months to $17\frac{1}{2}$ year-olds.[28] In 1977 weightlifting was included for three divisions. The elementary division was for the 13 to 14 year-olds, two to a team; second division was for the 15 to 18 year-olds, four to a team according to body weight; and third division was for the 19 to 20 year-olds, two to a team according to body weight.[29]

Department Order No. 50 s. 1976 provided that policemen, firemen and members of the Armed Forces are eligible as out-of-school youth only in individual events in track and field and swimming but not as a team, provided they are below twenty-five as of March 30 of every year of the meet. They should join the unit where they reside.

Special Programs

Aside from the many commercial leagues that import foreign players specially in basketball, the government invites outstanding coaches and teams from different countries to inspire the youth and improve the quality of sports in the country. Expert coaches train local coaches, hold sports clinics for teachers and referees to improve sports administration and coaching technics. Regional seminars and clinics are held to bring the new technics to the grassroots.

Peace Corps volunteers have shared their expertise wherever they were assigned. Special mention should be given to Peace Corps Philippines, Group 51 who were particularly requested to help in Physical Fitness Curriculum Development and Sports Development Program in 1972. These young men and women were fielded all over the country and worked closely with their Filipino counterparts.[30]

Another private group that has helped inspire the youth in the field of sports is the American Venture for Victory Teams that came yearly since 1952 to play against the national basketball teams and other college and provincial teams as they toured the country from June to August.[31] Once they brought a women's basketball team and a man's baseball team. Two of these women stayed behind for a month and helped organize and train the women's basketball team of Central Philippine University which later became champions in the Private Schools Interscholastic Athletic Association meet in Iloilo. In 1971 a team came to spend one year in the country which called themselves "Christ the Only Way Movement Team". They played basketball and held sports clinics all over the country. These fine Christian young men from different states of the United States and having different educational backgrounds brought a much needed refreshing experience by playing hard for fun and fellowship in the truest spirit of sportsmanship. Bud Schaeffer, one of the players of the first Venture for Victory Team who later became coach and recruiting officer, went to Australia to train similar teams who later came to do the same thing in the Philippines.

The President of the Philippines on October 25 announced a massive sports program involving all citizens, based on the barangay (smallest unit of society). At a mass rally on October 19, 1977 at the Rizal Memorial Coliseum launching the national physical fitness and sports development program, he inducted into office the two under-secretaries whom he designated through Presidential Decree 604, for the Department of Youth and Sports Development in 1975. The President himself is the secretary of this Department. He specifically named the Kabataan Barangay (organization of all youth in the barangays) as "the nucleus, the action unit" of the program "with full assistance and cooperation of various agencies and local governments." The government will tap the help of the private sectors if it will not be possible for it to fund overnight so far-reaching a program. The President also said that physical education teachers in schools will soon be barred from teaching other subjects than physical education because of the critical need of able instructors in physical fitness training and sports development. The first phase will be the training of public school physical education teachers through seminars and clinics. The second phase will be farming out able teachers throughout the 13 regions of the country. Other sectors included by the President in this program are the Departments of Health, Education and Culture, National Defense, the Government Corporations Athletic Association and even the Nutrition Center of the Philippines. The President promised the government will throw its full support to a nationwide sports program.[32]

## FOOTNOTES AND SELECTED REFERENCES

1. Ruiz, Josefina J. Unpublished materials, Boston University Graduate School. 1950.

2. National Census and Statistics Office. Manila. Vol. II. 1971.

3. NEDA STATISTICAL YEARBOOK OF THE PHILIPPINES 1975.

4. Ruiz, op. cit.

5. Bartolome, Candido C. Personal correspondence. August 16, 1970.

6. Bartolome, Candido C. "Evaluation of Teacher Training in P.E. and Sports Development in the Philippines". Unpublished, 1977.

7. Isidro, Antonio. "The Philippine Educational System". Bookman, Inc., Ch. V, p. 130. Manila. 1949.

8. Aldana, Benigno. "The Educational System of the Philippines". University Publication Co., Ch. XI, pp. 153-154. Manila. 1949.

9. Monroe, Paul. "Survey of the Educational System of the Philippines". P. 383. Bureau of Printing, Manila. 1925.

10. Bureau of Education, Bulletin No. 40, s. 1919, p. 480.

11. Monroe, op. cit.

12. Bureau of Education, Bulletin No. 46, Manila. October 23, 1937.

13. Bureau of Public Schools, Bulletin No. 25. "Description of Activities in P.E. for Elementary and Secondary Schools". Manila. 1960.

14. Board of National Education Order No. 10. Manila. 1970.

15. Department of Education. "Guide in P.E. for Secondary Schools". Manila. 1951.

16. U. S. Operation Mission to the Philippines, "A Survey of the Public Schools of the Philippines". Carmelo and Bauermann, Inc., Manila. 1960.

17. Department Order No. 15, s. 1973.

18. Department Order No. 31, s. 1973.

19. Board of Education, General Policies. "A Report of the Board of National Education", 1959-1961, M. Colcol and Co., Manila. 1962.

20. Bureau of Private Schools Circular No. 7. Manila. 1957.

21. Bartolome, op. cit.

22. Bureau of Private Schools, Memorandum No. 27. "The Revised Teacher Education Program". Manila. 1970.

23. Research of Mr. Serafin Aquino, former Executive Secretary of the PAAF and Director of the National College of Physical Education.

24. Bartolome, Candido C. "Sports Development in the Philippines". Unpublished. 1977.

25. Manual, Juan L. Secretary of Education and Culture, Bulletin Today. November 12, 1977.

26. Department Order No. 35, s. 1973.

27. Department Order No. 32, s. 1975.

28. Department Order No. 53, s. 1976.

29. Department Order No. 27, s. 1977.

30. Peace Corps Philippines, "Physical Fitness Curriculum Development and Sports Development Program". Group 51. 1972.

31. McCollum, Robert H. "Evangelism Through Sports in Asia". Cable Magazine, Box 66, Palo Alto, California. November-December, 1969, pp. 2-5.

32. Bulletin Today, October 30, 1977.

# SPORT AND PHYSICAL EDUCATION IN THE POLISH SCHOOL SYSTEM

by Andrezej Wohl

## Biographical Sketch

*Professor, Doctor hab. Andrzej Wohl* is a long time member of the sport and physical education faculty at the Academy of Physical Education of Warsaw, Poland. He has achieved worldwide recognition in the field of sport sociology and is the Editor-in-Chief of the Editorial Board of the International Review of Sport Sociology (I.C.S.P.E. Committee of Sport Sociology). For many years Professor Wohl has been a very cooperative resource person for colleagues from other lands visiting and studying the sport and physical education developments in Poland.

## Sport and Physical Education in the Polish School System

Primary schools in Poland are attended at present by 4,580,000 pupils, general education secondary schools by 490,000 pupils and vocational schools by 1,650,000 pupils. This means that the overall number of pupils amounts to 6,720,000 out of a population of 35,000,000. The pupils attend 21,500 schools. For the purpose of implementing their physical education syllabuses the schools have at their disposal 5,800 standard dimension gymnasia, 4,800 sub-standard gymnasia and 25,000 comprehensive sports fields. There are about 20,000 qualified physical education teachers. This means that every gymnasium caters to 634 pupils, every sports field to 268 pupils, and that every qualified physical education teacher has in his care 336 pupils.

These are, of course, general data which require many explanations concerning the training of physical education personnel for schools, sports facilities construction and syllabuses of physical education and its implementation.

### 1.  System of the Training of Personnel

Let us begin with the system of the training of personnel. According to the present regulations, physical education in forms from 1 to 4 is conducted by teachers of other subjects. This means that no qualified physical education teachers are employed in these forms. Beginning with form 4, however, only qualified teachers with the degree of master of physical education should be employed in all schools and at all levels. At present, however, the number of qualified physical education teachers is still insufficient for the implementation of these regulations. It is estimated that secondary general education and vocational schools employ 85 percent and 90 percent of teachers with the required qualifications, while primary schools have 55 percent of such teachers.

The most acute shortage of qualified teachers is felt by rural schools. The percentage of unqualified teachers in those schools is high and it reaches up to 70 percent. But the situation began to change three years ago with the liquidation of small schools employing 1-5 teachers and the creation of so-called comprehensive schools. At present, already more than 50 percent of rural schools are comprehensive schools with 10 forms each, equipped with gymnasia and employing qualified teachers.

According to the existing regulations of the employment of unqualified teachers in the school system, they should obtain the necessary qualification within the period of ten years. It is assumed, therefore, that schools of all levels, both in town and country, will employ qualified teachers by 1990. Since 1972, these teachers work a 22-hour week.

For the purpose of educating the indispensable number of physical education teachers, Poland has at present 6 colleges of physical education and 3 college branches which are training at 4-year studies 6,000 students under the day system and 4,000 under the extramural system. These schools graduate every year nearly 2,000 graduates. This means that in a period of 10 years they are capable of doubling the number of physical education teachers employed in the school system. Students of these schools receive, beside the degree of master of physical education, also the rights of coach and umpire in basic sport disciplines, of an instructor of recreation and an instructor of health education.

The 4-year program of studies consists of 2,713 hours of didactic lessons and lectures, of which 41 percent is occupied by subjects pertaining to the technique of motor exercises, 22 percent by biomedical subjects, 12 percent by social, psychological and pedagogical subjects, 10 percent by foreign languages and the rest by miscellaneous subjects. The studies are held at the following departments: teaching, coaching, recreation, motor rehabilitation (since 1973).

In our opinion the education of teachers of physical education and their distribution in schools are one of our biggest achievements in this field. We think that in this respect we are one of the leading countries of the world as regards the indices of the employment of college graduates. And I know from my own experience that the standard of our graduates is one of the highest. This achievement is all the more worth emphasizing that in 1945 we had begun with 180 graduates of higher schools of physical education.

## 2. Physical Education Syllabuses

The syllabuses of physical education in Poland includes:

1.  physical education lessons
2.  sports preparation
3.  school sports circles
4.  mid-lesson and inter-lesson breaks
5.  corrective exercises
6.  hours of sport.

Physical education lessons are obligatory for all children and are included in the school syllabus. Each lesson lasts 45 minutes. For many years the number of physical education lessons amounted for forms 1-4 to 2 hours a week, and for higher forms to 3 hours a week. Only in smaller countryside schools (1-2 teachers) the number of lessons amounted to 1 hour a week and in schools employing 3-6 teachers to 1-2 hours a week. Since 1976, there is a binding regulation on a successive introduction of 3 lessons per week for all pupils.

Apart from 3 physical education lessons there are usually 2-4 a week of sports preparation which is voluntary and held after lessons. The conduct of this preparation is obligatory for physical education teachers as a part of their weekly teaching duties.

Another form of facultative sports exercises is held in school sports circles and sports sections. These exercises are also conducted by physical education teachers. The number of hours for sports circles amounts to from 6 to 18 hours a week, depending on the size of a school and its possibilities. These hours are also included in the weekly duties of a physical education teacher. The circles were a nucleus of the School Sports Union, and interschool sports circles have been formed. In 1974, the Minister of Education and Upbringing gave the School Sports Union the status of the pilot organization in organizing the leisure of children and youth. At present, the School Sports Union has a membership of 1,400 thousand, that is about 30 percent of all pupils beginning with the 5th form.

For pupils of forms from 1 to 4, on the other hand, there were introduced so-called mid-hour breaks during all lessons. If the weather conditions are good, these exercises should be held out-of-doors. Long interlesson breaks should be also used for the purpose of motor exercises in accordance with regulations.

1973 saw the introduction of corrective exercises for children and youth with body build defects. The exercises are conducted by physical education teachers who had specialized in this field.

A so-called "sports hour" was introduced in schools in 1974. These exercises are conducted by youth sports activists in schools which received permission to conduct voluntary exercises within the framework of their sports club, and which decide to do this.

One should also add to this a well-developed system of youth holidays which cater at present to over 4 million pupils in 3-week summer camps and 10-day winter camps. Daily hours of physical education are held also in the holiday camps which are under the supervision of physical education teachers. And last but not least, there are also youth sports games, both summer and winter. Apart from games of a school and regional type which are attended by the entire youth, every two years there are central games which are attended by the best only. The latter were attended in recent years by nearly 50 thousand of the most talented youth aged up to 15 years. It may be said that they are really regional and Polish juvenile championships. They are reviews of the achievements of schools, clubs and regions in their sports work with youth. Their programs include the following sports disciplines: acrobatics, artistic and sports gymnastics, judo, kayak rowing, cycling, basketball, track and field events, archery, soccer, handball, swimming, volleyball, marksmanship, fencing, wrestling and yachting.

This shows that the system of physical education in Poland consists of obligatory physical education lessons and after-lesson and out-of-school forms. It is precisely these widely expanded after-lesson forms of exercises which embrace 20-60 percent of school pupils that are the biggest achievement of the school physical education in recent years. They open to youth interested in sport wide prospects of active recreation and physical fitness.

A very important role in the proper shape of the program of physical education is played by an energetic and all round editing activity. A monthly called "Wychowanie Fizyczne i Higiena Szkolna" ("Physical Education and School Hygiene"), as well as a number of specialized publications, such as "Sportowe Wakacje" ("Sports Vacations") and "Sportowa Zima" ("A Sports Winter") have published for many years to meet the needs of physical education at school. The publication of school textbooks of physical education for pupils began recently. A textbook for form 1 pupils published this year encourages the children to perform also simple physical exercises at home.

We note also a democratization of the school system of physical education. As a result of the liquidation of small rural schools which before 1945 constituted the majority of village schools and the transition to a system of 10-year comprehensive schools, we created equal opportunities for the implementation of physical education program in the countryside, the same as in towns.

Another important factor was the extension of general physical education to vocational schools and the whole system of schools of agricultural preparation. Another contribution was made by the system of vacation camps for children and youth extended to the entire school system, which are attended by the majority of youth at present. The uniformity of the system of physical education which embraces all levels of education in this country has become an inseparable element of its democratization.

### 3. Material Safeguards of the Process of Physical Education

In 1946, schools had at their disposal 600 gymnasia and 3,300 school playing grounds. The rest of the school sports facilities had been devastated during the war. In the course of the last 30 years we have not only rebuilt the devastated facilities, but we have also built many new ones. More than 3,600 gymnasia (standard dimensions) and over 15,000 ground were built in the years 1955–1975.

We have laid down standards according to which the area of gymnasia for primary schools with up to 320 pupils is to amount to 128 sq. m., for schools with up to 640 pupils - 162 sq. m., and for schools with up to 960 pupils - 178 sq. m. Standards of playing grounds with the surrounding green areas were laid down for these schools at the same time. For primary schools with up to 400 pupils - 3,600 sq. m., for schools with up to 600 pupils - 5,000 sq. m.

For general education secondary schools - gymnasia with an area of 242 sq. m., and playing grounds with an area of 6,000 sq. m., 8,000 sq. m. and 10,000 sq. m. depending on the number of pupils.

Standards for so-called School Sports Centers in towns, and local facilities centers in regions and towns set their area at 182.94 x 123.75$^m$ and sports gymnasia with the dimensions of 25 x 14 x 6 m. Standards of plots for small towns set their size at 1.6 hectare, for medium towns - 4 hectares and for towns with over 100,000 inhabitants

- 6 hectares, as well as a water sports center with an area of 1 hectare. The state of the supply of sports equipment at present as meeting the needs of the implementation of physical education syllabus in secondary schools in 90 percent in vocational schools in 85 percent and in the countryside in 60 percent.

## 4.  Problems for Solution

There is, however, also a number of weak aspects which require solution in the whole well-developed system of physical education at school.  There are also some question marks.  It is to be hoped that the school reform being introduced in Poland at present will solve a number of problems.  The reform consists in the transition from the system of 8-form primary schools to a compulsory 10-year education both in town and country, that is to a general education at the secondary school level.  This is accompanied by an appropriate change in syllabuses in which a stronger emphasis is laid on polytechnical education, including also physical education.

These weak sides of the present system of physical education may be said to include the absence of a full consistence between the planned effects and the means and conditions indispensable for their achievement.  These means and conditions are still very modest.  The centrally and uniformly laid down programs encounter a differentiated level of the equipment of schools and teaching personnel.  Among other things, forms from 1 to 4 have no qualified teaching personnel. The higher the level of education the higher the qualifications required from physical education teachers, while in practice bigger experience and higher qualifications are required from teachers of younger pupils.

Another loophole in the system of physical education is lack of intellectualization.  So far, children and youth acquire motor habits but cannot learn the biological and social process connected with the acquisition of these habits.

There is also a lack of correlation between physical education syllabus and the syllabuses of other subjects.  Physical education at school has no theoretical background at all.  There is a lack of proper textbooks of physical education, although there are methodical manuals for physical education teachers.  The problem still awaits solution. The first step has been taken by the publication of a textbook for 1-form pupils.

Still another loophole is a lack of organizational and programmatic solutions for pupils with impairment in their health condition, as well as for pupils whose physical fitness is subnormal for a given age group.  Solutions which meet these demands are found only in larger centers which have teachers specialized in rehabilitation.  Meanwhile it is necessary to pay to this part of the school population at least as much attention as to the need of the physically most talented youth. Attention should be also paid to the fact that there is no correlation between physical education and the school medical service.

It must be said finally that in spite of the numerous changes it had undergone in the course of the last thirty years the system is marked by a certain traditionalism. The changes which took place in the contents of teaching concerned most frequently only it's technical aspect, and to a much smaller extent the program itself. As a result of this, school equipment sets also did not change very much. It could be said generally that changes in the field of physical education were less essential than the changes which took place in the other didactic, program and pedagogical fields of the school. This gives rise to doubts whether the system is in its present form sufficiently progressive and whether it is consistent with the needs of the age of the scientific and technological revolution. One may doubt in particular whether the system achieves the goals contained in the school programs. The programs say: "Physical education constitutes an indispensable element of the overall development of the pupil, it permits an effective strengthening of the socio-moral influence of the school through the formation of such traits of the character of the pupil as discipline, activeness and endurance, ability of coexistence in a group and a sense of responsibility". Together with other subjects, physical education serves the cause of the preparation of the pupil for healthy, efficient and capable citizens.

The implementation of these program principles requires no doubt the consideration of at least two elements. First - the point is that the development of the modern technique of both production and transport requires from the working people a better sense of equilibrium, quicker reaction time, and increased variety and precision of movements. Besides his own actions and his own motor possibilities, a worker must take an ever greater account of the movements of machines. He frequently works at high altitudes, is exposed to a strong action of new stimuli, to increased noise, changes of temperature, exceptional nervous tension, changes of the rhythm and rate of work. Under these conditions, human organism must be able to adapt itself to a quick change of the work of all organs and systems of the human body participating in the metabolism and the environment.

This means that the human organism must be taught from the earliest youth to adapt itself to changing efforts, to a quick transition from one situation to another. Hence the necessity to expand the to-date repertoire of physical exercises and to introduce in school practice new and varied motor evolutions improving in particular reaction time and sense of equilibrium, and prepared for a strenuous although short effort. This calls no doubt for more sport in the programs of physical exercises, but this should be adjusted more than heretofore to the pedagogical atmosphere of the school.

All this calls also for a greater emphasis on the preparation of school youth for tourism. The social changes now taking place have increased leisure time. This increase will penetrate also into schools which will be able to devote one day every week to sports, excursions and motor games. These circumstances should exert an influence on the use of physical exercises during holidays. Particularly attractive for youth, sensitive to everything that is new and unusual, are hiking trips which should create new opportunities for a variety of physical exercises in fields, in the mountains, at the seaside and in forests and on the lakes. It should be also pointed out that no sufficient advantage has been taken so far of the changes taking place in human relations due to the process of the disappearance of discriminatory and customary barriers and the resulting greater sense of freedom. This should permit a higher rank of play and games culture and sports at school. The imparting of such a higher rank requires an increased number of mass events, motor play and games in the system of physical exercises, an increase of the activeness of the pupil himself in the assimilation of these exercises, a greater use of physical exercises for the creation of an atmosphere of relaxation and an increased sense of joy, that is complete departure from traditionalism in physical education. Only such a complete departure will create conditions for a full exploitation of physical exercises in the pedagogical process, to rid people of the ages-old prejudices concerning their own body.

We could call this the process of humanization of the teaching of physical exercises, for this process means the recognition of the principle according to which play and sports games are an authentic need of humans, and that physical exercises and sport are one of the universal means of leading man to his own road. The return of men to their own body and the extraction of its latent capabilities and possibilities is after all an expression of an ever more universal civilization tendency.

In this respect, the to-date physical education programs have numerous gaps and do not meet program requirements, particularly the requirement of the adaptation of pupils through physical exercises to the needs of life and the needs of work under conditions of an ever growing scientific and technological revolution and the building of a new and more human social order.

## 5. Diagnosis of the Motor Needs of a Developing Organism

And on the whole good diagnosis of the properties and motor needs of children and school youth is a considerable achievement of recent years. Higher schools of physical education have trained during that time a numerous staff of researchers who have undertaken intensive research in the field of human motorics, and particularly the motorics of youth. Thanks to this, physical education teachers could be equipped with knowledge on the development of a young human organism and its motor needs. Cooperation was established in this field with researchers in anthropology, rehabilitation, etc. Development was noted in the science on health education, physical education teachers have been supplied with research methods and techniques in this domain.

Much has been done with respect to the pedagogization of physical education lessens, to the verbal description of movements, methods of the demonstration of movements and individualization in the teaching of exercises. Thanks to the mass character of children's summer holidays it was possible to a certain extent to inculcate children not only with motor abilities as such, but also to combine them with an active attitude in life, with principles of a harmonious cooperation with others, with a sense of responsibility and the formation of an active social and civic attitude.

# SPORT AND PHYSICAL EDUCATION IN SAUDI ARABIA

Part I.    Physical Education by Kamal Saleh Abdou
Part II.   Sport by Carl B. "Berny" Wagner

## Biographical Sketches

*Kamal Saleh Abdou* was born in Egypt. After early education in his homeland, he studied and received his Doctorate at Indiana University, Bloomington, Indiana, U.S.A. While in the U.S.A. he was a member of Phi Epsilon Kappa (Men's Physical Education Honorary Fraternity) and contributed an article for its publication The Physical Educator. Dr. Saleh has been employed as an expert of physical education, Ministry of Education, Riyadh, Saudi Arabia for the past four years and will return to the Faculty of Physical Education, Alharam Str. Giza, Egypt after February 25, 1978.

*Carl B. "Berny" Wagner* was born in 1924 and received both his B.A. and M.A. degrees at Stanford University with additional graduate work taken at San Jose State, University of the Pacific, San Francisco State University, and at Stanford University. He coached for thirteen years at California high schools (Wheatland, Lodi, San Lorenzo, and San Mateo), then three at the College of San Mateo before starting a ten year period at Oregon State University, Corvallis, Oregon. He assisted the Mexican Government in preparation of coaches and officials for the 1968 Olympic Games and was the Athletics, Jumps Coach, 1976 U.S.A. Olympic Team. Presently, he is the Director of Training and Planning for the International Sports Program of Saudi Arabia.

Physical Education in Saudi Arabia

General Information

The present population of Saudi Arabia is approximately 6,870,000 people in an area of 2,149,690 square kilometers. There are 680 manufacturing enterprises which care only for domestic needs. Health care includes: 62 hospitals (plus the specialized King Faisal hospital), 372 health centers, 4,000 infirmaries, 215 clinics, and there are 2,000 physicians. Eight universities provide education for 15,600 male and 1,000 female students.

The Empty Quarter - A staggering geographical phenomenon, measuring 750 by 400 miles, that has been crossed by outsiders only within the last 40 years. The sands are of a rather complicated type. Dunes often climb one on the other until they form mountains attaining heights up to 1,000 feet.

The Great Nafud - In the North Central part of the country, an expanse of rolling sand dunes covering 22,000 square miles exists. Because of the presence of iron exides, the Nafud Sands have a reddish cast remarked on by generations of travellers.

Madayen Saleh - About 500 miles north of Jeddah, the main Saudi port on the west coast, old remains consisting of houses, some two stories high, are carved in the solid rock mountains. They were discovered 90 years ago and contain ornately carved tombs of the same Hellenistic influence as a Petra. Remains of wells suggest a large population was accommodated there.

The Bedouin's occupations - usually as camel breeders, hunters, or herdsmen - take them off the beaten track. There are 635,000 of them.

Historical Background of Physical Education

Before 1956, all the Saudi ministries and governmental offices were located in Mecca, the spiritual capital, including the ministry of education. In this ministry, physical education was born in a small office called the "department of activities". It was responsible for organizing and administering school physical education, scouting, arts, and social services. When the ministries were transferred to Riyadh, the capital of the Kingdom, there were about 36 teachers and superviros of physical education, who were at the same time in charge of scouting.

After 1956, the real growth of school physical education started ed wide steps. Furthermore, the school department was in charge of the national activities also. In 1961, a special department for national youth welfare was formed in the Ministry of Social Affairs (before 1956, the Ministry of Interior was in charge of national activities). Concerning school physical education, it began to spread and reach all male schools in the educational provinces. In 1957, special summer courses in physical education were organized in Taif, the summer capital. Its main objective was to prepare native teachers for the elementary schools. schools. Moreover, three school sports centers were opened in Mecca, Riyadh, and Jeddah. In 1959, the number of physical education teachers raised to 267 including 200 native teachers. The number of students who participated in school competitions - in soccer, basketball, and volleyball - was 3,286. In 1960, a special budget for physical education was approved. It was then that 561 thousand Riyals were added to 300 thousand Riyals for the summer courses for training teachers. This compares with the present budget of more than 174 million Riyals for school physical education.

In 1962, the school department of activities was changed to a general department including four departments (physical education, art education, scouting, and social services). In 1963, a mission of 12 native teachers was sent to study physical education in Egypt. At the same time the local preparation of native teachers continued and their number reached 600. Furthermore, new sports centers were opened in Medina, Taif, Kassim, and Damman (the Eastern port). In 1964, two plans were approved, the first was to establish a complete school stadium in the capital (Riyadh), and the second was opening of the only Institute of Physical Education - on the high school level - now, it graduates about 100 teachers annually.

The Recent Picture of School Physical Education

Saudi Arabian school physical education class
playing with the Big Ball (cage).

The aims and objectives of physical education at the Saudi institutions are attained through: physical education classes, school sports centers, intramurals and extramurals, and through international school competitions and leagues. These aspects are organized and administered by the department of physical education either directly or through the physical education units in the educational bureaus in the 23 provinces. The whole operating budget is derived completely from the Ministry of Education.

The physical education staff numbers 3,276 (a director, one expert, seven general supervisors, 30 provincial supervisors, and 3,237 teachers).

The number of male schools is now as follows:

2,485 elementary schools   -   438,027 students

525 intermediate schools  -    98,220 students

131 secondary schools     -    29,509 students

21 technical schools      -     4,063 students

34 retarded schools       -     1,804 students

30 teacher
institution schools  -    10,587 students

The number of annual school games include:

|  | elementary | | intermediate | | secondary | |
|---|---|---|---|---|---|---|
|  | intra-murals | extra-murals | intra-murals | extra-murals | intra-murals | extra-murals |
| soccer | 9,014 | 890 | 2,960 | 270 | 1,431 | 88 |
| basketball | 2,153 | 534 | 1,417 | 259 | 1,143 | 79 |
| handball (field) | 436 | 143 | 1,406 | 213 | 995 | 65 |
| volleyball | 9,081 | 1,143 | 3,662 | 323 | 1,464 | 98 |
| table tennis | 3,258 | 796 | 1,940 | 300 | 1,107 | 106 |
| track and field | 455 | 148 | 187 | 62 | 78 | 55 |

The Saudi sports selections participated in three of the Arabian school competitions which are held once every two years for school teams in Arabian countries for males and females. Some of the Saudi students got medals in swimming, table tennis, throwing the javelin and in soccer.

Marking in physical education - all physical education programs are compulsory and credit earning. Though the mark is added to the students whole general standing in school work, yet it has no minimum - it is a passing mark as a prerequisite to graduation. All capacities and limitations of every particular group of students are taken into account.

Evaluation - fortunately, the periodical and final reports from the provinces, besides the visits of the general supervisors furnish the needed data and information about the physical education programs. As a result of evaluating the curriculum of the institute of physical education was changed in 1974 in order to meet the needs of the elementary school level. Moreover, a book including the complete annual lessons for elementary classes was prepared in 1975, in order to help the high percentage of unqualified teachers.

Research - Saudi Arabia was the first Arabian country to apply the international battery of physical fitness. The tests were executed in ten provinces spread geographically all over the Kingdom. The sample was 2,301 students from the 4th grade in elementary schools to the last secondary level - age from 10 to 18 years of age. No doubt the results will lead to program adaptation and curricular development on both central and provincial levels. Furthermore, it may lead to the completion of the physical fitness picture of the Saudi students. Hence, they can participate fruitfully in establishing and developing the huge future plans of their nation.

Sports Development Program in Saudi Arabia

Whittaker International Sports has been assisting Saudi Arabia to build successful sports programs in Aquatics, Basketball, and Athletics (Track and Field) since the beginning of their contract with the Youth Welfare Organization twenty-one months ago. International sports success does not come quickly, however, a fact that has been learned around the world by Countries which have begun developing their sports programs in recent times.

In spite of this, rapid advances in sports have already been made in Saudi Arabia. It will take more time, however, until the concepts of consistent, long-range training; sequential scheduling; the need for widespread participation; and the necessity for public recognition of sportsmen's achievements in all sports are accepted in a country that is just beginning a serious effort in its sports program.

The contract lists as the objectives of our work:

(1) The planning and implementing of a comprehensive sports training program.
(2) Providing qualified training personnel.
(3) Providing the latest, modern training and competition equipment.

The on-going experience of the Whittaker Sports' staff and the Youth Welfare Organization has shown that more basic planning and many more facilities are necessary in order to carry out these objectives.

Within the three areas of responsibility outlined by the contract the following activities have been completed:

(1) An assessment of the sports resources was made. Appropriate developmental activities were initiated only after our staff had become familiar with the sports resources available. The structure of the newly organized Federations governing sports, the relative unavailability of young sports talent, and the lack of adequate facilities and training equipment were some of the information which became apparent to our staff. Program activities were then planned using the knowledge of the existing developmental requirements within the Kingdom.

Objectives for each sport, including short, medium, and long-range goals were planned. Activity plans to implement the objectives and goals were formulated and presented to the Federations. As the Federations became active, sequential scheduling was planned and budgeted in cooperation with them. This coordinated implementation is a new step for the Kingdom.

Selection and training camps have been conducted in all three sports along with many observations of club and school competitions to identify more potential national team athletes. The national team in Athletics was trained for competitions in the Mid-East, Europe and the Olympic Games. In Swimming, the national team was prepared for their successful performance in the Arabian Games in Damascus and is now beginning a new season of training and competition. In Basketball the national team was trained for the Arabian Games. Problems concerned with collecting the best players for the team kept this effort from being a successful (winning) one. At present, players are being assessed during the on-going in-Kingdom tournaments. New National players will be selected from this assessment, a selection camp will be held, and new National and Junior teams will be formed.

Seminars have been completed in several cities for over 40 coaches of basketball, athletics and swimming. Most of these coaches are citizens of other Arabic countries working in Saudi Arabia with Sports Clubs and the Youth Welfare Organization.

A program to create a selection of Saudi Arabian coaches in the three sports has been developed, because one of the primary needs identified by our staff is the necessity to develop Saudi Arabian coaches and sports officials. Curricula have been developed and Whittaker personnel will teach the clinic courses of the Department of Preparation and Training to potential Saudi Arabian coaches during their certification clinics in the summers.

Saudi Arabian coaches have been conducted on tours of facilities, training methods and competitions in the United States to widen their thoughts about what is possible within the Kingdom.

(2) Whittaker International Sports has assembled an experienced group of coaches; technical specialists such as physical therapists, audio-visual specialists, strength training specialists; and administrative and communications support personnel. Special expertise most suited to the developmental conditions found within the Kingdom were sought through the company's international recruiting capability. The current staff combines successful sports coaching, management, administrative and competitive experience.

(3) The necessary coaching devices for the three sports have been provided and have considerably aided performance levels. The purchase and installation of pool heaters for the swimming pool used by the Youth Welfare Organization for training, now allows year-round swimming training in Riyadh, the Kingdom's capital, our base of operations.

Films, pamphlets and books have been assembled in sports libraries for our three sports.

As the Federations of Athletics, Swimming and Basketball were formed and became active, the Whittaker personnel in these areas made their knowledge and experience available to them. The experience of the United States and of developing countries was incorporated into the reasoning and planning behind the training and competitive schedules. Programs were developed and presented to the Federations, for incorporation into their overall programs. Our coaches and administrative personnel continue to work with the Federations as technical resource people.

The occurrence of the XXIst Olympic Games within the initial year of the program was seen as an excellent opportunity for many Saudi Arabian sportsmen and officials to observe or compete in international sport as it is practiced at the highest level. It was felt that this was an invaluable opportunity to prepare and stimulate Saudi Arabians to participate successfully in the international environment of sports. This analysis was supported by the Youth Welfare Organization and a summer program for the coaches and athletes of nine sports was organized and administered by Whittaker Sports. The Athletics team competed in Montreal after a summer training program at the National Sports Center in Switzerland. The players of the other eight teams trained before, during and after the Olympic Games in the U.S., at Montreal and in Germany, and observed the world's most important sports event. The sportsmen and coaches participated in a one month training program at Springfield College, a fine school of physical education, following the Olympic Games.

A daily fifteen minute Olympic Games television program showing the activities of the Saudi Arabian delegation in Montreal was planned by our Audio-visual specialist and broad cast to the Kingdom via satellite.

A documentary film depicting the summer program in all its phases is being developed from film taken in Switzerland, Canada and the United States.

It is apparent that a realistic assessment of the physical fitness level of Saudi Arabian Youth is necessary to develop programs for widespread participation in sports and sports related recreation. A proposal for a needed testing program has been developed.

Facilities for training and competition in most sports are very few in the Kingdom. Plans for a top quality facility for training the national teams and suggestions for other facilities have been presented. An indoor facility, to be built in Riyadhl, with a 200 meter track, a 50 meters swimming pool, basketball courts and areas for other sports will allow training at any time of the year. Housing facilities for players and officials would be provided, as would medical, physical therapy, audio-visual, strength training and physiological testing complexes.

A strength training facility has been developed at Malaz Stadium in Riyadhl where sportsmen of many teams train daily. The same modern equipment which was purchased for the Malaz Stadium Strength Center has been purchased and is in storage while we await authorization to develop similar centers in other cities.

A complete physical therapy and training facility at the stadium was planned, equipped and stocked with supplies. Our three physical therapists and our doctor work out of this complex in the areas of injury prevention, nutrition, and treatment of injury.

Physiological testing of Saudi Arabian national team athletes has been conducted to determine further necessary aspects of their training programs. One of the world's foremost exercise physiologists tested the Athletics national team at the Swiss training camp. Basketball players and Swimmers were tested by a medical team at LeValle University of Montreal during the summer program. The sportsmen of the cycling, table tennis, fencing, volleyball, team-handball, and gymnastics teams were tested at Springfield College. The results of these tests are being used by Whittaker coaches and are available to the coaches of Youth Welfare Organization sports not coached by us.

The ultimate objective of a National Sports program is success in international competition. During the first year of the Whittaker International Sports Program, teams in Athletics, Swimming and Basketball were prepared as well as possible, within the constraints of a developing sports program, and the short time available, for the fifth Arabian Games in Damascus. Many of the Arabian countries have had on-going sports programs for many years. The ideas, concepts and procedures which Whittaker is suggesting for use within the Kingdom been planned and sequential; strength training has been used regularly; audio-visual aids have been employed. Even so, the Whittaker trained teams enjoyed success. The Saudi Arabian Athletics and Swimming teams dominated the Gulf countries (a sub-group of the total Arab world) in the Games. The Kingdom was represented twenty-nine times in the Athletics finals and won nine medals, two of which were gold. The Swimmers were represented twenty-five times in their finals and won four medals. The success in these sports was the Saudi Arabians' first. Since the beginning of our program, Saudi Arabian National records have been set in thirteen of the nineteen Athletics events competed in, and in all thirteen of the Swimming events contested.

Much remains to be done, but much has been accomplished in a short time.

# PHYSICAL EDUCATION AND SPORT IN SOUTH AFRICA
## by Stephanus F. du Toit

### Biographical Sketch

*Stephanus F. du Toit* was born in the Orange Free Free State in the Republic of South Africa on June 27, 1935. He graduated from high school in 1953 and obtained the Batchelor of Arts degree from the University of the Orange Free State in 1956. He also received the Senior Teachers Diploma in 1957, the B.A., Honors degree in 1959 and the Master of Arts degree in 1962 from the same institution.

Dr. du Toit taught physical education at the St. Andrews High School in Bloemfontein, South Africa from 1958-1959 and was junior lecturer in the department of physical education at the University of the Orange Free State from 1960-1962.

He was a graduate assistant in the department of physical education for men at the University of Illinois and received his Ph.D., degree in 1965-1966.

Upon his return to South Africa, Dr. du Toit has been engaged in teaching and research at the University level and is currently the Head of the Department of Physical Education at the University of Durban-Westville, Durban, Natal, South Africa.

## General Background

The Republic of South Africa is almost entirely within the southern tempearture zone, between 22°S and 35°S, at the southern end of the African Continent. Famous Cape of Good Hope separates the Indian and Atlantic Oceans on South Africa's eastern and western seaboards respectively. The Limpopo River in the north is its natural boundary with Rhodesia. South Africa's "mother" city, Cape Town, on the southwestern tip of the continent, is 9,600 kilometers by sea from London and 10,900 kilometers from New York. Sailing eastwards it is 12,500 kilometers from Wellington, New Zealand.

South Africa consists of four provinces; namely, the Cape Province, Transvaal, Orange Free State and Natal. The Republic also administers South West Africa, which is represented in its House of Assembly by six members.

Portugese seafarers first discovered South Africa in the late 15th century, while looking for a sea-route to the East. Jan van Riebeeck and his Dutch settlers sowed permanent seeds of Western civilization when they established a provisions' station at the Cape of Good Hope in 1652 for the fleets of the Dutch East India Company. Apart from Bushmen and small tribes of nomadic Hottentots, South Africa at that time was quite empty, When the first Whites settled at the Cape, the ancestors of Bantu peoples were still migrating south from the Great Lakes region of Central Africa.

At the time of the Napoleonic Wars, the Cape of Good Hope was taken over by Britain. In 1835-36 the Dutch Voortrekkers--pioneer farmers--became dissatisfied with British rule and began the Great Trek away from the Cape into the virtually unknown interior.

By the time of the Anglo-Boer War (1899-1902) the Whites had built up a prosperous land composed of English and Dutch speaking elements, reinforced by thousands of fortune seekers who flooded into the country after the discovery of diamonds in 1865 and gold in 1886. In 1910 when the four provinces were bound in union, the Union of South Africa was established, and a stable government inaugurated a period of progress and prosperity. The establishment of the Republic of South Africa on 31st May 1961 brought no visible changes, constitutionally or otherwise.

The population of South Africa is heterogeneous and multinational. Each large group has its own cultural heritage, its own language and hence its own educational and cultural institutions. The country has a total population of 22 million, consisting of Whites (3.8 million), Coloureds (2.1 million), Asians (0.6 million) and Bantu (15 million). The Bantu consist of several distinct nations, each with its own customs and traditions, namely the Zulu (4.0 million), Xhosa (3.9 million), Iswana (1.7 million), North and South Sotho (3.0 million), Shangaan (0.7 million), Swazi (0.5 million), Uanda (0.4 million), South and North Ndebele (0.4 million). Most of the Whites are descendants of Dutch, French, British and German settlers with smaller admixtures of other European peoples--mainly Portuguese, Greeks and Italians.

In view of the fact that South Africa's heterogeneous population groups have different ways of life, it is almost impossible to speak of a typical South African way of life. In general, however, it can be said that the South African way of life is largely the product of the country's sunny, healthy climate that has made the average South African a lover of outdoor life.

## Historical Background of Physical Education

It was only towards the end of the nineteenth and the beginning of the twentieth century, that a beginning was made with the actual teaching of physical education in schools and colleges in South Africa.

In the Cape Province, physical education was taught for the first time in schools towards the end of the nineteenth century, during the time of Dr. Thomas Muir, the third Superintendent-General of Education. Dr. Muir was personally interested in gymnastics and through his enthusiasm it was possible for teachers to take short courses during the holidays in Swedish Exercises. Until 1908 many such courses were organized in different towns with the result that more and more schools placed physical education in their curriculum. In a number of girls' schools, however, physical education was taught at that time by teachers from abroad. Dr. Muir also warned against the tendency which is still in existence today; namely, too much attention to the gifted child for the sake of extramural sport and not enough emphasis on the weaker child who needs physical education most.

In the other three provinces, namely the Transvaal, Free State and Natal, the introduction of physical education into the schools followed the same line of development. Physical Education came to these provinces toward the beginning of this century. Also in these provinces we find that training for teachers was provided for in short courses during holidays. Girls schools were again the first to appoint trained teachers from abroad.

The first actual training for women physical educators was started at the Cape Town Training College, where Miss M. C. Botha started to train her students according to the Swedish ideas in 1921. After a year of general education the students were able to take physical education for a year and for some time on a two-year basis. In 1936 a similar type of program was started for men in the Paarl. Shortly afterwards the teachers training colleges at Graff Reinett, Bloemfontein, Potchefstroom, Pretoria and Heidelberg Tv., started courses for the training of physical educators. The main purpose of this training was to provide teachers for elementary schools, but because of teacher shortages, many of these teachers were also appointed in high schools.

In 1938, the training of Coloured teachers in physical education was started at the Wesley Training School and in 1943 the training of Bantu physical educators at the Healdtown Native Training Institution.

The first university to start a department in physical education was the University of Stellenbosch in 1936, with Dr. Ernst Jokl as its first department head. Originally this was only a one-year course, but since 1940 a full degree course in physical education has been offered. Since the second World War, departments of physical education were also introduced at the universities of Grahamstown, Bloemfontein, Potchefstroom and Pretoria. Today it is possible to take an advanced degree in physical education at most of these universities.

A National Advisory Council for Physical Education was introduced in 1938. This helped a great deal to coordinate physical education and to put it on a firmer basis in the different provinces. Since 1943 this council produced a number of syllabi for use in schools, but, more exactly, produced a compilation of basic exercise material.

The South African magazine for physical education, health and recreation--"Vigor" which was originally called "Physical Education"-- was first published by the University of Stellenbosch from 1937-47. Since then it has been distributed by the Department of Education, Arts and Science.

The first Inspectors or Directors of physical education were appointed in 1938 by the Department of Education of the Cape Province. Although the Advisory Council proposed that three periods per week should be allocated to physical education, in most provinces only two periods of forty minutes are allowed.

The influence of a number of countries can be seen in the physical education programs in South Africa today. These influences came to South Africa through physical educators from abroad who were appointed in key positions as well as from many South Africans who rounded their studies off overseas, in England, the Netherlands, Germany, Denmark, Australia and the U.S.A. Visits of teams from abroad such as the Danish Gymnastic Team of Niels Bukh in 1939, the Swiss Gymnastic Team in 1947 and of influential people like Dr. and Mrs. Carl Diem 1959, and Dr. Dorothy S. Ainsworth in 1960 left a definite influence on physical education in South Africa.

In 1945 the first convention for physical education was held in Stellenbosch and Cape Town. Since then it has been held every two years. The South African Association for Physical Education and Recreation was formed in Cape Town in January 1950, to promote the interests of health-physical-and recreation education.

Probably the most significant development with respect to physical education and sport in South Africa over the past decade, if not in its whole history, was the establishment of a *Government Department of Sport and Recreation,* on the 1st July 1966.

This department, which was in fact the brainchild of the South African Association for Physical Education and Recreation, has its head office in Pretoria, with twelve regional offices all over the country. Well qualified physical educationists are in control of these offices. They establish liaison with sports and recreational bodies and give advice on technical and administrative matters.

The main aim of this department is to render service, not to exercise control. The administration of sport is in the hands of voluntary sports associations and in no way whatsoever does this department exercise control over the affairs of these sports bodies.

Furthermore, this department encourages activites which are aimed at the development of a strong and healthy nation, and where possible, to grant subsidies to promote such activities. Priority is given to coaching and training, through courses and clinics for the various sports, as well as recreational projects such as adventure courses where physical effort and moral development are emphasized. During 1973, 1077 training projects were subsidized and/or organized by the department. Over 53,000 participants, sports administrators, coaches and recreation leaders were directly involved.

The department also cooperates with sports bodies in organizing overseas tours by South African sportsmen and women and bringing world-class sportsmen and women to the Republic--to maintain the country's standing in international sport.

As the department developed it started to realize the great need for the provision of basic sport and recreation facilities for the masses. With this in mind, the department, since 1973, made substantial grants-in-aid to local authorities for the provision of these facilities.

One of the most recent gratifying developments in this department is the fact that funds have now been made available for the granting of financial assistance for scientific research in the field of sport and recreation.

This department was also responsible for the introduction of the State President's Sport Award. This decoration is awarded annually to individuals for sporting achievements at the highest international level, e.g., improving a world record or winning a world championship in an established sport.

The department also subsidizes the South African Federation for Youth and Sport. This Federation serves as coordinating and representative body of most national sport bodies in South Africa. It further endeavours to promote physical recreation among the youth, and launch youth projects such as National Fitness Schemes, in close collaboration with the Department of Sport.

Another outstanding feature of the past decade was the establishment of the *Sport Foundation of South Africa*, by a prominent public company. This non-profit organization endeavours to raise the standards in amateur sport by means of expert tuition and coaching. It advises sport bodies on modern training methods and assists in bringing overseas experts to the Republic. These services are available to all sections of the population. In 1973 the Foundation organized 175 coaching clinics with a total attendance of 16,450 participants.

The staff consists of five organizers and a general director in charge. A Dolphin Scheme was launched in 1973 with a grant of R50,000 from a well-known bottling company. In this scheme about 100,000 scholars are participating in a "learn to swim" campaign.

In collaboration with the South African Airways, the Foundation also awards the South African Airways Trophy annually to the sport which makes the greatest impact on the international sporting scene.

The Sport Foundation cooperates closely with the Department of Sport and Recreation as well as the South African Association for Physical Education and Recreation.

Through financial assistance received from the above two bodies, the *South African Association for Physical Education and Recreation* (S.A.A.P.E.R.) really made giant strides during the past ten years. This assistance not only enabled S.A.A.P.E.R. to organize its biannual Conferences on a more sophisticated level, but also to organize a host of other clinics and symposia in between. Furthermore, it enabled this association to invite prominent people from overseas as well as to send some of its own members overseas to attend international conferences.

This has made a tremendous impact on physical education and sport in South Africa, which becomes evident if we look at some of the names of people who lectured in South Africa during the past ten years.

In the field of physiology of exercise and fitness: Prof. O. O. Astrand (Sweden), Prof. E. Asmussen (Denmark), Prof. W. Van Huss (U. S. A.), Prof. A. H. Steinhaus (U.S.A.), Prof. T. K. Cureton (U.S.A.). In the field of recreation: Prof. N. P. Miller (U.S.A.).

In the field of psychology of sport and child development: Prof. B. Ogilvie (U.S.A.), Prof. A. Espenshade (U.S.A.), and Dr. J. Whiting (England).

Further international contact will take place when the Women's Section of S.A.A.P.E.R. will play host to the International Women's Physical Education Conference in South Africa in 1977.

## Administration of Physical Education in Schools

The administration of physical education in the public schools is in the hands of the Department of Education of each province. These departments have directors who guide and advise the teachers as to the programs to be followed.  Most of the necessary facilities, outdoor as well as indoor, are supplied or subsidized by the Department of Education, the remainder of the funds being provided by parent organizations.

The Department of National Education, which falls directly under the central government, administers physical education in technical schools and colleges, as well as in special schools which cater to blind, deaf, physically handicapped and cerebral palsied pupils.

Physical education is a compulsory non-examination subject in all schools, provided for by two periods of thirty minutes per week in primary schools and one period per week in secondary schools.

New National Syllabuses have been drawn up for boys and girls, but each educational department can adjust the program in such a way that it suits its local needs and conditions.

## Physical Education and Sport in Primary and Secondary Schools

In viewing the new syllabi for schools, it can now be said that there is a much more realistis, balanced and objective approach to the construction of these syllabi than what there was ten years ago.  The trend is to overemphasize certain aspects of the work in such a way that the child will come to realize the whole value spectrum of physical activity, so as to motivate him towards continued participation outside of the official class.  This motivational approach is based on the fact that with the limited time available, we cannot in any case fully realize our aims unless it is supplemented by extra curriculum work. Furthermore, specific attention is given to the fact that the activities are geared towards the physical-social-and-psychological characteristics of the children in the different age groups.

This is the basic philosophy underlying the work that is being done in the primary and secondary schools.  The means for achieving this is, especially in the primary school, to present the children with as large a variety of movement experiences as possible.  This is done with and without equipment and at different levels of intensity.  It is presented in such a way that children will come to realize why certain movements are performed as they are, as well as to make them realize the effects of activity and its value upon the human body.

In the secondary schools these activities are brought more and more in relation with specific sports and games. Again the activities are presented in such a way as to make the child realize the value of activity in a physical, social, emotional and intellectual context.

The standard of work ranges from excellent to poor, depending on the qualifications and enthusiasm of the teachers and the facilities available.

Sport is played in South African schools at all age levels and by both sexes on a competitive basis. Well organized and impressive are the provincial and interprovincial schools' swimming galas, and the track and field and gymnastic competitions in which as many as 1500 boys and girls from eight to eighteen years of age will compete in one single competition over a weekend. The other popular sports are rugby, cricket and soccer for boys, netball and field hockey for girls, and tennis.

## Physical Education at Universities and Colleges

Of the twenty-seven teachers' training colleges in South Africa, almost everyone offers two, three, or four year diploma courses in physical education. All these courses are teacher training oriented and directed towards teaching in primary schools. Of the sixteen universities, only six have departments of physical education: namely, Stellenbosch, Pretoria, Potchefstroom, Grahamstown, Orange Free State and the latest addition, the University of Durban-Westville.

The undergraduate student may either take a Bachelor or Arts, Science or Paedagogics degree, with physical education and one other subject of the student's choice, as majors. In general, the departments require from three to four subjects, physical education included on a one-year basis; then two to three subjects, physical education in included on a second-year basis, and finally the two major subjects in the third year, after which the degree is obtained. In the fourth year of study, those students who intend going into teaching take the University Education Diploma, which is an one-year course in general education and teacher preparation. Practice teaching in schools and method of teaching are the major areas emphasized during this course.

The next degree is a B.A. Honors, B.Sc. Honors or a B.Ed. This usually takes one year and includes only post-graduate courses in the field of physical education. These degrees are intended for which the only requirement is the presentation of a thesis. This is also the case with Ph.D. degrees.

Post graduate research has improved tremendously over the past ten years. Some really good studies have been completed and more can be expected in the near future.

The undergraduate programs are broad in nature and cover almost all areas in physical, health and recreation education. Specialization only starts with the B.A. Honors degree.

Sport competition is keen at the universities and colleges and excellent modern facilities exist at most of these instutitions.

Special Characteristics of South African Sport

Ideal climatic conditions, with an abundance of sunshine, encourages all forms of sport and outdoor recreation almost throughout the year. The famous bathing and surfing beaches of the Cape are a major attraction in summer. During the winter months, holiday makers flock to the subtropical coastal resorts in Natal. Hiking, camping, fishing, mountaineering--all these are popular activities.

Competitive sport is most popular. South Africans compete at the highest international levels and have frequently won international awards or held world records. Rugby is South Africa's national game and a game in which South African teams (The Springboks) are ranked with the best in the world. Cricket is the main summer sport for men, and field hockey and netball are the main winter games for women. Sports clubs, to which anyone can belong, are popular in South Africa with competitive participation in leagues every weekend.

In 1971 the South African Olympic Association was suspended from the I.O.C. for political considerations. South African competitors are now debarred from participating in the Olympic Games. This association, however, under its new name, *The South African Olympic and National Games Association,* (SAONGA), continues to function locally and takes a special interest in the organization of national festivals and games.

The 1973 South African Open International Games in Pretoria were by far the biggest international sports even ever staged in the country. They were the first multinational games in South Africa and will be remembered as the most significant recent development in the promotion of South African sport.

A brief historical review of the development of the games will show the tremendous recent development of sport in South Africa. The first South African Sports Festival was held in 1959 as part of the Johannesburg Festival. The program included 14 different sports, with no competitors from other countries. This event was so successful that the S.A.O.N.G.A. decided to have regular games of this kind.

In 1964 the first official South African Games were staged in Johannesburg. The program comprised 16 Olympic sports, with one overseas athlete competing.

In 1966 the second South African Games were staged in Bloemfontein. The program comprised 36 different sports, with 6000 competitors of whom 126 were from abroad.

The third South African Games in 1973, referred to above, drew 673 competitors and officials, representing 31 different sports, from 35 overseas countries. South African competitors of all races totalled 1652.

Most of the big national meetings in South Africa are now sponsored by business concerns. The first South African open championships in track and field for athletes from all population groups, were staged in 1974 and was also a sponsored meeting.

## SELECTED REFERENCES

1.    A Decade of Service 1964-1974, The Sport Foundation of South Africa. 1974.

2.    Postma, J. W. *Introduction to the Theory of Physical Education.* A. A. Balkama. 1968.

3.    South African Yearbook, South African Department of Information. Perskor Printers, Johannesburg. 1974.

# SPORT AND PHYSICAL EDUCATION IN TANZANIA
## by William Johnson

### Biographical Sketch

*William Johnson* was born at Clatskanie, Oregon
and received his B.S. degree from the University of
Oregon, Eugene in 1936. Additional graduate work was
taken at Stanford University, San Francisco State University, The University of California at Los Angeles, and
and the University of Southern California before the M.S.
and Ed.D. degrees were finally conferred at the University of Oregon in 1942 and 1955 respectively.

After twelve years in secondary teaching and
coaching at Hillsboro and Eugene, Oregon, Johnson entered college instruction first as a graduate assistant at
the University of Oregon in 1954; as Principal of the
College of Physical Education, East Pakistan in 1955-1957;
as coordinator of student teachers at Los Angeles State
University from 1958-1962; as department chairperson
and athletic director at the College of the Desert, Palm
Desert, California in 1963; and at Minot State College,
North Dakota in 1963-1965; and presently on the staff of
the Department of Physical Education, University of Illinois as an Associate Professor.

He has travelled extensively, first as a member of
of the U.S. Navy during World War II; then on the
A.A.H.P.E.R. Olympic Games tour to Helsinki, Finland
in 1956; as an employee of The Asia Foundation working
in East Pakistan and attending the Melbourne Olympics
with the Pakistan Olympic Team; to the Mexico City,
Munich, and Montreal Games; as a Fulbright-Hays Grant
recipient to the University of Dar es Salaam, Tanzania,
East Africa in 1973-1974; and finally on a sabbatical
leave to the U.S.S.R., Romania, Czechoslovakia, and
East Germany in 1976.

As a followup of this international interest he has
been Newsletter Editor of the International Relations
Council of A.A.H.P.E.R. for a period of ten years;
served two three-year terms as a Contributing Editor for
*JOHPERS* in the area of international relations; three
years on the Editorial Board of *The Physical Educator*
and is currently the Editor of the Department, "Elsewhere in the World" of the same publication. Seven
monographs entitled, "Physical Education Around the
World" have been edited by Dr. Johnson covering fifty-one

countries. Monograph articles are being updated for inclusion in the present book.

Dr. Johnson has been chairperson of the International Relations Sections of the States of California and and Illinois; of the Midwest District International Relations Section; of the International Relations Council of A.A.H.P.E.R.; of the NCPEAM International Relations Committee and of the Comparative Section of ICHPER.

## General Background

The United Republic of Tanzania, formerly an United Nations Trust Territory administered by Britain, is a 1964 merger of Tanganyika and the islands of Zanzibar and Pemba in East Africa. With a land area of 362,820 square miles, it is as large as the States of Texas and New Mexico combined and is the 19th largest country in the world. Its territory extends from the Indian Ocean on the east to Lake Tanganyika on the west, from Lake Victoria on the north to Lake Nyasa on the south. Mainland Tanzania is bordered on the north by Kenya, and Uganda; on the west by Rwanda, Burundi, and Zaire; on the south by Zamiba, Malawi, and Mozambigue; and on the east by the Indian Ocean.

Geographically, Tanzania's most renowned features is Mt. Kilimanjaro, the highest mountain on the African continent. Aside from the highlands, found mainly in the northeast and southwest, most of the country is open plateau. Many of Africa's big game roam these dry plains, and Serengeti National Park in northern Tanzania is where most African animal films are made. Along the edges of the plateau are trenchlike depressions characteristic of the Rift Valley System which extends through most of East Africa.

Climatically, the mainland may be divided into four areas: 1) the hot and humid coastal plains, 2) the hot, arid zone of the central plateau, 3) the high, moist lake regions, and 4) the temperate highland areas. Over half of the land area is either too arid or too infested by the tsetse fly for agricultural use. The climate of much of Tanzania is governed by two monsoons. The northeast monsoon from December to March brings the hottest temperatures of the year; when the wind shifts to the south from March through May, they bring heavy intermittent rains. The southwest monsoon extends from June through September bringing relatively cool weather. Light showers can be expected in November and December.

Population distribution in Tanzania is extremely uneven. Density varies from three persons per square mile in arid areas to 133 per square mile in the well-watered highlands of the mainland and 347

per square mile on Zanzibar. More than 90 percent of the total population is rural. With over 13 million people, Tanzania ranks approximately 40th in the world. Dar es Salaam is the capital and largest
city with around 500,000 and Dodoma is located in the center of the
nation and has been designated to become the new capital.

About 99% of the people are Africans consisting of more than
130 ethnic groups, only one of which (the Sukuma) exceeds one million members. The majority of Tanzanians, including such large tribes
as the Sukuma and the Nyamwezi, are of Bantu stock. Groups of
Nilotic or related origin include the nomadic Masai and the Luo, both
of which are found in greater numbers in neighboring Kenya. The
rest of the people are mainly Indians and Pakistanis, Arabs, and
Europeans.

All ethnic groups have their own language, but the national
language is Swahili, a Bantu-based tongue with strong Arabic borrow-
ings. English is also commonly in use. The African population is
mainly pagan, but includes a substantial number of Christians and
over two million Moslems.

## Historical Background

Northern Tanzania's famed Olduvai Gorge has provided rich
evidence of the area's prehistory, including some of the oldest known
fossil remains of man's early ancestors. The discoveries made by Dr.
and Mrs. L. S. B. Leakey suggest that East Africa rather than Asia
may have been the cradle of early man.

Little is as yet known of the history of Tanzania's interior
during the early centuries of the Christian era. The area is believed
to have been originally inhabited by ethnic groups using a click
tongue similar to that of southern Africa's Bushmen and Hottentots.
While remanants of these early tribes still exist, most were gradually
displaced by Bantu agriculturalists migrating from the west and south
and by Nilotes and related peoples coming from the north. A number
of these groups had well-organized societies and controlled extensive
areas by the time the Arab slavers and European explorers and missionaries penetrated the interior in the first half of the 19th century.

Although the coastal territory of Tanzania was long visited by
Arabs and Portugese sailors, it was not until the 19th century that
the interior began to be opened up by German and other European
missionaries. In 1871, the village of Ujiji on Lake Tanganyika, Living-
stone was found by Stanley. Ruled as a German colony from 1884,
the territory formed the major part of German East Africa until Germany's defeat in W.W.I. Development in the colony was slow until
after W.W. II. Then, under the proding of successive UN visiting
missions, Tanzania's economic, social, and political development was
accelerated. With the emergence of a strong African nationalist movement in the late 1950's, the territory proceeded rapidly along the road
to self-government (May 1961) and independence (1961).

## Government--Political Conditions--Economy

Tanzania is a *de jure* single-party with a strong central executive. The President is assisted by two Vice Presidents, one of whom is also designated Prime Minister. The President and the members of the National Assembly are elected concurrently by direct popular vote for five year terms. The unicameral National Assembly currently has 120 elected members. Mainland Tanzania has had, since 1964, a three-tiered judiciary which combines the jurisdictions of tribal, Islamic, and British common law. Appeal is from the primary courts through the district courts to the High Court. For administrative purposes the country is divided into 24 Regions.

The locus of political power in mainland Tanzania lies within the Tanganyika African National Union (Tanu), the dominant political organization since before independence. Constitutionally recognized as the only political party of the state, it is also the primary instigator of policy in the social, political, and economic fields. TANU functions as the bridge between the government and the people, provides nearly all top government leaders, and plays a leading role in the government scheme of nation-building. President Nyerere is President of TANU, and the party's control structure is closely interwoven with that of the government.

Tanzania's economy is predominantly agricultural and pastoral. The main cash crops for export are sisal (used for making rope), cotton and coffee representing 40 percent of all exports. The government has had some success in diversifying the country's agricultural base which now includes cashew nuts, tea, tobacco, pyrethrum (used in insecticides) and sugar. Livestock production is also expanding. The islands of Zanzibar and Pemba are known worldwide for their production of spices and cloves.

## Education

The official objective of education in Tanzania is a minimum of an eight-year primary course for all children. To this end every district in the country has a primary school, either government or voluntary, under the overall direction of the Ministry of National Education. About one-half of the country's youngsters can now be accommodated in the early primary grades, but facilities from grade five to grade eight are still very limited. The literacy rate is only five to ten percent and primarily results from economical reasons and lack of the understanding of the need for an education.

The system of elementary and secondary education leads to an examination equivalent to an American high school diploma. Two years of post-secondary education are required for university entrance; several colleges throughout the nation exist for professional and higher education preparation. The University of Dar es Salaam, formerly one branch of the University of East Africa (with Uganda and Kenya), is the major institution of higher education in Tanzania today.

The philosophy of Tanzania's educational system is to implement the country's policy of Socialism and Self-Reliance which was introduced in the Arusha Declaration of 1967. This means that the educational system fosters the social goals of living together and working together for the benefit of all. It is trying to prepare the young people to play a dynamic role and constructive part in the development of a society in which all members share fairly in the good of all the community. It emphasizes cooperative endeavor and stresses concepts of equality. In other words, the educational policy is well guided by President Nyerere's paper on "Education for Self-Reliance."

## Physical Education

Little documentary information is available on the development of physical education in Tanzania. However, three stages might be identified as follows: The cultural patterns found in pre-colonial tribes represent the first stage, where no formal education existed and physical activities were stressed as a means of informal education. This was seen in the dances that were organized by the natives to celebrate, mourn, and pay tribute. Dancing has always been the strongest expression of community feeling. The people dance before their leaders, they dance for special occasions—hunting, war, rain, and harvest, and they dance just because they feel like it.

The children were trained to be vigorous and strong before they were allowed to go into the bush on their own to herd cattle. During leisure time, the village youth performed dances and strenuous exercises such as tug-of-war, running, wrestling, swimming, and boating. Winners were given special recognition by their peers and by the adults of the tribe, providing motivation to excel.

The second stage of physical education and games development in Tanzania came during the colonial period. First, the Germans organized formal schools for the development of civil servants to carry on governmental functions. There was little emphasis on physical activities and even the indigenous activities of the people were neglected in favor of formal academic work. Although the German colonial administration brought cash crops, railroads, and roads to Tanzania, its harsh actions provoked African resistance which culminated in the Maji Maji rebellion of 1905.

When the British took over the United Nations Trust, following W. W. I., they came in large numbers and introduced their games and sports programs as an after school (work) release. Scholasticism and emphasis on the academic curriculum left little time in the school schedule for physical education instruction. The British introduced soccer, cricket, rugby, field hockey, lawn tennis, table tennis, netball, and badminton, with soccer becoming the nationals port of Tanzania. Instruction and play time were provided in after-school hours. Later there were some attempts to schedule physical education classes during the school day; activities were of a quite formal nature emphasizing disciplinary type exercises such as marching, gymnastics, and calisthenics, which were unpopular compared to the after school games program.

Since independence was achieved, the third stage of development of education and physical education has taken place. A large increase in school enrollment has resulted from the adoption of free education and from the abandonment of the colonial triparte system (schools for Europeans, Asians, and for Africans). Today, 48.6% of school age children are enrolled. Physical education in all primary schools, secondary schools and Colleges of National Education, where students are taught to become teachers, is run by the Ministry of National Education. The newly formed Ministry of National Culture and Youth gives technical assistance in sports and games during physical education seminars.

The Ministry of National Education has developed syllabi for primary schools and Colleges of National Education. Objectives are in accordance with the country's policy of Socialism and Self-Reliance:

1. To enable primary school children to achieve physical fitness and smartness.

2. To build the spirit of self-reliance and confidence.

3. To train the children or pupils in the Philosophy of Socialism and Self-Reliance, by playing together, making improvised physical education equipment, dancing together, etc.

4. To help the children achieve high standards of technique and skill in different sports and games.

5. To create a love of sports activities in the minds of pupils --their future participation in sports and games.

6. To train the pupils to become good athletes and sportsmen who can represent Tanzania in international competition.

7. To develop an inquiring mind and pupil's thinking approach to learning and to train them to think for themselves.

8. To build and maintain the national culture.

Physical education and sports programs have changed over the years and may be classified as eclectic. Popular activities of the colonists have been maintained and in addition the games and sports found in international competitions (the African, Commonwealth, and the Olympic Games) have been adopted to some extent. The physical education administrators in the Ministry of Education hope to develop a syllabus for secondary schools in the near future and believe that if the objectives of physical education outlined above are achieved, that Tanzania will be able to produce good sportsmen and women, strong and happy people, and a healthy nation in the future.

## Traditional (Indigenous) Activities

There has been an effort to bring back some of the indigenous games and dances that were so popular in the past tribal days. The Christian missionaries had discouraged many of the indigenous rituals as pagan and undesirable. New awakenings of nationalistic spirit and pride in traditional culture has led to the revival of such activities and the President has given his blessing to such a development. Some of the most known and liked were wrestling, archery, naga (the game resembling hockey), running, spear and club throwing, stick fighting, oro (throwing spears through a rolling hoop), tikli, dandi, naga, moto mlimani (fire on the mountain), tafuta nafasi (find a place), mbuzi no chui (a goat and a leopard), and dancing which includes gymnastic exercises. These were mainly played and enjoyed by men. The women folk had only minor games pertaining to their housework-- grinding and pounding grain, etc. They also did a lot of dancing to make their upper and lower body parts more flexible. Under the new system of Education for Self-Reliance women have equal status with men.

## Sports and Games

The priorities for sports are much higher than for physical education in Tanzania. Observing the tremendous prestige derived by neighboring Kenya after their Olympic Games track and field victories in Mexico City and Munich, Tanzania saw the value of a good sports program. Today, this sports emphasis has paid off handsomely as Filbert Bayi of 1500 meter fame has become a world-class athlete of whom Tanzania is justly proud.

In order to catch up with the world of sport, Tanzania has embarked on a sports development program supported by political leaders, with TANU (the only recognized political party) giving high priority to sports; treating it as a part of the national culture and putting sports development on the same status as other developmental projects. The Ministry of National Education had been entrusted by the government to run the sports program but this has been changed and added emphasis has been given by the formation of a new Minis- try--that of National Culture and Youth to carry out all sports of the nation.

The new Ministry of National Culture and Youth made immediate steps for improvement by posting sports officers in each of the 20 regions. These officers have a good knowledge of sports administra- tion with most of them having experience as sport and physical edu- cation teachers for some time. The government also plans to post district sport officers within a year's time. In line with the objective of "Sports for All", Tanzania is embarking on the formation of many sports associations as there are in the world of sports. In addition to the world sports, Tanzania is shortly reintroducing the traditional sports and games of the country. If everything goes as planned, sports will be played and enjoyed from the village level to the national level.  Many more talented sportsmen will be picked to represent Tanzania in international competitions and so put this nation in the world of today's sport scene.

The following is the present sport organization structure in Tanzania:

Ministry of National Culture and Youth

Department of Youth

Sport and Games

National Sports Council
(National Sports Associations)
(Tanzanian Olympic Committee)
(School & College Sport Committee)

Regional Sports Council
(Regional Sports Associations)

District Sports Council
(District Sports Associations)

Divisional Sports Council
(Divisional Sports Associations)

Ward Sports Council
(Ward Sports Associations)

Village Sports Council
(Village Sports Associations)

In rank order of their current popularity in Tanzania are the following sports:  football (soccer), athletics (track and field), boxing, basketball, volleyball, lawn tennis, table tennis, badminton, netball, cricket, swimming, field hockey, and rugby.  Because of the lack of good sports programs and qualified coaches in the primary schools, secondary schools, and colleges for the development of players, a feeder system as found in the schools of the United States does not exist as yet.  Sports associations and clubs have junior organizations to assist in player development and the newer development of the Ministry of National Culture and Youth is a long step toward sports program improvement.


Teacher Education and Coaches Training

Plans are being formulated for a long awaited Institute of Physical Education and Sport to provide for the preparation of physical education teachers and games coaches for all of Tanzania.  To date there are only a few adequately educated physical educators and even fewer qualified coaching specialists.  The country has been and still is sending teachers overseas to study physical education every year. Local physical education seminars are run once or twice a year nationally and some emphasis is given to physical education and games in the National Colleges of Education which prepares primary teachers. Some teacher-coach preparation efforts are being made at the University of Dar es Salaam. Sports leaders have identified major problems as:

1. Lack of sufficient facilities and sports.
2. Lack of knowledge of modern sport and games by the public.
3. The insufficiency of physical education teachers.
4. The insufficiency of qualified coaches.
5. Lack of funds.

It is not an easy matter to overcome the above problems but Tanzanian sport leaders feel that the problems can be resolved through their policy of "Freedom is work!", and through the motto of the Arusha Declaration, "Socialism and Self-reliance."

## University of Dar es Salaam

One of the first major decisions taken by the Government of Tanzania immediately after coming into power, was to establish a University College which would in due course develop into a fully fledged University. Five months later, the Government was ready with a draft bill to establish a Provisional Council for the planning, construction and establishment of a University College in Dar es Salaam. This action was to a large degree the "brain child" of the only President that Tanzania has had as he was a former teacher and greatly interested in promoting education in his new nation.

The University opened with a Faculty of Law and followed soon with Arts and Social Science, Science, Medicine, Agriculture, and Engineering. Education and Physical Education are included in the Faculty of Arts and Social Science and sports activities are in the Dean of Students area of responsibility.

Fourteen sports clubs provide a good intramural type program for the 2000 students at the University "Observation Hill Campus" and smaller programs are found at the Agriculture and Medicine Centers. Excellent outdoor facilities have been provided including a large swimming pool; two soccer fields; one rugby field; one cricket pitch; one field hockey area; one basketball court; two volleyball courts; two netball courts; four lawn tennis courts; and one badminton court. Boxing and weight training areas are also provided. Typically, hall (dormitory) competitions are held the first term and then all-star teams are selected to prepare for the All-University Games which are held annually just before Christmas. This program is quite successful and has developed a great deal of interest among the students.

The other aspects of the physical education program leaves much to be desired. Each student in the Education Department selects two major areas of interest (two primary areas) and then also indicates an optional area. Physical education is still categorized as an optional subject and is offered only once per week for the third year's program. This obviously is not enough time to cover minimum essentials of theory and practice for teacher-coaching preparation.

The present games coach, Erasto Zambi, studied for some time at the University of Guelph in Canada and is very active in the Tanzania National Sports Council and the Tanzanian Olympic Committee. The first coach, Savji Dusara, who was instrumental in developing the present program, just completed his master's degree in physical education at Brigham Young University, Provo, Utah and has started on his Ph.D. Four Fulbright grantees (Professor Dailey and McNeil of Oregon State University, Professor Adams of San Fernando Valley University and Professor Johnson of the University of Illinois) have assisted in the physical education and sports programs. Coaching specialists who have contributed a great deal to the sports programs included Mal Whitfield (former Olympic Gold Medal winner) of the United States who has been a sports diplomat in Africa for the Department of State for nearly two decades. Also in track and field was Werner Kramer of the Deutsches Democratic Republic of Germany who was successful in developing the abilities of Filbert Bayi. Victor Stanculescu of Rumania was a visiting soccer (football) coach, and Salvatore "Red" Verderame of the United States made several trips to assist in the development of basketball at the University of Dar es Salaam and in other countries in Africa.

## Acknowledgments

The writer is greatly indebted to Erasto Zambi, Director of Sports and Physical Education, University of Dar es Salaam, for providing material for this article. E. M. Sulus, Sports Official and Physical Education Tutor also provided information which was helpful for the completion of the section on the Ministry of National Culture and Youth. The students in the physical education and games class, 1973-74, were especially cooperative in submitting additional materials on topics such as indigenous games; special recognition is accorded to Miss Kosgei, and to Misters Mwangungulu, Ng'atigwa, Nyarunda, Seka, and Rugaihurza.

# SELECTED REFERENCES

1.  Dusara, Savji. University of Dar es Salaam, Tanzania. Correspondence with former Games Coach. Topic--The Development of the Physical Education and Sports Program. 1973. 1974.

2.  Johnson, William. "Physical Education and Sport in Tanzania." *JOHPER*, Washington, D. C. June 1974.

3.  Sulus, E. M. "The Development of Sport and Physical Education in Tanzania Since 1961." Paper presented at an International Sport and Physical Education Seminar at Long Beach State University. Summer Session, 1974.

4.  "Tanzania--Background Notes." *Department of State--United States*. Office of Media Services--Bureau of Public Affairs. Washington, D. C. Revised, December 1974.

5.  Thompson, E. M. "Other Lands Other Peoples." *National Education Association*. Washington, D. C. 1964.

6.  Zambi, Erasto. University of Dar es Salaam, Tanzania. Interviews. Topic--Physical Education and Sport in the Schools of Tanzania. 1973-1974.

# SPORT AND PHYSICAL EDUCATION IN TURKEY
by Oz Demir Karatun


## Biographical Sketch


*Oz Demir Karatun* was born in Afyon, Turkey in 1930. After completing his primary and secondary education, he graduated from the Turkish Naval College in 1950 and Gazi Teacher College and Educational Institute in 1953. Following his graduation he began teaching at the Turkish Naval Schools and also participated in several training programs of CISM (Conseil International du Sports Militaire) Academy in Sweden, France and West Germany. In 1959 he received a Degree of Merit in Physical Training and Sports from the Army School of Physical Training in Aldershot, England. He became one of the permanent members of the Turkish National Olympic Committee in 1969. Between the years of 1953-1970 he not only taught and administered sports and physical education in naval and other civilian schools at all educational levels, but also served in several sports federations and gained wide experience in physical education and sports both at national and international levels.

In 1971 he moved to the United States of America and completed a M.S. degree in 1972 and a Ph.D. in 1974, both with honors, in exercise physiology, at the University of Kansas, Lawrence, Kansas. During his doctoral study he became interested in a new and growing field: Cardiac Rehabilitation. In 1975 Dr. Karatun was the research fellow in the Cardiac Rehabilitation Program at the University of Wisconsin and Gundersen Clinic, La Crosse, Wisconsin. During the years of 1976-1977 he was the Director of Cardiac Rehabilitation and Evaluation Department at St. Mary's Hospital, Galesburg, Illinois. Dr. Karatun is presently the Associate Director of CAPRI - Cardio Pulmonary Research Institute in Seattle, Washington, which operates one of the largest cardiac rehabilitation programs in the United States.

## General Background

### History

Turkey's history goes back 7000 years. But recorded history begins with the Hittites. In the excavations carried out at the capital city of the Hittites in Central Anotolia, Bogozky, records have been found which illuminate a period of 4000 years. After the Hittites, the Phrygians, Lydians, Carrians, Dorians, Persians, Greeks, Romans, and Byzantines were seen in Anotolia. Following the Byzantines Seljuk Turks established a state in Anatolia; they were followed by the Ottoman Empire, which lasted from the 14th century to the 20th century.

The survival of Anatolian elements in modern Turkey is now beyond dispute. There is no need to assert that the Turks are Hittites or that the Hittites were Turks, but it is clear that there was a large measure of continuity. This becomes clear with the parallel progress of archaeological and anthropoligcal work in Anotolia today. The name "Turkey" has been given by Europeans to Turkish speaking Anotolia almost since its first conquest by the Turks. But the Turks themselves did not adopt it as the official name for their country and until 1923. When they did so, they used the form "Turkiye".

The recent history of Turkey starts with the Seljuk Turks, who originally came from the regions of Caspian Sea and first conquered parts of Persia, Mesopotamia, Syria and finally Anatolia. The Seljuks ruled Anatolia from the 11th century to the end of the 13th century and made an important contribution to Turkish culture and administration.

As Seljuk power declined after 1243, a number of smaller principalities arose. One of them, in northwestern Anatolia, ruled by Osman, emerged supreme in the local struggle for power and established the Ottoman state. After consolidating their rule in Anatolia, the Ottoman armies crossed into Europe in the middle of the 14th century and by 1400 were masters of Anatolia and part of the Balkans. Mehmet II (Fatih Sultan Mehmet) defeated the Byzantines and captured Constantinople (Istanbul) in 1453 and opened new horizons for the Turkish warriors.

Selim I, stopped the Persian influence definitely with the Chaldran Battle in 1514 and also defeated the Mamlukes of Egypt in 1517. The Empire reached its golden age during the rule of Suleyman the Magnificent (Kanuni Sultan Suleyman), whose tremendous fanfare of titles, given below, is enough to give the idea of the extent of the Ottoman power in that time:

I, who am Sultan of the Sultans of East and West, fortunate lord of the domains of the Romans, Persians and Arabs, Hero of creation, Champion of the earth and time, Padishah and Sultan of the Mediterranean and the Black Sea, of the extolled Kaaba and Madina the illustrious and Jerusalem the noble,

of the throne of Egypt and the province of Yemen, Aden
and San'a, of Baghdad and Basra and Lasha and Ctesiphon,
of the lands of Algiers and Azerbaijan, of the region of the
Kipchaks and the land of the Tartars, of Kurdistan and
Luristan and all Rumelia, Anatolia and Karaman, of Walla-
chia and Moldavia and Hungary and many kingdoms and
lands besides; the Sultan Suleyman Khan, son of the Sultan
Selim Khan.

At the end of the 17th century, external causes which were
the rise of new powerful empires in Europe, the overextension of
frontiers becoming difficult to defend, shifts in the trade routes of
the world from Mediterranean to the Atlantic, and the internal causes
which were the failure to modernize the main institutions of the empire
and not to participate in the industrial revolution, and most important,
the rise of separtist and nationalist movements; shook the very foundations of empire and started the decline. All the effort of the young
Turks' organization and the constitutional government trials did not
save the "sick man of Europe". At the end of the first world war
the empire collapsed and an armistice agreement was signed by British
and Turkish representatives on board "H.M.S. Agamemnon", at anchor
off Mudros, in the island of Lemnos, on 30 October, 1918, and the
partitioning of Turkey took place. While Sultan Mehmet VI (Vahdettin),
did not resist the occupation forces in order to keep his throne, the
Turkish nationalist forces led by Mustapa Kemal (Ataturk) fought a
war of Turkish Liberation known in Turkish as "Istiklal Harbi", or
the war of independence. Ataturk, Farther of the Turks, founded a
new state, new nation, a new country from the smoking ruins of the
old Empire. According to Lord Kinross he was an outstanding soldier-
statesman in the first half of the 20th century. When the Turkish
Republic was proclaimed on October 29, 1923, Ataturk became the
first President of the Turkish Republic. During his 15 year administration (1923-38) many basic reforms were introduced to transform
this islamic state into a modern westernized country. According to
many researchers his social and cultural reforms were much more in-
credible than his brilliant military career. He always believed in the
young generation and entrusted the Republic to their hands.

Ataturk reforms and ideas namely, Kemalism, have always been
a guiding light to this young progressive, open minded generation.
When there was a shadow on this young democratic republic on May 27,
1960, the officers of "his" trusted generation saved the country once
more and handed all the power to the constitutional elected government in one year.

Indeed, Turkey's political problems remain far from resolved.
She needs some time to complete her political achievements in modernization with social, economic and cultural accomplishments.

The personality, social and moral characteristics of the Turks
are probably the best analyzed and described by the British journalist,
Hotram, in the following passage from his recently published book:
"The Turks."

"To understand the Turks, it is essential to grasp two main
points: first, that the Turks are a people who have never
been conquered or colonized by other peoples, but historically
have always been themselves rulers; secondly, that unlike
most other peoples, they are neither purely European nor
purely non-European, but are a peculiar and interesting mixture of the two.........................Anybody who visits
Turkey for the first time is almost invariably struck by how
different the Turks are from preconceived notions of them:
kind, understanding, sincere, immensely hospitable, intuitive-
ly intelligent, and surprisingly artistic...."

## Geography

Modern Turkey occupies a small corner of the European Peninsula of Thrace, and the Asian Anatolian Peninsula also called Asia
Minor and lies between latitudes of 36° and 42° north. It is bounded
on the north by the Black Sea and south by the Mediterranean.
Turkey may be viewed as a western extension of the high mountains
and plateau of the Asian interior. Its total area, including lakes, is
780,576 square Km. (302,169 square miles.)

## Climate

In general terms, the climate of most of Turkey can be described as a dry, semi-continental variant of the Mediterranean type
or alternatively as transitional between the Mediterranean and temperate continental regimes. The population was 40 million in 1973.

## Language and Religion

Ninety percent of the population claim Turkish as their mother
tongue and the only sizable minorities are those speaking Kurdish
(2.2 million) and Arabic (.3 million). Ninety-nine percent of the
population professes adherence to Islam. There are 38,000 Jews and
206,000 Christians.

## Economy and Industry

According to official estimates, agriculture was responsible for
34.9 percent of the national income in 1967 and was dominant in
Turkish foreign trade. In 1967, at least 80 percent of the country's
exports were in the form of agricultural produce, with cotton (25 percent) and tobacco (23 percent) in the lead. Other important items
were raisins, figs, hazel nuts, olive oil, hides and skins. In 1967
machinery and transport equipment was the major part of the import
(42 percent). In 1965 there were about 13 million cattle of which
four million were dairy cattle, 20 million goats, including 5.5 million
of the "Angora" variety, and 33 million sheep. Turkey's mineral resources cover a wide range, including coal, chrome, copper, iron,

sulphur, manganese, mercury, bauxite and others.  As regards power, Turkey is fortunate in possessing sufficient coal for her present industrial needs.  But, oil has so far been discovered only in modest quantities.  The production of electricity, increased much in recent decades, is still very low.  The output of 7,830 million KWH in 1969 represented a supply of only 235 KWH per capita, about one-twentieth of that of Western Europe.  The most important branch of manufacturing industry is the production of textiles.

## Communication

The war of Independence showed up the inefficiency and poor condition of the roads and railways, when village women walked over the mountains of the Black Sea coast, carrying shells on their backs for the Nationalist guns in the interior.  But in 1969 the length of roads increased to 59,524 Km. and the railroads to 40,657 Km.  The gross tonnage of shipping increased to 3,500,000 while Turkish airlines have extended their routes worldwide in the last decade.

## Education

From the Seljuks to the Empire's last stage, the religious hierarchy controlled all education in Turkey.  The first western type educational institutions were military schools.  The Naval Engineering School (the origin of the Turkish Naval Academy) established in 1773 and the Military Academy in 1793.  In 1827, Sultan Mahmut, the reformer, established the Istanbul Medical School and later a military science school and brought a foreign, principally French, teaching staff from Europe.  The Ministry of Education was created in 1847 and western school adoptation was effectively started.  But as Nuri Eren said in "Turkey Today and Tomorrow", all these efforts remained fragmentary and dogmatic muslim scholasticism was broken completely only after the adoption of the Latin alphabet by Kemal Ataturk.  In less than a half century under the republic, educational progress leaped further ahead than all the advances in the five hundred years under the Ottomans.

The educational progress should be recognized as the highest achievement in the development and modernization struggle of the first fifty years of the republic.  Although the country's population has almost tripled, the goals which were set in 1923 for primary education had been 90% accomplished in 1973.  Table I shows this educational progress in the primary, secondary and higher educational institutions in terms of increased number of schools, teachers and students.

In the last 20 years, four new universities opened their doors for public service and the nation had achieved a more than tenfold increase in the number of schools and teachers.  Table II shows the progress rate of education between 1962 and 1969.

# Table I. Educational Progress in Last 50 Years.

| | Number of Schools | | Number of Teachers | | Number of Students | |
|---|---|---|---|---|---|---|
| | 1923 | 1973 | 1923 | 1973 | 1923 | 1973 |
| PRIMARY EDUCATION | 4,894 | 40,154 | 10,238 | 157,167 | 341,941 | 5,220,426 |
| SECONDARY EDUCATION | 159 | 6,267 | 1,891 | 75,597 | 13,493 | 2,778,910 |
| HIGHER EDUCATION | 9 | 123 | 307 | 9.818 | 2,914 | 174,774 |

# Table II. Flows to Upper Levels (Public and Private) in Education.

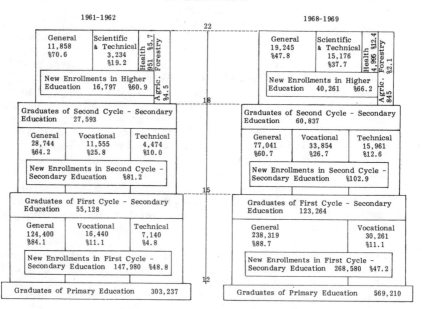

## History of Physical Education

Because of the wide boundaries of the empire, the Ottoman Sultans always paid a special attention to their army, and the young generation was kept as fit warriors, ready to fight. Therefore, the physical activities of military nature such as horsemanship, swordsmanship, archery and wrestling were the major sports during the old days.

Like all reforms, the army brought western type physical education into the country. As mentioned above the Naval Engineering School and the Military Academy were the first institutions which applied a western curriculum and employed European instructors. With this influence in mind, the physical education, especially German ecole showed an organized character in all higher educational institutions at the end of the 19th century. But, as a world influence, the Swedish ecole also affected physical education in Turkey in the first decade of the 20th century. Selim Sirri Tarcan who is accepted as the father of modern physical education in Turkey, was not only the only one who brought Swedish gymnastics to the country but he also made a tremendous effort to make it known to the people. When physical education became a requirement in the public schools in the early ages of the republic, Selim Sirri Tarcan and his Swedish colleague, Mr. Johnson, opened several short term courses to meet the physical education teacher needs of the country. These courses went on in the Chapa educational institute for several years. On the other hand extramural athletic activities developed in another direction during the same years. When the French and English occupation forces started their athletic practice to keep their soldiers fit in Istanbul, some Turkish teams were also formed to compete with these foreign forces teams, especially in soccer. The most popular sports clubs of Istanbul such as Fenerbahce and Galatasaray were officially formed in those days. In the republic reorganization, the sports clubs formed the Turkish Athletic Clubs Federation (Turkiye Idam Cemiyetleri Ittifaki) to administer the athletic activities country wide. The programs of this federation and the competitive atmosphere between the local sports clubs developed the physical education and sports concept highly in the country between 1920 and 1935.

In 1938, parliament discussed the first bill for physical education in detail. And from this date, physical education gained legality in the country. According to this law (No. 3550) the government would administer and control physical education. A country wide physical education organization was established. Every province (it was 63 in that time and 67 now) became a physical district and all these districts were administered from a central organization. General Directorate of Physical Education (Beden Terbiyesi Genel Mudurlugu), which was located in Anrara, was connected directly to the prime minister.

According to this law, which is still valid, all sports clubs of the country, were classified in four categories: (1) Youth Clubs, formed by the local communities; (2) Special Sports Clubs, formed and allowed only for one sportive area (for example, tennis club, swimming club); (3) Institutional Sports Clubs formed for the members or employers of an institution or factory; (4) Military Sports Clubs, formed by military units for military personnel.

The same law gave the obligation of instruction of physical education to the ministry of National Education for Schools, the Ministry of National Defense for the Armed Forces and the Ministry of Interior Affairs and Security, for police, gendarmery forces and prisoners.

One of the stipulations of this physical education law was the compulsory physical training for the Turkish citizens. Every institution or factory which employed more than 200 men had to set up a daily physical training program for its employees. These employees of each institution formed the physical training unit, and units formed the companies, and companies further formed the regiments in one region. The local regiments had periodic practices together under the responsibility and supervision of the provincial physical education department which was instructed and controlled by the central organization: General Directorate of Physical Education. This program seemed very much like the basic fitness training of the military troops.

The first General Director of Physical Education was a retired general, Cemal Taner. He did everything possible to make this program work. His efforts and physical education concepts should probably be seen as an effort to maintain the fitness and morale of the young generation following a successful revolution, War of Independence, under the leadership of a strong military leader, Kemal Ataturk.

After a short period of practice, this compulsory program was abandoned. It was not well received, neither by the participants nor the employers of the institutions. It was not only impractical, but its compulsory participation was a kind of violation of the new democratic constitutional rights of freedom of the citizens.

The same organization, the General Directorate of Physical Education administered physical education and sports in the country as a highest authority until 1970. The above mentioned law states that "the primary mission of the General Directorate of Physical Education, is to develop the physical and moral qualities of the Turkish citizens." Between 1939-71, this organization and its federations in 21 sportive branches increased the number of participations and meets every year gradually adding some modern facilities to the old ones, represented the country successfully in many international competitions; but, whether the main mission was accomplished or not, is still a matter of discussion in the country.

In 1970, the government decided to institute a reform in sports and physical education organizations in the country. This time "the Ministry of Youth and Sports" was established and the General Directorate of Physical Education was kept as an active part of this ministry to administer sportive activities. Table III and Table IV shows the present organization of the ministry of youth and sports and the directorate of physical education.

# Table III.   Ministry of Sports and Youth.

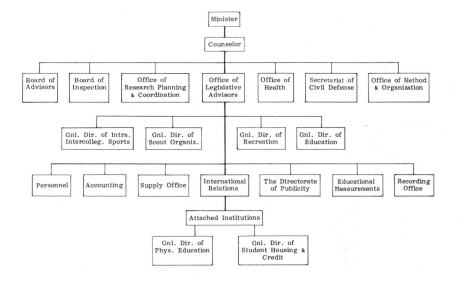

# Table IV.   General Directorate of Physical Education.

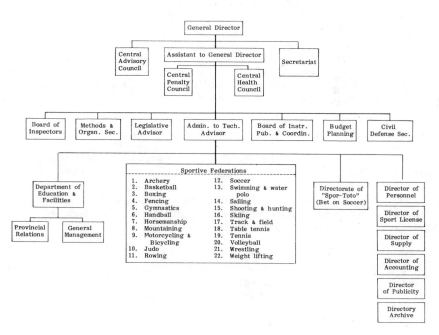

## Elementary School Physical Education

Elementary school education which is compulsory for every Turkish child, is required for five years. There are no public pre-school or kindergarten institutions. Nevertheless in the big cities many of the private elementary schools have opened kindergarten sections lately.

Generally, elementary school physical education is taught by the classroom teachers. Nevertheless, since 1970 some of the elementary school teachers attended a short, condensed training program offered by the Ministry of Sports and Youth and have been transferred to elementary school physical education teacher positions. The number of elementary school physical education teachers who were trained with this new program number 2000 at the present time. This ongoing procedure seems to be continued until the demand has been met and/or the teacher training institutions include the elementray school physical education teacher training program into their curriculum.

In the general curriculum, the physical education class is one hour a week, but the class teachers are encouraged to use every possibility to create game-like activities out of the classroom every day, during the one and one half hour rest period between the morning and afternoon class hours. In the first three years of elementary school education, physical education class activities include imitiative type body movements, minor games, basic postural and corrective positions and marching and running disciplines. In the last two years of this educational level the imitative exercises yield their place to more rhythmic, expressive and creative exercises, the games are more developed and include the mental progress of the child as well as the physical. Round dances and their folkloric type variations are practiced in (Yavru Kurt) young scout activities which are organized in almost every elementary school in the country.

## High School Physical Education and Sports

As it is shown in Table II the secondary education has two, three year cycles. According to their age and interest the physical education class programs show different characteristics. In both cycles the weekly class period is one hour. But every Wednesday afternoon is reserved for intramural and interschool athletic activities. In the first cycle, the basic class activities include:

a. Formative disciplinary walks and runs.
b. Calisthenics and rhythmic exercises.
c. Activities with and on apparatus.
d. Basic and preparatory skills of major athletic activities in relay form.

In the second cycle in addition to these activities some of the very popular athletic activities such as soccer, volleyball, basketball, wrestling are taught in the block education system.

One of the biggest problems in high school physical education is the lack of gymnasium or physical education classrooms. Only three persent of the high schools have gymnasia, in the other schools all physical education activities are carried out in the school yard if the weather permits.

Recent efforts of the Ministry of Sports and Youth seem to bring a practical solution to this problem. The construction sites for the public sports facilities are planned within a very close vicinity of the high school so that the same facilities could be used by the school during class hours and by the public after class hours.

Physical Education is taught by the physical education teachers. In the first cycle the classes are usually coeducational and taught by either male or female teachers. But in the second cycle, in spite of the fact that most of the schools are coeducational, physical education classes are taught separately and preferably the girls by female and the boys by male teachers. But another big problem of high school physical education in the country is the lack of physical education teachers.

According to the present curriculum and number of schools, 6000 physical education teachers are needed in the secondary education, but the number of active teachers is only 1600. Therefore 75% of the high school physical education classes are taught by substitute teachers. In the last 6 years, with the addition of five new teacher training colleges, the number of graduates has increased from 150 per year in 1971 to 575 per year in 1978. At least 8 years are necessary to close the present gap if all the present and new graduates remain within active teaching and do not desire to be transferred to administrative positions in the school system.

Preparation of the "May 19th" mass gymnastics demonstrations, which are held every year in every corner of the country, occupies an important place in physical education classes on the last month of the educational year. Activities for this mass demonstration are mostly rhythmical and are set up carefully by a special committee in every city or town and are carried out in company with the city bands.

Interscholastic athletic activities are very well organized both in the city and country levels, especially in the secondary cycle of the high schools. First every school selects their teams for intramural activities in soccer, volleyball, basketball, track and field and wrestling. Then those school teams meet each other for the provincial championship. The next step is the country wide championship which is organized and all participation expenses are paid by the ministry of youth and sports.

Almost every high school has a boys and girls scout organization and their drum and trumpet teams are used as a school band. Unfortunately all these teams participate more in demonstrative type activities than in ideal scout duties.

## College University Physical Education and Sports

Since physical education is not a requirement at the higher education level, none of the colleges offer physical education courses except the physical education teachers training colleges. Nevertheless, each of these colleges is supposed to have a faculty member in physical education for the organization, planning and conducting of extracurricular physical education and sports activities. In every university, most of the departments have their own sports clubs and teams in major athletic branches and participate in the amateur leagues of the local sports clubs in their province.

Similar to the high school championship, the country wide championship between the Turkish university and vocational college teams is held by the ministry of youth and sports. In fact, in addition to student senate budgets, the university sports clubs are financially supported with equipment, facilities and/or cash by the ministry of youth and sports.

## Teacher Education Programs in Physical Education

The influence of Swedish physical education, which was introduced by Selim Sirri Tarcan and his Swedish colleague, Mr. Johnson, formed the basic curriculum of Turkish physical education institutions at their foundation. In the following years this basic curriculum did not change much, because of the teaching and administration teams of these institutions, which included professors who graduated from Swedish physical education schools. Since this "ecole" was primarily accepted as corrective in nature, the curriculum was supplemented by biological science courses which are given in Table V. All physical education major students have to attend these courses full time.

Skiing, swimming and scout leadership are taught in special training camps opened in appropriate locations during the semester and/or summer breaks.

The Gazi Educational Institute, which has 100 gradutes per year, was the only physical education teacher training college until 1968. In the last ten years, the number of similar institutions has increased to seven and the number of graduates to 575 per year.

## Table V. The Curriculum of "Gazi" Physical Education Institute

| Subjects | First Year | Second Year | Third Year |
|---|:---:|:---:|:---:|
| Physiology | x | x | — |
| Anatomy | x | x | — |
| First Aid | x | — | — |
| Distinctive Pathology | — | — | x |
| Body Health | x | x | — |
| Medical Gym. and Massage | — | x | x |
| Theories of Gymnastics | — | x | x |
| Games and Sports | — | x | x |
| History of Physical Education | x | — | — |
| Psychology of Childhood and Adolescence | x | — | — |
| Education Psychology | x | — | — |
| Methods of Teaching | — | x | — |
| Organizations of Sports | — | — | x |
| Track and Field | — | x | x |
| Gymnastics | — | x | x |
| Recreational Activities & Games | — | x | x |
| The Knowledge of Facilities & Equipments | — | x | x |
| History of Turkish Revolution | — | — | x |
| Foreign Language | — | x | x |
| Music | — | x | x |

## Summary of the General Problems and Now the Improvements

The basic problems of the country in physical education and sports can be classified as facilities, personnel, general understanding of the physical education concept and cooperation among the institutions in this area.

### The Facilities

Within the normal economic problems of a developing country it was not possible either by the government or the local communities to spend money for sports facilities. The number of major sports facilities in 1971 were:

79 Stadia
71 Gymnasia (sport hall)
14 Outdoor swimming pools
3 Indoor swimming pools

It is obviously impossible to set up an ideal physical education program for a country with a 35 million population with these facilities.

The limited budget and import permission for the sportive equipment is another problem for some sports branches.

## Personnel

As was discussed before, the need of physical education teachers still exists. The total number of active physical education teachers was only around 900 for 395,436 secondary education students in 1969. (An average of 440 students for every physical education teacher). Ninety-five percent of the administrative personnel of the central and country wide organization of the ministry of youth and sports and its active organ, the General Directorate of Physical Education does not have any educational background in the field of physical education and sports. The same is true for the administration even of the coaching members of the sports clubs.

## General Understanding of Physical
## Education Concept

The educational reform of Kemal Ataturk was not enough to change the fanatic moslem understanding of the parents and allow their children to participate in physical education activities for a long time. Even the mass gymnastics demonstrations of "May 19th" met with resistance in several towns. But, the open minded new generation is aware of the needs and the efforts required in this area, and their new world concept is extremely favorable to physical education.

## Cooperation Between Institutions

The three basic highest authorities which were responsible for physical education and sports in the country were the General Directorate of Physical Education, the Turkish National Olympic Committee, and the Ministry of Education, and its scientific institutions examined the physical education and sports problem from different angles. They were not only lacking in cooperation but also blamed each other for the ignorance of problems. Without the support of the two others, the General Directorate of Physical Education became a target for all the criticism of the press and of public opinion for the problems or unsuccessful results in sports and caused the frequent replacement of the General Director. These rapid changes ruined the continuity of the programs, and the confidence of sportsmen, made this position a political chair, and finally prevented the rapid progress of physical education in the country.

## The New Improvements

1. The establishment of the Ministry of Youth and Sports has brought the solution to many problems automatically.

2. The financial sources for sports and physical education increased to a record level in 1971 (total of 19 million dollars for the Ministry and its active organ, the General Directorate of Physical Education).

3. The "Spor-toto" (bets on soccer) became a solid income for the construction of new sports faciliities (70,000,000 TL., $4.6 million in 1971).

4. The establishment of new General Directorates in the Ministry, such as Education in Physical Education, Recreation and School Sports, will promote the basic institutions and the activities of physical education which were not very well administered before.

5. The emphasis on the educational institutions, expansion of the existing teacher training colleges in physical education and the increase in their number from 2 to 7 in the last ten years looks very promising for solving one of the most important existing problems: the need for trained personnel in physical education and sports.

6. The establishment of the physical education health centers and clinics in big cities will not only control the basic physiological performance of athletes but also develop Turkish sports medicine.

As a final touch, the physical education and sports progress in the country has covered a big distance in the last five years and has made a good beginning toward solving the major problems for a hopeful future.

## SELECTED REFERENCES

1.  Bahrampout, Firouz. *Turkey: Political and Social Transformation*. Brooklyn: Theo. Gaus Sons. 1967.

2.  Basbakanlik, T. C. Deviet Planlama Teskilati, Yili Baslica egitim istatistiklen. 1969.

3.  Beden, Terbiyesi Genel Mudurlugo. Yili butce kanunu. 1972.

4.  Cohn, Edwin J. *Turkish Economic, Social and Political Change*. New York: Praeger Publishers, 1970.

5.  Davitson, Roderic H. *Turkey*. New Jersey: Prentice-Hall. 1968.

6.  Dewdney, John C. *Turkey*. London: Chotto and Windus. 1971.

7.  Eren, Nuri. *Turkey, Today and Tomorrow, An Experiment in Westernization*. London: Pall Mall Press. 1963.

8.  Gendik ve spor Bakanligi, butce Teklifi. 1972.

9.  Kazamias, Andreas M. *Education and the Quest for Modernity in Turkey*. Chicago: University of Chicago Press. 1966.

10. Kinross, John Patrick Douglas and Balfour, Baron. *Ataturk, a Biography of Mustafa Kemal, father of Modern Turkey*, by Lord Kinross. New York: W. Morrow. 1963.

11. Kinross, John Patrick Douglas and Balfour, Baron. *Ataturk, the Rebirth of a Nation*. London: Weidenfeld and Nicholson. 1961.

12. Lewis, Bernard. *The Emergence of Modern Turkey*. Royal Institute of International Affairs. London and New York: Oxford University Press. 1961.

13. Lewis, Geoffrey L. *Turkey*. London: E. Benn. 1965.

14. *Pocket Data Book of Turkey*. State Institute of Istatistik of Turkey, Ankara. 1969.

15. Türk kültürünü Aras. Ens., Türk Dünyasi El kitabi, Ayyildiz Matbaasi. 1976.

# SPORT AND PHYSICAL EDUCATION IN UNITED STATES
by C. Lynn Vendien

## Biographical Sketch

*C. Lynn Vendien* was born and raised in Michigan. She received her bachelor's degree from Eastern Michigan University, a master's degree from the University of Michigan, and a doctorate from Stanford University. Having taught in Michigan public schools for a good many years along with Michigan State University and Stanford University, she now is professor of professional preparation of physical education at the University of Massachusetts, Amherst.

Dr. Vendien has travelled extensively throughout the world serving as a consultant and participating on conference programs both nationally and internationally. She has served as chairperson for International Relations on the state, district, and national levels and has received state and national Honor Awards.

Dr. Vendien is co-author of two international textbooks, one with John E. Nixon, *The World Today in Health, Physical Education, and Recreation*, and the other with Sara S. Jernigan, *Playtime: A World Recreation Handbook*, along with authoring numerous articles in such periodicals as Gymnasion, JOHPER, Quest, and The Physical Educator. She also is the producer of many multi-media color-sound slide presentations that have been shown in many parts of the world.

Sport and physical education in the United States today seem to be undergoing the most rapid, exciting, and perhaps controversial changes in its history. However, because of state and local autonomy with very few national requirements, it is difficult to generalize about school programs. The United States is a land of great contrasts. Extremes of geography, climate, wealth, poverty, and distribution of population in urban and rural areas all add to the diversity.

Diversity in the academic world is additionally introduced through massive numbers of publications, with many interpretations of the contemporary scene, and what it should be. Probably never before has knowledge been in such demand. In today's competitive profession, not only are college professors faced with pressures to do research and/or publish, but many sport leaders and athletes are motivated to expand sport communication through various media. It also appears today that the consumer has an unlimited appetite not only for written or visual sport news, but for any literature relating to sport. Hundreds of books, reports, and papers come off the press annually on such topics as administration, curriculum, history, philosophy, principles, tests, measurement and evaluation, exercise science, professional preparation, women and men athletes, sport studies and sport. Consequently, only selected examples of typical programs will be presented (Vendien, 1970).

## Objectives

Although the major objectives of school physical education programs have been stated by many authorities in hundreds of different ways, most Americans today agree on certain essentials. First, physical education should help in developing and maintaining physical fitness through vigorous kinds of exercise. Many different kinds of movement, sport, dance, and conditioning programs contribute toward this goal. In a Youth Sports, Physical Education, and Recreation Participation Survey, 11,419,000 elementary-through-college age individuals were reported taking part in some form of scheduled physical fitness activity. Today's youth seem motivated to participate voluntarily in fitness programs. To "run for your life" is a popular slogan, and all ages are seen jogging and cycling. Americans believe these programs should provide mentally stimulating and socially gratifying experiences. They should contribute toward one's understanding of effective, efficient bodily movement, and toward self-awareness, which in turn contributes toward proficiency in motor skills. Americans believe it is important to teach a wide variety of skills and to develop competency in some selected activities such as sports, creative movements, swimming, outdoor pursuits, and gymnastics, some of which hopefully will be satisfying enough to pursue during leisure time (Vendien, 1970). Two other objectives can be added (Siedentop,1972), a developmental objective, which is to bring about a state of readiness for playing the activities of physical education, and a counseling objective, which is to provide, with the help of the teacher or coach, opportunities for players to match their interests and abilities to various activities.

## Facilities and Program

Although limited and poor programs with inadequate facilities and instruction are still found in some areas, most programs are improving, and many schools today offer some of the finest modern education programs in curriculum content and facilities. New large regional school districts serving communities are replacing many of the old small, and usually inadequate local schools, and students are transported by buses. Multi-purpose facilities are commonly used.

Activities generally found in most schools include games, fundamental skills, movement exploration, fitness programs, perceptual motor activities, gymnastics, rhythms, track and field, and aquatics at the primary level. The middle schools and high schools add dance, team and individual sports, combatives for boys, and some outdoor pursuits (Vendien, 1970). Although some activities have been stereotyped for men and boys such as football, baseball, ice hockey, wrestling, pole vaulting, men's gymnastics, and American handball, women are becoming challenged to be involved with and to compete in some of these activities.

Some activities taught in physical education classes are of such interest that students form clubs for learning more advance skills. They produce public performances such as dance concerts, gymnastic exhibitions, and aquatic art reviews. Some highly skilled groups go on tours throughout the United States and to other countries.

## Elementary School Programs

Probably one of the most rewarding trends in American physical education is the upsurge of interest in elementary school programs. The number of regular classes per week is increasing, more physical education specialists are doing the teaching, and more men are becoming interested in this level.

Games, stunts, folk dance, and creative rhythms are still taught at this level because they are fundamental skills and part of our cultural heritage. However, there is an increasing emphasis today on movement education, perceptual motor activities, track and field, and gymnastics. Use of large apparatus as well as a wide variety of small apparatus such as skipping ropes, hoops, and balls is increasing. New, interesting, and vigorous play experiences are provided for children with use of parachutes, large inner tubes, and endless kinds of creative handmade equipment and apparatus. The abundance of various good visual aids to improve the program is encouraging (Tanner, 1970). Some physical educators today are directing attention toward the need for preschool motor development and learning programs (Halverson, 1971). Some of these programs are found in institutions of professional preparation as well as some public schools and day care centers.

## Gymnastics

Gymnastic activites are now taught in most schools on all levels from kindgergarten through college, in another upsurge in American programs. Competition in gymnastics is increasing, as is the level of skill. More research is going into teaching of gymnastics and con-structing better equipment than ever before. Because of this nation-wide interest, the increase in competition, and great need for more and better officials, many rating and training programs, have been initiated at the local, state, and national levels.

## Special Education

Both in public schools and colleges, adapted programs for the handicapped and the mentally retarded have received much attention. Leaders in the field work closely with the medical profession to deter-mine appropriate programs for education, therapy, and development. Physical activity programs can be extremely important therapeutically for the handicapped and also for the instructor, in order to discover the amount of progress the handicapped can make. The Special Olym-pics and other special competitions have become increasingly popular today for both the handicapped and mentally retarded.

The Massachusetts Comprehensive Special Education Act of 1972, Chapter 766, is but one example of what some states are doing to assure that all children with special needs receive proper educa-tion, training, and assistance that is essentially right for them. Schools have a major role in seeing that children with special needs are identified and are given the necessary help (Chapter 766, 1974).

## Sport Camps

Fifty years ago some specialty sport camps were in existence, but in the last decade specialized sport camps have mushroomed in all parts of the country. The camp is usually housed at a camp site, (sometimes specially designed for the particular sport), a college cam-pus, or private school where the participants have board and room and easy access to facilities. Camps last for one week, two weeks, three weeks, or even two months or more. They feature specific pro-gressive skills of the sport each week, or during a short-term camp, specific or progressive skills are covered each day. Different camps cater to all ages of boys and girls as well as college men and women. Camps are staffed by highly qualified coaches, often Olympic and pro-fessional athletes or coaches, many nationally and internationally known. Many Olympic and All-American athletes have gotten their start during such a concentrated experience (Mann, 1974). Partici-pants pay their own expenses and enjoy the long days of skilled in-struction and supervised practices. Occasionally these specialization camps are called schools. Some of the most popular camps feature such sports as archery, basketball, baseball, field hockey, football, gymnastics, horseback riding, sailing, skiing, swimming, tennis, and volleyball.

In 1974, the United States Gymnastics Federation opened its first pre-Olympic summer camp at the University of Nebraska, August 12-21. Seven of the nation's outstanding high school gymnasts and seven of the best college sophomores attended this first camp. The goals of the camp were to provide stimulus, develop proper training methods, and teach the 1976 Olympic compulsories (Olympic, 1974).

## Competition for Women

Probably one of the most radical changes in sport and physical education in the United States has involved women in sport. Interscholastic, intercollegiate, national and international competitions for girls and women have not only been approved but are being promoted by local, state, and national leaders today. The Association for Intercollegiate Athletics for Women and Title IX have opened up an entirely new world of sport for the female athletes.

Today, more girls and women participate at a higher level of competition and in a wider variety of sports than ever before yet, according to Griffin, those female athletes or teachers of sport are still perceived as inconsistent with the desired role models for women (Griffin, 1973). However, the image of the female athlete has changed and women take a great pride in their female role. Most medical studies are centered around the effect of reproductive organs and the menstrual cycle. In general, conclusions are that regular exercise and competitive athletics do not have a harmful effect on pregnancy. Other studies focus on physiological demands, attitudes, and sociological aspects (Vendien, 1970).

As early as 1967, the Division on Girls and Women's Sports formed a Commission on Intercollegiate Athletics for Women (CIAW) to encourage organization of colleges and universities and/or women physical educators to govern intercollegiate competition for women at the local, state, or regional level and to hold national championships as needed. In 1972, the Association for Intercollegiate Athletics for Women (AIAW) was organized and replaced CIAW to provide a governing body and leadership for initiating and maintaining standards of excellence in women's intercollegiate athletic programs (NAGWS, 1974).

## Title IX

In 1972, Title IX was passed, which is that portion of the Education Amendments of 1972 which forbids discrimination on the basis of sex in educational programs or activities which receive Federal funds (HEW, 1975). In determining equal opportunities in athletics, consideration should be given to such factors as 1--whether the sports selected reflect the interests and competitive abilities of both sexes; 2--providing equal access to supplies and equipment, game and practice schedules, locker rooms and facilities; and 3--providing medical and training services, coaching and academic tutoring opportunities, publicity, housing and dining facilities as well as travel and per diem allowances.  Also the enrollment ratio of men and women students may be used as a criterion to determine equitable distribution of program dollars.

There have been a few court cases in which girls interested in a particular sport were allowed to play on a boys' team for which no girls' team existed (Felshin, 1974).  However, AIAW states these experiences are, and should be, judged acceptable only as an interim procedure for use until women's programs can be initiated (NAGWS, 1974).  It is apparent that there are more and more cases of men and women competing together, either as members of one team, or on separate teams in a joint competition.  Some schools have found running coeducational competitions have created great interest among competitors and spectators, whether the scoring is combined or not, and has advantages in terms of travel, facilities, and coaching.  Women have assumed roles in what were previously "men's" sports as both players and administrative personnel (Felshin, 1974).

If scholarships are given, schools today must provide reasonable opportunities for such awards to members of each sex in proportion to the number of students of each sex participating in either interscholastic or intercollegiate athletics (HEW, 1975).

Purses in national competitions are beginning to show change and equality as evidenced by the U.S. Open Tennis Tournament at Forest Hills in 1972.  Billie Jean King won $10,000 whereas her male counterpart, champion Ilie Nastase, collected $25,000 (Felshin, 1974).  However, in the 1975 U.S. Open Tennis Tournament at Forest Hills, champion Chris Evert collected $25,000, as did her male counterpart, champion, Manual Orantes (Kirkpatrick, 1975).  This in only one example of what is beginning to happen in male and female sport today.

School physical education programs, like all education across the country, are directly affected by Title IX.  According to the Health, Education, and Welfare documents on Title IX, a recipient of federal aid must not provide any education program or activity separately on the basis of sex.  With regard to physical education classes at the elementary level, recipients must comply with establishing coeducational classes not later than one year from the effective date of the regulation.  Secondary and post-secondary levels must comply with establishing such classes within three years.  The instructor of these classes are usually selected on the basis of special skill and ability, not sex.  Team teaching is often found.  This regulation does not prohibit grouping of students without regard to sex in some instances such as ability, participation in contact sports, or in portions of classes which deal exclusively with human sexuality (HEW, 1974).

Control and Promotion of Sport

Schools and colleges provide a broad base for sport participation in the U.S.A.  However, industry, commercial agencies, youth clubs, private clubs, churches, and civic recreation departments also provide opportunities for many athletes. Little League Baseball, Iddy-biddy Basketball, and Pop Warner Tackle Football are other examples of competition for children. Professional sports such as baseball, football, basketball, tennis, and ice hockey, are big business today and spectator attendance continues to set new records.

Each state has its own high school athletic association, which establishes policies for the control of secondary school athletics. Four-year colleges and universities are controlled by the National Collegiate Athletic Association (NCAA), along with the National Association of Intercollegiate Athletics (NAIA), usually associated with smaller institutions, and the Association for Intercollegiate Athletics for Women (AIAW). Junior and community colleges are under the National Junior College Athletic Association (NJCAA).

Athletes in schools and colleges are closely supervised by the above-mentioned associations but athletes who are not in school but retain an amateur status, participate under the Amateur Athletic Union (AAU). There continues to be a power struggle between the AAU and NCAA in selection of athletes to represent the U.S.A. in international competitions. On occasions the federal government has stepped in to mediate some of the bitter disputes (Bennett, Howell, Simri, 1975). In fact, on June 19, 1975, the president of the United States established a twenty-two member President's Commission on Olympic Sports to study 1--factors that impede or prevent the United States from obtaining the best amateur athletes for participation in the Olympic Games and other international amateur competitions, 2--methods of financing athletic teams which compete in Olympic sports, and 3--organizational structure of Olympic sports including the U.S. Olympic Committee and individual federations (Forker, 1975).

Today, however, American support for IFSU (Federation Internationale du Sports Universitaire) and the World University Games resides largely in the United States Collegiate Sports Council (USCSC), dedicated to promote international collegiate sport through the increased participation of American student athletes in international competition. The USCSC selects, makes arrangements for and manages United States teams at FISU-sponsored competitions. Charter members are NCAA, NAJCAA, and AIAW (Vendien, 1974).

Recently, the relatively new sport of "hang-gliding" has gained popularity. The hang-glider, buoyed up only by dacron wings, jumps off a mountain cliff and sails over the valley floor some thousand feet below. For safety reasons, examples of federal and state intervention in the sport in state and national parts include Mt. Tom in the East (Hampshire Gazette, 1975) and Yosemite in the West. Reports from Yosemite indicate of 700 recent flights only one bruised knee has been recorded (NBC News, 1975). The Federal Aviation Association is not so concerned about where hang-gliding is done as that safety controls are developed immediately.

## Professional Preparation

Today, 675 American colleges and universities offer a bachelor's degree in physical education, 251 offer a master's degree, and 60 offer a doctorate. The increase of interest and demand since 1965 is shown by these figures: 208 more institutions offer the bachelor's degree, 77 more offer the master's and 14 more offer the doctorate (Vendien, Nixon, 1968; JOHPER, 1974, JOHPER, 1975).

Many institutions are undergoing curriculum evaluation and change. Some schools are preparing specialists in comparison to the generalist. Specialized emphasis is given to such areas as elementary physical education, dance, gymnastics, aquatics, sport studies, sport administration, sport communication, and exercise science.

Some schools are successfully experimenting with flexible scheduling, allowing longer blocks of time for special classes such as golf to meet on golf courses, skiing on ski hills, bowling at bowling alleys, and horseback riding on riding trails. The time has come when community resources are being cooperatively used for facilities and instruction to expand the physical education and sport programs.

Physical education graduates today realize there are few positions for those qualified to teach only the traditional types of activities found in public schools. There seems to be an increasing interest and need for teachers capable of offering opportunities in such activities as the martial arts, yoga, water-based activities, and various outdoor pursuits.

Because competencies are beginning to be examined very carefully, it becomes necessary to assess the capabilities of incoming students and build upon the abilities possessed by the student at the time of entry (Professional Preparation, 1974). Curriculum committees today are addressing the issues of competency-based education where the competencies to be acquired by the student and the criteria to be applied in assessing the competence of the student are made explicit and the student is held accountable for meeting the criteria (Pelton, 1973). Although there is much literature and study done on competency-based education, a great deal of work is needed on evaluation systems before they can be effective. According to Jackson, the notion of accountability is predicated on the establishment of reliable and valid instrumentation, and the refinement of relevant criteria or standards, since the traditional program tends to be cognitively based, and the competency-based program is performance based (Jackson, 1973).

More emphasis today is being placed on the value of student teaching and the responsibilities involved in using the cooperating public schools. Much attention is given to careful preparation of student teachers, including ongoing field experiences beginning the first year of college and throughout their college years. Students are given opportunities of observing, assisting, and teaching at various levels and types of activities. Micro-teaching is an important phase in preparation. New techniques in supervising student teachers include use of audiovisual equipment. Many descriptive-analytic systems have been developed to classify events into meaningful categories so that the events may be tabulated to provide a concise picture of what has happened, and in an objective manner as opposed to judgmental (Anderson, 1975). Darst reports several of the objective recording instruments available today (Darst, 1975).

Physical education teachers in America are highly respected by most academic colleagues and have the same educational and financial status. Usually coaches receive supplementary pay. The annual mean salary for a public school physical education teacher ranges from $8,000 to $16,000 (HEW, 1974). The mean salary for college faculty ranges from $11,474 for an instructor to $18,609 for a professor (JOHPER, 1973).

## Research

More research is being conducted today than ever before. At the national AAHPER conventions, the research section arranges for continuous presentation of papers throughout the conventions. Most Master's degrees and all doctoral degrees require research. Very specialized research facilities are making possible various kind of research today that never existed a few years ago. The greatest attention has been given to exercise physiology, measurement, motor learning, motor integration, bio-mechanics, exercise therapy, and studies with the mentally retarded. However, now there is a counterbalancing increase of research in sport history, sociology, psychology, sport studies, and professional preparation.

## The Future

Sport is a mirror of American life, as it is reflected in national policies, used for rehabilitation, attracts millions of people through all forms of public media, becoming a common language, and develops sport habits and interests within family living. The same social and economic forces which have placed sport in this position in contemporary life will presumably continue to operate in the future.

Leaders of sport and physical education recognize that there is an immense challenge in the future to provide equal opportunities for all who wish to participate. Most leaders are optimistic that today's programs are making great strides toward identifying and implementing their contribution toward body development and total living. The kinds of programs that will be offered to our youth tomorrow depend upon the wise judgment and action of our leaders today.

SELECTED REFERENCES

Anderson, William G. "Videotape Data Bank." *Journal of Health, Physical Education, and Recreation.* September, 1975.

Belanger, Charles H. "Salaries of Physical Education Faculty in Selected Four-Year Institutions". Washington, D. C.: *Journal of Health, Physical Education, and Recreation.* April, 1973.

Bennett, Bruce L. Howell, Maxwell L. and Simri, Uriel. *Comparative Physical Education and Sport.* Philadelphia: Lea & Febiger, 1975.

Chapter 766, Massachusetts Comprehensive Special Education Act of 1972, "What Everyone Should Know About Chapter 766." Greenfield, Massachusetts: Channing L. Bete Co., Inc. 1974.

Darst, Paul W. "Student Teacher Supervision with Audiovisual Equipment." *Journal of Health, Physical Education, and Recreation.* September, 1975.

Felshin, Jan. Chapter 6, "The Status of Women and Sport," in Gerber, Ellen W., Felshin, Jan, Berlin, Pearl and Wyrick, Waneen. *The American Woman in Sport.* Reading, Massachusetts: Addison-Wesley Publishing Co. 1974.

Forker, Barbara E. "Amateur Sport and the Federal Government." Lecture presented at the University of Massachusetts. November 12, 1975.

Griffin, Patricia S. "What's a Nice Girl Like You Doing in a Profession Like This?" *Quest,* XIX, Perspectives for Sport. January, 1973.

Halverson, Lolas E. "A Real Look at the Young Child." *Journal of Health, Physical Education, and Recreation.* May, 1971.

Hampshire Gazette. "They Jump Off Cliffs—And Love It." Northampton, Massachusetts. September 30, 1975.

HEW. Department of Health, Education, and Welfare. General Administration. *Part 86 Non-Discrimination on the Basis of Sex in Education Programs and Activities Receiving or Benefiting From Federal Financial Assistance.* Washington, D.C.: Office of Civil Rights, HEW. 1975.

HEW. Department of Health, Education, and Welfare. General Administration. *Title IX Questions and Answers.* Washington, D.C.: Office of Civil Rights, HEW. 1975.

HEW. "Digest of Educational Statistics." Washington, D.C.: U.S. Department of Health, Education, and Welfare, Office of Education. 1974.

Jackson, Andrew S. "Prospects and Problems: Evaluation of Competency Based Education." *76th Annual Proceedings.* National College Physical Education Association for Men. C. E. Mueller (ed.). University of Minnesota. 1973.

JOHPER. "HPER Directory of Professional Preparation Institutions." Washington, D.C.: *Journal of Health, Physical Education, and Recreation.* September, 1974.

JOHPER. "HPER Directory of Professional Preparation Institutions." Washington, D.C.: *Journal of Health, Physical Education, and Recreation.* January 1975.

JOHPER. "HPER Directory of Professional Preparation Institutions." Washington, D.C.: *Journal of Health, Physical Education, and Recreation.* May, 1975.

Kirkpatrick, Curry. "A Big Home Victory at Last." *Sports Illustrated.* September 15, 1975.

Matt Mann Camps. "There Are Camps and There Are Camps." *The Swimming World.* Los Angeles, California. May 1974.

National Association for Girls and Women's Sports. *AIAW Handbook of Policies and Procedures, 1974-75.* Judith R. Holland (ed.). Washington, D.C.: American Alliance for Health, Physical Education, and Recreation. 1974.

NBC News. "6:30 P.M. NBC News, John Chancellor reporting." October 3, 1975.

Olympic. "Olympic Camp." *Gymnast.* October, 1974.

Pelton, Barry C. "Competency Based Teacher Education in Physical Education Prospects and Problems." *76th Annual Proceedings.* National College Physical Education Association for Men. C. E. Mueller (ed.). University of Minnesota, Minneapolis. 1973.

Professional Preparation. "Professional Preparation for Physical Education, Introduction." *Professional Preparation in Dance, Physical Education, Recreation, Safety Education, and School Health Education.* Harold M. Barrow, chairman of editorial committee, Washington, D.C.: American Alliance for Health, Physical Education, and Recreation. 1974.

Siedentop, Daryl. *Physical Education Introductory Analysis.* Dubuque, Iowa: Wm. C. Brown Publisher. 1972.

Tanner, Patricia. "Film Loops for Elementary School Physical Education." *Journal of Health, Physical Education, and Recreation.* June, 1970.

Vendien, C. Lynn. "FISU (Federation Internationale du Sports Universitair) and the World University Games." *Quest*, XXIX, World lof Sport. June, 1974.

Vendien, C. Lynn. "Traditional and Modern Forms of Physical Education in the U.S.A." *6th Congress Proceedings* of the International Association of Physical Education and Sport for Girls and Women. Tokyo: Organizing Committee of Japan for the 6th International Congress. 1970.

Vendien, C. Lynn and Nixon, John E. *The World Today in Health, Physical Education, and Recreation.* Englewood Cliffs, New Jersey: Prentice-Hall, Inc., 1958.

# SPORT AND PHYSICAL EDUCATION IN RUSSIA
by Russell L. Sturzebecker

## Biographical Sketch

*Dr. Sturzebecker* was born in Lansdale, Pennsylvania on March 5, 1916. After graduation from Lansdale High School he matriculated at West Chester State Teachers College in the Health and Physical Education program and by graduation in 1937 had secured additional certification in English and Science. He taught at both Penbrook and Stroudsburg, Pennsylvania during which time he received his Masters degree from Temple University. He entered the military service in 1942, serving in the United States Air Force, in New Guinea, the Philippine Islands and Okinawa as a member of the 312th Bombardment Group. By the time of his discharge to the Reserves in January, 1946, he had attained the rank of Captain. Currently he holds an Active Reserve Commission as Colonel in the United States Air Force.

He joined the Health and Physical Education Staff at West Chester in January, 1946, and served as Head Coach of Track and Gymnastics as well as assistant in Football. In February, 1949, he received his Doctor's Degree from Temple University. He was appointed Director of Health and Physical Education in 1950, serving in this capacity 17 years until August, 1966. He is currently Senior Teaching Professor at the College, serving mainly in the Graduate School.

He received the Honor Award in 1957 and the Elmer B. Cottrell Award in 1968 from the Pennsylvania State Associaton HPER. From 1955 to 1965 he promoted International Relations by bringing to the college the National Gymnastic teams from Sweden, West Germany, Finland, Denmark, Japan, the Soviet Union, Canada and Mexico. For these efforts in support of international exchange and the United States Olympic Games, he was cited by the Amateur Athletic Union of the United States in 1963 and 1964.

In 1961 he managed the United States National Men's and Women's Gymnastic Team tour for competition in Czechoslovakia, Poland and Russia. He received citations from both the Polish and Soviet Sports Federations. The Senate of Pennsylvania on August 14, 1961 presented him with a commendation for his work in bringing international sports to Pennsylvania.

He has been a delegate to the International Congresses of Health, Physical Education and Recreation in 1967, Vancouver, Canada, in 1968, Dublin, Ireland and in 1970, Warsaw, Poland. He was named delegate by the United States Olympic Committee to attend the International Olympic Academy at Olympia, Greece in the summer of 1969.

He has been a visiting lecturer in European and Middle Eastern Colleges and Universities from September, 1967, to January, 1968, and from September, 1969, to January, 1970. He participated in a lecture research tour of Europe, Africa and the Middle East in August and September, 1970, and attended the International Olympic Academy sessions in Greece for the second year. During these overseas tours he has undertaken extensive photographic studies of classical Greco-Roman athletics sites--gymnasia, palestra, stadia, amphitheaters and baths in Europe, Africa and the Middle East. This research is the basis of a future series of publications concerning Panhellenic and Roman game sites.

His specialization in "Comparative Physical Education and Sports" as well as "Olympic Games, Ancient and Modern" has resulted in his services being called on as a speaker at the national conventions of the American Association for Health, Physical Education and Recreation. On a number of occasions he has also appeared on television in support of the United States Olympic teams. His publications include articles and monographs on *Physical Education and Sport in Russia, Comparative Physical Education, Camp Athletics,* and *Technology in Physical Education.* He served as Education Director for the production of three physical education motion pictures for General Learning Corporation, a Division of Time Life, Inc.


Author's Note

Monograph Number one published in 1966, first of the current series, contains Glyn Roberts' report on the program in Russia based upon an extensive research of professional educational publications. The readers should use this as a background to the current publication based upon three tours to the Soviet Union in 1961, 1967 & 1969 and upon review of Soviet Books and Periodicals as well as conferences with officials, professors, athletes and citizens of the several Socialistic Republics. Insights have also been gained from discussions with foreign physical education leaders particularly in Poland, Czechoslovakia, Hungary, Romania, and Bulgaria who have had frequent professional interchange and visits with their Soviet contemporaries. The author is indebted to his friends in these countries who have given generously of their time and made their professional libraries available.


## History Background--Physical Education
## and Sports

In the Soviet Union today the term "physical culture" is broad in scope. It includes physical education for all children and young people, the improvement of health of the workers, training for labor and defense, strengthening of the body, development of will through physical exercises and a number of related areas. Sport as differentiated from physical culture concerns competition and the struggle for improved performances. Thus physical culture is the basis for sport and hopefully will involve many who in turn will provide vast pools of fine sportsmen. From this pool through graded competition the sportsman progresses upward to his highest level of attainment.

In the Russia of the Tsars, the principal involvement in physical culture and amateur sport was the prerogative of the well-to-do classes. The peasant class, illiterate in the mass, had limited folk activities on infrequent holidays.

In 1909 the Army in St. Petersburg opened the "Officer's General Gymnastic School." This as a research center would be the model for future Soviet physical culture institutes. Course content included anatomy, physiology, hygiene, history, methods and practical work in sports.

The most significant measure of a nation's interest in physical education and sports is shown in the degree of participation as measured against results in the Olympic Games. The Russian athletes made their first appearance in the 1908 games in London. There, three of the five entrants placed. Nikolai Panin-Kolemkin won the gold medal in figure skating; Nikolai Orlov, the silver medal in lightweight Greco-Roman wrestling; and Nikolai Petrov, the silver medal in the heavyweight division of the same sport. The official British Olympic Report of 1908 has a photograph of Panin opposite page 289 as well as on page 293 a diagram of the special figures he skated.

In 1911 the Russian Olympic Committee made an appeal for the several cities to organize their competitions so that the athletes could give a good account of themselves. However, leadership was apparently weak, rivalry among the cities for team membership became acute, training was poorly organized, and team selection was rather casual. As a result only two silver medals and two bronze were won by the Russian athletes. The official Swedish Olympic Report of 1912 on page

371, lists six Russians competing in the games. H. Blau took a
bronze medal in the clay bird shooting. Dr. Med. J. Shomaker took a
bronze medal in the 10 meter sailing in the GALLIA II with A. Wische-
gradsky listed as owner. In the group shooting with revolver or pis-
tol, two of the Russian team took silver medals but their names are
not listed. The report, however, does have two large photos. On
page 75 the Russian shooting group is shown and on page 315 the 10
meter sail boat GALLIA II is pictured.

The poor performances of their athletes inspired a number of
sportsmen to restudy the nature and extent of participation in the
games. Only in Kiev did their appeal strike a responsive note where
the sport enthusiasts promoted the building of the first stadium in the
country with a seating capacity of 10,000. A running track and field
event locations provided the means for 579 participants from eight
Russian cities to assemble in August 1913 for the competition in 10
events.

The following year in Riga the Olympiad held in July produced
900 participants from twenty cities. The organizing committee was an
impressive one having members of the royal family as well as high
Russian officials. The opening ceremony was marked by the absence
of the entire committee. These honors were performed by a spectator,
General Svechkin, who, by chance happened to be there.

The outbreak of the first World War closed the chapter of
physical education and sports under the Tsarist regime. A new day
was in the offing.

Both Marx and Lenin are quoted by Soviet writers as supporting physical education for the people. Marx included physical education as one of the three major parts of education. Lenin endorsed
Marx' view and further emphasized that healthful sport should be
combined with intellectual pursuits. Successive leaders since the revolution have continually echoed these thoughts.

The first indication of the Soviet interest in physical culture
was evidenced by the decree of April 1918 which placed military and
physical training under the responsibility of the Chief Administration
of Universal Military Training. This was prompted by the internal
situation existing after the October revolution of 1917.

The initial movement to replace the Bogatyr, the physical training society, with an institute of physical culture is marked by a marble tablet in the Lenin Institute of Physical Culture in Moscow. On
this is inscribed the original order of Vladimir Lenin establishing the
school in 1919.

In Moscow, April 1919, the first All-Russian Congress of Physical Culture Sport and Pre-Military Training introduced a two year
course of physical culture. This had a strong emphasis on para-
military sports. At Training Centers and factories sport clubs were
formed.

The Pre-Military Sports Administration (Vesvobuch) celebrated its first anniversary by a great parade in Moscow which was reviewed by Lenin. This demonstration would set the pace for the huge sport parades of the future.

The New Economic Policy of 1921 marked the appearance of a number of competing organizations interested in Soviet physical culture and sport. The two major groups were the Vsevobuch and the Konsomol. The latter, also known as the Young Communist League, was given the assignment of getting youth in factories into physical culture sections.

In 1923 the Dinamo sports club was organized to develop physical culture and sport among the members of the several security police forces. This society was one of the first producers of sports equipment.

Conflicts among the organizations desiring to maintain prime influence over Soviet physical culture and sport resulted in the establishment in April 1930 of the All Union Council of Physical Culture under the Central Executive Committee of the U.S.S.R.

In 1931 the GTO (GOTOV K TRUDU v OBORNE) Program was created at the start of the first Five Year Plan. The Konsomol was responsible for its introduction and management. By and large it consisted of physical fitness tests to evaluate military aptitude in general. Yearly physical culture parades were promoted in this year and by 1933 over one hundred thousand would march in Moscow. The official promotion during the 1930's developed sport holidays, mass runs, and demonstrations by the best athletes.

The Second World War brought immediate transfer of all physical cultural sport emphasis to the military effort. The response of the leaders, students and graduates of the institutes of physical culture was most significant. In 1937 the Lesgaft Institute in Leningrad had been awarded the Order of Lenin. After World War II it received a unique distinction--the only one of its kind. The highest Soviet decoration, the Order of the Red Banner, was presented to Lesgaft Institute for the contribution made by students and faculty during the war. One of the most singular accomplishments was the formation of a special regiment consisting of 300 students and faculty who formed a partisan "Black Death" group deep behind the German lines.

The Central Committee of the Communist party in December 1948 passed a resolution which to all intents and purposes set the pattern for the emergence of the Soviets as a ranking world power in physical culture and sports. Specifically the task of physical culture was to promote mass participation which in turn would raise the level of athletic performances. This in turn would provide the basis for the assumption of world leadership in sports by Soviet athletes.

In 1949 the All Union Sports Classification System was established. Achievement levels in forty-six sports were set up as targets for participating athletes. The Central Committee published levels of attainment in all sports including para-military ones. These levels must be attained in competition and are paired with attainment of the GTO standard for the sport. The classes starting with the lowest are *Class C, Class B, Class A, Master of Sport,* and *Honored Master of Sport.* The latter is the highest honor that can be given to an athlete. These are given to those who attain great success in international competition or to those who have passed the GTO levels in the highest percentile and who are professional physical culturalists directing youth programs for the Konsomol or Kollectiv. As in the GTO Program it is necessary for Classes C, B, and A to requalify biennially. This requalification is against the norms currently established. The Soviet periodical, "Physical Culture in Schools," regularly lists these. (The norms listed in the May 1970 issue cover the period 1969-1972.)

As higher levels of attainment are reached with the final accomplishment of "Honored Master of Sport" there is concurrent value for the person in both his work and his life. Although many writers of the Western world have been critical of the "benefits" accruing or seeming to come to top Soviet Athletes, a parallelism can be found in the United States in both the intrinsic and extrinsic "rewards" furnished athletes both in college and after graduation when they continue playing. Publicity in recent years concerning financial aid to promising athletes is not unlike that reported in the Soviet promotional program.

In Russia, a member of the physical education profession who attains a sports rank or title has a political-ideological obligation to act as an extended arm of the state. He must actively promote the Soviet philosophy to his charges and set an example in socialistic living. He is expected to be a member of a physical culture collective and to actively participate in the total program. Those who do not meet these requirements can have their title rescinded.

Though the promulgation of the Central Committee in 1948 brought little if any recognition from other countries of the world the ensuing four year period produced the greatest sports story of all times. At the end of the 1952 Olympic games, 332 men and 48 women had competed under the hammer and sickel banner and brought back 22 gold, 39 silver and 19 bronze medals. That this was not a freak was convincingly illustrated four years later at Melbourne, with the Soviets gathering 37 gold, 29 silver and 32 bronze medals. This fact, coupled with the scientific achievement of being the first nation to demonstrate the possibility of escaping the earth's orbit, placed the Soviets as a contender for world leadership.

Critical analyses of underlying causes for the emergence of this nation as a world leader in sports provides some very interesting observations. Philosophically physical culture and sports are an integral part of Soviet life. The communist's party goal of "everything for the sake of man, for the benefit of man" can be reached through physical culture and sport as a prime influence in health building, physical development and moral influence.

In essence, physical culture and sport are an extension of the state, politically and ideologically. The organization, administration, supervision, financial support, selection of leaders, construction of facilities, controls of award systems, and selections of athletes for international competition is considered just as important as any other function of government. Through central committees, the Soviets are involved in all levels of every activity in sport and physical culture.

## Kindergarten--Elementary Physical Education

The equality of men and women in the Soviet coupled with the work opportunities and economic considerations creates family situations with both husband and wife working. Thus the day nursery which accommodates all pre-school children is an important institution. Such institutions provide a doctor-nurse-physical education specialist cooperative program related to the capacity of the child. By and large the physical activity program coupled with environmental health as well as basic health practices form the core work of the pre-school program. Indirectly the freeing of the young mother provides a pool of trained women to take part in the labor and professional forces.

Personnel engaged in these programs receive professional training in the area of specialization including child psychology, methods, and hygiene. All such instutitons come under an inspection program of the state.

Both in the city and in rural kollectivs the child grows up in a "family" of many children and thus from his earliest years develops his relationship to groups.

The elementary schools have had compulsory physical education since 1929. In general as in other countries the room teacher in the primary grades conducts the program. In urban areas however, the trained specialists is engaged in assisting the teacher. Children of early years who develop aptitude or talent may have special instruction. This is particularly true in individual activities such as swimming, ice skating, dancing and gymnastics.

In the upper elementary grades gym classes forty-five minutes in length have content which parallels that of other countries. Pupil leadership is encouraged and patriotic-political indoctrination is thoroughly interwoven with the instruction.

Of particular interest and related directly to the indentification of the talented child is the referral to the children's sports schools. From ages seven to ten through sixteen candidates are accepted. The "schools" are under the direction of the Ministry of Education and voluntary sport societies who provide for facilities, equipment and trained personnel. Classes meet no less than twice a week after school hours. The program lasts three years and the entrant is expected to attain a rating in the sports classification system for his age level. There are over 2000 such sport schools in the Soviet Union.

An important extension of the formal school training is the free summer camp program open to each child for a month or more. There the physical culture program is extended and forms the major core of the experience.

### Secondary School--Physical Education

The physical education program is built upon the basic movement skills acquired in the elementary grades. Here the emphasis begins upon fitness and extends into furthering sports techniques. Teachers naturally try and prepare their charges for certification under the GTO system thus the test elements are practiced as part of required physical education. The GOT plan essentially has a paramilitary base which could provide a measurement of the individual's worth in terms of the needs of national security. The program is considered as the "road to sport."

Currently the GTO has 3 levels of attainment classified according to age groupings. The first level known as BGTO ("Getting ready for Labor and Defense"), is aimed at school children ages thirteen and fourteen. The events and concomitant tests include morning exercises, climbing ropes or poles, 60 meter dash, both high and broad jumps, a 25 meter swim, skiing, grenade throwing and hiking. The grenade is of simulated metal of the same size and weight of an actual one. The latter activity appears in the United States, only in military training, however, it is commonly found in European countries.

Qualification for the BGTO levels are as follows:

BGTO (Be Ready For Labor and Defense)

| Fitness Event | Boys | Girls |
|---|---|---|
| Rope or Pole Climbing | 3 meters | 2 meters |
| 60 Meter Run | 9.6 sec. | 10 sec. |
| Long Jump | 3.25 meters | 2.80 meters |
| Grenade Throw (500 gm. weight) | 25 meters | . . . . . . . . . . |
| 25 meter Swim | 27 sec. | 30 sec. |
| Skiing | 3 Kilometers in 22 minutes | 2 Kilometers in 18 minutes |
| Hiking (in districts without snow) | Walk 15 Kilometers or Cycle 20 Kilometers | Walk 12 Kilometers or Cycle 15 Kilometers |
| Games Standards | Play in 3 official games in one branch--football, basketball, volleyball, handball, hockey or tennis. | Play in 3 official games in one branch--basketball, volleyball, or tennis. |

The second category, *1st level GTO*, IS FOR THE GROUP SIX-
TEEN TO EIGHTEEN YEARS OF AGE. There is no distinguishment
as to sex, however, boys must meet riflery norms.

The third is titled *2nd level GTO* and is for those 19 years or
older. The tests are more difficult and include the basic requirement
of a grade of Excellent on the 1st and 2nd level GTO. Further,
there are certain utilitarian items such as experience with repairing
motors, or qualified to drive a vehicle on land or water, or elect to
pass either the parachute jumping or mountain climbing test. As a
matter of pride, it is not unusual to have a large percentage qualify
in all these requirements.

Once a person has secured a *GTO* badge, the system is like
that of American Red Cross Lifesaving certification in that it must be
renewed every three years. Badges are given to those attaining the
various levels. The political districts within the Soviet Socialist Republics are then allocated desirable quotas thus pushing physical culture or sport leaders to produce qualifiers from among those whom
they direct.

Observations of both indoor and outdoor programs reveal that
the discipline response is very high. By and large formalism is the
principal philosophy and the program is intensive in terms of utilization of instructional time. Apparatus, equipment, teaching aids,
particularly in urban areas, are in good supply. Thus, each student
is able to practice skills and stunts. This is particularly noticeable
in track and field where not only will there be sufficient equipment
but the space assigned to practice is also developed in multiples. It
is not uncommon to find a half dozen shotput circles or a number of
runways and jumping pits rather than the common American single
facility.

The periodical *"Physical Culture in Schools,"* one of the best
of its kind in this writer's opinion, offers a wealth of well illustrated
inservice materials including instructional aids, techniques of play,
and in particular, details for construction of teaching aids in many
activities. A typical issue will provide political history, basketball
fundamentals, exercises with wands and rubber ropes, floor exercises,
volleyball, ballet, elementary blocks, guarding in basketball. Greek
athletic races, barbells, children's games, bounce ball fundamentals,
free exercises, newest publications, coming sports events, effects of
alcohol, athletic mosaics from Piazza Armerina Sicily, sports records,
cartoons, and sports fiction are also included. It is particularly
interesting to note the timeliness of some articles. In November, 1966
issue page 15, there is a short illustrated article on a cosmonaut
"transference" test concerned with the recovery of inner ear balance
after a rotatory experience. Such exercise and test would have contemporary appeal. Drawings invariably are well done and most of the
materials immediately practicable.

Observation of schools in the remoter areas of the Ukraine gave evidence of the teachers' effective use of self-constructed aids to teaching. From a geographic view in terms of the rural population of the USSR such located schools can find ways to effectively implement the wealth of ideas suggested by the journal "Physical Culture in Schools."

Analagous to the Sports Schools for Children are those titled Sports Schools for Youth, ages seventeen to twenty. The main difference is in the admission requirements. Here the candidate must have a ranking in the first three sports categories for his age group. Such selectivity coupled with qualified instructors using school or factory or sports club facilities provides a strong link in the sports training hierarchy. These students in such schools enter regular sports meetings--district, regional, and national competitions. The watchful eye of individual coaches plus the chauvinistic recruiters of the sports clubs selects from the group those who will receive in turn more intensive training and competition.

Examples of "graduates" from such schools are Valery Brumel and Larissa Latynina, Olympic champions in the high jump and women's gymnastics, respectively.

Physical educators in the Soviet Union are self-critical just like their contemporaries in other European countries and the Western world. They press for more time, more equipment and improvement of both quantity and quality of facilities.

College and University Physical Education
and Sports

The college or university student may elect physical education or sports courses within the framework of his program. The required program is aimed at the entering student who must pass minimum level fitness tests.

The major emphasis in the Soviet Union is the use of Burevestnik or Student Sports Clubs as the collective center for student participation on the educational level. Burevestnik in Russian is translated as "stormy petrel," a symbol used to identify these clubs.

Unlike the United States there is no competition per se between universities or colleges with eligibility rules for a single all college team in a sport. The student club independent of the college is self-sustaining, arranges its own affairs, and students taking courses may be a member of the club for many years. Thus, there are no age or accumulated years of competition cut-offs for an athlete in a student club. A team from Moscow University competing in student games in perhaps Bucharest might have members whose ages and experience were quite divergent. In practice it is quite common, particularly in the Eastern Bloc, to have invitational student games or competition in every activity wherein geographic lines are crossed. The club in each case represents itself and its nation rather than the college or university. A typical student club in a Russian University will have a reception room wherein the walls will be well decorated with the typical triangular banners denoting student games in Warsaw, Prague, Amsterdam, Belgrade, Odessa and Leipzig.

The host university invariably makes low cost housing and meal arrangements for visiting teams. In larger competitions the host government frequently will underwrite part of the expenses.

Of particular note is the atmosphere existing on the site of such student games. The intense rivalry with its incipient hostility among the supporters of typical American college sports is not evident at the student games. The spirit that exists is more closely aligned with the British public school sports' ideals.

The student hosts at such physical education sports programs utilize the opportunity to exhibit the cultural aspects of their university or town. It is not uncommon to offer student tours, receptions, musical events or art exhibits as part of the total affair. At the same time newspapers, sports magazines, radio and television give generous coverage to their contests.

Notwithstanding the foregoing, there are significant numbers of Soviet students who like their contemporaries in Warsaw, Paris, London and Philadelphia consider neither participation in nor viewing of sports as particularly important in their lives.

From a comparative view the observation may be made that the nature and extent of program offering in both required physical education and sports program is much richer in the Soviet Union, the other socialist countries and the central-northern countries of Europe when compared with typical colleges in the United States. An examination of student sports instruction clubs open to membership in such colleges as Lenin Institute (Moscow), Lesgaft Institute (Leningrad), Pollock Institute (Edinburg), University of Brussels, University of Zurich, and the Universities of Cracow, Poznan, and Warsaw show a wide variety of activities openly sponsored seasonally and throughout the years.

Another point of departure in the rather common practice in colleges of the United States of assigning a partially trained faculty member or a graduate assistant to teach a required physical education class or to sponsor a sport is the European view that the specialist must be used. In the Soviet Union the Burevestnik may look outside the faculty to secure a qualified specialist from other schools, the factory or cooperative for the necessary trained leadership in a sport.

In the college and university level the question always asked is "what is your sport?" As in America, membership in the sports clubs open the door to socialization and contacts for employment opportunities.

It must be noted that women in the Soviet Union are not segregated to the extent they are in physical education and sports in the United States. It is not uncommon for scheduling of classes to be made without distinction as to sex.

The universities and colleges evince a great deal of pride in the accomplishment of their students in the field of athletics. In the case of the Institutes of Physical Culture, this has taken the form of memorial museums. In Moscow, Doctor Samokov, Professor of History, has developed an outstanding museum illustrating the development of the Lenin Institute of Physical Culture. Memorabilia on display include a marble tablet on which is inscribed the original order of Vladimir Lenin establishing the school in 1919. Sports equipment used in setting European and World Records as well as photos of the athletes are shown. A World War II memorial was created in honor of the graduates killed, numbering 50% of all those attending since its beginning in 1919.

A much closer relationship between the university-college sports clubs and the community-collective-factory-farm sports societies exists. Common exchange of instructors, utilization of common facilities and general close liaison is evident.

Teacher Education in Physical Education

Observations of classes in the Lesgav and in the Latin Institute reveal, on the whole, a serious attitude on the part of the Russian students toward their education. Pride is inculcated in both the profession and the achievement of Soviet athletes through the use of centralized historical display areas as well as specialized ones within the several sports disciplines.

In the Soviet Union there are a number of avenues for preparing leaders in the field of physical culture and sport. Professor Alexander Novikov of the Lenin Institute of Physical Culture in Moscow outlined the structure as follows: In higher education there are 17 Physical Culture Institutes as well as special departments of physical culture within 63 Pedagogical Institutes. On the secondary school level there are 14 Special Pedagogical Secondary Schools of Physical Culture.

The higher education programs administratively provide systems of matriculation not found in the United States. This is tripartite in nature with three tracks operating concurrently. The first is the *day study*, a four year program, analagous to the rather universally known system. The second is a *work-study program* wherein the student works in the day and attends evening classes. The third track is basically a *correspondence course* for those who cannot attend class sessions for geographic reasons. The two latter programs generally are of 5 year duration. In the Lenin Physical Culture Institute in the Fall of 1967 there were 1500 resident students and 4000 studying through evening courses or correspondence. Women make up 25% of the total enrollment. There were 450 faculty members including part-time ones servicing the three programs.

In the residency programs the courses are divided evenly between theory and practice. The syllabus for Sports Faculty approved, August 19, 1967, by the Vice-Minister of higher and special education is as follows:

Ministry of Specialized Secondary and
Higher Education of the USSR

Approved--Vice Minister of Higher and
Special High Education

Sports Faculty (coaches department)
Four Year's Duration

Subjects:

1. History of the Communist Party of the Soviet Union
2. Marxist-Leninist Philosophy Including Scientific Atheism
3. Political Economy
4. Foundations of Scientific Culture
5. Foreign Language
6. Biochemistry Including Fundamentals of Organic and Physical Chemistry
7. Anatomy
8. Physiology
9. Biomechanics Including Fundamentals of Sports Skills
10. Hygiene of Physical Exercises with Fundamentals of General Hygiene and Sports Facilities
11. Sports Medicine
12. General Psychology and Psychology of Coaching
13. Pedagogy and its History
14. History and Organization of Physical Education and Sports
15. Theory of Physical Education
16. Foundations of Sports Coaching
17. Specialization of Chosen Sport
18. Additional Sports
    (a) Track and Field Athletics and its Teaching Methods
    (b) Gymnastics and its Teaching Methods
    (c) Games and Their Teaching Methods
    (d) Swimming and its Teaching Methods
    (e) Skiing and its Teaching Methods
    (f) Weightlifting and its Teaching Methods
19. Special Seminars and Courses (free choice)
20. Photography and Motion Pictures
21. Civic Defense

Optional Subjects (Exemplary List)

1. Principles of Marxists Ethics
2. Principles of Marxists-Leninists Aesthetics
3. Improvement of Skill in Chosen Sport
4. Sports:
   Boxing, Wrestling, Cycling, Speed Skating, Rowing,
   Shooting, Chess, Moto-Sport
5. Therapeutic Exercises
6. Tourism
7. Musical and Rhythmic Education
8. Folk and Ball Dancing

Instructional Practical Work:

1. Winter Camps of Instruction
2. Summer Camps of Instruction

Work Practice:

1. Pedagocial, Organizational, and Methodolgy-Practice at
   School, Sports Clubs and Children Sports Schools
2. In Sports Organizations
3. In Arrangements of Mass Sports Outings

State Examination (must be passed in following subjects)

1. Foundations of Scientific Communism
2. Physiology
3. Specialization

An examination of the foregoing will reveal the significant pri-
macy of developing in each student political consciousness as to socialist ideology. From observations made in 1967 and in 1969, it is
quite evident that the nature and extent of the program compares
most favorably with those in comparatively structured professional
colleges in West Germany, Czechoslovakia, Poland and the United
States.

Professor Gromadsky outlines the Sports (coaches) Department
operations as follows:

EXEMPLARY LIST OF SPECIAL SEMINARS AND
COURSES (free choice)

1. Physiology
2. Special and Age Biochemistry of Sports
3. Morphology of Sport Skill
4. Biodynamics of Sport Skill
5. Medical and Pedagogical Control in Physical Training

6. Elements of Higher Mathematics and Statistics
7. Electronic and Optical Instrumentation and Registration of Movements
8. Practical Works in Research Methods

NOTES:

1. For rational use of climatic and other local conditions to study seasonal sports as well as for practical works in other towns and parts of the country, the Schedule Timetable for various Physical Training Institutes is fixed by the Head of the Institute in accordance with the Rebublican Union of Sport Societies and Organizations or with the Ministry (Committee) of Specialized Secondary and Higher Education (according to subordination of Institute). Thus, it is the Union of Sports Societies and Organizations of the USSR for the Moscow Institute of Physical Culture and Sports.

2. Academic hours for Track and Field Athletics, Swimming, Skiing and Games are planned by the Head of the Institute taking into consideration the climatic conditions in the limit of the academic hours fixed by the Syllabus and are carried out in the form of camp of instructions.

3. Specialization in one of the sports is carried out at free choice of studies. If for better mastering of the chosen sport it is practical to study some other sports which are not included in the Syllabus, the Institute may teach them during the academic hours fixed for specialization.

4. Annual theses in II, III, and IV year of study are made on specialization. In some cases annual theses may be carried out in other subjects of the Syllabus but on topics corresponding to the student's specialization.

5. Annual theses made according to the demands of diploma works may be presented on behalf of the Faculty (Department) to the State Examination Commission for defense instead of passing State Exams in specialization.

6. Training therapeutic exercise instructors (for women) is carried out during the academic hours fixed for the following subjects:

Sports Medicine..............100 academic hours
Weightlifting.................. 50 academic hours
Games (Football and Hockey).. 50 academic hours
Specialization ................160 academic hours

7. During their training at the Institute the students have to qualify second time for 2nd Grade GTO award (The initials GTO are

the Russian abbreviation for Ready for Labour and Defense), to pass
again or qualify for the title of First Class Athlete in chosen sport,
to have 3rd Class title in two other sports, and to get the title of
Referee or Judge in chosen sport.

Head of the P.T. Educational Institutions
(E. Gromadsky)

A rather unique requirement is promulgated in point 7 above
in terms of the five performance requirements. It would be interesting to observe the result of such a requirement, as a part of graduation, applied to students in the United States. Of particular interest was the use of cadavers by the undergraduate students in the
Moscow Institute Academy classes. In the United States it is rather
rare for physical education majors to have opportunity for dissection
on the human body whereas the Soviet student gets the actual experience.

Faculty in the institute are categorized into three levels: Department head--A professor or Doctor of Science, Chief Teacher--
Candidate for Science, and Assistant Teacher--sometimes a candidate
for science. Of the candidates only a small percentage, those most
capable and gifted, may aspire to the title of Doctor. The major area
of preparation for attainment in the higher ranks is in the scientific
area. This is also true in other countries in the Eastern Bloc.

Major Inspector Kuziminov, whose responsibility is the supervision of all teaching activities, outlined the general plan of practical
work for the student. In the second year opportunities are given for
teaching fellow students in the class on an informal basis. At the
end of each course the student must teach a complete formal lesson
which is observed by three tutors who critique the presentation.

In the third year, each student takes seven weeks of practice
on a full-time basis, in a nearby school. If the student has both
interest and ability in two specific activities which entail a geographic,
climatic or facility requirement, he may be sent to a school which can
support this activity. In the term visited, two were assigned to
schools having swimming, two to light athletics and two to sports and
games. On these assignments the student must organize a special activity section in the school. He also may be involved in a community
section.

In the fourth year, he spends eight weeks in a local sports
section in an industry, or factory or cooperative. There he provides
the leadership to the sports section just as he would in a school situation. He is supervised by a representative from the Institute as
well as a Supervisor of Sports from the factory or cooperative.

Both institutes experience an attrition of about 8% of their
students each year. Students have two examinations a year on all
subjects they are taking. Those who rank in the upper quarter of

the class may receive special scholarship stipends. Those who attain the best ratings may be matriculated into postgraduate work. All others must successfully complete two years of teaching before applying for advanced study. As in the United States there is a shortage of women in the profession. However it appears that the Soviets have an edge in enrolling girl majors as well as in holding them after marriage.

Dr. Alexander Novikov was asked to express his views concerning the future of the profession in the Soviet Union. He felt most optimistic with regard to the contributions made. Among his major observations were: the profession must dedicate itself to helping man attain the highest goals of health; in all countries all normal people want to become strong and healthy;--these worthwhile goals can be attained through the help and dedication of professionals in the field.

When broached with the question regarding the loss of folk activities in physical education, he spoke very strongly for the development of a total social culture. National traditions and folklore should be taken socialistic by meaning and nationally by shape or form. The various groups in the Soviet Socialist Republic have ancient forms of amusement and the physical educator's task is to choose and select progressively most suitable forms of games and amusements for the children. Traditional games and dances, which at present may only appear in folk festivals or in the repertoire of a professional group, should be supported as a part of the ethnographic physical culture.

## Soviet Sports

One of the most amazing phenomenon of the twentieth century has been the emergence of the Soviet Union as a major sports power. A significant difference between the United States and the Soviet Union is that of the latter's political involvement in the total field of sports. The Soviet program is a two pronged one which in the past twenty years is responsible for certain successes of its athletes.

GTO the first, originating in 1931, has been outlined to some extent. What is perhaps unique is the extension of GTO to age groups beyond those attending the ordinary schools. There are different standards for men ages 18-30, 31-40, 41-45 and 46 and above.

Men between the ages of 18 and 30 have minimal standards which if applied in some western countries would propose problems. These include climbing up a rope or pole 4 meters with hands alone, run 100 meters in 14 seconds, run cross country 1500 meters in 5 minutes 30 seconds, long jump 4.30 meters, throw the 700 gram grenade 35 meters to land within a 10 meter wide strip, swim 100 meters in 2 minutes, 20 seconds, and ski 10 kilometers in 1 hour 5 minutes. Small bore rifle experience is also required. If the candidate between the ages of 18 and 30 qualifies for the GTO Badge and wishes now to progress to the II Degree he faces more difficult levels. In the case of the four meter rope or pole climb, the legs must be at right angles to the body, i.e., parallel to the ground. The minimal times and distances for the other events are: 100 meters--13.4, five kilometer cross country run--21 minutes, long jump--5 meters, the grenade throw--45 meters, the 100 meter swim--1 minute 50 seconds, and the 15 kilometers on skiis in 1 hour and 30 minutes.

Standards for the GTO levels are evaluated and made more difficult at intervals. Today achievement in sport standards must be accomplished in competition.

A GTO badge holder must be able to perform eight morning exercises, answer questions on sports and physical culture in the USSR, know the details and importance of the GTO plan and have knowledge of hygiene and first aid.

Today in the Soviet Union the holder of a sports badge is referred to as a razryadnik--defined as a graded sportsman. The GTO Badges are distinguished by color and an inscribed numeral denoting the level achieved. The Master of sport is distinguished by a rectangular silver badge.

The Kollektiv, a primary physical culture group, is the basis of the sport society structure and by and large affects the mass of Russian people. These are organized as places of work, factories, offices, farms, schools, and universities. These groups use all available sports facilities at no cost. Membership dues average 40 Kopecks (43 cents) a year. The activities of all sport groups come under the supervision of the Communist Party and Konsomol primary organizations as well as trade union committees. They must arrange for training and coaching, keeping membership statistics, recruiting new candidates, publicizing the sports movement, arranging team study groups for the GTO tests, and institute active rest periods, during working hours. The Moscow radio station twice a day broadcasts exercises for the active rest period or work break referred to in Russian as ZARYADKI. In the case of large sport groups a complete organization structure is created to meet the demands outlined.

## Major Sports Societies

The basis of competition is identified through the structure of seven major sport societies, over one quarter million in number, whose groupings are universally applied across all fifteen Soviet republics. These groupings, based upon the work or professional association of the individual are:

| | |
|---|---|
| Dinamo | (Security Police) |
| Spartak | (Producer's Cooperative) |
| Burevestnik | (University Students) |
| Locomotive | (Transportation Workers) |
| Trud | (Labor) |

Vodnik                 (Maritime Employees)
Tsska                  (Central House of Soviet Army)

The cost of belonging to a society is approximately 30 Kopecks
(32 cents) a year. The motto is "play where you work."

Towns and cities will have clubs bearing the above titles and
concurrent competition takes place both intramural within the society
and extramural between societies. Such groups support the employment of physical culture coaches to direct their teams. Opportunities
for professional employment widely exist in the Konsomols or Kollectivs, however, recognition in coaching a championship sport society
team is the desired goal.

The Soviet's central committee organizes Spartakiades which
serve as a national mass sports competition for the republics. Internationalism is promoted in several ways. Soviet coaches are available
as instructors on call by other nations, particularly emerging ones.
Athletes participate on goodwill tours and in turn, student athletes
of other countries are encouraged to enroll in Soviet Physical Culture
Institutes. Sports instruction books are available everywhere, and
international competition in sought after.

### Books and Periodicals--Research Facilities

Statistically the Soviet Union leads the world in sheer volume
of publications. This leadership is particularly unique in that the
publications are multi-language in nature. There are limitations to
those available in English.

One of the areas in which the Western world has not been able
to compete is in the cost of such publications. This is illustrated by
the reference list which carries with it the price in roubles and
kopecks. Current rate of exchange is 1 rouble equals $1.10. There
are 100 Kopecks in a Rouble. It is not unusual to pay 40 and 75
cents for a physical education or sport book which could cost $2.50
to $5.00 in the Western world. Many books can be purchased in news-
paper kioaks in each town. The translations of such books into
foreign languages serves the purpose of sports-political ideology communication with other countries.

The libraries are generally well stocked and are heavily used
in the field of sports and physical culture. The general collection of
the Lenin Library in Moscow has 25,000,000 volumes representing over
132 languages. Within this is an extensive collection in Physical Culture and Sports. Research facilities exist in both Lenin and Lesgaft
Institutes. An examination of abstracts in a number of European
journals reveals the intensive and extensive nature of research going
on in the Soviet Union. Student research is both required and encouraged. The subjects for investigation are not limited to the school-
college age groups. It is noted that the physical culture institutes

proudly provide the visitor with a fixed display of all publications of their faculty.

## Sporting Goods

The merchandising of equipment and supplies is centrally controlled by the government. Sporting good stores, having stocks of identical items are widely distributed throughout the country. In some instances certain items are in short supply. Further, by American standards, the quality in certain products may be questioned; however, the cost of basic sports items is much less than the cost of other products in their economy. The dressing-up with color or chromeplating is missing and actually not essential to the ultimate user. The stores are heavily patronized by all age groups.

## Indigenous Activities

The Soviet Union made up of 15 diverse republics whose citizens speak 140 dialects had a rich reservoir of native sports and games. It has been the policy of the Central Committee to encourage not only the preservation of these activiteis by their presentation on holidays or at festivals, but also to organize official local or regional competitions with awards.

Examples of these native activities include the following: Georgiachidaoba (national style wrestling), lelo (soccer and rugby type game), Tskhenburti (polo-type game). Nentsi (reindeer races), Kazakhstan-Kyzkumai (co-ed equestrian game with a Nagaika or whip as the motivation), Yakuts-lasso. Buryat (archery) and of course Gordoki, a skittle-like game which draws over a half million Russians into competition.

The geographic ecological pattern of the socialist republics lends itself to the widest possible programs of sports and recreational activities of any country in the world. This fact undergirds the basic philosophy of equally recognizing all activities as part of the total Soviet sports program. Unlike the United States, where, unfortunately, commercial expediency may influence journals such as Sports Illustrated to cover principally the major spectator sports, Soviet general sports publications give coverage to all activities found within their boundaries.

As a further note it has been observed the popular European publications on individual sports subjects have greater depth, scientific investigation and pictorial development than their counterparts in America with the exception of the several major parts journals published in season. It must be reiterated that the European prefers to identify himself with his selected sport just as he does the brand of his beer with wine or tobacco. Such identification makes him a "hungry" devotee of publications related to his sport.

# RECENT OBSERVATIONS AND PUBLICATIONS

In the past several years there has been an increasing interest in both professional visitations and cultural sports interchanges. Dr. William Johnson, of Illinois University in the fall of 1976, made an extensive sabbatical trip which included considerable time in the Soviet Union. Through visits to a number of sport boarding schools, his observations are significantly important.

Physical education instructors recommend boys and girls with budding sports talent to attend the sports development schools. In addition, trainers in the 4,000 sport schools, as well as other specialists in the Pioneers and in Sport Clubs, make recommendations for candidates to attend. Dr. Johnson observed several of the 21 sports boarding schools which are conducting sports development programs. His report covers the age factors in attendance and the basic program of a day's activity in such schools.

Certain schools specialize in one activity while others offer several sports. His visit to the Leningrad school #62 showed a "student" population of 600, of which one half were boarders. The ratio of boys was 60% of the total and the program included swimming, gymnastics, track and field, and winter sports. The staff was made up of twenty-five regular teachers and thirty sports specialists. The facilities were very complete in that they offer all aspects of student life services.

His observations in Moscow made at both the Znamensky School and Pervomaisky District School parallel those of the Leningrad Sport School. These, however, provide an after school hours program generally for children starting at eleven years of age. He notes that of the over 42,000 full time physical education instructors and coaches, over one half work in these "special sport schools" in the afternoon.

Generally the sport facilities belonging to one of the seven Soviet societies is used as a center for these programs. Attendance as well as workout uniforms and equipment is free. This philosophy represents a most positive one producing many potential candidates for Soviet Olympic teams as well as being diametrically opposed to the American system, which carried a never ending price tag on student participation in sport development.

A third facet referred to previously, that of the Pioneer Palace contribution to sport development, was corroborated by Dr. Johnson's analysis. He notes that after age eighteen young men and women have several means of continuing their sport interest. The seven sport societies, twenty-three physical culture institutes, twenty-five sport colleges, and the eighty-five university of college physical education departments all provide paths to continuation in sport.

In essence, it is hoped that Dr. Johnson will develop a detailed monograph from his conferences and observations made in not only the Soviet Union but also in the neighboring eastern countries allied with the same philosophical view.

James Riordan in 1977 published his new book *Sport in Soviet Society - Development of Sport and Physical Education in Russia and USSR*. The publisher, Cambridge University Press in England, lists this under ISBN 0-521-21284-7. Professional physical educators and sport teachers will find an unusually extensive treatment in the 435 pages. The bibliography covering the period 1960 to 1975, contains 152 sources. Notwithstanding the lack of photographic support, he provides a number of revealing diagrams and charts which concretely furnish significant evidence as to the critical importance of sport and physical education in the growth of the Soviet Union.

Riordan describes a diverse account of many facets of Soviet sport. The section on folk activities include, in addition to those outlined earlier, a number of folk games. Described are lapta - related to rounders, lunki - a type of bowling, shariki - marbles, babki - a game with bones as implements of play, kila - a primitive football game, and svaika - spear throwing at a target.

The social aspects of sport, the relation of sport to foreign policy, classification of sport, and a detailed examination of contemporary organizations of Soviet sport provide both quantitative and qualitative analyses.

By the end of 1977, issue number 180 of the monthly *Sport in the USSR*, will be published. Printed in six languages - English, French, German, Hungarian, Russian, and Spanish, this periodical must be considered one of the finest of its type. The format and its contents over the past fifteen years provides a concisely illustrated journal of all physical education and sport administration in the Soviet Union. The thirty-two page issue furnished many points of view and includes an extensive coverage in philosophical ideas, international relations, indigenous folk activities in the several republics, cartoons, calendar schedules, history, human interest stories, award systems, sport stamps - in fact every possible direct and indirect relationship to physical activities.

Since 1955 The National Council of American Soviet Friendship has been sponsoring an extensive intercultural program in the United States. Mr. Richard Morford, executive director with headquarters at 156 Fifth Avenue, New York, N.Y. 10010, provides and extensive service in resource materials, guides, and student oriented trips to the Soviet Union. Of particular interest to the physical educator and sports teacher is the photograph loan display as well as list of rental motion pictures many in color.

Representative of the type of audiovisual sport and physical education motion pictures are the following:

| | Code Number and Date | Running Time in Minutes | Current Rental |
|---|---|---|---|
| The Champion (2 reels) | FP 403 (1953) | 60 | $ 7.50 |
| Fifty Years of Sports (2 reels) | FP 417 (1967) | 55 | $10.00 |
| Sports Rhythms | FP 414 (1970) | 20 | $ 5.00 |
| Three Interviews - Sports Champions | FP 415 (1970) | 25 | $ 5.00 |
| Yesterdays Champions Today | FP 413 (1968) | 20 | $ 5.00 |
| Two on the Track (cycle racing) | FP 416 (1970) | 12 | $ 5.00 |
| National School Games | FP 411 (1967) | 20 | $ 5.00 |
| The Russian Winter | FC 882 (1971) | 12 | $ 5.00 |
| We Invite You to the Olympiad | FP 420 (1974) | 20 | $ 7.00 |

Of this group the first was made following the 1952 Olympics and well qualifies the emergence of the Russians as top competitors in the games. The second furnishes an excellent visual anecdotal historical document of the Russian growth in becoming a leader in sports competition. The last one on the list was produced following the designation of the Russians as host of the XXII Olympiad.

THE USSR AND THE 1980 OLYMPIC GAMES - XXII OLYMPIAD

When the International Olympic Committee formally advised the Russians of their being selected to host the Olympics for 1980 the efforts of the total nation were brought into focus to prepare for the event. Both spectators as well as television observers will recall the closing display at the 1976 Olympics in Montreal - a welcome by the Soviets for all to attend the XXII Olympiad 1980.

If one examines the color photograph illustrated eight by twelve inch booklet *Sport - Moscow - Olympics* published by Novesti Press in 1975, a complete kaleidoscopic unveiling emerges. The congratulatory statment by Lord Killanin, chairman of International

Olympic Committee, is followed by a well-written review of the nature and extent of Soviet planning for 1980.

The initial motif in this monograph is the philosophy under-lining the Soviet view: "The USSR Games are a kind of review of the PT movement in the country involving 50 million people or every fifth citizen. The Games play an important role of bringing out the more gifted among the athletes and of introducing new thousands to sport . . . Altogether 66 sports are practiced in the Soviet Union."

Citing a membership of over 100 nationals with many local languages the Russian Federation holds championships in 26 national events "from Gordoki to the axe throw." A serious review of this booklet along with the continual articles in Sport in the USSR, reveal the intensity of planning going on new and continuing through 1980.

To cite but one of many, one issue made a detailed report of the three year course of study and examination requirements set up to be a Soviet official referee at the Olympic contest.

In *Soviet Life* August, 1977, pages 32 through 39, Ignati Novikov, chairman of the Olympiad - 80 Organization Committee, Vladimir Promystov, chairman of the Moscow City Executive Committee, and Anatoe Chaikovsky, Editor-in-Chief of Fizkultura i Sport magazine provided a question - answer review and excellent observations.

The five cities hosting the competition are Moscow, Leningrad, Kiev, Minsk and Tallinin. From July 19 to August 3, 1980, there will be 19 events. They expect 12,000 competitors and officials from more than 100 countries, 4000 referees, 850 guests of honor, more than 5,000 delegates to international congresses, 6000 press members and countless number of tourists.

From an architectural viewpoint the building program accom-panying the XXIId Olympiad reaches fantastic proportions. The range covers everything from a twenty-two story hotel to the building of twenty-six thousand new gyms. To much of the Western world the major gains from the Olympiad of 1980 will be intercultural growth, whether it be attendance at the games or sitting by a television set. In terms of the latter, a week ago the Soviet's announced that a con-tract was signed for Hungary to supply all studio equipment and acoustic systems for the Olympic IV and radio center and also with equipment for commentators' booths.

To close a seemingly inexhaustible topic the organizing com-mittee in Moscow is keeping all interested organizations and the press informed through form periodicals. These are, *Olympic Panorana*, *Olympiad-80*, *Express Information*, and *Focus on the Olympics*, pub-lished in five languages, including Russian, French, English, Spanish and German and sent free of charge to national Olympic committees.

The enthusiasm for Moscow 1980 Olympiad has traveled far and wide throughout the world. Perhaps to help those who plan on going or those who would simple like information, Collet's Publishers, Ltd. in London has prepared a hundred and ninety-seven page guide and information handbook titled *The Soviet Union*. This provides a "Baedeker" or guide with maps, history, travel hints, accommodations, driving routes, description of cities and interest sites plus even a list of basic English-Russian words and phrases.

## Summary

In terms of time, the Soviet Union has accomplished much since the creation of the present political system in 1917. In the past twenty years, their involvement in athletics and sports coupled with the scientific achievements has created international prestige.

From a comparative view, the system of Soviet physical culture and sport may be subject to a critical analyses as to goals, motivation for individual rewards, political chauvinism, emphases on winning, "professionalism", and other views expressed in recent years by sports writers of the Western World. The same writers can well direct their critiques toward their own doorstep. The methods taken by the USSR to promote and develop physical culture and sports have been emulated in part by a number of countries. The creation of National Sports Institutes such as in Lebanon, France, Tunisia, Switzerland and Spain provide for centers whose goals do include the promotion of physical culture and athletics, the development of demonstration teaching centers, the creation of research facilities and the identification of potential superior athletes with concomitant planned scientific training.

The Soviet philosophy accompanied by direct governmental implementation and promotion has brought this nation to the fore in the field of physical culture and sports in an eclipsed time span never before achieved by any country. This in turn presents the thesis that when a nation or any political body involves itself totally in motivating and supporting physical culture and sports with ancillary factors of free medical care and intrinsic-extrinsic awards, there will be an advancement in health and fitness for the citizens involved.

Russian Reference List

(Prices Shown In Roubles and Kopecks)

Books:

1.  Sveton, Alexander. *No Limits to Strength or Skill*. Novosti Press Agency. Moscow (English).

2.  _____. *Sport Calendar*. (Annual - Illustrated). (1 Rb.-40 Kop.)

3.  Yemshuk. I. F. and Sharev, N. B. *School Rowing*. Moscow 1969 (33 Kop.)

4.  Smolevski, V. *Master Gymnastics--Helps for Coaches*. Moscow 1969 (53 Kop.)

5.  Galinski, B. *Chernomorts--The Odessa Football Team*. Odessa 1969 (40 Kop.)

6.  Belits-Geman, G. *Techniques for Tennis*. Moscow 1966 (94 Kop.)

7.  Butovitsa, N. A. *Waterpolo*. Moscow 1967 (98 Kop.)

8.  Vorobeva, A. N. *Heavy Athletics*. Moscow 1967 (67 Kop.)

9.  Ukranian Konsomol. *Sports in the Ukraine Kiev*. 1968. (3 Rb.-15 Kop.)

10. Zdorovya. *Light Athletics*. Kiev 1967 (20 Kop.)

11. Kalinin, A. *Game Defenses--Football*. Moscow 1967 (14 Kop.)

12. Boldanov, M., Krakoviak, G. M. and Minsk, A. A. *Hygiene*. Moscow 1966 (1 Rb.)

13. Bulotsko, K. T. *Fencing*. Moscow 1967 (1 Rb.-2 Kop.)

14. Novikov, A. A. *Wrestling Guide*. Moscow 1963 (46 Kop.)

15. Korenberg, V. *Little Secrets of Gymnastics*. Moscow 1967 (25 Kop.)

16. Ukrana, M. L. *Sportswomen's Gymnastics*. Moscow 1965 (30 Kop.)

17. Gild, A. P. *Water Polo*. Moscow 1967 (24 Kop.)

18. Shelezniak, U. *120 Lessons in Volleyball*. Moscow 1965 (33 Kop.)

19.  Minenkov, B. *Primary Skiing*. Moscow 1966 (17 Kop.)

20.  Lukomski, I. *Secrets of Living Longer*. Moscow 1961 (6 Kop.)

21.  _____. *Leonid Shabutinski--Man of Steel*. Kiev 1969

22.  Chupanov, I. G. *History--Lenin Physical Culture Institute*. Moscow 1966 (68 Kop.)

23.  Shakverdov, G. G. *History Lesgaft Institute Physical Culture*. Leningrad 1958 (....)

24.  Metayev, L. A. *Physical Culture and Sport in the USSR*. (filmstrip--53 films) Moscow (3 Rb.)

25.  "Physical Culture and Sport." *Basketball*. Moscow 1967 (63 Kop.)

26.  "Physical Culture and Sport." *Physiological Characteristics of Sportsmen*. Moscow 1966 (80 Kop.)

27.  "Physical Culture and Sport." *Records of Soviet Sport*. Moscow 1967 (27 Kop.)

28.  "Physical Culture and Sport." *Physical Culture for the Family*. Moscow 1966 (2 Rb.-6 Kop.)

29.  "Physical Culture and Sport." *Encyclopedic Dictionary of Physical Culture and Sport*. Volumes I, II, III. Moscow 1963 (2 Rb.-5 Kop. per volume)

30.  "Sport Lessons." "Physical Culture and Sport." Moscow 1952 (Kozlova, M. C. Redaction).


Recommended Reading in English:

1.  Sobolev, P., Borodina, L. and Korobkov, C. *Sport in the USSR*. Moscow 1958 (1 Rb.)

2.  Tarasov, N. *Sport in the Soviet Union*. Moscow 1964 (1 Rb.- 80 Kop.)

3.  Belyakov, V. *Soviet Gymnasts*. Moscow .... (1 Rb.-52 Kop.)

4.  Morton, H. S. *Soviet Sport*. Collier Books, New York No. AS-588 (95c)

5.  *Holiday Magazine*. "An Entire Issue on Russia." October 1963.

6. *Newsweek.* "Life in Russia." 3 May 1966.

7. Look. "Russia Today." 3 October 1969.

8. Soviet Education--Bibliography No. 02-14101 U.S. Dept. of H.E.W. (20c)

9. "Yessis Translation Review." (Quarterly). Yessis, M. (California State College, Fullerton, California).

10. Collets Publishers, Ltd. Denington Estate, London Road, Wellingborough Northants, England. *The Soviet Union Guide and Information Handbook, 1976.* $2.00.

11. Johnson, William. "Olympic Sports Development Programs in the USSR and in Selected Eastern European Countries." Report of observations made and conferences held during a sabbatical leave. Fall 1976.

12. McDowell, Bart. *Journey Across Russia, The Soviet Union Today.* National Geographic Society, Washington, D. C. 1977. $12.95.

13. Novosti Press Agency Publishing House. *Sport-Moscow-Olympics.* 1975.

14. Riordan, James. *Sport in Soviet Society, Development of Sport and Physical Education in Russian and the USSR.* Cambridge University Press (first published in 1977). $21.50.

15. Riordan, J. "Pyotr Franzevich Lesgaft (1837-1909), Founder of Russian Physical Education." *Journal of Sport History.* Vol. 4, No. 2, pp. 229-241. Summer 1977.

# SPORT AND PHYSICAL EDUCATION IN YUGOSLAVIA
by Joe Rider Horn

## Biographical Sketch

*Joe Rider Horn* was born in Youngstown, Ohio in 1938, the son of a physical educator and coach. He received the A.B. degree in physical education from Oberlin College in 1960 and the M.Ed. degree in physical education from The Pennsylvania State University in 1961. In August of 1976 he received the Ph.D. in physical education from The Ohio State University.

In the summer of 1971 Dr. Horn traveled in Yugoslavia with twenty professors from the Great Lakes College Association (GLCA) as a participant in the GLCA ten week summer seminar in urban studies entitled "Human Values and Social Organization."

Dr. Horn taught Comparative Physical Education and International Sport and coached football, ice hockey and lacrosse at Oberlin College from 1963 to 1973. During the spring of 1973 he coached the varsity lacrosse team at Ohio Wesleyan University. During the 1974-75 academic years he served as chairman of the department of health, physical education and athletics at Urbana College, Urbana, Ohio. Dr. Horn and his wife Jean, are currently instructors of health and physical education at Wayne-Goshen Local Schools near Lima, Ohio where their two sons Jay, 16 and Jon, 14, are students.

## General Background

The Socialist Federal Republic of Yugoslavia is a rugged, heavily forested land located on the Balkan peninsula. This multinational state lies south of northern Italy, Austria and Hungary, west of Bulgaria and Rumania, north of Greece and Albania and east of the Adriatic Sea. Having an area of 98,766 square miles and a population of twenty million, Yugoslavia is divided into five major geographical zones:

1. The Slovenian Alps in the northwest.

2. The Pannonian lowland of the Sava and Danube River valleys.

3. The geologically unstable Morava-Vardar depression of east central Yugoslavia.

4. The Adriatic coastal belt.

5. The Dinaric Mountain chain lying island from the Adriatic Sea.

The wide variations in elevations give rise to a variety of climates. The Adriatic Coast enjoys a Mediterranean climate with warm summers and mild winters. The Slovenian and Dinaric Alps enjoy moderate summers and moderately cold winters, while the Pannonian lowland has a more continental climate of light precipitation and extreme temperatures in summer and winter.

Yugoslavia, a land of contrasts and cultural diversity, consists of the republics of Serbia, Croatia, Bosnia-Herzegovina, Slovenia, Montenegro, Macedonia and the autonomous provinces of Kosovo and Vojvodina. Major cities are Belgrade, the capital of Serbia, Zagreb (Croatia), Sarajevo (Bosnia-Herzegovina), Ljubljana (Slovenia), Skopje (Macedonia), Titograd (Montenegro), Novi Sad (Vojvodina) and Pristina (Kosovo).

In illustrating the cultural, ethnic and political diversity of Yugoslovia, Fisher stated:

> Yugoslavia is a state with two alphabets (Latin and Cyrillic), three major religions (Orthodox, Roman Catholic and Moslem), three major languages (Serbo-Croatian, Slovenian and Macedonian), four nationalities (Serbs, Croats, Slovenes and Macedonians), six republics (Serbia, Croatia, Macedonia, Slovenia, Montenegro and Bosnia-Herzegovina), and seven surrounding nations.[7]

According to Hamilton, internal physical disunity, a strategic location and easy accessibility by neighboring nations contributed to frequent invasions and domination by the Turks, Italians and the Hapsburgs.[4]

Following World War I, the Yugoslav state was constituted as the Kingdom of the Serbs, Croats and Slovenes. In 1929 under King Alexander I the Kingdom of Yugoslavia was established with an area slightly smaller than present. After routing the Germans in 1943 Josef Tito proclaimed the Federal People's Republic of Yugoslavia. In 1946 this action was formalized, the six republics were created and a section of Trieste was annexed from Italy. The Federal Socialist Republic of Yugoslavia was created following the acceptance of the April Constitution in 1963.

Concerning national goals under the 1963 Constitution, Fisher stated:

The Yugoslav goal is to obtain integration through controlled differences or ordered local diversity under an indirect mechanism of federal supervision. This goal is the distinguishing characteristic of the communal system and the fundamental philosophy of the April 1963 Constitution.[2]

The diverse ethnic composition and the intensity of nationalistic feeling by the various ethnic groups is an important question in future social and economic development in Yugoslavia.

Economically, large numbers of the population are being drawn into industry, but a majority of the people still engage in agriculture. Annual income ranges from $300 in Macedonia to $1,400 in Slovenia. In the last twenty years expenditures on industry, technological improvements in agriculture and federal reforms to decentralize industrial management and streamline production have contributed to a stronger economy. Metropolitan streets are jammed with automobiles and store fronts displaying modern clothing, appliances and foods.

In contrast grain in the fields of Macedonia and Kosovo is harvested largely by the labor of men and women using hand sickles. Transportation in most rural areas is mainly by horse or oxen.

Yugoslavia is governed by a President, a Federal Executive Council and a Federal Assembly. The Assembly is composed of six chambers which deal with federal, economic, political, nationality, health and cultural questions.

Education is free and compulsory from the ages of seven to fourteen. From the ages of fourteen to eighteen boys and girls may continue their education in a variety of free secondary schools. The secondary school diploma is becoming a prerequisite for most types of employment.

The Yugoslav elementary and secondary schools have their own self-management bodies consisting of the advisory board, management committee and teachers council. These bodies decide on educational matters in relation to statutes regulating self-management according to the constitution.[7] Schools in most areas are very crowded forcing three or four sessions of several hours daily.

There are universities for higher education in Belgrade, Zagreb, Sarajevo, Ljubljana, Skopje, Nis and Pristina, as well as individual faculties or high schools, in other industrial cities. The literacy rate is 75%.

## ELEMENTARY AND SECONDARY SCHOOL PHYSICAL EDUCATION

Physical and health education is supported by the federal government as an integral part of the school program. The objective of school physical education in Yugoslavia is:

> . . . the development of permanent interest and need for active engagement in the field of physical education and the development of interest for free sports activities in select-ed branches of physical education.[5]

As revealed by Slobodon Kostantinovic, administrator of elementary education for Belgrade, elementary school students receive physical education instruction three times per week with emphasis on physical training and ball games. These classes, which are sometimes coeduational, consist of thirty children, and the classes are usually directed by the classroom teacher.

In the secondary school and the later years of elementary school physical education classes are taught by physical education instructors. Mr. Konstantinovic further stated that every Belgrade school had a gymnasium which permitted a program where students receive physical training (strength and endurance exercise) one period per week and elect activities such as basketball, soccer, team handball or volleyball during the remaining two periods. Awards are given for outstanding performances on physical fitness tests. The system of high school physical education in Yugoslavia is based on the model applied in the USSR and other socialist countries.

After school hours the gymnasium, outdoor facilities and swimming pools are available for instruction for team activities, folk dance, gymnastics and swimming. Belgrade has thirty outdoor and five indoor pools.

## PROFESSIONAL PREPARATION

Physical education teachers are prepared at universities in Belgrade, Ljubljana, Zagreb and Sarajevo. There are high schools of physical education offering two years of preparation for elementary school teachers in Skopje, Pristina, Novi Sad, Belgrade and Split.

Admission to the university or high school is gained upon satisfactory completion of high school (general education) usually at the age of 18. Preparation at a university usually lasts for eight semesters with concentrations available in areas of physical education, coaching and physical therapy.

Dr. Ivan Aleksic and his staff at the University of Belgrade Faculty of Physical Education have developed a major curriculum under the following headings: Social Science and Humanities, Biological Sciences, Gymnastics, Sports and Games. The social science subjects include the history of physical education, psychology, pedagogy, methods of physical education, recreation and statistics. The biological sciences include anatomy, physiology, biomechanics, developmental biology, elements of sports medicine, hygiene and physical therapy. The gymnastics section covers physical conditioning, free calisthenics, dance and elements of music education. Sports include individual and dual competitive activities such as swimming, track and field, gymnastics, rowing, skiing and combative sports. The games section includes, besides games of low organization for elementary schools, the basic team sports such as soccer, basketball, volleyball and team handball. At the University of Belgrade fifty percent of a student's course load is given to biological and social studies while gymnastics, sports and games receive the remaining fifty percent. Each of the subjects is taught by a faculty member with complete academic qualifications. The biological sciences are taught by individuals with medical school diplomas. The social sciences are taught by professors with corresponding degrees in the various subject areas. Individuals with physical education diplomas teach in the areas of gymnastics, sports and games.

During the final year of preparation the student must choose to specialize in a specific sport or area of physical education as well as gain proficiencies in the area of physical therapy. Upon graduation from the university with a diploma in physical education the student may seek employment in elementary or secondary schools, as coaches of amateur and professional sports clubs, or as teaching fellows or professors at the various physical education faculties in Yugoslavia. In the late 1960's postgraduate studies were introduced at the University of Belgrade to prepare students for the Master of Arts degree in physical education. The doctoral dissertation in physical education may also be written and defended at the University of Belgrade.

The Faculty of Physical Education at the University of Belgrade enrolls approximately 150 new students each year, seventy percent of whom complete their studies in approximately four and one-half years. There are 34 male and six female instructors of physical education at the University of Belgrade.

Rusmir Sivcevic, a physical education student at the University of Belgrade, indicated that much emphasis is placed on the learning and teaching of sports skills. In the fourth year of study nearly seventy percent of the course work might be given to studying and mastering selected sports activities. Off campus experiences at summer youth camps on the Adriatic, or four week seminars on skiing in Slovenia or canoeing and kyaking on the rivers of central Yugoslavia are attended by students interested in developing these specialties.

Dr. Slavko Podkubovsek and his staff at the Faculty of Physical Education at the University of Sarajevo offer a similar preparation to approximately 170 men and 30 women. The recently created faculty of physical education at the University of Sarajevo has modern classrooms, a new gymnasium, modern gymnastics and apparatus facilities, spacious soccer fields and new team handball and volleyball courts.

## SCHOOL AND UNIVERSITY PHYSICAL EDUCATION FACILITIES

Each city appeared to have a school gymnasium. In rural areas gymnasiums were practically non-existent. The usual gymnasium observed by this writer in Split, Belgrade, Sarajevo, Zagreg, Ljubljana, and Skopje contained one basketball floor with floor markings for volleyball and team handball. Ropes, ladders, rings, and bars were available for gymnastics activities. It is this writer's observation that efforts are being made to improve the shortage of gymnasiums in Yugoslavia. New, well-equipped gymnasiums were seen in the smaller towns of Visegrad, Titovo Uzice and Ivangrad. Since most of these schools had two or more sessions per day, there is still a need for larger facilities and more instructors.

At the Faculty of Physical Education at the University of Belgrade, lush, well-groomed fields and well-maintained clay courts provided excellent instructional areas for physical education students. A six lane crushed brick and clay running track encircled a finely manicured soccer field. The gymnasium housed two pools, a gymnastics room, a basketball, team handball, volleyball teaching area plus dressing and shower facilities and several offices. Across the street from the gymnasium is located a modern classroom building including a physiology laboratory, physiotherapy room, offices and 17,000 volume physical education library.

## RESEARCH

The journal of the Association of Teachers of Physical Education is entitled *Fizika Kultura*. This journal contains scholarly articles and research in areas of philosophy, physical education, applied physiology and anatomy, and kinesiology.

Research in areas related to physical education such as sports medicine is undertaken at the universities of Belgrade, Zagreb, Ljubljana and Sarajevo. Sports medicine is being considered as an area of emphasis at the University of Belgrade, but at present no lecture course is offered. The Faculty of Physical Education, however, offers lectures in the areas of physiology of work and sport, hygiene of work and sport and traumatology of sport and physical exercise.

## SPORT

When traveling in Yugoslavia, one immediately realizes the high priority given to sport by the people and the government. Governmental assistance for sport is revealed in the large federal and industrial subsidies plus a percentage of the national lottery for the construction of stadiums, public sports fields and public camping facilities. Popular enthusiams for sport was seen in the wide participation at all ages in soccer, volleyball, team handball, basketball, gymnastics, swimming and camping. In Split this writer had the thrilling experience of witnessing 20,000 fans welcome the return of their national soccer championship team, Hajduk (pronounced hie-duke, meaning rebel) three days after an exciting come from behind 4-3 win over Belgrade Red Star. The local fans gave their team a ten minute standing ovation complete with smoke bombs, rockets and fireworks prior to the exhibition game with Real Madrid of Spain. Hajduk responded to the enthusiastic welcome with three goals in the first eighteen minutes to rout the visiting Spaniards 4-2.

Basketball is challenging soccer as the number one sport both in participation and in international competition. Yugoslavia won the 1970 world basketball championship competing against such established basketball countries as Brazil, United States and the Soviet Union. Yugoslavia won the silver medal in basketball in the 1976 Olympic Games. Yugoslav teams in water polo and men's team handball won European championships in 1976.

This writer observed the 1971 Balkan Gymnastics Championships in New Belgrade, Serbia. Men's and women's teams from Bulgaria, Greece, Romania and Yugoslavia competed in the two day event.

The Yugoalav Association of Organizations of Physical Culture (JSOFK) with offices in Belgrade promotes and coordinates popular and competitive participation in thirty-four sports. The Partisan Federation promotes popular participation on an amateur basis in gymnastics, track and field, cross country, swimming and camping.[6] Yugoslav youths participate competitively under the auspices of the JSOFK or Partisan. Interschool and interuniversity sports competition is beginning to appear in Yugoslavia.[1]

## SPORTS FACILITIES

Nearly every city that this writer visited from rural Prisren in Kosovo to metropolitan Belgrade had at least one stadium. The quality of the playing surfaces and seating varied greatly according to the size of the towns. Zagreb, Belgrade, Saravejo, Ljubljana, Skopje and Split had lighted stadiums with watered playing areas seating from twenty to sixty-five thousands spectators.

In smaller towns such as Pec, Ivangrad and Prisren in the south; Titovo Uzice and Prijepoli in central Yugoslavia and Kranj and Velenje in Slovenia, a complex which included a soccer field, a running track and a team handball-volleyball area was observed. For example in Velenje, a newly constructed mining town in Slovenia, a running track, soccer field and bleachers had been constructed with adjacent outdoor basketball, volleyball and team handball playing areas. Tennis courts and lawn bowling lanes were also included in this complex.

Many of the sports facilities are operated by local sports organizations, clubs or societies. An outdoor swimming pool and gymnastics hall operated by the Partizan Federation was visited in Ljubljana.

Most of the larger cities had one or two eight to ten lane outdoor fifty meter pools.

The monumental Sarajevo Sport and Cultural Center (Skenderije) seats eight thousand for conventions and boxing matches, five thousand for basketball and four thousand for ice hockey. The convention center, built at a cost of seven million dollars, includes a student center, theater in the round, lecture rooms, a practice basketball court, a practice volleyball court, a practice team handball court, a gymnastics room, an exercise room and dressing facilities. A modern shopping center is also housed under the convention center and future plans call for the addition of a swimming pool and a hotel.

Indoor skating rinks were visited in Ljubljana and Sarajevo. Outdoor skating rinks were visited in Skopje and Belgrade.

Generally, the existing facilities were of good quality, but more and better facilities are needed for general use by the public.

## INTERNATIONAL COMPETITION

The federal government of Yugoslavia is committed to supporting the growth of national teams through the organization of people's sports programs at all levels of competition. The Yugoslav Olympic Committee with offices in Belgrade is a member of the International Olympic Committee. In collaboration with the JSOFK, The Yugoslav Olympic Committee prepares and selects Olympic contestants, obtains funds to finance Olympic competition and disseminates literature and information to interested clubs and societies concerning Olympic competition.

# POPULAR RECREATION

The geography and climate of Yugoslavia make the country an excellent recreation land. Mountaineering ranks third in total participants as a recreational pursuit in Yugoslavia. The upper reaches of the crystal clear, fast flowing Radika River near Lake Mavrovo in south central Yugoslavia, the Lim east of Ivangrad and the Neretva north of Mostar provide excellent swimming and fishing. The central and lower reaches of these rivers are excellent for canoeing or kyaking. The Drina River near Visegrad provides good swimming, boating and fishing. Excellent camping facilities are found in Slovania at Lake Bled and Lake Bohinj. Asphalt bicycle paths edge many of the Slovenia highways.

Along the rock ledged Dalmatian coast, dotted with pebble bleached islands, camping, swimming, boating and skin diving abound.

Scenic metropolitan parks such as Ilidza in Sarajevo, Kalemagden and Tasmajdan in Belgrade, the promendates along the Vardar River in Skopje and Tivoli in Ljubljana are a few of the recreational areas available to citizens of these towns. This writers was awed by the quality and beauty of Tivoli in Ljubljana. Tivoli, a large metropolitan park, contained basketball, volleyball, team handball, tennis and lawn bowling courts, an indoor and outdoor skating rink, outdoor asphalt roller skating areas, a mini-golf course, a regulation public soccer field encircled by a good quality 400 meter running track, a fifty meter outdoor swimming pool, a tot play area and many bubbling fountains, miles of walkways and acres of lush green grass. Family activities at the parks included camping, informal soccer, volleyball and badminton games. Ping pong tables and chess boards received heavy play where available.

In the evenings during the warm summer months inhabitants of the cities and villages participate in the "corzo" or evening promenade. Traffic is halted on selected streets in cities and on main streets in the smaller towns. Families, children, teenagers, elderly matrons and young couples stroll down the street to the edge of town, turn around and walk back through town. This continuous evening stroll is a relaxed time of socializing and window shopping. The "corzo" may vary in length from a block or two as viewed in Ivangrad or Pec, to five or six blocks as observed in Visegrad, Titovo Uzice, Sarajevo and Belgrade.

Colorful folk dance performances were witnessed in Belgrade by the Yugoslav National Ballet. Performances by local folk dance groups were seen in Sarajevo and at Lake Bohinj in Slovenia. While in Visegrad this writer participated with patrons at a local hotel night club in a variation of the *kolo*, a popular Serbian folk dance.

Sport shops in Yugoslavia were well stocked with camping gear, skin and scuba diving equipment, hunting and fishing supplies, inflatable rafts and canoes and athletic equipment.

## ACKNOWLEDGEMENT

The author wishes to acknowledge the assistance given by Dr. Borivoje Todorovic, Associate Professor Physiology, Faculty of Physical Education, University of Belgrade. Dr. Todorovic served as a resource authority for the Professional Preparation section of this article.

## NOTES

1.   The Federal Committee for Information. *Facts About Yugoslavia.* (Belgrade: Belgrade Publishing Union, 1976). p. 78.

2.   Fisher, *op. cit.* p. 8.

3.   Fisher, Jack. *Yugoslavia - A Multinational State.* (San Francisco: Chandler Publishing Company, 1966). pp. 8-9.

4.   Hamilton, F. E. Ian. *Yugoslavia, Patterns of Economic Activity.* (New York: F. A. Praeger Publishers, 1968). p. 15.

5.   International Council on Health, Physical Education and Recreation. *Physical Education in the School Curriculum.* (Washington: ICHPER, 1969). p. 79.

6.   Jancovic, Ruzitan. Secretary to the Yugoslav Olympic Committee. Personal interview in Belgrade, June 29, 1971.

7.   The Secretariat for Information of the Federal Executive Council. *A Handbook of Yugoslavia.* (Belgrade: Belgrade Publishing Union, 1970). p. 203.

## BOOKS

The Federal Committee for Information. *Facts About Yugoslavia.* Belgrade: Belgrade Publishing Union. 1976.

Fisher, Jack. *Yugoslavia - A Multinational State.* San Francisco: Chandler Publishing Company. 1966.

Hamilton, F. E. Ian. *Yugoslavia, Patterns of Economic Activity.* New York: F. A. Praeger Publishers. 1968.

The International Council on Health, Physical Education and Recreation. *Physical Education in the School Curriculum.* Washington: ICHPER. 1969.

Partizan-Newa Publishing and Propaganda Enterprise. *Yugoslav Federation of Physical Culture Organization*. Belgrade: Budnucnost. 1964.

The Secretariat for Information of the Federal Executive Council. *A Handbook of Yugoslavia*. Belgrade: Belgrade Publishing Union. 1970.


## PERSONAL INTERVIEWS

Aleksic, Ivan. Vice Dean of the Faculty of Physical Education, University of Belgrade. June 25, 1971.

Jancovic, Ruzitan. Secretary to the Yugoslav Olympic Committee, Belgrade. June 23, 1971.

Janekelic, Jovan. Professor of Physical Education, University of Sarajevo. July 15, 1971.

Konstantinovic, Slobodan. Administrator of Belgrade Public School System. June 25, 1971.

Mihailovic, Rafailo. Teaching Fellow in Physiology, Faculty of Physical Education, University of Belgrade. June 25, 1971.

Podkubovsek, Slavko. Chairman of the Faculty of Physical Education, University of Sarajveo. July 16, 1971.

Sivecevic, Rusmir. Student, Faculty of Physical Education, University of Belgrade. June 20, 1971.

Todorovic, Borivoje. Associate Professor of Physiology, Faculty of Physical Education, University of Belgrade. June 25, 1971.

Visnar, Borut. Import-Export Employee, Ljubljana. July 25, 1971.